On the Frontier of Adulthood

The John D. and Catherine T. MacArthur Foundation
Series on Mental Health and Development
Research Network on Transitions to Adulthood and Public Policy

ON THE FRONTIER OF ADULTHOOD

Theory, Research, and Public Policy

RICHARD A. SETTERSTEN JR., FRANK F. FURSTENBERG JR.,
AND RUBÉN G. RUMBAUT, EDITORS

The University of Chicago Press • *Chicago & London*

RICHARD A. SETTERSTEN JR. is professor of sociology at Case Western Reserve University. He is the author of *Lives in Time and Place: The Problems and Promises of Developmental Science.* FRANK F. FURSTENBERG JR. is the Zellerbach Family Professor of Sociology at the University of Pennsylvania. He is author or coauthor of several previous books, including *Managing to Make It: Urban Families and Adolescent Success.* RUBÉN G. RUMBAUT is professor of sociology at the University of California, Irvine. He is the author or coauthor of several previous books, including *Immigrant America: A Portrait* and *Legacies: The Story of the Immigrant Second Generation.*

The University of Chicago Press, Chicago 60637
The University of Chicago Press, Ltd., London
© 2005 by The University of Chicago
All rights reserved. Published 2005
Printed in the United States of America

14 13 12 11 10 09 08 07 06 05   1 2 3 4 5

ISBN: 0–226–74889–8 (cloth)

Library of Congress Cataloging-in-Publication Data

On the frontier of adulthood : theory, research, and public policy / Richard A. Settersten, Jr., Frank F. Furstenberg, Jr., and Rubén G. Rumbaut, editors.
  p. cm. — (The John D. and Catherine T. Macarthur Foundation series on mental health and development. Research Network on Transitions to Adulthood and Public Policy)
Includes bibliographical references and index.
ISBN 0-226-74889-8 (cloth : alk. paper)
  1. Young adults.   2. Young adults—United States.   3. Youth.   4. Youth —United States.
5. Adolescence.   6. Adulthood.   I. Settersten, Richard A.   II. Furstenberg, Frank F.,
1940–   III. Rumbaut, Rubén G.   IV. Series.
  HQ799.5.O6 2005
  305.242—dc22

                                                    2004013686

Contents

PART FOUR
POLICY AND PRACTICE FOR LIVES IN TRANSITION

About the Editors and Contributors

EDITORS

Frank F. Furstenberg Jr., Ph.D., Zellerbach Family Professor of Sociology, Department of Sociology, University of Pennsylvania

Rubén G. Rumbaut, Ph.D., professor, Department of Sociology, and Codirector, Center for Research on Immigration, Population, and Public Policy, University of California, Irvine

Richard A. Settersten Jr., Ph.D., professor, Department of Sociology, Case Western Reserve University

CONTRIBUTORS

Jerald G. Bachman, Ph.D., distinguished research professor, Survey Research Center, Institute for Social Research, University of Michigan

Bonnie L. Barber, Ph.D., professor, Department of Family Studies and Human Development, University of Arizona

Mary Corcoran, Ph.D., professor, Department of Political Science, Social Work and Public Policy, University of Michigan

Jacquelynne S. Eccles, Ph.D., professor, Department of Psychology, University of Michigan

Jennifer Eggerling-Boeck, doctoral student, Department of Sociology, University of Wisconsin—Madison

Lance D. Erickson, doctoral student, Department of Sociology, University of North Carolina at Chapel Hill

E. Michael Foster, Ph.D., associate professor, Department of Health Policy and Administration, Pennsylvania State University

Frank F. Furstenberg Jr., Ph.D., Zellerbach Family Professor of Sociology, Department of Sociology, University of Pennsylvania

Elizabeth Fussell, Ph.D., assistant professor, Department of Sociology, Tulane University

Anne H. Gauthier, Ph.D., Canada Research Chair in Comparative Public Policy, Department of Sociology, University of Calgary

Elizabeth J. Gifford, doctoral student, Department of Health Policy and Administration, Pennsylvania State University

Jennifer Holdaway, Ph.D., program officer for International Migration, Social Science Research Council

Janis E. Jacobs, Ph.D., vice provost for Undergraduate Education and International Programs, and professor, Department of Human Development and Family Studies, Department of Psychology, Pennsylvania State University

Lloyd D. Johnston, Ph.D., distinguished research professor, Survey Research Center, Institute for Social Research, University of Michigan

Philip Kasinitz, Ph.D., associate director, Center for Urban Research, City University of New York Graduate Center

Jui-Chung Allen Li, doctoral student, Department of Sociology, University of Wisconsin—Madison

Jordan Matsudaira, doctoral student, Department of Public Policy and Economics, University of Michigan

John Mollenkopf, Ph.D., distinguished professor of political science, and director, Center for Urban Research, City University of New York Graduate Center

Jeylan T. Mortimer, Ph.D., professor, Department of Sociology, University of Minnesota

Ted Mouw, Ph.D., assistant professor, Department of Sociology, University of North Carolina at Chapel Hill

Patrick M. O'Malley, Ph.D., research professor, Survey Research Center, Institute for Social Research, University of Michigan

D. Wayne Osgood, Ph.D., professor, Department of Sociology, Pennsylvania State University

Hyunjoon Park, doctoral student, Department of Sociology, University of Wisconsin—Madison

Erik J. Porfeli, doctoral student, Department of Human Development and Family Studies, Pennsylvania State University

Karen Ross, doctoral student, Department of Sociology and School of Education, University of Michigan

Rubén G. Rumbaut, Ph.D., professor, Department of Sociology, and Codirector, Center for Research on Immigration, Population, and Public Policy, University of California, Irvine

Gretchen R. Ruth, doctoral student, Department of Sociology, Pennsylvania State University

Gary D. Sandefur, Ph.D., professor, Department of Sociology, University of Wisconsin—Madison

John E. Schulenberg, Ph.D., research professor, Survey Research Center, Institute for Social Research, and professor, Department of Psychology, University of Michigan

Robert F. Schoeni, Ph.D., senior associate research scientist, Institute for Social Research, and associate professor, Economics and Public Policy, University of Michigan

Richard A. Settersten Jr., Ph.D., professor, Department of Sociology, Case Western Reserve University

Michael J. Shanahan, Ph.D., associate professor, Department of Sociology, University of North Carolina at Chapel Hill

Tom W. Smith, Ph.D., director of the General Social Survey, National Opinion Research Center, University of Chicago

Mary C. Waters, Ph.D., Harvard College Professor, Department of Sociology, Harvard University

Lawrence L. Wu, Ph.D., professor, Department of Sociology, New York University

Acknowledgments

We wish to thank the individuals and organizations that follow for their important contributions to this project:

The John D. and Catherine T. MacArthur Foundation, for financing the Research Network on Transitions to Adulthood and Public Policy, including this book as its first major product. The network is composed of a group of interdisciplinary researchers whose mission is to understand the changing nature of early adulthood and how social institutions and public policies might better respond to the challenges of this life period. More information about the network and its initiatives can be found in chapter 1 and on the Web at www.pop.upenn.edu/transad.

Special thanks are due to Idy Gitelson, formerly our program officer at the MacArthur Foundation, for her constant support throughout the project and to Connie Yowell, who now serves in that capacity, for her encouragement and good advice.

Amy Wisniewski and Lynn Gannon, doctoral students at Case Western Reserve University; Jennifer Holdaway, of the Social Science Research Council and an associate of the network; and Sheela Kennedy, doctoral student at the University of Pennsylvania, for their exceptional assistance with reviewing, copyediting, and formatting.

Other members of the network, for their time, expertise, and intellectual stimulation: Gordon Berlin, Mark Courtney, Sheldon Danziger, Connie Flanagan, Vonnie McLoyd, Wayne Osgood, Jean Rhodes, Cecilia Rouse, and Mary Waters.

Lead authors and their collaborators, for meeting several times over three years to provide constructive feedback on early drafts of the chapters and harmonize data sets and analyses. The quality of this book ultimately rests on their fine skills.

Barbara Ray, for creating "Research and Policy Briefs" for the chapters of this book. The briefs can be found on the network Web site noted above.

The University of Chicago Press, especially David Brent, executive editor in the Books Division, Elizabeth Branch Dyson, editorial associate,

Yvonne Zipter, senior manuscript editor, and Peter Cavagnaro, promotions manager, for their enthusiasm about the project and for shepherding the book through the production process.

The anonymous reviewers assigned by the press for their thoughtful comments and criticism.

And to Patricia Miller, network administrator at the University of Pennsylvania, for her patience, kindness, persistence, and wisdom. Patricia has been our partner in this enterprise, and to her we extend our deepest appreciation.

PART ONE

ON THE FRONTIER OF ADULTHOOD

An Introduction

CHAPTER 1

ON THE FRONTIER
OF ADULTHOOD

Emerging Themes and New Directions

FRANK F. FURSTENBERG JR., RUBÉN G. RUMBAUT,
AND RICHARD A. SETTERSTEN JR.

Since the publication of Phillipe Ariès's *Centuries of Childhood* (1962), social historians and scholars of human development have debated how, when, and why distinct life "stages" are created and culturally defined. It is now commonly understood that economic and social conditions in tandem create categories such as childhood, adolescence, young adulthood, middle age, and old age that are recognized and reified in popular discourse. Ideas about life periods are rooted in social structural changes that give rise to new behaviors. They come about as inventions or solutions to structural dilemmas created when social change renders old practices unworkable or, in common parlance, out of fashion. In modern societies, these new patterns are often swiftly diffused in the form of new social norms, institutional arrangements, social affiliations, and personal identities.

This sort of change occurred in the early part of the last century when Stanley Hall (1904) "discovered" adolescence, a term applied to describe a "new life stage." The idea of a period of life between childhood and adulthood was quickly adopted in the United States because it seemed to fit the circumstances of young people at a time when public schooling was becoming universal, as the economic base of the nation moved away from agriculture toward industry, and as younger teens were no longer as readily suited to employment. These and other shifts in culture and society worked together to define adolescence as a meaningful life period separate from childhood and adulthood. Of course, many of the characteristics of adolescence had been recognized in the behaviors of young people long before the last century, but Hall suggested that these shifts resulted in an organized life stage that permitted young people to receive more schooling, explore options, and forge a sense of self.

We believe that similar forces are at work today to make early adulthood a distinct and socially recognized stage of life. In many respects, there is a direct parallel to what took place a century ago when the idea of a period called adolescence emerged in American culture. The seemingly seamless transition from childhood to adulthood that existed in preindustrial society became increasingly less plausible after industrialization, leaving many youth in the anomalous state of being neither a child nor an adult. Earlier puberty and later social development created a gap in the life course that initially took the form of what social historian Joseph Kett (1977) referred to as semiautonomy. In fact, Kett showed that young people experienced many of the manifestations of adolescence well before it was culturally accepted as a life period in its own right.

During the first few decades of the twentieth century, "adolescence" remained relatively brief, spanning the period from the early to the late teen years. By their late teens, only a very small fraction of the population was still in school. Most had left their natal households and entered the labor force, although marriage and childbearing often did not occur immediately thereafter. Yet as the century progressed, growing numbers of young people had formed families by their late teens or early twenties. The Great Depression slowed down the timing of family formation, but by the end of World War II, marriage and childbearing occurred almost in lockstep at the conclusion of schooling. In the postwar boom that followed, high-paying industrial jobs were plentiful, enabling most young people to become socially and economically independent by the end of their teens. By their early twenties, then, most young people were socially recognized as adults, more or less indistinguishable from men and women in their thirties or forties.

The high proportion of men in the military during the 1940s undoubtedly quickened entry into adulthood. War veterans were entitled to be considered adults and were granted economic support and job preferences that enabled them to marry and form families at young ages. In a family system that encouraged, if not insisted on, a gender-based division of labor, many women traded their fathers for husbands as sources of support. In the 1950s, close to half of all women were married by the age of twenty, many of them already pregnant on their wedding days. Thus, adulthood began after a relatively brief period of adolescence.

Social timetables that were widely observed a half century ago for accomplishing adult transitions no longer apply in the contemporary Western world. Adolescence now occurs earlier than in the past, moved up by earlier onset of puberty, increasing relevance of peer relationships, and new cultural understandings advanced by child development professionals about age-appropriate autonomy during the early teen years. The invention of the middle school, starting as early as the sixth grade, when children are typically eleven or twelve, marks the beginning of adolescence.

But as the chapters of this book clearly show, the end of adolescence has become a protracted affair. Entry into adulthood has become more ambiguous and generally occurs in a gradual, complex, and less uniform fashion. It is simply not possible for most young people to achieve economic and psychological autonomy as early as it was a half century ago. Thus, the term "adolescence" is becoming socially and psychologically inexact, including as it does twelve-year-olds and twenty-something-year-olds, who may be still living at home and are economically dependent on parents. There is an inclination to devise expressions like "emerging adulthood" (Arnett 2000) or the term "adultolescence," which was infelicitously coined by Tyre and associates (2002) in a recent *Newsweek* cover story about how young people are more dependent on parents than were previous generations. The notion that adolescence bridges the period between childhood and adulthood no longer works well to describe what happens as young people come of age in postindustrial economies. The timing and sequencing of traditional markers of adulthood—leaving home, finishing school, starting work, getting married, and having children—are less predictable and more prolonged, diverse, and disordered. The attendant quandaries are the stuff of leading stories in the popular media. For example, a recent cover of *Time* magazine (Gibbs 2002) shows a smiling baby lying on a pile of paperwork in an "in basket" at the office, with the headline "Babies vs. Career: Which Should Come First for Women Who Want Both?" Similarly, the results of a 2002 poll conducted by Monster.com, which showed that most people in their twenties said they would stay at or return home if they could not find employment, were widely reported in the print media.

The changing timetable for adulthood has given rise to a host of questions about whether current generations of young people are less interested in growing up, choosing to stay dependent on their parents, and more wary of making commitments. We do not think that any of these psychological explanations fit the facts described in the chapters of this book. The problem is not that young people are refusing to grow up or that parents are discouraging them from doing so. Nor do we believe that young people are unwilling to commit to future obligations. If anything, we might argue that the opposite is occurring. Young people are now much more aware of what it takes to be autonomous, and they tend to be disinclined to take on commitments that they cannot honor.

It is no great mystery why these changes have come about. Education and training are more valuable than ever before because jobs are less permanent and work careers have become more fluid. The demand for education and training has increased relentlessly during the past four decades, as have the economic returns to education. Teenagers continue to work, but a shrinking fraction enters full-time work before their early twenties and a growing number do so only toward the end of their twenties. We are just beginning to appreciate the full ramifications of the economic and social changes that have resulted from the extension of schooling and the delay of work and of the fact that family transitions now occur a decade or so later than in the past. Much as adolescence emerged as a distinct life period a century ago, early adulthood is now emerging as a unique period marked by cultural trappings that confer psychological identities and social affiliations.

We believe that public awareness and social policies have not yet caught up to the changes described in rigorous detail throughout the book. Indeed, we will return to this theme below and elaborate its implications in the final chapter. In particular, many features of American society operate on the assumption that the attainment of adulthood, at least in terms of the traditional markers noted earlier, occurs well before it actually does. Health insurance is but one obvious example. An awkward gap exists from the late teens through the twenties when many young people are insufficiently incorporated in social arrangements that provide the training and social support to sustain them during what has become a lengthy social hiatus. Consequently, natal families are required to fill in, but they frequently lack the resources and know-how to help young people negotiate the complex transition to adulthood.

The original papers commissioned for this book draw together information from a variety of sources to provide a more accurate and textured picture of early adulthood. It is not the first such description. Indeed, it builds on prior landmark research on this topic (e.g., Buchmann 1989; Modell 1989) and complements other recent research on this period (e.g., Booth, Crouter, and Shanahan 1999; Corijn and Klijzing 2001; Furstenberg 2002) and the adolescent years preceding it (e.g., Brown, Larson, and Saraswathi 2002; Larson, Brown and Mortimer 2002; Mortimer and Larson 2002). This book, however, is arguably the most thorough description of this period to date. As elaborated below, the authors draw on a wide range of large social surveys and censuses to analyze demographic, social, and economic transitions that occur as young people enter adult roles, and they use innovative methodological and statistical approaches to shed new light on these patterns.

Most prior work on this topic has generally examined these transitions singly, as isolated events and more or less independent of one another. Indeed, whole fields of research have been devoted to each of these transitions: completion of schooling, movement from the parental household, entrance into the labor force, formation of partnerships, and the onset of childbearing and parenting. One of the distinctive features of our contribution is that we have endeavored to examine multiple transitions simultaneously. While the aspirations to examine the multifaceted nature of the transition to adulthood often exceed the capacities of data or techniques for analysis, we believe that a great deal is lost when these transitions are examined one or even two at a time. Thus, we hope to gain a more coherent and complete understanding of this period by focusing on the interplay of multiple transitions across multiple life domains (such as education, work, family, and leisure). The time is ripe, we feel, to pioneer research efforts aimed at understanding the new frontiers of early adult life.

THE EVOLUTION AND ORGANIZATION OF THE BOOK

This book is the joint product of a working group of sociologists, demographers, economists, and psychologists brought together under the auspices of the Research Network on Transitions to Adulthood and Public Policy, a multidisciplinary research group initiated and funded by the John D. and Catherine T. MacArthur Foundation and directed by Frank Furstenberg.

This network, like all MacArthur networks, was established to foster research on human development that crosses the usual boundaries of the behavioral sciences. The MacArthur Foundation has a strong interest in promoting research that addresses public policy issues relating to human development, both those that are recognized as well as those not yet acknowledged. Over the past decade or so, the foundation has spawned a series of research networks on early childhood, middle childhood, the adolescent years, midlife, and successful aging, all of which yielded fresh information, novel perspectives, and policy prescriptions on these segments of the life span.

The Network on Transitions to Adulthood and Public Policy was initially formed in 1999 and funded for a three-year period beginning in 2000.

It immediately established as a first priority an investigation of large-scale, nationally representative surveys on young adults in the United States. We wanted to describe the changes that had taken place over time and among subgroups of the population in the postadolescent years that span roughly ages eighteen to thirty-four. We also wanted to see if the changes observed in the United States were happening in other nations with advanced economies as well. We gave high priority to longitudinal studies but also included census data and cross-sectional surveys that provided time-series comparisons. We wanted to draw on a wide range of nationally and internationally representative samples of young adults to describe in rich detail how young people negotiate the passage from adolescence to adulthood, to evaluate how the organization of that passage has changed over the past century, and, to the extent permitted by data, to examine whether and how the meanings of this period have shifted over the past few decades. This book is the result of these interests and intentions.

Beginning in 1999, members of the network contacted a number of scholars who work with some of the large data sets that contained longitudinal or time-series information on young adults. We met periodically over the next two years and together planned similar analyses that also capitalized on the strengths of various data sets. These fourteen data sets—arguably the best secondary sources available on this topic in the United States, Canada and Western Europe—include the U.S. Census, Current Population Surveys, Family and Fertility Survey, General Social Survey, High School and Beyond, Monitoring the Future, Multinational Time Use Survey, National Educational Longitudinal Study, National Longitudinal Survey of Youth, National Postsecondary Student Aid Study, and the Panel Study of Income Dynamics. Several high-quality regional studies from the United States are also included: the Michigan Study of Adolescent Life Transitions, the Immigrant Second Generation in Metropolitan New York Study, and the Youth Development Study.

These data sets are highlighted in table 1.1 and listed in alphabetical order. The table describes the sample size and composition, longitudinal or cross-sectional design and methods employed in the study, analytical foci, age range of respondents, time frame (one chapter covers a hundred years of American census data, another covers historical change in cohorts spanning more than fifty years, and others focus on single data points), and the countries where the surveys were carried out (two chapters report cross-national findings from, respectively, Canada, Sweden, Germany, and Italy and from Australia, Austria, Finland, Norway, the Netherlands, and the United Kingdom). The table also indicates which chapter uses particular data sets.

TABLE I.I

DATA SETS: SAMPLE CHARACTERISTICS, STUDY DESIGNS, AND ANALYTICAL FOCI

DATA SET	COUNTRIES	SAMPLE SIZE	SAMPLE DESCRIPTION	DESIGN AND METHODS	DATA POINTS	AGES OF FOCUS	CENTRAL DOMAINS OF FOCUS
Census of Population (chap. 2)	United States	4,019,768	• Nationally representative sample • Native-born white, black, and foreign-born men and women	• Cross-sectional data, patterns over time • Comparative historical cohort analyses	1900–2000 (2000 data are from Current Population Survey)	16–30 11 cohorts: 1876–85, 1886–95, 1896–1905, 1906–15, 1916–25, 1926–35, 1936–45, 1946–55, 1956–65, 1966–75, 1976–85	• Education • Work • Living arrangements • Family formation
Census of Population (chap. 12)	United States	Tens of thousands	• Nationally representative sample	• Cross-sectional data, patterns over time	1970–90	18–34	• Living arrangements

(continued)

TABLE 1.1

(CONTINUED)

DATA SET	COUNTRIES	SAMPLE SIZE	SAMPLE DESCRIPTION	DESIGN AND METHODS	DATA POINTS	AGES OF FOCUS	CENTRAL DOMAINS OF FOCUS
Current Population Surveys (chap. 4)	United States	132,797	• Nationally representative sample • Women	• Cross-sectional data • Sequence analysis of current and retrospective patterns	1980, 1985, 1990, 1995	Adolescence-midlife 6 cohorts: 1914–24, 1925–34, 1935–44, 1945–54, 1955–64, 1965–70	• Family formation
Family and Fertility Survey (chap. 3)	United States, Italy, Canada, West Germany, Sweden	26,476	• Sample design varies by country • Women from 5 countries	• Cross-sectional data, patterns over time • Comparative descriptive analyses of two cohorts	1990–95	20–35 2 cohorts: 1950–54, 1960–64	• Living arrangements • Family formation
General Social Survey (chap. 6)	United States	15,000	• National probability sample	• Cross-sectional data, patterns over time	1972–98	18–24 (vs. 5 older age groups)	• Wide range of political and social attitudes

Study	Country	Sample size	Sample	Method	Year	Age	Domains
High School and Beyond (chap. 9)	United States	12,000	• Nationally representative sample	• Longitudinal data • Latent class analysis of patterns	1992	20–28	• Family formation • Education • Work • Living arrangements
Immigrant Second Generation in Metropolitan New York Study (chap. 14)	United States	3,424 (364 in-depth interviews)	• Random sample of New York city area second generation immigrants	• Cross-sectional • Quantitative and qualitative analyses of domains by immigrant backgrounds	1998	18–32	• Education • Work • Family formation • Living arrangements
Michigan Study of Adolescent Life Transitions (chap. 10)	United States	1,410	• Sample from schools in a Midwestern city • White men and women from middle- and working-class backgrounds	• Longitudinal data • Latent class analyses of patterns	1990, 1996	18–24	• Education • Family formation • Work • Living arrangements • Time use

(continued)

TABLE I.I
(CONTINUED)

DATA SET	COUNTRIES	SAMPLE SIZE	SAMPLE DESCRIPTION	DESIGN AND METHODS	DATA POINTS	AGES OF FOCUS	CENTRAL DOMAINS OF FOCUS
Monitoring the Future (chap. 13)	United States	3,983	• Nationally representative sample	• Longitudinal data • Descriptive and repeated measures ANOVA of patterns	1977–95 (4 surveys per person over this time period)	18–24	• Education • Work and income • Family formation • Overall well-being • Substance use
Multinational Time Use Survey (chap. 5)	United States, Canada, Italy, Austria, Finland, Norway, Australia, Germany, Netherlands, Sweden, United Kingdom	192,824	• Nationally representative samples (for most data points)	• Cross-sectional data, patterns over time • Diary data of time use over a 24-hour period	23 surveys spanning 1971–98	18–34	• Education • Work • Leisure • Unpaid activities • Personal time

Study	Country	N	Sample	Design/Methods	Year(s)	Age	Topics
National Educational Longitudinal Study (chap. 9)	United States	13,500	• Nationally representative sample	• Longitudinal data • Latent class analysis of patterns	2000	20–26	• Family formation • Education • Work • Living arrangements
National Longitudinal Study of Youth (chap. 8)	United States	5,464	• Nationally representative sample	• Multiple quantitative strategies for analyzing sequence and timing patterns	1979–98	22–35	• Education • Work • Family formation • Living arrangements
National Postsecondary Student Aid Study (chap. 12)	United States	57,000	• Nationally representative sample	• Cross-sectional data on economic transfers	1992–93	18–22	• Economic transfers from parents to children during college
Panel Study of Income Dynamics (chap. 11)	United States	3,875	• Nationally representative sample	• Longitudinal data, patterns over time	1968–96	18–27 2 cohorts: 1952–59, 1962–69	• Education • Work and income • Living arrangements

(continued)

TABLE 1.1
(CONTINUED)

DATA SET	COUNTRIES	SAMPLE SIZE	SAMPLE DESCRIPTION	DESIGN AND METHODS	DATA POINTS	AGES OF FOCUS	CENTRAL DOMAINS OF FOCUS
Panel Study of Income Dynamics (chap. 12)	United States	6,661	• Nationally representative sample	• Cross-sectional data (from panel study), predictors of economic transfers	1988	18–34	• Economic transfers from parents to children by life statuses (e.g., becoming married, attending school)
Youth Development Study (chap. 7)	United States	1,010	• Random sample in a Midwestern city	• Cross-sectional data (from panel study) • Regression analyses	1999	25–26	Subjective evaluations of "adult" statuses in: • Work • School • Unpaid work • Family

It was not always possible to conduct comparable analyses because of the complex and diverse nature of data sets, but we always aimed at developing analyses that spoke to the multiple dimensions of adult transitions. Of course, some studies were better equipped to do this than others. As time went on, we also recognized that many data sets could not speak to the perspectives of young adults themselves. As a result, we added two chapters that begin to reveal how young people think about the transition to adulthood and experience it first-hand (Shanahan and colleagues, chap. 7; Mollenkopf and colleagues, chap. 14). The absence of attention to the subjective sides of early adult transitions led the network to sponsor a multisite qualitative study, of which Mollenkopf and colleagues' New York City project is part, to take a comprehensive look at the first-hand experiences of young people from a spectrum of rural to large urban environments (a small town in Iowa; Detroit, Mich.; Minneapolis, Minn.; San Diego, Calif.; and New York City). The results of these projects will begin to appear over the next few years.

As the chapters began to take shape, we encouraged the authors to address central theoretical issues posed by their research questions, use or develop new analytic strategies, and situate their empirical findings in appropriate social and historical contexts. The authors read and reacted to one another's work, and each chapter was later reviewed by at least two network members and the editors.

The book is organized into three major sections following this introduction, which makes up part 1. Part 2, "Comparisons over Time and Place: Cross-Sectional and Cross-National Studies," contains six empirical chapters that are based on cross-sectional and, in two cases, cross-national data sets. These chapters explicitly compare historical eras, cohorts, or nations. Chapter 2 (Fussell and Furstenberg) examines the experiences of American youth between ages sixteen and thirty over a hundred-year span and unearths patterns of multiple status transitions for men and women, blacks and whites, and native and foreign-born individuals. Chapter 3 (Fussell and Gauthier) compares the transition experiences of American women to women of four other nations (Canada, former West Germany, Italy, and Sweden), and chapter 4 (Wu and Li) focuses on the marital and childbearing trajectories of American women over fifty years. Chapter 5 (Gauthier and Furstenberg) explores historical trends in time use among young adults in eleven countries, while chapter 6 (Smith) tracks changes across three decades in a wide array of attitudes and values among age groups in the American population.

Part 3, "Passages to Adulthood: Findings from National and Regional Longitudinal Studies," consists of eight empirical chapters that are all based on American longitudinal studies—five national studies and three regional ones (St. Paul, Minn.; Detroit, Mich.; and New York City). Chapter 7 (Shanahan and colleagues) explores whether traditional social roles or subjective personal markers are more likely to denote adult status in the minds of young people. Chapter 8 (Mouw), like chapter 4 (Wu and Li), turns attention to the sequencing of traditional markers (leaving home, finishing education, entering employment, marrying, and having a child) and whether and how orderly or disorderly sequences matter for adult outcomes. Chapters 9 (Sandefur and colleagues) and 10 (Osgood and colleagues) emphasize the roles of education and family social class in shaping distinct pathways into adulthood. Chapters 11 (Corcoran and Matsudaira) and 12 (Schoeni and Ross) examine, respectively, economic attainments in early adulthood and the financial assistance that young people receive from natal families as they make the transition. Chapter 13 (Schulenberg and colleagues) explores how transitions patterns through age twenty-four relate to well-being and substance use. Chapter 14 (Mollenkopf and colleagues) compares transition experiences in New York City for second generation young people whose parents came from the Dominican Republic, the South American countries of Colombia, Ecuador, or Peru, the Anglophone Caribbean, China, Taiwan, Hong Kong, and the Chinese diaspora, and Russia, with those whose parents are native Puerto Ricans, blacks, and whites.

Part 4, "Policy and Practice for Lives in Transition," is composed of two chapters. Chapter 15 (Foster and Gifford) considers the challenges faced by three special populations: those in foster care, special education, or the juvenile justice system. Chapter 16 (Settersten) considers how institutions and policies might be strengthened to meet the needs of young people more appropriately and how the capacities of young people themselves might be strengthened so that they are better equipped to navigate the passage to adulthood. We will argue that it is in everyone's interest to share the load. In the next few sections of this introduction, we introduce just a few of the themes that cut across chapters.

LONGER, MORE COMPLEX—
AND SOMETIMES REVERSIBLE—TRANSITIONS

The chapters of this book show that the transition to adulthood looks very different today than it did fifty years ago—or hundred years ago, as revealed by Fussell and Furstenberg (chap. 2), which offers a broad overview of the experiences of youth between the ages of sixteen and thirty who lived between 1900 and 2000. Their chapter also serves to contextualize subsequent chapters because it ties its discussion of changing combinations of adult statuses to historical events and larger structural and cultural conditions. Curiously, adult transitions today resemble in certain respects some of the features that were present before industrialization, when most families earned a livelihood from the land rather than the job market. Most adults worked on farms or in agricultural jobs, as did their children, and young people often inherited land or found employment on farms or ranches. Attaining self-sufficiency then was a gradual process of semi-autonomy, just as it is now. The difference is that in the latter part of the last century, early adulthood became increasingly structured by social institutions outside the family, particularly higher education.

The growth of higher education has taken place in all postindustrial and emerging postindustrial societies. In an earlier time, this experience was reserved for the elite. But colleges and universities are now mainstream institutions, albeit delivering goods in different ways for the middle and working classes. Nonetheless, most youth now aspire to college (and beyond) because it is only through higher education that middle-class jobs are attainable. Without college or remunerative and relatively secure employment, it is not possible to manage other transitions associated with adulthood, such as gaining financial independence and setting up an independent household. Without the requisite human, cultural, and social capital, it is not possible to achieve a middle-class lifestyle.

The hope for and necessity, if not always the reality, of obtaining postsecondary education (or additional training through the military or an apprenticeship) has created the growing gap between the end of adolescence and the achievement of adult statuses. People in their late teens, as many parents (and young people themselves) are discovering, are simply not ready to be completely independent from their families. Many chapters attest to the lengthening of this period of dependency.

The evidence here also reveals a second hallmark of the early adult years: that entry into adulthood has become more complex and variable. The chapters of this book also demonstrate that experiences in early adulthood, like those in other periods, differ greatly by gender, race, ethnicity, and social class. For example, in contrast to the way adulthood was accomplished in the middle part of the last century, more young people, even those who are privileged, move back and forth between school and the labor force, do both at once or neither for a time. Growing numbers of young people give themselves an early sabbatical to travel and experience life or engage in a community service project before deciding what they are going to do with their lives. And while women's paths through marriage and childbearing have always been complicated, the range of available options for both men and women has made family patterns even more complicated.

Young people often start on one pathway and switch to another, which suggests that many transition experiences and pathways are flexible and sometimes reversible. Fewer and fewer people today expect a twenty-two-year old, much less someone in their late teens, to know what he or she is going to do in the next ten years than they did even a couple decades ago. Experimentation has become a more deliberate and self-conscious part of these years. We cannot easily define the end of early adulthood, but we can say with certainty that it is not the magic ages of eighteen or twenty-one that are most often used to define adulthood in social policies and the law.

The network has defined early adulthood as spanning the years from eighteen to thirty-four, recognizing at the same time that there is no simple way to distinctly or defensibly use chronological age to determine when adulthood begins or is fully achieved. However, to the extent that much of the pertinent action occurs in the early thirties—when a growing number of young people are concluding training, are marrying, and are having children or even departing from home—we cannot ignore the first part of the fourth decade of life. This is not pleasant news for families who are called on to bear an increasingly large burden of support. But it is a new and undeniable reality, especially for parents. Of course, parents were also raised under a very different set of conditions and expectations, and their lives followed courses that differ dramatically from those of their children. These chasms may also be fertile ground for family strain and tension between parents and children.

THE OVERBURDENED FAMILY?
PARENTAL SUPPORT IN EARLY ADULTHOOD

Despite much ado to the contrary, the age of home-leaving has not changed greatly in the past several decades in the United States. Poor recent economic times, however, may create pressure on families to house adult children. Young adults in the United States have traditionally left home at early ages, moving to group quarters (college, military, or, increasingly, incarceration) or shared living quarters. Residential independence has been and continues to be one of the markers of attaining adulthood (see chaps. 2 and 3 for national and cross-national evidence).

Nonetheless, there is reason to believe that young adults may be getting more help from their families than they did a generation ago when youth completed education and entered the labor force at younger ages than today. As the period of early adulthood becomes more protracted, the family is the primary institution that absorbs the costs of greater investment in the next generation. Questions related to why and how this is so are analyzed, for example, by Schoeni and Ross (chap. 12). Based on data from the 1988 Panel Study of Income Dynamics, these authors estimate that parents provide an average of some $38,000 in material assistance—housing, food, educational expenses, or direct cash assistance—as each child moves into adulthood. This breaks down to $2,200 for every year between eighteen and thirty-four, though in reality, support diminishes as the child grows older. It is clear, however, that many poor or broken families cannot and do not provide this level of support to young adult children. These findings also clearly show that inequities among social classes in available supports and resources matter not only when children are little but also when children are big, as advantages and disadvantages accumulate over time.

Two important implications follow from findings such as these. If families are called on to invest more in young adult children, parents may eventually feel greater pressure to limit family size. Demographers use such an argument to explain declining fertility in postindustrial nations. As the private costs of children grow, most parents can afford fewer of them. The tendency is to "invest" more in one or two "high-quality" children (if any at all) than produce more of lower quality. Or, to say it less abstractly, parents begin to think about how many children they can afford to send to college or help out when they purchase their first house. Parents must plan for their own futures at a time when they must also support adult children and, in many cases, provide care to elderly parents—resulting in a significant mid-life "squeeze."

Unfortunately, we know little about the upward flow of resources from children to parents as children enter adulthood. Do parents realize more than symbolic gains from investments in their children? Strong evidence from the ongoing qualitative studies of the network suggests that many children do, indeed, reciprocate by extending time and sometimes money to parents. Many young adult children of immigrants, in particular, stay in the parental home well into their twenties out of a sense of filial responsibility, rather than (just) the other way around. Instrumental and emotional supports to parents are especially common among first- and second-generation immigrants who feel strong obligations to reciprocate support (Fuligni and Pedersen 2002; Rumbaut 2003).

A significant proportion of parents, however, are largely absent from the lives of young adults and unavailable to provide the needed support to help youth make a successful transition to adulthood. We have referred to these populations as "vulnerable" because they have special needs that may be beyond the capacities of parents and other family members to provide or because parents are unavailable, unable, or in some cases unwilling to provide needed assistance. As noted earlier, the special concerns of vulnerable populations traditionally viewed as being "at risk" are addressed, to some extent, in this book (Foster and Gifford, chap. 15; Settersten, chap. 16). But we can also think about the uneven distribution of parental support owing to more troubled circumstances such as parental divorce, poverty and unemployment among families, and psychological estrangement of parents and young adult children. The ability of families to manage this long and complex period clearly varies greatly by the resources they possess or those they can access through formal or informal ties.

A PATCHWORK OF INSTITUTIONS AND POLICIES

The family, of course, is not the only institution that provides for young adults. One of the working assumptions of the network is that young people receive a patchwork of institutional support as they leave adolescence. Virtually all adolescents attend school and many receive support from youth organizations during the early and middle teens. In the late teens, these supports begin to diverge or disappear altogether.

Privileged youth typically attend four-year residential colleges and often go on to graduate and professional programs, which extend the period of education and training well into the twenties. Universities are the best example of a full-fledged social institution that shapes the lives of young adults. In a certain sense, they are virtually total institutions, which provide shelter, directed activities, adult and peer support, health care, and entertainment. They are explicitly designed to bridge the family and the wider society and, increasingly, have been tailored to provide the sort of semiautonomy that characterizes early adulthood.

Similarly, the military and some volunteer programs that offer service opportunities are designed to care for young adults by providing a setting in which they can live, work, and learn. These particular social arrangements are well suited to the needs of young adults because they couple expectations and demands with guidance, mentoring, and support to give young adults a chance to acquire skills and experiences that foster a sense of competence.

Some work settings that are less deliberately tailored for young adults may offer some of the same features of sponsored independence. Apprenticeships and training programs are designed to do so, but many professional, white-collar, and blue-collar occupations also recognize that the process of entering the world of work has changed. One cannot simply assume that people learn work roles through advanced schooling; it is necessary to train people on the job.

Unfortunately, many young people do not get the benefit of this kind of institutional support as they move into their twenties. Roughly one out of seven youth drop out of school, and these youth typically work intermittently if at all. Many individuals who graduate and move immediately into jobs are left to their own devices to manage the school-to-work transition. Others flounder as they experiment in the labor force or try to find secure and remunerative employment. For these young people, the process of becoming an adult appears haphazard and ill designed.

Worse yet, youth who have been in more or less protected environments, such as foster care, special education, or juvenile justice systems, find themselves without safety nets of any kind, and often abruptly so. Legal and welfare policy has generally deemed eighteen as the age at which the responsibilities of the state end. The evidence provided in this book leads us to question the wisdom of that age boundary, as do the practices of most families. It is simply too early to stop investing in young people; most cannot make it on their own as they might have done a half century ago. Housing and medical insurance alone, for example, cannot be afforded at typical starting wages for most high school graduates. In other words, the vast majority of young people are not in a position to live on their own, let alone live with a partner or start a family.

When families cannot help out, as is often the case with vulnerable populations, youth are left unprotected as they age out of foster care, leave special education programs, or exit from juvenile justice facilities. Some government programs are extending assistance through twenty-one, but unfortunately, institutional support for young adults is thin if it exists at all. Foster and Gifford (chap. 15) point to the striking special needs of youth with disabilities, emotional problems, those ensnared in the criminal justice system, or those who do not have a stable family or lack kinship support. They also highlight the fact that many standard surveys do not contain data on these populations and that we have much to learn about the special challenges they face as they move into adulthood. For this reason, the network has undertaken a separate but parallel examination of some of the largest and most vulnerable populations: young adults who were, as adolescents, in the mental health, foster care, juvenile justice, or criminal justice systems, homeless or runaways, in special education, or chronically ill or physically disabled. These findings will be published in the book *On Your Own without a Net: The Transition to Adulthood for Vulnerable Populations* (Osgood, Foster, Flanagan, and Ruth forthcoming).

Hovering just above vulnerable populations are youth caught in the middle—those whose families are middle-income but well short of affluent.

These youth are also often left to manage on their own, receiving no support from the state and only very modest help from their overburdened families and having to juggle both work and school responsibilities. As a result, they, too, remain in school into their late twenties and early thirties attempting to piece together adequate credentials.

TOWARD STRONGER INSTITUTIONS AND INDIVIDUAL CAPACITIES

The evidence documented in this book suggests that significant mismatches exist between the emerging and varied pathways to adulthood that are now taken and the institutions and policies that affect young people. How might the patchwork of often outdated institutions and policies be rewoven to smooth entry into adult life? How might the personal skills and resources of young people be improved so that they might better navigate the transition? These are the questions at the heart of the concluding chapter on social policy (Settersten, chap. 16). Effective institutions and policies must be responsive to both the longer and more complex nature of this juncture. Smoothing the transition will bring immediate payoffs for individuals, families, and societies and have cumulative payoffs over time. A significant challenge to overcome is to break up the lockstep nature of education and work emphasized in institutions and policies and develop strategies to better link and actively combine educational and work experiences.

Community colleges are a key institution for new interventions. They touch large numbers and a wide variety of young people, serve many purposes, are flexible, and offer connections to a range of potential career paths (see also Shaw and Jacobs 2003). Yet community colleges have been the stepchild of higher education, undernourished and largely invisible to most researchers. The network, in collaboration with Manpower Demonstration Research Corporation, has designed an experimental program to increase the financial, social, and psychological services offered at community colleges in an effort to provide these students with a set of services that more closely match those received by students at four-year residential colleges. We are especially interested in fostering attachment to community colleges so that they act less as "revolving doors" and more as routes to further education and employment. This will be a significant initiative of our network in the coming years, and it is an important response to the challenges faced by vulnerable populations.

What is also clear is that safety nets need to be constructed or strengthened for all young people. Some highly desirable outcomes, such as having relatively few young adults who are neither in education nor employed, or are in unstable or low-quality jobs, can only be achieved if young people are integrated and retained in mainstream education and training; if dropouts are closely tracked and intensely supported; and if strategies for responding to vulnerable populations include early intervention (see also Organization for Economic Co-Operation and Development 2000).

This chapter has repeatedly emphasized the fact that families of origin are a (if not the) central safety net for many young people—and a serious risk for many others. Significant efforts should therefore be aimed at building family relationships and resources—in both the families from which young people come and the families they create. Workplaces, too, must be restructured so that they allow young people—indeed, all adults—to better manage work and family responsibilities. Strategies such as on-site affordable child care; flextime; part-time parity in wages, benefits, training, and advancement opportunities; a handful of paid days for family and medical leave; and limits on mandatory overtime will go a long way toward easing the challenges of early adult transitions (see also Heymann 2000; Williams 2000).

In today's world, career information and guidance—in high schools, colleges and universities, workplaces, and families—must be viewed as essential for all young people. These services should provide accurate information on future educational options, develop young people's understanding and realistic knowledge of the world of work, assist them with job searches and choices, help them find high-quality child care, and identify strategies for balancing family, education, and work.

The new policy agenda outlined in the final chapter will require considerable public investment. It will also come with an understandable concern about immediate financial costs. These costs, however, must be considered against a recognition that low levels of investment up front will bring significant psychological, social, and economic costs in the long run (see also Cohen 1998; Coles 2002). Many of the changes evidenced in this book point to both new opportunities and risks in moving into adulthood. It is our hope that these chapters, taken singly or as a whole, will provide a fresh and deepened understanding of the complexity of early adult life and, at the same time, a humbling appreciation of the vast scope of the topic, how little we know, and how much work remains to be done if young people are to navigate successfully the new frontiers of adult life in the twenty-first century.

REFERENCES

Ariès, Phillipe. 1962. *Centuries of Childhood: A Social History of Family Life*. Translated by R. Baldick. New York: Random House.

Arnett, Jeffrey Jensen. 2000. Emerging Adulthood: A Theory of Development from the Late Teens through the Twenties. *American Psychologist* 55(5):469–80.

Booth, Alan, Ann C. Crouter, and Michael J. Shanahan, eds. 1999. *Transitions to Adulthood in a Changing Economy: No Work, No Family, No Future?* Westport, CT: Praeger Publishers.

Brown, B. Bradford, Reed W. Larson, and T. S. Saraswathi, eds. 2002. *The World's Youth: Adolescence in Eight Regions of the Globe.* New York: Cambridge University Press.

Buchmann, Marlis. 1989. *The Script of Life in Modern Society: Entry into Adulthood in a Changing World.* Chicago: University of Chicago Press.

Cohen, M. A. 1998. The Monetary Value of Saving a High-Risk Youth. *Journal of Quantitative Criminology,* 14(1):5–33.

Coles, Bob. 2002. *Youth and Social Policy: Youth Citizenship and Young Careers.* London: Routledge.

Corijn, Martine, and Erik Klijzing, eds. 2001. *Transitions to Adulthood in Europe.* Edited by Martine Corijn and Erik Klijzing. Boston: Kluwer Academic Publishers.

Fuligni, Andrew J., and Pedersen, Sara. 2002. Family Obligation and the Transition to Young Adulthood. *Developmental Psychology* 38(5):856–68.

Furstenberg, Frank F., Jr., ed. 2002. *Early Adulthood in Cross-National Perspective.* Annals of the American Academy of Political and Social Science 580, March. London: Sage Publications.

Gibbs, Nancy. 2002. Making Time for a Baby. *Time* April 15.

Hall, G. Stanley. 1904. *Adolescence: Its Psychology and Its Relations to Physiology, Anthropology, Sociology, Sex, Crime, Religion and Education.* New York: D. Appleton & Co.

Heymann, Jody. 2000. *The Widening Gap: Why America's Working Families Are in Jeopardy and What Can Be Done About It.* New York: Basic Books.

Kett, Joseph F. 1977. *Rites of Passage: Adolescence in America: 1790 to the Present.* New York: Basic Books.

Larson, Reed W., Bradford B. Brown, and Jeylan T. Mortimer, eds. 2002. *Adolescents' Preparation for the Future: Perils and Promises.* Ann Arbor, MI: Society for Research on Adolescence.

Modell, John. 1989. *Into One's Own: From Youth to Adulthood, 1920–1975.* Berkeley: University of California Press.

Mortimer, Jeylan T., and Reed W. Larson, eds. 2002. *The Changing Adolescent Experience: Societal Trends and the Transition to Adulthood.* New York: Cambridge University Press.

Organization for Economic Co-Operation and Development. 2000. *From Initial Education to Working Life: Making Transitions Work.* Danvers, MA: Organization for Economic Co-Operation and Development.

Osgood, D. Wayne, E. Michael Foster, Connie A. Flanagan, and Gretchen R. Ruth, eds. Forthcoming. *On Your Own without a Net: The Transition to Adulthood for Vulnerable Populations*. Chicago: University of Chicago Press.

Rumbaut, Rubén G. 2003. Legacies: The Story of the Immigrant Second Generation in Early Adulthood. The Sorokin Lecture, 74th annual meeting of the Pacific Sociological Association, Pasadena, California, April 5.

Shaw, Kathleen M., and Jerry A. Jacobs, eds. 2003. *Community Colleges: New Environments, New Directions*. Thousand Oaks, CA, and London: Sage Publications.

Tyre, Peg, with Karen Springer and Julie Scelfo. 2002. Bringing up Adultolescents. *Newsweek*, March 25.

Williams, Joan. 2000. *Unbending Gender: Why Work and Family Conflict and What to Do about It*. New York: Oxford University Press.

PART TWO

COMPARISONS OVER TIME AND PLACE

*Cross-Sectional and
Cross-National Studies*

CHAPTER 2

THE TRANSITION TO ADULTHOOD DURING THE TWENTIETH CENTURY

Race, Nativity, and Gender

ELIZABETH FUSSELL AND FRANK F. FURSTENBERG JR.

This chapter offers a broad overview of the experience of youth from 1900 up to the present and provides a context for the subsequent chapters in this volume. We will describe changes in the experience of youth between the ages of sixteen and thirty who lived between 1900 and 2000, distinguishing between men and women, native-born and foreign-born individuals, and native-born whites and blacks.[1] We relate changes in the combinations of adult statuses that average young people in these groups experience both to historical events and to structural and cultural change.

From the vantage point offered by U.S. census data, we can see that over the course of the century the ages at which young people fill the roles associated with adulthood have changed, generally moving toward later ages but also involving different combinations of statuses. Three trends are primarily responsible for the later transition to adulthood and the greater variety of status combinations held between ages sixteen and thirty: the prolongation of the period of education, the growth of a period of nonfamily living after leaving the parental household and before forming one's own family, and the delay in the age by which young people marry and have children. Furthermore, the small but growing percentage of women having

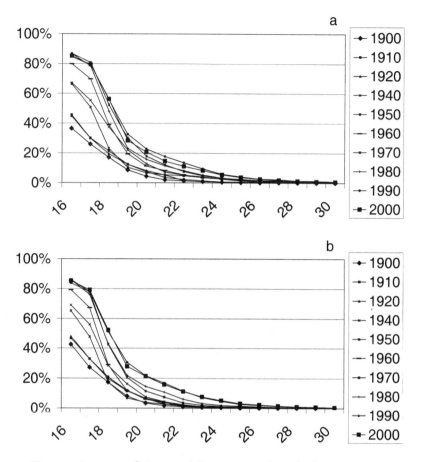

Figure 2.1. Percentage of (*a*) men and (*b*) women attending school who are living in their parent's household, are single, and are childless

children without marriage is also contributing to the greater variety of status combinations young people hold.

As more young people, regardless of gender, race, or nativity, participate in secondary education through their teens, young people leave home at later ages. This is evident from the growth in the percentage of single childless men and women living with their parents and attending school at all ages throughout the century but especially after 1960 (see fig. 2.1). In the second half of the century, young people took a greater variety of pathways after finishing secondary education than they did in the earlier half. This has been partially due to increasing participation in higher education, which offers young adults an alternative to employment that was not widely available in the first half of the century.

Furthermore, the norms surrounding the appropriate age for marriage and childbearing have changed radically over the century. At the beginning of the century the movement into marriage and childbearing was relatively late, especially for young men. This pattern shifted after World War II, when the economic prosperity that the country experienced from 1945 through the 1960s encouraged young men and women to enter into marriage and child-bearing at very early ages. Since then young people have increasingly been delaying marriage and childbearing (for a variety of reasons we will explore here and elsewhere throughout the vol.) so that by 1990 and 2000 the per-centage of young people reporting being married had diminished at all ages, shifting the timing of marriage into unprecedented older ages (see fig. 2.2).

As men and women delay marriage and childbearing but continue to leave their parents homes in their late teens or early twenties they are more likely to live in nonfamily situations, either as single heads of households or in-group living arrangements. Although living in nonfamily arrangements was not uncommon at the beginning of the century, particularly among the foreign born, the increase in this type of living arrangement has grown as-tonishingly since 1970 (see fig. 2.3). This phenomenon has caused some to identify a new stage in the life course in which nonfamily living is a norma-tive, though mostly temporary life stage (Arnett 2000).

While the aforementioned patterns of delayed marriage and child-bearing apply to more and more young people, a small but increasing num-ber, young women in particular, are forming families by having children without marrying. This represents just one of the ways, though certainly a controversial one, in which young people are pursuing new pathways to fam-ily formation since 1970 (see fig. 2.4). As young people adapt their lives to the more complex world in which we live, it becomes more difficult to say at which point or through which combination of statuses they have reached adulthood. There are more paths to take through life and few maps to guide young people, especially when they pursue nontraditional routes. In the re-mainder of this chapter, we will explore further the trends that we have il-lustrated in these introductory paragraphs.

STRUCTURING THE YOUNG ADULT LIFE COURSE

Sociologists and demographers have a tradition of studying the transition to adulthood according to the sociodemographic statuses a person has

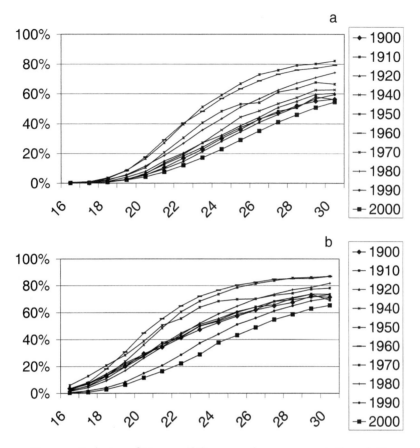

Figure 2.2. Percentage of (a) men and (b) women who are ever-married household heads with or without their own children in the household

achieved by a given age, such as student, worker, household head, spouse, and parent. Here and throughout much of the Western world, kinship arrangements have long favored independent living between the generations. Thus, growing up inevitably involves leaving the natal household, and doing so typically requires economic independence—the wherewithal to live in a separate domicile and to form a separate family unit. In turn, gaining a strong enough foothold in the economy to establish a separate residence or support a family requires completion of education and often some job experience. Thus, the life course is culturally scripted but structured in part by economic and social resources. Individuals acquire expectations, often early in life, of when and how these arrangements are to occur. A social timetable

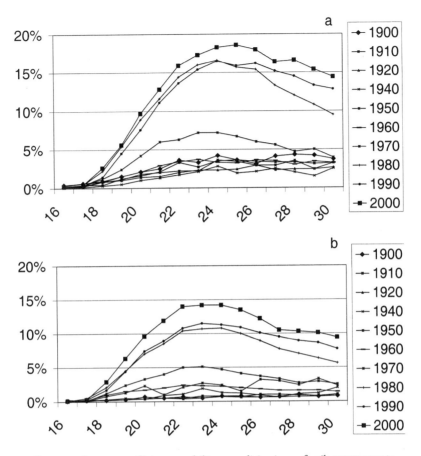

Figure 2.3. Percentage of (*a*) men and (*b*) women living in nonfamily arrangements who are single and childless

for growing up exists that is culturally prescribed but flexible enough to take account of economic and demographic vicissitudes. Individuals learn this timetable both by watching what others do and by taking cues from institutions that are gatekeepers of the life course (Heinz 2001).

The fluidity of the timing and sequence of the life course suggests that institutions and actors operate in a contingent fashion—forming provisional norms that may be altered under certain conditions. As we shall see later in this chapter, there are some remarkably rapid shifts in the timing and sequencing of the life course. Within a decade and certainly within the span of several decades, conventional ways of behaving can be radically revised. The dynamics of life-course reorganization, involving information ex-

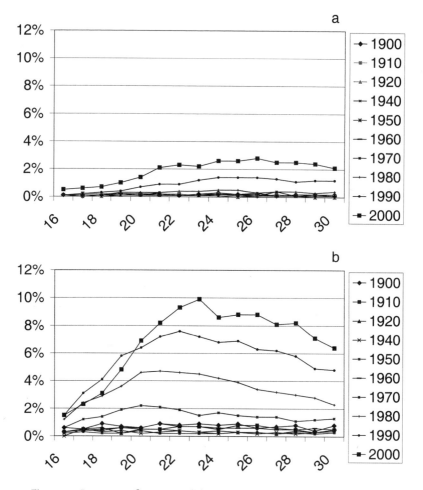

Figure 2.4. Percentage of (*a*) men and (*b*) women who are never-married with their own children in the household

change and situational adaptations, have not been adequately modeled. It is clear that this remains a great challenge for developing a genuine theory of the life course and the methodological tools to test such a theory.

Research on age structuring has attempted to understand why and how, on average, statuses at particular ages shift over time and differ between men and women and social groups based on race and nativity. Social institutions, such as schools and labor markets, structure the life course through age-based rules, as well as social norms. Families also structure the life course, though age-based rules are less easily observed or enforced. As the state and other social institutions have become more highly developed over the course of the twentieth century, people's lives have become more standardized (Kohli 1986; Settersten 1997, 2002). At the same time, more flexible institutions and less strict enforcement of age norms have allowed for more variation in the sequences of statuses one holds during the life course, particularly in early adulthood (Settersten 1997, 2002; Shanahan 2000). External shocks to the social structure, such as wars, economic depressions and booms, and ideological shifts also affect the age structure of lives. Furthermore, tensions within the age structure itself can cause shifts in the timing of social status acquisitions (Kertzer 1989; Modell, Furstenberg, and Hershberg 1976). Thus, in examining the changes in the organization of early adulthood during the past century we can begin to see how this period of life has been rearranged because of dramatic changes in education and family formation patterns (Ellwood and Jencks 2004).

Researchers have not yet developed a full repertoire of measures for describing the life course, however. Demography has provided most of what we know. The order, timing, duration, spacing, and density of life events are useful elements, but they have generally been applied to single transitions, typically one or two at a time. Leaving the parental home (Goldscheider and Goldscheider 1999), finishing school and starting employment (DiPrete and McManus 1996; Kerckhoff 1993, 2002; Mortimer and Johnson 1998), and marrying and having children (Thornton, Axinn and Teachman 1995; Tucker and Mitchell-Kernana 1995; Uhlenberg 1974) are the usual topics of study. Our first objective is to describe combinations of all of these statuses as a means of drawing a representative picture of youth and young adulthood throughout the twentieth century, linking historical moments with changes in the young adult life course. We look at statuses in conjunction with one another because we assume that each transition influences the probability of others occurring. Our second goal is to explore differences within the U.S. population in the combinations of adult transitions. In particular, we are interested in the separate and perhaps converging course of early adulthood among women and men, blacks and whites, foreign born and native born.

While our research follows in the tradition of understanding the timing and congruity of the acquisition of adult statuses, it opens up new terrain by using a standardized historical database not only to follow changes in the transition to adulthood over time but to compare groups that were typically excluded from life-course studies. Remarkably little research has focused on the experience of "average" black youth, instead, focusing on those at risk of delinquency (Maynard 1995). Likewise, few have looked at the experience of the foreign born, who experience the additional transition of international migration in their life course.[2] In addition, the life-course experiences of women, especially black women and foreign-born women, has been neglected except for issues relating to marriage and childbearing. By bringing race, nativity, and gender into the life-course perspective, this project advances our understanding of the similarities and differences in the transition to adulthood over the course of the century. In doing so we can also gauge the extent to which the young adult life course has become increasingly structured or more individualized by our social institutions.

DATA AND METHOD

To examine the experiences of youth in their transition to adulthood, we built a database from the 1900, 1910, 1920, 1940, 1950, 1960, 1970, 1980, 1990, and 2000 censuses, harmonized in the Integrated Public Use Microdata Series (IPUMS) (Ruggles and Sobek 1997).[3] The gender, nativity, and race composition of each of the censuses and surveys differs over the course of the century; therefore we examine six groups according to gender, nativity, and race (table 2.1). We look at the percentage of the gender/race/nativity group in a particular combination of statuses at a given age at one-decade intervals to follow change in the life course. For example, by examining sixteen-year-olds who are attending school, living in their parents' home, and remaining single and childless we see that in all groups the percentage in this status

TABLE 2.1

CENSUS AND SURVEY SAMPLE SIZES BY RACE AND NATIVITY

		MEN				WOMEN		
YEAR	NUMBER	% WHITE	% BLACK	% FOREIGN	NUMBER	% WHITE	% BLACK	% FOREIGN
1900	53,062	74.2	12.2	13.6	52,591	74.4	13.0	12.6
1910	53,648	71.1	10.4	18.5	51,300	74.3	12.1	13.6
1920	136,589	76.9	10.3	12.8	139,252	77.1	11.5	11.4
1940	24,191	86.7	9.8	3.5	24,844	85.7	10.7	3.6
1950	51,068	86.7	10.5	2.7	54,706	85.8	11.2	3.0
1960	168,628	86.9	10.5	2.7	174,199	85.3	11.5	3.1
1970	227,109	85.5	10.7	3.7	236,213	84.2	11.6	4.2
1980	300,329	81.5	11.8	6.7	301,953	80.6	13.0	6.4
1990	276,988	78.4	10.7	10.9	274,688	78.5	12.0	9.5
2000	260,460	71.1	12.1	16.7	253,440	71.7	13.4	14.9

combination has increased over the century. This represents a long-term standardization of the early life course so that by 2000 this combination describes nearly 90% of sixteen-year-olds. We examine youth in each decade at ages sixteen, twenty, twenty-five, and thirty to describe shifts in the young adult life course over the twentieth century.

Our analytic strategy is to capture as much variation in the combination of statuses experienced during the young adult life course as we can with as few categories as possible. We examine whether individuals are enrolled in school, in the labor force, living in their parents' household, living as a head of household, living in group quarters or a nonfamily household, whether they are ever married, and whether their own children live in the household.[4] We combine these statuses into ten different categories and a residual category that captures all those who do not fall into one of the others. The percentages of each of the age groups that have a particular combination of statuses exclusive of others are included in tabular form in the appendix (tables 2.A1–3 and 2.B1–3).

The census has measured a set of characteristics of individuals rather consistently, and the IPUMS data has harmonized the censuses to make them comparable. We have chosen to analyze groups based on race, nativity, and gender. These ascribed statuses are stable over the life course and therefore are a consistent way of measuring group differences. We do not use measures of acquired statuses, such as place or region of residence, educational attainment, and socioeconomic status, because they change over the life course and would lead to instability in our groups.

Life-course analysis typically uses longitudinal data that follows individuals over the life course. The advantage of this data set is continuity over the course of the century, something that longitudinal data sets lack. It is a comparative-historical analysis of life-course transitions rather than an analysis focused on a particular birth cohort during a particular period of history. As such, our questions differ from those of typical life-course analyses. Rather than focusing on the consequences of early life-course decisions for later individual outcomes, we ask about cohort experiences and differences between them. This allows us to view differences by gender, race, and nativity in the experience of the transition to adulthood.

KEY EVENTS AND TRENDS IN THE LIVES OF YOUTH

The World Trade Center attack, the political unrest of the 1960s, and World War II have all been important formative events for young people. Long-term changes that are more gradual and less easily recognized also shape the lives of young people. As we consider the changes in the transition to adulthood that occurred throughout the twentieth century, it is important to keep both of these phenomena in mind. In table 2.2 we show how ages, cohorts, and periods intersect in our data and describe briefly how these key events and trends may have influenced youth at a particular moment in our history. The social history of distinct generations is one that has been told before and will continue to be told (e.g., Elder [1974] 1999; Modell 1989; Shanahan 2000). Here, we suggest which events and trends have played a role in changing the transition to adulthood, ones that may influence how the story is told for recent generations of youth.

It is more difficult to recognize long-term trends than historical events that are fixed in time, and it is worth pointing out how some of these trends relate to the lives of youth. For example, life expectancy at birth has nearly doubled during the time period considered, rising from 47.3 years in 1900 to 77.1 years in 2000 (see "demographics," table 2.3). This is associated with the increased general health of the population but in particular, with the control of childhood infectious diseases in the first half of the century and the discovery of treatments for degenerative diseases of middle age during the second half. The population as a whole is much healthier today than ever before.

The lengthening of life is also associated with the lengthening of the period of preparation for adulthood, as youth spend more time in school. The percentages of the population age twenty-five and older who have completed high school or four years of college have increased steadily since 1940 when the government began collecting educational statistics ("educational attainment," table 2.3). Today's youth are more educated than any previous cohort: in 2000, among those aged twenty-five to twenty-nine, 88.1% had finished high school, and 29.1% had a bachelor's degree or more (National Center for Education Statistics 2001). This figure, however, masks persistent racial and ethnic inequalities in educational attainment. For native-born whites ages twenty-five to twenty-nine, 94% have completed high school and 34% have completed four or more years of college. The comparable figures for blacks are 86.8% and 17.8%, respectively, and even lower for Hispanic youth, 62.8% and 9.7%. Young people with higher levels of education have been able to take advantage of the technology revolution and the restructuring of the U.S. economy; but education, or lack thereof, also accounts for the growing divide between the middle class and the working class, as well as between racial and ethnic groups (Farley 1996; Levy 1998). Over the course of the century, the development of institutions to provide for the health and education of the population has fundamentally improved the lives of young people, though inequality in these basic entitlements continues.

The economic institutions shaping our daily lives have also been transformed in basic ways. Our economy has shifted from an agricultural base to a manufacturing base and, then, to a service base. Thus, young men and women have made their livings in very different ways from one generation to the next ("employment statistics," table 2.3). Agricultural employment has shrunk steadily to just 2.7% of the labor force in 2000, while manufacturing employment has been declining since the 1960s. The service sector and "other workers," including public employees, construction workers, and transportation workers, now account for two-thirds of the labor force. These structural shifts in the economy drew people to the cities; in 1900, 40% of the population lived in cities, compared with 80% in 2000 ("demographics," table 2.3). Obscured in these figures are the growth of suburban areas and the movement of the middle class out of central cities, a shift that residentially segregated the poor and the nonpoor, as well as blacks and whites. Throughout the century, we find the newest arrivals to this country concentrated in urban areas in just a few destinations, such as New York City, Chicago, Los Angeles, and Miami, making the racial and ethnic composition of the United States quite varied from region to region and city to city. In addition, women were drawn into the labor force as the economy grew and diversified, increasing their rate of participation from 18% in 1900 to 60% in 2000. Thus, as the economy changed and grew, the composition of the labor force became more diverse demographically.

The racial and ethnic diversity of the U.S. population is a natural outcome of its history as an immigrant-receiving nation. Western Europeans settled the country, also bringing Africans as slaves. Thus, prior to 1880 native-born whites and blacks made up most of the population, especially as Native American people were displaced and often died through war, disease, and famine. From 1880 to 1920, the United States experienced large waves of immigrant flows from southern and eastern Europe to feed the economy's demand for laborers. Between 1920 and 1965 immigration was severely limited to a small number of western European immigrants. After 1965 when migration policy was reformed, migration flows grew again, mostly coming from Asian and Latin American countries ("population composition," table 2.3). In the following analyses we see that native-born whites and blacks and the foreign born did not have equal access to health care, education, or employment. As we assess how the context of the transition to adulthood varied between periods, we must also bear in mind that the experience of becoming adult depends on one's group identity, as well as the historical period in which one comes of age. The trends described above help us to understand the social forces shaping the changes in the status

TABLE 2.2

COHORTS, PERIODS, AND AGES (ADAPTED FROM FARLEY 1996)

YEARS OF BIRTH	COHORT NAME	BECAME YOUNG ADULTS (16–30)	KEY EVENTS AT THAT TIME	AGES IN CENSUS YEAR										
				1900	1910	1920	1930	1940	1950	1960	1970	1980	1990	2000
1976– 85	Millennial generation	1992– 2015	The information era: economic growth and global politics											16–24
1966– 75	Gen X	1982– 2005	The Reagan era: economic polarization, political conservatism										16–24	25–30
1956– 65	Late baby boomers	1972– 95	The Watergate era: economic recession, employment restructuring									16–24	25–30	
1946– 55	Early baby boomers	1962– 85	The hippies: social movements, campus revolts								16–24	25–30		
1936– 45	Happy days generation	1952– 75	Family and conformity: the							16–24	25–30			

Birth years	Generation	Historical era	16–24	25–30
1926–35	Happy days/greatest generation	baby boom and the Cold War/McCarthy era		
1942–65		Family and conformity: the baby boom and the Cold War/McCarthy era	16–24	25–30
1916–25	Greatest generation/children of the great depression			
1932–55		Hard times: economic depression and World War II	16–24	25–30
1906–15	Children of the great depression			
1922–45		Hard times: economic depression and World War II	16–24	25–30
1896–1905	Lost generation			
1912–35		World War I and roaring twenties, prohibition	16–24	25–30
1886–95	. . .			
1902–25		The age of invention and World War I	16–24	25–30
1876–85	. . .			
1892–1915		The age of invention, urbanization	16–24	25–30

TABLE 2.3

LIFE AS THEY KNEW IT

	1900	1910	1920	1930	1940	1950	1960	1970	1980	1990	2000
Educational attainment:											
% completed high school (age 25+):											
All races[a]	...	13.5	16.4	19.1	24.5	34.3	41.1	55.2	68.6	77.6	83.4
Male[a]	...	...	...	...	22.7	32.6	39.6	55.0	69.2	77.7	83.5
Female[a]	...	...	...	...	26.3	36.0	42.5	55.4	68.1	77.5	83.4
White[a]	...	...	...	...	26.1	36.4	43.2	57.4	71.9	81.4	87.7
Male[a]	...	...	...	...	24.2	34.6	41.6	57.2	72.4	81.6	87.7
Female[a]	...	...	...	...	28.1	38.2	44.7	57.7	71.5	81.3	87.7
Black[a]	...	...	...	...	7.7	13.7	21.7	36.1	51.4	66.2	77.4
Male[a]	...	...	...	...	6.9	12.6	20.0	35.4	51.2	65.8	77.2
Female[a]	...	...	...	...	8.4	14.7	23.1	36.6	51.5	66.5	77.5
% completing college (age 25+):											
All races[a]	...	2.7	3.3	3.9	4.6	6.2	7.7	11.0	17.0	21.3	25.2
Male[a]	...	...	...	...	5.5	7.3	9.7	14.1	20.9	24.4	27.5
Female[a]	...	...	...	...	3.8	5.2	5.8	8.2	13.6	18.4	23.1
White[a]	...	...	...	...	4.9	6.6	8.1	11.6	18.4	23.1	27.7
Male[a]	...	...	...	...	5.9	7.9	10.3	15.0	22.8	26.7	30.6
Female[a]	...	...	...	...	4.0	5.4	6.0	8.6	14.4	19.8	25.0
Black[a]	...	...	...	...	1.3	2.2	3.5	6.1	7.9	11.3	15.5
Male[a]	...	...	...	...	1.4	2.1	3.5	6.8	7.7	11.9	14.3
Female[a]	...	...	...	...	1.2	2.4	3.6	5.6	8.1	10.8	16.5

Employment:											
Unemployment rate[b]	5.0	5.9	5.2	8.7	14.6	5.3	5.5	4.9	7.1[c]	5.6[c]	4.0[c]
Minimum wage (real dollars)[d]	...	...	...	...	.30	.75	1.00	1.60	3.10	3.80	5.15
% of women in labor force[e]	18.8	21.5	21.4	22.0	25.8	29.0	37.7	43.3	51.5	57.5	60.0
Household characteristics:											
Median family income (real dollars)[e]						3,319	5,620	9,867	21,023	35,353	48,950
White[e]	...	...	...	...	...	3,445	5,835	10,236	21,904	36,915	51,224
Black[e]	...	...	...	...	...	1,869	3,230	6,279	12,674	21,423	31,778
% children in single female headed households[f]	...	...	...	...	15.3	15.0	10.0	10.9	18.0	21.6	17.9
Demographics:											
Expectation of life at birth[e]	47.3	50.0	54.1	59.7	62.9	68.2	69.7	70.9	73.7	75.4	77.1
White[e]	47.6	50.3	54.9	61.4	64.2	69.1	70.6	71.7	74.4	76.1	77.7
Men[e]	46.6	48.6	54.4	59.7	62.1	66.5	67.4	68.0	70.7	72.7	74.8
Women[e]	48.7	52.0	55.6	63.5	66.6	72.2	74.1	75.6	78.7	79.4	80.4
Black[e]	33.0	35.6	45.3	48.1	53.1	60.8	63.6	61.4	68.1	69.1	72.4
Men[e]	32.5	33.8	45.5	47.3	51.5	59.1	61.1	60.0	63.8	64.5	68.9
Women[e]	33.5	37.5	45.2	49.2	54.9	62.9	66.3	68.3	72.5	73.6	75.6
Marriage rate per 1,000 population[e]	9.3	10.3	12.0	9.2	12.1	11.1	8.5	10.6	10.6	9.8	...
Divorce rate per 1,000 population[e]	.7	.8	1.6	1.6	2.0	2.6	2.2	3.5	5.2	4.7	...
Birth rate per 1,000 population[e]	32.3	30.1	23.7	18.9	17.9	24.1	23.7	18.4	15.9	16.7	14.5
White[e]	...	...	23.5	18.6	17.5	23.0	22.7	17.4	15.1	15.8	...
Black[e]	...	...	27.0	21.6	21.7	33.3	31.9	25.3	21.3	22.4	...
Immigration rate per 1,000 population[e]	...	10.4	5.7	3.5	.4	.7	1.5	1.7	2.1	3.1	3.6

TABLE 2.3

(CONTINUED)

	1900	1910	1920	1930	1940	1950	1960	1970	1980	1990	2000
Population characteristics:											
% urban[e]	39.6	45.6	51.2	56.1	56.5	64.0	69.9	73.6	73.7	75.2	80.3
% African-American, not Hispanic[e]	11.6	10.7	9.9	9.7	9.8	9.9	10.5	11.1	11.8	12.3	12.8
% Euro-American, not Hispanic[e]	87.9	88.9	89.7	89.8	89.8	89.3	88.6	87.6	85.9	83.9	82.9
% Hispanic[e]	LT	LT	LT	LT	LT	LT	LT	LT	6.4	9.0	11.9
% American Indian, Aleutian Islander[e]	.3	.3	.2	.3	.3	LT	LT	LT	.6	.8	.9
% Asian[e]	.1	.2	.2	.2	.2	LT	LT	LT	1.6	3.0	4.1
% foreign born[e]	13.6	14.7	13.2	11.6	8.8	6.9	5.4	4.8	6.2	7.9	. . .
Total population (millions)[e]	76.0	92.0	105.7	122.8	131.7	151.3	179.3	203.3	226.5	248.7	281.4

Note. LT = less than 0.1%. Ellipses dots indicate no information available.

[a] U.S. Department of Education 2001.

[b] U.S. Department of Commerce, Bureau of the Census 1995, 1900–2000.

[c] Littman 1998.

[d] Bureau of Labor Statistics 2002.

[e] U.S. Department of Commerce, Bureau of the Census 1900–2000.

[f] Littman 1998; U.S. Department of Commerce, Bureau of the Census 1900–2000.

combinations of men and women in different race and nativity groups at various ages. In the following analyses we also see the extent to which the life course for all groups has become more standardized at some ages and more individualized at other ages across the course of the century.

THE STANDARDIZATION OF THE LIFE COURSE
THROUGH SECONDARY EDUCATION: SIXTEEN-YEAR-OLDS

The lives of sixteen-year-olds in 1900 and 2000 could hardly be more different. In 1900 the term "adolescent" had barely been coined, much less popularized (Chudacoff 1989). Today, teens are often seen as a completely different "tribe" with their own culture, social institutions, and, some would argue, their own language (Hersch 1999). The evolution of this age group toward their present separate status has been supported by the institutionalization of secondary education, as well as the normative expectation that teenagers will continue living as dependents in their parents' home and not take on adult roles and responsibilities such as marriage and parenthood. Thus, we see that throughout the century, sixteen-year-olds are increasingly likely to be enrolled in school, living in their parents' home, single, and childless.

This standardization of adolescence has occurred for all gender/race/nativity groups but has reached different levels for each group (see the tables in the appendix). Progress toward the standardization of the life course of sixteen-year-old white men and women has been steady. The status combination of attending school, living in the parental home, and remaining single and childless characterized only 41% and 46% of white sixteen-year-old men and women, respectively, in 1900 but grew to about 70% of these groups by 1940, finally reaching about 90% by 2000.[5] Progress has been slower for native-born black sixteen-year-olds. In 1900 only 22% of single childless sixteen-year-old black men and 33% of such women lived at home and attended school. The percentages in this status combination grew steadily, especially after 1960 when the civil rights movement brought attention to the integration and improvement of public schools and emphasized the value of education for African Americans. However, in 1980 the percentage of sixteen-year-old black men and women in this status combination plateaued at around 81% and 78%, respectively, declining somewhat thereafter. Foreign-born sixteen-year-old men and women experienced rapid growth in this combination of statuses: they started from levels of about 9% and 15%, respectively, in 1900 and rose to more than 80% in 1970. Since 1970 the percentage of foreign-born sixteen-year-olds in this combination has decreased—a change that is associated with the arrival of the new wave of post-1965 immigrants, who are more likely to be non-European and therefore less easily integrated into American society than were the foreign-born sixteen-year-olds in the years between 1920 and 1970. In 2000, only 71% of foreign-born men and 76% of foreign-born women lived in their parents' homes while attending school and remaining single and childless. While levels vary in important ways between groups, this combination of statuses accounts for the majority of all sixteen-year-olds; only a few other combinations account for the remaining percentage.

Mandatory secondary education until the age of sixteen has meant that fewer and fewer sixteen-year-olds living in their parents' households are exclusively in the labor force or are neither in school nor at work. Furthermore, the percentage of single childless sixteen-year-olds who live in non-family households or institutions while working or attending school has nearly disappeared in the last third of the twentieth century. However, the percentage of sixteen-year-olds who do not fit into one of the ten predefined status combinations considered in this analysis persists at around 5% of native-born white men and women and has risen to between 15% and 20% among native-born black and foreign-born men and women. Apparently, the social institutions that structure the teenage years are not as effective at shaping the lives of young native-born black and foreign-born men and women as they are for native-born white men and women.

THE INDIVIDUALIZATION OF THE TRANSITION TO ADULTHOOD: TWENTY- AND TWENTY-FIVE-YEAR-OLDS

The twentieth century witnessed two revolutions that reorganized work and family life. First, the technology revolution raised the importance of technical knowledge in the labor market and increased demand for technical training. Second, the gender revolution lowered the barriers to entry into the workplace for women and created space for more egalitarian gender relationships within the home and work (Farley 1996; Levy 1998). These revolutions upset the institutions and social norms that had guided the transition to adulthood. For men of western European origin, the ability to support a family, in other words, stable employment, has been a necessary precursor to family formation (Modell 1989; Stone 1977). While most men were able to obtain such a situation by age twenty in the industrializing economy of the first half of the twentieth century, this became more difficult as the economy was transformed into a technology- and information-based economy, especially in the last three decades of the century. The expansion of education and the developing economy reinforced one another and demanded that young men, and increasingly young women, gain the education and skills necessary to participate productively in the changing, technology-driven economy.

The gendered division of labor, what work men and women perform, and where work occurs, has shifted along with changes in the economic structure of society. In colonial America, men and women were more likely to share family and productive work, which often occurred in the same location (Pleck 1987). As the United States industrialized, men went to work in factories and offices, away from their homes, and women specialized in domestic work (Welter 1966). This Victorian-era separation of male and female work lives dominated the growing middle class but was untenable for many families. The first wave of feminists in the 1910s and 1920s challenged the "separate spheres" ideology, and the Great Depression of the 1930s and World War II drew women into the labor force out of necessity (Goldin 1990). During the 1950s, the strict gender division of labor seemed to reemerge with the marriage and baby booms, but in the 1960s feminists again challenged this ideology. This social movement, and the decline of men's wages as the economic boom slowed, drew women into the labor force again. Since then, women's labor force participation has steadily increased. These gendered norms generally apply to the middle class and above but are more flexible under difficult economic circumstances.

These changes in work life had implications for young people's family decisions, though there is no consensus on the causal relationships between changes in work and family behaviors (Ellwood and Jencks 2004). Nevertheless, the long-term trends in marriage and fertility have been toward later average age at first marriage and lower lifetime fertility, in spite of the short-term reversal during the marriage and baby booms of the late 1940s and 1950s (Cherlin 1992). In the past three decades, the so-called retreat from marriage has been unprecedented, though it appears to be more of a delay than a rejection of marriage for most. Ellwood and Jencks (2004) find that most of the change in marriage patterns has occurred among the bottom two-thirds of women in terms of education. This is partly due to a delinking of marriage and childbearing in American society. In general, women with more education are postponing both marriage and childbearing, while women with less education are postponing marriage but not childbearing. This trend has been more pronounced among black women: there has been little change in the age at which they have children, but they are marrying at later ages or not at all. This helps us to understand the changes that have occurred for men and women in their twenties during the last half century. In the following sections, we examine both twenty- and twenty-five-year-olds, separating men and women to facilitate discussion.

CHANGES IN WORK AND FAMILY FORMATION: TWENTY- AND TWENTY-FIVE-YEAR-OLD MEN

Prior to 1950, for native-born white and black men, and 1960, for foreign-born men, the majority of twenty-year-olds were single childless working men (see tables in the appendix). Most young men were either training in their father's profession or craft or laboring in factories and building the growing cities, while a declining number worked in agriculture. Regardless of their occupation and skills, most were anticipating and perhaps even "saving up" for marriage and parenthood in the near future but not rushing in. This was especially true for twenty-year-old foreign-born men, many of whom delayed marriage since they were unlikely to meet potential coethnic marriage partners or were sojourners, living in the United States only temporarily. By age twenty-five, however, about half of native-born white and black men were working, married, household heads (with or without children). For foreign-born men, the percentages in this status combination were smaller, as more of them remained as single childless workers in their parents' homes or lived in other households or institutions.

The U.S. economy emerged from World War II as the leading industrial power in the world, growing as our markets expanded to rebuild Europe and Japan and further expanding into developing regions. This economic growth "lifted all boats" and enabled a growing middle class to send their children to college in greater numbers. In addition, returning GIs were able to attend college in droves with government support. Beginning in 1950, a growing percentage of single childless twenty-year-old men in all race and nativity groups were living in group quarters and attending school, as well as attending school while living in their parents' household. The extension of higher education has meant that it is an option for more young adults and is one reason why their pathways to adulthood have become more varied and individualized than those of their fathers, most of whom were in the labor force by their early twenties.

The period of prosperity that began after World War II is also associated with a boom in marriages and births. The boom refers to the fact that men and women of all ages were marrying in a concentrated period of time: those in their thirties who had come of age during the Great Depression and delayed marriage, young men and women in their twenties and thirties who had been separated as a result of the large deployment of young men during wartime, and young adults who felt they could afford to marry because of their growing wages and economic opportunities (Cherlin 1992; Rindfuss and Sweet 1979). Beginning in 1950 we see the results of this boom in the slight bulge in the percentages of married working twenty-year-old men in all race and nativity groups, with or without children, that peaks in 1960 and decreases to less than 5% thereafter. Among twenty-five-year-old men in all race and nativity groups, the post–World War II marriage and baby boom made a strong impact on the percentage distribution of statuses, especially for native-born blacks and whites. Between 1950 and 1970, more than 50% of twenty-five-year-old white men were employed, married household heads with or without children; more than 40% of native-born black men were in these status combinations, though the peak is not as obvious since this status combination had been common prior to 1950 as well. After 1970 these percentages decreased, declining to pre-1950s levels among white men and remarkably lower percentages among black men, marking the end of the marriage and baby boom periods. Among foreign-born men, the boom in marriage and childbearing is less apparent.

It is rare for men to begin a family while they are attending school, but some did so during the postwar period when the marriage boom, the baby boom, and the boom in education were occurring simultaneously. Among native-born white and black twenty-five-year-old men, small but significant proportions are ever-married household heads who attend school. Among foreign-born men, the percentages are higher, most likely due to the relatively large numbers of foreign students who come to the United States for professional training and higher education. While only a small percentage of men are in this status combination, it represents another way in which the life course has become more varied, especially for those obtaining higher levels of education and having the means to support a family.

Perhaps the most symbolically important status combination that emerged during the postwar period is that of single childless twenty-year-old native-born white and black men who head their own households or otherwise live independently of their families and are in school or in the labor force. This status combination began after 1950 for native-born white and black men and continues to increase up to the present day. Among foreign-born men this pattern is more common, since they often reside in the United States to attend school without bringing immediate family members. The rapid increase in single-person households results from increased earnings, an increase in affordable housing stock such as apartments for single-person households, and a growing preference for living alone (Sweet

1984). Here, those living in group quarters and in nonfamily or single-person households are combined, but the persistence of this pattern of living in nonfamily arrangements obscures the post–World War II shift from living in group quarters and boarding houses to living in single-person or nonfamily households. This status combination is an important alternative to the life-course pattern that was considered normative among the native-born populations in the earlier part of the century: that is, the pattern in which young men finish school, find gainful employment, and leave home to form a new family–but not to live alone. The possibility of living independently, even for a short time, marks a new sort of independence from family with significant social meaning (Goldscheider and Waite 1993).

The shift in the life-course pattern of twenty- and twenty-five-year-old men that began in the postwar period reflects the new opportunities created by an expanding economy, a growing system of higher education, and greater individual choice in the timing and selection of marriage partners. However, the pressure to finish school, enter the labor force, marry, and form an independent household between ages twenty and twenty-five put a great deal of pressure on young people—something had to give (Modell et al. 1976; Rindfuss 1991). After 1970, some of these stresses were resolved through the postponement of marriage and childbearing. Increasingly, twenty- and twenty-five-year-old men in all groups chose to remain single and childless. Some of these men became single childless household heads, living independently of their families. However, large percentages of men, especially native-born white and black men, continue to live in their parents' households, either while they are attending school or in the labor force. This trend toward prolonged family coresidence challenges conventional wisdom that young people will form independent households as soon as they are able.

The status combinations discussed above capture many of the ways in which the life course has become more individualized during the twentieth century. In 1900, eight of these categories describe 91% and 87%, respectively, of the status combinations of twenty-year-old native-born white and black men, and six categories describe those of 89% of foreign-born men. Over the century, the percentage captured by the status combinations used in this analysis has shrunk, reflecting the even greater variety of pathways to adulthood. In 2000, these ten categories described 87%, 72%, and 68%, respectively, of the status combinations of twenty-year-old native-born white men, black men and foreign-born men. In contrast to the experience of sixteen-year-olds, twenty-year-olds lives' are less standardized, especially among native-born black and foreign-born men. Evidently, race makes a difference in how likely one is to follow the standardized life course. Native-born white men carry a certain privileged position in negotiating the institutions that structure the life course, while native-born black and foreign-born men suffer disadvantages that cause them to fall "off course."

CHANGES IN WORK AND FAMILY FORMATION:
TWENTY- AND TWENTY-FIVE-YEAR-OLD WOMEN

In 1900, most twenty-year-old women were either single and possibly working or married and dedicated to domestic work. For twenty-year-old native-born white women and foreign-born women, there is a clear pattern of abstaining from paid employment after marriage (tables 2.B1 and 2.B3).[6] Thus, of the more than 55% of twenty-year-old native-born white women who were single and childless, about a third were living in their parents' homes and working or attending school, half were living in their parents' homes and neither in school nor working, and one-sixth were living in nonfamily households and working. For the foreign-born women, nearly half were living in nonfamily arrangements and working and a third lived with their parents and worked. Among the 28% of native-born white and 40% of foreign-born women who were already married, less than 1% were in the labor force or in school. White women who were twenty-five in 1900 display a similar pattern of exclusivity of work and marriage, but far more were married than single. For foreign-born twenty- and twenty-five-year-old women, the pattern was largely the same as for native-born white women, although more foreign-born women remained single and childless while working and most often lived in nonfamily households. These patterns persisted until 1940 for twenty- and twenty-five-year-old native-born white and foreign-born women.

Native-born black women experienced a somewhat different early adulthood in which marriage did not necessarily mean the end of paid employment. Forty percent of black twenty-year-old women were single and childless in 1900, three-quarters of whom were employed. Among the nearly 40% of twenty-year-old native-born black women who were married, nearly one-quarter were employed. This pattern also exists for twenty-five-year-old women, for whom nearly one-third of the 64% of married women worked. In spite of the prevailing ideology that married women attend solely to their own household's domestic work, it was not uncommon for married black women to find paid employment outside the home. Thus, the movement of married women into the labor force in the 1920s and 1930s and again in the 1970s that was so controversial for native-born white women and foreign-born women was old news for black women.

The increase in employment among twenty- and twenty-five-year-old married women was one of the most important ways in which women's transition to adulthood became more diverse in the twentieth century. This trend was driven in part by women seeking fulfillment outside of marriage and motherhood, as well as women seeking to support their families economically. In the 1930s economic necessity drove many single and married women, with or without children, into the labor force to help support their families during the Great Depression. Notably, these period-specific patterns are present but less pronounced among black women, for whom paid employment had been common prior to the women's movement and the Great Depression. The post–World War II marriage and baby boom significantly changed the early life course of young women by increasing the percentage of twenty- and twenty-five-year-old women who were married and had children. There was not a great need for these married women to work, given the economic good times the nation was experiencing. Consequently we see a greater percentage of twenty- and twenty-five-year-old women in all race and nativity groups who were married mothers and were neither employed nor in school in 1950 and 1960. This apparent return to female domesticity was fleeting, however. Among the many young wives and mothers, a small but growing percentage combined work and family, a trend that gained strength so that at the end of the century it is more common for ever-married mothers to work than not.

The postwar economic boom also facilitated an unprecedented enrollment of young women in colleges and universities as the middle class grew. Beginning in 1950 we see a growing percentage of single childless twenty-year-old women in all race and nativity groups living in nonfamily households (e.g., college dormitories, boarding houses, group homes) and attending school, especially among native-born white women. In 1950, 8% of twenty-year-old native-born white women fell into this status combination, and 7% of such foreign-born women did so, though only 3% of twenty-year-old native-born black women did so. As in the case of men, the race and nativity gaps in tertiary education narrowed gradually but still remained by 2000.

In addition to those who go away for college, a significant and growing percentage of single childless twenty-year-old women continue to live in their parents' homes while attending school. In 1950, about 6%–7% of all twenty-year-old women were doing so. Since then, living at home while attending school has become an increasingly attractive option, as more young people find higher education necessary to achieve their life goals and find it more affordable to do so while living with their parents. Throughout this period it has been more common for native-born black and foreign-born women to attend school while living at home than to live in nonfamily living arrangements.

While most twenty-year-old women attend school while they are single and childless, very small percentages of married women with or without children also attend school, a trend that began in the 1950s but has persisted. Notably, although most twenty-five-year-old women have completed their educations, after 1960 small but growing percentages of married women were attending school. Increased school attendance, both in the standard school ages and after, is one of the most important ways in which young women's life courses have become more diverse and individualized.

Beginning in 1970, as was the case for men, women began delaying marriage to later ages. This was due to the growing numbers of women and men attending college, a weakening in the marriage market as men's wages stagnated, women's growing interest in pursuing personal occupational goals, and changing preferences for marriage (Cherlin 1992). The prolongation of the period of semiautonomy that we saw for men is also evident for women: among native-born white twenty-five-year-old women, the fastest growing status combination is single childless women who are household heads and in the labor force. For native-born black women, this combination is exceeded somewhat by women who are single parents who are in the labor force. For foreign-born twenty-five-year-old women, the largest percentage who are not married and household heads are in other status combinations not included here, though those living with their parents or living in nonfamily arrangements and attending school are also growing. Like men their age, women are also delaying marriage and individualizing their pathway to adulthood.

Another trend apparent since 1970 is the small but growing percentage of single mothers in all race and nativity groups, but most notably among twenty- and twenty-five-year-old native-born black women. The percentage of twenty-year-old native-born black women who are single mothers grew from 2.5% in 1950 to 17% in 2000. Among their native-born white and foreign-born peers, the percentage has grown from less than 1% to 4% and from 0% to 2%, respectively. Some of these single mothers marry at later ages, and thus the percentages of single mothers decrease slightly, especially by age thirty, though less so among native-born black women. Among black women at age twenty-five, single parenthood is as common as ever-married parenthood. However, keep in mind that these single mothers are never-married mothers; separated and divorced mothers are included with married mothers in the category of ever-married. These data confirm other research that suggests that African Americans in particular, but Americans more generally, are moving away from limiting childbearing to within marriage and toward other family formation patterns and forms (Cherlin 1992; Ellwood and Jencks 2004; Taylor 2002).

Women's early life course has changed radically over the twentieth century, a fact shown by examining the greater number of status combinations in 2000 relative to 1900 for all race and nativity groups at age twenty. In 1900, these categories describe 87% of the status combinations of twenty-year-old native-born white women and foreign-born women and 83% of those of twenty-year-old native-born black women. Over the century, the percentage of women's status combinations described by these ten categories has decreased. In 2000, these categories describe 87%, 81% and 74%, respectively, of the status combinations of twenty-year-old native-born white, black, and foreign-born women. The difference for women age twenty-five is not as dramatic, suggesting that by this age the majority of women have returned to more typical status combinations.

Young women's lives have come to appear more like men's lives, in terms of the statuses they count. However, the meaning of these changes in status combinations for the content of their daily lives is quite distinct from that of men. Whereas men have held the roles of worker and parent simultaneously throughout the century, for women this combination is relatively new and more difficult to accommodate to the social institutions that structure their lives (Hochschild 1989; Spain and Bianchi 1996). Furthermore, being a working mother has meant different things for women in different times and contexts. Throughout the twentieth century black women and men have been struggling to improve their social and economic conditions in the face of racial segregation and discrimination. It is abundantly evident that they had less access to the social institutions that structure young people's lives—schools and jobs. Black families adapted to the social conditions as best they could—even if that meant they were labeled chaotic, matriarchal, pathological, or dysfunctional by society at large, as well as by some well-meaning family sociologists (Taylor 2002). Black women's combination of family and work roles is often an adaptive strategy to confront the difficult circumstances they encountered in American society.

Native-born white and foreign-born women and men have begun following the patterns of black women and men, suggesting an adaptive strategy on their part as well, although the specific reasons for these adaptations differ. Increasingly, the two-earner family is an adaptive strategy that married couples make regardless of their socioeconomic background. For some this may be considered a lifestyle choice, while for others it is an economic necessity. Separated, divorced, and single mothers work to support themselves and their children since they often cannot depend on the earnings of their childrens' fathers for their support. Indeed, the divorce revolution that began in the 1970s coincides closely with the rising employment rate of mothers. Greater instability in our family lives has made the specialization of men in paid work and of women in domestic work an idealized vision of the past (Coontz 1992).

This survey of men and women at ages twenty and twenty-five makes clear how much change occurs between the ages of twenty and twenty-five, especially in the period since the 1950s. During this five-year age span, many young people finish school, leave their parents' home, start employment, form independent households, marry, and begin having children. Considering the dynamism of this period in the life course, it is not unreasonable that young people are delaying family formation until later ages as a means of slowing down the transition to adulthood (Rindfuss 1991; Arnett 2000).

CONFORMITY AND CHANGE: THIRTY-YEAR-OLD MEN AND WOMEN

At age thirty, the status combinations of men and women in 1900 and 2000 do not look as different from one another as they did in their twenties. By this age throughout the century, the majority of thirty-year-olds have long since left their parents' homes and have gone on to marry and form families. For men in particular, life has not changed too much from this demographic perspective. In 1900 and 2000 alike, the modal status combination for thirty-year-old men of all race and nativity categories was ever-married, household heads, with children, and employed in the labor force. This category expanded during the 1950s, 1960s, and 1970s to include more than 70% of all native-born white men and about 60% of all foreign-born men. Among native-born black men this category was consistently around 60% of all men between 1900 and 1970, muting the effect of the postwar boom in family formation. Since then, the category has decreased as more men of this age in all race and nativity groups remain single and childless, though it still remains the modal category, accounting for 51% of thirty-year-old native-born white men, 30% of native-born black men, and 40% of foreign-born men. It is more difficult to argue that this movement away from marriage even at age thirty is attributable to the stresses brought on by other life transitions. Rather it suggests an increasing preference for remaining single and pursuing other nontraditional status combinations.

In some ways, this is a return to a pattern from the early part of the twentieth century. The period 1900–1940 saw nearly as many single childless thirty-year-old men as we see in 1980–2000. Within this group of men refraining from family formation at age thirty there are more attending school and living in nonfamily living arrangements. Only during the period from 1950 to 1970 were there fewer men who were single, childless, and living in nonfamily living arrangements.

While the status combinations of thirty-year-old men are more similar across time than those of men in their twenties, there is also evidence of growing diversity at this age. Throughout the century, the ten defined status combinations describe close to 90% or more of thirty-year-old native-born white men in most decades. However, among thirty-year-old native-born black men and foreign-born men these predefined status combinations account for a declining percentage of those populations, especially in 1990 and 2000. Clearly, the life course is becoming more individualized, and for native-born white men this occurs within the context of well-understood social institutions: families and households, schools, and labor markets. But for native-born black and foreign-born men, the institutions that shape their transition to adulthood send them into a greater variety of status combinations, meriting further investigation with less common status combinations.

Turning now to women, we see that their lives in 1900 and 2000 differ in one major respect: the presence of married women, especially those with children, in the labor force. While the percentage of thirty-year-old native-born white and foreign-born married women is not very different between 1900 and 2000, the majority of those women are in the labor force in 2000, whereas very few of them worked outside the home in 1900.[7] As discussed previously, through the course of the twentieth century the formal barriers to the employment of married women have nearly disappeared for all race and nativity groups. This occurred concomitantly with the growing tendency for women to remain single by age thirty, pursuing an independent life throughout their twenties, much like their male counterparts.

Thus, much of the shrinkage in the percentage of thirty-year-old women who are ever-married is due to an increase since 1970 in the percentage of women who remain single, head their own households, and work. For thirty-year-old white women, this group has increased from 3% in 1970 to 12% in 2000; from 3% in 1970 to 9% in 2000 for similar black women; and from 4% in 1970 to 7% in 2000 for similar foreign-born women.

Another trend that accounts for the shrinking percentage of ever-married women is the growing percentage of women who have children without marrying. Among all race and nativity groups the percentage of thirty-year-old women who are single and living with their own children has been growing. Notably, the percentage of these women who are in the labor force is larger than those who are outside of the labor force in all groups as well.

Among thirty-year-old white women, this trend has been gradual: in 1970 only 0.4% of these women were single mothers but this has increased to over 3% in 2000. The trend is similar for foreign-born women: in 1970 only 0.4% of foreign-born women were single mothers, while in 2000, nearly 3% are single mothers. For black women, single motherhood has been a small but enduring status combination throughout the century, though the percentage of women in this category has increased more rapidly since 1970. Then, 7% of thirty-year-old native-born black women were single mothers, whereas by 2000, 25% were. These single mothers may be living in cohabiting relationships with partners or living on their own. Either way, these never-married mothers represent another way in which young people are moving away from the traditional path of family formation through marriage.

These patterns suggest that while there is an increasingly varied set of patterns for becoming adult, most women have left their parents' homes, finished school, married, and had children by the time they are thirty. Furthermore, the majority of them are in the labor force. The ten status combinations presented here account for over 88% of thirty-year-old native-born white women throughout most of the century and an even greater percentage toward the end of the century. These combinations account for a smaller percentage of the status combinations of thirty-year-old native-born black women (76%–91%), especially between 1940 and 1960, but in recent decades they have accounted for relatively more. For foreign-born women, these combinations also have accounted for between 83% and 94% of the status combinations of thirty-year-old women, but this percentage has been decreasing in the past two decades (to 83%). It is the shifts within these ten categories that have been most remarkable, particularly married women's movement into the labor force, the delay in first marriages, and the increase in single motherhood. Thus, women's lives continue to be structured by the social institutions of education, employment, and marriage, but the combinations of these statuses have changed radically.

CONCLUSION

The portrait we have drawn here shows remarkable change in the age structuring of youth. Whereas in the first half of the twentieth century many adolescents were behaving as adults in the economy or in their households, by the end of the second half of the century, the vast majority of sixteen-year-olds are in educational institutions largely segregated from adult society. The expansion of higher education has prolonged the experience of semiautonomy from the natal family for some young adults, who rarely combine school attendance with family formation and frequently continue living with their natal families or in nonfamily or single individual households. For a growing proportion of youth, a period of economic and residential independence marks the break from dependence on the natal family but also a period in which they refrain from taking on new family roles. Residential independence is what distinguishes this late-twentieth-century pattern from the early-twentieth-century pattern of coresidence with parents prior to marriage. Despite this return to later age at first marriage, by age thirty, the majority of young adults have finished school, joined the labor force, left the parental home, and married, as they have done throughout the century. The pathways to that end state differ, but demographically speaking, the end state at age thirty looks similar.

Four major findings point to differences in the experience of the transition to adulthood over time and among gender, race, and nativity groups.

- In general, the span of life between ages twenty and twenty-five is the most turbulent in terms of changes in statuses, especially since 1950. After 1950 more youth in this age range had the option of being in school rather than the labor force. Furthermore, they had a greater range of options in terms of living arrangements as it became more common for single people to live in nonfamily households, college dormitories, or other group quarters. Since 1970, youth have taken more varied pathways to family formation, often staying single longer, as well as having children outside of marriage. Furthermore, among native-born black men and the foreign-born men and women there is a growing percentage in the unspecified combination category—a trend that merits further attention.

- Women and men's status combinations are more similar at the end of the twentieth century in all ages than at the beginning. This is a sign of growing gender egalitarianism in terms of the statuses they fill, although this apparent similarity may hide some of the stresses that young women experience in establishing themselves economically and/or juggling family and work commitments. This stress may underlie some of the changes in family formation patterns that we witness in the past several decades, particularly more single-parent households and more nonfamily households at later ages.

- Differences between native-born blacks and whites and the foreign-born have decreased as educational systems and labor markets have become less discriminatory and the economic status of native-born blacks and the foreign-born has improved. Nevertheless, fewer minority youth than native-born whites are participating in education and work, a fact deserving further investigation.

• The delay in age at first marriage in the last part of the century is not unlike the later age at first marriage experienced in the beginning of the century though it is now extending to even later ages. In other words, the marriage and baby boom was an aberration from a long-term trend. However, the explanations for the changes in family formation are quite different in the later third of the century than in the first third, and still not fully understood. Changes in the transition to adulthood are certainly part of the explanation.

This chapter has demonstrated the ways in which the transition to adulthood has become more complex in the later half of the twentieth century but also the greater similarity among gender, race, and nativity groups in the way in which the transition to adulthood is experienced in terms of sociodemographic status combinations. This is not to say that all groups have equal opportunities in life. A great deal of literature shows that inequalities between youth are more salient than ever, though they may not be manifest in their demographic status combinations (Portes and Rumbaut 2001; Zhou 1999). The intention of this chapter is to contextualize the chapters that follow, which further investigate the process of transition to adulthood and how this process shapes young people's life choices and life chances.

TABLE 2.AI

WHITE MEN'S STATUS COMBINATIONS AT AGES 16, 20, 25, AND 30

NATIVE-BORN WHITE MEN	SINGLE, NO CHILDREN					MARRIED, WITH OR WITHOUT OWN CHILDREN IN HOUSEHOLD; HOUSEHOLD HEAD OR SPOUSE OF HEAD			SINGLE WITH OWN CHILDREN; ANY TYPE OF LIVING ARRANGEMENT		IN OTHER STATUS COMBINATION	TOTAL
	LIVING IN PARENT'S HOUSEHOLD			LIVING IN NONFAMILY ARRANGEMENTS								
	IN SCHOOL	IN LABOR FORCE	NON-ACTIVE	IN SCHOOL	IN LABOR FORCE	IN SCHOOL	IN LABOR FORCE	NON-ACTIVE	IN LABOR FORCE	NON-ACTIVE		
Age 16:												
1900	40.92	38.32	7.06	1.72	5.11	.00	.00	.00	.03	.00	6.84	100.00
1910	49.43	33.22	6.62	2.16	3.29	.00	.00	.00	.00	.00	5.28	100.00
1920	46.62	32.44	11.59	1.36	1.88	.00	.01	.01	.01	.01	6.06	100.00
1940	69.69	15.93	6.65	1.14	.63	.00	.00	.01	.09	.00	5.85	100.00
1950	73.49	10.52	5.83	1.89	.55	.04	.00	.00	.00	.00	7.69	100.00
1960	82.05	5.68	5.13	1.60	.38	.06	.14	.00	.01	.00	4.95	100.00
1970	88.73	2.73	3.01	1.44	.11	.33	.15	.03	.02	.02	3.43	100.00
1980	88.49	3.03	2.64	1.73	.23	.05	.08	.03	.00	.01	3.72	100.00
1990	88.25	2.12	2.51	2.39	.17	.04	.06	.13	.00	.01	4.33	100.00
2000	89.73	1.10	1.17	2.31	.13	.06	.01	.00	.09	.01	5.39	100.00
Age 20:												
1900	5.31	55.17	5.96	1.26	18.24	.00	4.66	.11	.14	.00	9.14	100.00
1910	9.14	54.48	4.66	1.40	14.87	.07	5.95	.07	.04	.00	9.32	100.00
1920	9.12	51.04	7.40	1.12	12.32	.04	7.23	.09	.07	.01	11.56	100.00
1940	12.60	62.32	4.81	.88	5.41	.04	3.44	.00	.00	.07	10.42	100.00
1950	11.69	37.60	3.12	10.24	11.69	.91	9.55	.25	.07	.00	14.88	100.00
1960	11.42	26.88	3.35	13.91	14.49	2.12	16.43	.13	.03	.00	11.24	100.00
1970	18.61	18.32	3.65	17.92	14.82	2.71	14.20	.56	.05	.00	9.16	100.00

1980	15.92	30.36	3.07	16.80	12.99	1.01	11.53	.33	.23	.01	7.75	100.00
1990	23.96	25.43	2.45	20.72	11.47	.75	5.32	.38	.58	.03	8.90	100.00
2000	20.65	23.26	3.29	21.29	12.64	.85	3.59	.30	1.03	.05	13.05	100.00
Age 25:												
1900	.39	29.40	1.82	.58	19.98	.04	34.47	.70	.12	.00	12.51	100.00
1910	.90	26.43	1.11	.60	18.70	.09	39.71	.13	.13	.00	12.21	100.00
1920	.48	29.24	2.13	.22	13.70	.12	37.43	.45	.18	.03	16.02	100.00
1940	1.93	33.26	1.46	.41	7.23	.11	34.61	.57	.14	.00	20.27	100.00
1950	2.73	14.20	1.65	3.65	4.93	6.80	50.21	.92	.00	.00	14.90	100.00
1960	2.48	12.03	1.16	2.27	5.85	6.28	58.64	.86	.09	.00	10.35	100.00
1970	2.02	9.41	1.29	2.83	7.60	8.54	59.12	1.16	.11	.02	7.91	100.00
1980	2.26	11.75	1.37	4.75	17.43	5.55	47.45	.90	.27	.01	8.26	100.00
1990	3.83	16.89	1.58	6.61	19.95	5.14	32.69	1.15	.83	.08	11.25	100.00
2000	3.52	13.25	2.00	7.53	25.76	4.34	26.91	1.79	1.76	.21	12.94	100.00
Age 30:												
1900	.04	12.56	1.36	.12	16.10	.00	56.80	.62	.12	.08	12.19	100.00
1910	.35	13.33	.57	.18	14.87	.18	57.81	.26	.04	.00	12.40	100.00
1920	.05	12.88	.92	.03	10.43	.06	61.54	.52	.21	.00	13.35	100.00
1940	.17	15.20	.85	.17	5.04	.27	58.12	.52	.08	.00	19.56	100.00
1950	.00	7.81	.79	.00	4.16	.00	72.12	2.03	.06	.00	13.02	100.00
1960	.46	5.49	.70	.65	4.17	3.93	76.73	.70	.06	.01	7.10	100.00
1970	.28	4.16	.71	.52	4.30	5.26	77.50	1.33	.13	.01	5.81	100.00
1980	.28	3.90	.85	1.53	9.71	6.24	69.26	1.22	.13	.05	6.83	100.00
1990	.85	6.61	1.02	2.18	14.38	5.17	58.16	1.47	.63	.08	9.44	100.00
2000	.60	5.59	1.21	2.79	18.84	4.30	51.41	2.85	1.36	.11	10.94	100.00

Source. Author's calculations, IPUMS database of U.S. Censuses, 1900, 1910, 1920, 1940, 1950, 1960, 1970, 1980, 1990, 2000.

TABLE 2.A2

BLACK MEN'S STATUS COMBINATIONS AT AGES 16, 20, 25, AND 30

| NATIVE-BORN BLACK MEN | SINGLE, NO CHILDREN | | | | | MARRIED, WITH OR WITHOUT OWN CHILDREN IN HOUSEHOLD; HOUSEHOLD HEAD OR SPOUSE OF HEAD | | | SINGLE WITH OWN CHILDREN; ANY TYPE OF LIVING ARRANGEMENT | | IN OTHER STATUS COMBINATION | TOTAL |
| | LIVING IN PARENT'S HOUSEHOLD | | | LIVING IN NONFAMILY ARRANGEMENTS | | | | | | | | |
	IN SCHOOL	IN LABOR FORCE	NON-ACTIVE	IN SCHOOL	IN LABOR FORCE	IN SCHOOL	IN LABOR FORCE	NON-ACTIVE	IN LABOR FORCE	NON-ACTIVE		
Age 16:												
1900	22.16	48.70	5.99	1.80	9.98	.00	.00	.00	.20	.00	11.18	100.00
1910	28.21	42.66	5.59	2.10	7.23	.00	.00	.00	.00	.00	14.21	100.00
1920	37.48	32.70	10.24	1.39	4.08	.00	.20	.00	.20	.10	13.62	100.00
1940	44.63	32.33	5.66	0.20	3.03	.00	.00	.00	.00	.00	14.16	100.00
1950	55.09	13.57	5.48	4.18	2.61	.00	.00	.00	.26	.00	18.81	100.00
1960	64.05	8.35	6.72	3.33	.50	.06	.25	.06	.25	.13	16.30	100.00
1970	76.28	2.49	3.94	3.22	.28	.48	.24	.00	.00	.04	13.02	100.00
1980	81.37	1.60	3.57	2.96	.14	.07	.03	.03	.03	.00	10.20	100.00
1990	73.70	1.33	4.45	4.65	.19	.00	.03	.05	.03	.04	15.54	100.00
2000	74.05	.67	1.46	4.16	.04	.12	.02	.00	.26	.10	19.12	100.00
Age 20:												
1900	1.82	40.69	3.44	.20	29.15	.00	11.54	.20	.40	.00	12.55	100.00
1910	4.88	35.36	2.44	.31	22.56	.00	19.21	.00	.31	.00	14.95	100.00
1920	3.29	33.56	5.56	.34	18.71	.00	16.55	.11	.11	.00	21.77	100.00
1940	3.73	44.84	2.44	.14	8.88	.00	6.74	.00	.00	.00	33.24	100.00
1950	4.70	33.23	3.14	3.45	11.91	.00	10.03	.31	.63	.00	32.61	100.00
1960	10.50	27.83	6.19	4.67	11.40	.63	11.58	.09	.27	.27	26.57	100.00
1970	11.01	22.07	8.87	6.60	16.21	.94	10.70	.94	.37	.16	22.13	100.00

1980	13.96	29.50	9.82	9.82	12.58	.34	4.33	.30	.30	.15	18.90	100.00
1990	17.25	27.19	7.15	10.64	11.36	.32	2.57	.11	1.31	.38	21.72	100.00
2000	18.51	19.71	8.64	11.42	9.39	.51	1.61	.27	1.61	.54	27.78	100.00
Age 25:												
1900	.00	8.88	.59	.20	25.05	.00	50.30	.59	.79	.20	13.41	100.00
1910	.00	10.28	.00	.26	21.34	.00	47.81	.51	.51	.00	19.28	100.00
1920	.10	8.62	1.20	.10	18.04	.10	52.50	.50	.30	.00	18.53	100.00
1940	1.48	19.50	1.18	1.18	9.75	.30	41.21	.00	.00	.00	25.40	100.00
1950	1.48	10.65	.59	1.48	7.10	2.37	36.39	.89	.59	.00	38.47	100.00
1960	1.58	10.28	1.21	.93	7.03	3.15	46.56	1.58	.74	.28	26.67	100.00
1970	1.38	10.08	2.77	1.08	8.54	3.54	50.08	2.69	.62	.15	19.07	100.00
1980	2.82	15.57	4.48	3.70	15.43	3.09	30.72	1.76	1.39	.23	20.82	100.00
1990	4.32	21.36	4.94	4.83	15.67	2.14	16.67	1.41	2.03	.62	26.02	100.00
2000	3.79	14.91	4.91	5.21	17.32	2.66	13.31	2.28	3.24	1.31	31.07	100.00
Age 30:												
1900	.00	4.26	.24	.00	18.91	.00	63.83	.47	.00	.00	12.30	100.00
1910	.00	4.01	.24	.00	16.04	.00	65.33	.24	.71	.00	13.44	100.00
1920	.00	2.93	.43	.11	13.88	.00	61.27	1.19	.33	.11	19.75	100.00
1940	.00	5.80	.00	.00	8.91	.00	53.04	.85	.00	.00	31.40	100.00
1950	.00	2.78	1.01	.00	5.31	.00	60.85	2.78	.00	.00	27.28	100.00
1960	.28	4.37	.65	.28	7.35	2.14	59.63	2.23	.37	.09	22.60	100.00
1970	.41	4.69	1.48	.33	5.18	3.87	65.13	3.04	.49	.08	15.30	100.00
1980	.41	5.25	1.99	1.63	11.00	5.14	51.62	2.95	1.53	.10	18.39	100.00
1990	1.21	12.22	3.09	2.87	15.82	3.16	30.59	2.37	2.62	.66	25.40	100.00
2000	.64	7.36	2.69	2.29	16.98	3.27	30.32	4.87	4.50	.62	26.45	100.00

Source. Author's calculations, IPUMS database of U.S. Censuses, 1900, 1910, 1920, 1940, 1950, 1960, 1970, 1980, 1990, 2000.

TABLE 2.A3

FOREIGN-BORN MEN'S STATUS COMBINATIONS AT AGES 16, 20, 25, AND 30

FOREIGN-BORN MEN	SINGLE, NO CHILDREN					MARRIED, WITH OR WITHOUT OWN CHILDREN IN HOUSEHOLD; HOUSEHOLD HEAD OR SPOUSE OF HEAD			SINGLE WITH OWN CHILDREN; ANY TYPE OF LIVING ARRANGEMENT		IN OTHER STATUS COMBINATION	TOTAL
	LIVING IN PARENT'S HOUSEHOLD			LIVING IN NONFAMILY ARRANGEMENTS								
	IN SCHOOL	IN LABOR FORCE	NON-ACTIVE	IN SCHOOL	IN LABOR FORCE	IN SCHOOL	IN LABOR FORCE	NON-ACTIVE	IN LABOR FORCE	NON-ACTIVE		
Age 16:												
1900	8.93	57.59	9.82	3.13	12.50	.00	.00	.00	.00	.00	8.04	100.00
1910	23.36	40.19	6.08	3.27	16.82	.00	.00	.00	.00	.00	10.28	100.00
1920	30.85	46.48	11.33	2.35	4.49	.00	.00	.00	.20	.00	4.31	100.00
1940	71.58	15.74	4.57	8.11	.00	.00	.00	.00	.00	.00	.00	100.00
1950	58.49	7.55	1.89	15.10	3.77	.00	.00	.00	.00	.00	13.20	100.00
1960	77.62	7.76	3.20	4.12	.46	.00	.00	.00	.00	.00	6.84	100.00
1970	81.99	2.52	2.90	3.10	1.74	.97	.19	.00	.00	.00	6.58	100.00
1980	77.07	2.85	2.85	3.45	.98	.00	.30	.00	.00	.00	12.50	100.00
1990	72.37	3.12	3.12	5.16	1.88	.00	.09	.22	.00	.05	13.99	100.00
2000	71.19	2.44	1.91	3.72	2.52	.00	.04	.00	.07	.00	18.09	100.00
Age 20:												
1900	1.20	44.12	3.12	.00	37.17	.00	3.12	.24	.00	.00	11.04	100.00
1910	1.72	19.45	.86	2.24	61.10	.00	2.07	.00	.00	.00	12.57	100.00
1920	5.07	46.16	4.78	1.74	24.60	.00	3.76	.00	.00	.00	13.90	100.00
1940	16.88	62.99	1.30	.32	7.14	.00	.00	.00	.00	.00	11.36	100.00
1950	13.23	16.18	1.47	14.70	24.99	.00	5.89	.00	.00	.00	23.54	100.00
1960	13.28	23.22	2.84	21.34	15.65	.95	5.22	.00	.00	.00	17.51	100.00
1970	20.86	19.37	3.72	20.30	13.58	.93	8.57	.37	.00	.00	12.29	100.00

1980	17.44	18.03	3.84	15.90	15.00	1.11	7.91	.22	.30	.15	20.10	100.00
1990	21.79	12.71	2.15	15.50	13.36	.85	3.97	.15	.46	.00	29.07	100.00
2000	19.84	12.97	3.79	12.69	13.81	.65	3.06	.77	.52	.39	31.51	100.00
Age 25:												
1900	.00	16.58	1.22	.00	38.92	.00	27.23	.52	.00	.00	15.52	100.00
1910	.34	8.14	.34	.46	49.31	.00	26.26	.00	.00	.00	15.14	100.00
1920	.07	10.42	.55	.27	38.16	.14	32.30	.55	.00	.00	17.53	100.00
1940	2.91	36.91	1.46	.00	16.99	.00	21.36	.00	.00	.00	20.38	100.00
1950	.95	12.38	.00	6.67	23.81	3.81	31.43	.00	.00	.00	20.95	100.00
1960	3.18	8.10	.29	7.80	20.53	6.06	34.96	1.45	.29	.00	17.34	100.00
1970	3.53	6.56	.84	10.59	12.77	9.08	44.01	2.36	.00	.00	10.27	100.00
1980	2.97	7.20	1.45	10.63	15.57	5.55	38.29	1.25	.46	.00	16.63	100.00
1990	4.35	9.30	1.05	10.63	18.22	5.53	20.42	1.10	1.93	.11	27.36	100.00
2000	3.78	7.71	2.13	8.49	20.71	2.62	18.00	4.54	2.35	.61	29.08	100.00
Age 30:												
1900	.00	5.47	.12	.12	29.53	.00	49.53	.47	.12	.00	14.66	100.00
1910	.00	3.43	.19	.28	30.10	.37	47.40	.28	.00	.00	17.96	100.00
1920	.00	4.65	.09	.09	26.32	.14	53.38	.78	.00	.00	14.55	100.00
1940	.00	11.28	2.92	1.04	13.99	.63	48.43	.63	.00	.00	21.08	100.00
1950	.00	2.41	.00	.00	9.63	.00	51.82	3.01	.00	.00	33.12	100.00
1960	.49	2.96	.00	2.96	10.10	5.41	65.53	1.23	.24	.00	11.07	100.00
1970	.30	2.72	.75	1.51	7.85	6.94	68.32	1.36	.00	.00	10.26	100.00
1980	.21	1.95	.63	2.37	10.74	9.62	59.28	2.44	.42	.00	12.34	100.00
1990	.96	3.76	.62	4.39	13.17	7.68	43.96	1.87	1.77	.12	21.70	100.00
2000	.82	3.29	.92	3.57	13.69	4.46	40.07	8.37	1.60	.58	22.63	100.00

Source. Author's calculations. IPUMS database of U.S. Censuses, 1900, 1910, 1920, 1940, 1950, 1960, 1970, 1980, 1990, 2000.

TABLE 2.BI

WHITE WOMEN'S STATUS COMBINATIONS AT AGES 16, 20, 25, AND 30

NATIVE-BORN WHITE WOMEN	SINGLE, NO CHILDREN					MARRIED, WITH OR WITHOUT OWN CHILDREN IN HOUSEHOLD; HOUSEHOLD HEAD OR SPOUSE OF HEAD			SINGLE WITH OWN CHILDREN; ANY TYPE OF LIVING ARRANGEMENT		IN OTHER STATUS COMBINATION	TOTAL
	LIVING IN PARENT'S HOUSEHOLD			LIVING IN NONFAMILY ARRANGEMENTS								
	IN SCHOOL	IN LABOR FORCE	NON-ACTIVE	IN SCHOOL	IN LABOR FORCE	IN SCHOOL	IN LABOR FORCE	NON-ACTIVE	IN LABOR FORCE	NON-ACTIVE		
Age 16:												
1900	46.16	12.87	22.85	1.91	3.99	.13	.03	2.92	.10	.13	8.91	100.00
1910	50.14	16.63	18.55	2.02	2.72	.10	.19	2.37	.00	.13	7.15	100.00
1920	49.92	18.47	17.40	1.51	1.98	.16	.10	2.07	.02	.09	8.27	100.00
1940	71.95	5.88	12.58	1.29	.40	.05	.03	.91	.00	.00	6.91	100.00
1950	73.29	3.43	7.40	1.88	.36	.36	.29	2.71	.00	.00	10.28	100.00
1960	81.37	2.37	5.32	1.30	.07	.66	.39	2.38	.02	.02	6.10	100.00
1970	88.05	1.26	2.93	1.17	.02	.34	.37	1.38	.01	.08	4.39	100.00
1980	87.86	1.51	2.56	1.46	.21	.40	.40	.82	.11	.18	4.47	100.00
1990	87.07	1.55	2.54	2.29	.26	.14	.14	.34	.30	.22	5.16	100.00
2000	89.05	1.21	1.10	1.98	.17	.21	.07	.14	.38	.08	5.61	100.00
Age 20:												
1900	4.05	16.80	29.44	.79	7.70	.04	.39	27.22	.11	.21	13.25	100.00
1910	7.90	23.49	21.93	.62	7.59	.14	1.07	24.43	.14	.21	12.48	100.00
1920	7.24	27.46	16.21	.73	6.60	.37	1.22	24.59	.17	.08	15.33	100.00
1940	8.70	37.03	12.77	.72	5.24	.27	1.46	15.28	.21	.11	18.21	100.00
1950	5.92	22.42	4.76	8.08	4.14	1.20	9.07	27.11	.10	.07	17.14	100.00
1960	5.91	17.43	2.92	11.00	4.37	2.19	14.56	30.45	.08	.06	11.03	100.00
1970	11.59	17.25	2.79	15.20	5.18	2.51	16.08	18.72	.50	.45	9.73	100.00

1980	14.04	18.13	2.33	17.87	8.89	2.06	15.31	10.88	.99	1.12	8.38	100.00
1990	21.90	15.27	1.73	24.29	8.24	2.51	8.51	5.27	1.91	1.46	8.91	100.00
2000	21.67	11.37	2.21	27.12	8.92	2.50	5.75	3.41	3.33	.99	12.73	100.00
Age 25:											
1900	.15	10.31	12.70	.27	6.81	.08	1.41	54.43	.23	.30	13.32	100.00
1910	.53	12.03	8.51	.16	6.12	.20	3.12	55.47	.20	.24	13.42	100.00
1920	.24	13.80	7.04	.11	5.82	.06	3.32	55.24	.12	.04	14.21	100.00
1940	.77	18.56	5.88	.20	5.18	.15	5.62	43.98	.00	.00	19.67	100.00
1950	.65	8.09	1.67	.54	2.91	1.55	14.72	55.60	.03	.09	14.16	100.00
1960	.86	4.94	1.11	.50	3.34	1.86	22.59	58.48	.12	.10	6.10	100.00
1970	.89	4.88	.95	.95	4.92	3.29	31.88	45.67	.35	.19	6.03	100.00
1980	1.25	5.66	.75	3.50	11.75	5.16	39.08	23.65	.88	.62	7.70	100.00
1990	2.72	8.49	.84	4.64	14.22	6.47	35.84	13.55	2.12	1.54	9.59	100.00
2000	2.95	7.53	1.03	6.46	18.58	6.06	30.84	10.38	4.38	.97	10.82	100.00
Age 30:											
1900	.00	6.00	7.91	.00	4.14	.04	2.24	67.70	.08	.25	11.62	100.00
1910	.18	8.67	6.18	.09	5.69	.22	4.58	62.37	.13	.09	11.79	100.00
1920	.10	8.05	4.32	.03	4.61	.07	4.71	66.10	.23	.13	11.63	100.00
1940	.14	7.08	3.09	.20	2.20	.26	8.89	64.29	.00	.00	13.83	100.00
1950	.00	3.87	1.44	.00	2.40	.00	18.11	64.89	.09	.03	9.17	100.00
1960	.24	2.83	.73	.23	1.80	1.65	23.69	63.30	.14	.09	5.28	100.00
1970	.29	2.28	.74	.41	2.69	2.20	31.28	55.05	.37	.08	4.61	100.00
1980	.21	2.03	.63	1.13	5.82	5.24	45.67	33.26	.52	.33	5.18	100.00
1990	.45	3.06	.53	1.82	8.79	6.77	48.56	20.31	1.34	.64	7.74	100.00
2000	.52	2.80	.57	2.45	11.96	5.98	46.25	17.61	2.67	.58	8.61	100.00

Source. Author's calculations, IPUMS database of U.S. Censuses, 1900, 1910, 1920, 1940, 1950, 1960, 1970, 1980, 1990, 2000.

TABLE 2.B2

BLACK WOMEN'S STATUS COMBINATIONS AT AGES 16, 20, 25, AND 30

NATIVE-BORN BLACK WOMEN	SINGLE, NO CHILDREN					MARRIED, WITH OR WITHOUT OWN CHILDREN IN HOUSEHOLD; HOUSEHOLD HEAD OR SPOUSE OF HEAD			SINGLE WITH OWN CHILDREN; ANY TYPE OF LIVING ARRANGEMENT		IN OTHER STATUS COMBINATION	TOTAL
	LIVING IN PARENT'S HOUSEHOLD			LIVING IN NONFAMILY ARRANGEMENTS								
	IN SCHOOL	IN LABOR FORCE	NON-ACTIVE	IN SCHOOL	IN LABOR FORCE	IN SCHOOL	IN LABOR FORCE	NON-ACTIVE	IN LABOR FORCE	NON-ACTIVE		
Age 16:												
1900	33.21	24.91	14.34	1.32	4.72	.38	1.32	4.72	1.70	.38	13.01	100.00
1910	35.10	26.93	10.60	.88	4.63	.22	2.65	3.09	.44	.00	15.45	100.00
1920	41.81	14.83	16.22	2.20	2.12	.33	1.22	3.91	.57	.24	16.55	100.00
1940	56.37	11.80	13.20	1.22	.37	.28	.19	1.97	.00	.00	14.61	100.00
1950	53.34	4.14	8.97	3.45	.23	.00	.23	2.99	.23	.46	25.97	100.00
1960	64.44	3.29	7.84	1.96	.19	.70	.82	2.28	.19	.95	17.35	100.00
1970	74.02	1.28	5.35	1.61	.12	.58	.12	.91	.49	1.36	14.16	100.00
1980	78.40	.85	3.12	1.80	.10	.20	.00	.17	.68	1.02	13.67	100.00
1990	71.55	1.36	3.74	2.19	.48	.14	.05	.20	.97	.50	18.82	100.00
2000	74.00	.53	1.40	3.01	.13	.01	.00	.00	.82	.07	20.02	100.00
Age 20:												
1900	1.98	15.37	10.25	.33	12.40	.17	10.58	29.42	1.65	.66	17.19	100.00
1910	4.34	16.49	6.72	.87	10.41	.00	19.96	19.74	1.95	.22	19.30	100.00
1920	5.06	12.80	10.62	.67	5.22	.59	11.38	29.91	1.26	.59	21.89	100.00
1940	3.42	19.31	13.44	.00	3.42	.00	4.04	20.06	.00	.00	36.32	100.00
1950	5.91	10.40	10.17	3.07	2.36	1.18	10.17	19.86	.71	1.89	34.27	100.00
1960	6.61	12.22	8.92	5.22	4.46	1.23	7.92	20.98	1.92	1.77	28.75	100.00
1970	9.38	12.21	7.52	6.37	3.30	1.01	13.83	13.55	5.12	5.17	22.54	100.00

1980	15.80	14.20	7.60	11.62	4.78	1.22	6.63	4.81	7.60	9.56	16.18	100.00
1990	18.39	13.43	5.63	13.33	4.99	1.64	3.65	2.09	10.79	9.76	16.31	100.00
2000	17.82	12.28	5.61	15.34	6.41	1.33	3.45	1.14	12.09	5.20	19.34	100.00
Age 25:												
1900	.00	3.70	3.70	.00	9.44	.00	17.59	46.11	2.59	.56	16.30	100.00
1910	.22	6.65	1.78	.00	8.42	.00	31.71	30.82	2.88	.89	16.63	100.00
1920	.09	5.21	3.13	.09	6.96	.35	21.02	42.31	1.30	.09	19.46	100.00
1940	.00	5.54	1.84	.00	8.43	.00	11.99	41.89	1.19	1.58	27.55	100.00
1950	.23	4.75	1.13	.45	3.62	1.58	14.26	37.56	.45	1.36	34.61	100.00
1960	.63	4.55	2.04	.39	3.53	1.80	22.12	40.08	1.65	1.57	21.64	100.00
1970	.86	4.81	1.98	.33	4.35	2.83	33.29	28.41	4.94	4.35	13.85	100.00
1980	1.92	6.06	2.87	1.96	7.38	4.43	30.63	12.64	10.69	7.78	13.65	100.00
1990	2.92	11.52	2.21	3.10	9.92	3.71	18.86	5.82	15.48	11.30	15.15	100.00
2000	3.42	7.70	2.16	5.82	13.62	3.78	16.38	3.96	21.76	6.12	15.28	100.00
Age 30:												
1900	.00	1.86	2.06	.00	5.98	.00	24.33	48.04	3.30	.41	14.02	100.00
1910	.00	3.06	1.10	.00	8.97	.22	36.76	31.95	2.19	.22	15.54	100.00
1920	.00	1.72	1.37	.09	4.03	.17	28.47	47.17	1.54	.17	15.27	100.00
1940	.00	6.35	1.68	.91	4.79	.00	16.07	45.47	2.46	.39	21.88	100.00
1950	.00	1.27	1.06	.00	2.75	.00	30.51	38.99	.85	.85	23.72	100.00
1960	.29	2.33	.80	.15	3.13	1.82	33.50	38.52	1.39	1.31	16.76	100.00
1970	.21	1.93	1.04	.41	2.77	2.35	41.82	32.69	4.28	3.11	9.39	100.00
1980	.50	2.36	1.00	.68	5.67	5.95	44.17	16.34	7.90	3.99	11.44	100.00
1990	1.09	4.36	1.36	1.09	8.21	5.11	33.00	9.33	13.81	7.68	14.97	100.00
2000	.77	4.07	1.34	2.63	9.00	5.72	28.90	8.47	18.46	6.38	14.24	100.00

Source. Author's calculations, IPUMS database of U.S. Censuses, 1900, 1910, 1920, 1940, 1950, 1960, 1970, 1980, 1990, 2000.

TABLE 2.B3

FOREIGN-BORN WOMEN'S STATUS COMBINATIONS AT AGES 16, 20, 25, AND 30

| FOREIGN-BORN WOMEN | SINGLE, NO CHILDREN | | | | | MARRIED, WITH OR WITHOUT OWN CHILDREN IN HOUSEHOLD; HOUSEHOLD HEAD OR SPOUSE OF HEAD | | | SINGLE WITH OWN CHILDREN; ANY TYPE OF LIVING ARRANGEMENT | | IN OTHER STATUS COMBINATION | TOTAL |
| | LIVING IN PARENT'S HOUSEHOLD | | | LIVING IN NONFAMILY ARRANGEMENTS | | | | | | | | |
	IN SCHOOL	IN LABOR FORCE	NON-ACTIVE	IN SCHOOL	IN LABOR FORCE	IN SCHOOL	IN LABOR FORCE	NON-ACTIVE	IN LABOR FORCE	NON-ACTIVE		
Age 16:												
1900	15.38	36.75	18.38	1.28	16.24	.00	.00	2.14	.43	.00	9.40	100.00
1910	19.39	33.67	13.27	2.04	15.82	.51	.00	2.04	.00	.00	13.26	100.00
1920	31.02	36.99	18.11	1.54	3.66	.00	.00	.58	.00	.19	7.90	100.00
1940	65.38	4.49	14.10	4.49	3.85	.00	.00	.00	.00	.00	7.69	100.00
1950	56.60	3.78	5.66	13.21	1.89	.00	1.89	.00	.00	.00	16.98	100.00
1960	73.19	4.79	4.30	1.92	.00	.96	.48	2.87	.00	.00	11.51	100.00
1970	83.26	2.39	4.38	1.20	.20	.20	.00	.99	.00	.00	7.38	100.00
1980	78.72	2.20	3.30	3.20	.40	.50	.60	1.00	.00	.20	9.89	100.00
1990	78.36	1.17	2.46	4.21	.19	.16	.37	.57	.05	.19	12.29	100.00
2000	75.91	.93	3.04	4.57	.30	.26	.08	.57	.12	.07	14.15	100.00
Age 20:												
1900	1.10	19.74	11.84	.00	27.19	.00	.66	26.32	.22	.00	12.94	100.00
1910	1.30	17.14	4.99	.87	27.33	.00	3.25	27.11	.00	.00	18.01	100.00
1920	3.31	26.21	7.11	.64	10.44	2.42	1.91	30.65	.00	.00	17.31	100.00
1940	12.66	38.43	7.43	.00	3.06	.00	3.49	12.23	.00	.00	22.71	100.00
1950	7.14	12.85	2.86	7.14	12.85	.00	8.57	34.29	.00	.00	14.30	100.00
1960	5.92	17.07	2.78	10.45	8.71	2.09	8.72	28.23	.35	.00	15.68	100.00

1970	13.28	18.24	3.58	8.85	5.28	2.73	13.97	19.43	.68	.17	13.80	100.00
1980	17.38	15.23	3.71	12.44	5.52	2.72	12.02	13.67	1.15	.99	15.17	100.00
1990	24.71	9.40	2.83	15.16	6.06	3.35	6.09	7.53	2.06	1.13	21.69	100.00
2000	22.97	7.66	3.93	15.12	6.38	2.48	5.16	7.91	1.95	.69	25.75	100.00
Age 25:												
1900	.00	3.05	3.24	.00	22.86	.00	1.14	57.33	.19	.00	12.19	100.00
1910	.00	6.46	1.92	.17	18.50	.00	3.32	61.60	.00	.00	8.03	100.00
1920	.15	4.86	1.96	.00	11.77	.22	5.37	64.27	.07	.07	11.26	100.00
1940	3.69	13.94	5.74	.41	9.01	.00	10.65	33.20	.00	2.05	21.31	100.00
1950	.00	2.29	.76	.76	2.29	3.06	9.92	58.02	.00	.00	22.90	100.00
1960	.22	2.69	.45	2.46	8.06	2.24	19.46	53.47	.00	.00	10.96	100.00
1970	.93	4.94	.40	1.73	8.14	4.00	25.92	44.97	.80	.00	8.15	100.00
1980	1.43	5.32	1.01	4.53	8.98	5.96	29.38	25.86	1.29	1.22	15.03	100.00
1990	3.59	6.08	.93	6.24	8.86	8.13	23.83	16.19	3.10	1.35	21.70	100.00
2000	3.10	5.29	1.55	6.83	9.97	7.21	17.73	21.73	2.33	1.37	22.90	100.00
Age 30:												
1900	.00	2.28	1.22	.00	12.18	.15	1.98	73.36	.00	.30	8.52	100.00
1910	.00	3.57	.71	.00	10.14	.29	5.71	69.28	.00	.00	10.29	100.00
1920	.00	2.28	.71	.05	6.67	.11	7.43	74.94	.05	.00	7.76	100.00
1940	.00	4.87	1.99	.22	4.20	.66	8.64	64.81	.00	.00	14.60	100.00
1950	.00	2.98	.60	.00	4.17	.00	22.02	57.14	.00	.00	13.10	100.00
1960	.41	.82	.61	.61	4.29	1.43	25.51	59.80	.00	.00	6.52	100.00
1970	.25	2.10	.49	1.48	4.32	3.95	29.26	52.22	.37	.00	5.56	100.00
1980	.40	1.33	.20	1.53	4.32	6.37	41.41	33.04	1.19	.53	9.69	100.00
1990	.69	2.12	.29	2.06	6.03	10.00	35.54	23.54	2.66	1.03	16.04	100.00
2000	.79	2.15	.56	2.13	7.41	8.06	31.08	28.24	1.90	.94	16.75	100.00

Source. Author's calculations, IPUMS database of U.S. Censuses, 1900, 1910, 1920, 1940, 1950, 1960, 1970, 1980, 1990, 2000.

NOTES

1. We do not include those categorized as "other" since their numbers are too small to produce reliable statistics.

2. New research on the second generation looks at the children of immigrants. We are unable to do this with IPUMS because we are only able to identify immigrant youth through their birthplaces. While we can identify second-generation youth who are living at home, it is not possible to identify those in independent households.

3. It is the intention of IPUMS to integrate the 1930 censuses into the database in the near future.

4. Married men and women are considered heads of household, as are single men and women who identify themselves as such on the census form. And since we are focusing on the transition into adult roles, we look at whether an individual has ever been married. If they are widowed, separated, or divorced, they are counted as "ever-married." Finally, we use own children living in the household instead of whether the woman reports having any children since this is a more consistent variable from year to year and it applies to men as well as women. However, this indicator excludes men and women who are parents but are not living with their child(ren).

5. Those attending school may also be in the labor force, but we emphasize school over employment.

6. School attendance was not common for twenty-year-old men or women during this period.

7. In 1900, 70% of thirty-year-old native-born white women, 72% of such black women, and 75% of such foreign-born women were ever-married. In 2000 the numbers for thirty-year-old native-born white and foreign-born women are not so different, but those for native-born black women are quite different: 70% of white women, 44% of black women, and 67% of foreign-born women were ever-married.

REFERENCES

Arnett, Jeffrey Jensen. 2000. Emerging Adulthood: A Theory of Development from the Late Teens through the Twenties. *American Psychologist* 55 (5):469–80.

Bureau of Labor Statistics. 2002. *Value of the Federal Minimum Wage, 1938–2000.* U.S. Department of Labor, Washington, DC.

Cherlin, Andrew J. 1992. *Marriage, Divorce, Remarriage.* Rev. and enlarged ed. Cambridge, MA: Harvard University Press.

Chudacoff, Howard P. 1989. *How Old Are You? Age Consciousness in American Culture.* Princeton, NJ: Princeton University Press.

Coontz, Stephanie. 1992. *The Way We Never Were: American Families and the Nostalgia Trap.* New York: Basic Books.

DiPrete, Thomas A., and Patricia A. McManus. 1996. Institutions, Technical
Change, and Diverging Life Chances: Earnings Mobility in the United States
and Germany *American Journal of Sociology* 102 (1):34–79.

Elder, Glen H. Jr. [1974] 1999. *Children of the Great Depression: Social Change in Life
Experience*. Boulder, CO: Westview.

Ellwood, David T., and Christopher Jencks. 2004. The Uneven Spread of Single Parent Families: What Do We Know? Where Do We Look for Answers? In *Social
Inequality*, edited by Kathryn Neckerman. Cambridge, MA: Harvard University Press.

Farley, Reynolds. 1996. *The New American Reality: Who We Are, How We Got Here,
Where We Are Going*. New York: Russell Sage Foundation.

Goldin, Claudia. 1990. *Understanding the Gender Gap: An Economic History of American Women*. New York: Oxford University Press.

Goldscheider, Frances, and Calvin Goldscheider. 1999. *The Changing Transition
to Adulthood: Leaving and Returning Home*. Thousand Oaks, CA: Sage
Publications.

Goldscheider, Frances, and Linda J. Waite. 1993. *New Families, No Families: The
Transformation of the American Home*. Berkeley: University of California
Press.

Heinz, Walter R. 2001. Work and the Life Course: A Cosmopolitan-local Perspective. Pp. 3–22 in *Restructuring Work and the Life Course*, edited by Victor W.
Marshall, Walter R. Heinz, Helga Kruger, and Anil Verma. Toronto: University of Toronto Press.

Hersch, Patricia. 1999. *A Tribe Apart: A Journey into the Heart of American Adolescence*. New York: Ballantine Books.

Hochschild, Arlie. 1989. *The Second Shift*. New York: Avon Books.

Kerckhoff, Alan C. 1993. *Diverging Pathways: Social Structure and Career Deflections*.
New York and London: Cambridge University Press.

———. 2002. The Transition from School to Work. Pp. 52–87 in *The Changing
Adolescent Experience: Societal Trends and the Transition to Adulthood*, edited by
Jeylan Mortimer and Reed Larson. New York: Cambridge University Press.

Kertzer, David I. 1989. Age Structuring in Comparative and Historical Perspective.
Pp. 3–21 in *Age Structuring in Comparative and Historical Perspective*, edited
by David I. Kertzer and K. Warner Schaie. Hillsdale, NJ: Lawrence Erlbaum
Associates.

Kohli, Martin. 1986. The World We Forgot: A Historical Review of the Life Course.
Pp. 271–303 in *Later Life: The Social Psychology of Aging*, edited by Victor W.
Marshall. Beverly Hills, CA: Sage Publications.

Levy, Frank. 1998. *The New Dollars and Dreams: American Incomes and Economic
Change*. New York: Russell Sage Foundation.

Littman, Mark S. 1998. *A Statistical Portrait of the United States: Social Conditions and Trends*. Lanham, MD: Bernan Press.

Maynard, Rebecca. 1995. Teenage Childbearing and Welfare Reform: Lessons from a Decade of Demonstration and Evaluation Research. *Children and Youth Services Review* 17 (1–2):309–32.

Modell, John. 1989. *Into One's Own: From Youth to Adulthood, 1920–1975*. Berkeley: University of California Press.

Modell, John, Frank F. Furstenberg, and Theodore Hershberg. 1976. Social Change and the Transition to Adulthood in Historical Perspective. *Journal of Family History* 1:7–32.

Mortimer, Jeylan, and M. K. Johnson. 1998. New Perspectives on Adolescent Work and the Transition to Adulthood. Pp. 425–96 in *New Perspectives on Adolescent Risk Behaviors*, edited by R. Jessor. New York: Cambridge University Press.

National Center for Education Statistics. 2001. Table 8: Years of School Completed by Persons Age 25 and over and 25 to 29, by Race/Ethnicity and Sex: 1910 to 2000. *Digest of Education Statistics*. http://nces.ed.gov//pubs2002/digest2001/tables/dt008.asp.

Pleck, Joseph. 1987. American Fathering in Historical Perspective. Pp. 351–61 in *Changing Men: New Directions in Research on Men and Masculinity*, edited by Michael S. Kimmel. Beverly Hills, CA: Sage Publications.

Portes, Alejandro, and Ruben Rumbaut. 2001. *Legacies: The Story of the Second Generation*. Berkeley: University of California Press.

Rindfuss, Ronald R. 1991. The Young Adult Years: Diversity, Structural Change, and Fertility. *Demography* 28 (4):493–512.

Rindfuss, Ronald R., and James A. Sweet. 1979. Postwar Fertility Trends and Differentials in the United States. *Studies in Family Planning* 10 (2):69.

Ruggles, Steven, and Matthew Sobek. 1997. *Integrated Public Use Microdata Series*. Version 2.0 Minneapolis: Historical Census Projects, University of Minnesota.

Settersten, Richard A., Jr. 2002. Age Structuring and the Rhythm of the Life Course. Pp. 81–98 in *Handbook of the Life Course*, edited by Jeylan Mortimer and Michael Shanahan. New York: Kluwer Academic and Plenum Publishers.

———. 1997. The Salience of Age in the Life Course. *Human Development* 40: 257–81.

Shanahan, Michael J. 2000. Pathways to Adulthood in Changing Societies: Variability and Mechanisms in Life Course Perspective. *Annual Review of Sociology* 26: 667–92.

Spain, Daphne, and Suzanne M. Bianchi. 1996. *Balancing Act: Motherhood, Marriage, and Employment among American Women.* New York: Russell Sage Foundation.

Stone, Lawrence. 1977. *Family, Sex, and Marriage in England, 1500–1800.* New York: Harper & Row.

Sweet, James A. 1984. Components of Change in the Number of Households: 1970–1980. *Demography* 21 (2):129–40.

Taylor, Ronald L. 2002. Black American Families. Pp. 19–47 in *Minority Families in the United States: A Multicultural Perspective,* edited by Ronald L. Taylor. 3d ed. Upper Saddle River, NJ: Prentice Hall.

Thornton, Arland, William Axinn, and Jay D Teachman. 1995. The Influence of School Enrollment and Accumulation on Cohabitation and Marriage in Early Adulthood. *American Sociological Review* 60:762–74.

Tucker, M. Belinda, and Claudia Mitchell-Kernan. 1995. Trends in African American Family Formation: A Theoretical and Statistical Overview. Pp. 3–26 in *The Decline in Marriage among African Americans,* edited by M. Belinda Tucker and Claudia Mitchell-Kernana. New York: Russell Sage Foundation.

Uhlenberg, Peter. 1974. Cohort Variations in Family Life Cycle Experience of U.S. Females. *Journal of Marriage and the Family* 36:284–92.

U.S. Department of Commerce. Bureau of the Census. 1900–2000. *Statistical Abstract of the United States.* U.S. Government Printing Office, Washington, DC.

———. 1995. *Historical Statistics of the United States.* Washington, DC.

U.S. Department of Education. 2001. *Digest of Education Statistics 2000.* http://nces.ed.gov/pubs2002/digest2001/tables/dt008.asp.

Welter, Barbara. 1966. The Cult of True Womanhood: 1820–1860. *American Quarterly* 18 (2):151–74.

Zhou, Min. 1999. Segmented Assimilation: Issues, Controversies, and Recent Research on the New Second Generation. Pp. 196–211 in *The Handbook of International Migration: The American Experience,* edited by Charles Hirschman, Philip Kasinitz, and Josh DeWind. New York: Russell Sage Foundation.

CHAPTER 3

AMERICAN WOMEN'S TRANSITION TO ADULTHOOD IN COMPARATIVE PERSPECTIVE

ELIZABETH FUSSELL AND ANNE H. GAUTHIER

Throughout the Western world we are experiencing what demographers call the second demographic transition in which fertility levels hover near or below replacement level and young people are delaying or forgoing marriage (Ingelhart and Baker 2000; Lesthaeghe and Willems 1999; Van de Kaa 1994). This certainly reflects the more prolonged and individualized transition to adulthood, but some worry that it is also a rejection of the family as a central social institution of Western societies by new generations (Billari and Wilson 2001; Corijn and Klijzing 2001; Fussell and Furstenberg, this vol., chap. 2; Goldscheider 1997; Goldsheider and Waite 1991; Kiernan 2001; Ravanera, Rajulton, and Burch 2002; Simó and Golsch 2000).[1] We have seen that young adults have been leaving the parental home at older ages, prolonging their education, and delaying their entry into marriage and parenthood. Furthermore, they have altered the traditional sequence of these events, following more individualized and complex pathways (Corijn and Klijzing 2001; Shanahan 2000). Differences in the general patterns of family formation within developed countries suggest that young people's patterns of transition to adulthood are responding to evolving educational institutions and labor market regulations and uncertainties inherent in the postindustrial economies, in addition to new sets of values that are reformulating traditions surrounding marriage and childbearing. In this chapter we compare the timing and prevalence of transitions to independent living and family formation to investigate whether in fact young people are rejecting family formation and to ascertain how social structures that vary among a set of countries may be contributing to differences in the transition to adulthood.

An international perspective provides a unique vantage point for viewing the American transition to adulthood. In this chapter we describe the transition to adulthood for women in the United States and compare it with that of women in countries with contrasting social, economic, and policy contexts. We have chosen simple measures that impose an analytic framework on the data to illustrate differences in the timing of transitions and the degree of adherence to a "traditional" pattern of family formation between cohorts and nations. We use data from the U.S. National Survey of Family Growth and comparable data from the Family and Fertility Surveys carried out in Canada, Germany, Italy, and Sweden to compare the experience of two cohorts of women: one born in the early 1950s who came of age in the 1970s, and one born a decade later who came of age in the 1980s. We compare these cohorts in terms of the timing of their acquisition of family statuses (leaving the parental home, cohabitation, marriage, and childbearing), the prevalence of these transitions within cohorts, and the combinations of statuses acquired by a given age. In contrast to most of the comparative literature on this topic, our emphasis is on the combination of events that constitute the transition to adulthood instead of the analysis of single events.

We find that the American pattern of the transition to adulthood among women is similar to those of Canadian and German women but differs sharply from those of Swedish and Italian youth. The majority of women in the United States, Canada, and Germany follow the traditional sequence of leaving home followed by marriage and then childbearing. However, in these three countries, a small but growing proportion of women are breaking away from the traditional pattern and having children as single mothers or within cohabiting relationships. In addition, the pattern of premarital cohabitation followed by marriage and childbearing is becoming more common and accepted. In contrast to the pattern observed in these three countries, young women in Sweden display the least traditional pattern, with widespread cohabitation prior to marriage and a large proportion of children being born to cohabiting couples. Young women in Italy display the most traditional sequence, with a very low prevalence of cohabitation prior to marriage and very little nonmarital childbearing. We conclude that most young women in the United States still subscribe to the traditional pattern of family formation, although their age at family formation is later than the cohort that produced the post–World War II baby boom. Despite this adherence to tradition, a growing number of women are taking alternate routes to family formation. By comparing countries with different cultural patterns and welfare regimes we hope to gain insight into why these differences have emerged between advanced industrial countries.

The chapter is divided into five sections. In the first section, we review the comparative literature on the transition to adulthood to place the American experience in a comparative perspective. In the second section, we discuss some of the theoretical factors that have been posited to influence the transition to adulthood, including micro- and macrolevel factors. The data and methods are presented in the third section, with our main results in the fourth. In the final section, we offer our conclusions and discuss future avenues of research.

BACKGROUND

The transition to adulthood is a rapidly growing area of research, especially as the transition becomes more prolonged—a phenomenon with larger social and demographic implications than may be immediately apparent (Furstenberg 2000; Fussell 2002; Shanahan 2000). Studies have problematized the delay in the transition to adulthood since the 1970s, suggesting that the greater variation in the timing and sequence of transitions and the increasing individualization of trajectories are a response to the stress of undergoing multiple transitions in a short period of time (Liefbroer, Gierveld and De Jong 1995; Modell, Furstenberg and Hershberg 1976; Rindfuss 1991; Rindfuss, Swicegood and Rosenfeld 1987; Shanahan 2000). One consequence of the prolonged and complex transition to adulthood is greater uncertainty for young people navigating new pathways to adulthood (Buchmann 1989). These shifts in the pattern of transition to adulthood may present problems to individuals, insofar as they lack social support for their choices, and to societies in that they disrupt expected patterns of social reproduction (Fussell 2002). Some argue that this is the result of long-term secular change in advanced industrial countries (Lesthaeghe and Meekers 1986; Lesthaeghe and Willems 1999). Alternatively, the increased variation in patterns of transition to adulthood may be a short-term response to the economic transformations that have occurred in recent decades and may be resolved as governments adopt policies that support youth in their transition to adulthood.

Much of the literature on the transition to adulthood has been based on data from the United States, where a longer tradition of panel and other longitudinal surveys has allowed for more detailed analysis of the patterns of transition to adulthood. Initially this literature focused on the standardization of the sequence of life events that make up the transition to adulthood and the time it took to pass through the markers of that transition (Hogan 1981; Marini 1984; Modell et al. 1976; Rindfuss 1991; Uhlenberg 1969). Marini (1984) found that among a cohort of high school students from the class of 1957–58, the most common sequence of life-course events was to leave school, start full-time employment, marry and then have a child—a sequence completed by 40% of women and almost 38% of men by their early thirties. This cohort came of age at a time when secondary education was close to universal and higher education was becoming more widespread, thus extending the average number of years spent in school (Fussell and Furstenberg, this vol., chap. 2). The prolongation of education and the post–World War II patterns of early marriage and childbearing resulted in a concentration of transitions in the early twenties (Modell et al. 1976; Rindfuss 1991). Modell and his colleagues predicted that this amount of change early in the life course was untenable for many and would become decompressed as young people sought ways of spreading out the transitions that make up the pathway to adulthood.

Indeed, since the 1970s, the timing of events has become more dispersed. In particular, the length of time between the school to work transition and family formation has widened (Rindfuss, Morgan, and Offutt 1996; Stevens 1990). More recent research has focused on the individualization of the life course through the deconcentration of the timing of events that make up the transition to adulthood and the greater diversity in the sequencing of those events (Buchmann 1989; Shanahan 2000). Today, new research focuses on the social institutions that make the transition to adulthood more complex (Ellwood and Jencks 2004; Mortimer and Larson 2002).

In Europe, the recent European Household Panel Study and the Family and Fertility Surveys have provided new sources of data to study the transition to adulthood (Aassve et al. 2002; Billari et al. 2002; Corijn and Klijzing 2001; Iacovou 2002). Analyses of these data have revealed trends similar to those observed in the United States, including the prolongation of the transition to adulthood and the increasing disorderliness in the sequencing of transitions. In spite of these general trends, strong cross-national differences persist. For example, among the cohort of women born in the early 1960s, the median age at leaving the parental home has been found to vary between 18.4 years old in Sweden and 23.3 years old in Spain. The median age at entry into parenthood displays even greater cross-national variation, from a minimum of 21.7 years old in the Czech Republic to a maximum of

28.6 in Switzerland (authors' calculations). This cross-national information on the timing of key events suggests that the United States appears in a middle position, though we have yet to discern the structural, cultural, and attitudinal causes of variation between these countries.

Analyses of these cross-national differences have tended to focus on single events rather than on the combination of events that are part of the transition to adulthood. There are comparative analyses of the entry into sexual activity (Teitler 2002), the transition from school to work (Heinz 1999; Kerckoff 2002; Shavit and Muller 1998), the transition to independent living (Billari, Philipov, and Baizán 2001; Goldscheider 1997), union formation (Kiernan 2000; Sardon 1993), and the transition to parenthood (Lesthaeghe and Willems 1999), but few studies have attempted to capture and summarize the cross-national differences in the combination of these events (see Corijn and Klijzing [2001] for an exception).

In this chapter, we start filling in this gap by examining cross-national differences in the timing, prevalence, and combination of events in the transition to adulthood.[2] We are specifically interested in the timing and combination of those events related to family formation, including leaving the parental home, entering into a marriage, and having a first child. We consider this to be the traditional sequence of transitions. Cohabitation is an alternative route to family formation in most countries, though there is variation both in its prevalence and meaning. For example, cohabitation tends to be a much more permanent type of union in Sweden, while still being a sort of trial marriage in Germany, Canada, and the United States. In Italy, cohabitation is quite rare, except in the case of separated and divorced individuals who are prohibited from remarrying (Iacouva 2002). To examine cross-national differences we impose a framework on the data, measuring the percentage of the samples that has acquired sets of statuses by given ages. In this way we measure adherence to, and variation from, the traditional transition to adulthood using relatively simple measures.

We compare the timing and prevalence of these transitions in five countries: Canada, the former Federal Republic of Germany (referred to hereafter as West Germany), Italy, Sweden, and the United States.[3] These five countries were selected on the basis of their contrasting cultural and structural characteristics, as discussed in the next section. By examining the differences in the percentage of young adults in a combination of statuses at specific ages between two birth cohorts in the same country, and the related differences between countries, we place the transition to adulthood in the United States in a cross-national perspective.

THEORIES OF CROSS-NATIONAL DIFFERENCES
AND SIMILARITIES IN THE TRANSITION TO ADULTHOOD

The trends we identified in the previous section—later age at home leaving, a longer period of education, and delayed age at first marriage and giving birth—are commonly observed among advanced industrialized countries, but the underlying causes of these trends are not well understood. Social institutions, such as welfare regimes, labor and housing markets, religious and educational institutions, and cultural practices, ideologies, values and attitudes shape individual behavior. The most commonly identified set of changes that have taken place over the twentieth century in each of these countries is the rising standard of living associated with industrialization, women's increased labor force participation, and shifts in values orientations toward more expressive individualism (Becker 1981; Easterlin, Macdonald, and Macunovich 1990; Inglehart and Baker 2000; Lesthaeghe and Meekers 1986; Thornton 2001). These broadly construed changes are grounded in the social institutions that shape daily lives, particularly educational systems, welfare regimes, and labor market regulations (Breen and Buchmann 2002). Both culture and social institutions contribute to our understanding of differences between countries in their patterns of transition to adulthood, although as stated above, the links between microlevel behavior and macro-level institutions are still not well articulated.

In Europe, family norms and values largely follow the cultural-historical borders that coincide with nation-states as well as geopolitical boundaries. Hajnal (1965) identified an east-west divide drawn from Trieste, Italy, to St. Petersburg, Russia, that distinguished patterns of the timing of first marriage and norms surrounding the formation of households by newlyweds. Earlier ages at marriage were characteristic of Eastern European countries and were facilitated by the acceptance of the coresidence of the young couple with parents, whereas in western Europe marriage generally occurred at an older age, after a young man achieved financial independence and was able to form an independent household with his wife. This divide appears to have persisted over time (Ni Bhrolchain 1993). A north-south divide has also been identified by Iacovou (1998; 2002) and Reher (1998). Southern European countries have maintained low divorce levels and low rates of cohabitation and births outside marriage, while northern and western Europe have experienced greater levels of divorce, cohabitation, and non-marital births. In southern Europe, coresidence with parents both before and after marriage is also more common than elsewhere in Europe. This persistent divide in household formation patterns is mimicked by differences in values and attitudes. For instance, Ingelhart and Baker (2000) have shown the persistence of cross-national differences in values associated with trust, rationality, and tolerance—differences that characterize historically Catholic countries and historically Protestant countries. While the United States and Canada are not part of these schemas, they are most closely related to the northern and western European countries in terms of their historical origins.

The past century witnessed the growth of national-level social institutions that mold the young adult life course: mandatory secondary schooling, the growth of tertiary education, and regulated and hierarchical labor markets. States vary in the extent to which they subsidize or regulate these institutions and, consequently, provide young people greater or lesser access to education and employment. In addition, states offer varying degrees of direct support to families and children. Esping-Andersen (1990) characterized groups of countries according to their welfare regimes, a typology that subsequent scholars have modified and applied to understand differences between countries in terms of fertility, women's employment, and access to public resources (Gauthier 1996; Lewis 2000; Orloff 1993). We use these typologies both as a basis for selecting countries for analysis and in interpreting our findings. We chose five countries belonging to different welfare regimes; our choice of these countries allows us to relate our findings to other literature that contrasts welfare regimes and demonstrates how the United States stands apart from other industrialized countries.

Together with our knowledge of differences in cultural values that shape family values and household formation patterns, Esping-Andersen's (1990) typology of welfare regimes provides a basic explanatory framework for understanding differences between countries in terms of the transition to adulthood. We also add information on the educational systems and labor market structures to elaborate the differences between selected countries (Breen and Buchmann 2002; Cook and Furstenberg 2002). These help us to develop some hypotheses about cross-national differences and understand better how the characteristics of the United States shape the transition to adulthood there. Below, we briefly describe the characteristics of each of the countries we selected to compare with the United States. We use these typologies to predict three possible but not exclusive patterns: later family formation, adherence to traditional family formation patterns, and pursuit of nontraditional family formation patterns.

The former West Germany belongs to the so-called conservative regime characterized by policies promoting a relatively traditional gender division of labor and a system of support related to one's position in the labor market. In addition, West Germany's dual education-work system facilitates the school-to-work transition. Combined with highly regulated labor markets, this arrangement provides greater job security and relatively low youth unemployment (Breen and Buchmann 2002). Though the dual system facilitates economic independence, and therefore earlier home leaving and family formation, it has not kept pace with the transformation of the industrial economy to a postindustrial one (Heinz 2000). Therefore, young people in the 1990s were likely to experience labor market insecurities that might have delayed leaving the parental home and family formation, though we only capture a bit of this period since the German survey took place in 1992. The fact that West Germans are accustomed to turning to the state for support during the transition to adulthood, both in terms of employment and family formation, suggests that young people may be particularly frustrated by the obstacles they face in achieving economic independence and may therefore delay family formation, and childbearing in particular, more than young people in other countries. Furthermore, Germany lies to the west of the east-west cultural divide, suggesting that young people there may also be more likely to follow delayed and nontraditional paths to family formation.

Sweden belongs to the so-called social democratic regime characterized by a more egalitarian gender division of labor and a system of support based on the principle of universality. Here, students receive vocational training in schools, providing them with credentials that open doors to employment, though it is difficult for young people to find openings in a labor market that protects workers already on the job (Breen and Buchmann 2002). Young people also receive generous support in terms of unemployment benefits and subsidies to families with children. This strong welfare state support fosters egalitarianism in terms of parental involvement in child rearing and likely facilitates earlier independence and family formation, though not necessarily formal marriage (Moen 1989). Furthermore, Sweden's cultural context is unusual in that marriage in the church has not been as deeply engrained. Therefore, although we refer to cohabitation as a nontraditional route to family formation, in Sweden it is widely accepted as a context for raising children. Thus, we expect to find that the transition to family formation in Sweden would resemble more closely the traditional model if we were to combine cohabitation and marriage. Since we are keeping them separate for the purposes of comparison, we instead expect that cohabitation is a widely accepted alternative to marriage and an increasingly acceptable context for childbearing.

Canada and the United States belong to a third regime, the so-called liberal welfare regime. It is characterized by limited state support and a greater reliance on market forces. Here, secondary education is comprehensive, and young people must seek out further vocational or professional education or other means of entering into the labor market with occupation-specific skills. Since the labor market is also very open, offering the least employment protection, young people have greater opportunities, but those opportunities are conditioned on competing well in a highly competitive labor market. This market orientation results in greater self-reliance and less of a safety net for young people. We expect to find, therefore, a greater variety of pathways to family formation as young people confront financial uncertainties even as they forge ahead in the family domain. Young people are more accustomed to adapting their family situations to their economic circumstances, therefore we expect to see more single parents, more premarital cohabitation, and, to a lesser extent, more childbearing within cohabiting unions.

In some typologies Italy is said to belong to the conservative regime (Esping-Andersen 1990), while in others it is argued to belong to a distinct southern model characterized by a high degree of fragmentation along occupational lines and a mix of universal and private services and benefits. It is also a regime characterized by no national guaranteed minimum income (Ferrera 1996; Flaquer 2000; Rhodes 1996). Though the educational system in Italy has expanded in the past several decades, it has not become an effective mechanism for channeling youth into the labor market but, rather, a "parking lot" for young adults who have not found a way into the highly protected labor market (Breen and Buchmann 2002; Cook and Furstenberg 2002). Because Italy's welfare regime is so limited, and given Italy's history of extended family coresidence and adherence to Catholicism, families have continued to be the primary safety net for young people. We expect this situation to result in a more prolonged process of leaving the parental home and relatively later and less family formation. Therefore we expect to see later and lower levels of family formation and strict adherence to the traditional family form.

Because of these social, cultural, and welfare state differences, we expect to find important differences in the patterns of transition to adulthood in the five countries analyzed in this chapter.[4] In all countries except Sweden, we expect to see a later age at home leaving in the 1960–64 birth cohort than the in 1950–54 birth cohort, as young adults undergo a longer period of semiautonomy and face increased uncertainty in the labor market. In all countries, we expect that the transition to family formation has been delayed, leading to lower prevalence of marriage and parenthood throughout

the twenties for the younger cohorts. Furthermore, we expect some deviation from the "traditional" sequence of transitions to adulthood in the more
liberal welfare regimes in particular. This is expected to lead to greater percentages of the younger cohorts in nontraditional pathways, particularly in
Canada, the United States and Germany. This chapter adds to the literature
on transitions to adulthood by exploring the timing of status acquisition and
the combinations of statuses that constitute the transition to adulthood and
by situating the United States relative to other industrialized countries.

METHOD

To compare the transition to adulthood in the United States with those observed in Canada, Germany, Italy, and Sweden, we use data from the Family
and Fertility Surveys (FFS), an initiative coordinated by the Population Activities Unit of the United National Economic Commission for Europe (UN-
ECE). National statistical offices in twenty-five countries collected the data
between 1988 and 1999. There was some variation in the sampling design
and response rate. A standardized questionnaire was used in all countries,
asking retrospective questions about the occurrence of home leaving, education, employment, cohabitation, marriage, and births. In our analysis, we
used the harmonized version of the surveys made available by the Population Activities Unit of the UNECE. The United States did not use the same
standardized questionnaire but collected similar information as part of the
National Survey of Family Growth (NSFG). Discussion of the quality of the
data and their degree of cross-national comparability may be found in
Schoenmaeckers and Lodewijckx (1999) and Festy and Prioux (2002). In
general, the preliminary results are robust and point to regional differences
that are consistent with expectations. Basic information about sample size,
the data collection period, and response rates appears in table 3.1. Overall,
about 70% of the samples responded to the survey.

Our basic strategy is to describe changes over time within countries
and differences between countries in the progression of youth through the
traditional steps to adulthood. Our analysis focuses on women because the
NSFG sample is restricted to women, though the other FFS samples include
men. We look at women between ages twenty and thirty-five since women
are more likely to complete the transition to family formation by age thirty-
five due to biological constraints on childbearing. In addition, this allows us
to construct two birth cohorts within each country covering the same period
of time, those born between 1950 and 1954 and those born between 1960
and 1964. Although we would have liked to compare two birth cohorts cov-

TABLE 3.1

SURVEY DETAILS

COUNTRY	SAMPLE SIZE (WOMEN)	AGE RANGE	START	END	RESPONSE RATE (WOMEN)
Canada	4,482	15–54	January 1990	March 1990	75.8[a]
Germany (West)	3,005	20–39	May 1992	September 1992	71.0[a]
Italy	4,824	20–49	November 1995	January 1996	57.0
Sweden	3,318	23–43	October 1992	May 1993	75.4
United States	10,847	15–44	January 1995	October 1995	NA

Sources. Festy and Prioux (2002) and FFS online tables (http://www.unece.org/ead/pau/ffs/ffs_standtabframe.htm).

Note. NA = not available.

[a] Response rate for both men and women.

ering a greater time span, this was not possible with these cross-sectional surveys. Nevertheless, members of these two cohorts came of age at two very distinct periods; those in the earlier cohort reached their twenties in the early to mid-1970s and those in the later cohort in the early to mid-1980s. During this span of time, many young adults came to reject the traditional values of the post–World War II period in favor of more individualist values. These contrasting birth cohorts provide us with substantial information on the changes in the transition to adulthood experienced within countries. In addition to looking at changes within countries, we also compare the timing and prevalence of combinations of statuses between countries.

We define the traditional sequence of transitions to adulthood to be leaving the parental home, entering into marriage without prior cohabitation, and having a first child. We impose this structure as a way of measuring the diversification in pathways to family formation. The new pathways that we measure are home leaving followed by cohabitation, with or without children, and single motherhood.

RESULTS

To describe the patterns of transition to adulthood using simple descriptive statistics, we present the percentage of young women in a particular combination of statuses at ages twenty, twenty-five, thirty, and thirty-five. In doing so, we show the shifts over time in the prevalence of each status combination. In appendix A (table 3.A1), we examine the timing of home leaving and the combination of union and parental statuses associated with having left home at each age. In appendix B (table 3.B1), we use the sample of all those who have already left home and who have had a first child by age thirty-five. This allows us to see when young adults take on adult family statuses and what percentage of them do so in the traditional order (app. table 3.C1 provides the sample sizes for the groups in apps. A and B). Our purpose is to understand the extent to which the transition to family formation is being postponed or forgone and to describe the alternative pathways to family formation that are replacing the traditional one.

For the most part, women in the 1960–64 birth cohort are leaving home somewhat later than their 1950–54 counterparts, though they are more likely to have moved out by age twenty-five (see app. A and fig. 3.1). The exceptions are in Italy where more than 60% of twenty-year-old women were living at home in both the 1950–54 and 1960–64 birth cohorts and in Sweden where young women have left home at young ages in both cohorts. The delay in home leaving is likely due to greater participation in education for women at age twenty and, consequently, greater dependence on their parents for economic support. After education is completed and young people join the labor force, movement out of the household is more likely. This reflects the fact that young women now have more possible pathways out of the household: they can marry, the more traditional way out of the household

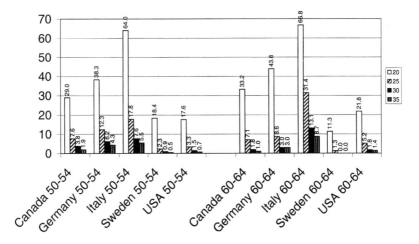

Figure 3.1. Women who have never left home, cohabited, married, or had kids—by age, country, and cohort (%)

for women, or they can cohabit with their romantic partner or live independently, both newer options.

Between these two cohorts, the number of individuals who leave their parents' household to live in nonfamily arrangements has increased at all ages everywhere but in Germany and Italy (fig. 3.2). At age twenty in the United States and Canada, this is likely to be associated with the North American practice of leaving home to attend university, whereas in Europe college students are more likely to live at home while pursuing higher education. At age twenty-five and older, living in nonfamily arrangements has a different meaning than it does for twenty-year olds, more likely reflecting a preference for nonfamily living, at least during this stage in the life course. However, this period of independent nonfamily living is of short duration for most.[5] By age thirty-five, only between 3% and 10% of women have left home but not begun to form their own family, registering a very slight increase in the later birth cohorts in all countries except the United States where the percentage has remained very low. Clearly women are not rejecting family formation, just delaying it. But those in the United States seem to be delaying less than in other countries.

The picture developed thus far—that there has been a shift in the timing of home leaving and family formation, but not a rejection of those transitions—is mirrored in figure 3.3. Although women in the 1960–64 cohort are less likely to have cohabited, married, or had children at ages twenty and twenty-five, by ages thirty and thirty-five the between-cohort, within-country

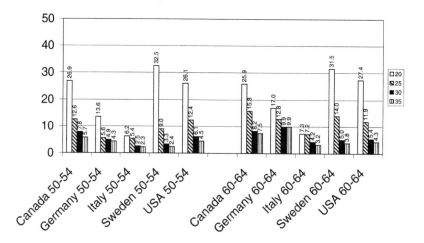

Figure 3.2. Women who have left home, but not cohabited, married, or had kids—by age, country, and cohort (%)

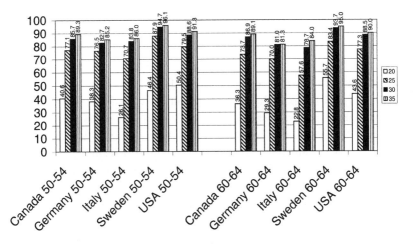

Figure 3.3. Women who have left home, cohabited or married, or had kids—by age, country, and cohort (%)

differences are very small. The only variation in this general trend is Sweden, which shows an increase in the percentage of twenty-year olds who had left home and cohabited, married, or had children between cohorts. There, it is most likely that young women left home and began cohabiting at this age. This suggests that young women are not rejecting the institution of the family but are creating a period of life in their early twenties in which they are living semiautonomously, not relying too much on their parents but refraining from taking on new family responsibilities.

The intercountry differences in the percentage of women who have left home and have cohabited, married, or had children are a test of our expectations that national employment and family policies may influence the timing and prevalence of family formation. In the United States, Canada, and Sweden, close to or more than 90% of thirty- and thirty-five-year-old women in the 1960–65 birth cohort had left home and begun family formation, but in Germany and Italy only about 80% of these women had done the same (fig. 3). We hypothesized that the Italian and German conservative corporatist states would discourage family formation since youth often have difficulty entering the highly protected labor market and since women with children have little support to continue working (Breen and Buchmann 2002; Orloff 1993). In countries where the population responds to the incentives and disincentives offered by the welfare state, these structures may make family formation more difficult and less attractive to young women and their partners. In Canada and the United States, we expect that the state's weaker interventions in terms of employment protection and family formation would result in a greater diversity of pathways to family formation but not necessarily to lower levels. In these countries, economic uncertainty in the early life course is common and not necessarily considered an impediment to family formation (Edin and Lein 1997; Ellwood and Jencks 2004; Smeeding and Philips 2002). In contrast to the four other countries, Sweden shows the greatest percentages of women leaving home and beginning family formation at ages twenty-five, thirty, and thirty-five in both cohorts. The generous welfare state and the cultural acceptability of cohabitation as a context for childbearing may support young women in their family formation by giving them a stronger economic safety net and allowing for more forms of family (Moen 1989). The continuity of these cross-national patterns across cohorts suggests that differences in welfare states partially account for differences in the timing and levels of family formation, though cultural patterns and value changes also play a role.

Having reviewed the transition out of the parental home as the first step in the transition to adulthood, our next step is to examine how the demographic transition to adulthood is completed—a process we define as becoming a parent (Elder 1985; Sandefur et al., this vol., chap. 9). We selected for analysis only those women who have left home and had a child and examined their union histories to see the couple arrangement in which they are raising their first child. This pares down our samples differently for each country (see app. table 3.C1) but allows us to focus on the variety of pathways to parenthood.

The traditional pathway to family formation—marrying and having kids without ever cohabiting—has decreased at all ages and in all countries, though more in some than in others (fig. 3.4). In Sweden, this pattern was already low in the 1950–54 birth cohort, and it further diminished in the 1960–64 birth cohort so that fewer than 10% of these women had married and had children without ever cohabiting by any age. In Canada, Germany, and the United States, there also have been decreases in the percentage of women following the traditional route, but more than 50% of young women who have had children by a given age have done so within the context of a marriage that was not preceded by cohabitation. Thus, for women in these countries there is still a great deal of adherence to the traditional pattern, though it is weakening. In contrast, for women in Italy the traditional path of marriage and childbearing is still the path most often taken among women with children at all ages.[6] The east-west family structure divide in Europe still influences the degree of adherence to the traditional pathway to

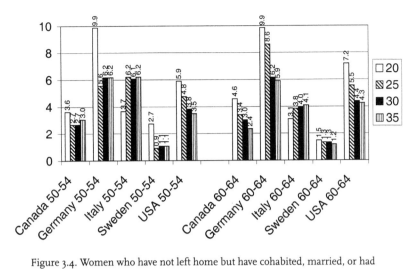

Figure 3.4. Women who have not left home but have cohabited, married, or had kids—by age, country, and cohort (%)

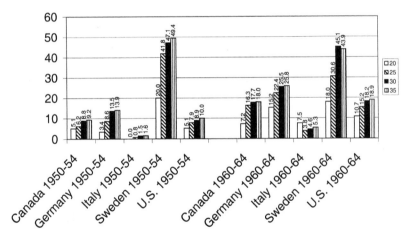

Figure 3.5. Women who have left home and cohabited, married, and had kids—by age, country, and cohort (%)

adulthood with Germany, Sweden, Canada, and the United States falling to the west and Italy falling to the east of this line.

An alternative to the traditional route to family formation involves premarital cohabitation, a practice that is becoming more common in many of these countries, though Sweden is the clear leader in this practice (fig. 3.5).

In the United States, Canada and Germany, there was a rise between the two cohorts in premarital cohabitation among women with children, accounting for a good deal of the decline in the traditional pattern in those countries. In Italy there is a negligible increase in premarital cohabitation. Clearly in most countries there has been a change in the degree to which young people believe that marriage is the only legitimate form of union formation, though in the United States, Canada, and Germany most women who cohabit later marry.

In Canada, Germany, and the United States, a small but growing minority of women have children within a cohabiting relationship and without marrying their partners by a given age, while in Sweden it is common in both cohorts, a pattern that continues to be on the rise (fig. 3.6). This is one of the more diverse ways in which women in these countries are pursuing family formation. However in Italy childbearing within cohabitation is still quite rare, less than 4% at all ages.

Perhaps the most controversial nontraditional route to family formation is having children without marrying and/or cohabiting (fig. 3.7). This is most common in Canada, Germany, and the United States, where the percentage of twenty-year-old mothers who are not cohabiting or married but have left home ranges from 14% to 24% of mothers in this age group in both birth cohorts and is increasing somewhat in the United States and Canada but decreasing in Germany. In Sweden and Italy, very small percentages of women with children are single mothers in each birth cohort. Despite these

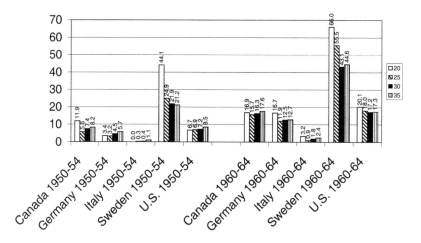

Figure 3.6. Women who have left home, cohabited, and had kids but never married—by age, country, and cohort (%)

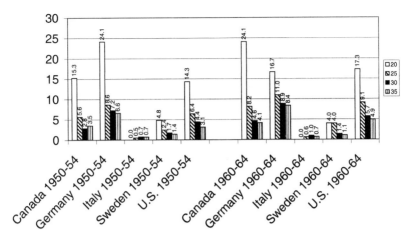

Figure 3.7. Women who have left home and had kids but not cohabited or married—by age, country, and cohort (%)

intercountry differences, the three countries in which single motherhood is significant all have in common the pattern of declining percentages of un-partnered mothers at older ages. These single mothers may go on to cohabit and/or marry, but they break from the traditional sequence by beginning family formation through childbearing. The fact that single motherhood is more common in the liberal welfare states, that is, the United States and Canada, supports our theory that childbearing in those states is more likely to occur in nontraditional patterns. The relatively high level of single moth-erhood in Germany is less expected but may be a result of the support that mothers are given in the German welfare state and the high level of accep-tance of single mothers living on their own. Again, the intersection of cul-ture and the welfare state plays out differently across contexts.

DISCUSSION

Home leaving is occurring later for young people in many advanced indus-trialized countries though generally it does not extend much beyond the early twenties. In the United States, Canada, Germany, and Sweden, the tim-ing of home leaving is tightly linked to longer periods of education. Home leaving occurs earliest in Sweden, where young people often receive un-employment benefits, higher starting wages, or financial aid for students, thus facilitating the transition to residential independence (Smeeding and Phillips 2002). Furthermore, cohabitation is a common practice among young people there, thus reducing the costs of establishing an independent household and making it a more attractive living arrangement than staying in the parental household. In Italy, in contrast, education is quite prolonged, in part because there is so little labor market opportunity and young people must search a long time before finding adequate employment. The later ages at home leaving may suggest initial difficulties in finding employment in most of these countries, but those obstacles are mostly overcome by age twenty-five in all countries except Italy.

Cross-national differences in the propensity to cohabit, either as a substitute for marriage or prior to marriage, are rooted in the culture of a society rather than in their welfare state typology, although the two certainly interact. The cultural divide between east and west that many scholars have noted coincides perfectly with the infrequency of cohabitation in Italy and its frequency in Sweden. In Germany, Canada, and the United States, while premarital cohabitation is becoming more acceptable, cohabitation is still considered less acceptable as an arrangement for childbearing (Rindfuss and VandenHeuvel 1990).

Differences between countries in the timing of childbearing are more closely related to the welfare regime. Italy and Sweden are distinct extremes in terms of the timing of home leaving and entry into cohabitation and/or marriage, although they share a tendency toward maintaining two-parent families as the context for child rearing. In Italy, child rearing is nearly always in the context of marriage, while in Sweden, child rearing also occurs within cohabiting unions. In neither country do we find significant levels of single mothers, but we believe that different explanations apply. Sweden's egalitarian welfare state has made financial supports to family a priority, facilitating the transition to family formation, particularly childbearing. In Italy, however, the conservative corporatist state has deemed family decisions to be private and, thus, offers little support for parents. Together with the highly protected labor market favoring those with longer job tenure, it is very difficult for young people to achieve financial stability and establish independent households, which are generally considered a prerequisite for marriage and childbearing. While women in both countries adhere to a norm of two-parent families, Sweden has a higher proportion of mothers by age thirty-five than does Italy (app. table 3.A1).

Family formation patterns within the remaining three countries, the United States, Canada, and Germany, are less distinct, but tentative interpretations can still be made. We expected that in the liberal welfare regimes, the tendency for young people to face greater uncertainties about their financial future would lead to more variation in the pathways to adulthood, especially family formation. This may also be the case in Germany, where the conservative corporatist state supports young people in the school-to-work transition but has not kept up with changes in the industrial structure of the economy. These uncertainties may lead young people to delay family formation but also to choose nontraditional routes to family formation, either through premarital cohabitation, cohabitation and childbearing, or single motherhood.

While changes in the timing of home leaving seem more clearly related to social structure and economic context, changes in patterns of family formation are based in both cultural patterns and welfare regime types. In Sweden, where the egalitarian welfare state is quite generous, we see less of a delay in family formation, more variation from the traditional pattern as more women cohabit instead of marrying, but very little single motherhood. In Italy, where the welfare state is weak, we see a quite prolonged delay in home leaving and family formation, perhaps as a result of the strict adherence to the traditional family formation pattern. Though we expected Germany to resemble somewhat the Italian case, it is closer to the North American pattern. The United States and Canada, with liberal welfare regimes and more heterogeneous cultures, show less delay in family formation but more variation from the traditional pattern, mostly through premarital cohabitation and, to a lesser degree, through single motherhood and childbearing within a cohabiting union.

By looking at the progression of women through home leaving, cohabitation, marriage, and childbearing, we see that several new pathways to family formation have been forged to varying extents in different countries. However, the majority still follow the traditional path: in the United States, 59% of women in the 1960–64 birth cohort who went on to have children by age thirty-five also married without ever cohabiting (Canada, 60%; Germany, 53%; Italy, 92%; Sweden, 10%).[7] The two outliers in this set of countries are instructive. In Italy, the small percentage of women who actually go on to have children (69%) suggests that the inflexibility of the marriage regime there may deter family formation. In Germany, where the marriage regime is more flexible but obstacles to stable employment are greater due to the corporate conservative welfare regime, the percentage of thirty-five-year-old women who have left home and had children is as low as that of Italy (68%). In contrast, a great number of women in Sweden's more flexible marriage regime, which includes cohabitation, go on to have children (80%) than in any other country in our study. The new pathways to family formation in the United States and Canada may also facilitate family formation; in these countries the percentage of women who have left home and had children by age thirty-five are 77% and 73% respectively. The challenge for social scientists is to understand the macrosocial circumstances that cause young women to follow new pathways to adulthood.

CONCLUSION

The anxiety parents express over their children's apparent reluctance to settle down and have a family may be just a matter of waiting long enough. Whether young people are waiting for the right partner, the right circumstances, or until fate intervenes is difficult to know for parents and social scientists alike. We are able to see, however, that the vast majority of young women in the United States and the other countries we have studied do marry and have children by age thirty-five. Young women in the United States are not so different from their counterparts in Canada and Germany; they are delaying leaving home slightly but not as much as young women in Italy, nor are they leaving as early as those in Sweden. This is part of a pattern of a more gradual transition into economic independence and the prolongation of the period of independence from family responsibilities. Throughout these countries women spend a growing period of time in nonfamily living arrangements after leaving the parental household and before forming their own families. But by age thirty-five, women who came of age in the 1980s are as likely to have married and had children as were their counterparts in the 1970s (note, however, that our analysis does not include separation or divorce, which may show nonnegligible differences between the two cohorts).

Nevertheless, there are a greater variety of pathways to reaching that point. More women are cohabiting prior to marriage in the United States as well as in Canada, Germany, and especially Sweden, where cohabitation is as accepted as marriage. On the one hand, as more young people pursue higher education or more intensive professional training, their interests may not be oriented toward marriage, even though they have not ruled it out, and cohabitation may be an attractive temporary living arrangement. On the other hand, many young people may feel thwarted in their efforts to achieve the economic independence they consider a prerequisite to family formation, and cohabitation may actually facilitate economic independence and family formation by reducing living costs. We cannot discern these motivations here. The overall trend, however, is for young women to increasingly delay, but not necessarily forgo, formal marriage and childbearing.

Substantial research suggests that the link between marriage and childbearing is weakening (Bumpass, Sweet, and Cherlin 1991; Ellwood and Jencks 2004; Lichter, McLaughlin, and Ribar 2002). While out-of-wedlock births were not unheard of among the earlier cohort in the United States, Canada, or Germany, the later cohort was more likely to have children without having cohabited or married, especially in their early twenties. In Germany, the percentage of women in their twenties and thirties who had children without having cohabited or married is greater than in the United States or Canada, perhaps due to the greater government benefits associated with childbearing there. In contrast, single motherhood is very rare and not increasing in Sweden and Italy. Clearly, the cultural and structural forces shaping these similar outcomes in Sweden and Italy are completely distinct. In Italy the institutions of marriage and childbearing remain tightly intertwined, while in Sweden cohabitation provides an alternative to marriage as a context for childbearing.

Our cross-national analysis suggests that young women adapt their family formation patterns to the macrosocial circumstances of a country through either delaying family formation or following nontraditional routes to family formation. While cultural patterns of family formation exert a strong influence, obstacles to employment among young adults also play a role. In the corporate conservative welfare states of Italy and Germany, we see that young people either delay family formation until quite late, in the case of Italy, or take different routes to getting there, in the case of Germany. In both countries, women are less likely to have left their parents' home and had children by age thirty-five than are women in other countries. In Sweden's egalitarian welfare state, the transition to family formation is facilitated by both the employment and family policies of the state, and more women complete the transition to family formation by having a first child. In the liberal welfare states of the United States and Canada, women are more likely to take alternative paths to family formation and more likely to have left home and had children by age thirty-five.

What does this tell us about the United States that we did not know before? Most important, it tells us that the delay in family formation in the United States is not "off the charts." On the contrary, it is part of a pattern common to advanced industrial countries. But it also tells us that the institutional supports and cultural guidelines that structure the transition to adulthood in some countries are not as strong in the United States. Indeed, the adaptations in family formation that young people in the United States make may be inevitable in a society as individualistic as is ours.

TABLE 3.AI

HOME-LEAVING PATTERNS

	AT AGE			
	20	25	30	35
Canada:				
1950–54:				
1. Never left home or cohabited or married or had kids	29.0	7.6	3.8	1.9
2. Left home but never cohabited or married or had kids	26.9	12.6	7.8	5.7
3. Never left home but has cohabited or married or had kids	3.6	2.7	2.7	3.0
4. Left home and has cohabited or married or had kids	40.6	77.1	85.7	89.3
N	525	525	525	525
1960–64:				
1. Never left home or cohabited or married or had kids	33.2	7.1	1.8	1.0
2. Left home but never cohabited or married or had kids	25.9	15.8	8.2	7.5
3. Never left home but has cohabited or married or had kids	4.6	3.4	3.0	2.4
4. Left home and has cohabited or married or had kids	36.3	73.7	86.9	89.1
N	764	764	764	764
Germany:				
1950–54:				
1. Never left home or cohabited or married or had kids	38.3	12.3	6.2	4.3
2. Left home but never cohabited or married or had kids	13.6	5.6	4.9	4.3
3. Never left home but has cohabited or married or had kids	9.9	5.6	6.2	6.2
4. Left home and has cohabited or married or had kids	38.3	76.5	82.7	85.2
N	162	162	162	162
1960–64:				
1. Never left home or cohabited or married or had kids	43.8	8.6	3.0	3.0
2. Left home but never cohabited or married or had kids	17.0	12.8	9.9	9.9

(continued)

TABLE 3.AI

(CONTINUED)

	AT AGE			
	20	25	30	35
3. Never left home but has cohabited or married or had kids	9.9	8.6	6.2	5.9
4. Left home and has cohabited or married or had kids	29.3	70.0	81.0	81.3
N	406	406	406	406
Italy:				
1950–54:				
1. Never left home or cohabited or married or had kids	64.0	17.8	7.6	5.5
2. Left home but never cohabited or married or had kids	6.2	5.4	2.5	2.3
3. Never left home but has cohabited or married or had kids	3.7	6.2	6.1	6.2
4. Left home and has cohabited or married or had kids	26.1	70.7	83.8	86.0
N	709	709	709	709
1960–64:				
1. Never left home or cohabited or married or had kids	66.8	31.4	13.1	8.7
2. Left home but never cohabited or married or had kids	7.3	7.2	4.2	3.2
3. Never left home but has cohabited or married or had kids	3.1	3.8	4.0	4.1
4. Left home and has cohabited or married or had kids	22.8	57.6	78.7	84.0
N	780	780	780	780
Sweden:				
1950–54:				
1. Never left home or cohabited or married or had kids	18.4	2.3	.9	.5
2. Left home but never cohabited or married or had kids	32.5	9.0	3.3	2.4
3. Never left home but has cohabited or married or had kids	2.7	.9	1.1	1.1
4. Left home and has cohabited or married or had kids	46.4	87.9	94.7	96.1
N	659	659	659	659

(continued)

TABLE 3.AI

(CONTINUED)

	AT AGE			
	20	25	30	35
1960–64:				
1. Never left home or cohabited or married or had kids	11.3	1.3	.0	.0
2. Left home but never cohabited or married or had kids	31.5	14.0	5.0	3.8
3. Never left home but has cohabited or married or had kids	1.5	1.3	1.3	1.2
4. Left home and has cohabited or married or had kids	55.7	83.4	93.7	95.0
N	679	679	679	679
United States:				
1950–54:				
1. Never left home or cohabited or married or had kids	17.6	3.3	1.5	.7
2. Left home but never cohabited or married or had kids	26.1	12.4	6.1	4.5
3. Never left home but has cohabited or married or had kids	5.9	4.8	3.8	3.5
4. Left home and has cohabited or married or had kids	50.4	79.5	88.6	91.3
N	1,493	1,493	1,493	1,493
1960–64:				
1. Never left home or cohabited or married or had kids	21.8	5.2	1.8	1.4
2. Left home but never cohabited or married or had kids	27.4	11.9	5.4	4.3
3. Never left home but has cohabited or married or had kids	7.2	5.5	4.4	4.3
4. Left home and has cohabited or married or had kids	43.6	77.3	88.5	90.0
N	2,163	2,163	2,163	2,163

Source. Fertility and Family Surveys.

TABLE 3.BI

PROGRESSION TO PARENTHOOD (FOR THOSE WHO LEFT HOME
AND BEGAN FAMILY FORMATION)

	AT AGE			
	20	25	30	35
Canada:				
1950–54:				
1. Cohabited and has kids but never married	11.9	5.6	7.4	8.2
2. Married and has kids but never cohabited	67.8	82.6	80.9	79.1
3. Cohabited and married and has kids	5.1	6.2	8.8	9.2
4. Has kids but never cohabited or married	15.3	5.6	2.8	3.5
N	59	195	351	401
1960–64:				
1. Cohabited and has kids but never married	16.9	15.7	16.3	17.6
2. Married and has kids but never cohabited	51.8	59.9	61.3	60.3
3. Cohabited and married and has kids	7.2	16.3	17.7	18.0
4. Has kids but never cohabited or married	24.1	8.2	4.6	4.1
N	83	319	496	557
Germany:				
1950–54:				
1. Cohabited and has kids but never married	3.4	3.2	4.5	5.7
2. Married and has kids but never cohabited	69.0	79.6	74.8	73.8
3. Cohabited and married and has kids	3.4	8.6	13.5	13.9
4. Has kids but never cohabited or married	24.1	8.6	7.2	6.6
N	29	93	111	122
1960–64:				
1. Cohabited and has kids but never married	16.7	11.9	12.5	12.7
2. Married and has kids but never cohabited	51.5	54.8	53.1	53.1
3. Cohabited and married and has kids	15.2	22.4	25.5	25.8
4. Has kids but never cohabited or married	16.7	11.0	8.9	8.4
N	66	219	271	275
Italy:				
1950–54:				
1. Cohabited and has kids but never married	.0	.3	.4	1.1
2. Married and has kids but never cohabited	100.0	98.5	97.4	96.7
3. Cohabited and married and has kids	.0	.8	1.5	1.6
4. Has kids but never cohabited or married	.0	.5	.7	.7
N	114	396	538	571

(continued)

TABLE 3.B1

(CONTINUED)

	AT AGE			
	20	25	30	35
1960–64:				
1. Cohabited and has kids but never married	3.2	.9	1.8	2.4
2. Married and has kids but never cohabited	89.2	94.6	92.6	91.6
3. Cohabited and married and has kids	7.5	3.8	4.6	5.3
4. Has kids but never cohabited or married	.0	.6	1.0	.7
N	93	316	502	580
Sweden:				
1950–54:				
1. Cohabited and has kids but never married	44.1	24.9	21.9	21.2
2. Married and has kids but never cohabited	31.0	30.8	29.3	28.1
3. Cohabited and married and has kids	20.0	41.8	47.1	49.4
4. Has kids but never cohabited or married	4.8	2.4	1.7	1.4
N	145	409	535	581
1960–64:				
1. Cohabited and has kids but never married	66.0	55.5	43.1	44.6
2. Married and has kids but never cohabited	12.0	10.0	10.4	10.4
3. Cohabited and married and has kids	18.0	30.6	45.1	43.9
4. Has kids but never cohabited or married	4.0	4.0	1.4	1.1
N	100	301	501	547
United States:				
1950–54:				
1. Cohabited and has kids but never married	6.7	6.9	7.2	8.5
2. Married and has kids but never cohabited	73.9	78.9	79.5	78.4
3. Cohabited and married and has kids	5.1	7.9	8.9	10.0
4. Has kids but never cohabited or married	14.3	6.4	4.4	3.1
N	448	815	1,067	1,188
1960–64:				
1. Cohabited and has kids but never married	20.1	18.0	17.2	17.3
2. Married and has kids but never cohabited	51.9	57.7	58.9	58.8
3. Cohabited and married and has kids	10.7	15.2	18.2	18.9
4. Has kids but never cohabited or married	17.7	9.1	5.7	4.9
N	532	1,142	1,554	1,663

Source. Fertility and Family Surveys.

TABLE 3.CI

SAMPLE SIZES FOR TABLES 3.AI AND 3.BI

		APPENDIX A					APPENDIX B (ALL WITH KIDS)			
COUNTRY/COHORT	TOTAL	NEVER LEFT HOME	LEFT HOME ONLY	NEVER LEFT BUT BEGAN FAMILY FORM	LEFT HOME AND BEGAN FORMING A FAMILY	TOTAL	COHABITED AND HAS KIDS	MARRIED AND HAS KIDS	COHABITED, MARRIED, AND HAS KIDS	HAS KIDS ONLY
Canada:										
1950–54	525	10	16	30	469	401	33	317	37	14
1960–64	764	8	18	57	681	557	98	336	100	23
Germany:										
1950–54	162	10	10	8	138	122	7	90	17	8
1960–64	406	12	25	40	330	275	35	146	71	23
Italy:										
1950–54	709	39	44	16	610	571	6	552	9	4
1960–64	780	68	32	25	655	580	14	531	31	4
Sweden:										
1950–54	659	3	7	16	633	581	123	163	287	8
1960–64	679	0	8	26	645	547	244	57	240	6
United States:										
1950–54	1,493	11	52	67	1,363	1,188	101	931	119	37
1960–64	2,163	31	92	93	1,947	1,663	288	978	315	82

NOTES

1. The demographic definition of the transition to adulthood typically considers the acquisition of measurable statuses—such as living independently, finishing school, engaging in steady full-time employment, marrying, and having children—as constituting adulthood, though other disciplines measure adulthood differently.

2. By focusing on combinations of statuses at given ages, we are not keeping track of the exact sequence in which these statuses were acquired. That will be examined in later work, using more sophisticated methods of analysis.

3. We excluded the former East Germany from the analysis in view of major political, social, and economic differences that shaped the transition to adulthood as compared to the other countries.

4. There are also important microlevel determinants of the transition to adulthood. In this chapter, we focus on macro- rather than microlevel factors since our objective is to compare countries and place the United States in a comparative perspective.

5. Using this cross-sectional approach, we don't register the actual percentage ever experiencing this combination of statuses, but this gives us an indication of how many experienced it at this particular age.

6. However, it is important to point out that the percentage of women who has children by age thirty-five is the smallest in Italy and the greatest in Sweden (see app. table 3.A1). Apparently conforming to the traditional path to family formation is not associated with higher levels of childbearing overall.

7. This increases to 54.9% if we include women who cohabited prior to marriage and had children.

REFERENCES

Aassve, Arnstein, Francesco C. Billari, Stefano Mazzuco, and Fausta Ongaro. 2002. Leaving Home: A Comparative Analysis of ECHP Data. *Journal of European Social Policy* 12 (4):259–75.

Becker, Gary S. 1981. *A Treatise on the Family.* Cambridge, MA: Harvard University Press.

Billari, Francesco C., Maria Castiglioni, Teresa Castro Martin, Francesca Michielin, and Fausta Ongaro. 2002. Household and Union Formation in a Mediterranean Fashion: Italy and Spain. Pp. 17–41 in *Dynamics of Fertility and Partnership in Europe: Insights and Lessons from Comparative Research,* vol. 2, edited by Erik Klijzing and Martine Corijn. Geneva and New York: United Nations.

Billari, Francesco C., Dimiter Philipov, and Pau Baizán. 2001. Leaving Home in Europe: The Experience of Cohorts Born around 1960. *International Journal of Population Geography* 7 (5):339–56.

Billari, Francesco C., and Chris Wilson. 2001. Convergence towards Diversity? Cohort Dynamics in the Transition to Adulthood in Contemporary Western Europe. Working Paper WP-2001–039. Max-Planck Institute for Demographic Research, Rostock.

Breen, Richard, and Marlis Buchmann. 2002. Institutional Variation and the Position of Young People: A Comparative Perspective. *Annals of the American Academy of Political and Social Sciences* 580:288–305.

Buchmann, Marlis. 1989. *The Script of Life in Modern Society: Entry into Adulthood in a Changing World*. Chicago: University of Chicago Press.

Bumpass, Larry L., James A. Sweet, and Andrew Cherlin. 1991. The Role of Cohabitation in the Declining Rates of Marriage. *Journal of Marriage and the Family* 53:535–51.

Cook, Thomas D., and Frank F. Furstenberg. 2002. Explaining Aspects of the Transition to Adulthood in Italy, Sweden, Germany, and the United States: A Cross-disciplinary, Case Synthesis Approach. *Annals of the American Academy of Political and Social Science* 580:257–87.

Corijn, Martine, and Erik Klijzing, eds. 2001. *Transitions to Adulthood in Europe*. London: Kluwer Academic Publishers.

Easterlin, Richard, Christine MacDonald, and Diane Macunovich. 1990. How Have the American Baby Boomers Fared? Earnings and Economic Well-being of Young Adults, 1964–1987. *Journal of Population Economics* 3 (4): 277–90.

Edin, Kathryn, and Laura Lein. 1997. *Making Ends Meet: How Single Mothers Survive Welfare and Low-Wage Work*. New York: Russell Sage Foundation.

Elder, Glen H. 1985. *Life Course Dynamics: Trajectories and Transitions, 1968–1980*. Ithaca, NY: Cornell University Press.

Ellwood, David T., and Christopher Jencks. 2004. "The Uneven Spread of Single Parent Families: What Do We Know? Where Do We Look for Answers?" In *Social Inequality*, edited by Kathryn Neckerman. Cambridge, MA: Harvard University Press.

Esping-Andersen, Gosta. 1990. *Three Worlds of Welfare Capitalism*. Cambridge: Polity Press.

Ferrera, Maurizio. 1996. The Southern Welfare State in Social Europe. *Journal of European Social Policy* 6 (1):17–37.

Festy, Patrick, and France Prioux. 2002. *An Evaluation of the Fertility and Family Surveys Project*. New York and Geneva: United Nations.

Flaquer, Lluís. 2000. Family Policy and Welfare State in Southern Europe. Working Paper 185. Institut de Ciències Polítiques i Socials, Universitat Autònoma de Barcelona. http://www.diba.es/icps/working_papers/docs/WP_I_185.htm.

Furstenberg, Frank F., Jr. 2000. The Sociology of Adolescence and Youth in the 1990s: A Critical Commentary. *Journal of Marriage and the Family* 62: 896–910.

Fussell, Elizabeth. 2002. The Transition to Adulthood in Aging Societies. *Annals of the American Academy of Political and Social Science* 580:16–39.

Gauthier, Anne H. 1996. *The State and the Family*. Oxford: Clarendon Press.

Goldscheider, Frances K. 1997. Recent Changes in U.S. Young Adults Living Arrangements in Comparative Perspective. *Journal of Family Issues* 18: 708–24.

Goldscheider, Frances K., and Linda J. Waite. 1991. *New Families, No Families? The Transformation of the American Home*. Berkeley: University of California Press.

Hajnal, John. 1965. European Marriage Patterns in Perspective. Pp. 101–43 in *Population in History: Essays in Historical Demography,* edited by David Victor Glass and David Edward Charles Eversley. Chicago: Aldine Publishing.

Heinz, Walter R. 1999. *From Education to Work: Cross-national Perspectives*. Cambridge: Cambridge University Press.

———. 2000. Youth Transitions and Employment in Germany. *International Social Science Journal* 52 (164):161–64.

Hogan, Dennis P. 1981. The Transition to Adulthood as a Career Contingency. *American Sociological Review* 45 (2):261–76.

Iacovou, Maria. 1998. Young People in Europe: Two Models of Household Formation. Working Paper, no. 98–13. University of Essex, Institute for Social and Economic Research.

———. 2002. Regional Differences in the Transition to Adulthood. *Annals of the American Academy of Political and Social Science* 580:40–69.

Ingelhart, Ronald, and Wayne R. Baker. 2000. Modernization, Cultural Change, and the Persistence of Traditional Values. *American Sociological Review* 65:19–51.

Kerckhoff, Alan C. 2002. The Transition from School to Work. Pp. 52–87 in *The Changing Adolescent Experience: Societal Trends and the Transition to Adulthood,* edited by Jeylan Mortimer and Reed W. Larson. New York: Cambridge University Press.

Kiernan, Kathleen. 2000. European Perspectives on Union Formation. Pp. 40–58 in *The Ties That Bind: Perspectives on Marriage and Cohabitation,* edited by Linda J. Waite, Christine Bachrach, Michelle H. Hindin, Elizabeth Thomson, and Arland Thornton. New York: Aldine de Gruyter.

————. 2001. The Rise of Cohabitation and Childbearing outside Marriage in Western Europe. *International Journal of Law, Policy and the Family* 15 (1): 1–21.

Lesthaeghe, Ron, and Dominique Meekers. 1986. Value Changes and the Dimensions of Familism in the European Community. *European Journal of Population* 2 (3–4):225–68.

Lesthaeghe, Ron, and Paul Willems. 1999. Is Low Fertility a Temporary Phenomenon in the European Union? *Population and Development Review* 25 (2): 211–28.

Lewis, June. 2000. Gender and Welfare Regimes. Pp. 37–51 in *Rethinking Social Policy*, edited by Gail Lewis, Susan Geewirtz, and John Clarke. New York: Sage Publications.

Lichter, Daniel T., Diane K. McLaughlin, and David C. Ribar. 2002. Economic Restructuring and the Retreat from Marriage. *Social Science Research* 31: 230–56.

Liefbroer, Aat C., and Jenny de Jong Gierveld. 1995. Standardization and Individualization: The Transition from Youth to Adulthood among Cohorts Born between 1903 and 1965. Pp. 57–79 in *Population and Family in the Low Countries*, edited by Hans van den Brekel and Fred Deven. Dordrecht: Kluwer Academic Publishers.

Marini, Margaret M. 1984. The Order of Events in the Transition to Adulthood. *Sociology of Education* 57:64–84.

Modell, John, Frank F. Furstenberg Jr., and Theodore Hershberg. 1976. Social Change and Transitions to Adulthood in Historical Perspective. *Journal of Family History* 1:7–32.

Moen, Phyllis. 1989. *Working Parents: Transformations in Gender Roles and Public Policies in Sweden*. Madison: University of Wisconsin Press.

Mortimer, Jeylan, and Reed Larson. 2002. The Changing Adolescent Experience: Societal Trends and the Transition to Adulthood. New York: Cambridge University Press.

Ni Bhrolchain, Maire. 1993. East-West Marriage Contrasts, Old and New. Pp. 461–479 in *European Population*. Vol. 2, *Demographic Dynamics*, edited by A. Blum and J. L. Rallu. Montrouge: John Libbey Eurotext.

Orloff, Ann S. 1993. Gender and the Social Rights of Citizenship: The Comparative Analysis of Gender Relations and Welfare States. *American Sociological Review* 58 (3):303–28.

Ravanera, Zenaida R., Fernando Rajulton, and Thomas K. Burch. 2002. Effects of Community and Family Characteristics on Early Life Transitions of Canadian Youth. Paper Presented at the 2002 Population Association of America Annual Meeting, Atlanta, May 9–11.

Reher, David. 1998. Family Ties in Western Europe: Persistent Contrasts. *Population and Development Review* 24 (2):203–34.

Rhodes, Martin. 1996. Southern European Welfare States: Between Crisis and Reform. *South European Society and Politics* 1 (3):1–22.

Rindfuss, Ronald R. 1991. The Young Adult Years: Diversity, Structural Change, and Fertility. *Demography* 28 (4):493–512.

Rindfuss, Ronald R., P. S. Morgan, and Kate Offutt. 1996. Education and the Changing Age Pattern of Fertility: 1963–1989. *Demography* 33 (3):277–90.

Rindfuss, Ronald R., C. Gray Swicegood, and Rachel A. Rosenfeld. 1987. Disorder in the Life Course: How Common and Does It Matter? *Annual Sociological Review* 52:785–801.

Rindfuss, Ronald R., and Audrey VandenHeuvel. 1990. Cohabitation: A Precursor to Marriage or an Alternative to Being Single? *Population and Development Review* 16:703–26.

Sardon, Jean-Paul. 1993. Women's First Marriage Rates in Europe: Elements for a Typology. *Population: An English Selection* 5:119–52.

Schoenmaeckers, Ronald, and Edith Lodewijckx. 1999. Changes in Demographic Behavior in Europe: Some Results from FFS-Country Reports and Suggestions for Further Research. *European Journal of Population* 15:207–40.

Shanahan, Michael J. 2000. Pathways to Adulthood: Variability and Mechanisms in Life Course Perspective. *Annual Review of Sociology* 26:667–92.

Shavit, Yossi, and Walter Muller. 1998. *From School to Work: A Comparative Study of Education Qualifications and Occupational Destinations.* Oxford: Clarendon Press.

Simó, Carles, and Katrin Golsch. 2000. The Transition to Motherhood under the Globalization Process—an Attempt to Study the Consequences of the Globalization Process in the Transition to Motherhood by Means of Rational Choice Models. GLOBALIFE Working Paper Series, no. 04, Faculty of Sociology, University of Bielefeld. http://alia.soziologie.uni-bielefeld.de/~globalife/abstracts_workingpapers/abs004.html.

Smeeding, Timothy M., and Katherin R. Phillips. 2002. Cross-national Differences in Employment and Economic Sufficiency. *Annals of the American Academy of Political and Social Science* 580:103–33.

Stevens, David A. 1990. New Evidence on the Timing of Early Life Course Transitions: The United States, 1900 to 1980. *Journal of Family History* 15 (2):163–78.

Teitler, Julien. 2002. Trends in Youth Sexual Initiation and Fertility in Developed Countries: 1960–1995. *Annals of the American Academy of Political and Social Science* 580:134–52.

Thornton, Arland. 2001. The Developmental Paradigm, Reading History Sideways, and Family Change. *Demography* 38:449–66.

Uhlenberg, Peter. 1969. A Study of Cohort Life Cycles: Cohorts of Native-Born Massachusetts Women, 1830–1920. *Population Studies* 23 (3):407–20.

Van de Kaa, Dirk J. 1994. The Second Demographic Transition Revisited: Theories and Expectations. Pp. 81–126 in *Population and Family in the Low Countries, 1993: Late Fertility and Other Current Issues,* edited by G. C. N. Beets, J. C. van den Brekel, R. L. Cliquet, G. Dhooghe and J. De Jong Gierveld. Lisse: Swets & Zeitlinger.

CHAPTER 4

HISTORICAL ROOTS OF FAMILY DIVERSITY

Marital and Childbearing Trajectories of American Women

LAWRENCE L. WU AND JUI-CHUNG ALLEN LI

Are modern family forms more diverse now than in the past? Conventional wisdom takes the answer to be yes, while in this chapter we provide evidence suggesting that the answer is more nearly no. This question is not merely of academic interest but is of considerable importance to several ongoing debates. For example, family diversity is central to the recent "culture wars" over the family, with some authors viewing recent changes in the family as simply reflecting new and more diverse family forms (Demo, Allen, and Fine 2000; Stacey 1991), and others seeing these changes as heralding a serious and fundamental decline in the institution of the family (Gilder 1986; Popenoe 1993; Whitehead 1993).

The conventional viewpoint is also adopted by several authors in this volume (see e.g., Fussell and Furstenberg; chap. 2; Fussell and Gauthier, chap. 3), in which the traditional markers of adulthood are seen as having shifted dramatically with the changing social landscape of the past several decades, with young adults today possessing far more options as they move through adulthood than in the past. These changes are seen as having been particularly consequential for women, who have a markedly wider range of options relative to what was available to them in decades past. Moreover, the consequences of these greater options are widely argued not to be confined only to women's employment opportunities but to reach even further to influence many realms of women's lives, including childbearing and marriage.

Logically, the arguments encapsulated in the conventional view would imply greater diversity in the family patterns over time, with some women continuing to follow traditional trajectories of marriage and childbearing but others increasingly following nontraditional patterns. Examples of non-traditional patterns include delaying childbearing and marriage, bearing children outside of marriage, or retreating from marriage altogether. Thus conventional wisdom holds that because women early in the twentieth century had relatively fewer life options, their pathways through marriage and childbearing were simpler than those for women born later in the twentieth century. Diversity in women's family lives, thus, should have increased dramatically over time, with much of what we regard as new, diverse, and "nontraditional" in patterns of marriage and childbearing emerging only recently.

Our findings contradict this assumption with respect to women's patterns of marriage and childbearing. We find that diversity in women's patterns of marriage and childbearing is not confined to recent generations and that family diversity has not increased over time. These findings suggest not only that can we detect a diverse set of family experiences for women born early in the century but also that the diversity in women's trajectories through marriage and childbearing differs little then and now. We conclude from this that there are deep historical roots to what is typically regarded as "modern" diversity in the family.

Our answers to these questions come from analyses of women's behaviors in two domains—childbearing and marriage—for women in the United States born between 1914 and 1970. Our focus on women's pathways through childbearing and marriage can be seen as providing stylized demographic biographies (Settersten and Mayer 1997), or what we call "demo-biographies," for successive birth cohorts of women—stylized in the sense that what our data provide is only a small part of the subjective biographical accounts that these women might have actually told us about themselves (Mills [1959] 2002). Although stylized, our data and methods provide descriptions of the childbearing and marital trajectories of women over an unusually long historical period—for birth cohorts spanning more than fifty years. Another distinctive aspect of our analyses is that they take seriously the idea that marriage and childbearing are interrelated. In doing so, we move beyond usual descriptions that supply snapshots of women's marital behaviors separately from women's childbearing behaviors and instead provide analyses based on the view that women's life courses are best seen as processes unfolding continuously in time and across multiple behavioral domains.

As Fussell and Furstenberg note (this vol., chap. 2), when social scientists describe trends, they almost always focus on changes in averages—for example, trends in women's mean age at marriage or a first birth, changes in the proportion who have separated or divorced, shifts in the average number of children a woman has during her reproductive years, and so forth. Our interest in family diversity requires something different. It requires that we look not only at the mean or modal family experiences of women but also at how varied women's family experiences are and whether such "diversity" has changed over time. Asking about diversity in family experience also requires acknowledging that family structure may not be fixed for a given woman but, instead, may be fluid, as when a woman marries, has children, divorces, remarries, and bears children in the remarriage. Thus, a truer, more accurate account of the diversity of family experience requires moving beyond snapshots of family experience and asking instead about *trajectories* of family experience.

To achieve these goals, we focus on the order and sequence of life events for women in two behavioral domains—marriage and childbearing. We then use these data to distinguish between "traditional" and "nontraditional" trajectories through marital and childbearing statuses, for example, by contrasting pathways in which all childbearing occurs within an enduring first marriage and "nontraditional" pathways in which a divorce or separation has occurred or in which one or more children are born outside of marriage. We then ask how diverse are women's pathways and whether this diversity has varied for successive cohorts of women.

As noted above, we follow the marital and childbearing behaviors of U.S. women born between 1914 and 1970. Our analyses thus span a relatively long and unusually eventful historical period in which successive generations of women became adults, bore children, married, divorced, and remarried under a very diverse set of historical contexts: the Great Depression, World War II, the postwar baby boom years of economic prosperity, the economic recession and sexual revolution in the 1970s, the Reagan years of the 1980s, and a period of rapid economic expansion during the early 1990s.

Our chapter is organized as follows. First, we outline our questions and the changes we expect to observe in women's lives when we look at trajectories of childbearing and marriage across successive birth cohorts of women. We then provide some detail about the data we use and about the descriptive methods we employ. This section is followed by our empirical results and some concluding remarks.

THEORY

Although social scientists have often construed marital and childbearing behaviors as tightly connected (Becker 1991; Bumpass 1990), there is often a
surprising disjuncture between theoretical and empirical research, with most
empirical studies documenting historical trends in marriage separately from
historical trends in childbearing. As a result, we know much about evolving
patterns of marriage in terms of delayed age at first marriage, increased marital instability and remarriage, the rise of cohabiting unions, and so forth
(Bumpass and Sweet 1989; Casper and Bianchi 2002; Castro-Martin and
Bumpass 1989; Cherlin 1992; Preston and McDonald 1979; Spain and
Bianchi 1996). Likewise, we know much about evolving patterns of marital
fertility (Bumpass 1990; Cherlin 1992; Martin 2000; Rindfuss, Morgan, and
Offut 1996; Ryder 1980) and nonmarital fertility (Ventura et al. 1995; Wu,
Bumpass, and Musick 2001). We know, however, surprisingly little about
how marriage and childbearing have coevolved during the twentieth century.

Historical patterns of change show a clear upward trend in age at first
marriage (Spain and Bianchi 1996), although social scientists continue to
debate whether this reflects a postponement of marriage (Oppenheimer
1988) or a retreat from marriage altogether (Becker 1991; Goldstein and
Kenney 2001). Similarly, divorce rates have increased steadily, with annual
(Cherlin 1992, 21) and cohort (Preston and McDonald 1979) divorce rates
rising steadily since the mid-nineteenth century, leveling off at historically
high levels only in the 1990s (Goldstein 1999). Because of this, the proportion of marriages ending in divorce has increased steadily (Cherlin 1992;
Preston and McDonald 1979), and it is estimated that more than half of all
recently contracted marriages will dissolve (Castro-Martin and Bumpass
1989). Although these trends have often been interpreted as evidence of
family decline (Gilder 1986; Popenoe 1993; Whitehead 1993), it is the case
that remarriage occurs frequently following divorce (Bumpass, Sweet, and
Castro-Martin 1990). Thus, high levels of both divorce and remarriage have
led some to conclude that individuals in the United States are following a
pattern of serial marriage rather than abandoning the social institution of
marriage altogether (Cherlin 1992).

Accompanying these changes have been important shifts in norms
and attitudes concerning family and gender roles as both men and women
have adopted more egalitarian views. For example, Thornton (1989, 873) has
argued that between the late 1950s and the 1980s, there has been "an important weakening of the normative imperative to marry, to remain married,
to have children, to restrict intimate relations to marriage, and to maintain

separate roles for males and females." Important shifts also occurred in attitudes about the sexual activity of young adults, with increasingly less social stigma attached to sexual activity prior to marriage. These shifts in attitudes may have also increased public acceptance for forms of emotional intimacy and sexual activity that were once expected to occur only within marriage.

There have also been important shifts in fertility in the United States. Fertility rates have declined steadily during the past two centuries, save for the baby boom period during the mid-1940s and 1950s, with fertility now slightly less than two children per woman (Bumpass 1990; Casper and Bianchi 2002; Ryder 1980). As a result, the average size of U.S. families has declined markedly, with some noting a convergence to a two-child norm (David and Sanderson 1987). While much childbearing continues to take place within first marriages, increases in divorce and remarriage have given rise to a research literature on remarital fertility (Griffith, Koo, and Suchindran 1985; Stewart 2002; Thomson and Li 2002; Thornton 1978). Remarriage is of particular interest to us in this chapter not only because it will complicate women's pathways through marital statuses but also because patterns of childbearing in a first marriage, between marriages, and within a marital union will, on average, lead women who remarry to have diverse marital and childbearing trajectories. (Although social scientists have just started to understand fertility dynamics in remarriages, findings in various studies buttress these expectations.) For example, couples in a remarriage who have children from previous marital or cohabiting unions are less likely to desire or bear another child (Stewart 2002), but they also have more children on average than typical couples. After adjusting for these differences, Thomson and Li (2002) find that such couples are more, not less, likely to desire and to bear another child than couples in a first marriage.

Another major shift in U.S. fertility has been a steady increase in births to unmarried women. The proportion of births to unmarried women in the United States, which had increased steadily over the course of the twentieth century, has recently plateaued at historically high levels since 1995 (Ventura and Bachrach 2000; Wu, Bumpass, and Musick 2001). The characteristics of women having nonmarital births has changed as well, from first births to teenage women in the 1960s to higher-order births to older mothers, and from births to women in neither a marital nor cohabiting union to births to cohabiting women (Bumpass and Lu 2000; Wu, Bumpass, and Musick 2001). Although we know relatively little about the marital and childbearing trajectories of women who have one or more children outside of marriage, findings from a handful of studies suggest that the lives of such women are quite varied (Furstenberg, Brooks-Gunn, and Morgan 1987; Wu, Bumpass, and Musick 2001; Wu and Martin 2002).

Do studies of the life course shed any light on whether women's marital and childbearing trajectories have become more or less complicated over time? An ongoing debate among life-course researchers has been whether there has been a trend toward greater standardization in the transition to adulthood or whether this transition has been subject to increasing variability (Shanahan 2000).

As Settersten (1997) notes, proponents of the so-called standardization thesis tend to emphasize life-course transitions in the domains of education and work, placing great importance, for example, on the rising educational attainment of both men and women and on the increasing importance of education in the transition from school to work. From this perspective, the dictates of modern occupational systems and accompanying educational institutions are seen as standardizing the life course during the period of adolescence and early adulthood (Mayer and Muller 1986; Mayer and Schoepflin 1989; Meyer 1986). For example, Mayer and Schoepflin (1989) note that social welfare provisions are typically organized around strict age categories that define young adult responsibilities and entitlements. Thus, in most Western industrialized nations, there are strict age criteria governing compulsory schooling, permissible work, driving, drinking, military service, and voting. Similarly, Bertaux and Kohli (1984) argue that the cognitive "map" of the life course for modern individuals is organized into three periods: a period in which children, adolescents, and young adults are enrolled in school; a lengthy period spanning early to late adulthood in which the life course is structured by work activities; and a retirement period in which individuals engage in postwork activities.

By contrast, proponents of the so-called individualization thesis point to long-term secular developments, particularly in the area of familial and intimate relationships, which they argue have caused life-course trajectories to become more complex and diverse (e.g., Buchman 1989; Giddens 1993). Thus, for example, strict religious, community, and family norms regarding the permanence of marriage and strictures against sexual activity outside of marriage have eroded in the face of the sexual revolution of the 1960s and 1970s (Laumann et al. 1994), the increasing instability of marriage (Cherlin 1992), the rapid rise of cohabitation (Bumpass and Lu 2000; Bumpass and Sweet 1989), and the equally rapid rise in nonmarital fertility (Wu, Bumpass, and Musick 2001).

Overall, then, the broad theoretical arguments and empirical trends reviewed do not provide straightforward predictions about the direction of historical change in women's joint pathways through marriage and child-bearing. Although declining fertility may have simplified married women's trajectories of childbearing, with many women "standardizing" their fertil-ity around two-child norms (David and Sanderson 1987), women's pathways through marriage may have become more complicated and hence more var-ied over time. Considering these two trends jointly yields ambiguous pre-dictions. If the increasing complexity of marriage has outpaced standard-izing patterns of childbearing, then women's trajectories through marriage and childbearing may have become more varied and complex over time. But if increasingly standardized trajectories of childbearing offset the increasing complexity of marital patterns then trajectories of family experience may ac-tually have become less complex. The third possibility is that the two trends offset one another and that there is therefore little net change.

DATA AND METHOD

To describe trajectories of marriage and childbearing, we use retrospective data on the marital and fertility experiences of U.S. women available in the June 1980, 1985, 1990, and 1995 Current Population Surveys (CPSs). In these data, married women aged fifteen or older and never-married women aged eighteen or older were asked the dates of birth (to the nearest month and year) for their first four and most recent children. Similar information was obtained for the dates of the first two and most recent marriages—data on when their marriage began and, if a marriage ended, the dates (as rele-vant) of widowhood, separation, and divorce in the 1980, 1985, and 1990 June CPS. In June 1995, these marriage data were expanded slightly to en-compass the first three and most recent marriages. With these data, we can determine when a woman's marriage began, when it ended, how it ended, and whether she bore children prior to a first marriage, within a first mar-riage, between marriages, or in second or later marriages.

One advantage of these data is that they provide very large samples for women born between 1914 and 1980. One difficulty is that women born in the late 1970s and early 1980s are very young at last survey—for example, women born in 1980 were at most fifteen years old in June 1995. As a result, we restrict our attention to six birth cohorts of women: those born 1914–24, 1925–34, 1935–44, 1945–54, 1955–64, and 1965–70. In all, these birth co-horts span more than fifty years and cover an unusually interesting period of U.S. history. Women born between 1914 and 1924 reached their early adult years during the Depression era, while women born between 1925 and 1934 were in their early twenties during the prosperous post–World War II years. Similarly, women born 1945–54 comprise the main portion of the baby boom generation who reached their early twenties during the late 1960s and early 1970s, a period marked by the Vietnam War. The oldest of the women born 1955–64 represent the tail-end of the baby boom generation, while those born 1965–70 were in their teen years and early twenties during the Reagan and Bush administrations.

Because these data are retrospective, the oldest women interviewed will supply data on their marriage and childbearing experiences over many more years than the youngest women—a woman aged sixty-five in 1990 will be providing us with 65 years of life experience, while a woman aged forty will obviously be able to provide us with only forty years. These differences mean that we will observe a greater number of life events among older women—with the passage of time, we might expect more of them to have experienced a divorce or widowhood, a remarriage, and so forth—than among their younger counterparts. To adjust for these differences, we chose to examine only the first thirty-five years of life experience for the first four birth cohorts—that is, for women born 1914–24, 1925–34, 1935–44, and 1945–54. Restricting the sample to only those women for whom we can observe at least thirty-five years of life experience is not possible for the last birth cohort (women born 1965–70), since the oldest of them would be at most thirty years old in June 1995, the date of the most recent survey. Similarly, imposing this restriction substantially reduces our sample size for those women born 1955–64, since only women born between 1955 and 1960 could be thirty-five years or older in June 1995 and only women born in 1955 could be thirty-five years or older in June 1990. To deal with this problem for these last two birth cohorts, we chose to include only those women who were at least twenty-five years old.

Another reason for restricting our attention to the first thirty-five years of life is that this age range covers the period during which individuals move from adolescence into early and mid-adult statuses. Furthermore, the age cutoff should not significantly impair our ability to track childbearing; for these cohorts of women, virtually all childbearing will have been completed by age thirty-five. Clearly, though, this restriction will exclude some marital experiences—some women may marry for the first time after age thirty-five, and larger numbers of women may experience a marital separation, divorce, or remarriage after age thirty-five. Widowhood, especially, is affected by our decision to restrict our attention to the first thirty-five years of life. In any case, our estimates for the first four cohorts tells us what happened during the first thirty-five years of life for women born during these years, while our estimates for the last two cohorts tells us what happened during their first twenty-five to thirty-five years of life.

Our main goal in this chapter is to describe the life-course trajectories of marriage and childbearing jointly. As noted above, we do so by constructing what we call "demo-biographies" that provide simple descriptions of the observed trajectories of marriage and childbearing, in which we ignore the timing of marital and childbearing events available in these data. For example, consider a woman who enters a first marriage at age twenty and has two children, the first at age twenty-two and the second at age twenty-seven; at age thirty-five, we observe her in this first marriage with two children. Similarly, consider a woman who is observed to enter a first marriage at age twenty-nine and who also has two children, the first at thirty-one and the second at thirty-four; at age thirty-five, we also observe her in this marriage and with two children. In our analyses, we regard both women as having identical demo-biographies since they followed identical trajectories of marriage and childbearing: entry into a first marriage, followed by two children. Thus, descriptions of this sort focus attention on the order and sequencing of events defined by childbearing and marital statuses but ignores variation in the age at which these events occurred.

The main advantage of ignoring the timing information available in these data is that the resulting sequences of marriage and childbearing clarify how the ordering of marriage and childbearing events varies across successive cohorts of U.S. women. Yet another advantage is that this technique can be applied not only to single statuses—fertility or marriage in isolation—but also to multiple statuses—in our case, the joint trajectories of marriage and childbearing available in our data. And while demographers have traditionally paid much attention to the age at which marital and childbearing events occur, our approach may more closely correspond to the sort of verbal descriptions that many of us would give in describing our lives— that we married, had two children, divorced, remarried, and so forth—in which we typically emphasize the order and sequencing of events.

Table 4.1 gives sample sizes for the data used in our analyses. We restrict our attention to three racial and ethnic groups: non-Hispanic white women, non-Hispanic black women, and Hispanic women. As noted above, one of the advantages of the June 1980, 1985, 1990, and 1995 CPSs is that these data both provide very large samples and contain women born over a period spanning more than five decades. Table 4.1 also provides breakdowns of available sample sizes by race and ethnicity, birth cohort, and survey. Thus, in the first panel of table 4.1, we see that these data provide us with in-

TABLE 4.1

DESCRIPTIVE STATISTICS FOR WOMEN BORN 1914–70

	1914–24	1925–34	1935–44	1945–54	1955–64	1965–70	TOTAL
Whites:							
1980	8,007	7,543	8,247	426	525	0	24,748
1985	3,430	6,049	6,440	4,708	4,543	0	25,170
1990	316	5,603	6,341	8,962	9,945	401	31,568
1995	0	2,616	5,526	8,161	9,068	3,965	29,336
Total	11,753	21,811	26,554	22,257	24,081	4,366	110,822
Blacks:							
1980	746	862	970	44	82	0	2,704
1985	328	710	736	507	480	0	2,761
1990	35	617	778	1,231	1,540	64	4,265
1995	0	333	703	1,101	1,337	626	4,100
Total	1,109	2,522	3,187	2,883	3,439	690	13,830
Hispanics:							
1980	246	391	569	27	38	0	1,271
1985	129	306	404	336	379	0	1,554
1990	10	310	436	696	1,073	38	2,563
1995	0	162	370	674	968	583	2,757
Total	385	1,169	1,779	1,733	2,458	621	8,145
All women:							
1980	8,999	8,796	9,786	497	645	0	28,723
1985	3,887	7,065	7,580	5,551	5,402	0	29,485
1990	361	6,530	7,555	10,889	12,558	503	38,396
1995	0	3,111	6,599	9,936	11,373	5,174	36,193
Total	13,247	25,502	31,520	26,873	29,978	5,677	132,797

Source. June 1980, 1985, 1990, and 1995 Current Population Surveys.

formation on 11,753 white women born between 1914 and 1925. Of these 11,753 women, 8,007 were interviewed in June 1980, 3,430 in June 1985, and 316 in June 1990.

The other panels in table 4.1 provide sample sizes by birth cohort and survey for black women, Hispanic women, and for women of all three race and ethnic groups. In all, we have data on 110,822 white women, 13,830 black women, and 8,145 Hispanic women. Combining data across these three racial and ethnic groups yields a sample totaling 132,797 women.

As table 4.1 makes clear, data for the more recent cohorts tend to come from the more recent surveys, while data on older cohorts tend to come from the less recent surveys. Thus, the number of women sampled from the 1980 survey tends to decrease for more recent cohorts, while the number of women sampled from the 1995 survey increases. An exception to this overall pattern occurs for the last two cohorts, in which we chose to include women for whom we observe at least twenty-five years of life experience, as opposed to the thirty-five years of experience that we imposed for the other four cohorts.

RESULTS

As noted above, some social scientists have argued that life-course patterns have become more standardized over time as, for example, education has become both more widespread and more standardized for both men and women (Mayer and Muller 1986; Meyer 1986). Still others have argued, by contrast, that changing economic circumstances or the progressive loosening of norms concerning the appropriate ages at which to marry and to have children could well imply increasing variability in life-course trajectories over time (Settersten 2002; Shanahan 2000). Although often posed as competing hypotheses, it is in fact possible, and perhaps even plausible, that both increasing standardization and progressive loosening of age norms may have taken place. If so, expectations concerning trends in the variability of life-course patterns will no longer be clear-cut. That is, life-course patterns could have become less varied over time if increasing standardization outpaced changes in economic circumstances and loosening norms; conversely, life-course patterns could have become more varied over time if the opposite took place. There is also a third possibility—little trend in the variability of life-course patterns—which could occur if these trends offset each other. As a result, these sorts of theoretical arguments may in fact provide little real guidance on whether we might expect more or less diversity over time in women's life-course trajectories.

Posing the problem in terms of our specific outcomes—marriage and childbearing—also does not yield unambiguous predictions. Past research would lead us to expect decreasing variability over time in women's childbearing patterns as well as increasing variability in marriage patterns. But when childbearing and marriage patterns are considered jointly, it is not clear what we might expect: the amount of diversity over time in women's joint marital and childbearing trajectories could increase, decrease, or exhibit little trend. Thus, prior empirical work that has examined trends in each domain separately in fact provides us with little guidance for what we might expect for women's life trajectories when we think about marriage and childbearing jointly.

We have structured our analyses with these considerations in mind. We begin our analyses by considering women's childbearing trajectories and ignoring all information on their marital statuses. We then examine trajectories of marital statuses for successive cohorts, ignoring all information on their childbearing. This allows us to compare the trends we observe with previous research. We then examine sequences that take childbearing and marriage jointly to see what we learn by considering the two domains simultaneously rather than one at a time.

Childbearing

Table 4.2 shows childbearing trajectories for successive cohorts, ignoring all information on marital status. These trajectories are based on observed fertility through age thirty-five for the first four birth cohorts and for women aged twenty-five or older for the last two birth cohorts. We present results through the first five births. Results are shown for white, black, and Hispanic women.

The impact of the Depression on the transition to adulthood can be seen in the relatively high levels of childlessness for women born between 1914 and 1924. Table 4.2 shows that roughly one of every six white and Hispanic women was childless at age thirty-five. Childlessness was even more prevalent for the Depression cohort of black women, with 28.7%, or roughly two in seven, of black women remaining childless at age thirty-five. Thus, what is striking is the long reach of the Depression, which occurred when these women were in their teens and early twenties, but which appears to have had consequences extending into the midthirties for many of these women.

Overall, trends in childlessness followed a U-shaped pattern, with childlessness least prevalent for the cohort of women reaching adulthood after the Depression and then rising sharply for more recent cohorts of women. For white women, childlessness reached its lowest levels for the next two cohorts, with 12.2% and 11.6% remaining childless by age thirty-five for the 1925–34 and 1935–44 cohorts of white women, respectively. Childlessness then increased substantially to 18.4% and 29.8% for, respectively, the 1945–54 and 1955–64 cohorts of white women, levels that exceeded those for Depression-era white women. Note, however, that the quite

TABLE 4.2

SEQUENCES OF CHILDBEARING THROUGH AGE 35 FOR WOMEN BORN 1914–70

	1914–24	1925–34	1935–44	1945–54	1955–64	1965–70
Whites:						
0	17.0	12.2	11.6	18.4	29.8	49.1
0→1	16.5	11.0	11.5	17.9	22.2	21.9
0→1→2	26.5	24.8	30.1	36.5	30.0	18.6
0→1→2→3	19.0	22.8	23.3	17.4	12.2	7.2
0→1→2→3→4	16.3	22.1	17.0	6.8	3.5	1.8
0→1→2→3→						
4→5	2.7	5.2	4.6	1.4	.8	.3
All other sequences	2.0	1.9	1.9	1.6	1.5	1.1
Number of						
sequences	19	22	24	22	18	18
Sample size	11,753	21,811	26,554	22,257	24,081	4,366
Blacks:						
0	28.7	16.6	13.0	14.4	20.1	29.6
0→1	19.7	14.7	15.1	20.1	24.3	23.9
0→1→2	12.1	14.8	19.2	29.0	27.9	21.9
0→1→2→3	10.6	14.3	17.4	17.3	15.6	15.4
0→1→2→3→4	24.7	32.2	26.0	13.5	7.7	5.2
0→1→2→3→						
4→5	2.8	5.9	6.7	3.6	2.4	1.7
All other sequences	1.4	1.5	2.6	2.1	2.0	2.3
Number of						
sequences	13	14	21	19	20	12
Sample size	1,109	2,522	3,187	2,883	3,439	690
Hispanics:						
0	16.6	15.2	12.5	11.2	19.7	28.2
0→1	13.2	12.7	11.5	15.5	18.4	26.9
0→1→2	19.2	17.5	22.6	28.4	29.1	25.1
0→1→2→3	13.8	15.7	18.9	20.1	17.8	11.4
0→1→2→3→4	33.2	29.2	25.9	16.4	10.3	5.0
0→1→2→3→						
4→5	2.1	7.8	6.9	3.8	3.1	1.4
All other sequences	1.9	1.9	1.7	4.6	1.6	2.0
Number of						
sequences	10	15	17	17	15	13
Sample size	385	1,169	1,779	1,733	2,458	621

Source. June 1980, 1985, 1990, and 1995 Current Population Surveys.

high levels of childlessness for the two most recent cohorts of white women is due partly to the fact that we do not observe these women through age thirty-five; hence, the results in table 4.2 overstate levels of childlessness among women in these two cohorts. This is particularly true for the last cohort of white women, most of whom are under age thirty in these data. Compared to white women, childlessness was higher in the earliest cohorts of black and Hispanic women and less prevalent in later cohorts.

Table 4.2 also shows that women have increasingly followed patterns suggestive of a two-child norm (David and Sanderson 1987). Having only two children is the modal pattern for all three racial and ethnic groups, both for the 1945–54 cohort of women, for whom we have complete information through age thirty-five, and for the 1955–64 cohort of women, many of whom were younger than thirty-five in our last survey. Trends, however, differ noticeably by race and ethnicity. While having just two children is the modal pattern in all birth cohorts for white women, for black and Hispanic women the modal pattern shifts from high levels of childbearing in early cohorts to two children in later cohorts.

A more striking finding is that fewer women than might be expected have only two children. Even for women born between 1945 and 1954, where this pattern is most prevalent, just over one out of three white women, and somewhat fewer than one out of three black and Hispanic women, follow this pathway; hence, by age thirty-five, the vast majority of women in the 1945–54 cohort—roughly two out of three white, black, and Hispanic women—deviated from what we often think of as a two-child norm. Moreover, this pattern is even less characteristic of trajectories of childbearing in earlier cohorts of women. Thus, what is commonly presumed to have occurred historically—that childbearing typically stopped at two children—is on the one hand the most typical pattern that we observe, but it is also true that throughout this century, more women have deviated from this "norm" than have followed it.

If what is often considered to be "normative" is in fact not "typical" statistically, what might we say about childbearing trajectories that are both nonnormative and statistically atypical? The percentage of women with pathways that do not fall into one of six trajectories for childbearing and the total number of sequences we observe by race and ethnicity and birth cohort are also reported in table 4.2. For white women born between 1914 and 1924, 2.0% follow sequences not reported in table 4.2. Thus, the six sequences displayed in table 4.2 summarize the fertility trajectories of 98% of women in this cohort. Conversely, 2.0% of women in this cohort follow one of the thirteen trajectories that fall outside the patterns reported in table 4.2. (These more complicated trajectories consist of patterns involving twin or higher-order multiple births, i.e., sequences such as $0 \rightarrow 2$ or $0 \rightarrow 1 \rightarrow 3$.) Looking across table 4.2, we see that relatively few women have childbearing trajectories that are not explicitly represented by the six trajectories in table 4.2, with the percentage of women not falling into one of these six trajectories ranging from 1.1% to 4.6%. These results show, too, that most of the diversity in childbearing patterns also lies in this very small group of women.[1] Thus, while most women follow relatively straightforward childbearing trajectories, a small proportion of women have much more complicated patterns.

Overall, table 4.2 also suggests a general trend toward fewer children, although the patterns involved are complicated. For both black and white women, the proportion who have four children by age thirty-five peaks for the 1925–34 cohort and declines steadily for each cohort thereafter, while for Hispanic women, the proportion who have four children declines steadily across all cohorts, beginning with that of 1914–24. But trends in the proportions who have three children by age thirty-five are somewhat different, with a modest increase over the first four cohorts of black and Hispanic women and a similar increase over the first three cohorts of white women.

This trend toward smaller families can be seen more clearly in table 4.3, in which we repeat the first three childbearing sequences of table 4.2 but combine all others into a single residual category. How quickly this trend occurred differs modestly by race and ethnicity. The percentage of white women having more than two children drops from 52.0% for the 1925–34 cohort to 46.8% for the 1935–1944 cohort and declines even more steeply, to 27.2%, for the 1945–1954 cohort. For black women, the decline in family size is less rapid, with slightly more than one in three black women in recent cohorts having more than two children by age thirty-five, compared to more than one in two black women born between 1925 and 1944. Note that for Hispanic women such a trend is much less evident: table 4.3 shows declines of only 10 percentage points across the 1935–44 cohort and the 1945–54 cohorts among women who had more than two children.

The patterns in tables 4.2 and 4.3 thus suggest a general shift away from women bearing large numbers of children toward their bearing no children, one child, or two children. Although not consistent with perhaps naive expectations about strong two-child norms, these patterns are consistent with expectations that women's trajectories of childbearing have become more uniform with time, with women in earlier birth cohorts having more varied trajectories of childbearing relative to their counterparts born in later years.

TABLE 4.3

SEQUENCES OF CHILDBEARING THROUGH PARITY 2 AND AGE 35

FOR WOMEN BORN 1914–70

	1914–24	1925–34	1935–44	1945–54	1955–64	1965–70
Whites:						
0	17.0	12.2	11.6	18.4	29.8	49.1
0→1	16.5	11.0	11.5	17.9	22.2	21.9
0→1→2	26.5	24.8	30.1	36.5	30.0	18.6
All other						
sequences	40.0	52.0	46.8	27.2	18.0	10.4
Blacks:						
0	28.7	16.6	13.0	14.4	20.1	29.6
0→1	19.7	14.7	15.1	20.1	24.3	23.9
0→1→2	12.1	14.8	19.2	29.0	27.9	21.9
All other						
sequences	39.5	53.9	52.7	36.5	27.7	24.6
Hispanics:						
0	16.6	15.2	12.5	11.2	19.7	28.2
0→1	13.2	12.7	11.5	15.5	18.4	26.9
0→1→2	19.2	17.5	22.6	28.4	29.1	25.1
All other						
sequences	51.0	54.6	53.4	44.9	32.8	19.8

Source. June 1980, 1985, 1990, and 1995 Current Population Surveys.

Marriage

We now turn to the sequences of marital statuses for successive cohorts of women, ignoring information on childbearing. Table 4.4 presents results that parallel our analyses in tables 4.2 and 4.3. The first row for each ethnic group gives the percentage of women who are never-married at age thirty-five. For white women in the first four cohorts, the percentage of women who are never-married at age thirty-five shows relatively little change, fluctuating from a low of 4.5% for the 1935–44 cohort to a high of 6.9% for the 1945–55 cohort. Compared to white women, roughly twice as many Hispanic women are never-married at age thirty-five; in the first four cohorts of Hispanic women, the percentage of those never-married rises modestly from a low of 8.6% for the 1914–24 cohort to 11.9% for the 1945–54 cohort. As in tables 4.2 and 4.3, interpreting the percentages for the two most recent cohorts is confounded by age truncation in these cohorts; thus, increases in

TABLE 4.4

SEQUENCES OF MARITAL STATUSES THROUGH AGE 35 FOR WOMEN BORN 1914–70

	1914–24	1925–34	1935–44	1945–54	1955–64	1965–70
Whites:						
N	6.1	4.6	4.5	6.9	12.7	32.5
$N \rightarrow M$	79.8	80.3	72.6	62.2	60.8	51.0
$N \rightarrow M \rightarrow S$	.7	1.1	1.7	1.8	2.3	2.5
$N \rightarrow M \rightarrow D$	.5	.5	.7	1.2	1.0	1.2
$N \rightarrow M \rightarrow S \rightarrow D$	2.3	3.1	5.9	8.4	7.9	5.7
$N \rightarrow M \rightarrow W$	1.2	1.0	.9	.7	.5	.3
$N \rightarrow M \rightarrow S \rightarrow D \rightarrow M$	4.9	5.1	7.7	11.2	9.3	4.6
$N \rightarrow M \rightarrow D \rightarrow M$	1.5	1.3	1.4	1.6	1.2	.5
$N \rightarrow M \rightarrow W \rightarrow M$	1.5	1.0	.8	.6	.2	.1
All other sequences	1.5	2.0	3.8	5.4	4.1	1.6
Sample size	11,753	21,811	26,554	22,257	24,081	4,366
Number of sequences	30	40	52	50	49	24
Blacks:						
N	11.6	9.6	11.0	18.9	37.2	60.9
$N \rightarrow M$	60.5	63.2	54.1	44.4	35.9	26.7
$N \rightarrow M \rightarrow S$	5.0	6.7	9.2	8.2	9.7	5.2
$N \rightarrow M \rightarrow D$	1.1	1.4	1.2	1.6	1.2	.9
$N \rightarrow M \rightarrow S \rightarrow D$	4.9	5.6	10.3	12.8	8.2	4.1
$N \rightarrow M \rightarrow W$	4.2	3.2	3.2	2.5	1.3	.3
$N \rightarrow M \rightarrow S \rightarrow D \rightarrow M$	5.6	5.7	6.2	6.9	3.7	1.2
$N \rightarrow M \rightarrow D \rightarrow M$	2.3	1.2	1.0	1.0	.3	.3
$N \rightarrow M \rightarrow W \rightarrow M$	2.1	1.3	.8	.6	.1	.0
All other sequences	2.7	2.1	3.0	3.1	2.4	.4
Sample size	1,109	2,522	3,187	2,883	3,439	690
Number of sequences	27	25	24	27	30	11
Hispanics:						
N	8.6	10.6	10.1	11.9	16.2	30.9
$N \rightarrow M$	75.3	73.5	67.9	60.2	59.4	54.6
$N \rightarrow M \rightarrow S$	2.1	1.6	4.5	4.4	6.1	5.0
$N \rightarrow M \rightarrow D$	1.3	1.1	1.2	1.7	1.5	1.8
$N \rightarrow M \rightarrow S \rightarrow D$	2.3	3.8	5.1	8.7	6.6	4.0
$N \rightarrow M \rightarrow W$	2.9	1.5	2.3	1.4	.9	.0
$N \rightarrow M \rightarrow S \rightarrow D \rightarrow M$	2.6	4.4	4.8	6.8	5.7	2.3
$N \rightarrow M \rightarrow D \rightarrow M$	2.6	.9	1.0	.6	.2	.2

(continued)

TABLE 4.4

(CONTINUED)

	1914–24	1925–34	1935–44	1945–54	1955–64	1965–70
$N{\to}M{\to}W{\to}M$	2.9	1.5	2.3	1.4	.9	.0
All other sequences	1.3	1.7	1.8	2.9	2.3	.6
Sample size	385	1,169	1,779	1,733	2,458	621
Number of sequences	14	17	22	24	26	11

Source. June 1980, 1985, 1990, and 1995 Current Population Surveys.

these percentages, relative to earlier cohorts, could reflect a tendency either to delay or to forgo marriage.[2]

The patterns are somewhat different for black women. Table 4.4 suggests an increase across successive cohorts of black women in the percentage who have never married by age thirty-five, with this percentage reaching 18.9% for black women in the 1945–54 cohort. This increase is also mirrored in a widening black/white gap. For women in the earliest cohort, the percentage of black women who have never married by age thirty-five is roughly twice that of white women, a pattern observed also for the earliest cohort of Hispanic women. This ratio widens substantially for the last three cohorts of black and white women. Table 4.4 suggests that entry into first marriage has decreased more rapidly for successive cohorts of black women than for their white counterparts, a result consistent with observations made by Wilson (1987).[3] The black/white gap, however, widens for successive cohorts.

The percentage of women who have married and who have not left that marriage by age thirty-five (table 4.4) captures the most common experience of women, irrespective of birth cohort or race and ethnicity. One might thus regard this trajectory as "normative" in two senses: it is in accord with norms concerning the permanence of marriage and it is the statistical norm. But like others (Bennett, Bloom, and Craig 1989), we find substantial movement away from this trajectory. For white women born in the first quarter of the twentieth century, about 80% remained in their first marriages at age thirty-five. This percentage steadily declines, by about 20 percentage points, for successive cohorts of white women, with about three in five women in the 1945–54 or 1955–64 cohorts still in their first marriages at age thirty-five. We observe an even sharper decline, by about 27 percentage points, for black women, from a maximum of 63.2% in the 1925–34 cohort to 35.9% for the

1955–64 cohort. The trend for Hispanic women falls between that for whites and blacks, with percentages somewhat more similar to those of whites.

Table 4.4 also presents trajectories through age thirty-five that are associated with the dissolution of a first marriage, a first remarriage, and higher-order dissolutions or remarriages. There are modest increases in the percentage of women experiencing dissolution of their first marriage via separation or divorce and a modest decrease in the percentage who experience widowhood—patterns that hold for all three race/ethnic groups. Although trends toward dissolution are subject to slight increases over time, it is harder to discern clear trends in the trajectories involving first or later remarriages or higher-order dissolutions.

Overall, table 4.4 clearly illustrates what others have also found: a substantial increase in the instability of marriage. One way to view this is to note that those at risk of marital instability or who have experienced marital instability are women who fall into all categories save for the first. Of these women, only those with the second trajectory ($N \rightarrow M$) have not experienced a marital dissolution. Table 4.4 provides clear evidence, then, of an increase in marital dissolution for successive cohorts of women across all three race/ethnic groups. More generally, there is also a clear trend toward more complicated marital trajectories. Thus in addition to increases across cohorts in the dissolution of a first marriage, women in later cohorts were more likely to experience more than one marital disruption by age thirty-five. These results suggest that women's marital life-course trajectories have become more diverse over time.[4]

Table 4.4 also says something about trends in how marriages end. Note that while the percentage of women widowed in a first marriage is generally small, these widowhood percentages decline for all three racial and ethnic groups. (The larger percentage of black women falling into this category is likely to reflect the higher mortality of black males during early and mid-adulthood.) Turning this trend on its head implies an increasing trend for first marriages to be dissolved voluntarily. Among such voluntary dissolutions we observe higher percentages of black women separated but not divorced from their first marriage, relative to their white and Hispanic counterparts.

Joint Sequences of Marriage and Childbearing

Thus far, we have analyzed marriage and fertility one domain at a time. Not surprisingly, our results are consistent with those of previous studies. For example, Cherlin (1992) and Casper and Bianchi (2002) report a general trend toward smaller family size, with the exception of the baby boom period. Similarly, both sets of authors report evidence suggestive of an emerging two-child norm. Thus, both their findings and ours suggest that the American family, when viewed in terms of childbearing patterns, has become more uniform over successive birth cohorts. Similarly, our results, like those of others, show a clear trend away from marriage, a finding that has often been interpreted as showing that the American family is in decline (e.g., Gilder 1986; Popenoe 1993; Whitehead 1993). By contrast, our results show increasing diversity in women's marital experiences, which would, in turn, support the views of those who see the family not as collapsing but simply as diversifying (e.g., Coontz 1992; Demo et al. 2000; Stacey 1991). As noted earlier, however, increasing marital diversity coupled with increasing uniformity in childbearing yields ambiguous predictions for trends in women's joint trajectories in marriage and childbearing. Moreover, there is strikingly little empirical evidence on this point, despite considerable agreement among social scientists that marriage and childbearing involve tightly interwoven behaviors and decisions (Becker 1991; Bumpass 1990).

We address these issues in table 4.5. One advantage of the simple descriptive techniques used in tables 4.2 – 4.4 is that they are easily adapted to describing joint marital and childbearing statuses. For example, we use $(N, 0)$ in table 4.5 to denote women who are childless and never married at age thirty-five and $(N, 0) \rightarrow (M, 0)$ to denote women who, at age thirty-five, move from being childless and never-married to being childless and married. The trajectories for other rows are defined similarly.

A dramatic complexity in women's joint trajectories of marriage and childbearing can be seen in table 4.5. For example, we have listed fourteen separate trajectories there, representative of women's marriages and childbearing by age thirty-five, but these fourteen trajectories do not begin to exhaust the range observed in these data. For example, for white women born between 1914 and 1924, fully 30.8% do not fall into one of these trajectories, with even larger percentages—ranging from 31.6% to 38.9%—observed for the next three cohorts of white women. Even more black and Hispanic women follow pathways that fall outside of those represented in table 4.5. For black women, between 40.3% and 57.6% of women in the first five birth cohorts follow pathways other than those listed; for Hispanic women, the corresponding figures are 35.6% to 48.4%.

As in previous tables, diversity in women's marital and childbearing pathways occurs in trajectories that fall outside the table—in the so-called tail of the distribution. But unlike previous tables, the percentage of women

TABLE 4.5

SELECTED SEQUENCES OF JOINT MARITAL AND CHILDBEARING STATUSES

THROUGH AGE 35 FOR WOMEN BORN 1914–70

	1914–24	1925–34	1935–44	1945–54	1955–64	1965–70
Whites:						
$(N,0)$	5.6	4.1	4.0	5.8	10.7	27.3
$(N,0) \rightarrow (M,0)$	9.3	6.5	5.4	7.6	13.7	18.2
$(N,0) \rightarrow (M,0) \rightarrow (M,1)$	12.9	8.3	7.6	9.7	13.1	12.6
$(N,0) \rightarrow (M,0) \rightarrow (M,1) \rightarrow (S,1) \rightarrow (D,1)$	.4	.4	.9	1.7	1.6	1.0
$(N,0) \rightarrow (M,0) \rightarrow (M,1) \rightarrow (M,2)$	22.4	20.4	22.6	24.2	18.9	10.4
$(N,0) \rightarrow (M,0) \rightarrow (M,1) \rightarrow (M,2) \rightarrow (S,2) \rightarrow (D,2)$	.4	.6	1.5	2.0	1.2	.4
$(N,0) \rightarrow (M,0) \rightarrow (M,1) \rightarrow (M,2) \rightarrow (M,3)$	15.6	18.7	17.3	10.9	6.8	2.9
$(N,0) \rightarrow (M,0) \rightarrow (S,0) \rightarrow (D,0)$	.4	.4	.8	2.0	2.4	1.5
$(N,0) \rightarrow (M,0) \rightarrow (S,0) \rightarrow (D,0) \rightarrow (M,0)$	.7	.4	.6	1.4	1.5	.8
$(N,0) \rightarrow (N,1)$	.2	.2	.2	.6	1.1	3.3
$(N,0) \rightarrow (N,1) \rightarrow (M,1)$	.5	.4	.4	.7	1.1	1.5
$(N,0) \rightarrow (N,1) \rightarrow (M,1) \rightarrow (M,2)$	.5	.4	.7	1.0	1.4	1.9
$(N,0) \rightarrow (N,1) \rightarrow (N,2)$	.2	.1	.1	.3	.6	.9
$(N,0) \rightarrow (N,1) \rightarrow (N,2) \rightarrow (M,2)$	.1	.2	.3	.5	.7	.5
All other sequences	30.8	38.9	37.6	31.6	25.2	16.8
Sample size	11,753	21,811	26,554	22,257	24,081	4,366
Number of sequences	487	831	1,236	1,098	1,013	269

Blacks:

(N,0)	7.1	4.5	4.3	6.6	11.5	23.9
(N,0)→(M,0)	15.5	8.3	5.5	4.3	5.4	5.1
(N,0)→(M,0)→(M,1)	8.1	6.7	6.0	4.7	5.2	4.6
(N,0)→(M,0)→(M,1)→(S,1)→(D,1)	.3	.4	1.1	1.4	.9	.6
(N,0)→(M,0)→(M,1)→(M,2)	5.5	7.6	7.8	8.9	6.3	2.6
(N,0)→(M,0)→(M,1)→(M,2)→(S,2)→(D,2)	.0	.4	1.3	1.7	.6	.4
(N,0)→(M,0)→(M,1)→(M,2)→(M,3)	5.2	6.9	6.5	4.8	2.1	1.3
(N,0)→(M,0)→(S,0)→(D,0)	1.9	.7	1.2	1.3	1.0	.3
(N,0)→(M,0)→(S,0)→(D,0)→(M,0)	.5	.6	.5	.6	.3	.0
(N,0)→(N,1)	2.4	1.5	2.0	4.4	9.8	12.5
(N,0)→(N,1)→(M,1)	2.3	2.1	2.0	3.1	3.5	3.5
(N,0)→(N,1)→(M,1)→(M,2)	1.4	1.3	2.1	3.7	2.9	3.2
(N,0)→(N,1)→(N,2)	.9	.8	1.5	3.2	8.0	10.0
(N,0)→(N,1)→(N,2)→(M,2)	.9	.6	1.3	1.8	2.2	2.3
All other sequences	48.0	57.6	56.9	49.5	40.3	29.7
Sample size	1,109	2,522	3,187	2,883	3,439	690
Number of sequences	206	361	468	416	358	91

(continued)

TABLE 4.5

(CONTINUED)

	1914–24	1925–34	1935–44	1945–54	1955–64	1965–70
Hispanics:						
(N,0)	5.7	6.7	6.0	5.4	8.1	16.6
(N,0)→(M,0)	8.1	6.9	5.1	3.5	8.8	9.8
(N,0)→(M,0)→(M,1)	8.6	8.9	6.8	6.9	9.5	14.3
(N,0)→(M,0)→(M,1)→(S,1)→(D,1)	.3	.4	.3	1.6	1.0	1.0
(N,0)→(M,0)→(M,1)→(M,2)	13.8	11.7	14.2	16.5	14.7	11.6
(N,0)→(M,0)→(M,1)→(M,2)→(S,2)→(D,2)	.3	.4	.7	1.2	1.0	.2
(N,0)→(M,0)→(M,1)→(M,2)→(M,3)	10.6	11.2	13.4	12.2	8.7	4.0
(N,0)→(M,0)→(S,0)→(D,0)	.5	.6	.2	1.1	.8	.8
(N,0)→(M,0)→(S,0)→(D,0)→(M,0)	.3	.4	.2	.6	.9	.2
(N,0)→(N,1)	1.3	1.2	1.3	2.6	2.6	5.0
(N,0)→(N,1)→(M,1)	1.0	.5	.8	1.2	1.5	3.2
(N,0)→(N,1)→(M,1)→(M,2)	.8	1.1	1.1	1.9	2.3	3.2
(N,0)→(N,1)→(N,2)	.8	1.1	.9	1.6	2.7	4.8
(N,0)→(N,1)→(N,2)→(M,2)	.5	.5	.7	.9	1.8	1.4
All other sequences	47.4	48.4	48.3	42.8	35.6	23.9
Sample size	385	1,169	1,779	1,733	2,458	621
Number of sequences	78	164	246	271	289	94

Source. June 1980, 1985, 1990, and 1995 Current Population Surveys.

who fall into the distributional tail is large. For example, in tables 4.2 and 4.4, no more than 5.4% of women in any cohort, race, or ethnicity fell outside the trajectories depicted in those tables. In table 4.5, by contrast, this percentage is 30.8% or higher for the first four cohorts of white, black, and Hispanic women; even for the most recent two cohorts of white, black, and Hispanic women, this percentage never falls below 16.8%. Thus, an inescapable conclusion from table 4.5 is that the seemingly simple move from one to two behavioral domains uncovers a substantial amount of complexity in women's lives that is hidden in analyses that proceed one domain at a time.

Our other measure of diversity—the number of distinct trajectories observed—again shows substantially more variation in table 4.5 than in previous tables. For example, there are 487 distinct pathways through marriage and childbearing for white women in the 1914–24 cohort displayed in table 4.5. By contrast, we observed nineteen pathways through childbearing and thirty distinct trajectories through marriage for this same cohort; hence, the number of distinct trajectories we observe when considering marriage and childbearing jointly is more than sixteen times the number of distinct trajectories when we consider either marriage or childbearing in isolation. The results are even more dramatic for the next three cohorts of white women, in which we observe 831, 1,226, and 1,098 distinct pathways through marriage and childbearing. Thus, for these cohorts, the number of distinct trajectories we observe when considering marriage and childbearing jointly is more than twenty times greater than the number of distinct trajectories when we consider either marriage or childbearing in isolation. Results are similar for black and Hispanic women, with the number of distinct trajectories when considering marriage and childbearing jointly more than seven and five times greater for black and Hispanic women, respectively, than the number of distinct trajectories when we consider either marriage or childbearing in isolation. These results thus also show that proceeding one domain at a time substantially understates the complexity of women's life-course trajectories.

Table 4.5 contains other surprises. Social scientists have often speculated that several aspects of modern life are likely to have made people's lives more complicated, and that these resulting complications should have resulted in increasingly diverse life-course patterns. Because our data speak only to two behavioral domains, we, like others, cannot test these speculations in a rigorous way. Our results, however, make clear that for the two behavioral domains we observe, the life-course pathways through marriage

and childbearing for women early in the twentieth century were just as complex as those for women much later in the twentieth century. Thus, what is
often viewed as a modern phenomenon—complex and diverse patterns of
family life—can in fact be observed to a surprising extent even for women
born in the 1910s and 1920s.

Another surprise is how few women follow even the most common
pathways. Consider, for example, the trajectory in which a woman enters a
first marriage, bears two children within this marriage, and remains in this
marriage when we observe her at age thirty-five. We might regard this trajectory as "normative," in that it conforms to stereotypical notions concerning marriage and childbearing; moreover, it also coincides with the modal
trajectory we observe for all cohorts of white women, save for the most recent cohort. But as in previous tables, that a trajectory represents a modal
pattern does not necessarily imply that many women actually follow it. This
is also true in table 4.5. Thus, this "normative" path through marriage and
childbearing characterizes between 20.4% and 24.2% of the first four birth
cohorts of white women. Of the first four birth cohorts of black and Hispanic
women, the corresponding percentages are even smaller, with between
11.7% and 16.5% of Hispanic women and between 5.5% and 8.9% of black
women following this trajectory. Hence, for women between 1914 and 1954,
more than three of four white, five of six Hispanic, and ten of eleven black
women follow marital and childbearing trajectories through age thirty-five
that depart from the pathway of two children born within an enduring first
marriage.

In table 4.5, we have identified all distinct trajectories for a given birth
cohort of women and then computed the percentage of women falling into
these trajectories. But doing so imposes a specific set of substantive distinctions, thus answering some questions but not others. In table 4.6, we reas-
semble our results by grouping together all trajectories in which childbearing occurs within an enduring first marriage. These trajectories are those of
women who, by age thirty-five, have had one or more children within an enduring first marriage, following the "traditional" trajectory of marriage and
childbearing (e.g., Uhlenberg 1969). This allows us to distinguish four types
of trajectories: for women who are single and never married, for women who
marry once but remain childless, for those who have one or more children
in an enduring first marriage, and all other trajectories. Note that women in
the last category will include women who had children in a first marriage but
who experienced a marital separation or divorce, as well as those who bear
children in a remarriage or outside of marriage altogether—trajectories of

TABLE 4.6

JOINT MARITAL AND CHILDBEARING STATUSES THROUGH AGE 35 FOR WOMEN BORN 1914–70

	1914–24	1925–34	1935–44	1945–54	1955–64	1965–70
Whites:						
1. Never-married, childless	5.6	4.1	4.0	5.8	10.7	27.3
2. First marriage, childless	9.3	6.5	5.4	7.6	13.7	18.2
3. First marriage with children	67.6	70.6	63.6	50.6	41.8	26.9
4. All other sequences	17.5	18.8	27.0	36.0	33.9	27.6
Number of sequences in 3	18	20	21	19	15	12
Number of sequences in 4	467	809	1213	1077	996	255
Number of sequences, total	487	831	1236	1098	1013	269
(n of seq in 4)/(n of seq, total)	95.9	97.4	98.1	98.1	98.3	94.8
Sample size	11,753	21,811	26,554	22,257	24,081	4,366
Blacks:						
1. Never-married, childless	7.1	4.5	4.3	6.6	11.5	23.9
2. First marriage, childless	15.5	8.3	5.5	4.3	5.4	5.1
3. First marriage with children	31.8	39.8	31.5	22.6	14.8	9.1
4. All other sequences	45.5	47.4	58.7	66.6	68.2	61.9
Number of sequences in 3	9	12	13	9	12	6
Number of sequences in 4	195	347	453	405	344	83
Number of sequences, total	206	361	468	416	358	91
(n of seq in 4)/(n of seq, total)	94.7	96.1	96.8	97.4	96.1	91.2
Sample size	1,109	2,522	3,187	2,883	3,439	690

(continued)

TABLE 4.6
(CONTINUED)

	1914–24	1925–34	1935–44	1945–54	1955–64	1965–70
Hispanics:						
1. Never-married, childless	5.7	6.7	6.0	5.4	8.1	16.6
2. First marriage, childless	8.1	6.9	5.1	3.5	8.8	9.8
3. First marriage with children	58.4	57.8	54.4	47.5	38.8	33.5
4. All other sequences	27.8	28.6	34.5	43.6	44.3	40.1
Number of sequences in 3	9	13	14	15	10	10
Number of sequences in 4	67	149	230	254	277	82
Number of sequences, total	78	164	246	271	289	94
(n of seq in 4)/(n of seq, total)	85.9	90.9	93.5	93.7	95.8	87.2
Sample size	385	1,169	1,779	1,733	2,458	621

Source. June 1980, 1985, 1990, and 1995 Current Population Surveys.

marriage and childbearing that are taken by commentators and researchers alike to represent "nontraditional" family forms.

Table 4.6 shows a dramatic gap in the life-course trajectories of white and black women. For white women, the typical pathway through age thirty-five is one in which a woman has one or more children within a first marriage; for black women, the typical pathway through age thirty-five is one in which a woman either has one or more children outside of marriage or has experienced the disruption of a first marriage. More than 50% of white women born between 1914 and 1954 followed a trajectory through age thirty-five in which we observe them having one or more children within an enduring first marriage, which drops to 41.8% for white women born between 1955 and 1964. Thus, for white women born over a fifty-year span, this trajectory comprised the statistical norm and conformed to common images of traditional family life as well. Over the same fifty-year span, what was typical for black women were nontraditional family forms that involved trajectories either in which one or more children were born outside of marriage or in which a first marriage ended via separation or divorce. The percentage of black women following such nontraditional life-course trajectories rose by more than 20 percentage points, from 45.5% in the 1914–24 cohort to 68.2% in the 1955–64 cohort. Conversely, the percentage of black women following traditional trajectories declined steadily, from 31.8% in the 1914–24 cohort to 22.6% in the 1955–64 cohort.

From Table 4.6 we can therefore see that what constituted a typical pathway through marriage and childbearing differed greatly for white and black women. "Traditional" trajectories of childbearing and marriage were indeed typical for white women born over a fifty-year span. However, for black women born during this same time period, "nontraditional" trajectories, in which women experienced the dissolution of one or more marriages or bore one or more children outside of marriage, were in fact typical. Moreover, while there is clear movement away from traditional trajectories of marriage and childbearing for women in all three racial and ethnic groups, substantial numbers of women followed nontraditional pathways. Thus for women born between 1914 and 1924, trajectories involving one or more marital disruptions or one or more nonmarital births were followed by more than one in six white women, more than one in four Hispanic women, and nearly one in two black women. This suggests that what we often regard as modern family developments are in fact not modern at all but, instead, have deep historical roots in the life experiences of white, black, and Hispanic women born as far back as the 1910s and 1920s.

What might the data in table 4.6 indicate about historical diversity in women's marriage and childbearing experiences? As in table 4.5, an enormous degree of diversity has been characteristic of the marital and childbearing trajectories of substantial numbers of women. To see this, consider the trajectories represented in the first two rows for each ethnic group in table 4.6. In the first row, we report percentages for women who remained childless at age thirty-five; in the second row, we report percentages for women who, by age thirty-five, entered a first marriage and remained in it but did not have children. The first row, thus, corresponds to the trajectory $(N, 0)$ and the second row to the trajectory $(N, 0) \rightarrow (M, 0)$. Similarly, the third row in each case gives percentages for women who, at age thirty-five, were observed in a first marriage with one or more children. Women falling into this category thus span a number of possible trajectories, for example, $(N, 0) \rightarrow (M, 0) \rightarrow (M, 1), (N, 0) \rightarrow (M, 0) \rightarrow (M, 1) \rightarrow (M, 2), (N, 0) \rightarrow (M, 0) \rightarrow (M, 1) \rightarrow (M, 2) \rightarrow (M, 3)$, and so forth. For white women born between 1914 and 1924, we observe eighteen distinct trajectories corresponding to childbearing within an enduring first marriage; for other cohorts, the number of distinct trajectories varies between twelve and twenty-one. Thus across all birth cohorts of white women, we observe a considerable degree of diversity even within this traditional pattern of marriage and childbearing, with the diversity of experience generated solely by different patterns of childbearing within a first marriage.[5]

Diversity in family life is also commonly regarded as a modern phenomenon, but our results suggest instead that family diversity has deep historical roots. As can be seen in table 4.6, substantial numbers of women have always followed pathways involving nontraditional patterns of marriage and childbearing. The trajectories followed by such women are enormously diverse, yet the diversity in such nontraditional trajectories varies remarkably little across time. For example, for white women born between 1914 and 1924, we observe 487 distinct trajectories of marriage and childbearing, 467 of which fall into the nontraditional category. Thus, 95.9% of the trajectories observed for white women in this cohort are nontraditional in nature, an astonishingly high number. Moreover, this degree of diversity remains just as high in subsequent cohorts, ranging between a low of 94.8% for the most recent cohort of white women to a high of 98.3% for white women born between 1955 and 1964. A similar extremely high degree of diversity—typically more than 90%—is observed in the nontraditional trajectories for black and Hispanic women. Thus, we observe enormous variation in the life-course trajectories of women who follow nontraditional pathways; moreover, the proportion of all trajectories that are "nontraditional" has been relatively constant over time.[6]

What characterizes these nontraditional trajectories? Table 4.7 provides one look at this question by examining specific trajectories for women who follow a nontraditional pathway through marriage and childbearing. For example, we observe 17.5% of white women born between 1914 and 1924 following a nontraditional trajectory of childbearing and marriage, with 11.3% of white women in this cohort following a nontraditional trajectory in which we observe no nonmarital fertility and 6.2% following a trajectory in which we observe some nonmarital fertility—that is, with the woman bearing one or more of her children outside of marriage. Thus of this 17.5%, roughly one out of three women have borne one or more children outside of marriage; in this cohort therefore, the vast majority of women with nontraditional pathways have trajectories in which we observe no nonmarital fertility. But table 4.7 also shows that 49% of the nontraditional trajectories observed for this cohort occur to women who have borne one or more children outside of marriage; hence, while nonmarital fertility makes up only about a third of women who follow a nontraditional pathway, the trajectories of women with some nonmarital fertility account for about half of the distinct nontraditional trajectories observed for this cohort. Surprisingly, there is little trend in this percentage across all cohorts of white women. Thus, nonmarital fertility accounts for about half of the diversity in the trajectories through marriage and childbearing of all of cohorts of white women in our data.

The next set of rows, for each ethnic grouping, repeats these calculations for women who we observe giving birth in a second or higher-order marriage versus women with no such remarital fertility. The percent with any remarital fertility rises from 3.7 to 6.5 for white women born between 1914 and 1954; hence, for these cohorts, women with any nonmarital fertility comprise only a fraction of those with nontraditional trajectories and account for between 33.8% and 39.4% of the diversity in nontraditional trajectories that we observe.

The last set of rows presents results for women who do not bear any children following the dissolution of a first marriage versus those women who have children either prior to a first marriage or following the dissolution of their first marriage. The proportion with no fertility following a first marital dissolution rises steadily across the first four cohorts of white women, from 6.0% to 14.2%, with the distinct trajectories observed for these women accounting for between 26% and 27% of the distinct

TABLE 4.7

DECOMPOSITION OF THE CATEGORY "ALL OTHER SEQUENCES," IN TABLE 4.6, FOR WHITE, BLACK, AND HISPANIC WOMEN BORN 1914–70

	1914–24	1925–34	1935–44	1945–54	1955–64	1965–70
Whites:						
4. All other sequences	17.5	18.8	27.0	36.0	33.9	27.6
Number of sequences in 4	467	809	1213	1077	996	255
4.1 Any nonmarital fertility	6.2	6.9	8.9	11.1	13.5	16.2
4.2 No nonmarital fertility	11.3	11.9	18.1	24.9	20.3	11.4
Number of sequences in 4.1	229	407	610	549	540	140
(num seq 4.1)/(num seq 4)	49.0	50.3	50.3	51.0	54.2	54.9
4.3 Any remarital fertility	3.7	4.7	5.6	6.5	5.3	2.4
4.4 No remarital fertility	13.8	14.1	21.4	29.5	28.6	25.2
Number of sequences in 4.3	158	319	491	403	332	53
(num seq 4.3)/(num seq 4)	33.8	39.4	34.5	37.4	33.3	20.8
4.5 No fertility after end of 1st marriage	6.0	6.2	11.0	14.2	10.3	6.3
4.6 Fertility pre or post 1st marriage	11.5	12.6	16.0	21.8	23.6	21.3
Number of sequences in 4.5	127	211	316	295	271	80
(num seq 4.5)/(num seq 4)	27.2	26.1	26.1	27.4	27.2	31.4
Blacks:						
4. All other sequences	45.5	47.4	58.7	66.6	68.2	61.9
Number of sequences in 4	195	347	453	405	344	83
4.1 Any nonmarital fertility	26.7	30.8	37.9	46.0	55.7	55.8
4.2 No nonmarital fertility	18.8	16.6	10.8	20.6	12.5	6.1
Number of sequences in 4.1	108	217	275	254	237	53
(num seq 4.1)/(num seq 4)	55.4	62.5	60.7	62.7	68.9	63.9

4.3 Any remarital fertility	4.1	3.8	3.8	3.3	.6
4.4 No remarital fertility	41.4	43.6	54.9	63.3	61.3
Number of sequences in 4.3	37	68	89	68	4
(num seq 4.3)/(num seq 4)	19.0	19.6	19.6	16.8	4.8
4.5 No fertility after end of 1st marriage	11.7	10.5	15.4	17.9	4.9
4.6 Fertility pre or post 1st marriage	33.8	36.9	43.3	48.7	57.0
Number of sequences in 4.5	60	108	145	149	24
(num seq 4.5)/(num seq 4)	30.8	31.1	32.0	36.8	28.9
Hispanics:					
4. All other sequences	27.8	28.6	34.5	43.6	40.1
Number of sequences in 4	67	149	230	254	82
4.1 Any nonmarital fertility	15.6	17.2	20.0	24.9	30.8
4.2 No nonmarital fertility	12.2	11.4	14.5	18.7	9.3
Number of sequences in 4.1	31	72	133	140	50
(num seq 4.1)/(num seq 4)	46.3	48.3	57.8	55.1	61.0
4.3 Any remarital fertility	2.9	4.0	4.2	3.9	1.4
4.4 No remarital fertility	24.9	24.6	30.3	39.7	38.7
Number of sequences in 4.3	11	39	57	54	9
(num seq 4.3)/(num seq 4)	16.4	26.2	24.8	21.3	11.0
4.5 No fertility after end of 1st marriage	6.5	6.2	9.1	13.1	4.3
4.6 Fertility pre or post 1st marriage	21.3	22.4	25.4	30.5	35.8
Number of sequences in 4.5	17	43	69	84	17
(num seq 4.5)/(num seq 4)	25.4	28.6	30.0	33.1	20.7

Source. June 1980, 1985, 1990, and 1995 Current Population Surveys.

sequences observed for women following a nontraditional pathway through marriage and childbearing.[7]

The proportion of black women following what we have termed "nontraditional" pathways is so large across all cohorts that calling these pathways nontraditional might well be regarded a misnomer for this population: close to half of all black women born between 1914 and 1934—between 45.5% and 47.4%—and well over half of all black women born 1935 or later—between 58.7% and 68.2%—followed such nontraditional pathways. This suggests what continues to be a minority experience for white women has historically been extremely common for black women. Moreover, table 4.7 makes clear that across all cohorts of black women, more than half of women who we observe following a nontraditional trajectory have borne one or more child outside of marriage.

DISCUSSION

In an often-cited passage, C. Wright Mills ([1959] 2002) argued that social scientists should study how biography and history intersect. We have taken his dictum seriously. In this chapter, we have reconstructed women's pathways through marriage and childbearing, focusing on the order and sequencing of marital and childbearing events as they unfold in women's lives. This is the biography part of Mills's dictum. To be sure, our demo-biographic approach depicts a woman's life course in a highly stylized way, focusing only on the demographic bare bones of marriage and childbearing, but it also hews closely to the sort of verbal descriptions that many of us would give in describing our lives—that we married, had two children, divorced, remarried, and so forth.

What becomes immediately apparent in taking such an approach is that family experience can be highly fluid for some women and much less fluid for other women. As a result, the term often used by social scientists—"family structure"—is a useful metaphor for the family lives of some women—those for whom family experience is less fluid—but may not be as apt for other women—those for whom family experience is highly fluid.

Finding that some women's family lives are highly fluid and others are not also implies that what is interesting is not only what might be typical and that the range of variation in women's family lives might be of equal importance as an object of study. This, in turn, carries many consequences. Focusing on the range of variation in women's family lives provided us with a way to examine diversity in family experience; it also let us quantify the idea of "family diversity" in a straightforward and simple way. And because our data spanned a good portion of the twentieth century, we could ask if family life is more diverse now than in the past—a question that takes seriously both the history and biography parts of Mill's dictum.

Focusing on women's pathways through marriage and childbearing also lets us pursue empirically the idea that the transition to adulthood is better conceptualized as a constellation of multiple roles and statuses, a viewpoint often articulated, but rarely followed, by life-course researchers. We thus contrasted our approach from more conventional analyses that examine trends in marriage separately from trends in childbearing. This turned out to matter a great deal, with conventional approaches obscuring substantial diversity in women's lives that is revealed when examining trends in these two behaviors jointly. What emerges, then, is a much richer and far more complex picture of women's pathways through marriage and childbearing.

Our analyses show that while most women have followed so-called traditional pathways involving childbearing within an enduring first marriage, a surprising and substantial minority—more than one in six for white women born in the 1910s and 1920s—has followed nontraditional pathways involving marital disruption or nonmarital fertility. For white women born around 1950, even more women—more than one in three—are observed to exhibit such nontraditional trajectories. Thus, our analyses reveal that surprisingly large proportions of women born in the early twentieth century had already moved away from traditional pathways through marriage and childbearing.

How might we characterize this diversity of family experience? Because most white women have followed traditional pathways involving childbearing within an enduring first marriage, one might appropriately regard their trajectories as being normative, both statistically and socially. But the trajectories we observe for women following such traditional pathways are also relatively simple, while those for women following nontraditional pathways are extremely diverse. Thus, for white women born in the 1910s and 1920s, one in six follow nontraditional pathways through marriage and childbearing, but the number of different pathways for such women makes up more than 95% of the distinct pathways observed for white women born in the 1910s and 1920s. Similarly, 98% of the diversity in the trajectories of white women born around 1950 comes from the one in three white women who followed a nontraditional pathway through marriage and childbearing. Our results are strikingly similar for black and Hispanic women, with between 86% and 97% of the diversity in marriage and childbearing coming from women who followed nontraditional pathways.

As a result, these findings provide much more specific detail about patterns of historical change than other studies to date. On the one hand, we observe relatively simple trajectories through marriage and childbearing for women following traditional patterns of marriage and childbearing; while on the other hand, the trajectories for those who depart from these patterns are extremely diverse and complicated. Moreover, while growing numbers of women have followed such nontraditional trajectories, there is also remarkably little variation over time in the amount of diversity observed for such nontraditional trajectories. Thus, the overall rise in diversity in women's trajectories through marriage and childbearing is an example of what social scientists term a "compositional shift" in the population, with *more* women following nontraditional patterns of marriage and childbearing but with the diversity in the trajectories *among* such women remaining relatively constant over time.

Our overall finding—that there has always been substantial diversity in women's pathways through marriage and childbearing—echoes Coontz's (1992) observation that much of what has been termed the "traditional family" might best be understood as specific to the family patterns of white, middle-class women during a specific period—the 1950s. However, our findings complement Coontz's findings in several ways. Coontz's work is based primarily on secondary historical sources that typically provide snapshots of a woman's family situation; by contrast, our data provide retrospective life histories from four large nationally representative surveys of women that let us estimate the proportions of women born in different periods who follow traditional and nontraditional pathways through marriage and childbearing.

In addition, our findings depart somewhat from Coontz's account. For example, our estimates suggest that nearly one out of five white women in the 1950s followed a nontraditional pathway through marriage and childbearing in which there was a marital disruption or childbearing outside of marriage. Perhaps more important, our findings show that diversity in family experience holds to a remarkable extent not only across time but also across women of different racial and ethnic backgrounds. For example, because nontraditional pathways involve either divorce or nonmarital fertility, we can further characterize diversity in women's trajectories by asking if, on average, diversity is greater among those women who experience divorce or for those who bear one or more children outside of marriage. Our results suggest that diversity is greatest among women who have a child outside of marriage— roughly 40%–70% of the diversity among women taking a nontraditional pathway through marriage and childbearing occurred among those who have had one or more children outside of marriage. This finding—that nonmarital fertility gives rise to the most diverse trajectories through marriage and childbearing—holds with equal force both across time and race and ethnicity. It is thus characteristic of white, black, and Hispanic women and, within each racial and ethnic group, for cohorts of women born over a period of fifty years.

More generally, our results suggest that what has often been characterized as a modern rise in family diversity in fact has deep historical roots. Thus, like others, we observe steady increases in the proportion of women who have experienced a marital disruption or who have had one or more children outside of marriage, but we also find little change in the diversity of experience among those who divorce or who bear one or more children outside of marriage. These latter findings provide a marked contrast to how most social scientists have interpreted historical change in the family, with rapid increases in divorce and nonmarital fertility prompting many to proclaim these changes as marking a fundamental decline in the family (Gilder 1986; Popenoe 1993; Whitehead 1993), and others seeing these transformations as merely giving rise to modern, albeit highly diverse, family forms (Demo et al. 2000; Stacey 1991). Our analyses, by contrast, reveal an astonishing degree of diversity in women's lives, particularly among those who follow nontraditional pathways through marriage and childbearing. Of greater importance, however, is that diversity in women's pathways through marriage and childbearing was as great for women born in the 1910s and 1920s as for women born in the 1960s and 1970s. "New" forms of family diversity are in fact not new at all.

NOTES

Funding for this research was provided by the National Institute of Child Health and Human Development (HD 29550), with additional research facilities provided under HD 05876 to the Center for Demography and Ecology, University of Wisconsin—Madison. We thank Cheryl Knobeloch for expert programming assistance and Larry Bumpass and the volume editors for helpful comments.

1. We note that a quantity such as the number of distinct trajectories falls into a class of extreme value statistics, whose value will typically rise with sample size.

2. It is important to emphasize that the percentages for earlier cohorts should be interpreted as the percentage we observe to be never married at age thirty-five—clearly, some of those who we observe to be never married at age thirty-five may marry at some later age.

3. A drawback of the CPS data is that they do not provide retrospective data on cohabitation. Raley (1996) finds that when cohabitation is taken into account, the black/white gap is narrowed substantially. More generally, it is unclear how our lack of cohabitation data will affect our main finding about diversity across cohorts. For

example, were we able to include cohabitation, diversity may have increased across cohorts. Alternatively, it is also possible that diversity would show little trend as family patterns involving common-law marriage were replaced by informal cohabiting unions in later periods.

4. Note, moreover, that because the two most recent cohorts have delayed entry into marriage, our estimates will understate the actual diversity of marital sequences for these two cohorts, relative to earlier cohorts, since we do not observe women in these cohorts through age thirty-five. Thus, table 4.4 is likely to somewhat understate trends in the increasing diversity of women's marital trajectories.

5. As noted in our discussion of childbearing trajectories in tables 4.2 and 4.3, the large number of distinct trajectories is due to women with twin and higher-order multiple births. Examples of childbearing trajectories including multiple births are $(N, 0) \rightarrow (M, 0) \rightarrow (M, 2)$, $(N, 0) \rightarrow (M, 0) \rightarrow (M, 3)$, $(N, 0) \rightarrow (M, 0) \rightarrow (M, 1) \rightarrow (M, 3)$, and so forth.

6. Some of the diversity that we observe for such nontraditional trajectories may be due to measurement error—e.g., errors by women when providing retrospective reports of the timing of a marital separation or divorce. However, the quality of retrospective reports of marriage and fertility in the June CPS has been shown to be quite high (see, e.g., Pendleton, McCarthy, and Cherlin 1989; Wu, Martin, and Long 2001); hence, while measurement error is present and will contribute to some of this diversity, it is extremely unlikely that it is responsible for all of the diversity we observe.

7. We present and discuss the three panels of table 4.7 separately since these groups of women are not mutually exclusive. Thus, a woman could fall into the first two categories—i.e., some nonmarital fertility and some remarital fertility—if, e.g., she bore her first child before a first marriage and if she bore her second child in a second marriage. Similar overlap can occur between all three groups.

REFERENCES

Becker, Gary S. 1991. *A Treatise on the Family.* Enlarged ed. Cambridge, MA: Harvard University Press.

Bennett, Neil G., David E. Bloom, and Patricia H. Craig. 1989. The Divergence of Black and White Marriage Patterns. *American Journal of Sociology* 95 (3): 692–722.

Bertaux, Daniel, and Martin Kohli. 1984. The Life Story Approach: A Continental View. *Annual Review of Sociology* 10: 215–37.

Buchman, Marlis. 1989. *The Script of Life in Modern Society.* Chicago: University of Chicago Press.

Bumpass, Larry L. 1990. What's Happening to the Family: Interaction between Demographic and Institutional Change. *Demography* 27 (4):483–98.

Bumpass, Larry L., and Hsien-Hen Lu. 2000. Trends in Cohabitation and Implications for Children's Family Contexts. *Population Studies* 54 (1):29–41.

Bumpass, Larry L., and James A. Sweet. 1989. National Estimates of Cohabitation. *Demography* 26 (4):615–25.

Bumpass, Larry, James Sweet, and Teresa Castro-Martin. 1990. Changing Patterns of Remarriage. *Demography* 52:747–56.

Casper, Lynne M., and Suzanne M. Bianchi. 2002. *Continuity and Change in the American Family*. Thousand Oaks, CA: Sage Publications.

Castro-Martin, Teresa, and Larry L. Bumpass. 1989. Recent Trends in Marital Disruption. *Demography* 26 (1):37–51.

Cherlin, Andrew J. 1992. *Marriage, Divorce, Remarriage*. Rev. and enlarged ed. Cambridge, MA: Harvard University Press.

Coontz, Stephanie. 1992. *The Way We Never Were: American Families and the Nostalgia Trap*. New York: Basic Books.

David, Paul A., and Warren C. Sanderson. 1987. The Emergence of a Two-Child Norm among American Birth-Controllers. *Population and Development Review* 13 (1):1–41.

Demo, David H., Katherine R. Allen, and Mark A. Fine. 2000. *Handbook of Family Diversity*. New York: Oxford University Press.

Furstenberg, Frank F., Jr., J. Brooks-Gunn, and S. Philip Morgan. 1987. *Adolescent Mothers in Later Life*. New York: Cambridge University Press.

Giddens, Anthony. 1993. *Modernity and Self-Identity: Self and Society in the Late Modern Age*. Stanford, CA: Stanford University Press.

Gilder, George F. 1986. *Men and Marriage*. Gretna, LA: Pelican.

Goldstein, Joshua R. 1999. The Leveling of Divorce in the United States. *Demography* 36:409–14.

Goldstein, Joshua R., and Catherine T. Kenney. 2001. Marriage Delayed or Marriage Forgone? New Cohort Forecasts of First Marriage for U.S. Women. *American Sociological Review* 66:506–19.

Griffith, Janet D., Helen P. Koo, and C. M. Suchindran. 1985. Childbearing and Family in Remarriage. *Demography* 22:73–88.

Laumann, Edward O., John H. Gagnon, Robert T. Michael, and Stuart Michaels. 1994. *The Social Organization of Sexuality: Sexual Practices in the United States*. Chicago: University of Chicago Press.

Martin, Steven P. 2000. Diverging Fertility among U.S. Women Who Delay Childbearing Past Age 30. *Demography* 37:523–33.

Mayer, Karl Ulrich, and Walter Muller. 1986. The State and the Structure of the Life Course. Pp. 217–45 in *Human Development and the Life Course: Multidisciplinary Perspectives*, edited by Aage B. Sorensen, Franz E. Weinert, and Lonnie R. Sherrod. Hillsdale, NJ: Erlbaum Associates.

Mayer, Karl Ulrich, and Urs Schoepflin. 1989. The State and the Life Course. *Annual Review of Sociology* 15:187–209.

Meyer, John W. 1986. The Self and the Life Course: Institutionalization and Its Effects. Pp. 199–216 in *Human Development and the Life Course: Multidisciplinary Perspectives,* edited by Aage B. Sorensen, Franz E. Weinert, and Lonnie R. Sherrod. Hillsdale, NJ: Erlbaum Associates.

Mills, C. Wright. [1959] 2002. *The Sociological Imagination.* New York: Oxford University Press.

Oppenheimer, Valerie K. 1988. A Theory of Marriage Timing. *American Journal of Sociology* 94:563–91.

Pendleton, Audrey J., James McCarthy, and Andrew Cherlin. 1989. The Quality of Marriage and Divorce Data from Surveys. U.S. National Center for Health Statistics, PHS 90–1241. *Challenges for Public Health Statistics in the 1990s: Proceedings of the 1989 Public Health Conference on Records and Statistics.* Washington D.C.: U.S. Government Printing Office.

Popenoe, David. 1993. American Family Decline, 1960–1990: A Review and Appraisal. *Journal of Marriage and the Family* 55 (3):527–55.

Preston, Samuel H., and John McDonald. 1979. The Incidence of Divorce within Cohorts of American Marriages Contracted since the Civil War. *Demography* 16:1–25.

Raley, R. Kelly. 1996. A Shortage of Marriageable Men? A Note on the Role of Cohabitation in Black-White Differences in Marriage Rates. *American Sociological Review* 61:973–83.

Rindfuss, Ronald R., S. Philip Morgan, and Kate Offut. 1996. Education and the Changing Age Patterns of American Fertility: 1963–89. *Demography* 33:277–90.

Ryder, Norman B. 1980. Components of Temporal Variations in American Fertility. Pp. 15–45 in *Demographic Patterns in Developed Societies,* edited by R. W. Hiorns. London: Taylor & Francis.

Settersten, Richard A., Jr. 1997. The Salience of Age in the Life Course. *Human Development* 40:257–81.

———. 2002. Socialization and the Life Course: New Frontiers in Theory and Research. Pp. 13–40 in *Advances in Life-Course Research: New Frontiers in Socialization,* edited by Richard A. Settersten Jr., and Timothy Owens. London: Elsevier Science, Ltd.

Settersten, Richard A., Jr., and Karl Ulrich Mayer. 1997. The Measurement of Age, Age Structuring, and the Life Course. *Annual Review of Sociology* 23:233–61.

Shanahan, Michael J. 2000. Pathways to Adulthood in Changing Societies: Variability and Mechanisms in Life Course Perspective. *Annual Review of Sociology* 26:667–92.

Spain, Daphne, and Suzanne M. Bianchi. 1996. *Balancing Act: Motherhood, Marriage and Employment among American Women*. Thousand Oaks, CA: Sage Publications.

Stacey, Judith. 1991. *Brave New Families: Stories of Domestic Upheaval in Late Twentieth Century America*. New York: Basic Books.

Stewart, Susan D. 2002. The Effects of Stepchildren on Childbearing Intentions and Births. *Demography* 39:181–97.

Thomson, Elizabeth, and Jui-Chung Allen Li. 2002. Her, His, and Their Children: Childbearing Intentions and Births in Stepfamilies. NSFH working paper No. 89, National Survey of Families and Households, Center for Demography, University of Wisconsin, Madison.

Thornton, Arland. 1977. Decomposing the Re-Marriage Process. *Population Studies* 31:383–92.

———. 1978. Marital Dissolution, Remarriage, and Childbearing. *Demography* 15: 361–80.

———. 1989. Changing Attitudes toward Family Issues in the United States. *Journal of Marriage and the Family* 51 (4):873–93.

Uhlenberg, Peter R. 1969. A Study of Cohort Life Cycles: Cohorts of Native-Born Massachusetts Women, 1830–1920. *Population Studies* 23:407–20.

Ventura, Stephanie J., and Christine A. Bachrach. 2000. *Nonmarital Childbearing in the United States, 1940–99*. National Vital Statistics and Reports, vol. 48, no. 16. Washington, DC: National Center for Health Statistics.

Ventura, Stephanie, Christine A. Bachrach, Laura Hill, Kelleen Kaye, Pamela Holcomb, and Elisa Koff. 1995. The Demography of Nonmarital Childbearing. Pp. 3–133 in *Report to Congress on Out-of-Wedlock Childbearing*, edited by U.S. Department of Health and Human Services. Hyattsville, MD: National Center for Health Statistics.

Whitehead, Barbara Dafoe. 1993. Dan Quayle Was Right. *Atlantic Monthly* 4:47–84.

Wilson, William Julius. 1987. *The Truly Disadvantaged: The Inner City, the Underclass, and Public Policy*. Chicago: University of Chicago Press.

Wu, Lawrence L., Larry L. Bumpass, and Kelly Musick. 2001. Historical and Life Course Trajectories of Nonmarital Childbearing. Pp. 3–48 in *Out of Wedlock: Trends and Consequences of Nonmarital Fertility*, edited by Lawrence L. Wu and Barbara Wolfe. New York: Russell Sage Foundation.

Wu, Lawrence L., and Steven P. Martin. 2002. Is There an Engine of Nonmarital Fertility? CDE Working Paper No. 2002–14, Center for Demography and Ecology, University of Wisconsin—Madison.

Wu, Lawrence L., Steven P. Martin, and Daniel A. Long. 2001. Comparing Data Quality of Fertility and First Sexual Intercourse Histories. *Journal of Human Resources* 36 (3):520–55.

CHAPTER 5
HISTORICAL TRENDS IN PATTERNS OF TIME USE AMONG YOUNG ADULTS IN DEVELOPED COUNTRIES

ANNE H. GAUTHIER AND FRANK F. FURSTENBERG JR.

Time use among young people varies greatly during the transition to adulthood. But it is their stage in the transition, rather than their age, that governs the allocation of time (Gauthier and Furstenberg 2002). Time spent on education, paid work, housework, child care, and leisure varies with the transition from school to work, the transition to residential independence, and the transition to parenthood. For instance, young people who reside with their parents tend to devote less time to housework than do their counterparts who have achieved residential independence, while fathers tend to devote more time to housework than all other subgroups of men. As such, young people's patterns of time use are strongly regulated by social roles, constraints, and obligations. Yet, time use has not been one of the indicators traditionally used by scholars to examine the transition to adulthood. Scholars have relied on key demographic markers and, more recently, on subjective indicators (Saetermoe, Beneli, and Busch 1999), while time-use research has been incompletely integrated into the literature on the transition to adulthood.

This chapter continues our efforts to fill this void (Gauthier and Furstenberg 2002) by examining broad historical trends in patterns of time use among young adults as they make their transition to adulthood. We pose two main questions: whether patterns of time use among young adults have changed since the 1970s and whether there has been a convergence in the patterns of time use of men and women. To answer these questions, we use a series of time-use surveys carried out in eleven industrialized countries since the 1970s. Our approach is primarily descriptive and examines how young adults reallocate time as they pass through different stages of their transition to adulthood.

The chapter is divided in four sections. In the introduction, we set the stage by reviewing the empirical and theoretical literature on historical changes in patterns of time use among young adults. We also report the scanty evidence linking the transition to adulthood and the corresponding changes in patterns of time use. We then present our data and methods. In the third section we report the cross-national results. Finally, we discuss some of the implications of our findings and identify future avenues of research.

THEORETICAL CONSIDERATIONS

The demographic composition of the young adult population has changed significantly since the 1960s. Because young people are delaying marriage and parenthood and attaining financial and residential independence later than they used to, the population of young adults contains a larger proportion of students, unattached individuals, and childless adults today than thirty years ago (Fussell 2002). Because the transition status of young people is associated with specific time-use patterns (Gauthier and Furstenberg 2002), we can expect these changes in the demographic composition of the young adult population to have resulted in major changes in patterns of time use at the aggregate level. For this reason, our theoretical and empirical approach in this chapter is to examine subgroups of young adults who have reached various transition statuses, rather than to examine the whole young adult population. In other words, a disaggregated rather than an aggregated analysis is required to understand fully the changes that have taken place in time use during this stage of life.

Various macrolevel factors may have affected patterns of time use among young adults since the 1960s, including changes in the economic circumstances and opportunities facing young adults and changes in social norms, especially regarding gender equality. Regarding the first factor, the economic context and the availability of jobs for young people have changed substantially since the 1960s. Youth unemployment, for instance, was much higher in the early 1980s and early 1990s than it was in the 1960s (National

Center for Education Statistics [NCSE] 1996). During the past decades, entry-level job opportunities and advancement possibilities for young adults have deteriorated, especially for less skilled workers (Hill and Yeung 1999). The economic position of young adults has also deteriorated. While the median income of full-time year-round workers aged twenty to twenty-four in the United States was $22,141 in 1965, it was $16,276 in 1994 (in constant 1994 dollars) (NCSE 1996). At the same time, the cost of higher education has significantly increased since the 1960s, at more than twice the rate of inflation between the 1970s and 1990s (Hauptman 2000).

These changes in work opportunities and economic circumstances may have motivated young people to make a greater investment in human capital–building activities. Facing fiercer competition in the job market, they may have decided not only to delay the transition from school to work but also to increase the amount of time that they devote to education (including time spent studying). The worsening economic environment young adults encountered may also have motivated (or obliged) them to devote more time to paid work. Overall, then, we may expect to find employed people working more, and students more often combining school with paid work. The same changes in employment opportunities and the general economic situation facing young adults may also have led them to delay marriage, if not partnering, and especially parenthood, and, in some countries, to postpone leaving their parents' home (Furstenberg, Cook, Sampson, and Slap 2002).

Social norms concerning gender equality have also changed since the 1970s. As women's labor force participation has increased, societies have been placing more emphasis on gender equality. If we assume that young people's allocation of time is influenced by such norms, we would expect young partnered men (cohabiting or married) to have been spending more time on housework over the past few decades and reaching a more equal division of labor with their partners. Such a trend was in fact observed among working-age adults (Gershuny 2000).

The literature notes at least two other societal changes that may have altered young people's allocation of time. First, young people's material aspirations have been rising. Among college freshmen in the United States, being well-off financially is now the primary life goal. While 45% of young people thought that being well-off financially was an important life goal in 1974, this figure had risen to 75% by 1989 (Easterlin and Crimmins 1991). This increase in materialism may have enhanced the wish (or need) to make more money in order to afford more goods and, if so, we would expect this to translate into more time being devoted to paid work, even at the expense of leisure.

Finally, there are indications that societal expectations concerning time devoted to child care have been increasing since the 1970s, for both men and women. Numerous studies have shown the importance of parent-child activities for children's cognitive development, and parents have been reminded of the importance of playing with and reading to their children (Child Trends 1999; Garrett 2002). This social pressure may have led parents to spend more time on child-care activities.

In sum, changes in the social and economic situations of young adults since the 1970s have not only restructured the transition to adulthood but may also have altered patterns of time use among young adults at different transition stages.[1] This chapter can be viewed as a companion piece to the previous chapters on historical and cross-national changes in early adulthood. However, our focus is not on the restructuring of this period but on how this restructuring has affected young people's experience during discrete stages of the early adulthood transition.

DATA AND METHOD

In this chapter we analyze a series of cross-sectional time-use surveys carried out since the 1970s in eleven countries: Australia, Austria, Canada, Finland, Germany, Italy, the Netherlands, Norway, Sweden, the United Kingdom, and the United States. Some of these countries have conducted more than one time-use survey since the 1970s, bringing our sample to a total of twenty-three surveys. These surveys are part of the Multinational Time Use Study Archive and have all been recoded into a common set of variables.[2]

Geographically, this sample covers a wide set of countries, though only a relatively small fraction of the industrialized world. The limited sample restricts our ability to generalize beyond the eleven countries. Moreover, although the surveys cover the period of the 1970s–90s, the surveys are not equally distributed over this period: four were carried out in the 1970s, eight in the 1980s, and eleven in the 1990s (see table 5.A1 in the appendix for details). Most of the data are therefore concentrated in the later part of the 1970s–90s, limiting the conclusions that we can draw about historical trends in time use. Even recognizing these shortcomings, this data set offers a unique opportunity to examine historical and cross-national variations in patterns of time use among young adults.

All surveys included in this analysis used the same instrument to collect data on time use, namely, the twenty-four-hour diary. The literature suggests that this instrument provides more accurate estimates of time than the stylized technique, which consists of asking respondents how much time they have spent on specific activities during a specific recall period (Robinson and Godbey 1999). In all surveys, the collection period encompassed each of the seven days of the week in order to capture daily variations. Recent surveys also spread the data collection over the twelve months of the year. The surveys included in this analysis vary largely in terms of their collection period, sample size, and response rate (detail on all surveys is reported in table 5.A1). In particular, the small sample sizes will restrict our analysis of specific subgroups of young adults.[3]

Our empirical analysis is focused on the young adult population aged eighteen to thirty-four. While one may worry that such a large age range could result in a very heterogeneous sample, the literature suggests that the transition status of young adults, rather than their age itself, tends to account for most of the variation in their patterns of time use (Converse 1972; Gauthier and Furstenberg 2002). We consequently organized our analysis around six main subgroups of young adults:

1. Students (nonpartnered students without children);[4]
2. Employed singles (nonpartnered employed people without children);[5]
3. Employed partnered (cohabiting or married employed people without children);
4. Employed parents (cohabiting or married employed people with children);
5. Disengaged (nonpartnered and nonemployed people without children); and
6. At-home parents (cohabiting or married nonemployed people with children).

These subgroups were selected to capture some of the key transitions to adulthood, namely, the transition from school to work (comparison of subgroups 1 and 2), the transition to partnership (comparison of subgroups 2 and 3), and the transition to parenthood (comparison of subgroups 3 and 4).[6] Together these subgroups represent about 80%–95% of all young adults. The excluded cases correspond to students who are cohabiting or married and/or have children, single parents, and unemployed men with children. For the purpose of this analysis, we also excluded from the subgroup analysis any survey that had fewer than twenty-five cases.

For each of these subgroups of young adults, we distinguish seven broad categories of time use:

• Education (including time spent attending classes, studying, and doing homework);
• Paid work (including coffee breaks);

- Housework (including cleaning, cooking, and house maintenance);
- Child care (including playing with and caring for children);
- Leisure (including socializing, volunteering, watching television, etc.);
- Personal activities (including eating, sleeping, bathing, dressing); and
- Travel to and from school and/or work.

The sum of these seven activities is twenty-four hours. It should be pointed out that the analysis is restricted to primary activities and excludes secondary (or simultaneous) activities. This restriction likely underestimates the total time spent on child care, as many child-care activities are carried out at the same time as another activity, such as cooking.

In the next section, we examine the mean patterns of time use for each of the subgroups of young adults. The data have been weighted to correct for over- or undersampling, including the sampling of the day of the week.[7] We restrict the analysis to the mean weekly patterns of time use averaged over the seven days of the week. As such, the multinational data set provides us with twenty-three survey means that, when used as unit of analysis, allows us to capture any linear historical trend. We then test the statistical significance of this trend by fitting a bivariate regression using the year of the survey as covariate.

Before turning to the results, we should point out that the central aim of this analysis is to provide a general picture of historical trends in time use among young adults over the past several decades. Consequently, relatively little will be said about cross-national differences apart from noting particularly wide disparities among countries when they exist. Explaining cross-national differences is beyond the scope of this chapter; subsequent papers will address the sources of variations in the time-use patterns observed here.

RESULTS

We first explore patterns of time use among young adults for the entire 1970s–90s period. We then examine the patterns by subgroup of young adults, focusing on historical trends and gender differences. When applicable, we also comment on changes in the patterns of time use associated with changes in transition status.

Overall Patterns of Time Use of Young Adults

Young people ages eighteen to thirty-four devote an average of 4.5 hours per day to paid work and education (including related travel), 3.4 hours to housework and child care, 5.8 hours to leisure, and 10.2 hours to personal activities (average across all twenty-three surveys). As can be seen in table 5.1, the pattern of time use among young adults varies strongly by employment and family status, as well as by gender. Among all subgroups, fathers devote the highest number of hours to paid work (6.2 hours per day or about forty-three hours a week), while students, disengaged young adults, and at-home parents devote, not surprisingly, the least time to paid work.[8] It is also worth noting that women of all subgroups devote less time to paid work than their male counterparts. The gender difference is especially large when children are present. Conversely, women of all subgroups devote more time to child care and housework than men. It is particularly interesting that this gender difference is observable even among students and employed singles. Women's tendency to spend time on housework appears to be deeply ingrained in the Western societies included in our sample.

As for leisure, it varies between a minimum of 4.5 hours per day for employed mothers and a maximum of 8.9 hours for disengaged young men. This large variation is almost entirely accounted for by differences in the amount of time spent on paid and unpaid work. Women, furthermore, devote less time to leisure activities than men among all subgroups. Finally, time spent on personal activities varies much less across subgroups, from a minimum of 9.6 hours per day for employed fathers to a maximum of 11.7 hours for disengaged men. In contrast to leisure, women tend to devote slightly more time to this activity than men.

The above results are based on averages across all data sets. We now turn to a finer analysis and examine patterns of time use among young adults by subgroup, gender, and year.

Students

Results for students appear in figure 5.1. We should again stress that the student subgroup is restricted for the purpose of this analysis to nonpartnered students without children. It includes, however, both students living with their parents and students living independently, as not all surveys included information on residential status. For each subcategory of activities, we plotted the mean value for each survey and computed the regression line in order to summarize the overall historical trend.

Contrary to what one might expect, students in the 1990s are not devoting more time to education than did earlier cohorts. If anything, they spent less time than in the 1980s.[9] The trends, however, are not statistically significant and instead reveal a wide dispersion in the data. Students in dif-

TABLE 5.1

MEAN PATTERNS OF TIME USE OF YOUNG ADULTS AGED 18–34,

1970S–90S (HOURS PER DAY)

GENDER/GROUPS	PAID	EDUC	HOUS	CCARE	FREE	PERS	TRAV
All							
Students	2.5	2.4	1.7	.1	6.4	10.3	.6
Singles	5.7	.1	1.5	.0	5.9	10.1	.6
Partnered	5.2	.1	2.7	.1	5.5	10.0	.5
Parents	4.7	.0	2.8	1.6	4.7	9.7	.4
Disengaged	.7	.1	2.5	.4	8.6	11.5	.2
At-home	.1	.0	4.9	3.2	5.4	10.3	.0
All	3.6	.5	2.6	.8	5.8	10.2	.4
Men							
Students	2.7	2.4	1.5	.0	6.5	10.2	.7
Singles	5.8	.1	1.3	.0	6.2	9.9	.6
Partnered	5.7	.0	2.2	.0	5.5	9.9	.5
Parents	6.2	.0	1.8	.8	4.9	9.6	.6
Disengaged	.8	.2	2.1	.1	8.9	11.7	.2
All	4.7	.6	1.8	.3	6.0	10.1	.6
Women							
Students	2.3	2.3	1.9	.1	6.3	10.4	.6
Singles	5.4	.1	1.9	.1	5.6	10.4	.6
Partnered	4.6	.1	3.1	.2	5.4	10.2	.4
Parents	2.5	.0	4.4	2.6	4.5	9.8	.2
Disengaged	.5	.0	3.0	.8	8.2	11.3	.1
At-home	.0	.0	4.9	3.5	5.3	10.2	.0
All	2.6	.5	3.4	1.3	5.6	10.3	.3

Note. The sum of all activities may not exactly add up to 24 hours because of rounding and a resid-ual category composed of unclassifiable activities (representing less than 0.1 hour per day). The gen-der/groups totals refer to all young people aged 18–34 and not only those belonging to the subgroups reported in the table. The "at-home parent" category for men is not reported in this table because of too few cases. Variables refer to time spent as follows: PAID—paid work (excluding travel to/from work); EDUC—education (including classes, study, and homework and excluding travel to/from school); HOUS—housework (including shopping); CCARE—childcare; FREE—leisure activities (including volunteering); PERS—personal activities (including eating, sleeping, bathing, and dressing); and TRAV—travel to/from work and school.

ferent countries devote, somewhat surprisingly, very different amounts of time to education, with values ranging from less than three hours per day to more than six hours per day. These cross-national differences likely reflect institutional differences in the number of days and hours of school.[10]

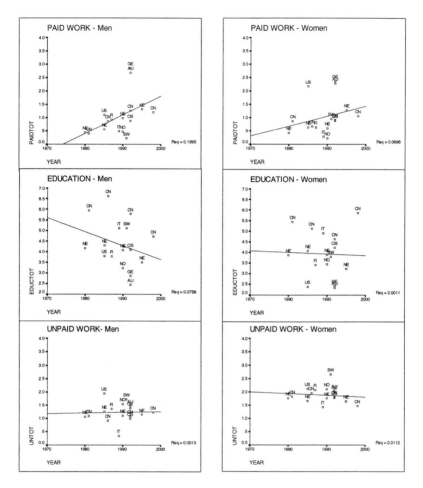

Figure 5.1. Patterns of time use of students (unpartnered and childless). *AU:* Australia; *CN:* Canada; *FI:* Finland; *GE:* Germany; *IT:* Italy; *NE:* Netherlands; *NO:* Norway; *OS:* Austria; *SW:* Sweden; *UK:* United Kingdom; *US:* United States. Time spent traveling to/from school and/or work does not appear in these graphs because a relatively small amount of time was devoted to this activity by the various subgroups and did not reveal any historical trend. For consistency, the vertical axis on all graphs covers four hours—but with different beginning and endpoints. The only exceptions are time spent on education by men and women for students, which instead covers five hours. The trend for time spent on paid work for men results in out-of-bound results for the early 1970s (i.e. negative time spent on paid work). This is caused by the fact that our time series starts in 1971 and suggests a relatively strong increase during the following years. For students, only two trends appear to be statistically significant: time spent on paid work by men and time spent on leisure by men.

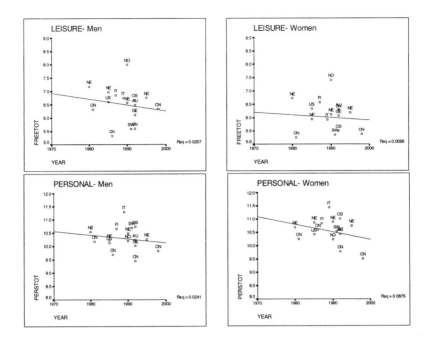

Figure 5.1. (continued)

In contrast to education, students appear to have increased the time they spend on paid work since the 1980s. As suggested in our theoretical discussion, worsening economic circumstances may have motivated or forced young adults to devote more time to paid work. In countries where the data are available, tuition fees appear to have increased (in constant value), therefore adding further incentives for young adults to combine work and education.[11] The cross-national variation in time spent on paid work by students is again relatively wide, especially in view of the large amount of time devoted to paid work by German students. This unusual situation in Germany most likely results from the apprenticeship system there. This increase in time spent on paid work by students is consistent with data from the United States, which show an increase in the employment rates of students since the 1970s. Among college students, employment rates increased from 45% in 1976 to 53% in 1993 (Rones, Ilg, and Gardner 1997).

For unpaid work (child care and housework), no trend is visible apart from a small decrease for women. As noted above, female students devote more time to housework than their male counterparts, although a small convergence is visible. Furthermore, students spend less time doing housework than any other subgroup of young adults: perhaps because they are more likely to be living with their parents or to have fewer material possessions (or less interest in cleaning!).

Students devote relatively large amounts of time to leisure, especially compared to employed young adults, a difference of about a half-hour per day. And while female students devote more time to housework than do their male counterparts, they conversely spend less time on leisure activities. Overall, a small decrease in time devoted to leisure is observed for both men and women, but the trend is not statistically significant. Large cross-national variations are also observed, with time devoted to leisure exceeding seven hours per day in Norway and the Netherlands (although not for all years), while averaging less than six hours per day in Canada and Sweden. Gender differences appear to be relatively large in Austria and Italy. Finally, time spent on personal activities reveals a downward trend for both men and women (but not a statistically significant one). Most likely, this decrease in personal time compensates for the observed increase in time devoted to paid work. Figure 5.1 also reveals the large difference in time devoted to personal activities between Italy (high) and Canada (low).

Employed Singles

The transition from school to work is associated with a major reallocation of time for young adults. Obviously, this transition is associated with less time devoted to school. More interestingly, the transition from school to work is associated with an increase in time devoted to the combined education and paid work categories. In other words, employed singles devote more time to human capital and income generating activities than do their student counterparts. The only exceptions are Canadian men and women, where the opposite trend is observed for some surveys (but not all). For most young men and women, the transition from school to work is also associated with a decrease in time devoted to leisure and personal activities (table 5.1).

Cross-national and historical data for employed singles are reported in figure 5.2. Time devoted to paid work shows an increase for both men and women during the 1970s–90s (it is statistically significant, however, only for men).[12] As discussed earlier, this could be a reaction to the worsening economic circumstances of young adults. Interestingly, single women in all countries devote less time to paid work than do men. The difference is relatively large in the Netherlands, Finland, and Sweden. These cross-national differences likely capture differences in social expectations concerning the role of men and women and in the prevalence of part-time work.

Conversely, single women devote more time to housework than men do. The difference is especially large in Austria and Italy. As for leisure,

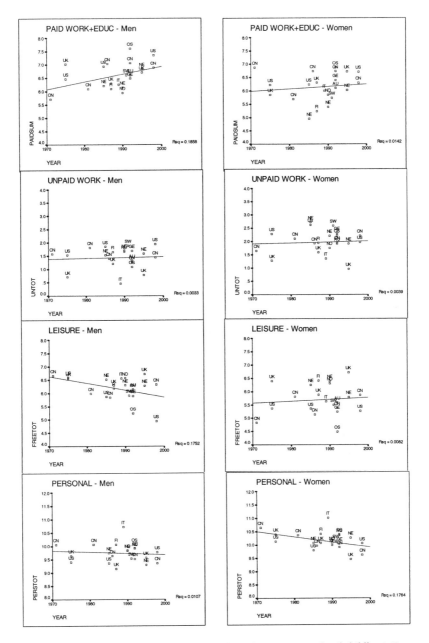

Figure 5.2. Patterns of time use of employed singles (unpartnered and childless). For employed singles, the following trends appear to be statistically significant: time spent on paid work and education by men, time spent on leisure by men, and time spent on personal activities by women.

single men display a decrease in time spent on this activity, which parallels to some extent the increase in time devoted to paid work. Finally, time devoted to personal activities reveals no strong historical trend for men and a slight decrease for women.

Overall, the patterns of time use for students and employed singles appear to have been relatively stable since the 1970s, apart from the increase in paid work and the decrease in leisure (for men). But more important, these results reveal different patterns of time use for men and women despite the same marital status (single) and same parenthood status (childless). Gender differences appear to manifest themselves throughout the different adult transition stages. As we will see below, the gendered nature of early adult experiences becomes more pronounced once children are born.

Employed Partnered

To what extent does the transition to partnership (i.e., cohabitation or marriage) alter patterns of time use among young people? Traditionally, we would expect young women to withdraw from the labor market after marriage. However, our analysis is confined to employed partnered people and does not completely capture this pattern of withdrawal from the labor market. It does, however, reveal partial reductions in work, such as the switch from full-time to part-time employment. Our data suggest that the transition to partnership tends to be associated with an increase in time devoted to paid work by most men and with a decrease for women. The decrease is particularly strong in the Netherlands and Italy, likely reflecting relatively traditional views of male and female roles. As for housework, the transition to partnership is associated with an increase in time spent on this activity for both men and women, although the increase is larger for women. It is particularly large for Italian women, reaching more than two hours per day. Over historical time, the gender gap appears to have been slightly reduced. The transition to partnership is also associated with a decrease in time devoted to leisure, a likely counterpart to the increase in time devoted to paid and unpaid work by men and the increase in time devoted to unpaid work by women.

Figure 5.3 presents the mean patterns of time use for employed partnered adults. It reveals trends that were not visible when simply comparing the changes associated with the transition to partnership. In particular, the data reveal a relatively strong increase in time devoted to paid work by both men and women. The increase is particularly strong for men, resulting in a divergence in the amount of time devoted to paid work by men and women. In contrast, there is a convergence between men and women in the amount of time spent on housework, with women spending slightly less time and

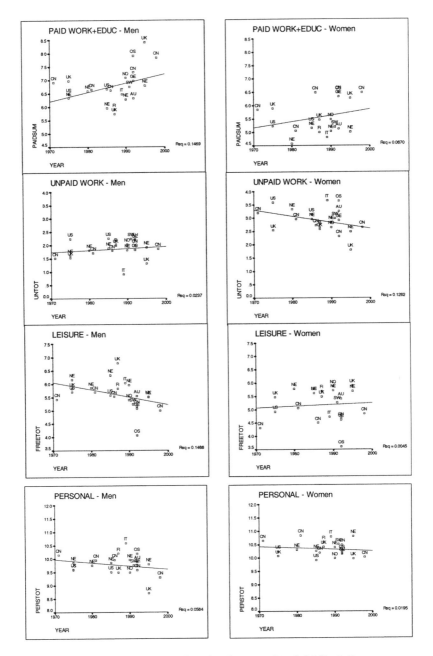

Figure 5.3. Patterns of time use of employed partnered (and childless). For employed partnered, the following historical trends appear to be statistically significant: time spent on paid work and on education by both men and women and time spent on leisure by men.

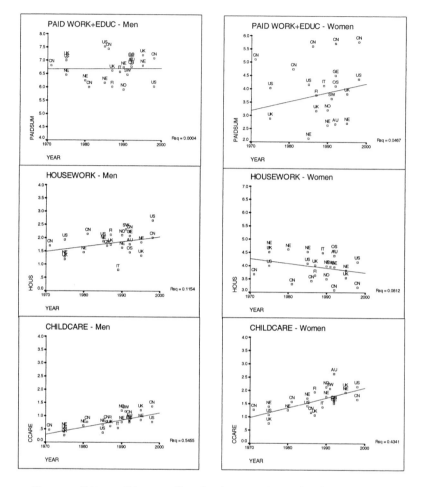

Figure 5.4. Patterns of time use of employed parents. For employed parents, the following historical trends appear to be statistically significant: time spent on housework by both men and women, time spent on child care by both men and women, time spent on leisure by both men and women, and time spent on personal activities by men.

men slightly more. This trend was not visible for students and employed singles, but it is in line with other studies of time use (see, e.g., Gershuny 2000). Women still devote more time to housework than men do, but the gap has been considerably reduced. As a result, when both paid and unpaid work are combined, men and women tend to devote the same amount of time to these activities. As for leisure and personal activities, men have slightly decreased the time devoted to these activities, while no significant changes were observed for women.

Overall, the transition to partnership does bring about changes in pat-

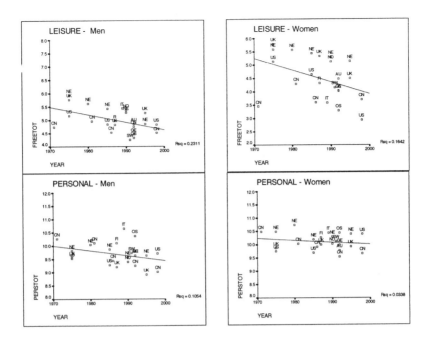

Figure 5.4. (continued)

terns of time use among young adults, especially with regard to paid and unpaid work. These changes are not gender neutral but, rather, enlarge the gap
between men and women. At the same time, historically, the gap has diminished somewhat, especially with regard to the gender division of unpaid work.

Employed Parents

Of all three transitions examined in this chapter, the transition to parenthood is associated with the largest changes in patterns of time use. It corresponds to a substantial decrease in time devoted to paid work among
employed mothers: a decrease of about two hours per day. This decrease is
observed in all surveys, although to varying degrees (it tends to be smallest
in Canada and largest in the Netherlands). In contrast, the transition to fatherhood is associated with an overall increase in time devoted to paid work
of about a half-hour per day (although a decrease is observed in some countries). For both men and women, becoming a parent is also associated with
an increase in time devoted to unpaid work (housework and child care) and
a decrease in time devoted to leisure and personal activities.

Cross-national and historical results appear in figure 5.4. In contrast
to the trend for employed singles and the partnered, time devoted to paid

work appears to have remained relatively constant since the 1970s for employed fathers. And although fathers have been increasingly given the opportunity to take time off to look after their children, the change in the countries' family policies does not appear to have led to a decrease in time devoted
to paid work. In fact, it is well known that the take-up rate of parental leave
among fathers (i.e., the rate at which they take advantage of a parental leave
program) is still very small (Moss and Deven 1999). As for women, the data
on time devoted to paid work reveal a large dispersion across surveys with
an upward trend (although not a statistically significant one). Canadian
mothers appear to be devoting relatively large amounts of time to paid work
(more than five hours per day), while Dutch mothers devote fewer than three
hours per day.

As for unpaid work, there is a clear upward trend in child care and
housework for men. Women, in contrast, appear to have increased time spent
on child care but decreased time spent on housework. As pointed out above,
time devoted to housework by women has also decreased for employed partnered women. The result is a clear reduction of the gender gap for housework, although women still continue to devote more time to this activity than
men. As for child care, during the 1970s–90s period men devoted 0.8 hours
per day to child care, compared with 2.6 for women. These figures are obviously small and most likely underestimate the total amount of time devoted
to children. As stressed in the previous section, this is because the analysis
is restricted to primary activities. Nonetheless, the increase in time devoted
to child care is unmistakable and confirms trends observed in other studies
(Bianchi 2000; Sandberg and Hofferth 2001).

This increase in time spent on unpaid work appears to have been
"financed" by a reduction in leisure time, a trend that is observed for both
men and women. Part of this leisure time may have been spent with children
(with child care as secondary activity), but it has decreased since the 1970s.
Time devoted to personal activities also appears to have decreased since the
1970s for men and remained constant for women.

Nonemployed Mothers

The share of nonemployed mothers has decreased over time as a result of the
increase in female labor force participation, including women with young
children. Cross-national variation remains nevertheless large with employment participation rates of mothers with children under the age of six ranging from less than 50% in Italy and Australia (in 1999) to more than 75%
in Sweden (Organization for Economic Co-Operation and Development
[OECD] 2001). In figure 5.5, we report the trends in patterns of time use

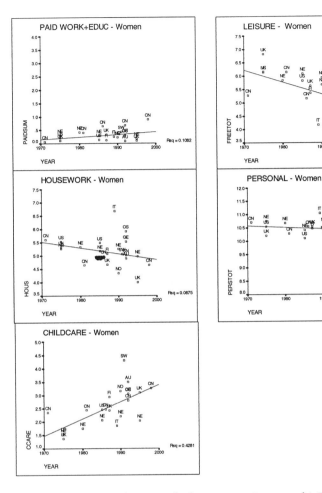

Figure 5.5. Patterns of time use of at-home parents (women only). For at-home mothers, the following historical trends appear to be statistically significant: time spent on paid work and on education, time spent on child care, and time spent on leisure.

among nonemployed mothers.[13] It should be pointed out that this group of nonemployed mothers includes mothers who have had work experience at some point in their lives and some that have had none. The data set does not include the information necessary to distinguish these two groups.

Results in figure 5.5 show a small increase in time devoted to paid work and education (though still with very little time devoted to these two activities), a strong increase in time devoted to child care, and a decrease in time devoted to housework. These trends parallel those observed for employed mothers. Italian mothers stand out in devoting a large amount of

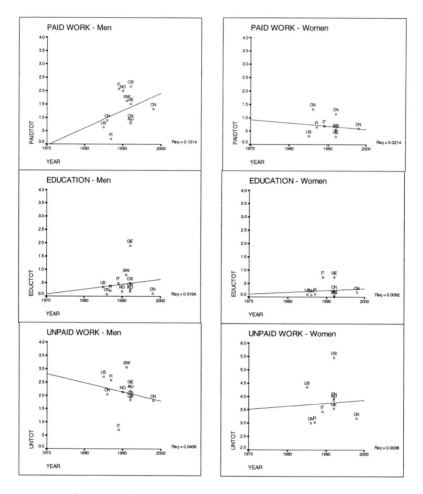

Figure 5.6. Patterns of time use of the disengaged (unpartnered and childless). None of the historical trends for disengaged young adults appear to be statistically significant, a situation likely due to the short time series, the small number of cases, and the heterogeneous situation of disengaged young adults.

time to housework, a situation that is not unrelated to the fact that Italian fathers spend the least amount of time on housework. Also worth noting is the large amount of time devoted to child care by Swedish at-home mothers. Turning to leisure time, we observe a strong decrease since the 1970s. Time devoted to leisure is particularly low in Sweden, Italy, and Austria, a reflection of the relatively high amount of time devoted to unpaid work (child care and housework) by at-home mothers in these countries.

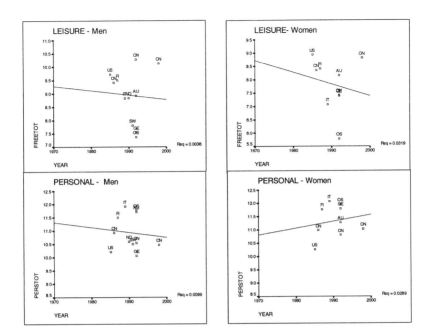

Figure 5.6. (continued)

Disengaged Young Adults

Finally, our last subgroup is composed of so-called disengaged young adults, defined as being out of school, nonemployed, nonpartnered and childless. In other words, these are young people who have left school but not made any other transitions to adulthood.[14] Some of these young people may have obtained educational qualifications (such as a high school diploma or its equivalent), others may not; some may have had work experience, others not. Again, the data do not allow us to distinguish these various groups. Moreover, the sample size is relatively small and would not allow further breakdown of the subgroup. Results in figure 5.6 are in fact reduced to a subset of surveys and a period starting from 1981 (although for comparative purposes, we started the x-axis in the figures at 1970 as for the other subgroups).

Young disengaged adults clearly spend very little time on paid work. Most of them, however, do work a little, around one hour per day. This is most likely irregular employment, as these young people said they were not employed when asked about their main activity during the week prior to the survey. It may also be time devoted to looking for work, which is unfortunately classified as paid work in the multinational data set. The trends are difficult to establish considering the small number of cases. They neverthe-less suggest an increase since the 1980s in time devoted to paid work for men (although not a statistically significant trend). Possible explanations in-clude increased restrictions on the receipt of social assistance (thus forcing people to seek paid work) and the increase in casual paid work (Booth, Dolado, and Frank 2002).

As for unpaid work, the data suggest that disengaged young men de-vote about the same time to this activity as other young men, around two hours per day. Disengaged women, in contrast, devote more time to this ac-tivity than other childless women. The cross-national differences are again large, possibly reflecting the fact that the category of disengaged includes young people with a wide range of experience.

Time spent on leisure activities is conspicuously high among these young adults, although with large cross-national variations. It is beyond the scope of this chapter to examine exactly what young people do during these seven to ten hours per day. It would, however, be interesting to explore the extent to which they volunteer, spend time actively, or spend time more pas-sively. Finally, time devoted to personal activities by young disengaged adults is just slightly higher than that devoted by other subgroups.

CONCLUSION

Let us first summarize the key findings. Undoubtedly, the way young people use their time is primarily determined by their transition status, that is, the statuses that they hold as they move from being a dependent in their natal household to economic independence, partnership, and parenthood. Child-less students not only devote more time to education than other subgroups of young adults (an obvious fact), but they also devote less time to the com-bined education and paid work categories, devote less time to housework, and enjoy more leisure and personal time. These findings are likely ex-plained by a low level of family responsibilities and the fact that a nonnegli-gible proportion of students still live in their parental home (and thus face fewer household-related responsibilities). Childless students also display more gender equality in their patterns of time use than young people who are further along in their transition to adulthood.

Results also indicate that, of all the transitions to adulthood, the tran-sition to parenthood most significantly affects patterns of time use among young adults. The transition to parenthood is associated with a decrease in time devoted to paid work by women and with a substantial increase in time devoted to housework and child care by both men and women. Employed parents also display the largest degree of gender inequality in terms of their allocation of time use.

Finally, we find some changes since the 1970s in young people's patterns of time use, including an increase in time devoted to paid work and a corresponding decrease in time devoted to leisure. Results also suggest an increase in time devoted to housework by men and a slight decrease for women. Overall, the patterns of time use among men and women have become more similar since the 1970s, but some important gender differences nevertheless persist, especially among employed parents.

Do these results match our theoretical expectations? We started the chapter by identifying two major trends that we expected to have affected the way young adults use their time: changes in economic opportunities for young adults and changes in social norms concerning gender equality, materialism, and child care.

With regard to the first of these factors, we expected the worsening of economic opportunities for young adults to have led to an increase in time devoted to human-capital and income-generating activities—that is, education and paid work. We found some increase in time devoted to paid work by students and by employed adults but not in education, although it is important to remember that more young adults are full-time students than in previous decades. Among employed adults, the increase in time devoted to paid work was larger for employed people without children than for those with children.

With regard to changing norms regarding gender equality, we expected to observe a convergence in the patterns of time use by men and women, with more time being devoted to paid work by women and to child care and housework by men. Gender convergence was most clearly observed for employed people without children. For employed people with children, a gender convergence also took place but did not bring about complete gender equality. This result is in line with that observed by Gershuny and Robinson (1988) for the total adult population. As to changing norms regarding child care, time devoted to child care increased for both men and women and for both employed and nonemployed mothers, thus seemingly capturing a general behavioral trend. It would seem that young adults are having fewer children but investing more time in raising them (Gauthier, Smeeding, and Furstenberg, in press).

Overall, this chapter clearly demonstrates the usefulness of time-use data as an indicator in studying the transition to adulthood. Although young people are "free" to use their time as they wish, social norms and family responsibilities partly dictate on what they actually spend it. This type of analysis opens up many avenues of research. For instance, it would be particularly interesting to examine variations within subgroups of young adults instead of focusing on the means as we did in this chapter. It would be interesting to examine the differences in the patterns of time use of young adults across socioeconomic groups and how these differences have changed over time. We hope to address some of these topics in future work.

TABLE 5.A1

TECHNICAL INFORMATION ON THE SURVEYS

COUNTRY AND YEAR	AGE	N OF CASES	RESPONSE RATE (%)	DIARY	SURVEY PERIOD (MONTHS)
Australia:					
1992	15+	13,086	83	2-day	11
Austria:					
1992	10+	25,162	47	1-day	2
Canada:					
1971–72	18–64	2,000	72	1-day	1
1981	15+	2,631	46	1-day	3
1986	15+	9,618	80	1-day	2
1992	15+	8,936	77	1-day	12
1998	15+	10,726	78	1-day	12
Finland:					
1987–88	10+	15,219	74	2-day	12
Germany:					
1991–92	12+	25,775	Quota	2-day	4
Italy:					
1988–89	3+	37,764	70	1-day	12
Netherlands:					
1975	12+	1,292	79	7-day	1
1980	12+	2,727	54	7-day	1
1985	12+	3,263	54	7-day	1
1990	12+	3,158	49	7-day	1
1995	12+	3,227	20	7-day	1
Norway:					
1990	16+	6,129	64	2-day	12
Sweden:					
1991	20–64	7,065	75	2-day	9
United Kingdom:					
1975	5+	3,423	60	7-day	4
1987	16+	1,225	70	7-day	1
1995	16+	1,906	70	1-day	1

(continued)

TABLE 5.A1

(CONTINUED)

COUNTRY AND YEAR	AGE	N OF CASES	RESPONSE RATE (%)	DIARY	SURVEY PERIOD (MONTHS)
United States:					
1975	18+	2,406	72	1-day	3
1985	18+	4,935	56	1-day	12
1998	18+	1,151	56	1-day	12

Sources. Authors' tabulation from information contained in Fisher (2002) and various country-specific documents.

Note. More countries than those listed here have carried out time-use surveys. A complete list is available at the Multinational Time Use Study (MTUS) Web site (http://www.iser.essex.ac.uk/mtus/technical.php). The actual number of respondents is smaller than the number of cases shown here in surveys for which 2- or 3-day diaries were collected. The figures furthermore refer only to complete diaries and to diaries that contained less than one hour of nonclassifiable activities (the total number of diaries is slightly larger). The survey period in column 5 refers to different collection periods throughout the year. The 1991–92 German survey used a quota sample. No information on the corresponding nonresponse rate is available. Regarding the 1987 United Kingdom figures, in the first version of the MTUS data set, United Kingdom 1983–84 and 1987 were combined and called United Kingdom 1985; we use here only the 1987 survey. For the United Kingdom 1995 figures, the response rate of the time-use module was high (93%), but we report here the overall response rate of the Omnibus survey. The U.S. 1975 data includes only data from the main respondents and from the first wave of this longitudinal data set and the U.S. 1985 data were collected on individuals aged twelve, but only the sample for the population eighteen and over has been publicly released.

NOTES

The data for this chapter were obtained through the Multinational Time Use Study (MTUS). We are grateful to Jonathan Gershuny and Kimberly Fisher for their assistance regarding access to the data and to Cara Fedick and Tyler Frederick for their assistance with the data analysis. We are also grateful to Statistics Finland, Statistics Sweden, and the Australian Bureau of Statistics for granting access to data. This work was supported by a grant from the Canadian Social Sciences and Humanities Research Council of Canada, by the Canada Research Chair program, and by the MacArthur Research Network on the Transitions to Adulthood and Public Policy. We bear all responsibilities for errors and omissions.

1. There is an additional factor that we do not address here, namely, the claim made by Putnam (2000) that people have been participating in fewer socially engaged activities and have been spending more time on their own. In the context of this chapter, we do not distinguish different types of leisure activities and do not provide data on time spent alone. Putnam's theory could be tested with the MTUS data, but we do not do this here.

2. The Web site for the Multinational Time Use Study is http://www.iser .essex.ac.uk/mtus/index.php. The archive contains more surveys, but we restrict the analysis here to surveys that were recently documented and checked and that included new variables such as student status.

3. While some of the response rates fall below an acceptable range, they are nevertheless included in the analysis in order to maximize the number of surveys. While we may worry about the inclusion of surveys with low response rates, results presented in this chapter often reveal remarkable similarities across surveys and countries.

4. The data set tells us whether there are children residing in the respondents' household but does not tell us if these children are the respondents' own children or younger siblings of the respondents (a very likely situation if the respondent still resides in his or her natal home). Because a large proportion of students still reside in their natal home, excluding those residing in households where there are younger children would have meant excluding a nonnegligible fraction of students. For this reason, we did not impose a selection criterion based on the presence of children for students and assumed that most nonpartnered students are childless.

5. Because of the data limitation outlined in the previous footnote, we confined the "employed singles" category to respondents who did not reside in households with children. This criterion therefore excludes respondents who are employed and singles but who still reside in their natal home and have younger siblings.

6. We do not distinguish in this chapter the residential status of young adults (living in parental home versus living independently) because the relevant variable is not available in all surveys.

7. We used the weights provided by the statistical agencies in charge of the surveys when available. If none were provided, we used post hoc weights computed by MTUS to mirror the age and gender distribution of the populations (based on United Nations' estimates) and to ensure an equal number for every day of the week. When the sample of respondents of all ages is analyzed, the weights ensure an equal representation of every day of the week. The distribution across the seven days of the week is not perfect when smaller subsamples are used.

8. The figure of forty-three hours per week devoted to paid work may appear unrealistically high in view of current thirty-five to forty hours per week contracts found in industrialized countries. The figure represents the historical average over the 1970–98 period and includes overtime and time spent on meals at work.

9. When Australia and Germany are excluded from the analysis, the decrease for men is less steep, while for women the trend is reversed, suggesting a small increase.

10. We were not able to locate cross-national information concerning tertiary education. But data on the number of teaching hours per year in upper secondary general education programs suggest very large differences across countries, with

lower values in Continental Europe and high values in non-European countries (Australia and the United States) (OECD 2001).

11. There are other possible explanations, including an increase in the material desires of young adults, as well as an increase in the cost of housing and a possible decrease in government subsidies to students.

12. Education is included here with paid work because this subgroup of young adults devotes so little time to this activity.

13. The results for stay-at-home fathers are not reported here because of the small number of cases.

14. They may have made the residential transition out of their parental home, but our data do not allow us to examine this.

REFERENCES

Bianchi, Suzanne. 2000. Maternal Employment and Time with Children: Dramatic Change or Surprising Continuity? *Demography* 37 (4):401–14.

Booth, Allison L., Juan J. Dolado, and Jeff Frank. 2002. Symposium on Temporary Work: Introduction. *Economic Journal* 112 (480):F181–88.

Child Trends. 1999. What Do Fathers Contribute to Children's Well-being? *Child Trends Research Brief.*

Converse, Philip E. 1972. Country Differences in Time Use. Pp. 145–78 in *The Use of Time: Daily Activities of Urban and Suburban Populations in Twelve Countries,* edited by A. Szalai. Paris: Mouton.

Easterlin, Richard A., and Eileen M. Crimmins. 1991. Private Materialism, Personal Self-fulfillment, Family Life, and Public Interest: The Nature, Effects, and Causes of Recent Changes in the Values of American Youth. *Public Opinion Quarterly* 55:499–533.

Fisher, Kimberly. 2002. Technical Details of Time Use Studies. Release 3. 30 June 2002. Institute for Social and Economic Research, University of Essex. http://www.iser.essex.ac.uk/mtus/technical.php.

Furstenberg, Frank F., Jr., Thomas D. Cook, Rob Sampson, and Gail Slap. 2002. Introduction. *Annals of the American Academy of Political and Social Science* 580 (3):2–15.

Fussell, Elizabeth. 2002. The Transition to Adulthood in Aging Societies. *Annals of the American Academy of Political and Social Science* 580 (3):16–39.

Garrett Joan A. 2002. Parental Involvement Contributes to Child's Success in School. Ohio State University Extension FactSheet. http://ohioline.osu.edu/hyg-fact/5000/5304.html.

Gauthier, Anne H., and Frank F. Furstenberg Jr. 2002. The Transition to Adulthood: A Time Use Perspective. *Annals of the American Academy of Political and Social Science* 580 (3):153–71.

Gauthier, Anne H., Timothy Smeeding, and Frank F. Furstenberg Jr. In press. Are We Investing Less in Children? Historical Trends in Parental Time. *Population and Development Review.*

Gershuny, Jonathan. 2000. *Changing Times: Work and Leisure in Postindustrial Society.* Oxford: Oxford University Press.

Gershuny, Jonathan, and John P. Robinson. 1988. Historical Changes in the Household Division of Labor. *Demography* 25 (4):537–52.

Hauptman, Arthur M. 2000. Key Policy Issues in the United States. *International Higher Education,* vol. 18 (winter). http://www.bc.edu/bc_org/avp/soe/cihe/newsletter/News18/text15.html.

Hill, Martha S., and W. Jean Yeung. 1999. How Has the Changing Structure of Opportunities Affected Transitions to Adulthood? Pp. 3–39 in *Transitions to Adulthood in a Changing Economy: No Work, No Family, No Future?* edited by A. Booth, A. C. Crouter, and M. J. Shanahan. Westport, CT: Praeger.

Moss, Peter, and Fred Deven, eds. 1999. *Parental Leave: Progress or Pitfall? Research and Policy Issues in Europe.* Brussels: NIDI/CBGS Publications.

National Center for Education Statistics. 1996. Youth Indicators 1996: Trends in the Well-being of American Youth. http://nces.ed.gov/pubs98/yi/.

Organization for Economic Co-Operation and Development. 2001. Balancing Work and Family Life: Helping Parents into Paid Employment. Pp. 129–66 in *OECD Employment Outlook.* Paris: OECD.

Putnam, Robert D. 2000. *Bowling Alone: The Collapse and Revival of American Community.* New York: Touchstone.

Robinson, John P., and Geoffrey Godbey. 1999. *Time for Life: The Surprising Ways Americans Use Their Time.* University Park: Pennsylvania State University Press.

Rones, Phillip L., Randy E. Ilg,, and Jennifer M. Gardner. 1997. Trends in Hours of Work since the Mid-1970s. *BLS Monthly Labor Review Online,* vol. 120, no. 4. http://www.bls.gov/opub/mlr/1997/04/art1abs.htm.

Saetermoe, Carrie L., Iris Beneli, and Robyn M. Busch. 1999. Perceptions of Adulthood among Anglo and Latino Parents. *Current Psychology: Developmental, Learning, Personality, Social* 18 (2):171–84.

Sandberg, John F., and Sandra L. Hofferth. 2001. Changes in Children's Time with Parents, U.S. 1981–1997. *Demography* 38 (3):423–36.

CHAPTER 6

GENERATION GAPS IN ATTITUDES AND VALUES FROM THE 1970S TO THE 1990S

TOM W. SMITH

The transition to adulthood is as old as humankind and as new as today. Each new generation travels the pathways of physical and mental maturation, attending school, forming new households, starting families, and taking the many other steps that lead from childhood to adulthood. But while each generation's path shares many milestones and processes in common, each generation's journey is unique. Social conditions continually change and new historical events occur that distinguish one generation's transition from that of preceding and succeeding cohorts. To understand the transition to adulthood one needs both to examine the experiences of past generations and to determine how well those examples apply to the current, entry generation.[1]

To examine the contemporary transition to adulthood, this chapter places the process in perspective by comparing the current entry generation (those eighteen to twenty-four) both to earlier emerging generations and to older age groups at the same point in time. This provides two perspectives for assessing the contemporary transition to adulthood: the current entering generation compared to earlier entering generations and today's young adults compared to older generations at present. First, the changing demographic composition of age groups in 1973, 1985, and 1997 is examined, highlighting differences in ethnic background, family structure, religious affiliation, and educational and employment patterns. Differences in values, attitudes, and behaviors across time and age groups are analyzed to draw a profile of the emerging generation of young adults. This includes attitudes toward abortion, civil liberties, crime, social policy, family and gender roles, and intergroup relations, as well as levels of confidence in political, economic, and social institutions, religious beliefs, and sense of personal and financial well-being. In evaluating these differences, the following are considered: (1) how age groups differ at each of the three time points, (2) how the same age groups compare across time points, and (3) how the generation gap changed from the 1970s to the 1990s. Special focus is placed on how the adult entry group differs across time and from older adult age groups.

DATA

This analysis uses the General Social Surveys (GSSs) of the National Opinion Research Center, University of Chicago. The GSSs are full-probability samples of adults living in households in the United States (for details on the GSS, see Davis, Smith, and Marsden [2001]). This research mainly uses eight of the twenty-two GSSs conducted between 1972 and 1998. The 1972, 1973, and 1974 surveys are combined to represent the data point referred to as 1973; the 1984, 1985, and 1986 surveys are combined for the 1985 point; the 1996 and 1998 surveys are combined for the 1997 point. This study will compare young adults (defined as eighteen- to twenty-four-year-olds) to five other age groups: (1) twenty-five- to thirty-four-year-olds, (2) thirty-five- to forty-four-year-olds, (3) forty-five- to fifty-four-year-olds, (4) fifty-five- to sixty-four-year-olds, and (5) those sixty-five and older. Many demographic and attitudinal measures will be described, with an emphasis on exploring how young adults have changed over the three time periods and how they are similar to or different from other age groups. To compare across age groups, a generation gap for measures has been calculated, which is based on the average of the absolute difference on a measure across age groups.

RESULTS

Demographics

Demographic change is usually small and slow, but there have been some important shifts in the profile of age groups over the past three decades (details can be found in app. A). During this period the young (i.e., those eighteen to twenty-four) have become more diverse in terms of race, ethnicity, and nativity. In 1997 the young were more likely than before to be black, Hispanic, immigrants, and multiethnic, with the highest share of individuals from these backgrounds of any age group. Older age groups have shown similar shifts in terms of race, ethnicity, and ethnic identity but on nativity and ancestral nativity there has been differential change across age groups. Younger age groups have increased their share of the foreign born, those with foreign-born parents, and those with all grandparents foreign born. But for older age groups current and ancestral foreign nativity has decreased. Thus, immigrant origins have shifted from being an attribute of the old to being one more common among the young.

In terms of family structure, the young are more likely to have grown up in broken homes, to have gone through a parental divorce, and to have fewer brothers and sisters than previously. In 1997 they were the age group with the most broken homes, the highest incidence of parental divorces, and the fewest siblings. The rise in broken homes and parental divorce has been mostly among those under forty-five, and the difference between age groups on family instability has grown. In fact, the young were the age group least likely to have been raised in a broken home in 1973 (20.0%) but were the most likely in 1997 (39.1%).

Young people also display different patterns of family formation. They are less likely to be married than previous cohorts, have had fewer children, and live in smaller households than they used to. In 1997 they were the age group least likely to be married and had the fewest children. Young people had the largest household size, but this is because many of them were still living with their parents. Most of the changes in current family structure reflect shifts occurring across all age groups. As the average age at first marriage has risen in recent decades (Smith 1999), however, there has been a widening age difference in marital status. The percentage of the young who have never married rose from 60.5 in 1973 to 73.8 in 1985 and to 77.1 in 1997. Compared to the most married age group (either the forty-five- to fifty-four-year olds or the fifty-five to sixty-four-year-olds, depending on the year), this meant a widening difference in the percentage of the never married of 57.9 percentage points in 1973, 71.4 in 1985, and 73.9 in 1997. The young have always had by far the smallest mean number of children. The difference between them and the old increased (from 2.3 children in 1973 to 2.5 children in 1997), but the differences in mean number of children between the young and all age groups, twenty-five to sixty-four, declined over time.

In terms of both the religion they were raised in and current religion, the young have become less Protestant over time and are the least likely of all age groups across time to be Protestant. This is partly because a growing percentage of young people belong to non-Judeo-Christian religions (Smith 2002), but most of the change stems from the fact that fewer young people have any religious preference (Hout and Fischer [2001], and see discussion below on religious change).

The young score slightly higher on educational and cognitive measures than previously. On years of schooling and interviewer evaluation of comprehension during the interview, the young fall in the middle, lower than several middle-aged groups but above the older groups. On vocabulary, however, the young get the lowest scores in all years. For all three measures, a clear cohort pattern emerges. In 1973 those twenty-five to thirty-four had the most years of schooling, the highest comprehension ratings, and the top vocabulary scores. The same cohort continued to have the highest scores on these variables in 1985 when they were thirty-five to forty-four and in 1997 when they were forty-five to fifty-four. The young have fallen further behind the leading age group in years of schooling and vocabulary. But compared to those twenty-five to thirty-four the pattern is mixed. The difference in years of schooling has widened (since many of the young have not completed their education), but their lower comprehension ratings narrowed somewhat and differences in verbal ability closed appreciably. This occurred because those twenty-five to thirty-four lost more ground both absolutely and relatively over time than the young did.[2]

Mixed trends exist on other measures of socioeconomic status. The young are less likely to classify themselves as middle or upper class. They report lower real incomes than in 1973, but higher than in 1985, and have about the same occupational prestige in 1997 as in 1973. On social class, the young placed themselves in the middle in 1973 and 1985 but had the lowest self-rated class position across age groups in 1997. On earned income they are the lowest in all years. On household income they are the second lowest behind those sixty-five and older (the "old") in all years. They have lost ground on both social-class rank and occupational prestige. From being only 2.3 points below the top age group on social class in 1973, they fell behind by 13.3 in 1985 and 21.4 in 1997. Self-assessments of social class rose for age groups forty-five and older, held steady for those thirty-five to forty-four, and fell for those under thirty-five. On occupational prestige, all age groups over twenty-five increased their scores at least marginally from 1973 to 1997, while the scores of the young fell slightly. Furthermore, occupational prestige shows the same cohort effect as the educational and cognitive measures. The age groups with the highest occupational prestige were those who were twenty-five to thirty-four in 1973, those who were thirty-five to forty-four in 1985, and those who were forty-five to fifty-four in 1997. On housing, all age groups under sixty-five are less likely to live in a detached single-family house in 1997 than in 1985, and most age groups under sixty-five showed a small decline in home ownership. The young were the age group least likely to live in or own a house in both 1985 and 1997.

In terms of labor force measures, young adults experience less long-term unemployment and are more likely to be in full- and part-time employment than previous cohorts of young adults. The biggest change from 1973 to 1997 was an increase from 10.9% to 24.5% in part-time employment. Of all the age groups, the young are the age group least likely to be self-employed, are the most likely (in 1997) to have suffered extended unemployment, have the second lowest level of full-time employment (after the mostly retired old), and have the highest level of part-time employment. Their lagging in self-employment increased as their level essentially held steady, while all other age groups from twenty-five to sixty-four increased their rates of self-employment. Differences also widened on part-time employment as the levels of the young climbed much more than for any other age group. Experiences of long-term unemployment, however, narrowed as the level among the young fell while it rose for all other age groups (twenty-five to sixty-four).

The young are less likely to have been raised in a large central city or to currently live in one than they used to be and show slightly greater geographic mobility (since age sixteen) than in the past. They were the age group most likely to live in a central city in 1973 and 1985 and are the second most likely in 1997 (behind those twenty-five to thirty-four). In all years they show the least geographic mobility (since age sixteen). Both their shift from central cities and their greater geographic mobility reflect trends that all age groups experienced.

In sum, the entering adult generation of the late 1990s is distinguished from past cohorts of the young and from older age groups in several ways. First, the young are more racially and ethnically diverse, but this reflects a change across the population in general. The young, however, also increased their share of foreign born and having foreign-born parents and grandparents, while these declined among the old. Second, due to the rise in divorce, the young are much less likely to have been raised in an intact two-parent home than previously and are now much less likely than those in older age groups to have grown up in a stable two-parent family. Third, because of the rise of cohabitation and the delay of first marriage, the young are more likely never to have married, and the marriage gap between them and older adults is greater than in the past. Fourth, on most socioeconomic measures the young were the worst-off age group in 1997, and the gap has widened between their standing and that of the top age group. Moreover, since the top socioeconomic status group has aged over time, the young are also further away from the top in terms of years as well as in terms of status. Fifth, full-time and, especially, part-time employment has increased among the young. The latter comes in part because more are combining work and higher education.

The Generation Gap in Attitudes, Behaviors, and Values

Table 6.1 provides the overall mean generational gap for each of the attitudinal and behavioral topics that will be discussed in this section, while table 6.2 ranks the overall categories of attitudes from largest to smallest generation gap for each of the three time periods considered. Overall, the generation gap in attitudes, behaviors, and values has narrowed over the past three decades, with the biggest change taking place between 1973 and 1985.[3] This is not surprising if one considers that the 1960s saw a transformation in many social attitudes and behaviors and that people who grew up during or after this time can be expected to have more in common with each other than those who were raised before, regardless of their age or generation. In 1973 the average generation gap was 19.4 percentage points. This fell to 16.7 points in 1985 and 15.2 in 1997.[4] Accompanying this overall decline was a sharp reduction in the number of topics on which there was a large or defining gap between the generations. In 1973, there was a generation gap of forty points or more on twelve of 101 attitudes or behaviors, but in 1985 and 1997 there were only three gaps this large. Looking at variables appearing in 1985 and 1997 only, the generation gap declined slightly from 14.3 to 13.8 points. Sixty-six percent of trends in attitudes, values, and behaviors showed convergence, or a smaller generation gap in 1997 than in 1973.[5] And 34% of the trends showed divergence.[6]

   The pattern of change was quite different across topical areas (the twenty areas are described in app. B). Showing declines in the generation gap across all three time points were items relating to abortion, civil liberties, crime, gender roles, sex and sexually explicit materials, and socializing. For the three topics that had additional trends for 1985 and 1997 (civil liberties, gender roles, and sex), each also had a decline in the generation gap for these items. Similarly, among topics with items asked only during the two most recent time points, declines occurred for social welfare and suicide/euthanasia. Five topics (confidence, government spending and taxes, intergroup relations, well-being, and work and finance) had an increase in the generation gap from 1973 to 1985, followed by a decline from 1985 to 1997. Most of the changes were small and in each case the 1985–97 decline exceeded the 1973–85 gain. Four topics (family, miscellaneous, politics, and religion) had drops in the generation gap from 1973 to 1985 and increases

TABLE 6.1

MEAN GENERATION GAP BY TOPICS BY YEAR BY

NUMBER OF DATA POINTS

	YEARS		
TOPICS	1973	1985	1997
Abortion:			
All	.119	.062	.049
Two	. . .	. . .	. . .
Civil liberties:			
All	.431	.300	.239
Two	. . .	.209	.163
Combined	.431	.264	.209
Confidence in institutions:			
All	.087	.090	.049
Two	. . .	.052	.059
Combined	.087	.086	.050
Crime:			
All	.121	.065	.057
Two	. . .	. . .	. . .
Family:			
All	.210	.195	.216
Two	. . .	.053	.067
Combined	.210	.100	.117
Firearms:			
All	.012	.017	.109
Two	. . .	.163	.106
Combined	.012	.114	.107
Gender roles:			
All	.282	.252	.142
Two	. . .	.370	.329
Combined	.282	.311	.235
Government spending/taxes:			
All	.105	.126	.094
Two	. . .	.118	.120
Combined	.105	.123	.102
Intergroup relations:			
All	.235	.238	.216
Two	. . .	.133	.095
Combined	.235	.200	.173

(*continued*)

TABLE 6.1

(CONTINUED)

| TOPICS | YEARS | | |
	1973	1985	1997
Misanthropy:			
All	.119	.134	.246
Two	. . .	. . .	. . .
Miscellaneous:			
All	.168	.163	.216
Two	. . .	.035	.142
Combined	.168	.121	.191
Politics:			
All	.193	.176	.240
Two	. . .	. . .	. . .
Religion:			
All	.155	.140	.162
Two	. . .	.110	.110
Combined	.155	.123	.132
Sex:			
All	.320	.237	.217
Two	. . .	.355	.293
Combined	.320	.276	.242
Sexually explicit material:			
All	.513	.419	.410
Two	. . .	. . .	. . .
Socializing:			
All	.334	.272	.243
Two	. . .	. . .	. . .
Social welfare:			
All	. . .	. . .	. . .
Two	. . .	.108	.090
Suicide/euthanasia:			
All	. . .	. . .	. . .
Two	. . .	.122	.086
Well-being:			
All	.149	.153	.139
Two	. . .	. . .	. . .

(continued)

TABLE 6.1

(CONTINUED)

	YEARS		
TOPICS	1973	1985	1997
Work/finances:			
All	.147	.163	.112
Two	. . .	.185	.290
Combined	. . .	.170	.171
All topics:			
All	.194	.167	.152
Two	. . .	.143	.138
Combined	.194	.155	.148

Source. GSS.

Note. There are 101 trends covering all three time points, plus an additional fifty-two trends for 1985 and 1997, for a total of 153 trends overall. These have been subdivided into twenty topics. These twenty topics contain between two and sixteen variables.

thereafter. The changes were typically small and the gains after 1985 were larger than the prior declines. Only one topic (misanthropy) unambiguously showed the opposite pattern of a widening generation gap across all three periods.[7] The changes across time and the differences across age groups are presented below (see app. B for details).

ABORTION. The generation gap fell from 11.7 in 1973 to 6.2 in 1985 and then to 4.9 in 1997. The young were generally the most in favor of abortion rights in 1973 (on five of the six items), but in later years were the most pro-abortion on only two items (for rape in 1985 and 1997, for a birth defect in 1985, and for poverty in 1997). The generation gap declined mostly because of joint convergence: the young became less supportive of abortion rights (on all but abortions resulting from rape), while the old generally showed little change or a small rise in support for abortions.

CIVIL LIBERTIES. The generation gap dropped from 43.1 in 1973 to 30.0 in 1985, and 23.9 in 1997 regarding freedom of speech, college teaching, and books in libraries for the antireligious, Communists, and homosexuals. The generation gap concerning civil liberties for racists and militarists fell from 20.9 to 16.3 from 1985 to 1997. The young were generally the most favorable toward civil liberties in 1973 and 1997 but were mostly toward the middle

TABLE 6.2

CHANGES IN THE RELATIVE RANKING OF THE GENERATION GAP BY TOPICS FOR 1973–97

	YEAR					
	1973		1985		1997	
RANK	TOPIC	AVERAGE PERCENTAGE POINT DIFFERENCES	TOPIC	AVERAGE PERCENTAGE POINT DIFFERENCES	TOPIC	AVERAGE PERCENTAGE POINT DIFFERENCES
1	Sexual matters	51.3	Sexual matters	41.9	Sexual matters	41.0
2	Civil liberties	43.1	Civil liberties	30.0	Misanthropy	24.6
3	Socializing	33.4	Socializing	27.2	Socializing	24.3
4	Sex	32.0	Gender Roles	25.2	Politics	24.0
5	Gender roles	28.2	Intergroup	23.8	Civil liberties	23.9
6	Intergroup	23.5	Sex	23.7	Sex	21.7
7	Family	21.0	Family	19.5	Miscellaneous	21.6
8	ALL	19.4	Politics	17.6	Family	21.6
9	Politics	19.3	ALL	16.7	Race	21.6
10	Miscellaneous	16.8	Miscellaneous	16.3	Religion	16.2
11	Religion	15.5	Work/finance	16.3	ALL	15.2
12	Well-being	14.9	Well-being	15.3	Gender roles	14.2
13	Work/finance	14.7	Religion	14.0	Well-being	13.0
14	Crime	12.1	Misanthropy	13.4	Work/finance	11.2
15	Misanthropy	11.9	Government spending	12.6	Firearms	10.9
16	Abortion	11.7	Confidence	9.0	Government spending	9.4
17	Government spending	10.5	Crime	6.5	Crime	5.7
18	Confidence	8.7	Abortion	6.2	Abortion	4.9
19	Firearms	1.2	Firearms	1.7	Confidence	4.9

in 1985. Their net change from 1973 to 1997 was typically quite small except for views on homosexuals. Support for the rights of homosexuals rose by 6.5 to 13.9 points on the three measures from 1973 to 1997 and by 14.7 to 16.8 points from 1985 to 1997. The convergence came mostly from gains in tolerance among the old or, for items on homosexuals, from even larger gains in tolerance among the old than among the young.

CONFIDENCE. The GSS has measured confidence in a number of key institutions, including corporations and banks, organized religion, education, government, the media, and medicine. The generation gap in overall confidence levels changed little from 1973 (8.7) to 1985 (9.0), and then fell to 4.9 in 1997. The one added item, confidence in banks, had gaps of 5.2 and 5.9 in 1985 and 1997. In 1973 the young generally had middling confidence (most confident on two, least confident on three, and intermediate on seven). But in 1985 and 1997 their relative position shifted markedly, and they were the most confident on nine or ten and least confident on none. The generation gap narrowed after 1985 for two reasons. First, a curvilinear relationship developed, with the young and the old being first or second in confidence on ten of the thirteen institutions. For example, 39% of the young had a great deal of confidence in education, followed by 32.9% of the old, with those thirty-five to forty-four the least confident (19.2%). Second, the difference between the young and old switched directions from 1973 to 1997 for eight institutions considered. The young were less confident than the old in 1973 but more confident than them in 1997 regarding business, the armed forces, education, the executive branch, labor, and, to a lesser degree, television, the Supreme Court, and Congress. This pattern occurred mostly because the old lost more confidence over time than the young did. In recent years, the biggest changes among the young were their dropping confidence in the Supreme Court (−15.3 points), the executive branch (−14.5), the Congress (−14.2), the press (−11.3), and science (−10.5).

CRIME. Attitudes toward crime and the criminal justice system were ascertained, including whether courts were harsh enough, views on capital punishment and gun control, individual fear of crime, and attitudes regarding the use of force by police. The overall generation gap on crime-related issues declined from 12.1 in 1973 to 6.5 in 1985, and 5.7 in 1997. The young tended to be the least punitive age group in 1973 (on six of nine items) and in 1997 (on four of nine) but not in 1985 (on one of nine). Across periods, the young were the most punitive in 1985 (on seven of nine). For example, 61.0% of the young thought courts were too lenient in 1973. This rose to

81.5% in 1985 and then fell to 78.1% in 1997. The narrowing of the modest
generation gap came mostly from the young, who moved toward the more
punitive position of the old by 1985.

FAMILY. These variables measured attitudes toward divorce, child rearing, and responsibility for caring for elderly parents. The overall generation
gap on these issues has changed little over the years, from 21.0 in 1973 to
19.5 in 1985 and back to 21.6 in 1997. For the added items on children, the
gap was 5.3 in 1985 and 6.7 in 1997. The young have been the age group
most supportive of elderly parents living with their children and of easier divorce laws, but their views on both have become more traditional over time.
Since the old did not change their low level of support for elderly parents
living with their children, the generation gap on this almost doubled from
17.5 to 32.6 from 1973 to 1997.

On values for children, the generation gap is largest regarding the importance of obedience. In both 1985 and 1997 the young were least likely to
rank this as the most important trait for children, while the old were the
most likely to do so. The young were also the least supportive of spanking
children in 1997, but the age differences were small. Moreover, support for
obedience and spanking both dropped among the young from 1985 to 1997.
However, the young are not uniformly for "modern" values for children.
From 1985 to 1997, mentions of hard work as the most important trait for
children rose from 14.0% to 24.2% among the young, and in 1997 the young
were the age group most likely to mention this traditional value.

FIREARMS. For the sole item appearing in this category in all three
years, having a gun in the household, there was virtually no generation gap
in 1973 and 1985 (respectively, 1.2 and 1.7) and a moderate gap in 1997
(10.9). For the added measures on personal gun ownership and hunting, the
generation gaps were 16.3 in 1985 and 10.6 in 1997. The young are the least
likely to personally own a gun, but the most likely to hunt. The generation
gap slightly increased on gun ownership but markedly declined for hunting.
All gun-related behaviors have declined among the young.

GENDER ROLES. Variables measuring gender roles included attitudes
toward women's involvement in politics and attitudes toward women working after marriage and parenthood. The overall generation gap has closed
from 28.2 in 1973 to 25.2 in 1985 and to 14.2 in 1997. Likewise, for the added
measures on the impact of women's work on children and the family, the
generation gap declined from 37.0 in 1985 to 32.9 in 1997. The young are
generally more supportive of modern or egalitarian gender roles than older

age groups and have generally become more modern over time (on seven of eight items). The gap between their views and those of older people is declining mostly because older age groups have moved toward the modern perspective even more than the young have. For example, 26.1% of the young in 1973 agreed that women should stay home and men should run the country, as did 60.2% of the old, giving a generation gap of 34.1. By 1997 agreement among the young fell to 11.8% while among the old it declined to 33.1%, yielding a much reduced generation gap of 21.3.

GOVERNMENT SPENDING/TAXES. These variables measure support for taxation and government spending on space, racial equality, the environment, health, big cities, crime and drug prevention, education, defense, welfare, foreign aid, transportation, and social security. The overall generation gap in attitudes toward government spending has never been large and has changed little over time (10.5 in 1973, 12.6 in 1985, and 9.4 in 1997). The added items on transportation, social security, and federal taxation also show moderate differences and little change (11.8 in 1985 and 12.0 in 1997). The one large difference (near to or above 30.0 in all years) is on the environment, with the young more pro-spending than the old. The generation gaps on most items have shown no consistent direction across the three time periods. Only the generation gap for the environment and drugs has fallen across each time interval. The young are the age group most in favor of increased spending for the environment and foreign aid and the least in favor of increased spending against drugs at all three time points.

INTERGROUP RELATIONS. Variables for intergroup relations measure attitudes toward the integration of housing and education, intermarriage and social contacts, and opinions about the causes of racial differences. The overall generation gap in attitudes toward intergroup relations has been quite large and has changed little (23.5 in 1973, 23.8 in 1985, and 21.6 in 1997). The added items show a smaller generation gap and more of a decline (13.3 in 1985 and 9.5 in 1997). The young have been most supportive of racial equality and integration on almost all items in all years. On most measures (eleven of fourteen) the young have become more egalitarian across time. The average generation gap has not altered much in part because the old and young have moved in parallel. The modest overall change in the generation gap was also a result of offsetting trends by different items. Items on school busing, blacks not pushing for integration, having a neighbor of another race, and school integration saw large increases in the generation gaps (+8.9 to +14.7), but items on whites maintaining segregated neighborhoods, racial intermarriage laws, and voting for a black for president showed declines (ranging from −6.2 to −20.7). On specific items, where the generation gap narrowed markedly (interracial marriage, voting for a black for president, and keeping segregated neighborhoods), the closure occurred because the old converged toward the young.

MISANTHROPY. These variables measure whether people consider others trustworthy, fair, and helpful. The generation gap in misanthropy has grown over time from 11.9 in 1973 to 13.4 in 1985 and 24.6 in 1997, and it has grown in both absolute and relative terms. As table 6.2 indicates, misanthropy moved from having the fourteenth largest generation gap in 1973 to having the second largest in 1997. The biggest change has been a drop in judgments that people are trustworthy, helpful, and fair from 1985 to 1997. The young have always been the most misanthropic and have become more so; the decline was almost perfectly inversely related to age, with the largest drops among the young and the smallest among the old.

MISCELLANEOUS. This category includes whether the respondent was cooperative with the interviewer, support for legalizing marijuana, newspaper reading, union membership, hours of TV watching, and whether the respondent expects another world war. The overall generation gap was stable in 1973 and 1985 (respectively, 16.8 and 16.3) and then grew (21.6 in 1997). Likewise, the generation gap for the added items on TV watching and expectations of war increased from 3.5 in 1985 to 14.2 in 1997. The biggest change was in newspaper readership. Daily newspaper reading has been lowest among the young. Across time, newspaper readership has fallen for all age groups but has fallen furthest among the young and least among the old. This increased the generation gap from 27.3 in 1973 to 51.2 in 1997. Support for the legalization of marijuana also showed large changes. The young have generally been the most in favor of legalization. The generation gap dropped from 38.4 in 1973 to 17.2 in 1985 as support fell among the young while gaining among the old. Then the generation gap widened again in 1997 as support among the young rebounded even more than the continued rise in backing among the old.

POLITICS. These variables cover party identification, political ideology, and voting. The generation gap on politics changed little from 1973 to 1985 (respectively, 19.3 and 17.6) and then rose moderately to 24.0 in 1997. With most topics showing declines, however, this was enough to move politics up from eighth place in 1973 to fourth largest in 1997 in the overall ranking of generation gaps (table 6.2).

The political leanings of the young have shown some notable zigzags.

In 1973, they were the age group least likely to identify as Democratic or Republican and the most independent, the most likely to self-identify as liberal, and the most likely to vote Democratic in the 1972 election. In 1985 they were the least likely to be Democratic, tied with those ages twenty-five to thirty-four as most independent, and more Republican than most other age groups. They were second, behind those twenty-five to thirty-four, in identifying as liberals, but least likely to vote Democratic in the 1984 election.[8] In 1997 the young were again the least Democratic or Republican and the most independent on party identification, the most liberal, and the most likely to have voted Democratic in the 1996 election. They have been the age group least likely to have voted, and the generation gap has widened as voting rates have increased among the old and decreased among the young.[9]

RELIGION. These variables measure religious belief, affiliation, and practice, views about life after death and the nature of God, and opinions about school prayer. The generation gap on religion has varied little over time (15.5 in 1973, 14.0 in 1985, and 16.2 in 1997 and 11.0 in both 1985 and 1997 for the added items on the nature of God and school prayer). On almost all items, the young have been the least religious, and they became less religious between 1985 and 1997. For example, the young now attend weekly religious services less often (−7.1 points) and are less likely to identify with a religion (−10.9 points). They are also less likely to believe that the world reflects God's goodness (−10.1 points). An exception is a rise among the young in belief in an afterlife from 69.9% in 1973 to 79.5% in 1985 and to 82.3% in 1997. This increase also moved them from being 15.0 points less likely to believe in life after death than the old in 1973 to 2.0 more likely in 1997. This is the only item on which the young are more religious than the old.[10]

SEX AND SEXUALLY EXPLICIT MATERIAL. These variables measure attitudes toward extramarital, premarital, and homosexual sex, sex education, teenage sex and contraception for teenagers, and pornography. The generation gap on sex fell from 32.0 in 1973 to 23.7 in 1985 and 21.7 in 1997. Likewise, the generation gap on the added items on contraception for teenagers and attitudes toward teenage sex declined from 35.5 in 1985 to 29.3 in 1997. Similarly, the generation gap on sexually explicit material dropped from 51.3 in 1973 to 41.9 in 1985 and to 41.0 in 1997. This was the largest generation gap for any topic at all three time points (table 6.2). Between 1973 and 1997, the young became less permissive regarding extramarital sex, watching x-rated movies, legalizing pornography, and premarital sex (and between 1985 and 1997 on teenage sex and birth control for teens). More permissive positions were taken on sex education in schools and, after 1985, on homo-sexuality. The young have been the most permissive or modern age group in their sexual attitudes and behaviors for most items. The moderate decrease in the generation gap has been influenced by several factors. The generation gap in attitudes toward extramarital sex has virtually disappeared (falling from 29.9 in 1973 to 1.6 in 1997) mostly because the young moved toward the less accepting position of the old. The generation gap in approval of sex education narrowed as the positions of both the young and old liberalized, but the old moved more and began to catch up with the young. The genera-tion gap on approval of homosexuality showed a third pattern. It narrowed in 1985 as the young increased their disapproval and moved toward the old. Then the trend reversed. All age groups became less disapproving, with the greatest change among the young. On watching x-rated films the narrowing came from joint convergence—a rise in watching among the old and a de-cline in viewing among the young.

SOCIALIZING. The generation gap on socializing has moderately de-creased over time (from 33.4 in 1973 to 27.2 in 1985 and to 24.3 in 1997). The young almost always report the highest level of all forms of socializing (vis-its to bars and with friends, neighbors, and relatives). The generation gaps are especially large regarding going to bars and seeing friends. The young showed declines in visits to bars, neighbors, and relatives, while visits with friends had a small increase. On visits to bars the declining generation gap came from the young and old moving in opposite directions toward the middle.

SOCIAL WELFARE. The generation gap on attitudes toward social welfare policy changed little from 1985 to 1997 (respectively, 10.8 and 9.0). The young tend to be more supportive of government social welfare policies than other age groups are. Among the young, support slightly increased for health care and slightly decreased for assistance to the poor and equalizing wealth. The one large change was the drop from 44.2% saying that the gov-ernment should do more, in 1985, to 25.7% saying so in 1997. This shift brought the position of the young into almost complete convergence with that of the old and reduced the generation gap from 22.8 to 3.4.

SUICIDE AND EUTHANASIA. The generation gap on opinions regarding suicide and euthanasia declined moderately from 12.2 in 1985 to 8.6 in 1997. The young tend to be most approving of suicide and euthanasia (on three of five measures in both years). The decline in the generation gap occurred mostly due to the old moving toward the more accepting position of the young on suicides and euthanasia involving incurable diseases. Regarding suicides relating to bankruptcies, dishonorable conduct, and being tired of living, there are small generation gaps and little shift in attitudes over time.

WELL-BEING. The generation gap in overall perceptions of well-being changed little over time (from 14.9 in 1973 to 15.3 in 1985 and to 13.9 in 1997). It widened for financial satisfaction and narrowed for job satisfaction and excitement in life. The young have been consistently the most negative age group in their evaluations of general happiness and job satisfaction and generally (but not always) the most likely to rate their health as excellent and their lives as exciting. Marital happiness has tended to be lowest among the middle-aged (thirty-five to fifty-four). The generation gap between the young and old has been small but has flipped direction with the young being slightly happier in 1973 and 1985 and the old happier in 1997. Over time, the young have changed little in their ratings of general happiness, health, or job satisfaction. There was a small decline among the young in financial satisfaction (−4.2 points) and larger decreases for excitement (−7.3 points) and marital happiness (−8.3 points).

WORK AND FINANCES. These variables measure people's assessment of their financial situation, whether they would work if they were rich, whether they feel hard work will lead to success, and job security. The overall generation gap for these variables shows no clear trend across time. Across all years it rose from 14.7 in 1973 to 16.3 in 1985 and then fell to 11.2 in 1997. However, the added items on job security and likelihood of finding another job show an increase in the generation gap from 18.5 in 1985 to 29.0 in 1997. The old are the most likely to see themselves as above average in terms of finances, with the middle-aged the least likely. However, the old are least likely to report a recent improvement in their financial situation. The old thus tend to see finances as good and stable. Those twenty-five to thirty-four report the most gains, followed by the young. In terms of job security, those fifty-five to sixty-four are least likely to think they might lose their job (relatively few of those over sixty-five are still in the workforce), while the young see the least job security. When it comes to thinking one could find as good a job if one did become unemployed, however, optimism is highest among the young and lowest among the old or those fifty-five to sixty-four. On work values, the young are the most likely to say they would continue working even if they became rich, while the old are the least likely to say they would stay employed. On whether one gets ahead in life mainly by hard work, the young are most likely to endorse this idea, but the age differences are quite small.

Few notable changes have occurred among the young over time in their outlooks toward work and finances. They have gained more faith in the utility of hard work (+6.4 points) and, as noted above, are more likely to rate hard work as the top value for children (+10.2 points). They are also more positive about their financial condition (+8.1 points feeling above average) and have mixed judgments on job security since 1985 (−6.3 points on not likely to lose their job, but +9.5 points in saying it would be easy to find an equally good job).

Overall Assessment of Young Adults' Attitudes

Looking broadly across all the topics and issue areas above, three general, substantive changes distinguish the emerging adults of the late 1990s both from their earlier counterparts and from older contemporaries. First, the young are more disconnected from society. They are less likely to read a newspaper, attend church, belong to a religion or a union, vote for president or identify with a political party than previously. Moreover, on all of these measures the generation gap increased from 1985 to 1997. This growing disconnectedness among the young is consistent with arguments about declining social capital (Putnam 2000, but see also Ladd 1999.)

Another indication of disconnection comes from an analysis of the "don't know" (DK) responses to opinion questions, which shows that the young today are less opinionated than they used to be. On a scale created from 100 items appearing in all years, the general pattern is for the strength of respondents' opinions to decline with age, with DKs low among those under sixty-five and increasing markedly among those over sixty-five. However, while 20.1% of those eighteen to twenty-four in 1973 gave two or more DKs (to the 100 items), this fell to 17.3% in 1985, and rose to 27.4% in 1997. For those over sixty-five, the DKs levels were 40.1% in 1973, 32.9% in 1985, and 40.3% in 1997. The generation gap thus closed from 20.0 in 1973 to 15.6 in 1985 and to 12.9 in 1997, with the young both less opinionated and less different from the old.

Second, the young are more cynical or negative about people than previously. This is most clearly evidenced by the decline in the belief that people are trustworthy, helpful, and fair, that humans are naturally good, and that the world reflects God's goodness. It may also partly explain the greater expectation of a world war. In all of these cases the declines since 1985 are greatest among the young and the young are the most negative.

The young have also lost confidence in institutions (a net decline from 1973 to 1997 on ten of thirteen), but decreases also occurred across most age groups. The generation gaps are neither large nor increasing for most confidence items, and usually the middle-aged group has the least confidence in institutions.

Moreover, the negativism apparent among the young does not extend to personal evaluations of well-being. Only financial satisfaction showed both a monotonic decline in optimism and a widening generation gap across time. Job satisfaction and financial position both had the opposite trend, with assessments more positive and the generation gaps down. Happiness and other measures showed a mixed pattern involving mostly small changes. Thus, although the young have become especially negative about people and human nature and have, along with those of other age groups, lost confidence in most institutions, they are not generally more pessimistic about their personal lives.

Third, on balance the young have moved in a liberal direction (e.g., for civil liberties, modern gender roles, racial equality, and secularism). Of one hundred trends that could be classified as tapping the liberal/conservative dimension, seventy-one moved in a liberal direction and twenty-nine had a conservative shift. For the sixty-five trends covering the whole period from 1973 to 1997, the shift from 1973 to 1985 was mostly in the conservative direction (forty-five conservative to twenty liberal), but from 1985 to 1997 liberal trends predominated (fifteen conservative to fifty liberal). Thus, as noted in the previous topic-by-topic discussion (e.g., on politics and civil liberties), the young veered to the right from 1973 to 1985 and then moved back to the left thereafter. Overall, the young have generally been the most liberal age group (on two-thirds of the items in 1973, half in 1985, and three-fifths in 1997). However, the liberal shift among the young was not distinctive as most age groups also moved in the same direction. Thus, the young tend to be liberal and continue moving in a liberal direction, but the age differences have not changed much over time.

While these are important changes that distinguish the current entering generation from past generations and other age groups, the young are not more distinctive than in the past nor are the young especially distinctive among age groups. First, the generation gap was smaller in 1997 than in 1973 or 1985. Second, the difference between the young and those aged twenty-five to thirty-four was also smaller in 1997 than in previous years. Third, the difference between the young and those ages twenty-five to thirty-four has never been the largest gap between adjoining age groups. In both 1985 and 1997 the gap between the two youngest age groups was in the middle compared to differences between other adjoining age groups. Thus, while the young are distinctive from other adults, the differences are not more pronounced than those between other age groups.

CONCLUSION

The generation gap has narrowed from the 1970s to the 1990s (1973, 19.4; 1985, 16.7; 1997, 15.2). Today's entering cohort of adults differs less from older age groups than their counterparts did in the 1970s and 1980s. Declines in the generation gap have been largest and most sustained within the areas of abortion, civil liberties, crime, gender roles, sex and sexually explicit materials, and socializing. Smaller and/or shorter-term declines have occurred for confidence in institutions, government spending, intergroup relations, social welfare, suicide/euthanasia, well-being, and work and finances. Countering this overall trend were increases in the generation gap since the 1980s for family, miscellaneous, political, and religious perspectives and across all years for misanthropy.

To some extent this decline is a diminishing echo from the social changes of the 1960s. Generation gaps come from a combination of differences across life stages and differences across birth cohorts. The latter will be greater during and immediately following periods of rapid social change and especially when the social change disproportionately affects the young. Both situations prevailed during the 1960s. This is clearly demonstrated by the large generational gaps in the early 1970s on sex and drugs, two of the major shifts of the 1960s, and by the decline in these gaps over the following decades.[11]

The latest entering generation differs most from the past in being (1) more disconnected, (2) more pessimistic about society in general and people in particular, and (3) more liberal on a wide range of social and political measures. Moreover, on disconnectedness and negativism the young are more sharply differentiated from older adults than in the past.

The young also differ from past generations in having less stable and settled family circumstances. Twice as many in 1997 as in 1973 came from broken homes, and many more have never married. There has also been some slippage in the socioeconomic status of the young relative to that of older adults. The young are somewhat further behind older cohorts than their counterparts used to be.

Succeeding generations of adults go through a largely similar process of maturation involving the same key institutions (e.g., families, schools, employers) and similar processes. But each new generation also matures and comes of age during a unique historical period. Their collective familial and historical socialization creates a point-of-view distinctive from that of earlier cohorts and changing social conditions affect how the transition to adulthood is achieved.

TABLE 6.AI

DEMOGRAPHIC CHANGES AMONG AGE GROUPS

	AGE						
	18–24	25–34	35–44	45–54	55–64	65+	N
Gender (SEX/male):							
1973	.555	.475	.433	.482	.527	.536	4,596
1985	.476	.438	.442	.465	.471	.396	4,461
1997	.500	.449	.458	.462	.478	.422	5,730
Race (RACE/black):							
1973	.145	.122	.127	.150	.125	.147	4,596
1985	.123	.121	.085	.130	.100	.097	4,461
1997	.149	.136	.137	.138	.121	.100	5,730
Ethnicity (ETHNIC/Hispanic):							
1973	.072	.049	.054	.046	.035	.026	4,596
1985	.093	.109	.079	.083	.067	.027	4,461
1997	.131	.106	.102	.058	.054	.036	5,730
Residence at 16 (REG16/foreign):							
1973	.015	.032	.047	.041	.026	.072	4,596
1985	.017	.045	.063	.051	.038	.040	4,461
1997	.041	.080	.080	.078	.077	.030	5,730
Born in United States (BORN/no):							
1985	.059	.071	.080	.067	.045	.065	4,445
1997	.088	.113	.107	.091	.079	.042	5,705
Parents born in United States (PARBORN/neither):							
1985	.053	.073	.088	.093	.162	.196	4,433
1997	.115	.133	.109	.101	.104	.140	5,674
Grandparents born in United States (GRANBORN/none):							
1985	.103	.150	.190	.226	.295	.313	4,199
1997	.144	.167	.159	.189	.226	.238	5,338
Ethnic identity (ETHNUM/one group):							
1973	.556	.554	.546	.604	.606	.627	4,560
1985	.472	.436	.409	.470	.467	.477	4,452
1997	.443	.500	.487	.507	.505	.515	5,693
Family of origin (FAMILY16/intact):							
1973	.800	.776	.773	.766	.756	.738	4,594
1985	.720	.755	.773	.763	.777	.722	4,460
1997	.609	.626	.729	.757	.755	.738	5,728
Family of origin (FAMDIF16/disrupted due to divorce):							
1973	.076	.056	.067	.027	.027	.022	4,594
1985	.171	.127	.097	.066	.044	.048	4,460
1997	.268	.231	.134	.100	.082	.056	5,728

(continued)

TABLE 6.AI

(CONTINUED)

	18–24	25–34	35–44	45–54	55–64	65+	N
				AGE			

Siblings (SIBS/mean no.):

	18–24	25–34	35–44	45–54	55–64	65+	N
1973	3.74	3.61	3.88	4.21	4.70	5.30	4,586
1985	3.64	3.90	3.79	4.28	4.44	4.91	4,443
1997	2.95	3.50	4.07	4.05	4.39	4.55	5,708

Marital status (MARITAL/married):

1973	.352	.786	.883	.887	.829	.666	4,596
1985	.235	.641	.765	.792	.771	.565	4,461
1997	.188	.501	.650	.697	.703	.545	5,729

Ever divorced (MARITAL&DIVORCE/yes):

1973	.033	.121	.175	.172	.175	.166	4,596
1985	.032	.174	.316	.280	.223	.164	4,461
1997	.028	.153	.311	.422	.383	.232	5,730

Children (CHILDS/mean no.):

1973	0.41	1.72	3.26	3.24	2.66	2.67	4,574
1985	0.28	1.26	2.24	3.28	3.09	2.62	4,439
1997	0.35	1.13	1.88	2.23	2.87	2.89	5,708

Adults in household (ADULTS/mean no.):

1973	3.03	2.27	2.35	2.76	2.49	2.18	4,596
1985	2.77	2.10	2.18	2.68	2.32	1.88	4,461
1997	2.69	2.09	2.04	2.31	2.10	1.80	5,730

Household size (HHSIZE/mean no.):

1973	4.17	3.95	4.83	3.98	2.90	2.34	4,586
1985	3.46	3.28	3.79	3.46	2.49	1.98	4,461
1997	3.42	3.09	3.33	2.92	2.29	1.85	5,730

Religion raised in (RELIG16/Protestant):

1973	.585	.591	.647	.648	.703	748	2,981
1985	.586	.613	.606	.684	.653	730	4,434
1997	.496	.509	.553	.630	676	688	5,693

Religion (RELIG/Protestant):

1973	.533	.564	.615	.645	.704	.729	4,583
1985	.552	.602	.577	.666	.652	.702	4,441
1997	.415	.484	.530	.585	.649	.686	5,410

Degree (DEGREE/college+):

1973	.062	.219	.144	.118	.088	.085	4,554
1985	.074	.212	.264	.164	.142	.090	4,460
1997	.075	.256	.280	.327	.249	.141	5,714

Years of schooling (EDUC/mean years):

1973	12.5	12.9	12.1	11.4	10.6	9.3	4,584
1985	12.6	13.2	13.4	12.2	11.7	10.4	4,460
1997	12.7	13.7	13.7	13.9	13.1	11.9	5,707

(continued)

TABLE 6.A1

(CONTINUED)

	AGE						
	18–24	25–34	35–44	45–54	55–64	65+	N
Interview comprehension (COMPREND/good):							
1973	.812	.879	.818	.816	.721	.566	4,565
1985	.835	.877	.892	.808	.782	.688	4,370
1997	.845	.871	.877	.885	.823	.730	5,676
Vocabulary (WORDSUM/mean correct words):							
1973	5.46	6.30	6.17	6.22	6.02	5.53	1,452
1985	5.47	5.87	6.43	6.17	6.00	6.14	1,403
1997	5.49	5.71	6.15	6.57	6.33	5.80	3,176
Social class (CLASS/middle+):							
1973	.468	.491	.479	.477	.446	.491	3,823
1985	.485	.411	.508	.483	.563	.618	4,434
1997	.399	.412	.471	.513	.589	.613	5,697
Real household income (REALINC/mean $):							
1973	30,133	33,510	38,319	39,822	30,472	18,189	4,193
1985	24,456	29,822	39,920	40,463	35,343	19,766	4,074
1997	27,447	29,551	39,596	44,517	41,709	23,210	2,546
Real earned income, self (REALRINC/mean $):							
1973	10,103	20,203	28,048	31,786	24,287	16,775	850
1985	7,516	17,117	23,828	24,622	25,746	20,701	2,878
1997	9,093	17,125	24,298	27,219	29,668	18,847	1,997
Occupational prestige (PRESTIGE&PRESTG80/mean score):							
1973	34.6	41.3	40.7	38.2	37.5	37.0	4,098
1985	33.6	40.0	43.2	40.7	40.2	39.0	4,172
1997	34.4	41.4	42.8	43.5	43.2	40.8	5,463
Housing tenure (DWELOWN/owns):							
1985	.445	.500	.726	.804	.832	.776	2,956
1997	.455	.485	.693	.773	.784	.784	3,783
Dwelling type (DWELLING/detached house):							
1985	.555	.590	.748	.785	.781	.702	4,413
1997	.497	.498	.681	.730	.717	.697	5,662
Self-employed (WRKSELF/yes):							
1973	.031	.060	.084	.120	.136	.171	4,115
1985	.049	.113	.161	.151	.138	.170	4,176
1997	.034	.099	.127	.174	.160	.150	5,410
Unemployed, last 10 years (UNEMP/yes):							
1973	.514	.390	.248	.207	.157	.079	2,984
1985	.559	.484	.316	.288	.154	.068	2,922
1997	.452	.453	.381	.285	.205	.055	3,777

(continued)

TABLE 6.AI

(CONTINUED)

	\		AGE				
	18–24	25–34	35–44	45–54	55–64	65+	N
Labor force status (WRKSTAT/student):							
1973	.234	.040	.014	.005	.000	.000	4,596
1985	.190	.018	.010	.007	.004	.000	4,461
1997	.176	.030	.014	.008	.003	.002	5,729
Labor force status (WRKSTAT/employed, full time):							
1973	.401	.514	.526	.567	.480	.081	4,596
1985	.418	.624	.658	.614	.424	.066	4,461
1997	.448	.678	.688	.730	.529	.074	5,729
Labor force status (WRKSTAT/employed, part time):							
1973	.109	.085	.097	.069	.072	.055	4,596
1985	.204	.120	.125	.087	.080	.061	4,461
1997	.245	.115	.106	.083	.085	.087	5,729
Residence at 16 (RES16/big city):							
1973	.191	.214	.189	.187	.146	.130	4,587
1985	.134	.138	.152	.169	.138	.117	4,450
1997	.137	.164	.152	.138	.132	.130	5,720
Residence (SRCBELT/central city, 100 largest metro areas):							
1973	.337	.305	.272	.243	.248	.304	4,596
1985	.220	.207	.185	.166	.184	.189	4,461
1997	.249	.294	.222	.225	.196	.195	5,730
Residence (SRCBELT/suburb, 100 largest metro areas):							
1973	.237	.223	.248	.257	.212	.167	4,596
1985	.312	.308	.329	.357	.292	.258	4,461
1997	.228	.261	.280	.271	.281	.201	5,730
Geographic mobility (MOBILE16/same city):							
1973	.652	.446	.412	.418	.448	.376	4,461
1985	.624	.460	.379	.349	.346	.378	4,429
1997	.609	.425	.350	.337	.334	.336	5,701

Source. GSS.

Note. The 1973 cases are from the 1972, 1973, and 1974 GSSs, 1985 cases are from the 1984, 1985, and 1987 GSSs, and 1997 cases are from the 1996 and 1998 GSSs. For each variable the item is briefly described and then in parentheses the GSS mnemonic and the category that the proportions represent are given for each age group and time point. The gain in Hispanics from 1973 to 1985 is exaggerated because the 1973 data are based on ethnicity items that produce lower figures for the proportion of people with ethnic identifications (Hispanics and other groups as well). The 1973 method for all years yields 4.8% Hispanic in 1973, 6.3% in 1985, and 6.8% in 1997. The revised method produces 7.9% Hispanic in 1985 and 8.4% in 1997.

TABLE 6.BI

GENERATION GAP ON ATTITUDES AND BEHAVIORS BY GROUPS

	AGE						
	18–24	25–34	35–44	45–54	55–64	65+	N
Abortion:							
Abortion if defect (ABDEFECT/Legal):							
1973	.855	.855	.853	.812	.779	.761	4,425
1985	.823	.807	.812	.767	.777	.756	2,902
1997	.782	.806	.785	.790	.781	.804	3,652
Abortion if no more children wanted (ABNOMORE/Legal):							
1973	.538	.483	.440	.464	.387	.354	4,394
1985	.373	.459	.474	.423	.355	.322	2,904
1997	.428	.466	.452	.471	.359	.387	3,626
Abortion if mother's health endangered (ABHLTH/Legal):							
1973	.945	.928	.908	.906	.880	.843	4,463
1985	.923	.900	.929	.890	.881	.846	2,918
1997	.914	.925	.882	.897	.875	.865	3,646
Abortion if too poor (ABPOOR/Legal):							
1973	.594	.551	.515	.529	.465	.452	4,372
1985	.458	.477	.493	.440	.381	.383	2,899
1997	.490	.471	.448	.465	.368	.381	3,619
Abortion if raped (ABRAPE/Legal):							
1973	.845	.849	.836	.821	.807	.805	4,371
1985	.852	.822	.804	.756	.788	.795	2,872
1997	.861	.858	.804	.788	.797	.793	3,638
Abortion if doesn't want to marry (ABSINGLE/Legal):							
1973	.543	.489	.468	.484	.438	.403	4,376
1985	.412	.442	.478	.435	.372	.365	2,905
1997	.398	.431	.444	.466	.379	.402	3,637
Civil liberties:							
Public speech by atheist (SPKATH/Allow):							
1973	.827	.897	.738	.728	.488	.372	4,527
1985	.703	.759	.757	.664	.620	.477	2,963
1997	.812	.807	.788	.762	.713	.573	3,750
Atheist teach in college (COLATH/Allow):							
1973	.692	.615	.445	.339	.238	.198	4,413
1985	.608	.643	.563	.380	.301	.215	2,897
1997	.692	.654	.656	.611	.513	.357	3,616

(*continued*)

TABLE 6.BI

(CONTINUED)

	AGE						
	18–24	25–34	35–44	45–54	55–64	65+	N
Atheist's book in library (LIBATH/Allow):							
1973	.815	.751	.682	.591	.450	.396	4,463
1985	.711	.731	.726	.634	.555	.432	2,925
1997	.822	.778	.724	.722	.673	.524	3,667
Public speech by communist (SPKCOM/Allow):							
1973	.768	.702	.649	.559	.435	.343	4,457
1985	.650	.681	.675	.571	.528	.434	2,916
1997	.674	.724	.710	.705	.609	.518	3,705
Communist teach in college (COLCOM/Allow):							
1973	.620	.520	.428	.345	.229	.242	4,285
1985	.613	.614	.551	.414	.350	.243	2,844
1997	.639	.713	.621	.639	.536	.439	3,555
Communist's book in library (LIBCOM/Allow):							
1973	.748	.708	.655	.571	.418	.362	4,423
1985	.705	.712	.707	.581	.492	.375	2,887
1997	.754	.741	.712	.715	.621	.530	3,634
Public speech by homosexual (SPKHOMO/Allow):							
1973	.782	.781	.696	.647	.530	.339	2,867
1985	.719	.781	.770	.683	.644	.514	2,895
1997	.887	.882	.850	.825	.774	.713	3,712
Homosexual teach in college (COLHOMO/Allow):							
1973	.707	.670	.646	.483	.360	.259	2,855
1985	.698	.730	.692	.539	.478	.345	2,888
1997	.846	.840	.813	.797	.670	.682	3,676
Homosexual's book in library (LIBHOMO/Allow):							
1973	.736	.676	.630	.558	.409	.304	2,891
1985	.654	.710	.677	.593	.495	.327	2,911
1997	.801	.776	.749	.746	.662	.538	3,662
Public speech by militarist (SPKMIL/Allow):							
1985	.635	.711	.645	.528	.471	.316	2,936
1997	.739	.710	.703	.682	.596	.481	3,725
Militarist teach in college (COLMIL/Allow):							
1985	.557	.583	.508	.310	.244	.183	2,898
1997	.549	.590	.561	.546	.448	.342	3,617
Militarist's book in library (LIBMIL/Allow):							
1985	.648	.722	.703	.550	.461	.354	2,930
1997	.764	.748	.708	.685	.620	.512	3,650

(continued)

TABLE 6.BI

(CONTINUED)

	18–24	25–34	35–44	45–54	55–64	65+	N
				AGE			

Public speech by racist (SPKRAC/Allow):

	18–24	25–34	35–44	45–54	55–64	65+	N
1985	.520	.642	.659	.611	.524	.444	2,926
1997	.616	.631	.672	.653	.607	.548	3,270

Racist teach in college (COLRAC/Allow):

1985	.441	.492	.486	.386	.313	.332	2,891
1997	.454	.499	.494	.507	.486	.402	3,640

Racist's book in library (LIBRAC/Allow):

1985	.623	.652	.726	.668	.592	.500	2,912
1997	.702	.679	.658	.681	.646	.559	3,659

Confidence in institutions:

Confidence in major companies (CONBUS/Great Deal):

1973	.240	.241	.310	.359	.423	.372	2,841
1985	.300	.244	.285	.259	.300	.317	2,353
1997	.289	.280	.222	.252	.309	.264	3,643

Confidence in organized religion (CONCLERG/Great Deal):

1973	.335	.348	.361	.400	.504	.535	2,900
1985	.266	.268	.251	.243	.309	.369	2,353
1997	.317	.232	.216	.244	.300	.399	3,642

Confidence in education (CONEDUC/Great Deal):

1973	.399	.396	.399	.414	.502	.526	2,943
1985	.390	.258	.222	.259	.300	.335	2,391
1997	.390	.231	.192	.215	.259	.329	3,750

Confidence in executive branch of federal Government (CONFED/Great Deal):

1973	.168	.175	.196	.225	.285	.288	2,921
1985	.286	.183	.200	.173	.204	.228	2,376
1997	.141	.109	.090	.112	.129	.129	3,675

Confidence in organized labor (CONLABOR/Great Deal):

1973	.196	.123	.131	.172	.231	.255	2,886
1985	.133	.110	.052	.063	.048	.109	2,340
1997	.180	.136	.086	.104	.079	.154	3,493

Confidence in the press (CONPRESS/Great Deal):

1973	.265	.255	.209	.225	.259	.258	2,944
1985	.269	.181	.157	.193	.159	.177	2,388
1997	.156	.098	.090	.079	.088	.116	3,699

Confidence in medicine (CONMEDIC/Great Deal):

1973	.705	.627	.554	.543	.522	.504	2,947
1985	.649	.519	.455	.461	.395	.470	2,404
1997	.568	.475	.435	.416	.432	.446	3,740

(continued)

TABLE 6.BI

(CONTINUED)

	18–24	25–34	35–44	45–54	55–64	65+	N
				AGE			

	18–24	25–34	35–44	45–54	55–64	65+	N
Confidence in TV (CONTV/Great Deal):							
1973	.254	.181	.178	.181	.222	.255	2,948
1985	.229	.145	.102	.126	.139	.147	2,399
1997	.169	.118	.072	.088	.093	.115	3,720
Confidence in Supreme Court (CONJUDGE/Great Deal):							
1973	.343	.301	.336	.350	.318	.346	2,873
1985	.537	.332	.299	.271	.260	.299	2,350
1997	.384	.303	.280	.302	.290	.349	3,609
Confidence in Congress (CONLEGIS/Great Deal):							
1973	.202	.163	.231	.208	.232	.221	2,899
1985	.259	.149	.119	.112	.135	.162	2,377
1997	.117	.091	.086	.076	.079	.103	3,670
Confidence in the armed forces (CONARMY/Great Deal):							
1973	.326	.306	.375	.348	.433	.436	2,907
1985	.398	.351	.253	.320	.369	.403	2,370
1997	.472	.341	.350	.337	.443	.468	3,684
Confidence in scientific community (CONSCI/Great Deal):							
1973	.488	.480	.418	.431	.490	.422	2,687
1985	.489	.482	.455	.447	.353	.362	2,299
1997	.384	.303	.280	.302	.290	.349	3,510
Confidence in banks (CONFINAN/Great Deal):							
1985	.328	.215	.178	.247	.209	.380	2,381
1997	.390	.245	.198	.213	.259	.331	3,705
Crime:							
Courts (COURTS/Not Harsh Enough):							
1973	.610	.740	.852	.799	.849	.833	3,486
1985	.815	.859	.868	.911	.875	.899	4,279
1997	.781	.822	.831	.810	.847	.820	5,331
Afraid to walk at night (FEAR/Yes):							
1973	.365	.412	.401	.421	.452	.467	2,961
1985	.338	.404	.335	.381	.427	.514	2,961
1997	.362	.412	.395	.361	.382	.490	3,764
Capital punishment (CAPPUN/Favor):							
1973	.475	.593	.647	.667	.694	.674	4,312
1985	.751	.775	.767	.798	.767	.555	4,222
1997	.746	.771	.753	.749	.783	.732	5,309

(continued)

TABLE 6.B1

(CONTINUED)

| | \multicolumn{6}{c}{AGE} | | | | | | |
	18–24	25–34	35–44	45–54	55–64	65+	N
\multicolumn{8}{l}{Police permit before buying gun (GUNLAW/Favor):}							
1973	.756	.756	.725	.722	.723	.797	4,489
1985	.737	.768	.692	.699	.714	.743	2,835
1997	.804	.840	.830	.847	.800	.821	3,727
\multicolumn{8}{l}{Police hitting person (POLHITOK/Disapproves):}							
1973	.336	.212	.254	.270	.239	.318	1,469
1985	.292	.228	.234	.284	.289	.377	2,835
1997	.340	.283	.293	.259	.315	.372	3,633
\multicolumn{8}{l}{Police hitting attacker (POLATTAK/Disapproves):}							
1973	.026	.107	.205	.025	.022	.072	1,074
1985	.023	.029	.023	.007	.024	.043	2,046
1997	.026	.019	.017	.013	.011	.009	2,527
\multicolumn{8}{l}{Police hitting murder suspect (POLMURDR/Disapproves):}							
1973	.980	.967	.928	.888	.888	.837	1,060
1985	.941	.948	.934	.922	.893	.840	2,021
1997	.960	.965	.956	.962	.963	.893	2,497
\multicolumn{8}{l}{Police hitting escapee (POLESCAP/Disapproves):}							
1973	.121	.086	.108	.111	.107	.183	1,060
1985	.157	.184	.167	.160	.112	.143	1,996
1997	.207	.198	.168	.154	.140	.150	2,442
\multicolumn{8}{l}{Police hitting verbal abuser (POLABUSE/Disapproves):}							
1973	.905	.844	.834	.741	.659	.649	1,061
1985	.869	.908	.880	.848	.808	.788	2,020
1997	.970	.927	.944	.912	.925	.829	2,500
\multicolumn{8}{l}{Family:}							
\multicolumn{8}{l}{Care for elderly parents (AGED/In Children's Homes):}							
1973	.422	.357	.360	.276	.280	.247	1,493
1985	.599	.544	.504	.465	.353	.276	2,907
1997	.591	.537	.544	.444	.386	.265	3,738
\multicolumn{8}{l}{Divorces (DIVLAW/Make Easier):}							
1973	.526	.456	.281	.232	.227	.248	1,409
1985	.324	.320	.294	.227	.190	.165	2,867
1997	.390	.289	.262	.264	.177	.169	3,621
\multicolumn{8}{l}{Ideal number of children (CHLDIDEL/3+):}							
1973	.466	.452	.603	.550	.610	.644	2,993
1985	.449	.381	.355	.429	.475	.552	2,929
1997	.398	.347	.386	.361	.390	.500	3,710

(continued)

TABLE 6.BI

(CONTINUED)

	AGE						
	18–24	25–34	35–44	45–54	55–64	65+	N
Child value: obeying (OBEY/Most Important):							
1985	.183	.190	.195	.184	.396	.319	737
1997	.142	.156	.161	.146	.243	.312	3,745
Child value: popular (POPULAR/Most Important):							
1985	.000	.000	.007	.013	.005	.005	737
1997	.006	.003	.007	.012	.004	.108	3,745
Child value: think for self (THNKSELF/Most Important):							
1985	.524	.497	.623	.598	.370	.408	737
1997	.442	.483	.551	.561	.524	.393	3,745
Child value: work hard (WORKHARD/Most Important):							
1985	.140	.148	.091	.126	.136	.108	737
1997	.242	.213	.150	.167	.146	.149	3,745
Child value: help others (HELPOTH/Most Important):							
1985	.152	.165	.984	.079	.193	.160	737
1997	.167	.146	.131	.114	.083	.128	3,745
Spanking children (SPANKING/Agree with):							
1985	.836	.838	.831	.830	.860	.815	1,454
1997	.724	.729	.739	.741	.779	.762	3,785
Firearms:							
Gun in household (OWNGUN/Yes):							
1973	.433	.504	.504	.521	.511	.421	2,970
1985	.414	.414	.520	.597	.558	.431	2,984
1997	.310	.328	.400	.475	.507	.419	3,797
Personally owns gun (ROWNGUN/Yes):							
1985	.175	.224	.298	.376	.353	.299	2,978
1997	.146	.201	.234	.294	.350	.297	3,787
Hunts (HUNT/Yes):							
1985	.274	.210	.197	.202	.142	.059	2,989
1997	.184	.160	.153	.153	.167	.105	3,800
Gender roles:							
Women stay home, men run country (FEHOME/Agree):							
1973	.261	.221	.298	.381	.447	.602	1,435
1985	.135	.151	.200	.278	.313	.466	2,898
1997	.118	.103	.134	.120	.202	.331	3,725
Men better at politics than women are (FEPOL/Agree):							
1973	.377	.354	.444	.530	.534	.602	694
1985	.309	.282	.345	.390	.440	.586	2,871
1997	.228	.176	.182	.192	.262	.380	3,632

(continued)

TABLE 6.BI

(CONTINUED)

	18–24	25–34	35–44	45–54	55–64	65+	N
			AGE				
Vote for woman for president (FEPRES/No):							
1973	.163	.163	.193	.253	.316	.338	2,969
1985	.112	.090	.110	.164	.186	.298	2,901
1997	.048	.052	.048	.055	.083	.127	3,726
Wife works if husband can support her (FEWORK/Disapproves):							
1973	.181	.210	.286	.322	.409	.569	3,028
1985	.104	.120	.138	.182	.181	.318	2,919
1997	.150	.148	.139	.164	.194	.272	3,779
Working mother as close to child (FECHLD/Agree):							
1985	.665	.710	.715	.585	.524	.433	2,964
1997	.762	.710	.701	.653	.617	.528	4,266
Wife give priority to husband's career (FEHELP/Disagree):							
1985	.819	.781	.752	.592	.449	.324	2,890
1997	.865	.876	.849	.855	.759	.518	4,182
Preschoolers suffer if mother works (FEPRESCH/Disagree):							
1985	.582	.607	.533	.394	.327	.295	2,932
1997	.654	.657	.566	.531	.479	.360	4,185
Better if wife takes care of family (FEFAM/Disagree):							
1985	.711	.678	.635	.439	.337	.244	2,934
1997	.774	.750	.667	.662	.539	.323	4,201
Government spending/taxes:							
Spending for space (NATSPAC&NATSPACY/Too Little):							
1973	.094	.070	.105	.080	.051	.048	2,867
1985	.140	.138	.146	.124	.062	.045	3,791
1997	.139	.139	.122	.153	.102	.058	5,281
Spending for blacks (NATRACE/Too Little):							
1973	.401	.392	.355	.332	.256	.304	2,788
1985	.413	.375	.342	.360	.330	.311	1,805
1997	.395	.390	.416	.332	.299	.290	2,563
Spending on the environment (NATENVIR&NATENVIY/Too Little):							
1973	.825	.748	.626	.608	.506	.451	2,806
1985	.774	.691	.666	.571	.526	.443	3,747
1997	.732	.720	.658	.629	.540	.438	5,420
Spending on health (NATHEAL&NATHEALY/Too Little):							
1973	.620	.720	.681	.667	.623	.553	2,878
1985	.511	.606	.636	.633	.578	.542	3,818
1997	.647	.690	.689	.723	.677	.586	5,507

(continued)

TABLE 6.B1

(CONTINUED)

	18–24	25–34	35–44	45–54	55–64	65+	N
				AGE			

	18–24	25–34	35–44	45–54	55–64	65+	N
Spending on big cities (NATCITY/Too Little):							
1973	.641	.633	.558	.550	.503	.489	2,595
1985	.569	.505	.483	.488	.461	.351	1,729
1997	.593	.595	.568	.644	.502	.481	2,526
Spending on halting crime (NATCRIME/Too Little):							
1973	.644	.676	.690	.718	.768	.688	2,818
1985	.741	.669	.623	.703	.741	.600	1,869
1997	.663	.687	.667	.648	.667	.651	2,749
Spending against drugs (NATDRUG/Too Little):							
1973	.612	.687	.654	.675	.719	.685	2,808
1985	.568	.625	.644	.707	.647	.601	1,864
1997	.581	.600	.609	.622	.621	.603	2,722
Spending on education (NATEDUC&NATEDUCY/Too Little):							
1973	.566	.590	.569	.513	.442	.414	2,851
1985	.678	.730	.724	.645	.554	.480	3,864
1997	.730	.807	.779	.730	.641	.585	5,563
Spending on defense (NATARMS&NATARMSY/Too Little):							
1973	.116	.109	.127	.183	.221	.162	2,801
1985	.145	.154	.176	.157	.190	.180	3,795
1997	.129	.129	.172	.194	.270	.264	5,342
Spending on welfare (NATFARE/Too Little):							
1973	.254	.250	.204	.224	.191	.201	2,852
1985	.242	.253	.206	.200	.267	.152	1,877
1997	.166	.151	.160	.167	.138	.149	2,725
Spending on foreign aid (NATAID&NATAIDY/Too Little):							
1973	.076	.043	.043	.029	.025	.021	2,847
1985	.128	.084	.050	.039	.037	.019	3,792
1997	.085	.065	.056	.048	.038	.035	5,379
Spending for roads and bridges (NATROAD/Too Little):							
1985	.392	.388	.427	.436	.462	.466	3,767
1997	.284	.340	.377	.430	.481	.479	5,386
Spending on social security (NATSOC/Too Little):							
1985	.585	.641	.565	.565	.471	.439	3,800
1997	.537	.597	.594	.556	.542	.466	5,338
Spending on parks and recreation (NATPARK/Too Little):							
1985	.403	.366	.339	.282	.252	.232	3,791
1997	.397	.417	.362	.317	.292	.264	5,433

(continued)

TABLE 6.B1

(CONTINUED)

	AGE						
	18–24	25–34	35–44	45–54	55–64	65+	N
Spending on mass transit (NATMASS/Too Little):							
1985	.240	.323	.359	.348	.336	.339	3,580
1997	.259	.301	.375	.414	.370	.360	5,056
Federal income taxes (TAX/Too High):							
1985	.611	.673	.674	.714	.523	.509	2,911
1997	.642	.648	.712	.737	.705	.544	3,648
Intergroup relations:							
Dinner guest of another race (RACHOME/Had):							
1973	.277	.281	.226	.228	.147	.103	2,616
1985	.374	.342	.344	.319	.240	.157	2,977
1997	.525	.426	.429	.416	.389	.295	941
School busing (BUSING/Favor):							
1973	.313	.224	.180	.200	.158	.188	2,968
1985	.402	.342	.221	.217	.194	.188	2,900
1997	.541	.521	.356	.274	.241	.327	928
Open housing law: Nonblacks (RACOPEN/For):							
1973	.537	.422	.367	.220	.296	.229	1,293
1985	.614	.604	.453	.449	.388	.285	2,558
1997	.762	.727	.695	.683	.513	.542	840
Vote for black for president: nonblacks (RACPRES/Yes):							
1973	.870	.848	.816	.778	.707	.642	2,513
1985	.845	.886	.898	.877	.853	.723	2,562
1997	.897	.954	.943	.931	.909	.876	837
Blacks shouldn't push: nonblacks (RACPUSH/Agree):							
1973	.592	.645	.718	.818	.831	.861	2,543
1985	.449	.509	.540	.663	.726	.749	1,928
1997	.282	.310	.378	.415	.522	.644	3,144
Integrated schools: nonblacks (RACFEW&RACHAF&RACMOST/Not Object):							
1973	.470	.416	.376	.350	.396	.362	2,618
1985	.419	.390	.386	.381	.399	.321	2,650
1997	.665	.455	.512	.466	.467	.410	843
Has neighbor of other race: nonblacks only (RACLIVE/Yes):							
1973	.427	.410	.442	.351	.347	.323	3,822
1985	.566	.488	.472	.449	.431	.387	3,810
1997	.730	.697	.617	.625	.594	.517	4,671

(*continued*)

TABLE 6.BI

(CONTINUED)

	AGE						
	18–24	25–34	35–44	45–54	55–64	65+	N
Black-white marriages: nonblacks only (RACMAR/Make Illegal):							
1973	.186	.236	.326	.400	.463	.623	3,876
1985	.131	.180	.153	.358	.371	.517	2,596
1997	.035	.068	.067	.117	.198	.269	3,230
Whites keep segregated neighborhoods: nonblacks only (RACSEG/Agree):							
1973	.225	.296	.401	.397	.511	.583	1,240
1985	.145	.189	.191	.318	.322	.439	2,617
1997	.063	.073	.105	.088	.188	.259	809
Discrimination cause of racial differences (RACDIF1/Yes):							
1985	.522	.469	.447	.402	.412	.435	2,886
1997	.393	.348	.369	.385	.368	.432	3,614
In-born ability cause of racial differences (RACDIF2/Yes):							
1985	.117	.113	.138	.228	.288	.404	2,871
1997	.047	.060	.078	.088	.132	.207	3,707
Education cause of racial differences (RACDIF3/Yes):							
1985	.512	.554	.568	.497	.512	.503	2,920
1997	.432	.423	.453	.448	.456	.478	3,693
Motivation cause of racial differences (RACDIF4/Yes):							
1985	.455	.522	.577	.633	.692	.717	2,851
1997	.456	.464	.446	.466	.556	.618	3,555
Special efforts to help blacks (HELPBLK/Oppose, 4,5):							
1985	.473	.530	.542	.518	.505	.494	2,820
1997	.451	.539	.518	.579	.511	.522	3,649
Misanthropy:							
People trustworthy (TRUST/Yes):							
1973	.364	.464	.533	.508	.481	.421	3,090
1985	.355	.376	.492	.484	.488	.422	2,920
1997	.202	.254	.373	.465	.492	.372	4,224
People fair (FAIR/Yes):							
1973	.431	.573	.640	.621	.648	.588	3,080
1985	.515	.571	.650	.675	.708	.695	2,913
1997	.338	.430	.534	.566	.618	.606	3,744
People helpful (HELPFUL/Yes):							
1973	.340	.443	.526	.510	.476	.483	3,075
1985	.467	.481	.566	.562	.591	.623	2,914
1997	.318	.361	.438	.490	.562	.602	3,777

(*continued*)

TABLE 6.BI

(CONTINUED)

	18–24	25–34	35–44	45–54	55–64	65+	N
				AGE			

Miscellaneous:

Cooperation with interview (COOP/Friendly & Interested):

1973	.771	.867	.841	.850	.831	.771	2,968
1985	.783	.823	.823	.815	.804	.796	4,423
1997	.661	.710	.725	.743	.722	.691	5,671

Legalize marijuana (GRASS/Yes):

1973	.445	.261	.145	.150	.007	.061	1,469
1985	.276	.293	.214	.124	.117	.104	2,835
1997	.370	.316	.293	.313	.177	.150	3,760

Newspaper reading (NEWS/Every Day):

1973	.470	.593	.777	.804	.780	.743	2,928
1985	.260	.396	.538	.641	.698	.708	2,988
1997	.205	.244	.381	.521	.600	.717	3,850

Union (UNION/Doesn't Belong To):

1973	.800	.734	.685	.640	.660	.814	1,493
1985	.893	.804	.745	.746	.751	.873	3,572
1997	.945	.847	.803	.744	.801	.844	3,771

Watches TV (TVHOURS/Less Than 3 Hours a Day):

| 1985 | .453 | .478 | .586 | .567 | .465 | .385 | 2,979 |
| 1997 | .512 | .577 | .616 | .593 | .486 | .364 | 4,309 |

Expect world war (USWAR/Yes):

| 1985 | .464 | .506 | .409 | .482 | .493 | .462 | 2,122 |
| 1997 | .556 | .466 | .450 | .386 | .440 | .421 | 3,519 |

Politics:

Party identification (PARTYID/Democratic):

1973	.351	.379	.448	.500	.463	.498	4,553
1985	.302	.342	.369	.396	.452	.455	4,477
1997	.265	.280	.299	.350	.367	.440	5,714

Political ideology (POLVIEWS/Liberal):

1973	.427	.394	.267	.224	.220	.259	1,416
1985	.280	.287	.252	.191	.178	.206	4,271
1997	.298	.291	.279	.267	.196	.197	5,424

Presidential vote (PRES72&PRES84&PRES96/Democratic Vote):

1973	.538	.477	.344	.348	.297	.361	2,002
1985	.314	.392	.332	.398	.349	.424	2,001
1997	.704	.563	.465	.531	.498	.554	1,692

(continued)

TABLE 6.BI

(CONTINUED)

	AGE						
	18–24	25–34	35–44	45–54	55–64	65+	N
Presidential vote (VOTE72&VOTE84&VOTE96/Voted):							
1973	.469	.663	.741	.740	.792	.750	2,970
1985	.417	.599	.737	.730	.800	.784	2,921
1997	.271	.525	.658	.716	.791	.805	2,748
Religion:							
Religion (RELIG/None):							
1973	.131	.088	.042	.038	.032	.034	4,583
1985	.117	.089	.089	.042	.034	.032	4,441
1997	.226	.173	.129	.103	.068	.050	5,686
Religion (FUND/Fundamentalist):							
1973	.267	.268	.273	.286	.293	.284	4,596
1985	.301	.312	.313	.367	.345	.365	4,461
1997	.277	.301	.285	.313	.323	.300	5,730
Church attendance (ATTEND/Weekly+):							
1973	.212	.262	.358	.346	.364	.378	4,575
1985	.231	.250	.323	.356	.437	.438	4,443
1997	.140	.177	.264	.271	.308	.395	5,606
Religious attachment (RELITEN/Strong):							
1973	.284	.321	.449	.403	.508	.511	1,465
1985	.304	.358	.400	.424	.518	.564	4,269
1997	.274	.307	.308	.384	.418	.526	5,451
Life after death (POSTLIFE/Believes In):							
1973	.699	.771	.770	.739	.776	.849	1,362
1985	.795	.837	.804	.813	.805	.812	2,715
1997	.823	.807	.838	.830	.812	.803	3,832
Ban on school prayer (PRAYER/Approves):							
1973	.539	.368	.292	.230	.216	.267	722
1985	.533	.502	.437	.380	.332	.327	2,179
1997	.564	.514	.416	.410	.328	.317	3,678
Bible (BIBLE/Word of God):							
1985	.380	.307	.334	.351	.431	.510	1,679
1997	.290	.291	.294	.295	.361	.385	4,232
Pray (PRAY/Daily):							
1985	.421	.478	.519	.594	.638	.715	2,953
1997	.393	.435	.592	.586	.574	.717	2,431

(continued)

TABLE 6.BI

(CONTINUED)

| | \multicolumn{6}{c}{AGE} | |
	18–24	25–34	35–44	45–54	55–64	65+	N
God like master/spouse (MASTERSP/Spouse, 5–7):							
1985	.128	.089	.091	.092	.126	.124	3,765
1997	.094	.113	.076	.087	.116	.102	2,324
God like judge/lover (JUDGELUV/Lover, 5–7):							
1985	.146	.144	.148	.158	.221	.247	3,777
1997	.182	.167	.145	.173	.177	.169	2,335
God like friend/king (FRNDKING/Friend, 1–3):							
1985	.469	.434	.432	.420	.440	.446	3,806
1997	.394	.333	.319	.341	.317	.418	2,354
God like mother/father (MAPA/Mother, 1–3):							
1985	.059	.053	.044	.074	.068	.114	3,801
1997	.059	.078	.060	.089	.057	.058	2,349
World reflects God's goodness (WORLD1/Agree, 5–7):							
1985	.468	.473	.573	.590	.538	.612	1,504
1997	.367	.480	.535	.604	.574	.616	4,292
Human nature is good (WORLD4/Agree, 1–3):							
1985	.620	.641	.684	.709	.635	.713	1,501
1997	.435	.530	.535	.634	.576	.599	2,425
Sex:							
Extramarital sex (XMARSEX/Always Wrong):							
1973	.569	.632	.708	.753	.807	.868	2,953
1985	.663	.696	.681	.726	.829	.857	2,954
1997	.805	.777	.792	.773	.834	.821	3,742
Premarital sex (PREMARSX/Not Wrong at All):							
1973	.497	.410	.256	.199	.164	.149	2,962
1985	.500	.544	.489	.413	.263	.191	2,899
1997	.479	.527	.474	.488	.330	.184	3,728
Homosexual sex (HOMOSEX/Always Wrong):							
1973	.551	.604	.732	.728	.829	.881	2,859
1985	.695	.668	.693	.803	.849	.890	2,892
1997	.449	.506	.615	.582	.701	.787	3,534
Sex education in schools (SEXEDUC/For):							
1973	.888	.904	.863	.854	.743	.585	1,438
1985	.927	.910	.897	.862	.776	.677	2,906
1997	.948	.919	.881	.878	.834	.731	3,756

(continued)

TABLE 6.B1

(CONTINUED)

| | \multicolumn{6}{c|}{AGE} | |
	18–24	25–34	35–44	45–54	55–64	65+	N
Contraceptives for teenagers (PILLOK/Agree):							
1985	.719	.660	.599	.527	.465	.421	1,426
1997	.692	.682	.599	.594	.456	.411	3,720
Teenagers having sex (TEENSEX/Always Wrong):							
1985	.449	.547	.663	.731	.836	.860	1,438
1997	.545	.617	.716	.748	.813	.850	3,800
Sexually explicit material:							
Pornography (PORNLAW/Illegal to All):							
1973	.153	.257	.421	.492	.606	.650	1,468
1985	.199	.320	.324	.490	.583	.695	2,893
1997	.215	.260	.328	.389	.501	.645	3,755
Seen X-rated movies (XMOVIE/Yes):							
1973	.551	.346	.276	.198	.118	.022	1,488
1985	.400	.311	.298	.209	.123	.057	2,916
1997	.460	.370	.261	.209	.160	.070	3,770
Socializing:							
Go to bar (SOCBAR/Never):							
1973	.308	.323	.509	.551	.700	.890	1,462
1985	.341	.307	.410	.536	.727	.878	2,982
1997	.416	.316	.409	.536	.639	.801	3,837
Spend evening with friends (SOCFREND/Several Times a Week+):							
1973	.505	.290	.163	.135	.125	.098	1,481
1985	.441	.271	.190	.152	.127	.112	2,987
1997	.533	.278	.215	.140	.113	.153	3,827
Spend evening with neighbor (SOCOMMUN/Several Times a Week+):							
1973	.439	.355	.260	.201	.262	.268	1,479
1985	.422	.271	.199	.203	.180	.268	2,986
1997	.326	.227	.171	.163	.136	.238	3,839
Spend evening with relative (SOCREL/Several Times a Week+):							
1973	.521	.370	.298	.407	.376	.346	1,484
1985	.420	.397	.330	.338	.366	.353	2,981
1997	.461	.390	.329	.354	.268	.343	3,845
Social welfare:							
Equalize wealth (EQWLTH/Favors, 1,2):							
1985	.332	.330	.265	.313	.353	.369	2,880
1997	.303	.259	.266	.257	.245	.255	3,711
Government should do more (HELPNOT/Agree, 1,2):							
1985	.442	.307	.233	.259	.207	.214	2,756
1997	.257	.275	.257	.225	.215	.223	3,594

(continued)

TABLE 6.BI

(CONTINUED)

	AGE						
	18−24	25−34	35−44	45−54	55−64	65+	N
Government should help sick (HELPSICK/Agree, 1,2):							
1985	.556	.518	.474	.436	.341	.426	2,835
1997	.576	.519	.503	.477	.442	.385	3,680
Government should help poor (HELPPOOR/Agree, 1,2):							
1985	.330	.333	.280	.285	.261	.290	2,834
1997	.296	.294	.254	.239	.239	.210	3,650
Suicide and euthanasia:							
Right to suicide if has incurable disease (SUICIDE1/Yes):							
1985	.609	.610	.543	.447	.384	.302	2,887
1997	.614	.702	.639	.653	.601	.517	3,667
Right to suicide if bankrupt (SUICIDE2/Yes):							
1985	.077	.084	.072	.065	.056	.050	2,951
1997	.115	.111	.096	.079	.099	.058	3,780
Right to suicide if dishonored family (SUICIDE3/Yes):							
1985	.088	.084	.070	.060	.041	.046	2,936
1997	.129	.121	.089	.079	.101	.055	3,775
Right to suicide if tired of living (SUICIDE/Yes):							
1985	.162	.145	.153	.116	.090	.129	2,932
1997	.209	.200	.148	.146	.154	.141	3,720
Euthanasia (LETDIE/Approves of):							
1985	.759	.743	.720	.590	.621	.559	2,895
1997	.745	.758	.694	.722	.691	.609	3,663
Well-being:							
Happiness (HAPPY/Very Happy):							
1973	.243	.347	.346	.391	.376	.381	4,580
1985	.279	.292	.320	.330	.376	.407	4,412
1997	.224	.337	.306	.320	.403	.387	5,689
Marital happiness (HAPMAR/Very Happy):							
1973	.719	.680	.646	.657	.724	.692	2,217
1985	.720	.591	.590	.600	.641	.671	2,828
1997	.636	.681	.580	.576	.676	.687	3,210
Health (HEALTH/Excellent):							
1973	.388	.455	.376	.281	.197	.138	4,586
1985	.394	.362	.363	.336	.281	.159	4,412
1997	.393	.376	.338	.313	.273	.174	5,231
Life is . . . (LIFE/Exciting):							
1973	.555	.479	.445	.419	.398	.376	2,928
1985	.566	.485	.490	.467	.450	.381	2,971
1997	.482	.492	.503	.482	.488	.420	3,765

(continued)

TABLE 6.BI

(CONTINUED)

	AGE						
	18–24	25–34	35–44	45–54	55–64	65+	N
Satisfaction with job (SATJOB/Satisfied):							
1973	.756	.818	.865	.914	.922	.950	3,326
1985	.781	.844	.848	.881	.868	.940	3,659
1997	.783	.868	.864	.856	.916	.931	4,645
Satisfaction with finances (SATFIN/Satisfied):							
1973	.294	.237	.270	.346	.400	.399	4,584
1985	.272	.209	.240	.302	.414	.432	4,437
1997	.252	.212	.260	.302	.358	.445	5,716
Work and finances:							
Financial position (FINRELA/Above Average):							
1973	.225	.223	.176	.212	.245	.338	4,556
1985	.280	.268	.222	.264	.282	.314	4,430
1997	.306	.296	.252	.250	.267	.341	5,697
Continue to work if rich (RICHWORK/Yes):							
1973	.751	.725	.707	.658	.532	.500	1,669
1985	.807	.798	.738	.681	.570	.511	1,965
1997	.765	.740	.696	.629	.582	.594	2,709
Getting ahead (GETAHEAD/By Hard Work):							
1973	.645	.606	.661	.586	.643	.630	2,996
1985	.687	.715	.635	.649	.661	.646	2,965
1997	.709	.705	.687	.668	.644	.697	3,760
Financial situation (FINALTER/Better):							
1973	.472	.515	.439	.405	.372	.263	4,528
1985	.490	.498	.453	.386	.294	.208	4,431
1997	.467	.559	.447	.406	.368	.236	5,697
Likely to lose job (JOBLOSE/Not Likely):							
1985	.636	.660	.643	.690	.761	.685	1,823
1997	.573	.617	.618	.658	.712	.690	2,647
Get a job if lost job (JOBFIND/Not Easy):							
1985	.271	.343	.373	.457	.660	.591	1,821
1997	.176	.231	.380	.444	.560	.638	2,632

Source. GSS.

Note. Items are grouped into the twenty topics introduced above. First those items with three time points are presented and then those from only 1985 and 1997. For each variable, the item is briefly described and then in parentheses the GSS mnemonic for the variable and the category that the proportions represent are given for each age group and time point. The full wording of the items can be found in Davis, Smith, and Marsden (2001) or at www.icpsr.umich.edu/gss.

Some figures for intergroup relations are based only on nonblacks because the items were not asked of blacks in early years.

NOTES

1. On the role of generations in social change, see Friedenberg (1969); Kertzer (1983); Laufer and Bengtson (1974); and Roberts and Lang (1985).

2. For information about trends in verbal ability over time, see Alwin (1991); Alwin and McCammon (1999); Glenn (1994, 1999); and Wilson and Gove (1999a, 1999b).

3. With the six age groups used in this report, there are fifteen possible "generation gaps" that could be looked at (age1 vs. age2, 2 vs. 3, 3 vs. 4, 4 vs. 5, 5 vs. 6, 1 vs. 3. 1 vs. 4, 1 vs. 5, 1 vs. 6, 2 vs. 4, 2 vs. 5, 2 vs. 6, 3 vs. 5, 3 vs. 6, 4 vs. 6). While some attention is given to several of these comparisons, the standard measure of the generation gap used here is the youngest to oldest comparison (eighteen to twenty-four to sixty-five and older). While for some variables in some years alternative comparisons show larger differences (particularly when curvilinear relationships appear), on average this youngest to oldest comparison represents the maximum difference across age groups.

4. On the generation gap of the late 1960s/early 1970s, see Booth (1976); Borelli (1971); Brunswick (1970); Cutler (1977); Cutler and Kaufman (1975); Erskine (1972–73); Friedman, Gold, and Christie (1972); Fritz (1969); Ginandes (1969); Holsti and Rosenau (1980); Jeffries (1974); Jennings and Niemi (1975); Keeley (1976); Klecka (1971); Mauss and Garland (1971); Payne (1973); Roskin (1974); Starr (1974); Thomas (1974); Wright (1972); and Zey-Ferrell, Tolone, and Walsh (1978). For more information about the situation in the 1990s, see Barnes (1991); Carr (2000); Coupland (1996); Epstein (1998); Howe (1993); Howe and Strauss (2000); Ortner (1998); Sacks (1996); Sberna and Gay (2000); Strauss (1998); Strauss and Howe (1991); and Williams et al. (1997).

5. Thirty-five percent had a monotonic decline, 11.9% showed a wider gap in 1985 and then a narrowing in 1997 for a net convergence from 1973 to 1997, and 19.8% had a narrower gap in 1985 with a widening from 1985 to 1997 and a net convergence across the three time points.

6. Monotonic increases were found in 17.8%, and 15.9% had a mixed pattern, but there was a net divergence.

7. The single item in the firearms topic asked at each time point (gun in the household) showed an increasing generation gap, but the two other items (personal ownership of a gun and hunting) had a decline from 1985 to 1997, as did the combined three items.

8. They were referred to at the time as the "Reagan generation" (see Smith 1989).

9. Voting levels among the young are especially sensitive to the interval between the last election and survey and to how ineligibles are handled. Looking at a constant two-year interval the generation gap in reported voting was largest after the

1996 election compared to all presidential elections from 1972 to 1996 (53.4 with ineligibles retained and 41.4 with them excluded). Only 38.3% of those eligible to vote
in 1996 reported doing so. This was the lowest level across these elections but only
slightly lower than the levels in 1976 (39.3%) and 1988 (40.4%).

    10. On trends in belief in an afterlife, see Greeley and Hout (1999).

    11. Besides large differences on sex and drugs, these generations also differed
greatly about rock and roll. However, since there is only a measure of musical preferences on the 1993 GSS, this cannot be followed across both time and age groups (see
Smith 1995).

REFERENCES

Alwin, Duane F. 1991. Family of Origin and Cohort Differences in Verbal Ability.
    American Sociological Review 56:625–38.

Alwin, Duane F., and Ryan J. McCammon 1999. Aging versus Cohort Interpreta-
    tions of Intracohort Differences in GSS Vocabulary Scores. *American Socio-
    logical Review* 64:272–86.

Barnes, James A. 1991. Age-Old Strife: It's Been Years since the "Generation Gap"
    Was a Topical American Phrase . . . *National Journal* 23 (January 26): 216–19.

Booth, Norman J. 1976. The Generation Gap: A Cross-Generational Study of Selected
    Social Attitudes and Alienation. PhD diss., Southern Illinois University.

Borelli, Kenneth. 1971. The Generation Gap: Age or Issue? *Social Work* 16:91–96.

Brunswick, Ann F. 1970. What Generation Gap? A Comparison of Some Genera-
    tional Differences among Blacks and Whites. *Social Problems* 17:358–71.

Carr, Deborah S. 2000. Perceptions of Workplace Inequities and Mental Health
    across Three Cohorts: Do Rising Expectations Lead to Lower Well-being? Pa-
    per presented at the American Sociological Association, Chicago, August.

Coupland, Douglas. 1996. *Generation X: Tales of an Accelerated Culture.* London:
    Abacus.

Cutler, Neil A. 1977. Demographic, Socio-Psychological, and Political Factors in the
    Politics of Aging: A Foundation of Research in "Political Gerontology." *Ameri-
    can Political Science Review* 71:1011–25.

Cutler, Steven J., and Robert L. Kaufman. 1975. Cohort Changes in Political Atti-
    tudes: Tolerance of Ideological Nonconformity. *Public Opinion Quarterly*
    39:69–81.

Davis, James A., Tom W. Smith, and Peter V. Marsden. 2001. *General Social Survey,
    1972–2000: Cumulative Codebook.* Chicago: NORC.

Epstein, Jonathon S. 1998. Introduction: Generation X, Youth Culture, and Iden-
    tity. Pp. 1–23 in *Youth Culture: Identity in a Postmodern World,* edited by J. S.
    Epstein. Maldem, MA: Blackwell.

Erskine, Hazel. 1972–73. The Polls: Pacifism and the Generation Gap. *Public Opinion Quarterly* 36:616–27.

Friedenberg, Edgar Z. 1969. The Generation Gap. *Annals of the American Academy of Political and Social Science* 382:32–42.

Friedman, Lucy N., Alice F.Gold, and Richard Christie. 1972. Dissecting the Generation Gap: Intergenerational and Intrafamilial Similarities and Differences. *Public Opinion Quarterly* 36:334–46.

Fritz, Donald L. 1969. The Generation Gap in Current Attitudes toward Religion. PhD diss., Ohio State University.

Ginandes, Shepard. 1969. The Generation Gap Widens in America. *International Journal of Offender Therapy and Comparative Criminology* 13:18–20.

Glenn, Norval D. 1994. Television Watching, Newspaper Reading, and Cohort Differences in Verbal Ability. *Sociology of Education* 67:216–30.

———. 1999. Further Discussion of the Evidence for an Intracohort Decline in Education-adjusted Vocabulary. *American Sociological Review* 64:267–71.

Greeley, Andrew M., and Michael Hout. 1999. Americans' Increasing Belief in Life after Death: Religious Competition and Acculturation. *American Sociological Review* 64:813–35.

Holsti, Ole R., and James N. Rosenau. 1980. Does Where You Stand Depend on When You Where Were Born? The Impact of Generation on Post-Vietnam Foreign Policy Beliefs. *Public Opinion Quarterly* 44:1–22.

Hout, Michael, and Claude S. Fischer. 2001. Explaining the Rise of Americans with No Religious Preference: Politics and Generations. GSS Social Change Report No. 46. NORC, Chicago.

Howe, Neil. 1993. *13th Gen: Abort, Retry, Ignore, Fail?* New York: Vintage Books.

Howe, Neil, and William Strauss. 2000. *Millennials Rising: The Next Great Generation.* New York: Vintage Books.

Jeffries, Vincent. 1974. Political Generations and the Acceptance or Rejection of Nuclear Warfare. *Journal of Social Issues* 30:119–36.

Jennings, M. Kent, and Richard G. Niemi. 1975. Continuity and Change in Political Orientations: A Longitudinal Study of Two Generations. *American Political Science Review* 69:1316–35.

Keeley, Benjamin J. 1976. Generations in Tension: Intergenerational Differences and Continuities in Religion and Religion-Related Behavior. *Review of Religious Research* 17:221–31.

Kertzer, David I. 1983. Generation as a Sociological Problem. *Annual Review of Sociology* 9:125–49.

Klecka, William R. 1971. Applying Political Generations to the Study of Political Behavior: A Cohort Analysis. *Public Opinion Quarterly* 35:358–73.

Ladd, Everett C. 1999. *The Ladd Report.* New York: Free Press.

Laufer, Robert S., and Vern L. Bengtson. 1974 Generations, Aging, and Social Stratification: On the Development of Generational Units. *Journal of Social Issues* 30:181–205.

Mauss, Armand L., and William E. Garland Jr. 1971 The Myth of the Generation Gap. Paper presented at the American Sociological Association, Denver, CO, August.

Ortner, Sherry B. 1998. Generation X: Anthropology in a Media-Saturated World. *Cultural Anthropology* 13:414–40.

Payne, Eleanor H. 1973. Study of a Generation Gap: The Effects of Age, Race, and Sex on Values. PhD diss., University of Colorado.

Putnam, Robert D. 2000. *Bowling Alone: The Collapse and Revival of American Community.* New York: Simon & Schuster.

Roberts, Carl W., and Kurt Lang. 1985. Generations and Ideological Change: Some Observations. *Public Opinion Quarterly* 49:460–73.

Roskin, Michael. 1974. From Pearl Harbor to Vietnam: Shifting Generational Paradigms and Foreign Policy. *Political Science Quarterly* 89:563–88.

Sacks, Peter. 1996. *Generation X Goes to College: An Eye-Opening Account of Teaching in Post-Modern America.* Chicago: Open Court.

Sberna, Melanie, and David Gay. 2000. Cohort Membership and Trends in Political Tolerance: Baby Busters, Baby Boomers, and Generation X. Paper presented at the Southern Sociological Society, New Orleans, April.

Smith, Tom W. 1989. The Reagan Generation? *GSS News* 3:2.

———. 1995. Generational Differences in Musical Preferences. *Popular Music and Society* 18:43–59.

———. 1999. The Emerging Twenty-First Century American Family. GSS Social Change Report No. 42. NORC, Chicago.

———. 2002. Religious Diversity in America: The Emergence of Muslims, Buddhists, Hindus, and Others. *Journal for the Scientific Study of Religion* 41:577–85.

Starr, Jerold M. 1974. The Peace and Love Generation: Changing Attitudes toward Sex and Violence among College Youth. *Journal of Social Issues* 30:73–106.

Strauss, William. 1998. *The Fourth Turning: An American Prophecy.* New York: Broadway Books.

Strauss, William, and Neil Howe. 1991. *Generations: The History of America's Future, 1584 to 2069.* New York: William Morrow.

Thomas, L. Eugene. 1974. Generational Discontinuity in Beliefs: An Exploration of the Generation Gap. *Journal of Social Issues* 30:1–22.

Williams, Angie, Justine Coupland, Annette Folwell, and Lisa Sparks. 1997. Talking about Generation X: Defining Them as They Define Themselves. *Journal of Language and Social Psychology* 16:251–77.

Wilson, James A., and Walter R.Gove. 1999a. The Age-Period Conundrum and Verbal Ability: Empirical Relations and Their Interpretation. *American Sociological Review* 64:287–302.

———. 1999b.The Intercohort Decline in Verbal Ability: Does It Exist? *American Sociological Review* 64:253–66.

Wright, Burton, II. 1972. The Generation Gap: An Intergenerational Comparison of Values. PhD diss., Florida State University.

Zey-Ferrell, Mary, William L. Tolone, and Robert H.Walsh. 1978. The Intergenerational Socialization of Sex-Role Attitudes: A Gender or Generation Gap? *Adolescence* 13:95–108.

PART THREE

PASSAGES
TO ADULTHOOD

*Findings from National and
Regional Longitudinal Studies*

CHAPTER 7

SUBJECTIVE AGE IDENTITY AND THE TRANSITION TO ADULTHOOD

When Do Adolescents Become Adults?

MICHAEL J. SHANAHAN, ERIK J. PORFELI, JEYLAN T. MORTIMER, AND LANCE D. ERICKSON

At what point in life does a young person become an adult? For many decades, scholars held that five transition markers delineated entry into adulthood: completing school, leaving home, beginning one's career, marrying, and becoming a parent. By assuming these roles, youth were thought to relinquish the hallmarks of adolescence, including dependency on parents, "immature" behaviors that reflect experimentation with roles, and indecision about one's identity. In turn, the newly acquired adult roles brought with them strong expectations for "adult" behaviors. Indeed, most adults at mid-twentieth century held expectations about the timing of these transitions and about the inappropriateness of being "off time" (Neugarten, Moore, and Lowe 1965).

Based on these five criteria, however, the percentage of youth in their twenties and thirties who would qualify as adult has decreased significantly in recent decades (Fussell and Furstenberg, this vol., chap. 2; Mortimer and Aronson 2001; Shanahan 2000). For a considerable segment of the population, education has extended into the late twenties and early thirties, family formation has been postponed, and many young people plan on remaining single and childless well into their thirties, if not indefinitely (e.g., Casper and Bianchi 2002). Moreover, at century's end, most adults hold expectations about the timing of these markers, but they do not view off-time transitions as deserving of disapprobation (Settersten 2003; Settersten and Hagestad 1996).

In turn, these social changes have prompted new views of what constitutes adulthood. Arnett (2001) argues that "emerging adulthood" now constitutes a phase of the life course that extends between adolescence and adulthood. Emerging adulthood is characterized by relative independence from age-normative tasks, by experimentation with social roles, and by little meaningful commitment to one's relationships and organizational involvements. In the context of emerging adulthood, young people identify individualistic indicators of maturity (e.g., independent decision making) as the new markers of whether one is an adult and, according to this view, the demographic markers are deemed substantially less important by youth. Similarly, Côtè (2000) suggests "youthhood" as a new phase of life during which "psychological adulthood" is hopefully attained through personal strivings. Côtè likewise maintains that the importance of the traditional markers has declined significantly, largely replaced by emotional and cognitive maturity and an advanced sense of ethics.

The possibility that adulthood is now viewed by young people primarily as a reflection of individualistic criteria is intriguing to life-course sociologists, who have assumed, based on research by Neugarten and her colleagues (1965), that adult identity is founded on the assumption of related social roles. Perhaps with increasing variability in the timing of transition markers, the criteria that define adulthood have become individualized, now resting primarily on subjective self-evaluations. Yet surprisingly little empirical research has examined the extent to which youth view their adult status as a reflection of individualistic criteria and transition markers. In this chapter, we draw on data from the Youth Development Study to examine the importance of the traditional transition markers and personal qualities in predicting whether young people view themselves as adult. We begin by briefly examining the conceptual and empirical basis for claims about the changing nature of adult identity.

CHANGING SOCIETIES, CHANGING CONCEPTIONS OF ADULTHOOD?

The Conceptual Basis of "Emerging Adulthood" and Subjective Age Identity

According to Arnett and Taber (1994), the contrast between the traditional conception of adulthood and "emerging adulthood" reflects the distinction between broad and narrow socialization. Broad socialization—which characterizes large segments of the contemporary West, including Europe, Canada, and the United States—refers to the encouragement of multiple routes through the life course, consistent with values emphasizing independence, individualism, and self-expression. Narrow socialization—which characterizes preindustrialized societies—refers to the restriction of life-course patterns to a narrowly defined range. Emphasis is placed on conformity to expectations, with punitive measures for unconventional life-course patterns. Arnett and Taber argue that this distinction is crucial for understanding the transition to adulthood according to cognitive, emotional, and behavioral trajectories.

In preindustrialized societies, the acquisition and application of knowledge begins in early childhood and continues to accumulate through the early life course. The vast majority of youth in these societies are heavily involved in work, which is performed under the supervision of adults. In these circumstances, according to Arnett and Taber, youth vary little in their cognitive activities, which are relatively continuous trajectories that reflect a concern for others and a sense of interdependence beginning in early childhood. In such societies, cognitive skills are not crucial indicators of adulthood because interdependence and responsibility do not emerge in an abrupt manner. In contrast, youth in societies with broad socialization attend schools, which foster individualism and independence. In these circumstances, one observes substantial variability in when youth actually achieve responsibility and interdependence, and these factors distinguish adolescents from adults.

Emotionally, Westerners hold that adulthood is indicated by autonomy from parents and intimacy in a committed love relationship. According to Arnett and Taber, this pattern is not observed, however, in societies characterized by narrow socialization, which typically emphasize rigid conformity to gender roles and marriage based on agreement. That is, marriage often reflects practical considerations rather than romantic love. In the case of males, narrow emotional socialization often involves intense rituals marking manhood and then marriage, which is infrequently based on love. In the case of women, dependence is transferred from the family of origin to the family of procreation, but love is irrelevant. In contrast, in societies marked by broad socialization, intimacy and autonomy are valued, but these desired outcomes are not the assured result of socialization. In such societies, the achievement of autonomy and intimacy is based on circumstances of personal development.

Behaviorally, contemporary adulthood is indicated by self-control and

compliance with social conventions. Under conditions of narrow socialization, with its emphasis on intergenerational interdependence through daily
interactions in work and play, youth rarely engage in reckless behavior. Self-
control and compliance are exhibited early in life because of intolerance
for behaviors that do not conform to expectations. In contrast, the youth of
broad socialization exhibit comparatively high levels of reckless behavior.
Pressures to conform are comparatively low, and many youth experiment
with various forms of deviance. The cessation of reckless behavior and acts
of deviance is thus thought to indicate the onset of adulthood in societies
characterized by broad socialization.

In sum, for youth growing up in societies marked by narrow socialization, autonomy, interdependence, and conformist behavior are exhibited
early in life and thus are not good markers of a discontinuous break between
adolescence and adulthood. Moreover, these skills culminate in marriage,
which, coupled with the abilities "to provide, protect, and procreate," are
regarded as indicating adulthood (Arnett 1998). In contrast, among contemporary youth, individualistic criteria—a sense of autonomy and interdependence, the achievement of intimacy in a close and enduring relationship, and the cessation of reckless behaviors—distinguish adolescence from
adulthood.

While this conception of emerging adulthood places a heavy emphasis
on individualistic criteria in postindustrial societies, it likewise maintains
that the demographic transition markers have become much less important
because of delays in marriage and parenthood. In the case of the United
States, the latter half of the twentieth century is thought to correspond to a
shift from narrow to broad socialization, which in turn led to greater variance
in how youth entered adult roles and the postponement of family transitions.
In turn, "this rise [in age of marriage between 1960 and 1990], along with
the corresponding strength in American individualism . . . led ultimately to
the demise of marriage as a significant marker of the transition to adulthood,
in favor of the individualistic character qualities" (Arnett 1998, 301).

Yet historical considerations suggest that combinations of individual
characteristics and transition markers have defined adult status in many
times and places, and the contemporary United States would not appear exceptional. Schlegel (1998) observes that significant groups of youth who delayed marriage or simply never married have characterized much of history
in Europe and America. These groups include youth who were financially independent but too poor to marry, and youth from aristocratic or patrician
families without adequate resources to provide for the marriage of all of their
sons and daughters. Given that financial independence might begin as early

as age fourteen, for the considerable number of older youth who did not enter into marriage, the transition to adulthood was ambiguous and almost
certainly hinged on personal qualities indicative of maturity. In contrast,
youth fortunate enough to marry were not likely to be accorded adult status
immediately by the community without basic indications of maturity, which
could encompass personal qualities and skills.

These historical observations suggest that the use of individualistic
criteria to determine adulthood is not likely new or limited to societies characterized by broad socialization.[1] This has been true when marriage was delayed or not possible (as is presently the case in the United States). A myriad
of combinations of individual attributes and transition experiences probably
lead to feeling unambiguously like an adult.

By implication, prior experiences are salient to one's self-perceptions,
independent of one's current situation. The importance of both past and
present experiences seems especially plausible with respect to transition
markers, since contemporary young people move in and out of adult statuses with some frequency. That is, many of the transition markers are "reversible," meaning that an adult status marker can be acquired (e.g., spouse,
full-time worker, independent householder) and then relinquished as youth
return to their prior status (respectively, unmarried, part-time worker or unemployed, and living with parents). Perhaps such past experiences with
adult roles encourage self-perceptions of adulthood even when these roles
may have been relinquished.

Empirical Evidence for Conceptions of Adulthood

Do people in fact rank "individualistic" criteria high and the demographic
transition markers low in their judgment of what constitutes "adulthood?"
No empirical research actually assesses the factors that contribute to self-
perceived adulthood in societies characterized by narrow socialization or
even prior to the 1960s in the United States. Strictly speaking, therefore, arguments for a shift in the way adulthood is defined are necessarily impres-
sionistic: without knowing how the narrowly socialized young adults of earlier America would rank individualistic criteria and transition markers,
responses from current cohorts cannot be used to make statements about social change. Nevertheless, some empirical research has assessed the criteria
used by more recent cohorts of Americans.

In a series of studies, Arnett has asked respondents to "indicate
whether you think the following [criteria] must be achieved before a person
can be considered an adult" from a list of about forty items. That is, the ques-

tion asks respondents to identify the requirements for adulthood for a hypothetical person. In an early study, a convenience sample of 346 students enrolled in an introduction to communication course at a large Midwestern university were asked this question and generally ranked the demographic markers low in importance (Arnett 1994). While 57% of the respondents indicated "move out of parents' house," the other markers were identified as necessary for adult status by less than 30% of youth. More likely, respondents chose items indicating cognitive, emotional, and behavioral maturity, such as independent decision making, establishing a relationship with parents as an equal, and avoiding petty crime.

In subsequent papers, this question was asked of 140 twenty-one- to twenty-eight-year-olds (Arnett 1997), and then 171 adolescents, 179 "emerging adults" (twenty-one to twenty-eight years of age), and 651 adults (thirty to fifty-five years of age) (Arnett 2001); all of these studies are therefore based on convenience samples of people "intercepted" in public places. The univariate results from these studies are consistent with the earlier study of college students: people were considerably more likely to indicate cognitive, emotional, and behavioral requirements for adulthood—whether for a hypothetical adult or oneself—than the transition markers.

Clearly, these results suggest the importance of individualistic criteria and the irrelevance of the demographic markers (see also Greene, Wheatley, and Aldava [1992] for a study of a convenience sample of high school and college students and Scheer and Palkovitz [1994] for a study of a convenience sample of 248 youth ranging from fifteen to twenty-eight years of age). Indeed, Arnett (2000, 472) concludes that "these demographic transitions have little to do with emerging adults' conceptions of what it means to reach adulthood" (see also, e.g., Arnett 1994, 222; 1997, 15; 1998, 296; Arnett and Taber 1994, abstract and 533).

Yet do these standards reflect the respondents' own experiences? Very little evidence bears on this question. Arnett (1997) summarizes cross-tabulations from the 140 twenty-one- to twenty-eight-year-olds showing that whether or not one is in school, married, full-time employed, or a parent is not significantly related to whether these criteria are viewed as necessary for a hypothetical person. Yet standards and interpretative frames applied to "the Other" are not always the same standards and frames applied to oneself (Neugarten 1996). How are people's actual experiences and dispositions predictive of their self-conception of adult status? The 140 twenty-one- to twenty-eight-year-olds were also asked, "Do you feel like you have reached adulthood? In what ways do you feel you and have and have not?" The criteria mentioned were than ranked and, consistent with results for the hypothetical person, people viewed their own adult status as reflecting acceptance of responsibility for one's self, financial independence, and independent decision making (Arnett 1998). "Becoming a parent" was ranked sixth, with full-time employment and marriage ranked eighth and eleventh, with 15% and 8% mentioning them, respectively. Such an analysis, however, does not interrelate actual transition experiences and individualistic criteria with self-perceived adulthood in a multivariate framework.

Another piece of evidence comes from a study of a convenience sample of ethnically diverse youth ages eighteen to twenty-nine in the San Francisco area. Youth who were parents in this sample were more likely to indicate that they felt like an adult and that role transitions were necessary for a hypothetical adult (Arnett 2003). Only two role transitions (marriage and parenthood) were entered as covariates in the ANCOVAs, however, and no indicators of psychological or behavioral maturity were considered. Thus, the extent to which one's own psychological and behavioral maturity and experiences are associated with one's self-perception of adult status has not been systematically studied in a multivariate framework.

Based on these considerations, we test two broadly stated expectations about self-perceived adulthood. First, self-perceived adulthood reflects both objective transition markers and personal indicators of maturity. Second, prior experiences with adult roles and present role occupancies may both contribute to feeling like an adult. We consider the merits of these ideas by drawing on the Youth Development Study (YDS), a longitudinal investigation into early work experiences and their effects through the adolescent and adult life course.

DATA AND MEASURES

The Youth Development Study

The target population consisted of all ninth-grade students enrolled in the St. Paul, Minnesota, public school district who would not be prevented from filling out a questionnaire due to a disability ($n = 2,321$). A random selection of 1,785 students and their parents were invited to participate in the research; consent to participate was obtained from 1,139 parents and their adolescent child, resulting in a 64% response to invitation rate. The present analyses focus on the 1,010 students who were initially surveyed in the early months of 1988.

The local character of this panel poses certain advantages (facilitating the logistics of the research and enhancing respondent commitment), although it also raises issues of generalizability. The panel has been shown to represent well the St. Paul community and its student body at the initiation of the study (Mortimer et al. 1992), but how does this population compare to a nationally representative population? To answer this question, we compare population characteristics of the United States and St. Paul from the 1980 U.S. Census and the St. Paul public school district. The St. Paul public school population is more racially diverse than the nation as a whole. Although the representation of African Americans and Native Americans is comparable (e.g., among the former, 11.7% in the United States, 9.8% in St. Paul), St. Paul has a greater percentage of Asians and Pacific Islanders (3.9%) when compared with the United States (1.6%). The greatest difference can be found between the "other" designation from the U.S. Census (2.6%) and the local sample's other and mixed race categories (6.8%). Comparisons of economic indicators suggest that St. Paul is somewhat more well-off than the country: Per capita income is slightly higher ($7,694 in St. Paul, $7,298 in the United States), unemployment is lower (4.7% in St. Paul, 6.5% in the United States), and the number of families classified as impoverished is lower (8.0% in St. Paul, 9.6% in the United States). Thus, St. Paul is more racially and ethnically diverse than the U.S. population, but in socioeconomic terms, the two groups are similar.

The YDS panel has been surveyed annually from the ninth (1988) to the twelfth (1991) grades in high school, with excellent panel retention (93%) through this period. Yearly questionnaires, administered in school, included a large battery of items tapping experiences in work, occupationally relevant attitudes, and plans for the future. After the young people left high school, they were surveyed annually by mail. The questionnaires again addressed work experiences and orientations and obtained detailed monthly records (via life-history calendars [Freedman et al. 1988]) of residential arrangements, educational attendance, and both part- and full-time labor force participation.

Data for this paper come primarily from the eleventh wave, collected in 1999, when the participants were twenty-five or twenty-six years old. The eleven-year retention rate was 72.4%. Though males and socioeconomically disadvantaged young people were more likely to leave the study, the social background of first-wave and twelfth-wave panel members, and their work-related attitudes and plans (measured in the ninth grade), were quite similar.

Self-Perceived Adulthood

In 1999 (wave 11), respondents were asked how they "usually feel in the following situations," with response options "not at all like an adult," "somewhat like an adult," "entirely like an adult," and "does not apply." Ten situations that relate to school, work, family, and recreation were then listed. An eleventh option, "most of the time," was provided to assess a global self-perception of adult status. (See app. A for the instrument as it appears in the survey.) The instrument is similar to that used in previous attempts to measure self-perceived adulthood, although it also addresses both global and domain-specific self-perceptions. Prior research in self-conceptions suggests that people distinguish between global and domain-specific views of the self (e.g., Grabowski, Call, and Mortimer 2001), and so this possibility was examined with respect to self-perceived adulthood.

The response patterns are shown in table 7.1. Generally speaking, less than 5% of respondents report feeling "not at all like an adult" in the listed contexts, the exceptions being participating in active sports (7.5%), time spent with friends (12.4%), and time spent with parents (7.2%). Even with these exceptions, however, all of the variables are noticeably bimodal, with youth choosing the "somewhat" or "entirely" options. All of the variables were thus recoded to contrast "entirely" with the combined categories "not at all" and "somewhat." Our analyses will focus on these dichotomized versions of the subjective age identity variable.

Table 7.2 reports the descriptive statistics and degree of association among the subjective age identity items. With respondents in the "does not apply" category eliminated from consideration, the means show that respondents are most likely to report feeling entirely like an adult in their private lives (78% at home, 75% with their child, and 70% with their romantic partner) and at work (72%). Respondents are least likely to report feeling entirely like an adult with friends (37%) and with their parents (43%). The other responses are rather evenly split. Sixty percent of those in the sample report feeling entirely like an adult most of the time; this figure may seem surprisingly low given that these respondents are twenty-five or twenty-six years old.

The table also reports phi coefficients, which can be interpreted as a simple bivariate correlation between two dichotomous variables, indicating the propensity for someone who claims to feel entirely like an adult in one domain to report feeling entirely like an adult in another domain. The correlations show that the dimensions of self-perceived adulthood are moderately and significantly correlated (excepting the relationship between school and child). This is especially true for the relationships between "most of the time" and "romantic partner" with the various other dimensions. Nevertheless, the range of means and the moderate values of the correlations indicate that people do distinguish among the dimensions: people who report feeling entirely like an adult on one dimension have an increased propensity to

TABLE 7.1

OBSERVED FREQUENCIES FOR SUBJECTIVE AGE IDENTITY ITEMS: YOUTH DEVELOPMENT STUDY

	DOES NOT APPLY		NOT AT ALL LIKE AN ADULT		SOMEWHAT LIKE AN ADULT		ENTIRELY LIKE AN ADULT	
	n	% REPORTED	n	% REPORTED	n	% REPORTED	n	% REPORTED
At school	472	67.6	13	1.9	99	14.2	114	16.3
At work	48	6.8	5	.7	181	25.8	468	66.7
In community organizations	292	41.5	9	1.3	126	17.9	276	39.3
Doing active sports	84	12.0	53	7.5	244	34.7	321	45.7
Other recreations	64	9.1	30	4.3	271	38.7	335	47.9
With friends	8	1.1	87	12.4	351	49.9	257	36.6
Taking care of house	23	3.3	17	2.4	132	18.8	530	75.5
With my children, child	399	57.3	13	1.9	60	8.6	224	32.2
With my parent(s)	25	3.6	51	7.2	335	47.6	293	41.6
With romantic partner	66	9.4	15	2.1	177	25.2	444	63.2
Most of the time	7	1.0	15	2.1	260	37.1	419	59.8

TABLE 7.2

DIMENSIONS OF SELF-PERCEIVED ADULTHOOD: DESCRIPTIVE STATISTICS, BIVARIATE ASSOCIATIONS: YOUTH DEVELOPMENT STUDY

	n	X̄	SD	SELF-PERCEIVED ADULTHOOD DIMENSIONS									
				SCHOOL	WORK	COMMUNITY	EXERCISE	RECREATION	FRIENDS	HOME	CHILD	PARENTS	PARTNER
School	226	.50	.50										
Work	654	.72	.45	.41***									
Community	411	.67	.47	.25**	.44***								
Exercise	618	.52	.50	.23***	.15***	.21***							
Recreation	636	.53	.50	.27***	.24***	.29***	.51***						
Friends	695	.37	.48	.23***	.26***	.27***	.39***	.42***					
Home	679	.78	.41	.29***	.29***	.34***	.23***	.28***	.25***				
Child	297	.75	.43	.13	.25***	.24***	.24***	.33***	.25***	.37***			
Parents	679	.43	.50	.27***	.29***	.36***	.21***	.28***	.38***	.24***	.23***		
Partner	636	.70	.46	.37***	.36***	.32***	.31***	.42***	.40***	.43***	.36***	.31***	
Most of the time	694	.60	.49	.44***	.53***	.49***	.38***	.49***	.45***	.44***	.48***	.44***	.53***

**p < .01.
***p < .001.

report feeling the same way on another dimension, but this relationship is clearly not determinative.

Objective Transition Markers

The data set allows us to examine measures of the demographic transition markers, whether these events had ever occurred, and whether the respondent is currently occupying a role associated with a specific marker (e.g., parenthood). In 1999 (wave 11), respondents were asked, "has this event happened?" followed by "live with partner or spouse," "get married," "own a home," "become a parent," "complete school," and "started a career." The cohabiting and married items were combined into a single indicator reflecting whether the respondent had ever married or cohabited. These items were used to create the variables indicating whether a respondent had ever experienced any of the demographic transition markers.

For present status, respondents were asked "if you are married or cohabiting," "do you rent or own the place that you are currently living in?" and "do you have any children?" Additionally, respondents completed a life-history calendar that indicated whether they were employed for thirty-five hours per week or more. Their reported status in April of 1999 was used to indicate whether they were presently employed full-time. Respondents also reported how much time they spent studying or in class. Any nonzero response was taken to mean that the person was presently a student in some capacity. These items were used to create variables indicating the current adult role set occupied by each respondent. Note that there are some discrepancies between the ever experienced and currently experiences role sets, the former, for example, referring to owning a home, while the latter refers to owning or renting.

In order to examine the possible effects of configurations of these statuses, four dummy variables were created. Two variables reflect whether respondents ever experienced or presently are experiencing the family role transitions (own home or rent apartment, cohabiting/marriage, parenthood). The other two dummy variables reflect whether respondents ever experienced or presently experience the attainment roles (school completion and full-time employment).

Table 7.3 shows the descriptive statistics and associations among these variables. The means for the markers that have ever been experienced show that many people have launched a career (61%) and cohabited or married (73%) at some point in their lives. Few people have experienced all of the family transitions (18%) and about one in three respondents have ever

TABLE 7.3

DEMOGRAPHIC TRANSITION MARKERS: DESCRIPTIVE STATISTICS, PAIRWISE BIVARIATE ASSOCIATIONS: YOUTH DEVELOPMENT STUDY

	$\bar{x}$	SD	1	2	3	4	5	6	7	8	9	10	11	12	13	14
Ever:																
1. Cohabited/married	.73	.44	1.00													
2. Own home	.34	.47	.28	1.00												
3. Parent	.41	.49	.38	.18	1.00											
4. School complete	.58	.49	-.05	.05	.05	1.00										
5. Career	.61	.49	.02	.20	-.07	.27	1.00									
6. Family	.18	.38	.28	.65	.55	.05	.10	1.00								
7. Attainment	.42	.49	-.03	.11	-.05	.72	.68	.07	1.00							
Present:																
8. Cohabited/married	.54	.50	.66	.40	.27	-.04	.07	.35	.03	1.00						
9. Own, rent	.88	.33	.15	.16	.16	.03	.12	.09	.07	.23	1.00					
10. Parent	.39	.49	.36	.14	.96	.05	-.08	.52	-.05	.26	.15	1.00				
11. Not in school	.80	.40	.08	.09	.18	.14	.10	.10	.11	.03	.08	.19	1.00			
12. Full-time work	.72	.45	.00	.04	-.18	.05	.29	-.11	.22	.00	.05	-.18	.13	1.00		
13. Family	.26	.44	.36	.25	.72	.00	.01	.59	-.00	.55	.22	.75	.11	-.11	1.00	
14. Attainment	.60	.49	.01	.05	-.06	.10	.27	-.06	.23	.02	.07	-.05	.60	.77	-.03	1.00

Note. Correlations $> .07$ or $< -.07$ are significant at $p < .05$.

owned a home (34%). The means for the markers that are presently experienced indicate that most people own a home or rent an apartment (88%) and are full-time employed (72%); most have begun their careers and are no longer students (60%). Few youth currently have their own home, are married or cohabiting, and have children, however (26%). (The present role set is similar to Arnett's [1997] sample of twenty-one- to twenty-eight-year-olds, with roughly 50% married, 25% parents, and 66% employed full time.)

The correlations reveal that ever cohabited/married is moderately related to ever own a home or become a parent and that, as would be expected, the family and attainment dummy variables are related to their components. Otherwise, the correlations are low in magnitude, indicating that the attainment transitions ever experienced are not strongly interrelated or related to family transitions (e.g., a young person may or may not marry and/or become a parent before completing school). The correlations for transitions presently experienced reveal the same pattern.

Ever experiencing a transition may or may not be related to its "present" counterpart, as would be expected. Parenthood is almost perfectly related ($r = .96$), and the correlations for ever-present cohabiting/marriage and the family composite are substantial ($r = .66$ and $r = .59$, respectively). The other correlations are moderate in size, which likely reflects differences in wording (e.g., ever owning a home versus presently renting or owning). Ever completing school and presently not in school have a low correlation ($r = .14$). Further analyses suggest that some youth are not presently enrolled in any educational setting but consider themselves "students" because they have not attained their final educational goals. Of 224 students answering the self-perceived adulthood in school item, one hundred reported no time at school or studying, and about seventy people have not been enrolled in school in the past sixteen months and have not achieved their educational goal yet. Given the hypothetical nature of self-perceptions at school among those students not attending school, the analysis of this item will be restricted to those who report nonzero time at school or studying.

Individualistic Criteria

While the Youth Development Study offers greater coverage of objective marker transitions than of subjective criteria of adulthood, the data set does provide some indicators of individualistic qualities that are emphasized in the literature on emerging adulthood. In 1999 (wave 11), the respondents were asked: "During the past year, what share of your living expenses were covered by each of the following sources? Do not include educational expenses." The percentage of contributions by the parents and relatives were then summed (other sources include "your own earnings or savings," "spouse or partner," "governmental assistance," and "other."). This summed percentage was then subtracted from one to arrive at a measure of financial independence, which reflects the percentage of living expenses not covered by one's family of origin.[2] As defined, this variable is highly skewed, with a mean of 94.29 and a standard deviation of 16.62. In fact, almost 80% of the sample reports receiving no contributions from any members of the family of origin, and only about 5% of the sample reports having at least half of their living expenses covered by parents or relatives. In this situation, no common transformation will improve matters. Therefore, the variable was dichotomized to contrast those respondents who received less than and more than 15% of their living expenses (coded as 0 and 1, respectively) from relatives.

A second criterion frequently mentioned is accepting responsibility for one's self. In 1998 (wave 10), respondents were asked, "What happens in the future mostly depends on me" (with responses ranging from 1 = strongly disagree to 4 = strong agree). Although this item is used as part of the Pearlin Mastery Scale, it does reflect a dimension of personal responsibility. The observed values for this variable are also skewed, with only 3.25% of the sample strongly disagreeing or disagreeing with this statement ($\bar{X} =$ 3.45; SD = .58). The most effective transformation (the square root) hardly improves on identity, so the variable is not recoded.

FINDINGS

Our primary focus is determining whether both the objective transition markers and individualistic criteria predict self-perceived adulthood. The model of emerging adulthood suggests that individualistic criteria will be associated with self-perceived adulthood to a much greater degree than, or to the exclusion of, the demographic transition markers. We begin by examining simple measures of bivariate associations among the potential predictors and the subjective age identity variables. We then build multivariate models that interrelate the predictors and subjective age identity. Prior research suggests that these models would not differ by gender, and preliminary analyses of these data confirm this lack of difference. The analyses thus focus on the total sample.

Several limitations should be noted when interpreting these findings. First, because of the design of the study (with subjective age measured on just one occasion), no attempt can be made to develop causal explanations or to address dynamic processes of self-identification through time. We highlight associations among the variables. In fact, it seems likely that individualistic criteria and adult roles and subjective age identity are reciprocally interrelated. That is, even under ideal circumstances involving longitudinal data, it would be difficult to identify the unique effects of each set of variables. Second, our analyses do not include a wide range of individualistic criteria, only a single measure of each of two constructs that are frequently mentioned as salient individualistic criteria. Furthermore, the measure of personal responsibility is assessed one year prior to self-perceived adulthood. If we do not observe significant associations between these criteria and subjective age identity, it may reflect a lack of sufficiently complex measures. If we do observe associations, however, then it may be concluded that individualistic criteria are relevant.

Transition Markers, Individualistic Criteria, and Adulthood

Table 7.4 shows the bivariate associations among the domains of self-perceived adulthood, on the one hand, and the transition markers and individualistic criteria, on the other. Several patterns emerge from these results.

First, the family transitions are often significantly correlated with dimensions of perceived adulthood. Cohabiting/marriage and parenthood—whether ever experienced or presently experienced—are significantly, weakly related to several dimensions of adulthood, particularly feeling entirely like an adult at work, when engaged in sports, at home, with romantic partner, and most of the time. Second, the family dummy variable index—indicating whether the respondent is an independent householder, cohabited or married, and a parent—is significantly related to numerous dimensions of perceived adulthood, and this relationship appears stronger if ever experienced when compared to currently experienced transitions. Third, financial independence is significantly, weakly related to several domains of adulthood, including at work, with romantic partners or parents, and most of the time. Finally, the associations are generally weak in magnitude, suggesting that few, if any, of these variables are important predictors of self-perceived adulthood.

Table 7.5 shows multivariate logistic regression models that interrelate the individualistic criteria and transition markers ever experienced (as predictors) to the dimensions of self-perceived adulthood. Several conclusions can be drawn from this table. First, respondents who have ever cohabited or married are more likely to report feeling entirely like an adult when taking care of their house or apartment (odds ratio = 2.2) and when spending time with their romantic partner (odds ratio = 1.6, marginally significant).

TABLE 7.4

SELF-PERCEIVED ADULTHOOD, TRANSITION MARKERS, AND INDIVIDUALISTIC CRITERIA: BIVARIATE ASSOCIATIONS—YOUTH DEVELOPMENT STUDY

	SELF-PERCEIVED ADULTHOOD DIMENSIONS										
	SCHOOL	WORK	COMMUNITY	SPORTS	RECREATION	FRIENDS	HOME	CHILD	PARENTS	PARTNER	MOST OF THE TIME
Ever:											
Cohabited/married	.24***	.11**	.09+	.07	.07+	.05	.19***	.04	.03	.11**	.09*
Own home	.02	.06	.06	.02	.08*	-.00	.11**	.10+	.03	.09*	.04
Parent	.13+	.12**	.09+	.09*	.03	.08*	.11**	...	.05	.11**	.12**
School complete	...	.04	-.06	-.03	-.06	-.00	.00	.10+	-.02	.01	.04
Career	.07	.08+	.06	.00	-.00	-.03	.04	.03	-.03	-.11**	.06
Family	.06	.13**	.09+	.12**	.13**	.07+	.11**	...	.08*	.11**	.11**
Attainment	...	.06	-.05	.01	-.02	-.04	.03	.04	-.06	.05	.02
Present:											
Cohabited/married	.15*	.10*	.03	-.02	.08+	.01	.13***	.04	.04	.10*	.05
Own, rent	.03	.03	.02	.02	-.02	-.00	.11**	.06	-.01	.07+	.04
Parent	.09	.10**	.08+	.09*	.03	.10**	.09*	...	.08*	.10**	.12**
Not in school	...	-.03	.01	.00	-.05	.03	-.02	.05	-.19***	-.00	-.00
Full-time work	.01	.06	.04	.03	.01	-.03	.03	.02	.00	-.00	.01
Family	.06	.08*	.05	.07+	.09*	.07+	.12**	...	.07+	.12**	.10**
Attainment	...	-.02	.01	.03	-.02	-.03	-.01	.00	-.05*	-.02	.00
Financial independence	.11+	.10*	.03	.01	.05	-.01	.04	.11+	.11**	.08*	.08*
Personal responsibility	.03	.04	.05	.08+	.07+	.03	-.01	-.04	-.01	-.01	.06
n (range)	206–26	592–652	374–416	561–616	578–634	631–93	615–77	269–97	618–78	575–636	631–92

+p < .10.
*p < .05.
**p < .01.
***p < .001.

TABLE 7.5

MODELS OF SELF-PERCEIVED ADULTHOOD, EVER EXPERIENCED ADULT ROLES, AND INDIVIDUALISTIC CRITERIA: YOUTH DEVELOPMENT STUDY

| PREDICTORS | SELF-PERCEIVED ADULTHOOD DIMENSIONS | | | | | | | | | | |
	SCHOOL	WORK	COMMUNITY	SPORTS	RECREATION	FRIENDS	HOME	CHILD	PARENTS	PARTNER	MOST OF THE TIME
Financial independence	.39	.33	-.25	-.27	-.19	-.32	-.23	.18	.51	.01	.10
	(.63)	(.31)	(.43)	(.31)	(.30)	(.30)	(.38)	(.63)	(.31)	(.35)	(.29)
Personal responsibility	.13	.11	.20	.24	.27	.15	.16	-.14	.02	-.02	.16
	(.37)	(.17)	(.21)	(.16)	(.16)	(.16)	(.14)	(.27)	(.15)	(.17)	(.15)
Cohabited/married	.79	.32	.09	.17	.36	.29	.79**	.06	.20	.46+	.22
	(.49)	(.23)	(.30)	(.23)	(.22)	(.23)	(.25)	(.71)	(.22)	(.24)	(.22)
Own home	-.26	.15	.18	.11	.24	-.12	.17	.33	.02	.16	.00
	(.56)	(.23)	(.27)	(.20)	(.20)	(.20)	(.25)	(.35)	(.20)	(.22)	(.20)
Become parent	.58	.43+	.66*	.44*	.14	.35+	.37	...	.24	.42+	.52**
	(.56)	(.23)	(.28)	(.20)	(.20)	(.20)	(.24)		(.19)	(.22)	(.20)
Complete school	...	.16	-.29	-.17	-.30	-.19	-.02	.36	-.12	-.18	.00
		(.21)	(.25)	(.19)	(.19)	(.19)	(.22)	(.34)	(.18)	(.21)	(.19)
Start career	.32	.23	.24	.09	-.06	.04	.09	.01	-.15	.48*	.20
	(.42)	(.22)	(.27)	(.20)	(.20)	(.20)	(.24)	(.35)	(.19)	(.22)	(.19)
Constant	-1.07	-.47	-.13	-.90	-.83	-1.07	.23	1.09	-.92	.14	-.72
	(1.39)	(.67)	(.87)	(.66)	(.64)	(.65)	(.75)	(1.37)	(.62)	(.74)	(.62)
n	107	524	332	501	514	557	543	218	546	511	559
χ^2, df	7.3, 6	16.3, 7	11.3, 7	11.0, 7	13.2, 7	9.2, 7	21.8, 7	2.9, 6	9.1, 7	18.3, 7	14.3, 7
p	.29	.02	.13	.14	.07	.24	.00	.83	.25	.01	.05
Pseudo R^2	.05	.03	.03	.02	.02	.01	.04	.01	.01	.02	.02

Note. Unstandardized effects, with standard errors in parentheses.

+ $p < .10$.

* $p < .05$.

** $p < .01$.

Second, starting a career increases the likelihood of self-perceived adulthood when spending time with a romantic partner (odds ratio = 1.62).

Third, respondents who have ever had a child are more likely to report feeling entirely like an adult when engaged in work (odds ratio = 1.5), when spending time with partner (odds ratio = 1.53), and most of the time (odds ratio = 1.69). Parenthood is also associated with self-perceived adulthood when participating in the community and in sports, and when spending time with friends, but these equations are insignificant in their overall fit. Indeed, no other patterns emerge in table 7.5, suggesting that family transitions—particularly parenthood—are important predictors that are significantly associated with feeling entirely like an adult. Finally, however, the models have very low explanatory value, as indicated by the pseudo-R^2, and indeed many do not have significant overall explanatory value.

In order to examine whether constellations of family and attainment transitions are important, we reestimated the models presented in table 7.5. The family-related transitions (cohabited/married, own home, and become parent) were replaced with a dummy variable that indicates whether the person ever experienced all three transitions. Similarly, the attainment-related transitions (complete school and full-time job) were replaced with a dummy variable indicating whether the person ever experienced both transitions. (The models for school and children are not considered given that the attainment dummy includes school completion and that the family dummy includes becoming a parent.) The results are shown in table 7.6 and confirm the importance of the family transitions. Young people who have cohabited or married, had at least one child, and have owned their home or rented their own apartment are significantly more likely to report feeling entirely like an adult along every dimension of the dependent variable. The magnitude of these odds ratios ranges from 1.5 (with parents) to 2.4 (work, community, home). (Two models, feeling like an adult among friends and with partner, were not statistically significant overall, and two models—community and house—were overall marginally significant, $p < .10$).

The model also shows that respondents who had ever left school and started their careers were less likely to feel entirely like an adult with parents ($b = -.42$, $p < .05$, odds ratio = 0.66). This is consistent with the bivariate findings, which showed a negative, significant zero-order relationship between the two variables. Follow-up analyses revealed that the effect is being driven by school completion. Youth who were not in school were less likely to view themselves entirely like an adult. Although this result is unexpected, perhaps youth still in school are acquiring advanced educational degrees and are thus not inclined to think of themselves as only somewhat of an adult; in

TABLE 7.6

MODELS OF SELF-PERCEIVED ADULTHOOD, EVER EXPERIENCED ADULT ROLE CONFIGURATIONS,
AND INDIVIDUALISTIC CRITERIA: YOUTH DEVELOPMENT STUDY

PREDICTORS	SELF-PERCEIVED ADULTHOOD DIMENSIONS								
	WORK	COMMUNITY	SPORTS	RECREATION	FRIENDS	HOME	PARENTS	PARTNER	MOST OF THE TIME
Financial independence	.45	−.13	−.22	−.10	−.23	−.09	.59[+]	.18	.24
	(.30)	(.43)	(.30)	(.29)	(.29)	(.36)	(.30)	(.34)	(.28)
Personal responsibility	.10	.17	.24	.27[+]	.14	.12	.02	.05	.15
	(.17)	(.21)	(.16)	(.16)	(.16)	(.19)	(.15)	(.17)	(.15)
Family sum	.87**	.86**	.75**	.77**	.46*	.86*	.41[+]	.62*	.67**
	(.30)	(.33)	(.24)	(.25)	(.23)	(.33)	(.23)	(.27)	(.24)
Attainment sum	.16	−.31	.02	−.20	−.30	−.03	−.42*	.10	−.10
	(.20)	(.24)	(.18)	(.18)	(.18)	(.21)	(.18)	(.20)	(.18)
Constant	−.09	.21	−.77	−.76	−.86	.82	−.77	.69	−.40
	(.65)	(.83)	(.64)	(.63)	(.63)	(.73)	(.60)	(.70)	(.59)
n	524	332	501	514	557	543	546	511	559
X^2, df	14.2, 4	9.0, 4	11.5, 4	13.3, 4	7.4, 4	8.1, 4	12.0, 4	6.8, 4	9.8, 4
p	.01	.06	.02	.01	.12	.09	.02	.15	.04
Pseudo R^2	.02	.02	.02	.02	.01	.01	.01	.02	.02

Note. Unstandardized effects, with standard errors in parentheses.

[+] $p < .10$.

* $p < .05$.

** $p < .01$.

contrast, youth who have left school may be just starting their occupational careers and inclined to view themselves as not entirely an adult around their parents, who may have well-established professional careers. It could also be that the school dropouts—those who start college but don't finish—feel less like an adult (and because these are very numerous, determine the negative coefficient) than those who complete high school and do not go on further.

The analytic sequence reported in tables 7.5 and 7.6 was repeated for one's present roles in tables 7.7 and 7.8. That is, table 7.7 interrelates the individualistic criteria and presently occupied roles (e.g., presently cohabiting or married) with self-perceived adulthood. Being presently married or cohabiting significantly increases the likelihood of reporting feeling entirely like an adult when taking care of the house or apartment (odds ratio = 1.6); this variable also predicts self-perceived adulthood when engaged in recreation, although the overall model is not significant. Also, consistent with the previous tables, currently being a parent is significantly related to feeling entirely like an adult across a wide range of dimensions, including work (odds ratio = 1.6), when engaged in sports (odds ratio = 1.7; equation is not significant), spending time with friends (odds ratio = 1.5; equation is not significant), interacting with parents (odds ratio = 1.6), and most of the time (odds ratio = 1.7; equation is marginally significant, $p = .09$). Thus, specific family-related roles are significantly associated with self-perceived adulthood.

Also, finishing school is negatively related to feeling like an adult when with parents (odds ratio = 0.60) and when at home (odds ratio = 0.60; marginally significant). This is, once again, likely due to students pursuing advanced degrees thinking of themselves as entirely adult, while new graduates just entering labor markets may view themselves as somewhat adult.

With respect to the individualistic criteria, financial independence is positively associated with self-perceived adulthood when with parents (marginally significant, odds ratio = 1.8, $p = .053$). On the one hand, these results make intuitive sense, particularly since financial independence is largely a function of not relying on one's parents for money. Yet these same variables were unrelated to self-perceived adulthood in tables 7.5 and 7.6, suggesting that the statistical significance of this effect is contingent on the model's specification. Personal responsibility is not significantly related to any dimensions of self-perceived adulthood.

Table 7.8 shows the results for the models that replace the transition markers with dummy variables indicating whether all of the family or attainment transitions are currently completed. Financial independence is positively associated with self-perceived adulthood while at work (odds

TABLE 7.7

MODELS OF SELF-PERCEIVED ADULTHOOD, CURRENTLY EXPERIENCED ADULT ROLES, AND INDIVIDUALISTIC CRITERIA: YOUTH DEVELOPMENT STUDY

PREDICTORS	SELF-PERCEIVED ADULTHOOD DIMENSIONS										
	SCHOOL	WORK	COMMUNITY	SPORTS	RECREATION	FRIENDS	HOME	CHILD	PARENTS	PARTNER	MOST OF THE TIME
Financial independence	.32	.49	.00	-.29	-.02	-.12	-.28	.51	.61[+]	.04	.23
	(.71)	(.31)	(.43)	(.31)	(.30)	(.30)	(.36)	(.58)	(.31)	(.34)	(.29)
Personal responsibility	.26	.15	.23	.23	.25	.09	-.00	-.15	-.03	-.07	.20
	(.37)	(.17)	(.21)	(.16)	(.15)	(.15)	(.18)	(.27)	(.15)	(.16)	(.15)
Cohabited/married	.63	.23	.04	-.21	.33[+]	-.03	.47*	-.14	.08	.30	-.04
	(.46)	(.21)	(.25)	(.19)	(.19)	(.19)	(.22)	(.37)	(.18)	(.20)	(.18)
Own, rent	-.65	-.09	-.16	.29	-.22	-.20	.58	.05	-.33	.32	.02
	(.64)	(.32)	(.43)	(.30)	(.29)	(.28)	(.32)	(.68)	(.28)	(.33)	(.28)
Become parent	.94	.45*	.53	.55**	.23	.41*	.37	...	.46*	.38	.52**
	(.59)	(.22)	(.27)	(.20)	(.19)	(.19)	(.23)		(.19)	(.21)	(.19)
Complete school	...	-.34	-.19	-.17	-.28	-.05	-.53[+]	-.07	-.53*	-.14	-.23
		(.26)	(.29)	(.23)	(.22)	(.22)	(.28)	(.50)	(.22)	(.25)	(.22)
Full-time job	.42	.37	.18	.17	.04	-.07	.33	-.02	.07	.07	.09
	(.43)	(.23)	(.28)	(.21)	(.21)	(.20)	(.24)	(.34)	(.20)	(.23)	(.20)
Constant	-.87	-.21	-.10	.84	-.64	-.65	.82	1.34	-.30	.48	-.62
	(1.44)	(.71)	(.88)	(.68)	(.64)	(.64)	(.75)	(1.40)	(.63)	(.73)	(.61)
n	109	559	351	512	547	595	580	223	585	547	596
χ^2, df	8.0, 6	14.9, 7	5.4, 7	11.6, 7	9.4, 7	6.2, 7	17.0, 7	1.3, 6	16.9, 7	10.3, 7	11.9, 7
p	.24	.03	.61	.12	.22	.51	.02	.97	.02	.17	.10
Pseudo R^2	.06	.02	.01	.02	.01	.01	.03	.00	.02	.02	.01

Note. Unstandardized effects, with standard errors in parentheses.

[+] $p < .10$.
* $p < .05$.
** $p < .01$.

TABLE 7.8

MODELS OF SELF-PERCEIVED ADULTHOOD, CURRENTLY EXPERIENCED ADULT ROLE CONFIGURATIONS,

AND INDIVIDUALISTIC CRITERIA: YOUTH DEVELOPMENT STUDY

PREDICTORS	SELF-PERCEIVED ADULTHOOD DIMENSIONS								
	WORK	COMMUNITY	SPORTS	RECREATION	FRIENDS	HOME	PARENTS	PARTNER	MOST OF THE TIME
Financial independence	.64*	.04	-.22	.03	-.16	.08	.63*	.21	.30
	(.29)	(.41)	(.29)	(.28)	(.28)	(.34)	(.30)	(.33)	(.27)
Personal responsibility	.14	.21	.24	.25	.08	-.00	-.02	-.09	.19
	(.16)	(.20)	(.16)	(.15)	(.15)	(.18)	(.14)	(.16)	(.14)
Family sum	.27	.38	.40+	.51*	.31	.60	.32	.56**	.43*
	(.23)	(.27)	(.20)	(.20)	(.19)	(.25)	(.19)	(.22)	(.20)
Attainment sum	-.08	-.07	.08	-.09	-.14	-.14	-.28*	-.02	-.02
	(.20)	(.24)	(.18)	(.18)	(.18)	(.21)	(.17)	(.19)	(.17)
Constant	-.11	-.06	-.75	-.85	-.70	1.11	-.74	.81	-.63
	(.64)	(.79)	(.63)	(.59)	(.59)	(.68)	(.57)	(.66)	(.56)
n	559	351	532	547	595	580	585	547	596
χ^2, df	7.0, 4	2.98, 4	6.6, 4	9.1, 4	3.8, 4	7.0, 4	10.5, 4	8.2, 4	8.1, 4
p	.13	.56	.16	.06	.43	.13	.03	.08	.09
Pseudo R^2	.01	.01	.01	.01	.00	.01	.01	.01	.01

Note. Unstandardized effects, with standard errors in parentheses.

$+p < .10$.

$*p < .05$.

$**p < .01$.

ratio = 1.77; equation insignificant) and with parents (odds ratio = 1.90). The family composite is positively associated with feeling like an adult when engaged in sports and recreation, when with a romantic partner, and most of the time. However, these equations are insignificant or marginally insignificant in their overall fit. Like the results shown in table 7.5, the attainment dummy likewise is significantly, negatively predictive of feeling entirely like an adult with parents.

Thus far, the results suggest that the family transitions are positively, significantly related to feeling entirely like an adult, and this pattern may be stronger for the ever experienced than currently experienced transitions. Can the relative importance of the past and present transitions be tested directly? Because of collinearity, all ten past and present demographic markers cannot be entered into one equation. The composite variables, however, are less strongly related and analyses suggest that collinearity is much less of an issue. The models in tables 7.6 and 7.8 were thus combined such that both past and current family and attainment composites predicted each dimension of self-perceived adulthood. The results (not shown) suggest that ever experiencing the family transitions is decisive in many cases: youth are more likely to report feeling completely like an adult if they have ever experienced all three family-related transitions at work (odds ratio = 2.7), participating in community affairs (odds ratio = 2.2), while exercising (odds ratio = 1.9), while engaged in recreation (odds ratio = 1.8), and most of the time (odds ratio = 1.9), controlling presently experienced roles and past and present attainment transitions. Given small cell sizes (i.e., most youth have never experienced all of the transitions in the past or present), the results should be viewed with caution. Nevertheless, they suggest an interesting possibility for future research: that ever experiencing family-related transitions, regardless of one's present status with respect to those roles, may be important predictors of feeling like an adult.

Do these transitions interact with the individualistic criteria to predict self-perceived adulthood? That is, are youth who have experienced the family transitions and achieved financial independence more likely to view themselves entirely like an adult when compared to youth who have achieved only one? Unfortunately, this is a difficult question to answer because very few young people have achieved all three family transition markers and yet remain financially dependent on their family of origin (four such cases are observed in the sample). Virtually all of the respondents who have achieved the family transitions are financially independent. (This does not mean that the two variables are highly interrelated, since, among those who have not experienced the three markers, a substantial majority is also financially independent.) Similarly, except for one case, all youth who have achieved all three markers report being somewhat or completely personally responsible for their future. Thus, the distributions of the variables do not allow for good tests of interactions among the family transition dummy variable and the individualistic criteria.

DISCUSSION

At what point in life does a young person become an adult? Prior research on "emerging adulthood" suggests that contemporary American youth now rely on individualist criteria (i.e., indicators of emotional, cognitive, and behavioral maturity) to the exclusion of demographic transition markers. Yet that research is based on convenience samples; rarely has this question been considered in a multivariate framework that simultaneously examines the relative importance of individualistic criteria and demographic transition markers; and rarely have youth been asked about their own maturity, experiences, and sense of adulthood. Drawing on a community sample and appropriate methods, our analyses warrant several conclusions.

First, the respondents distinguish among dimensions of self-perceived adulthood. In some respects, youth are quite apt to report feeling entirely like an adult (especially at work, at home, with their children, and with their romantic partner). Yet, in other respects, and, not surprisingly, these same respondents are much less likely to report feeling entirely like an adult (particularly among friends and parents). In situations involving other people that confirm adult roles—with co-workers in the workplace, with one's partner and children at home, with a romantic partner—people are apt to feel entirely like an adult. Parents, in contrast, may still treat adult children as "children," making it hard to get out of the child role. The friends' variable is especially interesting. Presumably, friends would be age-graded, likely the same age, and so mutually struggling with adult status. Perhaps interacting with other youth, with similar doubts or less well-confirmed adult statuses, does not promote or confirm one's own sense of identity. Moreover, young adults may engage in behaviors while with friends that are quite similar to their adolescent pursuits—staying out late, partying, and so forth—that would not confirm an adult identity.

Second, the multivariate models suggest that the family transitions significantly distinguish youth who feel not at all or somewhat like an adult from those that feel entirely like an adult. Youth who have experienced all of the family transitions—establishing an independent household, getting married or cohabiting, and becoming a parent—are typically about twice as likely to report feeling like an adult compared to youth who have not experienced all of these transitions. With respect to one's present roles, it is specific roles—especially being a parent but also cohabiting/married—that make youth feel entirely like an adult.

Third, financial independence significantly, positively predicted self-perceived adulthood. Youth who were financially independent from their families of origin were more likely to view themselves as adults at work and with parents. These results make intuitive sense, since the variable largely refers to independence from parents, which would typically be explained by one's earnings from work. At the same time, these results are sensitive to model specification; with different control variables (namely, the "ever" transition markers as opposed to the "present" transition markers), these effects are no longer significant. Nevertheless, they constitute the sole evidence from this study that the individualistic criteria may be associated with feeling like an adult.

Taken together, these results support the expectation that family transition markers and self-perceived adulthood are interrelated. Nevertheless, care must be exercised in interpreting these results. It may be that stronger support for the individualistic criteria was not obtained because of constrained variability in financial responsibility and personal responsibility. Both variables were skewed, meaning that a very large percentage of respondents were essentially financially independent and accepting of personally responsibility.

The possibility of constrained variability in turn raises two issues. It may be that better measures of these constructs would have yielded greater variability; in turn, the measures might have had stronger relationships with self-perceived adulthood. This is not terribly persuasive with respect to the measure of financial independence, however, which has good validity, reflecting the percentage of living expenses covered by the family of origin. Perhaps the argument has merit for the measure of personal responsibility, an item taken from a standard, widely used scale (the Pearlin Mastery scale). Thus, the relative lack of importance of the individualistic criteria may reflect a methodological artifact. An alternative explanation, however, is that these measures simply reflect reality: financial independence was achieved by the vast majority of respondents, who likewise reported high levels of personal responsibility. In this case, any sensitive, valid instrument would find these patterns. That is, such individualistic factors cannot explain variance in self-perceived adulthood because they simply do not vary sufficiently.[3]

Perhaps such factors are more important in late adolescence and into the early twenties. Or perhaps these criteria are important for "emerging adults" as well, but it is a mistake to think that a sample of youth in their midtwenties are all emerging adults. On the one hand, Arnett (2001) refers to a sample of twenty-one- to twenty-eight-year-olds as "emerging adults." On the other hand, emerging adulthood is defined by exploration of and serious lack of commitment to adult roles and relationships, and these characteristics have never been measured in a study of emerging adults. Perhaps among youth who are appropriately classified as emerging adults—as opposed to being presumed emerging adults because of their age—individualistic criteria are more salient.

An additional caveat to observe when interpreting these results is that the explanatory value of the models is very low. In part, this may reflect an incomplete consideration of the factors that are associated with self-perceived adulthood. For example, it may be that the number of negative life events (e.g., death of a loved one, losing one's job) leads to feeling more adult-like. In part, however, this low explanatory power is likely to reflect constrained variability in the dependent variable, self-perceived adulthood. Given the distributions of the dimensions of self-perceived adulthood, the models attempt to explain how people who view themselves as "somewhat adult" differ from people who viewed themselves as "entirely adult." In reality, such a difference may be substantively quite small and unimportant (i.e., of little consequence to the respondents themselves), due to idiosyncratic considerations that are poorly understood, or a combination of these factors.

Once again, there are two possible ways to evaluate this constrained variability. Perhaps it reflects poor measurement. This is a difficult argument to assess because so few attempts have been made to measure this construct with survey data. In the alternative, perhaps any measure would yield this result, reflecting the fact that most youth view themselves as at least somewhat of an adult by age twenty-five or twenty-six.[4]

Nevertheless, in this sample, the family transition markers are the most consistent predictors of self-perceived adulthood. Given limitations of measurement and design, we acknowledge that individualistic criteria may be important as well: Adult status is likely based on a combination of personal qualities and social roles. As historians and anthropologists suggest, such has always and everywhere been the case, and the current cohorts coming of age in the United States are not likely to be an exception. Future research can build on this study and prior research by studying representative samples, by employing appropriate multivariate techniques, by improving measures of the individualistic criteria, and by actually assessing issues of exploration and commitment, which determine whether youth are in fact "emerging adults."

TABLE 7.AI

MEASUREMENT OF SUBJECTIVE AGE IDENTITY VARIABLES

Young people often feel more or less like "an adult" in different situations or areas of their lives. We would like to know more about your experience of becoming an adult. In answering the following questions, please consider how you usually feel in these situations and place an "X" in the appropriate box.

	NOT AT ALL LIKE AN ADULT	SOMEWHAT LIKE AN ADULT	ENTIRELY LIKE AN ADULT	DOES NOT APPLY
When I am at school				
When I am at work				
When I am participating in a community organization (civic, religious, etc.)				
When I am doing active sports or exercising				
When I am involved in other recreational activities (going to a museum, concert, sports event, etc.)				
When I am with my friends				
When I am taking care of my house/apartment				
When I am with my child/children				
When I am with my parent(s)				
When I am with a romantic partner				
Most of the time				

NOTES

This chapter draws on data from the Youth Development Study, which is supported by grants (titled "Work Experience and Mental Health: A Panel Study of Youth") from the National Institute of Child Health and Human Development (HD44138) and the National Institute of Mental Health (MH42843).

1. Indeed, Modell (1998) suggests that emerging adulthood is a "cultural-political" construction that has been devised by contemporary behavioral scientists to create a youth that resonates with the ethos of the times—including volition, subjectivity, and pluralism—in much the same way that Kenneth Keniston (1968) created a youth for the 1960s and 1970s.

2. In creating this variable, two cases were deleted from the analysis because the summed percentages did not equal 100.

3. Indeed, the personal responsibility item appears to be constrained in its variability across adolescence and young adulthood. The Youth Development Study asked the same question in wave 4 (ages seventeen to eighteen) and wave 8 (ages twenty-one to twenty-two). The distribution of this item hardly changed across the years, with means of 3.43 in wave 4, 3.48 in wave 8, and 3.45 in wave 10. That is, at least in this sample, this item has always been skewed. A similar pattern is observed in the National Longitudinal Survey of Youth (NLSY) among non-Hispanic whites, although this trend is observed among a somewhat older group than the Youth Development Study's respondents.

4. In fact, wave 3 of the National Longitudinal Study of Adolescent Health Add Health data set asks respondents, "How often do you think of yourself as an adult?" Responses ranged from 0 = never to 4 = all of the time. Among non-Hispanic whites who were twenty-six-years-old, none of the youth reported "never" and 4.3% reported "seldom." Almost 96% of these twenty-six-year-olds view themselves as adults at least sometimes. Thus, an analysis of nationally representative data comparable to those used in this study also yields a skewed distribution.

REFERENCES

Arnett, Jeffrey Jensen. 1994. Are College Students Adults? Their Conceptions of the Transition to Adulthood. *Journal of Adult Development* 1:213–24.

———. 1997. Young People's Conceptions of the Transition to Adulthood. *Youth and Society* 29:3–23.

———. 1998. Learning to Stand Alone: The Contemporary American Transition to Adulthood in Cultural and Historical Context. *Human Development* 41: 295–315.

———. 2000. Emerging Adulthood: A Theory of Development from the Late Teens through the Twenties. *American Psychologist* 55:469–80.

———. 2001. *Adolescence and Emerging Adulthood: A Cultural Approach.* Upper Saddle River, NJ: Prentice Hall.

———. 2003. Conceptions of the Transition to Adulthood among Emerging Adults in American Ethnic Groups. Pp. 63–75 in *Exploring Cultural Conceptions of the Transition to Adulthood,* edited by Jeffrey Jensen Arnett and Nancy Galambos. New Directions for Child and Adolescent Development, vol. 100. San Francisco: Jossey-Bass.

Arnett, Jeffrey Jensen, and Susan Taber. 1994. Adolescence Terminable and Interminable: When Does Adolescence End? *Journal of Youth and Adolescence* 23: 517–37.

Casper, Lynne M., and Suzanne M. Bianchi. 2002. *Continuity and Change in the American Family.* Thousand Oaks, CA: Sage.

Côtè, James E. 2000. *Arrested Adulthood: The Changing Nature of Maturity and Identity.* New York: New York University Press.

Freedman, Deborah, Arland Thornton, Donald Camburn, Duane Alwin, and Linda Young-DeMarco. 1988. The Life History Calendar: A Technique for Collecting Retrospective Data. *Sociological Methodology* 18:37–68.

Grabowski, Lori J. S., Kathleen T. Call, and Jeylan T. Mortimer. 2001. Global and Economic Self-sufficiency in the Educational Attainment Process. *Social Psychology Quarterly* 64:164–79.

Greene, A. L., Susan M. Wheatley, and John F. Aldava IV. 1992. Stages on Life's Way: Adolescents' Implicit Theories of the Life Course. *Journal of Adolescent Research* 7:364–81.

Keniston, Kenneth. 1968. *Young Radicals: Notes on Committed Youth.* New York: Harcourt, Brace & World.

Modell, John. 1998. Responsibility and Self-respect: How Alone Do Americans Stand? *Human Development* 41:316–20.

Mortimer, Jeylan T., and Pamela Aronson. 2001. Adulthood. Pp. 25–41 in *Encyclopedia of Sociology,* edited by Edgar Borgatta and Rhonda J. V. Montgomery. 2d ed.. New York: Macmillan.

Mortimer, Jeylan T., Michael Finch, Michael Shanahan, and Seongryeol Ryu. 1992. Adolescent Work History and Behavioral Adjustment. *Journal of Research on Adolescence* 2 (1):25–57.

Neugarten, Bernice L., Joan W. Moore, and John C. Lowe. 1965. Age Norms, Age Constraints, and Adult Socialization. *American Journal of Sociology* 70: 710–17.

Neugarten, Dail A., ed. 1996. *The Meanings of Age: Selected Papers of Bernice L. Neugarten.* Chicago: University of Chicago Press.

Scheer, Scott D., and Rob Palkovitz. 1994. Adolescent-to-Adult Transitions: Social Status and Cognitive Factors. *Sociological Studies of Children* 6:125–40.

Schlegel, Alice. 1998. The Social Criteria of Adulthood. *Human Development* 41:323–25.

Settersten, Richard A., Jr. 2003. Age Structuring and the Rhythm of the Life Course. Pp. 81–98 in *Handbook of the Life Course,* edited by Jeylan Mortimer and Michael J. Shanahan. New York: Kluwer Academic/Plenum Publishers.

Settersten, Richard A., Jr., and Gunhild Hagestad. 1996. What's the Latest? Cultural Age Deadlines for Family Transitions. *Gerontologist* 36:178–88.

Shanahan, Michael J. 2000. Pathways to Adulthood in Changing Societies: Variability and Mechanisms in Life Course Perspective. *Annual Review of Sociology* 26:667–92.

CHAPTER 8

SEQUENCES OF EARLY
ADULT TRANSITIONS

A Look at Variability and Consequences

TED MOUW

The transition from adolescence to adulthood is "demographically dense" (Rindfuss 1991) in that it involves a number of significant demographic transitions: leaving home, finishing school, starting work, getting married, and becoming a parent. The evidence suggests that over the first half of the twentieth century the transition to adulthood became more age stratified and occurred over a shorter period of time (Buchman 1989; Shanahan 2000). Recent evidence, however, suggests that since 1970 it has taken birth cohorts longer to achieve these demographic markers of adulthood (Buchman 1989). Stevens (1990) uses synthetic cohorts constructed from decennial census data to find the age difference between the time 25% and 75% of a cohort have achieved a particular adult transition. He finds that the time it took the twenty-fifth through seventy-fifth percentiles to achieve the transitions declined from 1900 to 1960 and that the transitions were more likely to happen at the same time. Importantly, his data suggest that these trends had begun to reverse in 1980. In addition, some authors have argued that the pathways to "adulthood" have become more diverse and disordered as the age at which individuals finish school, find stable employment, get married, and have children has increased and the sequential order in which these things occur has become less predictable (Buchman 1989; Rindfuss, Swicegood, and Rosenfeld 1987). The popular image of the "Generation X" twenty-something living a prolonged adolescence by delaying serious employment and family responsibility gained widespread currency in the 1990s and lends credence and imagery to the raw demographic data suggesting a delayed and chaotic path toward adulthood. One suspects, however, that every adult generation expresses public concern (or consternation) about the presumed inability of the next generation to live up to itself.

In this chapter I use longitudinal data from the 1979 National Longitudinal Survey of Youth (NLSY) to address two sets of questions. In the first part of the chapter, I focus on determining how many different pathways to adulthood there are and whether the transition has become less structured over time. I ask whether the transition to adulthood can be characterized by diverse pathways and is "disordered" compared to some normative sequence of events. Despite the valuable evidence that can be obtained from repeated cross-sectional surveys, such as the decennial census (Stevens 1990), only longitudinal data can really indicate the sequence of steps through which individuals become adults.

The second question is whether the different pathways affect adult outcomes. Does the mutual timing of the individual transitions contribute anything to our understanding of adult outcomes? In other words, does the timing of individual transitions, such as the age at first birth, leaving home, or starting work have an additive effect on adult outcomes—in which case the sequence does not matter—or are there significant interaction effects among the timing of these transitions? In order to answer this question, I test whether the pathways to adulthood identified in the first part of the chapter are correlated with adult outcomes even after controlling for relevant background factors and the additive effect of the timing of the individual adult transitions.

METHOD

I use life-history data for those aged twenty-two to thirty-five from the 1979–98 waves of the National Longitudinal Survey of Youth (NLSY79). The NLSY79 is an annual (biannual after 1994) survey of 12,685 individuals who were between fourteen and twenty-two years old in 1979. I use responses for all respondents who were at least thirty-five years old in 1998 (i.e., those who were between sixteen and twenty-two in 1979) and were interviewed in each survey year between the ages of twenty-two and thirty-five.[1] This results in a sample of 5,464 respondents with complete life-history data from the age of twenty-two to thirty-five.[2] The demographic transitions I analyze here are

(1) not living in the same household with parents, (2) completing full-time schooling, (3) starting full-time work, (4) marriage, and (5) having children. I could define "adulthood" as the point at which one has achieved each of these states. However, despite the fact that these are common indicators of adulthood, I make no normative evaluation about what adulthood actually means. If anything, I would argue that adulthood is better understood as the completion of the nonfamilial transitions of leaving home, finishing school, and finding work. Taking the endpoint of the process of becoming an adult to be the arbitrary but reasonable age of thirty-five, I attempt to determine the interrelationships among the different demographic transitions mentioned above and assess the degree to which there are multiple pathways or sequences of transitions that seem to be particularly salient. Certainly, by the age of thirty-five one is an "adult" whether one has achieved all of these demographic transitions (and whether or not, in our youth-oriented culture, one is willing to admit to being an adult).

WHAT IS THE SEQUENCE OF THE TRANSITION TO ADULTHOOD?

One of the advantages of longitudinal data is that it makes it possible to study movement in and out of "adult" states. For example, while repeated cross-sectional data can determine the percentage of a cohort who live with their parents at particular points in time, only longitudinal data can reveal whether individuals who leave home return to live with their parents at a later date. Table 8.1 depicts the transition variables used in this chapter, and

TABLE 8.1

VARIABLE NAMES AND DEFINITIONS

VARIABLE NAME	DEFINITIONS
Pa	Currently not living with parents.
P	Completed transition from parental home: not currently living with parents and does not live with parents from current age to age 35.
Ea	Not currently enrolled in school.
E	Competed schooling: does not return to school from current age to age 35.
L	Full-time employment: respondent or respondent's spouse worked at least 1,500 hours during the year.
Ma	Currently married.
M	Ever married.
B	First birth: has had at least one child.

TABLE 8.2

PERCENTAGE OF MEN COMPLETING TRANSITION, BY AGE

AGE	PA	*P*	EA	*E*	*L*	MA	*M*	*B*
22	53.3	37.0	77.0	61.6	54.6	23.1	23.1	19.3
23	62.1	46.4	83.7	67.9	64.0	30.1	32.0	24.2
24	67.9	53.7	88.2	72.9	70.6	36.7	39.8	29.5
25	75.4	61.4	89.2	77.0	75.7	42.6	47.3	33.5
26	78.6	66.1	91.4	81.1	79.3	47.6	53.7	38.6
27	81.3	71.1	94.4	84.6	80.8	52.2	59.5	43.0
28	84.5	74.9	95.0	86.6	84.0	55.3	64.2	48.2
29	86.7	78.1	95.7	88.8	85.3	59.0	68.1	53.0
30	87.5	80.4	95.9	90.5	85.7	61.1	71.2	56.7
31	87.4	82.3	95.7	92.3	85.0	62.2	73.1	59.5
32	89.0	85.0	96.6	94.0	86.0	63.3	75.3	62.3
33	89.1	86.9	96.6	95.4	86.6	64.1	77.2	64.5
34	89.6	88.7	97.3	96.8	88.2	64.9	78.5	66.5
35	90.5	90.5	97.8	97.8	89.0	65.4	79.6	67.6

Note. See Table 8.1 for definitions of variables.

tables 8.2 and 8.3 present basic data on the percentage of men and women in the NLSY79 who had completed these transitions between the ages of twenty-two and thirty-five. For reversible variables such as leaving home, enrollment in school, and marital status, I have included two measures: a variable indicating the current status of the transition, and a second variable showing whether the transition is "permanent" in the sense that the respondent remains in that state until the age of thirty-five. For example, from table 8.1 we see that the variable Pa indicates whether the respondent is living with his or her parents at a particular point in time, while the variable *P* indicates the age at which the respondent has completed this transition (i.e., he or she does not subsequently return to the parents' household). In table 8.2, Pa is 53.5% for twenty-two-year-old males and *P* is 37.2%. The difference between the current measure of not living with parents, Pa, and the completed transition measure, *P*, indicates that 16.2% of the 53.5% of men not living with their parents at the age of twenty-two return home at some point before the age of thirty-five. Clearly there is a difference between the age at which individuals first leave home and the age at which they permanently establish their own independent household. This means that if we focus exclusively on cross-sectional data, we will overestimate the rate at which reversible adult transitions—such as leaving home, finishing school, and getting married—have been completed.

TABLE 8.3

PERCENTAGE OF WOMEN COMPLETING TRANSITION, BY AGE

AGE	PA	P	EA	E	L	MA	M	B
22	64.7	48.8	81.9	59.8	59.8	38.5	38.5	36.2
23	73.7	57.9	87.2	66.1	66.7	44.2	47.2	41.2
24	78.9	64.1	89.7	70.1	75.0	48.1	53.5	45.7
25	82.7	70.2	91.1	73.4	77.5	52.1	59.9	50.0
26	85.8	74.8	91.1	75.7	78.7	55.4	64.7	55.3
27	87.2	78.2	92.8	79.4	79.5	58.7	69.1	59.1
28	88.4	80.9	94.7	82.1	82.4	61.4	72.3	62.7
29	90.1	83.9	95.3	84.0	82.7	63.1	75.2	65.4
30	91.9	86.3	95.0	86.0	82.9	63.6	77.5	68.8
31	92.2	88.2	95.2	88.5	83.8	65.1	79.5	72.0
32	92.9	89.9	95.0	90.6	83.9	65.7	81.0	74.6
33	93.0	91.1	95.3	92.6	85.3	66.0	81.9	75.8
34	92.9	92.3	95.8	94.2	85.5	65.8	82.9	77.1
35	93.6	93.6	95.2	95.2	86.1	66.4	83.9	78.4

Note. See Table 8.1 for definitions of variables.

Even with the added insight on reversible transitions from longitudinal data, the basic results from tables 8.2 and 8.3 are not surprising. Tables 8.2 and 8.3 show that men leave home earlier than women do (Pa and P are higher for men than women for each age), but even using the restrictive notion of completing this transition, P, 75% of men and women have left their parents' home by age twenty-seven and twenty-eight, respectively. Next, comparison of tables 8.2 and 8.3 shows that women complete their education sooner than men do. Interestingly, education is a variable where there is a substantial difference between current enrollment (Ea) and transition completion (E): 91.1% of women are out of school at the age of twenty-five, but 26.6% will enroll in school again before the age of thirty-five (73.4% will not enroll). This seems to capture the increasing tendency of individuals to return to school for additional education; provided this return to school in the late twenties does not substantially delay the familial transitions of marriage and childbirth, this would indicate one way in which the life course is becoming increasingly diverse as familial and nonfamilial transitions overlap in nontraditional ways. The final nonfamilial transition, full-time work (L), indicates whether the respondent, or the respondent's spouse, worked at least 1,500 hours during the interview year. Similar to Pa and Ea, the data for both men and women show a rapid transition to economic independence for the majority of respondents; 75% of men and women are working full time (or supported by a full-time spouse) by twenty-four to twenty-five. At first glance, the relationship between leaving home, finishing school, and full-time employment seems consistent with the conventional notion of the transition to adulthood. I will have more to say on this issue when considering the relationship between these transitions in detail.

Compared to leaving home, finishing school, and starting work, the familial transitions of marriage and childbirth occur at later ages, and both the male and female cohorts pass through these transitions slowly. Table 8.2 shows that only 65.4% of men are married at the age of thirty-five (Ma) and only 79.6% have ever been married (M). A higher percentage of women marry in their early twenties than men (38.5% are married at age twenty-two vs. 23.1% of men), but the male/female gap shrinks over time. The timing of first birth—the final transition to adulthood according to the traditional modal sequence—occurs last and has the most "spread" in terms of the interquartile range of cohort progression (i.e., the age difference between the twenty-fifth and seventy-fifth percentiles). While tables 8.2 and 8.3 depict the basic rate of transition through each of these adult statuses, a similar picture could be obtained from repeated cross-sectional data sets, such as the census, either by following cohorts over time (Fussell and Furstenberg, this vol., chap. 2) or by constructing synthetic cohorts from each census year (Stevens 1990). The advantage of longitudinal data is that it allows us to inspect the relationship between the timing of these events for individuals, which is what we turn to next.

The remainder of this section describes the relationship between the timing of these five adult transitions. Figures 8.1–8.5 visually depict the relationship between the timing of pairs of transitions for groups of individuals who experienced one of the transitions at a certain same age. Next, I look at the sequential order of the adult transitions between the ages of twenty-two to thirty-five and compare the NLSY data to illustrative data from the 1950s (Marini 1984). Finally, I utilize a clustering algorithm to categorize the life-history data into groups. I show that this algorithm may be useful in comparative analysis of whether the "paths" to adulthood have changed or become less ordered over time.

Figures 8.1–8.5: Transition Timing for Pairs of Events

While tables 8.2 and 8.3 depict the timing of individual transitions for men and women, they do not tell us anything about the relationship between timing of other transitions. For instance, the normative relationship between marriage and childbirth suggests that birth of one's first child is not just age dependent, as depicted in tables 8.2 and 8.3 but also contingent on marriage. To what degree does the NLSY cohort follow the "normative" pattern of marriage and childbirth? Figures 8.1–8.5 allow us to investigate these sequential relationships in detail. For each of the demographic events, I have selected three groups of individuals who experienced the transition at different ages and graphed the proportion of each group that has achieved the other transitions for ages twenty-two to thirty-five.

The easy way to read these graphs is to recognize that a lot of space between the lines on the graph indicates a relationship between the timing of the two transitions. For example, in figure 8.1 I have graphed individuals who left home (P) at the age of twenty-three (462 cases from table 8.4) and twenty-eight (191 cases) and those who were still living with their parents at the age of thirty-five (545 cases). Evidence that the timing of leaving home is associated with making one of the other transitions at different ages would be represented by the separation between the graphs of the three groups. Figure 8.1D shows the proportion currently married (Ma). The strong association suggested in table 8.4 between age of leaving home and marriage is evident again in figure 8.1D as the separation between the lines indicates a sharply demarcated effect of leaving home on the probability of marriage. The proportion of the first group (those who left home at twenty-three) who are married jumps significantly at twenty-three, and the proportion of the second group (who left home at twenty-eight) who are married increases substantially at twenty-eight and twenty-nine years old. In figure 8.1E, a similar effect is apparent for group 2 on childbirth, as B increases from about 0.35 to about 0.6 between the ages of twenty-seven and twenty-nine. In contrast, among those who are still living at home by age thirty-five, the proportion of individuals who have had children is higher than that of group 1 and group 2 until the midtwenties. Finally, there is some separation between the three groups for figure 8.1B and 8.1C, which shows that although the median age may be fairly similar, there is a relationship between the age of leaving home and the upper percentiles of the other two nonfamilial transitions. For example, although the median age for full-time work is similar for the three groups, full-time work is nearly universal for groups 1 ($P = 23$) and 2 ($P = 28$) by the age of thirty, but only 90% or so of those still living with their parents at thirty-five are working by the age of thirty.

Figure 8.2 shows the relationship between completing education at ages twenty-three, twenty-six, and thirty and the timing of the other transitions. The smaller effect of E versus P on the median age at marriage is evi-

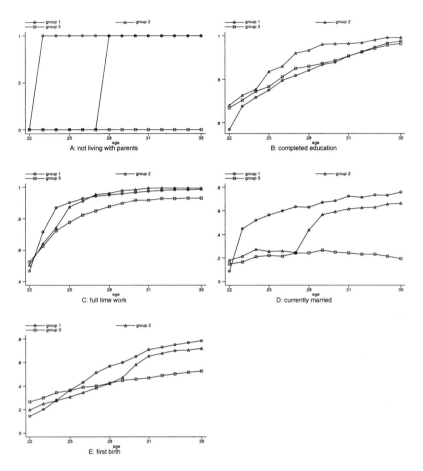

Figure 8.1. Timing of transitions by age of leaving home. Group 1 = left home at age 23; group 2 = left home at age 27; group 3 = living with parents at age 35. *A,* Not living with parents; *B,* completed education; *C,* full-time work; *D,* currently married; *E,* first birth.

dent in a comparison of figures 8.1*D* and 8.2*D.* While figure 8.1*D* shows clearly demarcated jumps, figure 8.2*D* shows little separation between the three groups. In contrast, a stronger relationship is evident between *E* and *B* in figure 8.2*E.* In figure 8.2*E,* however, the paths cross, making interpretation more complicated: individuals who did not complete their education until the age of thirty were more likely to have had children between ages twenty-two and twenty-six, while a higher proportion of those who finished their education at age twenty-three had become parents by age twenty-eight.

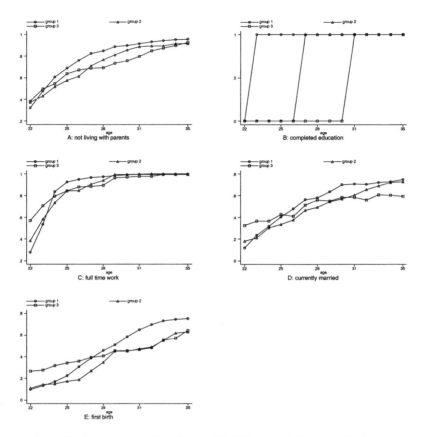

Figure 8.2. Timing of transitions by age of finishing school. Group 1 = finished school at age 23; group 2 = finished school at age 26; group 3 = finished school at age 29. *A*, Not living with parents; *B*, completed education; *C*, full-time work; *D*, currently married; *E*, first birth.

In other words, while table 8.2 documents a linear effect (b = .153, *p* < .001), figure 8.2*E* suggests a more complicated relationship between leaving school and childbirth.

Figure 8.3 depicts the transition rates for individuals who started full-time work at age twenty-three (group 1, 807 cases), those who started at twenty-seven (group 2, 123 cases), and those who had not worked full-time by the age of thirty-five (group 3, 197 cases). Several interesting relationships are evident. First, there is a lot of separation among the three groups in figure 8.3*A*, with a clear jump apparent for group 2 between ages twenty-six and twenty-nine. This suggests that leaving home and working are clearly temporally related even if the sequential order may not be clear (i.e., the increase in the proportion not living with parents between age twenty-six and twenty-seven for group 2 may indicate that *P* and *L* occurred simultaneously, while the large jump between twenty-eight and twenty-nine indicates that *P* occurred after the respondent started full-time work). Second, in figure 8.3*B* there appears to be a relationship between timing of work and completing education—at least prior to the age of twenty-seven to twenty-eight, when the three lines coincide. Third, in figure 8.3*D* the effect on marriage seems similar to the effect noted in figure 8.1*D*; that is, there is evidence of a linear effect of the timing of *L* and marriage. Finally, the effect of working on childbirth appears to be more complicated in figure 8.3*E*. At least on the basis of

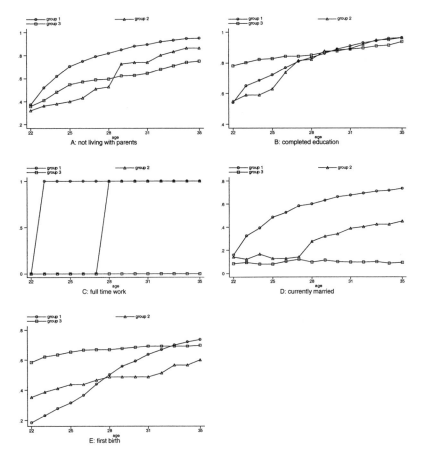

Figure 8.3. Timing of transitions by age of starting full-time work (*L*). Group 1 = *L* at age 23; group 2 = *L* at age 27; group 3 = *L* > 35. *A*, Not living with parents; *B*, completed education; *C*, full-time work; *D*, currently married; *E*, first birth.

these three groups, there is a clear negative relationship between the age of beginning work and the proportion of men and women that have had a child (i.e., $B = 1$) between twenty-two and twenty-five. However, this initial negative relationship becomes complicated as the proportion of group 1 (started work at age twenty-three) that has had a child increases rapidly with age, while the slopes for the other groups are fairly flat; among the 197 individuals in group 3 who do not start work by the age of thirty-five, almost all of them who have children have had at least one child by the age of twenty-two, while the opposite is the case for group 1.

Figures 8.4 and 8.5 show the effects of familial transitions (marriage and childbirth) on the timing of other transitions. Figure 8.4—the timing of

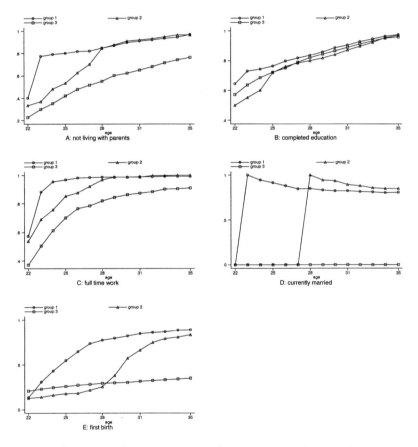

Figure 8.4. Timing of transitions by age at first marriage (M). Group 1 = M at age 23; group 2 = M at age 28; group 3 = $M > 35$. A, Not living with parents; B, completed education; C, full-time work; D, currently married; E, first birth.

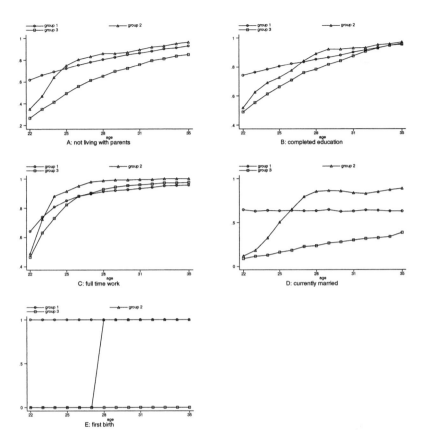

Figure 8.5. Timing of transitions by age at first birth (*B*). Group 1 = *B* ≤ 22; group 2 = *B* at age 28; group 3 = *B* > 35. *A*, Not living with parents; *B*, completed education; *C*, full-time work; *D*, currently married; *E*, first birth.

first marriage for those who married at twenty-three, those who married at twenty-eight, and those who did not marry by age thirty-five—shows more "separation" among the trajectories of the other transitions than any of the other graphs. We can see the relationship between leaving home, working full time, and the timing of first births and the age at first marriage. Figure 8.4*A*, for example, shows that in group 1 (married at twenty-three) there is a big jump in the proportion of individuals who leave home between twenty-two and twenty-three. A similar jump is apparent for group 2 (married at age twenty-eight), although the size of the marriage-induced jump is smaller. In addition to sharply demarcated changes in the proportion in adult states associated with the timing of marriage, there is evidence of sustained differences in the years prior to the event. Individuals who eventually get married at twenty-eight make a more rapid transition to establish their own residence (fig. 8.4*A*) to work (fig. 8.4*C*) prior to the age of twenty-eight than those who are unmarried by thirty-five. Finally, figure 8.4*E* shows a substantial relationship between marriage and childbirth. Although the proportion of individuals in all three groups who have children prior to marriage is notable, the overall pattern of figure 8.4*E* clearly suggests that the modal pattern is marriage before childbirth. Indeed, the results in figure 8.5*D* are also consistent with this pattern, as marriage rates for individuals who gave birth at the age of twenty-seven rises substantially between the ages of twenty-two and twenty-seven.

Overall, the descriptive information on the relationship between the different adult transitions presented in figures 8.1–8.5 is an important addition to the basic information on the timing of the transitions depicted in tables 8.2 and 8.3. One advantage of these graphs is that the type of relationship between the transitions is visibly apparent. One can see the difference between a sharp transition, such as the relationship between leaving home and getting married (fig. 8.1*D*), and a gradual one, such as the relationship between marriage and full-time work (fig. 8.4*C*). However, while these graphs provide useful insights into the temporal nature of the relationships among the transitions, the amount of information can be overwhelming. In order to test hypotheses about the "orderliness" of the sequences of transitions, we need to reduce the complexity of the data. In the next two parts of this chapter, I attempt to compress the information inherent in these individual life histories in order to determine the number of pathways that exist in the transition to adulthood and the degree to which the transition is ordered or disordered.

Descriptive Analysis of Sequences

How many pathways are there to adulthood? To what degree does the transition to adulthood follow a standard sequence of transitions? One way to answer these questions is simply to look at the order in which the transitions occurred. For instance, we might imagine that leaving home, finishing school, finding work, getting married, and having children is the normative or standard life-course sequence. This sequence can be represented as *P, E, L, M, B* based on the transition variables described in table 8.1. Notice that this sequence ignores the age of the events and just focuses on their relative ordering. In other words, it compresses the age-specific event history information depicted in figures 8.1–8.5 into a single sequence for each individual. Someone who leaves home at twenty-two but completes the other transitions in normative order at the age of thirty is represented by the same sequence as someone who completes them all in order at the age of twenty-three.

Previous research on the sequence of transitions to adulthood has been limited by lack of available longitudinal data. Most empirical studies have used repeated cross-sectional datasets, such as the decennial census. Marini (1984) and Rindfuss and colleagues (1987) both analyze life-course sequences. Marini analyzes the relative sequences of events as suggested above, while Rindfuss and colleagues (1987, 789) measure the life-history sequences as the time spent in each state. I focus on the relative sequence of events in this section and discuss the complete life-history approach of Rindfuss and colleagues in the next.

First, we will compare the frequency of the standard pattern of transitions to evidence from an earlier survey of a cohort that went through their twenties in the 1960s. Marini (1984) describes the sequencing patterns of transitions for a cohort of individuals from ten Illinois high schools in 1957–58 who were interviewed in a follow-up survey fifteen years later in 1973–74. Marini (1984) studies four transitions: finishing education, starting work (defined as the first full-time job held for at least six months), first marriage, and childbirth. She finds that the sequence *E, L, M, B* occurs 40.4% of the time for women and 37.7% of the time for men. The next largest category (*L, E, M, B*) was experienced by 7% of women and 11.6% of men. In other words, in data from a cohort that made the transition to adulthood in the 1960s, there is substantial evidence that there was a standard pathway to adulthood, one that was experienced by a substantial percentage of the cohort.

Table 8.4 shows the results for a similar analysis using the NLSY79 data for ages twenty-two to thirty-five for the top thirty sequences. Sixty-two sequences were observed in the data (allowing for ties and transitions that did not occur by age thirty-five). For each of the sequences listed in this table, the numbers refer to the position in which the transitions occurred, for *E, L, M,* and *B*, in that order. For example, the sequence 1234 corresponds to the normative ordering of events, while the sequence 4321 would mean that the events occurred in reverse order (*B, M, L,* and *E*). One difficulty in reconciling my results with Marini's is that I only know the year in which a particular event occurred, so ties are possible. For instance, if all the events occurred at the age of twenty-three, the sequence would be "1111." Table 8.4 shows that the normative sequence "1234" occurs only 2.9% of the time among men and 2.4% of the time among women. To make these results consistent with Marini's, I combine all the possible sequences that could be "1234" if we had continuous time data. To do this, I resolve all ties in favor of the normative

TABLE 8.4

THE 30 MOST PREVALENT TRANSITION SEQUENCES,

BY GENDER

RANK	SEQUENCE E, L, M, B	MALE %	FEMALE %
1	1111	7.7	13.5
2	1134	7.2	5.1
3	1114	4.6	5.5
4	12..	6.4	2.6
5	1141	4.5	3.2
6	13.1	2.2	4.2
7	4111	1.8	4.4
8	1411	3.0	3.0
9	11..	3.6	2.0
10	1234	2.9	2.4
11	21..	2.6	2.6
12	113	3.1	1.6
13	123	2.8	1.4
14	1133	2.4	1.3
15	1341	1.7	1.9
16	1331	1.3	2.3
17	1..1	.9	2.5
18	11.1	1.8	1.5
19	1143	2.3	.9
20	11.3	1.6	1.4
21	2134	1.4	1.4
22	1224	1.6	1.0
23	312	1.0	1.4
24	111	.9	1.4
25	4123	1.5	.8
26	4113	.9	1.2
27	12.3	1.2	.8
28	4311	.9	1.1
29	3114	.6	1.2
30	1...	1.1	.6
31	All other	24.7	25.7

Note. Sequence refers to the timing in which the events *E, L, M, B*
occurred.

"." Indicates that the event has not occurred by age 35.

sequence. For example, "1111" could be "1234," so I add it to the "1234" total. If I do this for men and women, then 28.7% of women and 25% of men have the sequence "1234."[3] Of course, this must be taken as an upper bound, as I have combined sequences that are consistent with the *E, L, M, B,* even though they may not be. Nevertheless, a comparison with Marini's results shows that the percentage of individuals who follow this path to adulthood has certainly declined from the 1960s to the 1980s. 37%–40% followed the modal path in Marini's cohort compared with a maximum of 25%–29% in the NLSY79 data. In other words, this suggests that there has been a breakdown in the normative ordering of adult transitions and that the young adult life course has become more diverse or disordered since 1960. This would lend credence to the over-time cross-sectional data that suggests that the age congruity of the timing of adult transitions has decreased since the 1960s (e.g., Stevens 1990).

However, it turns out that it is difficult to make definitive statements about the sequencing patterns. Of primary concern here is the possibility that adding an irrelevant (or substantively uninteresting) transition multiplies the complexity of the data and makes it less likely that a single sequence will represent the data. For example, if we added a fifth transition to this data that occurred randomly between the ages of twenty-two and thirty-five then the sequences 12345, 2341, 13452, 12453, and 12354 may all be substantively equivalent but they would appear in the raw data as independent sequences. A related difficulty might be whether we care about the relative ordering of any pair of transitions. For instance, if someone starts working full time while in college, resulting in a "2134" sequence rather than "1234," is this really a nonnormative sequence? I would argue that it is not. What about "4111" which is working, marriage, and childbirth all in the same year, followed by leaving home? This pattern corresponds to 1.8% of males and 4.4% of females. I would argue that the raw sequence data presented in table 8.4 is useful for a comparison of the relative frequency of the modal category—school, work, marriage and childbirth—but its validity rests on the assumption that similar sequences actually represent different pathways. In addition, it is difficult to suggest how many "pathways" to adulthood exist without reducing or editing the data in some way.

In other words, given that sixty-two sequences were observed with this data, we need to reduce the data to a manageable size by combining substantively similar sequences in order to produce a table of sequences representing genuinely different pathways to adulthood. Otherwise it is difficult to distinguish between apparent disorder in the life course (aside from the

13.5% of women in "1111" in table 8.4, no single sequence represents more than 7% of the sample) and the possibility that a large number of similar pathways have simply divided the sample between them (i.e., the six sequences that are consistent with the normative ordering "1234" in n. 4 below). In general, as the number of transitions increases, the complexity of the observed sequences increases rapidly. Sequence analysis (Abbott 1995; Abbott and Tsay 2000) attempts to make sense of complex patterns in the data by clustering similar sequences together, where the number of additions, deletions, or insertions it would take to transform one sequence into another determines the degree of similarity between sequences. For the sequence data in table 8.4, for instance, we could define the difference between two sequences to be the absolute value of the difference in the ranking order of each position. The difference between "1234" and "2134" would be 2 ($|1 - 2| + |2 - 1|$). If we calculated the "difference" between all sequences, we could cluster sequences together one at a time by taking the least prevalent sequence and aggregating it to the sequence that was the most similar to it. We could then repeat this process of absorbing the least likely sequence into a neighboring sequence until we were left with a manageable number of sequences.

While sequence analysis seems like a useful method to analyze the existence of pathways to adulthood, it has yet to be convincingly applied to social science data (Abbott and Tsay 2000; Levine 2001). A basic criticism is that the rules used to calculate the similarity or difference between pairs of sequences—and hence to cluster them together—are arbitrary (Wu 2000). To the degree that slightly different rules result in substantively different clusters, the results of sequence analysis may be misleading. Moreover, the complexity involved in specifying how sequences are similar to each other means that the process may not be transparent to the reader. Modified forms of sequence analysis may well turn out to enjoy widespread use in sociology (Abbott and Tsay 2000)—and similar techniques modeled after data-mining algorithms already in use in other fields seem promising (Billari, Furnkranz, and Prskawetz 2000). Indeed, as a form of descriptive analysis I do not have any qualms about sequence analysis, provided that clustering rules can be made transparent to the reader. However, I believe that the specific questions posed by this book—How many pathways to adulthood are there? How well does the observed data fit these pathways?—call for a slightly different approach. In the next part of the chapter, I discuss and apply an alternative clustering method that can classify life histories in a small number of steps.

A Monothetic Divisive Algorithm for the Analysis of Life-History Data

As discussed above, sequence analysis clusters sequences together in order to provide a basic typology. Sequence analysis is a "ground-up"—or agglomerative—clustering algorithm because it groups individual sequences together into larger groups. As such, many sequences must be combined to result in manageable groups. For example, Rindfuss, Swicegood, and Rosenfeld (1987) study life-history data for five different states (working, in school, homemaker, military, and other) over an eight-year period after high school. For a sample of 6,700 young men and 7,000 women they observe a total of 1,100 and 1,800 different sequences, respectively—an average of six men and four women for each sequence. Even with eight years of life-history data this is an enormous amount of complexity. In order to collapse these observed sequences into a manageable number—say, eight to ten different "pathways"—we would have to aggregate several hundred actual sequences together into these larger groups. While this could be done, the sheer number of decisions that would have to be made would mean that the reader would have to take the aggregated pathways as a given because the actual process would be hidden. Supposing we end up with four pathways to describe Rindfuss and colleagues' data—does this mean that the life course is "ordered" or that we have merely aggregated dissimilar life histories together? Ultimately, clustering decisions must be evaluated on substantive and statistical grounds, and the number of decisions that must be made in an agglomerative clustering algorithm, such as optimal sequence analysis, renders it unattractive given our interest in determining the number of pathways and the degree of order within them.

In this section I use a monothetic divisive algorithm (MDA) that was recently proposed by Piccarreta (1998) and Billari and Piccarreta (2001). In contrast to sequence analysis, which groups the data together beginning with individual sequences, this approach is a "top-down" (i.e., divisive) approach because it starts with the data all grouped together and then proceeds to divide it into smaller groups one variable at a time. It chooses the grouping variables in order to minimize differences within groups and maximize differences across groups. As will soon be clear, the advantage of the MDA approach is that the data can be grouped on the basis of a relatively small number of binary divisions that makes the clustering process explicit to the reader and relatively easy to interpret. In addition, a simple measure of global fit allows us to evaluate the success of the clustering process. Following Billari and Piccarreta (2001), I represent the life-history data for the vari-

TABLE 8.5

EXAMPLE SEQUENCE

	AGE													
VARIABLE	22	23	24	25	26	27	28	29	30	31	32	33	34	35
P	0	1	1	1	1	1	1	1	1	1	1	1	1	1
E	0	0	0	1	1	1	1	1	1	1	1	1	1	1
L	0	0	0	0	1	1	1	1	1	1	1	1	1	1
M	0	0	0	0	0	0	0	0	1	1	1	1	1	1
B	0	0	0	0	0	0	0	0	0	0	1	1	1	1

ables *P, E, L, M,* and *B* from table 8.1 as a sequence of 1s and 0s for each variable for ages twenty-two to thirty-five. For example, the sequence in table 8.5 would represent an individual who left home at twenty-three, finished school at twenty-five, entered the labor force at twenty-six, got married at thirty, and had his or her first child at age thirty-two.

The MDA approach works by taking all of the life histories in the sample—coded as above—and dividing them into groups one variable at a time in such a way that minimizes the heterogeneity in life histories within the group and maximizes it across groups. For example, in the first step, the algorithm may find that that dividing the entire sample on the basis of whether the respondent was married by age twenty-eight ($M = 1$ at age twenty-eight, or the seventh position on the *M* sequence) results in two groups with the most explanatory power compared to all the other possible choices (such as whether they are working at age twenty-five or done with school at twenty-nine).

To measure within- and cross-group heterogeneity, we need some measure of qualitative variability. Here, replicating the derivation of Piccarreta (1998), we use the Gini heterogeneity measure. For a qualitative variable *Y* with two categories and with proportions p_1 and p_2, the Gini heterogeneity is $E(Y) = 1 - \sum_j p_j^2$. For *N* individuals and *Q* binary variables (in the case of life-history data for the ages twenty-two to thirty-five with five transitions, we have $15 \times 5 = 70$ binary variables), the measure of total variability is

$$I_1(1) = N \sum_q E(Y_q), \tag{1}$$

which is the sum of the Gini variability for each variable in the life-history data. If the sample is divided into G groups, then

$$I_g(G) = N_g \sum_q E(Y_q | g) \tag{2}$$

is the total variation of the gth group. Given a division of the data into G groups, a measure of the explanatory power of those groups can be defined as

$$R_G^* = \frac{I_1(1) - \sum_g I_g(G)}{I_1(1)}, \tag{3}$$

that is, R_G^* is the proportion of the total Gini variability that is "explained" by membership in the G groups (for further details on this derivation, see Billari and Piccarreta [2001]).

The MDA algorithm works sequentially, choosing a single variable at each step that results in the highest overall measure of fit, R_G^*. If, as in the above hypothetical example, the best R_G^* was when the data was divided on the basis of marriage at age twenty-eight, then in the next step the algorithm would divide the data again, finding a single variable to split one of the two existing groups (married and not married at twenty-eight) into two smaller groups, based on maximization of R_G^*. This process continues—resulting in a decision tree of sequential divisions of the data—until the incremental increase in explanatory power falls below a certain threshold.

I ran this algorithm on the life-history data for ages twenty-two to thirty-five separately for men and women. I programmed the algorithm to work step by step, choosing the variable that maximized the explanatory power of the groups, until the incremental increase in R_G^* dropped below 0.02. Figures 8.6 and 8.7 show the resulting decision trees, and table 8.6 reports the fit of the model by step. For example, figure 8.6 indicates that for men, the MDA selected B30—whether the individual had a child by age thirty—as the best variable to divide the data in the first step (i.e., it was the variable that maximized R_G^*). This first step divided the data into two groups composed of 993 cases of B30 = 0 and 1,532 cases of B30 = 1 and resulted in an incremental increase in R of 0.211. Next, in step 2, the algorithm divided the second group (B30 = 1) into two smaller groups based on M30. This resulted in an increase of R_G^* of 0.081. This process continues until step 5. After this point, there was no variable that could divide any existing group and result in an increase of R_G^* of more than 0.02. As a result,

TABLE 8.6

RESULTS FROM THE MONOTHETIC DIVISIVE ALGORITHM
FOR THE NLSY LIFE-HISTORY DATA

STEP	R_G^*	CHANGE	VARIABLE
Men:			
1	.211	.211	B30
2	.299	.081	M30
3	.349	.056	M32
4	.389	.040	B24
5	.416	.027	P29
Women:			
1	.194	.194	B28
2	.313	.119	M29
3	.364	.051	M32
4	.393	.029	B24
5	.418	.024	L33

figure 8.6 shows that these five steps divide the data into six groups. Group 1, for example, consists of 212 men who had no children by thirty, were unmarried by thirty-two, and were still living at home at twenty-nine. We could call them the "slacker" group (not to ascribe any normative meaning to these life-course transitions). In contrast, group 6 is composed of men who had a child by twenty-four and were married by thirty (clearly, this group consists of earnest family starters). The nice thing about the MDA approach is that we have achieved a succinct clustering of the data as the result of five binary divisions. Moreover, the clustering is the product a process of sequential maximization of the ability of the groups to "explain" heterogeneity in the life-course data. Recall that the life-course data is the sequence of 1s and 0s associated with each of the adult states over time. Finally, because the formula for R_G^* is explicitly defined, the process is accessible to the reader who might want to repeat the analysis.

Figure 8.8 shows the transition rates for these six groups for men over time. The group numbers are displayed directly on the graphs. If you wish to interpret the groups in terms of the other variables, figure 8.8 aids in making such an interpretation. For example, group 1 (the slacker group, unmarried <32, no baby <30, live with parents <29) is indeed less likely to enter into full-time work (fig. 8.8C), while the reverse is true for group 6 (married ≤30, baby ≤24). Group 1 also has delayed exit from education compared to

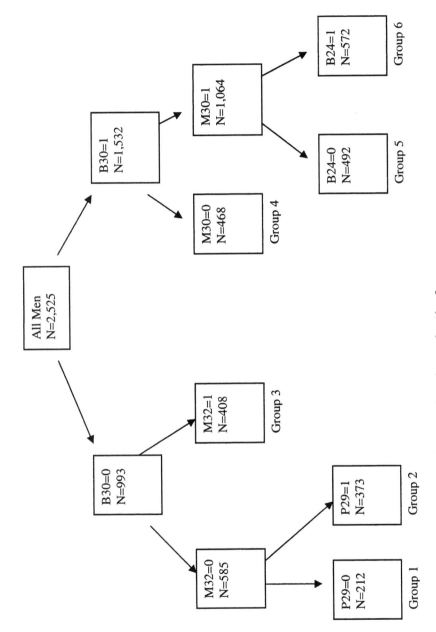

Figure 8.6. Tree representation of the monothetic divisive algorithm for men

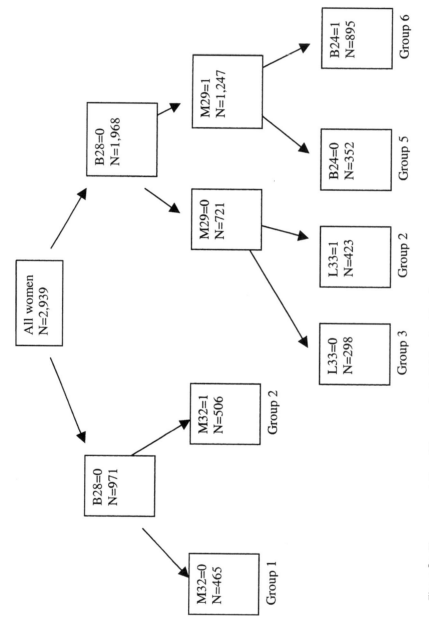

Figure 8.7. Tree representation of the monothetic divisive algorithm for women

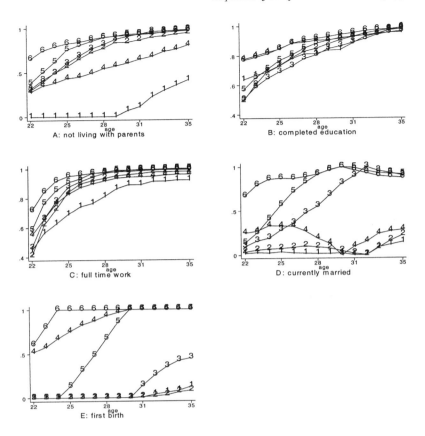

Figure 8.8. Results of the MDA clustering for men, life-history transitions by group. (Numbers on the graph refer to the MDA group number, see figure 8.6.) *A*, Not living with parents; *B*, completed education; *C*, full-time work; *D*, currently married; *E*, first birth.

group 6. One thing that is apparent is that the differences in *E* and *L* between the groups are smaller than the differences in *M* and *B*. Obviously, this is partly a function of the fact that the MDA method divided the groups explicitly on the basis of *M* and *B*. We could, of course, arbitrarily define groups on the basis of other variables, but such a clustering would not fit as well as the clustering obtained by MDA.[4] It might be substantively more interest-ing, but it would not be as efficient an explanation for variability in the life course.

The question remains as to what to make of all of this. My personal opinion is that one should not attach too much importance to the groups as representing specific pathways—instead, as I argue below, the benefit is in thinking of the number of pathways and the degree of "order" in the life course. In other words, I believe that the purpose of using a divisive clustering algorithm is not to derive "ideal" type pathways. As Wu (2000) points out, if you stare at clusters of sequences long enough, you can find reason-able labels for them. In this sense, a comparison of figure 8.6 (men) and figure 8.7 (women) is instructive. The clustering tree for women in figure 8.7 is slightly different. Although group 1 is composed of individuals who are childless at twenty-eight and unmarried at thirty-two, it says nothing about living with parents and hence doesn't necessarily match up with group 1 for males. In contrast, groups 3 and 4 incorporate full-time employment (re-spondent or spouse), which is something that did not show up in the male groups. So, you could interpret these as different pathways. However, when I used the female decision tree to group the male data, the measure of fit, R_G^*, was 0.391 which is only 0.025 lower than the fit obtained by the decision tree in figure 8.6 (see table 8.6). Likewise, when I used the female decision tree to group the male data, the measure of fit, R_G^*, was 0.410, which is almost the same as the fit found from the MDA in figure 8.6 and reported in table 8.6. The upshot of this is that both figure 8.6 and figure 8.7 fit the data for either men or women equally well, and interpretations of the trajectories of indi-vidual groups should be general enough to accommodate this fact.

The real benefit of the MDA approach is in comparing the structure and organization of the life course across time, space, and demographic groups. Table 8.6 shows that both men and women in the NLSY data can be characterized by six groups (five binary divisions) before the incremental im-provement in explanatory power becomes small and we are really explaining noise or "disorder" in the life course. In addition, the measure of fit is about the same for both men and women, indicating that they are equally ordered or organized by the resultant groups. As a useful point of comparison, imag-ine the following example of an "ordered" life course. In the hypothetical so-ciety of Pleasantville, individuals leave home at age eighteen and complete their education between the ages of eighteen and twenty-four. They start work the same year they finish school, get married two years after starting work, and have children one year after getting married. In Pleasantville, the only thing that differentiates sequences is what age you finish school (there are seven possibilities, eighteen . . . twenty-four). As a result, the MDA algo-rithm would end up with seven groups that would explain all of the variation in life-course trajectories (R_G^* would equal 1). A comparison of these results with the NLSY79 results would indicate that the life course of American men and women in the 1980s was less ordered by identifiable pathways to adulthood than the Pleasantville data. In contrast, imagine data from Slack-erville, where *P, E, L, M,* and *B* occurred randomly between twenty-two and thirty-five. Although the MDA would undoubtedly find some random order in the data, the incremental increase in R_G^* would likely fall below 0.02

quickly, and the overall fit to this random life-course data would be very poor. In this case, comparison with the NLSY79 data would conclude that NLSY data consisted of more recognizable pathways and more overall order in the early adult life course. At this point it is important to point out that the algorithm is agnostic about what constitutes order. Any group that can be identified in the data that has high internal similarity will result in an increase in the overall fit. For example, if the Pleasantville data also consisted of an additional 30% of the population that followed a nonnormative sequence such as give birth at twenty-two, start work at age twenty-five, leave home at twenty-seven, finish education at thirty, and get married at thirty-five, then this group—because of its internal similarity—would not diminish the overall perception that Pleasantville had a set of well-organized pathways to adulthood.

As a point of actual comparison, Billari and Piccarreta (2001) apply this MDA algorithm to Italian data for the ages of twenty to thirty-five with six transitions (including sexual intercourse). In seven steps they divide the data into eight groups and find they can explain 50.5% of the total heterogeneity.[5] While standard errors could be bootstrapped to test the difference in fit explicitly, I would conclude that the Italian transition to adulthood is more ordered than that of Americans, with the caveat that they have six transitions while the NLSY data analyzed above included only five. Again, further inspection would be necessary to conclude that this higher fit for the Italian data corresponds to what we mean by structure or order in that the identified pathways make some substantive sense. Certainly, however, in terms of what the algorithm is designed to do—find groups based on binary divisions of the data that explain the overall dispersion in life history—one could argue that the results do indicate a higher predictability to the Italian versus the American life course. Finally, one must stress that a mechanical clustering procedure is not intended to uncover causality. The fact that having a child by age thirty ($B30$) was chosen as the first variable to divide the data in figure 8.6 does not indicate that it is causally linked to the other transitions but, rather, that it has a higher degree of association with patterns in the data than the other variables.

In sum, I have presented here a variety of descriptive analyses of the relationship among five demographic transitions: leaving home, finishing school, starting work, getting married, and having children. I would argue that figures 8.1–8.5 suggest that the American young adult life course is indeed age-stratified and ordered. Most important, there seems to be a clear link between the timing of the nonfamilial transitions and the timing of the family transitions, even though the temporal ordering of the individual nonfamilial transitions is largely uncoupled. Of course, the age ordering and sequencing of the transitions can only be properly interpreted in a comparative framework. The results of a simple comparison of sequences between the NLSY79 data, as depicted in table 8.4, and data from the 1960s suggests that fewer individuals followed the normative sequence of *E, L, M, B* (finish education, start work, marry, have a baby) in the 1980s than they did in the 1960s. Of course, repeated cross-sectional data suggest that the 1960s were something of an aberration in terms of the age congruity of these adult transitions, so we are left to wonder what result we would have with other cross-time comparisons. Nonetheless, several basic problems in analyzing sequences have emerged. In particular, with so many observed sequences (sixty-two), some form of data reduction is necessary for a more formal comparison of transition sequences between Marini's data from the 1960s and the NLSY data from the 1980s and 1990s. As a possible solution to this impasse, I employed a simple divisive algorithm (Billari and Piccarreta 2001) to provide an accessible top-down clustering of the life-history data. Results from this clustering process indicate that about 42% of the overall heterogeneity in the life course can be explained by classifying the data into six groups. Nonetheless, this result can perhaps be interpreted only in comparison to other cohorts over time or in different societies. Taken as a whole, however, this chapter presents several different descriptive tools—tables of medians, graphs of transitions, frequency tables of sequences, and clustering of life histories—that may prove to be useful in undertaking a more complete comparison of longitudinal data from several different cohorts.

DOES THE SEQUENCE MATTER?

In this part of the chapter, I consider whether the different pathways to adulthood affect adult outcomes. I use the groups resulting from the MDA cluster analysis listed in figures 8.6 and 8.7 to represent different pathways to adulthood. The MDA analysis divides the data into six pathways for both men and women. As described above, these pathways explain 41.6% of the variance in life-course transitions for men and 41.8% for women. Additional groups would each explain less than 2% of the variance. It is clear, therefore, that these groups are a succinct explanation of the variation in the timing and sequence of the transition to adulthood among twenty-two- to thirty-five-year-olds. The next question is whether these different pathways are associated in some way with adult outcomes.

In order to depict the relationship between the life-course pathways and adult outcomes, table 8.7 shows the average education, poverty rate, family income, poverty ratio, and self-reported happiness and depression of individuals in each of the different groups. These measures capture a broad range of outcomes depicting socioeconomic and psychological well-being. In order to control for the number of family members when looking at income, the "poverty ratio" is the ratio of the family's income to the poverty line for the family, which controls for the number of and age of the individuals in the household. All the variables are measured at age thirty-five except for happiness and depression.[6] Self-reported happiness is a question in the NLSY in 1992 (when the respondents were between twenty-nine- and thirty-five-years-old), which asked respondents how happy they were in the past week (coded 0–3, 0 is "rarely/none of the time" and 3 is "most/all of the time"), and self-reported depression (in the 1994 NLSY questionnaire) was based on the question of how often the respondent felt depressed in the past week (coded 0–3, 0 is "rarely/none of the time" and 3 is "most/all the time").

Table 8.7 suggests substantial differences in these outcomes by age thirty-five. Among men, those in group 3 (married ≤32, no baby <30) have higher levels of education, lower poverty rates, higher incomes, and appear to be happier and less depressed. In contrast, men in group 1 (unmarried <32, no baby <30, live with parents <29), have higher poverty rates (0.144) and lower incomes ($33,797 annually). The highest poverty rate is among men in group 4 who were unmarried by thirty but had a child before age thirty. For women, those in group 2 (no baby by age twenty-eight and married by age thirty-two) had the lowest poverty rate (0.023) and the highest family income ($86,855 annually). In contrast, women in group 3 (baby by twenty-eight, unmarried by twenty-nine, and no one in the household in the labor force full-time by age thirty-three) had a poverty rate of 0.518. Women in group 6 (first child between twenty-four and twenty-eight, married by twenty-nine) were the happiest (2.56) and the least likely to be depressed (0.387).

Overall, table 8.7 depicts substantial variance in the outcome measures among the different pathways to adulthood. Nevertheless, one might ask whether this association is attributable to factors other than the timing and sequence of the demographic indicators of adulthood. Indeed, there is a large literature on the predictors of each of the outcome variables in table 8.7; what we want to know is what the life-course perspective can add to our understanding of the causes of poverty, income inequality, and psychological well-being. In order to test for the effect of the pathways in table 8.7, I model the relationship between the groups and the outcomes, controlling for other

TABLE 8.7

DESCRIPTIVE STATISTICS FOR DIFFERENT PATHWAYS TO ADULTHOOD

GROUP	n	MEAN EDUCATION	POVERTY RATE	HOUSEHOLD INCOME ($)	POVERTY RATIO	HAPPINESS	DEPRESSION
Men:							
1—Unmarried (<32), no baby (<30), live with parents (<29)	212	12.6	.144	33,797	3.24	2.42	.331
2—Unmarried (<32), no baby (<30), not with parents (≤29)	373	13.9	.090	43,575	5.23	2.41	.357
3—Married (≤32), no baby (<30)	408	14.4	.018	74,969	6.22	2.63	.210
4—Unmarried (<30), baby (≤30)	468	12.1	.160	49,153	4.14	2.20	.436
5—Married (≤30), baby (≤30)	492	14.0	.019	71,828	4.80	2.58	.239
6—Married (≤30), baby (≤24)	572	12.5	.065	51,650	3.48	2.49	.233
Women:							
1—No baby (<28), unmarried (<32)	465	14.3	.104	50,957	5.47	2.42	.601
2—No baby (<28), married (≤32)	506	14.7	.023	86,855	6.91	2.46	.456
3—Baby (≤28), unmarried (29), household not working (<33)	298	11.8	.518	26,081	1.79	2.06	.876
4—Baby (≤28), unmarried (<29), household working (≤33)	423	12.5	.164	38,832	2.82	2.30	.600
5—Baby (between 24 & 28), married (≤29)	352	14.2	.032	73,221	4.67	2.56	.387
6—Baby (≤24), married (≤29)	895	12.5	.101	47,178	3.00	2.44	.513

TABLE 8.8

ESTIMATION RESULTS: EFFECT OF PATHWAYS TO ADULTHOOD FOR MEN

GROUP	POVERTY (1)	POVERTY RATIO (FAMILY INCOME/ POVERTY LINE) (2)	SELF-REPORTED HAPPINESS (3)	SELF-REPORTED DEPRESSION (4)
2—Unmarried (<32), no baby	.242	.750	−.266	.375
(<30), not w/parents (≤29)	(.400)	(.930)	(.130)*	(.146)**
3—Married (≤32), no baby	−1.278	1.332	.010	.223
(<30)	(.559)*	(1.052)	(.153)	(.171)
4—Unmarried (<30), baby	.813	1.638	−.400	.659
(≤30)	(.827)	(1.280)	(.190)*	(.214)**
5—Married (≤30), baby (≤30)	−.716	−.061	−.254	.482
	(.840)	(1.185)	(.179)	(.203)*
6—Married (≤30), baby (≤24)	.377	.944	−.142	.290
	(.909)	(1.442)	(.216)	(.245)
Constant	−1.119	−.767		
	(1.080)	(2.133)		
Dummy variables for additive				
effects of transitions	Yes	Yes	Yes	Yes
Log-likelihood (R^2)	−388.9	(.055)	−2,145.4	−1,481.5
Model df	24	24	24	24
Observations	2,203	1,923	2,326	2,332
Log-likelihood ratio test of				
significance of group				
variables (df)	19.7 (5)**	10.24 (5)	20.43 (5)**	24.63 (5)**

Note. Group 1—Unmarried (<32), no baby (<30), live with parents (<29)—is excluded. Standard errors in parentheses. All models include dummy variables for the additive effects of the timing of the individual demographic transitions, as well as race, Armed Forces Qualification Test scores, and parents' education (see text, coefficients not shown).

*Significant at 5% level.
**Significant at 1% level.

relevant demographic variables. In order to control for relevant background factors that might affect these outcomes, the models in tables 8.8 and 8.9 include control for parent's education, race, and Armed Forces Qualification Test (AFQT, an achievement test) scores. In addition, all the models also include dummy variables indicating the timing of each of the demographic

TABLE 8.9

ESTIMATION RESULTS: EFFECT OF PATHWAYS TO ADULTHOOD FOR WOMEN

GROUP	POVERTY (1)	POVERTY RATIO (FAMILY INCOME/POVERTY LINE) (2)	SELF-REPORTED HAPPINESS (3)	SELF-REPORTED DEPRESSION (4)
1—No baby (<28), unmarried (<32)	.810 (.549)	.149 (1.118)	−.002 (.163)	−.007 (.163)
2—No baby (<28), married (≤32)	−.297 (.547)	1.327 (.985)	−.022 (.146)	−.183 (.147)
3—Baby (≤28), unmarried (29), household not working (<33)	1.352 (.255)**	−.512 (.845)	−.174 (.114)	.360 (.114)**
5—Baby (between 24 & 28), married (≤29)	−.411 (.432)	.814 (.870)	.107 (.129)	−.153 (.129)
6—Baby (≤24), married (≤29)	−.074 (.239)	−.498 (.605)	.145 (.087)	−.120 (.089)
Constant	−.885 (.403)*	.853 (1.009)		
Dummy variables for additive effects of transitions	Yes	Yes	Yes	Yes
Log-likelihood (R^2)	−659.4	(.092)	−2,734.6	−2,621.4
Model df	24	24	24	24
Observations	2,680	2,336	2,801	2,792
Log-likelihood ratio test of significance of group variables (df)	45.51 (5)**	6.30 (5)	10.39 (5)	21.37 (5)**

Note. Group 4—Baby (≤28), unmarried (<29), household working (≤33)—is excluded.

Standard errors in parentheses. All models include dummy variables for the additive effects of the timing of the individual demographic transitions, as well as race, AFQT scores, and parents' education (see text, coefficients not shown).

*Significant at 5% level.

**Significant at 1% level.

transitions.[7] I do this because each pathway may be thought of as an inter-action effect between variables measuring the timing of different transitions. I argue that in order to demonstrate that the pathway matters, we must find significant effects of the pathways above and beyond the additive effects of the timing of each of the individual transitions. By modeling the effect of the transitions and including dummy variables for the timing of each individual transition we test for the significance of the pathways as "interaction effects." In other words, having a baby by age twenty-eight and being un-married by age twenty-nine may each have a separate effect on poverty rates at age thirty-five. Does the effect of having both of these things happen (baby by twenty-eight, unmarried by twenty-nine) differ from the sum of the indi-vidual effects? If we find that there are interaction effects—in the form of the hypothesized pathways—then we may conclude that our understanding of the causes of these outcomes is improved by organizing the timing of in-dividual transitions into sequential pathways.

Tables 8.8 and 8.9 show estimation results of the effects of the pro-posed pathways on measures of adult well-being. As discussed above, each of the models includes controls for race, achievement test scores, parents' education, and dummy variables for the timing of each of the individual transitions. (These coefficients are not included in the models; contact me for full results.) In addition, each model performs a likelihood-ratio test for the joint significance of the pathways.

Table 8.8 shows estimation results for men. In all the models, group 1 (unmarried <32, no baby <30, live with parents <29) is the comparison cat-egory. Model 1 uses a logit model to estimate the poverty status at age thirty-five. Controlling for background variables that would affect adult socioeco-nomic status and the timing of the individual transitions, only group 3 (married ≤32, no baby <30) has a significantly different probability of being poor compared to group 1. Nonetheless, the log-likelihood ratio test does in-dicate that including the group (pathway) variables represents a significant improvement in fit over a model with just the additive effects of the timing of the different transitions and the background variables ($\chi^2 = 19.7$, 5 df). Nonetheless, the explanatory power of the groups was reduced by about 60% by including the additive effect of transition timing (additional models not shown). In other words, over half of the explanatory power of the path-ways in table 8.7 for men can be explained away by simple additive effects of the timing of each transition, and about 40% of the apparent effect may be due to interaction effects.

Moreover, in contrast to the results for poverty, a regression model of the poverty ratio fails the log-likelihood ratio test (χ^2 = 10.24, 5 df). This indicates that we do not improve the analysis of family income (as measured by poverty ratios) by considering the sequential timing of the demographic indicators of adulthood, as represented by the six pathways depicted in figure 8.6 and table 8.7. When we turn to the measures of psychological well-being, we do find a significant effect for the pathways. Groups 2 and 4 are significantly less happy and more depressed than we would predict based just on their background variables and the timing of their adult transitions. This suggests that the sequence of adult transitions matters for adult psychological well-being. Again, however, the important caveat to this result is that the coefficients in models 3 and 4 are substantially smaller than models that exclude the dummy variables for transition timing; not all of the descriptive result in table 8.7 is due to the interaction effect represented by the pathways.

The results for women in table 8.9 correspond to the same pattern as the result for men. The pathway variables appear to have a significant explanatory effect on poverty and depression, but no significant effect on either the poverty ratio or happiness.

In sum, tables 8.7–8.9 show that the pathways to adulthood identified in the first part of this chapter do correlate with adult outcomes that researchers might care about. However, I argue that to demonstrate that the sequence of the transitions matters, the correlation with outcomes must hold even after controlling for the additive effect of the individual transitions and background variables. With the exception of the poverty ratio for men and women—used here as a measure of household income controlling for household size—and self-reported happiness for women, the pathways do have explanatory power. However, the effect is substantially smaller than suggested by table 8.6, and I have made no attempt to include an exhaustive list of background variables that might explain both the outcomes and one's placement on the various pathways.

A reasonable interpretation of the results in tables 8.8 and 8.9 is that the pathway to adulthood has little meaningful impact on poverty, income, happiness, and depression above and beyond the effects of the individual transitions themselves. Only a few of the coefficients estimating the effects of pathways in tables 8.8 and 8.9 have significant correlations with the outcome variables. I would place the most emphasis on the results for income (as measured by the household's poverty ratio) in model 2 of tables 8.8 and 8.9. There is no evidence that any of the different pathways to adulthood affect income at age thirty-five. To be sure, there are significant effects of the timing of each of the transitions themselves, such as age at marriage and when you started work, but there is no evidence of interaction effects between the timing of these transitions, as represented by the different pathways identified in table 8.6 and figures 8.6 and 8.7. In practical terms, this suggests that policy concerned with income maintenance, for example, can focus on these transitions separately (i.e., increasing education, increasing hours of work, and decreasing the rate of teenage pregnancy) rather than focusing on the simultaneous timing of several transitions at once.

It is certainly possible to argue that the pathways themselves could be constructed differently to get at the "social problems" aspect of the transition to adulthood. In other words, what sequences of transitions seem most likely to be associated with negative adult outcomes? That, however, runs the danger of making selections on the basis of the dependent variable.[8] The approach here, utilizing the MDA algorithm from the first part of the chapter, has been to describe the complexity of the transition data as concisely and as effectively as possible and then see whether the life-course data, clustered into six groups for both men and women, explains much of the variance in the measures of well-being listed in table 8.7. The goal has not been to replicate the large literature on the causes of each of these dependent variables but to suggest a framework for evaluating the contribution of sequence data—the demographic pathways identified in figures 8.6 and 8.7—to our understanding of poverty, income, and psychological well being. The results suggest that there is no additional effect of the major pathways to adulthood on family income (as measured by the poverty ratio) and a small effect on poverty rates, happiness, and the prevalence of depression.

NOTES

1. The survey has been conducted every other year since 1994: 1994, 1996, and 1998. For those respondents who turned thirty-five after 1994 (sixteen to eighteen years old in 1979), data for 1995 and 1997 were interpolated by randomly taking $x_t = x_{t-1}$ for half the respondents and $x_t = x_{t+1}$ for the other half.

2. Of the original 12,685 cases, only sixteen- to twenty-two-year-olds were used, which eliminates 2,514 fourteen- and fifteen-year-olds. Another 3,349 were lost due to sample attrition, 1,351 cases that are still in the survey were eliminated because they are missing one or more years of data (this could be included following the strategy of n. 1 above), and 7 were lost because of missing data.

3. In particular, I combine the following sequences into the "1234" category: 1111, 1134, 1224, 1233, 1114, and 1222.

4. This is not entirely true. As the MDA algorithm is a process of sequential maximization, it is possible that it does not select the best overall fit. More complicated models could attempt to minimize this possibility.

5. The final step explains 2.5% of the variability (>2%), consistent with the approach I have adopted here.

6. For respondents who turned thirty-five in-between NLSY interviews, the variables are measured at age thirty-four or age thirty-six.

7. Each of the transitions is grouped into four categories to prevent multicollinearity problems. The categories are P (22, 25, 30, >35), B (19, 25, 34, >35), E (22, 25, 30, >35), L (22, 24, 27, >35), and M (22, 26, 34, >35). Using individual-year dummy variables does not affect the conclusions.

8. In additional to results not presented here, I estimated two-way interaction models for the timing of the transitions (using the four category variables described in n. 7 above). None of the two-way interactions represented an improvement in fit over the model with simple additive effects of the transitions. This qualifies, but does not negate, the results for the MDA-identified pathways presented in tables 8.8 and 8.9, as the pathways represent more complicated sets of sequences.

REFERENCES

Abbott, Andrew. 1995. Sequence Analysis: New Methods for Old Ideas. *Annual Review of Sociology* 21:93–113.

Abbott, Andrew, and Angela Tsay. 2000. Sequence Analysis and Optimal Matching Methods in Sociology. *Sociological Methods and Research* 29 (1):3–33.

Billari, Francesco, Johannes Furnkranz, and Alexia Prskawetz. 2000. Timing, Sequencing, and Quantum of Life Course Events: A Machine Learning Approach. Working Paper 2000–010. Max-Planck Institute for Demographic Research, Munich.

Billari, Francesco, and Raffaella Piccarreta. 2001. Life Courses as Sequences: An Experiment in Clustering via Monothetic Divisive Algorithms. Pp. 351–58 in *Advances in Classification and Data Analysis*, edited by Simone Borra, Vichi Rocci, and Martin Schader. New York: Springer.

Buchman, Marlis. 1989. *The Script of Life in Modern Society*. Chicago: University of Chicago Press.

Levine, Joel H. 2001. But What Have You Done for Us Lately. *Sociological Methods and Research* 29 (1):34–40.

Marini, Margaret. 1984. The Order of Events in the Transition to Adulthood. *Sociology of Education* 57:63–84.

Piccarreta, Raffaella. 1998. Divisive Monothetic Algorithms for Clustering Binary Data: A Proposal. http://citeseer.nj.nec.com/282936.html.

Rindfuss, Ronald. 1991. The Young Adult Years: Diversity, Structural Change, and Fertility. *Demography* 28 (4):483–512.

Rindfuss, Ronald, C. Gary Swicegood, and Rachel A. Rosenfeld. 1987. Disorder in the Life Course: How Common and Does it Matter? *American Sociological Review* 52:785–801.

Shanahan, Michael. 2000. Pathways to Adulthood in Changing Societies: Variability and Mechanisms in Life Course Perspective. *Annual Review of Sociology* 26:667–92.

Stevens, David. 1990. New Evidence on the Timing of Early Life Course Transitions: The United States, 1900–1980. *Journal of Family History* 15 (2): 163–78.

Wu, Lawrence L. 2000. Some Comments on "Sequence Analysis and Optimal Matching Methods in Sociology: Review and Prospect." *Sociological Methods and Research* 29 (1):41–64.

CHAPTER 9

OFF TO A GOOD START?

Postsecondary Education and Early Adult Life

GARY D. SANDEFUR, JENNIFER EGGERLING-BOECK,
AND HYUNJOON PARK

The transition to adulthood is a critical period in the lives of individuals as they move from being dependent on their parents to supporting themselves financially and forming their own families. Many sociologists and social demographers have approached the study of this period by looking at various "markers" of the transition to adulthood (Hogan 1978; Hogan and Astone 1986; Marini 1984; Modell, Furstenberg, and Hershberg 1976; Rindfuss, Swicegood, and Rosenfeld 1987).[1] These include completing full-time education, entering the labor market, living away from home, getting married, and having children. A good deal of work has focused on the order of events during this transitional period (Hogan 1978; Marini 1984). Yet while most Americans have in mind a fairly orderly transition from full-time schooling to work and then to marriage and childbearing, research suggests that such orderly transitions are less common than one might think (Hogan 1978; Rindfuss et al. 1987). Many individuals marry or have children prior to completing their education and intermingle periods of full-time work and full-time education.

A smaller body of research has explored how individuals entering or going through this transitional period see it themselves (e.g., Arnett 1994, 1998; Arnett and Taber 1994; Aronson 2001). This research suggests that marriage is no longer a marker that is important to adolescents as an indicator of being an adult. Instead, they tend to focus on individualistic criteria, such as accepting responsibility for one's self, making independent decisions, and achieving financial independence from their parents. This suggests that, of the traditional markers of adulthood, living independently and working are the most important to contemporary youth because they are outward signs of financial independence from their parents. However, in her interviews with twenty-one- and twenty-two-year-old women who had been ninth graders in St. Paul, Minnesota, in 1988, Aronson (2001) found some respondents, especially those who had children, who viewed becoming a parent and financial independence as markers of the transition to adulthood. These women did not see beginning full-time work or getting married as essential in order to be considered an adult.[2]

Although it is useful to consider how individuals entering, going through, or completing the transition to adulthood view the experience, it is not clear that we should be more concerned with their perceptions than with their actions. Whether a woman becomes a parent during or right after high school and before marriage has societal as well as personal implications, quite possibly creating a demand for public services that would not occur if she were to delay childbearing until she had completed more education and obtained a full-time job. Consequently, we are interested in how much education people receive, when they marry, and when they have children, even if the individuals concerned do not see these as critical markers of adulthood. As Settersten (2003, and this vol., chap. 16; Furstenberg, Rumbaut, and Settersten, this vol., chap. 1) points out, understanding the developmental aspects of this transitional period could better inform social policies designed to maximize individual and social benefits during this time.

In this chapter, we focus specifically on getting off to a good start in the transition to adulthood by examining two key dimensions of the early transition to adulthood: educational attainment and avoiding early out-of-wedlock childbearing. We focus on these for both scientific and policy reasons. As a great deal of social science research has demonstrated over the years, educational attainment is one key to much of what happens to people later in their lives (Hogan and Astone 1986). The amount and quality of education that a person achieves affects her occupation and career, her lifetime earnings, income, and wealth accumulation, and whom she marries as well as many other features of early, mid-, and late life. Educational attainment also is strongly associated with the well-being of an individual's children, affecting their lives as well as the parent's. A more educated citizenry also has benefits for the country as a whole. A number of social policies at the local, state, and federal levels are designed to enhance educational attainment. Research on these outcomes can help inform social policies designed to increase the ability of individuals to be economically successful in early adulthood.

We also examine the relationship between some critical components of social structure—family and school characteristics—and educational attainment. Better understanding the role that families and schools play in eventual educational attainment not only enriches our scientific understanding of this critical phase, it also provides some guidance as to where social policy might be most effective in helping young people obtain as much education as possible. If, for example, family economic resources are critical in assisting individuals in obtaining postsecondary education, we can devise ways of assisting young people whose families lack these resources to pursue postsecondary education nonetheless. If graduates of private schools have significant advantages over those from public schools, we can attempt to use social policy to create more opportunities for students to benefit from the aspects of the private school experience that are most important for preparing them for postsecondary education.

Just as obtaining a college degree can open doors for young adults and have implications for all stages of the life course, early out-of-wedlock childbearing can be a devastating experience for young people, especially young women. Having a child outside marriage early in life can prevent a young woman from pursuing postsecondary education. In addition to this indirect effect through education, if she cannot find adequate and affordable child care, it can also limit the kind of occupation or career she can pursue. For this reason, policymakers are very concerned with both the level of out-of-wedlock childbearing and the factors that are associated with it. Again, it is important to understand the roles of families and schools in helping young women avoid out-of-wedlock childbearing early in their lives.

Because experiencing or avoiding early childbearing and pursuing postsecondary education occur in the context of other decisions and events that are important parts of the transition to adulthood, we also examine leaving home, work, and marriage. Our approach is guided by the assumption that one pattern of events during the early twenties clearly has negative consequences: having a child out-of-wedlock and attaining little or no postsecondary education. Characterizing this as a negative pattern involves making a value judgment—that is, that people are better off if they do not have a child by themselves early in life and if they get at least some postsecondary education. We, however, feel this is an appropriate value judgment to make. We also assume that another pattern clearly has positive consequences: obtaining a four-year degree, moving away from home, and working full-time.

These turn out to be fairly common patterns among recent cohorts of American young people, although there are other common patterns as well.

We examine two cohorts: the High School and Beyond Survey (HSB) of people born in 1964; and the National Educational Longitudinal Study (NELS) of people born in 1974. Chapter 2 in this volume looks at a more extensive set of cohorts, but the data used in that chapter do not permit the examination of as much family information as we are able to look at in our data. We examine the very early stages of the transition to adulthood at age twenty-eight in the HSB and age twenty-six in the NELS, focusing on these five major markers: postsecondary education, employment, living away from home, marriage, and childbearing. We examine out-of-wedlock childbearing by looking at the combination of marriage and childbearing at ages twenty-six and twenty-eight. The overall trends in out-of-wedlock childbearing and educational attainment that span the early adult lives of these two cohorts are in different directions. The trend in educational attainment was a positive one as the availability of opportunities for postsecondary education expanded and as the percentage of individuals with college degrees increased. During the same period, however, the fertility rate of unmarried women increased and so did the proportion of children born outside marriage.

This chapter is organized as follows. We develop a model of how individuals make decisions that are part of the transition to adulthood, drawing on simple rational choice models of decision making, previous work on the association between race and ethnicity and the transition to adulthood, and the theoretical model underlying the work of Furstenberg and colleagues (1999) that suggests some of the ways in which families and schools can influence this critical period of life. We then use the HSB and NELS data to examine the educational attainment, employment, residential independence, childbearing, and marital status of individuals at ages twenty-eight and twenty-six, respectively. We are particularly interested in patterns of statuses, so we use latent class analysis to examine how educational attainment is associated with marriage and childbearing, as well as with work and living independently. Finally we look at the association between some key social structural variables—race and ethnicity, parental education, family type, and the type of school—and these markers of the transition to adulthood.

A MODEL OF HOW PEOPLE MAKE THE TRANSITION TO ADULTHOOD

One way to view the early transition to adulthood is as a sequence of decisions that individuals make to prepare themselves for full adult status. Research suggests that social structure—including families and schools—

creates a set of opportunities and constraints within which people make decisions. Within this context, we assume that individuals act rationally in a way they think will maximize their short-term and long-term happiness and that they base their decisions on the perceived costs and benefits of alternative choices.[3] For example, when it comes to deciding whether to work or enter postsecondary education after high school, what we know about the financial benefits of attending postsecondary education suggests that this is the best choice. But for some people the costs of postsecondary education may be too high for them or their families to bear, or the combination of an immediate income and the lower costs associated with working may make it a more attractive option than going to school. The costs of pursuing postsecondary education also vary with the type of institution and whether the student lives away from home while attending school.

Of course people sometimes make poor choices. This may be the result of bad information as, for example, in the case of someone who thinks the long-run benefits of going to work immediately are higher than those of completing postsecondary education and then working. Or, someone may be unfamiliar with financial aid and other ways of reducing the cost of postsecondary education. Having a child out-of-wedlock early in life, to cite another example, is often due to a decision to have sex without contraception, resulting in an unintended pregnancy that is carried to term.

Previous research suggests that members of different racial and ethnic groups have different probabilities of experiencing each of the events that make up a part of the transition to adulthood and that, on average, they experience these events at different ages. Asians and whites, for example, are more likely to obtain a college degree than are American Indians, Hispanics, or blacks. Blacks are more likely to experience an early out-of-wedlock birth than are any of the other groups, while Asians and whites are the least likely to do so. Latinos marry and have children within wedlock earlier in life than any of the other groups. (See Sandefur et al. [2001] for a discussion of racial and ethnic differences in these and other demographic markers and trends in these differences over time. Chapter 14 in this volume also explores some of the racial and ethnic variations in the transition to adulthood.) Based on previous research, we expect that whites and Asians will be more likely to have four-year degrees by their midtwenties than American Indians, blacks, and Hispanics and that black women will be more likely than other women to have children out-of-wedlock by their midtwenties, while Asian and white women will be least likely to do so.

No research has carefully examined racial and ethnic differences in the joint achievement of education, marriage, childbearing, living independently, and work. We know for example, that whites and Asians are more likely to be employed in their midtwenties than are members of the other groups, but we do not know about racial and ethnic differences in having the joint statuses of a four-year degree, work, living independently, marriage, and children—all of the major markers associated with adult status. The HSB and NELS data permit us to do this since they have sizable samples of American Indians, Asians, and Latinos, as well as blacks and whites.

In addition to racial and ethnic differences in educational attainment, out-of-wedlock childbearing, and the full transition to adulthood, we are also interested in some of the ways in which families and schools facilitate or impede the successful transition to adulthood. Furstenberg and colleagues (1999) suggest a conceptual framework for the influences on children and adolescents that includes both the community and family, and we incorporate this with our simple model of decision making to develop a model of how family and community resources influence decisions during the early transition to adulthood.

It is beyond the scope of this chapter to investigate all the ways in which families and communities can influence the development of individuals from adolescents into adults. Here we focus on a few key aspects of family and community life. Families can provide at least two important resources that assist young people in making good choices as they leave high school. First, some families are in a position to help cover the costs of attending college and living outside the family home if this is necessary to attend a good university. Second, some families are more able to provide good information to young adults about the choices they are making. This information may come in the form of role modeling, as with the children of college-educated parents, who know this route is open to them, or it may come in the form of direct information and advice about the choice between school and work.

We look at parental education, family type, and family income as key indicators of the ability of families to facilitate the successful transition of adolescents to adulthood. Parental education influences individual decisions in two ways: through role modeling and as an indicator of lifetime family income. Measured family income is also important, but it suffers from the disadvantage of being measured in only one year, and so in some ways parental education is a better indicator of actual family income over the whole period of childhood and adolescence. Different family structures (two-parent, single-parent, stepparent, or other) may also expose the adolescent to different options for early family formation, as well as providing different social and economic resources that influence the transition to adulthood.

The aspect of the community we focus on is the high school that an individual attended.[4] Although schools do not provide resources to assist students in pursuing secondary education, some schools are better than others at providing information about postsecondary educational opportunities and sources of financial assistance, and some are better at providing training in responsible decision making about sexual activity, childbearing, and marriage. The work of Bryk, Lee, and Holland (1993) and others has suggested that Catholic schools are particularly adept at creating a sense of community and providing a functioning social community of parents, teachers, and students that provides an environment in which students may excel. The type of school—public, Catholic, or other private—is indicative of a number of factors, including the cohesiveness of the adult community, class size, and other school resources.

Our model predicts, then, that we will find racial and ethnic variations in making a successful transition to adulthood and that these differences will persist after controlling for family characteristics and type of school. Previous research on family formation and educational attainment suggests that whites and Asians will have particularly successful early transitions to adulthood while blacks will be the least successful.[5] However, almost no research has examined racial and ethnic differences in the joint occurrence of the different events associated with a successful transition to adulthood. Our model predicts that parental education and family income will be positively associated with making a successful transition to adulthood and avoiding an early mistake, such as out-of-wedlock childbearing. Individuals who come from intact families will have more successful transitions to adulthood than those from other types of families. Finally, individuals who attend Catholic schools will have more successful transitions to adulthood than those who attend other types of schools.

SAMPLE AND DATA

Our data on the early transition to adulthood come from the sophomore cohort of the High School and Beyond Study (HSB) and the eighth graders in the National Educational Longitudinal Study (NELS). Table 9.1 contains some basic information on the two cohorts. The HSB sophomore cohort was born in 1964 and reached age twenty in 1984, while the NELS cohort was born in 1974 and reached age twenty in 1994. In certain important respects, the NELS cohort faced more favorable life circumstances during their childhood, adolescence, and early adulthood than did the HSB cohort. The child

TABLE 9.1

THE WORLD AS THEY KNEW IT

	HSB	NELS
Important dates/event:		
Birth	1964	1974
Grade 8	1978	1988
Grade 12	1982	1992
Age 20	1984	1994
Last interview[a]	1992 (28)	2000 (26)
Birth cohort size	4.0M	3.2M
Immigration	7.8M	11.8M
	(1961–80)	(1971–90)

	DATES						
	1964	1974	1982	1984	1992	1994	2000
Key indicators:							
Unemployment (%)	5.2	5.4	9.6	7.2	7.8	6.1	4.0
Child poverty	23	15	21	21	19	21	16
Expenditures/pupil							
(1999 $)	3,000	5,000	5,500	6,000	7,500	N.A.	N.A.
Pupil/teacher							
(public schools)	25	20	19	18	17	N.A.	N.A.
Children in two-parent							
families (%)	87	83	75	75	71	69	69

Sources. Data from various governmental publications.

Note. HSB is the High School and Beyond Survey; NELS is the National Educational Longitudinal Study. N.A. = not available.

[a]Numbers in parentheses are respondents' ages at last interview.

poverty rate was slightly higher for the HSB cohort in the year of their birth, and expenditures per pupil and class size were less favorable than for the NELS cohort. In addition, the unemployment rate was lower when the NELS cohort reached age twenty-six than when the HSB cohort reached age twenty-eight. In contrast, the evidence on fertility suggests that some conditions were less favorable for the NELS cohort than for the HSB cohort. The teen fertility rate in 1980 when the HSB cohort was in the tenth grade was fifty-three per thousand teenaged women, while in 1990 when the NELS cohort was in the tenth grade it was 59.1 per thousand teenaged women. The out-of-wedlock fertility rate in 1985 when the HSB cohort members were twenty-one was thirty-three per thousand unmarried women, ages fifteen to forty-four, while it was forty-five per thousand in 1985 when the NELS cohort was twenty-one (Sandefur et al. 2001).

Table 9.2 contains information on family characteristics, school type, and key outcomes for the HSB cohort at age twenty-eight and the NELS cohort at age twenty-six. There are a few important differences. As one would expect, the NELS cohort has a smaller percentage of non-Hispanic whites, and larger percentages of Hispanics and Asians, reflecting immigration and changes in the racial and ethnic composition of the general population. The parents of the NELS cohort are more educated on average than the parents of the HSB cohort. This is reflected most clearly in the "some college" category, which includes individuals with any postsecondary education (who have spent some time in a technical college, community college, or four-year college but not obtained a BA degree). In contrast, those in the NELS cohort were less likely to grow up in an intact family. Family income is higher for the NELS cohort, but this is not adjusted for inflation. Roughly equal percentages of the two cohorts went to private schools.

Members of the NELS cohort were more likely to have obtained a four-year college degree than were members of the HSB cohort. Members of the NELS cohort, especially the women, were also more likely to be working than were members of the HSB cohort. On the contrary, the percentage that was living independently was higher in the HSB cohort than in the NELS cohort, but this may be due to the two-year age difference between the two cohorts when last observed. In both cohorts, more than 80% of the men and women were living independently.

Comparing marital status and childbearing across the two cohorts yields even more ambiguous results given the age differences. The statistics show that the percentage of both men and women who were ever married declined across cohorts. Part of this is due to the differences in age while part of it is due to the delays in age at first marriage over time. The percentage of men and women who reported ever having a child also decreased over time—a reflection of the age differences in the two cohorts when last observed. The information on these individuals at age twenty (not shown in the table) shows that the percentage of individuals who were ever married decreased across cohorts while the percentage of individuals who ever had a child at age twenty increased across cohorts.

These comparisons of the two cohorts in their midtwenties indicate that much of what we see reflects trends in other data sets, including an increase in the percentage of individuals who pursue postsecondary

TABLE 9.2

CHARACTERISTICS OF TWO COHORTS OF YOUNG ADULTS

CHARACTERISTIC	HSB 1992 (AGE = 28)		NELS 2000 (AGE = 26)	
	MEN	WOMEN	MEN	WOMEN
Individual and family:				
Race:				
Hispanic	8.6	7.5	9.9	11.2
Black	12.7	14.0	12.0	12.3
Native American	1.6	1.1	1.0	.9
Asian	1.4	1.2	3.5	3.1
White, non-Hispanic	75.7	76.3	72.6	70.8
Parent education:				
Less than high school	10.3	12.7	9.2	11.2
High school	32.8	31.1	19.1	20.2
Some college	29.0	31.5	40.6	41.7
4-yr degree	13.6	11.7	16.3	14.1
Beyond BA/BS	14.3	13.0	14.8	12.1
Family type (12th grade):				
Intact	68.9	64.9	62.9	59.6
Step	7.0	9.0	14.5	13.3
Single	17.3	18.7	19.3	21.4
Other	6.7	7.4	3.3	5.8
Family income (12th grade):				
Less than $20,000	35.1	37.3	30.0	34.7
$20,000–$49,999	53.6	53.7	36.1	33.6
$50,000 or more	11.3	9.0	34.0	31.6
School type (12th grade):				
Catholic	5.6	6.5	5.6	4.8
Private	3.2	3.2	3.9	3.8
Public	91.2	90.3	90.3	91.4
Outcomes:				
BA or more	23.6	24.0	28.3	33.2
Ever married	54.4	68.4	39.6	53.2
Ever gave birth	43.3	58.2	31.7	47.5
Live independently	83.7	89.2	81.0	86.4
Working	90.1	76.3	91.9	81.4

Source. Authors' calculations using the 1992 HSB and 2000 NELS.

Note. HSB is the High School and Beyond Survey; NELS is the National Educational Longitudinal Survey. Family type, family income, and school type were measured in the ways when most individuals were in the twelfth grade.

education. The data also reveal that a substantial majority of young people are moving toward what qualitative research has shown to be the major demographic markers of adult status in the minds of young adults: financial and residential independence from their parents.

The percentages that have achieved each of these five demographic markers do not tell us much about the patterns of statuses in each cohort or variations in these patterns across cohorts. One way to look at patterns of statuses is to use latent class analysis, which allows us to examine the associations among categorical variables and identify both patterns in the data and the characteristics of individuals who fit the patterns.[6] We are most interested in patterns that reflect a successful transition to adulthood (postsecondary education, employment, and delayed childbearing) and those that reflect an unsuccessful transition to adulthood (little or no postsecondary education and early childbearing).

RESULTS

Identifying Patterns of Early Adult Life

We divided the two cohorts into men and women and performed latent class analysis for four samples (HSB men, HSB women, NELS men, and NELS women) to identify sets of latent classes characterizing the associations among educational attainment, work, marriage, childbearing, and living independently and to test how well the alternative sets of classes fit the data. Latent class analysis is also used by Osgood and colleagues (chap. 10, this vol.). The classes that are discussed in that chapter are somewhat different since we are using very different data sets. The relative advantages of the data in this chapter is that they come from racially and ethnically diverse national samples, while the relative advantage of the data in chapter 10 is that they contain detailed information on family and community inputs for a Michigan sample of mostly white individuals. The results show that a four-class model fits the data well for each group but that the nature of these classes varies across men and women. For both men and women the extent to which individuals have pursued postsecondary education and have formed families are the most critical demographic markers distinguishing the four latent classes.[7]

Table 9.3 shows the composition of the four latent classes for men and women in the HSB and NELS data. The four latent classes among the men include a group we call limited postsecondary education/family (LPSE/

FAM): most did not attend college, have married, and have children. This group is the largest group among the HSB men, making up just over a third or 36% of this cohort of men; it is the third largest group among NELS men, constituting just over a fourth or 26% of the NELS men. The second class in table 9.3 is a group we call limited postsecondary education/no family (LPSE/NOF): most did not attend college and have not started a family. This class constitutes just under a quarter or 24% of the HSB men and 29% of the NELS men. The third group in table 9.3 is a group we call BA/no family (BA/NOF): most completed four years of college and most have not started a family. They are the third largest group among the HSB men (22%) but the largest group among the NELS men (30%). The final group is one we call BA/family (BA/FAM): most have completed or at least attended college and have started a family.[8] This group makes up a slightly higher percentage of the HSB men (18%) than of the NELS men (16%). Overall the results reflect the lower level of family formation among the NELS men than among the HSB men; 54% of the HSB men are in the two FAM categories compared to 42% of the NELS men. They also reflect the expansion of higher education that occurred between the two cohorts: 46% of the NELS men are in the two BA cohorts compared to 40% of the HSB men. Although we use these descriptive labels in table 9.3, as we point out below, one should not confuse the short descriptive labels for what are actually more complicated latent classes.

Among women, the four latent classes are LPSE/FAM, which is very similar to the group with the same name among men: most did not attend college and most have married and have at least one child. This group is larger in the HSB cohort, making up 40% of the women, than in the NELS cohort where it makes up 28% of the women. The second group is one we call limited postsecondary education/children (LPSE/CHI)—it does not appear among the men: most did not attend college, most are not married, and most have children. This group is larger among the NELS women, where it makes up 22% of the sample, than among the HSB women where it constitutes 14%. The third group is similar to that among men, BA/NOF: most have a four-year degree or higher and have not started a family. This group makes up 23% of the HSB women and 29% of the NELS women. The final group is also similar to that among the men, BA/FAM: most have a four-year degree or higher and have married. The percentage of each cohort in this class is relatively equal. If we look at the two "marriage" classes, we find that 63% of the HSB women are in one of them, compared to 50% of the NELS women, a pattern similar to what we found in our comparison of the two

TABLE 9.3
LATENT CLASSES IN THE TWO COHORTS OF MEN AND WOMEN

	MEN				WOMEN			
	LPSE/FAM	LPSE/NOF	BA/NOF	BA/FAM	LPSE/FAM	LPSE/CHI	BA/NOF	BA/FAM
HSB:								
PR	.36	.24	.22	.18	.40	.14	.23	.23
Education:								
No postsecondary education	.82	.79	.17	.21	.78	.69	.26	.20
Some postsecondary education	.17	.18	.09	.18	.21	.26	.18	.21
BA	.01	.02	.74	.60	.01	.04	.57	.59
Married:								
No	.07	.98	.96	.01	.01	.74	.95	.04
Yes	.92	.02	.04	.99	.99	.26	.05	.96
Kids:								
No	.19	.85	.99	.56	.09	.33	1.00	.60
Yes	.81	.15	.01	.44	.91	.67	.00	.40
Independent:								
No	.08	.41	.24	.01	.04	.25	.33	.03
Yes	.92	.59	.76	.99	.96	.75	.67	.97
Working:								
No	.07	.16	.10	.04	.33	.68	.08	.10
Yes	.93	.84	.90	.96	.67	.32	.92	.90

NELS:

PR	.26	.29	.30	.16	.28	.22	.29	.22
Education:								
No postsecondary education	.53	.28	.00	.00	.40	.30	.00	.00
Some postsecondary education	.46	.66	.22	.48	.59	.67	.23	.34
BA	.00	.06	.78	.51	.02	.03	.77	.66
Married:								
No	.13	.97	.98	.03	.03	.86	.99	.02
Yes	.87	.03	.02	.97	.97	.14	.01	.98
Kids:								
No	.22	.84	1.00	.71	.13	.45	.98	.26
Yes	.78	.16	.00	.29	.87	.55	.02	.74
Independent:								
No	.06	.39	.19	.01	.05	.29	.23	.01
Yes	.94	.61	.81	.99	.95	.71	.77	.99
Working:								
No	.05	.10	.12	.06	.32	.16	.10	.11
Yes	.95	.90	.88	.94	.68	.84	.90	.89

Source. Authors' calculations using the 1992 HSB and 2000 NELS.

Note. LPSE/FAM = limited postsecondary education and family; LPSE/NOF = limited postsecondary education and no family; BA/NOF = BA or higher and no family; BA/FAM = BA or higher and family; LPSE/CHI = limited postsecondary education and a child or children; HSB = High School and Beyond Survey; NELS = National Educational Longitudinal Survey; PR = probability of being in a latent class.

cohorts of men. At the same time, just as with the men, a higher percentage of the NELS women than the HSB women are in one of the BA categories (51% and 46%, respectively). The classes for women and men are very similar with one major difference: there is a group of men with little postsecondary education who have not started family life, and there is a group of women with little postsecondary education who have had at least one child, mostly outside marriage.

Most individuals in all groups are working and living independently. The people least likely to be living independently (59% in HSB and 61% in NELS) are men in the LPSE/NOF category, who have little postsecondary education and have not started families. The lowest percentage for working (32%) is among women in the LPSE/CHI class in the HSB cohort, who are mostly unmarried women with little postsecondary education and a child. In the NELS cohort, 84% of the women in this category are working. Some of the reasons for the different levels of labor force participation in this class in the two cohorts are apparent from looking at the distribution of the other markers in the two classes. Higher percentages of members of this class in HSB than in NELS have children and are married, while a higher percentage of the members of this class in NELS have some postsecondary education. Overall the results of the latent class analysis reveal that most individuals are working to achieve financial independence and are living independently.

Latent class analysis is a useful tool for revealing patterns in the data based on the association among categorical variables of interest. But as the discussion of the differences in the LPSE/CHI class between the two cohorts above suggests, we should be careful not to overinterpret or reify these categories. To give another example of how misuse of these categories can lead to an oversimplified view of the world, in table 9.3, the percentage of HSB men (LPSE/FAM) who are married is 92% rather than 100%, and the percentage with children is 81%, not 100%. This is because values on the other three variables—education, living independently, and employment—also enter into the assignment of an individual to this class.

Consequently an analysis of the association of family resources and school characteristics with being in one of the latent classes in table 9.3 is different from an analysis that looks only at whether individuals pursued postsecondary education or married by their midtwenties. Latent class analysis reveals some interesting patterns in the association of our five categorical variables, but an analysis of who is in these latent classes draws on a combination of all five variables rather than just the distinctions that seem to be most important in distinguishing the classes from one another.

With these caveats in mind, the results in table 9.3 are still informative about whether individuals are moving toward a successful start to their adult lives and about how they are doing in terms of statuses that policymakers regard as important. To reiterate, the percentage of men in either of the BA categories went from 40% to 46% between the HSB and NELS cohorts, while the percentage of women increased from 46% to 51%. These are the people who seem to be most poised for continued success in the labor market over the course of their adult lives. In contrast, the percentage of men in either of the FAM categories declined from 54% in the HSB cohort to 42% in the NELS cohort, while the percentage of women declined from 63% to 50%. The percentage of women in the most problematic category in table 9.3— LPSE/CHI—increased from 14% in the HSB cohort to 22% in the NELS cohort. These changes reflect the increases in postsecondary educational attainment across cohorts, the declines in marriage, and the increases in childbearing outside marriage.

The Influence of Families and Schools on Early Adult Life Patterns

In addition to analyzing the patterns of early adult statuses, we used multinomial logistic regression analysis to examine the relationship between family and school characteristics and membership in the latent classes shown in table 9.3 for men and women in each cohort. We used one of the classes as the reference class in each of the four sets of multinomial logistic regressions. This yields three distinct coefficients for each variable in each set of analyses, one for each of the contrasts between the reference class and the other three classes. Consequently, these analyses yield a large number of estimated coefficients, twelve coefficients for each variable or category of the categorical variables. In order to ease the presentation of results, we converted these results into predicted probabilities for two selected latent classes.

Tables 9.4 and 9.5 summarize the results of this analysis by presenting the predicted probabilities of being in two latent classes—BA/no family in table 9.4 and limited postsecondary education/children in table 9.5—that are crucial in terms of setting the stage for later success in life. The members of the latent class BA/NOF completed a four-year degree or more and delayed family formation until education was completed. The members of the latent class LPSE/CHI, found only among women, have had little exposure to postsecondary education and have had a child outside marriage. We look at how these predicted probabilities are associated with four key

TABLE 9.4

PROBABILITIES OF BEING IN LATENT CLASS BA/NO FAMILY BY

CHARACTERISTICS

	HSB		NELS	
CHARACTERISTIC	MEN	WOMEN	MEN	WOMEN
Overall PR	.22	.23	.30	.29
Race:				
White	[.46]	[.61]	[.47]	[.53]
Native American	.43	.43*	.04*	.31*
Asian	.68*	.73*	.69*	.74*
Black	.42	.57	.38*	.61*
Hispanic	.43	.76	.39*	.44*
Parental education:				
Less than high school	.44	.55	.30*	.55
High school	[.46]	[.61]	[.47]	[.53]
Some college	.55*	.67*	.53	.62*
BA/BS	.67*	.77*	.74*	.75*
More than BA/BS	.73*	.78*	.86*	.83*
Family structure:				
Two parents	[.46]	[.61]	[.47]	[.53]
Step	.41	.48*	.41	.44*
Single	.44	.57*	.50	.55
Other	.27*	.46*	.24*	.27*
School:				
Public	[.46]	[.61]	[.47]	[.53]
Catholic	.60*	.73*	.74*	.68*
Other private	.74*	.70*	.76*	.73*

Note: The baseline probability, shown in brackets, is for a white individual from a two-parent family with high school–educated parents, two or fewer siblings, and the lowest category of family income who lived in an urban area in the Northeast and attended public schools. HSB is the High School and Beyond Survey; NELS is the National Educational Longitudinal Survey; PR = probability of being in a latent class.

*This probability is associated with a coefficient that differs significantly from the baseline coefficient at or below the .05 level.

variables: race/ethnicity, parental education, family structure, and type of school.[9] Previous research and theoretical models of the transition to adulthood discussed above suggest that these variables will be strongly associated with the probabilities of successful and unsuccessful early transitions to adulthood. We expect that blacks, Native Americans, and Latinos will have

TABLE 9.5

PROBABILITIES OF WOMEN BEING IN THE LATENT CLASS OF

LITTLE POSTSECONDARY EDUCATION AND CHILDREN

(LPSE/CHILDREN) BY CHARACTERISTICS

CHARACTERISTIC	HSB	NELS
Overall PR	.14	.22
Race:		
White	[.26]	[.55]
Native American	.67*	.80*
Asian	.30	.45
Black	.72*	.83*
Hispanic	.44*	.70*
Parental education:		
Less than high school	.23	.61
High school	[.26]	[.55]
Some college	.17*	.47*
BA/BS	.10*	.32*
More than BA/BS	.12*	.33*
Family structure:		
Two parents	[.26]	[.55]
Step	.42*	.64*
Single	.36*	.61*
Other	.47*	.70*
School:		
Public	[.26]	[.55]
Catholic	.19*	.44*
Other private	.21	.22*

Note: The baseline probability, shown in brackets, is for a white individual from a two-parent family with high school–educated parents, two
or fewer siblings, and the lowest category of family income who lived in
an urban area in the Northeast and attended public schools. HSB is the
High School and Beyond Survey; NELS is the National Educational Longitudinal Survey; PR = probability of being in a latent class.

*This probability is associated with a coefficient that differs
significantly from the baseline coefficient at or below the .05 level.

less successful early transitional periods than whites and Asians. The likelihood of successful transitions should increase with parental education and
be highest for those who grew up in an intact family relative to other type of
families. Those who attended Catholic schools should also have a greater
likelihood of successful early transitions to adulthood.

Race/Ethnicity and Getting Off to a Good Start

Table 9.4 presents the predicted probabilities of being in the BA/NOF class for individuals in different categories of race/ethnicity, parental education, family structure, and type of school. These probabilities are first computed for a "baseline" individual: a white man, with high school–educated parents, living in an intact family, and who attended public school in the twelfth grade. The first column of predicted probabilities is for the HSB men. The only group that differs significantly from white men in the HSB cohort is the Asian group, with a probability of .68. This reflects other research that shows that Asians are more likely to obtain four-year or higher degrees than white Americans are. The other HSB male groups have slightly lower, but not statistically significantly different, probabilities compared to whites.

Among the HSB women, Asians are also significantly more likely than whites to obtain a four-year degree, while Native Americans are less likely to do so. Among the NELS cohorts, all groups differ significantly from whites, with Asians being the most likely to be in the BA/NOF category and Native Americans the least likely. Among the NELS men, blacks are less likely than whites to be in the BA/NOF class, while among the NELS women, blacks are more likely than whites to be in the BA/NOF category.

These differences are those that occur after controlling for the effects of the other variables in the model. In many studies of educational attainment, African Americans have higher levels of attainment than whites after controlling for other characteristics of individuals and families such as family income and parental education. It is therefore not surprising that African Americans do not differ from whites in terms of being in the BA/NOF category within the HSB men and women or that African American women are more likely than white women to be in this category in the NELS cohort. The findings for black men in the NELS cohort suggest that there is something very different about their experiences relative to white men in that group. The very low probability (.04) for Native Americans should be regarded with caution given the relatively small numbers of American Indians in the sample.

The results do not tell us why Asians are more likely to get off to a good start than are the other groups, or why Native Americans, black men, and Latinos fare less well than whites do. This could be due to unmeasured differences in the resources available to individuals for pursuing higher education, in the opportunities that are available generally to individuals, or in preparation for higher education. The results, however, suggest that members of three minority groups are at greater risk of not getting off to a good start and that the risks may have been more pronounced for the cohort born in 1974 than for the cohort born in 1964.

Family Resources and Getting Off to a Good Start

Parental education may affect the early life course both through role modeling and socialization and also as a measure of lifetime income for the family. The results in table 9.4 show that the probability of getting off to a good start varies significantly with parental education in each cohort. The baseline category for parental education is high school graduation, so an asterisk indicates that individuals in the other categories differ significantly from those whose parents had a high school diploma but no more. The difference in probabilities between the lowest (less than high school) and highest (education beyond a BA/BS) parental educational categories ranges from .23 among the HSB women (.78—.55) to .56 among the NELS men (.86—.30), and the probability of getting off to a good start increases dramatically with the educational level of one's parents. The difference between those whose parents had less than a high school diploma and those whose parents had a high school diploma is significant only in the NELS-men group. Within this same group the difference between those whose parents had some college and those whose parents had a high school diploma is not significant, but a significant difference exists between these categories for each of the other three groups. These results strongly suggest that family resources play a significant role in determining whether individuals get off to a good start in their early adult lives.

Family Structure and Getting Off to a Good Start

Research has shown that individuals who grow up with two parents attain higher levels of education and are less likely to form families in early adulthood than those who grow up in other types of family situations (McLanahan and Sandefur 1994). This is partly due to differences in family income, and we control for this in the analysis reported in table 9.4. Other factors that are associated with the effects of family structure include differences in parental time and energy across types of families and differences in the involvement of stepparents as opposed to biological parents in the lives of their children.

The reference category for family structure is those residing with two biological or adoptive parents in the twelfth grade. The results show that the only category that differs significantly from the two-parent category in all

four groups is the "other" category. These are unusual families in that neither parent resides in the household. These families make up less than 10%
of all families in the four cohorts. Individuals who grew up with a single parent differ from those who grew up with both parents only among the HSB-
women group, while those who grew up with a parent and a stepparent differ from those living with two parents in the twelfth grade among the female
groups in both the HSB and NELS.

These results reflect the fact that family structure tends to have more
pronounced effects on outcomes involving early family formation than it
does on educational attainment in these four data sets. It has especially
strong effects on having a child prior to marriage, as we will discuss further
below.

Schools and Getting Off to a Good Start

The final panel in table 9.4 shows the effect of the type of school attended
during senior year on membership in the latent class BA/NOF. Individuals
who attended a Catholic or other private high school are significantly more
likely to be in this category than are individuals who attended public school.
Among all groups except the HSB women, the probabilities are highest for
those who attended other private high schools. These results show that another aspect of social structure—the kind of high school one attends—is associated with whether one gets off to a good start. Our results, of course, do
not allow us to control for any selectivity into type of high school or to explore
what factors are associated with these differences. Bryk, Lee, and Holland
(1993) argue that Catholic schools provide a strong community of parents,
teachers, and fellow students who encourage students to do well in school
and provide emotional support and social control that promotes doing well.
If this is the case, the results in table 9.4 also suggest that other types of private schools may provide similar kinds of social capital.

Race/Ethnicity and Making Early Mistakes

Table 9.5 shows the predicted probabilities of being in the latent class of
those having little postsecondary education in conjunction with having a
child out of wedlock, LPSE/CHI. This is the latent class category that is most
clearly associated with not getting off to a good start. Women in this latent
class have limited future opportunities for obtaining additional postsecondary education, and their economic prospects via marriage or work are
also more limited than those of women who are not in this latent class. The
overall probability in the two samples shows that the probability of being in

this latent class increased from .14 to .22 between the 1964 and 1974 birth cohorts (table 9.3). This is due in part to the increase in age at marriage and in childbearing outside marriage across the two cohorts.

Asian and white women are not very likely, but equally so, to be in this latent class. Native Americans, blacks, and Hispanics, on the contrary, have significantly higher probabilities of being in this latent class, with blacks the most likely to be there in both cohorts. These results suggest that black, Hispanic, and Native American women are at a greater risk of getting off to a bad start than are Asian and white women. Although membership in this latent class involves five markers, much of the racial and ethnic difference is accounted for by the greater likelihood of black women bearing a child out-of-wedlock. Vital statistics data indicate that black women have historically experienced much higher levels of out-of-wedlock childbearing than white and Asian women have, and Hispanics and Native Americans have had levels intermediate between blacks and whites (Ventura and Bachrach 2000).

Parental Education and Making Early Mistakes

Parental education also plays a role in membership in the LPSE/CHI latent class. Among the HSB women, those whose parents have education beyond a BA/BS have a probability of being in this latent class that is .11 less than those whose parents have less than a high school education (.23−.12). Among the NELS women, the difference is higher, .28 (.61−.33). There are no significant differences among women whose parents have less than high school and those whose parents have only high school. But those whose parents have some college are significantly less likely to be in this latent class than those whose parents have only high school. Women whose parents are in the highest two educational categories have roughly equal probabilities of being in this latent class, but in both cases the probability is significantly lower than for those whose parents have a high school education only.

The effects of parental education again illustrate the role of social structure in influencing the early aspects of the transition to adulthood. There is, of course, both randomness and explicit choice involved in having a child prior to marriage, but the results illustrate that this adverse event is more likely to happen to individuals from less-privileged families.

Family Structure and Making Early Mistakes

Women from two-parent families are significantly less likely to be in the latent class LPSE/CHI than are women from the other three types of families. Women who were living with neither of their parents at the time of the interview in their senior year are the most likely to be in this category. The effects of family structure could be due to role modeling or socialization, but they could also be due to differences in economic resources or parental time across different types of families. The results here and elsewhere suggest that family structure has stronger influences on family formation associated with the early transition to adulthood than with educational attainment. Parental education, conversely, emerges as an important influence on both educational attainment and early family formation.

Schools and Making Early Mistakes

In both cohorts, individuals who attended Catholic schools are less likely to be in the latent class LPSE/CHI than are individuals who attended public schools. In the NELS cohort, women who attended some other type of private school are also less likely to be in this latent class. This is consistent with the argument of Bryk and colleagues (1993) that Catholic schools provide a community that encourages and supports behaviors and decisions that lead to successful early transitions to adulthood.

As a group, the results in table 9.5 clearly show that social structure—as reflected in race and ethnicity, parental education, family structure, and the type of school attended—exerts significant and powerful effects on whether individuals get off to a bad start in the early transition to adulthood.

DISCUSSION

The early transition to adulthood—the time during which young people complete their education, begin their work lives, and start their families—is a critical period in which individuals are making choices that will affect their lives in both the short run and the long run. These choices will also affect the lives of their children. Each individual has some control over his or her choices, but a large body of social science research also shows that social structure, including the families, communities, and schools in which people spend childhood and adolescence, has a powerful impact on whether adolescents have a successful or unsuccessful early transition to adulthood.

Previous quantitative research suggests that there is a great deal of disorder to the life course. Young people do not necessarily follow a normative route of completing their education, going to work, establishing independent residences, marriage, and then childbearing in the context of marriage. Instead, many young people have children prior to marriage, or they marry before they complete their education. The results of previous qualitative work by other researchers suggests that young people think a good deal about the events of their lives, and the way in which these events lead to the transition from being an adolescent to being an adult. Most of this qualitative work suggests that financial and social independence from parents is seen as the key marker of being an adult. A college education is a route to becoming an adult since it helps develop work-related and social skills that enable young people to achieve independence. Our multivariate analyses suggested that social structure, reflected in the social circumstances of childhood and adolescence, plays an important role in the early transition to adulthood. Young people who are white, have highly educated parents, and who attended private schools are more likely to start off well during the early adult period than are those who are black, Native American, or Hispanic, have less educated parents, and who attended public schools. The type of family one resided in during the senior year of high school was also significantly related to demographic markers during the early adult period, especially to whether a young woman had little postsecondary education and gave birth to a child out-of-wedlock.

Our comparisons of the cohorts in the High School and Beyond and National Educational Longitudinal Study show that the statuses of these cohorts in their midtwenties reflect what we know from other research on trends in social and demographic behaviors over time. A higher percentage of the NELS cohort had attained a four-year college degree or higher by their midtwenties. At the same time, a smaller percentage of them had begun their families by their midtwenties, although this difference is in part due to the fact that the HSB cohort was last observed at age twenty-eight while the NELS cohort was last observed at age twenty-six. In comparing the cohorts at age twenty, the NELS women were more likely to have had a child out-of-wedlock and were less likely to be married than were the HSB women. Most members of both cohorts were living independently and working by their midtwenties. The percentage of the NELS women who were working was noticeably higher than the percentage of HSB women who were working, reflecting the growing labor force participation of women across cohorts during this period.

When we examined the patterns of demographic markers among men and women in the two cohorts, we found a similar set of patterns with some gender differences. Among the men, four major patterns fit the data well: (1) little postsecondary education and the initiation of family life, (2) little postsecondary education without the beginning of family life, (3) a four-year degree or higher and no family, and (4) a four-year degree or higher and the initiation of family life. Among the women, the four major patterns were the same with the exception that a class of little postsecondary education and not beginning family life (LPSE / NOF) is not really present in the data. Instead, we find a class of little postsecondary education and a child outside marriage (LPSE/CHI).

The analyses illustrate both the strengths and limitations of latent class analysis. Latent class analysis provides a mechanism for exploring the interconnections among a set of categorical variables. In the case of schooling and family formation, it shows that associations between these two statuses are also associated with work and residential independence. The principal limitation of latent class analysis lies in the temptation to attach too much meaning to a latent class. In some ways the existence of four latent classes in each of the four groups suggests an order to the early transition to adulthood that runs counter to what we know about the many paths individuals may take from late adolescence to adulthood.

Nonetheless, both ways of looking at this critical period in the lives of individuals have merit. We know that the paths individuals take in their late teens and early twenties vary widely, but by their midtwenties many of them have arrived at points that are similar to many other people of the same age. The results suggest that families and schools not only influence the separate dimensions of educational attainment and early family formation but they also influence the joint distribution of these and other dimensions of the transition to adulthood. Exploring the mechanisms through which parental education and type of school influence the transition to adulthood was beyond the scope of this chapter. We know, however, that parental education reflects a number of factors that are critical in shaping peoples lives— including the lifetime income of the family of origin, the role modeling of the parents, and the parents' knowledge of secondary and higher education. Since we cannot directly change the educational levels of our current generation of parents in the same way that we might change family income through public assistance or progressive taxation and redistribution, this finding suggests that we might try to increase the availability of aid for higher education and improve the information available to middle school and high school students about higher education. The important role of private schools in facilitating the successful transition to adulthood suggests the need for further research on the differences between private schools and public schools that account for this.

All in all, the results suggest that most young people in both cohorts were able to achieve the two demographic markers that are most associated with the financial, residential, and personal independence craved by the subjects of qualitative research: living away from home and working. So most

American young people in these two cohorts must have felt that in their midtwenties they were adults or close to adult status. However, other choices they made or were forced to make about education and early family formation would continue to affect their ability to be economically successful throughout their adult lives.

NOTES

This work was supported by the MacArthur Foundation and by grant HD57366 to Gary Sandefur from the National Institute for Child Health and Human Development.

1. Fussell and Furstenberg (this vol., chap. 2) review this research, so we will not repeat a review in this chapter.

2. We must be careful, of course, in reaching too many conclusions based on small samples from one city. Aronson's sample was actually a subsample of a larger sample selected randomly from ninth graders in St. Paul. She selected her sample by targeting and sampling three groups: (1) those who had spent a significant amount of time in postsecondary education, (2) those who became parents, and (3) those who had considerable investment in full-time work. This was done to insure that she would have examples of different trajectories of experience.

3. This is, of course, a very simple economic or rational choice model of the transition to adulthood. Although it has its limitations, it nonetheless can be used to suggest ways in which family and community resources are associated with successful and unsuccessful transitions to adulthood.

4. We focus on schools because the data we are using, the High School and Beyond Study and the National Educational Longitudinal Study, contain information about schools but no real information about the neighborhoods in which the respondents were living.

5. In our analysis we use the pan-ethnic categories of white, black, Hispanic, Asian, and American Indian. This pan-ethnic grouping masks a great deal of heterogeneity within these groups. The Hispanic group, e.g, consists of Mexicans and Cubans, who have very different levels of educational attainment. Within the Asian category, the Japanese and Indian groups have much higher levels of education than the Vietnamese.

6. The basic approach to the latent class analysis used in this chapter is similar to that used in Wells, Sandefur, and Hogan (2003) where the focus is on adolescents with disabilities. We use a program known as Latent Gold 2.0 to estimate these models. This program is available from Statistical Innovations located in Belmont, MA. See Clogg (1995) for a straightforward overview of the main principles and possible applications.

7. We chose the four-class model for each group based on the Bayesian information criteria (BIC) statistics for each model. The BIC statistic takes both goodness of fit and degrees of freedom into account. The complete set of fit statistics and other results from the latent class analysis are available from us on request.

8. We are using "attended college" loosely here. The variable actually indicates whether the individual pursued any postsecondary education since completing high school.

9. Each model also included a set of control variables available in both the HSB and NELS data. These were number of siblings, family income in the base year of the survey, whether the individual lived in a rural, suburban, or urban area in the base year, and region of the country in the base year.

REFERENCES

Arnett, Jeffrey Jensen. 1994. Are College Students Adults? Their Conceptions of the Transition to Adulthood. *Journal of Adult Development* 1:154–68.

———. 1998. Learning to Stand Alone: The Contemporary American Transition to Adulthood in Cultural and Historical Context. *Human Development* 41: 295–315.

Arnett, Jeffrey Jensen, and Susan Taber. 1994. Adolescence Terminable and Interminable: When Does Adolescence End? *Journal of Youth and Adolescence* 23:1–21.

Aronson, Pamela. 2001. The Markers and Meanings of Growing Up: Contemporary Young Women's Transition from Adolescence to Adulthood. Paper presented at the 2001 Annual Meeting of the American Sociological Association, Anaheim, CA, August 18–21.

Bryk, Anthony S., Valerie E. Lee, and Peter B. Holland. 1993. *Catholic Schools and the Common Good.* Cambridge, MA: Harvard University Press.

Clogg, Clifford C. 1995. Latent Class Models. Pp. 311–59 in *Handbook of Statistical Modeling for the Social and Behavioral Sciences,* edited by Gerhard Arminger, Clifford C. Clogg, and Michael Sobel. New York: Plenum.

Furstenberg, Frank F., Jr., Thomas D. Cook, Jacquelynne Eccles, Glen H. Elder Jr., and Arnold Sameroff. 1999. *Managing to Make It: Urban Families and Adolescent Success.* Chicago: University of Chicago Press.

Hogan, Dennis. 1978. The Variable Order of Events in the Life Course. *American Sociological Review* 43:573–86.

Hogan, Dennis, and Nan Marie Astone. 1986. The Transition to Adulthood. *Annual Review of Sociology* 12:109–30.

Marini, Margaret Mooney. 1984. The Order of Events in the Transition to Adulthood. *Sociology of Education* 57:63–84.

McLanahan, Sara, and Gary Sandefur. 1994. *Growing Up with a Single Parent: What Hurts? What Helps?* Cambridge, MA: Harvard University Press.

Modell, John, Frank Furstenberg Jr., and Theodore Hershberg. 1976. Social Change and Transitions to Adulthood in Historical Perspective. *Journal of Family History* 1:7–31.

Rindfuss, Ronald, C. Gray Swicegood, and Rachel Rosenfeld. 1987. Disorder in the Life Course: How Common and Does It Matter? *American Sociological Review* 52:785–801.

Sandefur, Gary D., Molly Martin, Jennifer Eggerling-Boeck, Susan Mannon, and Ann Meier. 2001. An Overview of Racial and Ethnic Demographic Trends. Pp. 40–102 in *America Becoming: Racial Trends and Their Consequences,* edited by Neil J. Smelser, William Julius Wilson, and Faith Mitchell. Washington, DC: National Academy Press.

Settersten, Richard. A. Jr. 2003. Rethinking Social Policy: Lessons of a Life-Course Perspective. Pp. 191–222 in *Invitation to the Life Course,* edited by Richard A. Settersten Jr. Amityville, NY: Baywood Publishing.

Ventura, Serra J., and Christine A. Bachrach. 2000. Nonmarital Childbearing in the United States, 1940–1999. *National Vital Statistics Reports: From the Centers for Disease Control and Prevention, National Center for Health Statistics, National Vital Statistics System* (Hyattsville, MD), vol. 48, no. 16.

Wells, Thomas, Gary Sandefur, and Dennis Hogan. 2003. What Happens after the High School Years for Young Persons with Disabilities? *Social Forces* 82 (2): 803–23.

CHAPTER 10

SIX PATHS TO ADULTHOOD

Fast Starters, Parents without Careers,
Educated Partners, Educated Singles,
Working Singles, and Slow Starters

D. WAYNE OSGOOD, GRETCHEN RUTH, JACQUELYNNE S. ECCLES,
JANIS E. JACOBS, AND BONNIE L. BARBER

The transition to adulthood is most obviously characterized by movement from the roles of childhood and adolescence to those of adulthood. Youth leave their parents' homes to live on their own, they marry or cohabit with romantic partners, and they become parents themselves. They finish their schooling and take full-time employment. Completing most, if not all, of these role transitions is often considered to be the standard for reaching adulthood. As the other chapters in this volume demonstrate, however, this set of changes does not come as an organized "package" or standard sequence. Rather, young people today take many varied paths through these transitions.

The purpose of this volume is to move beyond existing research in order to gain a more coherent understanding of this period of life. Most research on transitions to these adult roles has concentrated on only one at a time, such as research on the predictors and consequences of marriage or of college completion. Research of that sort is of limited value for learning how these different aspects of the transition to adulthood weave together in people's lives.

We attempt to move beyond prior research by taking a largely descriptive person-oriented approach (Magnusson 1988). Our work is person-oriented in that it attempts to identify the different ways that these roles do and do not combine for different people. We seek to elaborate the meaning of these distinct patterns of transition by comparing several groups on a wide variety of information that was gathered from them during the transition to adulthood. We also examine how factors earlier in life predict these divergent paths during the transition. In these ways we attempt to put flesh on the bones of the basic facts about transitions into adult roles.

Our primary focus is on information gathered at age twenty-four, an approximate midpoint in the transition to adulthood falling roughly halfway between the completion of high school and the end of the twenties. To consider several role transitions jointly, we begin by classifying respondents into groups on the basis of simple facts about their transitions in five major role domains: romantic relationships, residence, parenthood, employment, and education. These groups represent distinct paths through the transition to adulthood, at least as viewed through one snapshot in time, and they are comparable to those that Sandefur and colleagues distinguish in their chapter of this volume (chap. 9), using similar measures of adult role statuses. Together, our chapters provide a rich picture of how these roles intersect during this transitional period, and we will be especially attentive to how our groups compare to theirs.

After defining the groups that represent the distinct paths, we consider the relationship of group membership to other variables in order to address two types of questions. First, we seek to enrich our understanding of what it means to be on one path rather than another by comparing members of different groups on other measures collected at age twenty-four. We examine patterns of time use, the degree to which respondents feel that they are carrying out various adult responsibilities, and more detailed information about each of the five role domains. Second, we investigate whether the path a youth will take at age twenty-four is foreshadowed by various factors, including demographic characteristics of the individuals and their families of origin, as well as information gathered from the respondents at age eighteen, including their attitudes toward marriage and family, employment, and education. There are other things that it would be useful to know about these groups, such as their stability over time and the relative outcomes for the different groups as they progress through the transition and on into adulthood. For now, those topics await future research.

SAMPLE

Our data come from the Michigan Study of Adolescent Life Transitions (MSALT [Eccles et al. 1989]). This project began in 1984, when the respondents were in the sixth grade and approximately age twelve. They were then students in 143 math classes located in twelve school districts. The study continues today; a ninth wave of data was collected in 1999.

The sample came from white middle- and working-class suburbs in the Detroit metropolitan area. Only 5% of the respondents are minority group members, and the largest share of the respondents' parents worked in the auto industry. Through the 1970s, labor unions were strong in Michigan, allowing working-class families to reach a comfortable standard of living. At the beginning of this study, Michigan was in the midst of its auto crisis of the 1980s. Many auto plants closed, never to reopen. Since that time, new jobs in the auto industry have almost always gone elsewhere. Long-term auto workers, such as many of these respondents' parents, were able to retain their jobs and continue their relative financial success, but the employment prospects for their children were bleak, and they were unlikely to obtain working-class jobs with comparable pay and benefits. This is the world that our respondents faced as we found them on these several paths through the transition to adulthood.

METHOD

We used latent class analysis (Clogg 1995; Lazarsfeld and Henry 1968) to identify clusters of respondents that we use to illustrate alternative paths through the transition to adulthood. The method defines these groups or clusters by the proportion of members that have each of the characteristics included in the analysis. For instance, most members of one cluster might be married parents with high levels of education, while members of another might be predominantly cohabiting nonparents with a moderate amount of schooling. Latent class analysis derives a set of profiles of characteristics that best account for patterns of association in the data.

The groups resulting from a latent class analysis are, of course, dependent on the variables considered in the analysis, and table 10.1 summarizes the measures we used for this purpose. The nature of this statistical method limits us to about five multiple-category variables for our sample of 1,410. Accordingly, our latent class analysis used one measure for each of the five primary domains of the transition to adulthood: romantic relationships, residence, parenthood, employment, and education.

We distinguished four categories of romantic relationships, classifying respondents as either married, cohabiting with a partner, steadily dating someone (with whom they did not reside), or single (with no steady dating relationship). As table 10.1 shows, the portion of respondents falling into

TABLE 10.1

VARIABLES DEFINING CLUSTERS IN LATENT CLASS ANALYSIS

	PERCENTAGE
Romantic relationship:	
Single	28
Steady dating	33
Cohabiting	15
Married	24
Residence:	
With parents or other relatives	38
Renting or temporary	44
Home owner	18
Parenthood:	
No	80
Yes	20
Employment:	
Not employed	15
Short-term job	29
Job is step on career path	36
Long-term job	21
Education:	
No more than high school degree	21
Some college	47
Bachelor's degree or more	33

Note. n = 1,410.

these categories ranged from 15% who were cohabiting to 33% who were steadily dating.

Our measure of residence embodies two useful distinctions. First, we separated respondents who had left their parents' households to live on their own from the substantial portion of the sample who had not (38%). Second, among respondents who were not living with their parents (or other relatives), we distinguished the smaller group of respondents who were independent and financially stable enough to purchase their own homes (18%) from the plurality (44%) who either rented or lived in temporary arrangements (e.g., military housing, with friends). This data set did not allow us to make further distinctions about household composition, such as identifying those who lived alone versus with friends.

Our last measure in the realm of family and relationships is whether respondents were serving in the role of parent. Twenty percent of our respondents indicated that they had children. Of the children, 93% were biological or adopted, and 7% were stepchildren. Only 12% of these parents reported having children who did not live with them, and only 1% of parents reported that they did not regularly interact with their children.

Because our focus is on paths through the transition to adulthood, when considering employment we took into account how respondents thought their current work related to their future plans. All but a small portion of the sample (15%) was employed when we contacted them at age twenty-four. At this point in their lives, relatively few of the respondents (21%) felt that they would hold their current jobs for the long term, without moving on to some other position. Many reported that their current jobs were either steps on a career path (36%) or short-term positions of little relevance to their futures (29%).

By age twenty-four, respondents who were enrolled in school were more often engaged in part-time than full-time study. Their programs varied from the highest academic level (e.g., doctoral students and medical residents) to the lowest (e.g., students in literacy and GED programs). Accordingly, current student status did not prove a useful basis for defining the transition groups, but the amount of schooling completed did. For our latent class analysis, we categorized level of education as (1) no more than high school completion (21%), (2) some college or postsecondary training (47%), or (3) bachelor's degree or beyond (33%).

We used the latent class analysis to identify six classes or clusters representing distinct paths through the transition to adulthood. Appendix A provides technical information about that analysis. We present this set of six paths as a heuristic summary of common life situations midway through the period of transition to adulthood. It would be a mistake to view these groupings as "natural," "true," or somehow representing a deeper reality more fundamental than this set of measures. The number of groups is also subjective because statistical criteria did not give a clear-cut answer about the "correct" number of groups. We chose to present the results for six groups because, among the statistically plausible choices, that typology generated the most interesting and informative results. We have labeled the six groups: fast starters (12% of the sample), parents without careers (10%), educated partners (19%), educated singles (37%), working singles (7%), and slow starters (14%).

The classes are latent in the sense that they are not directly observable. Instead they are inferred from the data as a set of ideal types that would most plausibly produce the set of cases we observed. Some individuals clearly exemplify a single class, while others plausibly fit two or more of the classes. A large share of our respondents are relatively clear matches to one or another of the groups, but others are not: 57% have a probability of at least .8 of belonging to some cluster, while 38% have a probability of .5–.8, and 5% have a probability less than .5 of belonging to any single cluster. As it is impossible to "correctly identify" to which latent class each individual belongs, we more accurately represent the latent classes by treating individual group membership as probabilistic. Appendix A describes our statistical approach to the problem of classifying respondents into these groups.

RESULTS

Figure 10.1 compares the six paths through the transition to adulthood on the variables used to define them. The first path or group we designated as the fast starters because these respondents occupied the greatest number of adult roles at age twenty-four. All but 10% of this group were married (73%) or were cohabiting with a partner (17%). Accordingly, very few lived with parents or other relatives (12%), while more than half already owned their own homes (55%). Indeed, the majority of these fast starters were parents by age twenty-four (57%). This group was also advanced in the world of work, with 70% in jobs they considered long term and 28% in jobs they viewed as steps on a career path. Given the fast starters' early commitments in these realms, it was not surprising that their investments in education were more limited, with only 6% having earned bachelor's degrees. The majority had some college or postsecondary training (57%). Twelve percent of our sample fell into this fast starter cluster.

Our label for the second cluster is parents without careers. This 10% of the sample was distinct in their combination of extensive commitments in the realm of family and relationships but limited involvement in employment. Most notably, virtually all were parents (94%). They were either married (72%) or cohabiting (27%), and all but 6% resided in their own households rather than with parents. Almost all members of this group were either not employed (55%) or regarded their jobs as short-term employment (36%). The parents without careers had the most limited educational achievement, with 57% having no education beyond a high school degree.

The respondents we call educated partners had also made the transition from their parents' homes to living with romantic partners, but in contrast, none had become parents. Cohabiting was especially common in this group, occurring as often as marriage (43% each). Employment was quite variable, but the highest proportion viewed their current jobs as steps on a

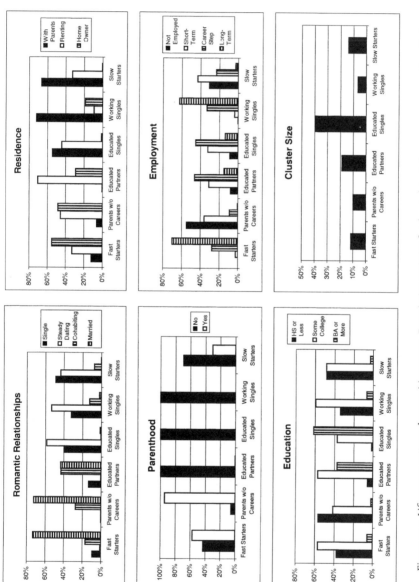

Figure 10.1. Life-course patterns by transition group. Descriptive statistics for the six latent class groups representing distinct pathways through the transition to adulthood.

career track (46%). Respondents in this group had made considerably greater investment in education than the first two groups, with 94% obtaining at least some postsecondary education, and 37% earning bachelor's degrees. The educated partners comprised 19% of the sample.

The most common path by far was the 37% of the sample we designated the educated singles. They differed from the first three clusters in that they did not live with romantic partners. About half lived with their parents or other relatives (55%), and almost all the rest rented rather than owned their homes (44%). In other respects, the educated singles were very similar to the educated partners. None were parents, and the largest proportion viewed their jobs as career steps (45%). This was the most highly educated group of respondents, with 61% having bachelor's degrees. The large size of this group is consistent with Fussell and Furstenberg's (this vol., chap. 2) depiction of the increasing prominence of education over the past century combined with delays in marriage and parenthood.

The working singles, the smallest cluster in the sample (7%), were similar to the educated singles in that they did not live with romantic partners and they were not parents, but they differed in other respects. The working singles were especially likely to live with their parents (72%). They were advanced in the world of work, with 63% in long-term jobs. Few had graduated from college (7%), but many had obtained lower levels of postsecondary education (59%).

We labeled the final cluster the slow starters because this 14% of the sample had made the fewest transitions to adult roles by age twenty-four. These respondents rarely lived with romantic partners (8%), two-thirds lived with their parents, and none owned homes. The majority were either not employed (31%) or worked in short-term jobs (43%). Almost none had jobs they considered long term (3%). This group was also among the least educated, with 48% having no postsecondary schooling. The slow starters were more "advanced" in the area of parenthood, with 30% becoming parents by age twenty-four.

These six transition groups at age twenty-four relate well to the four groups that resulted from the latent class analysis conducted by Sandefur and colleagues (this vol., chap. 9) using the National Educational Longitudinal Study (NELS) of individuals at age twenty-six and the High School and Beyond survey (HSB) of individuals at age twenty-eight. Both our and Sandefur's analyses yield two groups distinguished by college education. At age twenty-four, it is a completed degree that distinguishes the educated partners and educated singles from other groups. Similarly, higher levels of education also distinguish two of Sandefur's groups at ages twenty-six or twenty-eight

(BA/no family and BA/family) from the other two groups identified (limited postsecondary education/family and limited postsecondary education/no family).

Starting a family early is also important in both analyses. Members of Sandefur's limited postsecondary education/family group lived independently, and they were the most likely to be married and parents. The males in this group were typically employed full-time, while the employment of the females was quite mixed. This group is similar to both the fast starters and our parents without careers at age twenty-four, who are distinguished by whether their employment becomes more career-oriented. Sandefur also found a highly educated group that is married by ages twenty-six or twenty-eight, some of whom are also parents (BA/family). We did not find a group of individuals, by age twenty-four, who have achieved high levels of education and have both married and begun to have children. The closest group is the educated partners, who have high levels of education and who are partnered, although many are not yet married and none have had children. This group may foreshadow the BA/family group.

Our final group, the slow starters, was not found among Sandefur and colleagues' analysis of twenty-six- and twenty-eight-year-olds. However, their limited postsecondary education/children group, which was found for women only, may be the most closely linked to our slow starters. The former group was largely not highly educated, not married, and mixed in its employment status and were parents. Similarly, at age twenty-four, our slow starters had limited education, most had not married, many were unemployed, and almost one-third had become parents.

Demographics and Family of Origin

Before turning to a more detailed characterization of life at age twenty-four for these six groups, it is useful to consider basic information about their backgrounds. Table 10.2 compares the six groups in terms of gender, race/ethnicity, and several characteristics of their families of origin. Females were overrepresented in two of the groups of respondents who lived with romantic partners: parents without careers and educated partners. In contrast, males were overrepresented among the working singles. It is interesting that nonwhite respondents were considerably more common among the slow starters than in any of the other groups, but the difference is not statistically reliable given the small number of minority respondents in this sample.

Table 10.2 shows that membership in a transition group is strongly related to the social class of one's natal family. The groups with the most education and job prestige, the educated partners and educated singles, came

TABLE 10.2

PRECURSORS OF ALTERNATIVE PATHWAYS THROUGH THE TRANSITION TO ADULTHOOD:

DEMOGRAPHICS AND FAMILY OF ORIGIN (%)

	FAST STARTERS	PARENTS WITHOUT CAREERS	EDUCATED PARTNERS	EDUCATED SINGLES	WORKING SINGLES	SLOW STARTERS
Gender:						
Female	55	71	66	53	47	56
Race/ethnicity:						
Nonwhite	4	6	2	5	3	11
Family of origin income:						
>$40,000/year	54	55	68	74	62	54
Father's education:						
High school or less	63	64	38	28	47	55
Some postsecondary	21	21	26	24	24	23
Bachelors or more	16	15	36	48	29	22
Mother's education:						
High school or less	63	67	47	41	55	60
Some postsecondary	23	19	23	21	27	20
Bachelors or more	14	14	30	38	18	21
Parent's marital status:						
Not married	34	40	30	24	40	37

from families with considerably higher incomes and education. In contrast, these indicators of social class in the natal family were lowest for all three groups that included parents at age twenty-four (fast starters, parents without careers, and slow starters). Educated partners and educated singles were also more likely to have parents who were still married when respondents were age twenty-four. These patterns suggest that differences in the social-class resources of parents are likely to be replicated in the social-class assets of the young people in this sample, both through greater educational attainment early in adulthood and through delayed entry into marriage and parenthood. This pattern was also evident in the analyses reported by Sandefur and his colleagues in their chapter in this volume.

Six Versions of Life Midway through the Transition to Adulthood

As expected, we found that there is not one path into adulthood, but rather, there were interesting differences between the six transition groups on the five variables included in the latent class analysis. This statistical technique allowed us to model and describe how the traditional markers of adulthood can be experienced differently across individuals. It must be remembered, however, that these are not empirical relations in the usual sense. The five measures are not simply related to group membership but, rather, define groups in much the same way that answers to a series of attitude items define scores on the scale that they comprise. This next section of our chapter moves beyond the definition of the latent classes to draw a richer picture of their lives at age twenty-four. In other words, we seek to better understand what it means for individuals to take each of the six paths by describing other aspects of their lives that extend beyond their basic status on these five traditional role domains. To do so we compare the six classes on a number of additional lifestyle variables measured at the same point in time. Table 10.B1 (app. B) lists the specific measures used in this analysis. We report only differences between groups that meet the conventional standards of statistical significance (two-tailed $p < .05$), except in a few cases when we note otherwise.

THE FAST STARTERS. The fast starters are the respondents who had gone the farthest in entering adult roles. As noted above, they had the highest rates of marriage, home ownership, and employment in jobs they saw as long term; most of the fast starters were parents as well.

More detailed information about the fast starters' employment supports the impression that they were the group most firmly established in the world of work. They worked more hours per week than most of the other groups (forty-two hours per week compared to an overall mean of thirty-five), and their average earnings per week were the highest of the six ($674 compared with an overall mean of $471).[1] Yet their employment profile also showed the limits of their education. Only 26% held jobs with prestige ratings above the midpoint of the scale, compared to 42% for the entire sample. Furthermore, few fast starters held professional positions (9% vs. 22% overall), while jobs in skilled and technical trades were especially common (35% vs. 24% overall). Few of the fast starters were taking steps to gain the post-secondary education they had lacked so far. Only 9% were currently enrolled in college-level courses, compared to 23% for the entire sample.

In the realm of romantic or family relationships, there were no reliable differences among the six groups on average levels of satisfaction with marital, cohabiting, or steady dating relationships. There were slight differences across groups, however, with respect to whether they thought the relationship was in trouble or had thought about ending the relationship. Fast starters were less likely to view their romantic relationships negatively. When asked if they had ever felt that their relationship was in trouble, only 55% of this group agreed versus 68% for the full sample. Fast starters were also less likely ever to have suggested ending their relationship, at 23% compared to 34% in the full sample. Yet fast starters were significantly more likely to indicate being involved in physically abusive relationships, reporting the highest number of times their partners had thrown something at them.

The length of time respondents had been married and cohabiting did vary across these six groups, with the fast starters falling near the sample mean for both. At age twenty-four, the average length of their marriages was twenty-six months (vs. twenty-five for the entire sample) and the average length of their cohabitations was twenty-four months (vs. twenty-one). Before marrying, the fast starters had dated their future spouses an average of thirty-five months (also the overall sample mean), while their period of dating before cohabiting was on average twenty-one months (compared to nineteen for the entire sample). This indicates that married and cohabiting fast starters had typically been with the same partner since ages nineteen and twenty, respectively. Thus, the fast starters had entered long-term romantic relationships quite early in the transition to adulthood.

There was considerable variation across the groups in patterns of time use, and this variation corresponded to differences in romantic relationships and patterns of residence. As was typical of the groups that lived with romantic partners and away from parents, the fast starters devoted a great deal of their time to household and family-oriented activities, such as housework, yard work, and child care. Seventy-two percent of the fast starters spent more than twenty hours per week in such activities, compared to only 50% for the sample as a whole. Conversely, while 70% of the entire sample spent more than twenty hours per week in leisure pursuits, this was true for only 58% of the fast starters. The lower level of leisure time for fast starters held across physical activities (e.g., fitness, sports), skill-oriented activities (e.g., hobbies, reading), and hedonistic activities (e.g., hanging out with friends, going to bars and nightclubs, playing games). The fast starters also had low rates of illegal behavior, with only 42% engaging in any of a set of activities including illicit drug use, assault, and vandalism in the past six months, compared to 51% of the entire sample.

We asked respondents how much of the responsibility they took for a set of four adult tasks: earning their own living, paying rent, paying their other bills, and making sure that their household ran smoothly. Interestingly, although the fast starters had made more transitions into adult roles than the other groups, they were no more inclined than the average respondent to indicate that they had taken each of these adult responsibilities. With a few notable exceptions, members of all the six groups felt highly responsible in all of these areas. Only with regard to running the household did the fast starters feel somewhat more responsible than the average respondent

(73% reported they did so most of the time, compared to 66% for the total sample).

To summarize, as our label implies, the fast starters had the most adult-like lives at age twenty-four. They were heavily invested in work and family, working full-time at jobs they saw as long term and living in romantic partnerships that they saw as stable and that had already lasted for several years. These commitments also translated to devoting more time to home and family and less time to leisure pursuits. The trade-off for these early transitions was less education, which brought less prestigious employment and weaker prospects for long-term occupational advancement.

PARENTS WITHOUT CAREERS. Virtually all of the respondents on this path were parents who lived with romantic partners or spouses and who either did not work or held a job they regarded as short term. A high proportion of the parents without careers were female (71% vs. 58% for the entire sample). Most members of this group were housewives or mothers who worked at jobs in which they were not heavily invested. Even so, more than a quarter of the group were men, typically fathers who held short-term jobs.

The employment of the parents without careers was much more limited than those of the other groups. On average they worked only twenty-three hours per week and earned an average of only $239 per week, both figures the lowest of the six groups. The men in the group averaged many more hours of work per week than the women (forty-two vs. sixteen) and, accordingly, had far higher incomes ($476 per week vs. $154). Compared to other groups, the parents without careers were more likely to have jobs in sales, low-level service, and skilled trades and less likely to have jobs classified as professional or office work. Very few respondents on this pathway held positions with prestige rankings above the midpoint of the scale (18% vs. 42% overall). Furthermore, it is likely that many of the parents without careers will be in a weak position to raise the quality of their employment in the future. Not only did this group have the lowest level of previous education, at age twenty-four they were unlikely to be building on it by taking college-level courses (12% vs. 23% for the entire sample).

The marriages and cohabiting relationships of the parents without careers had lasted longer, and thus had begun at an earlier age, than those of the other groups. The average length of their marriages was thirty-three months, versus twenty-nine for the entire sample, and the average length of their cohabiting relationships was thirty-four months, versus twenty-nine for the entire sample. Parents without careers had a shorter period of dating before marriage (a mean of twenty-nine months vs. thirty-five overall). Thus, the length of their relationships with their spouses was effectively the same as the other groups, but they had married earlier. This pattern did not hold for cohabitation, however, so that the parents without careers had been involved in longer cohabiting relationships than respondents in the other five groups. Some differences appeared, however, with respect to the quality of partnerships, with 77% of this group feeling that their relationship was in trouble, compared to only 68% of the full sample. The parents without careers also reported a high number of times that their partner had thrown something at them compared to other groups (with the exception of fast starters, who had a slightly higher rate of abuse), indicating that their relationships may be more problematic than those in other groups.

The time use of the parents without careers also showed a greater emphasis on home and family: 82% spent more than twenty hours per week on activities in this domain, compared to 50% for the entire sample. Though this figure may be partly due to the high concentration of females in this group, the pattern holds for both sexes: 91% for females versus 59% overall and 74% for males versus 35% overall. Correspondingly, the parents without careers spent less time than all other groups in leisure activities, with only 20% reporting more than twenty hours per week, compared to 70% for the entire sample. They were also the group that spent the least time in the specific leisure domains of physical and hedonistic activities and the second lowest for time in skill-oriented activities. Relatively few committed any of the illegal acts assessed in this study.

Oddly enough, this high investment in home and family was associated with reporting relatively low levels in the assumption of some adult responsibilities. On average, parents without careers were the least likely to report that were responsible for earning their own living (54% vs. 84% for the entire sample) and paying their own bills (64% vs. 85% overall). It seems likely that this reflects a gender division in the household rather than a delayed transition to adulthood. Because many of these primarily female respondents either did not work or held poorly paying short-term jobs, they may have been indicating that their spouses or partners carried these responsibilities. Correspondingly, parents without careers were especially likely to report that they took most of the responsibility for seeing that their households ran smoothly (87% vs. 66% overall).

It is simplest to summarize the situation of parents without careers at age twenty-four by comparing them to the fast starters. These were the two groups with the deepest involvement in adult family roles. With their high rate of parenthood and heavy time investments, family may have been even more prominent in the lives of the partners without careers than in the lives of the fast starters. Yet these two groups are quite distinct when it comes to employment. Many parents without careers do not work, and those who do have jobs work few hours and earn little.

EDUCATED PARTNERS. The profile of educated partners is quite distinct from those of fast starters and parents without careers. Although all three groups lived with romantic partners, the educated partners had much higher levels of education and none were parents by age twenty-four. Like the parents without careers, females were overrepresented among the educated partners (66% vs. 58% for the sample as a whole).

Figure 10.1 showed that the employment situation of the educated partners was quite variable. A more detailed examination of their employment reveals both strengths and weaknesses. Educated partners held jobs with higher average prestige ratings (45% over the scale midpoint) than all other groups except the educated singles. Both of these groups also had the highest proportions of members employed in professional positions (24% for educated partners vs. 8% for all other groups except the educated singles). But other office work, including administrative support positions such as office supervisors, secretaries, typists, and clerks, was also especially common in this group. The educated partners worked a few more hours per week than the total sample on average (thirty-eight vs. thirty-five) and earned the same weekly wage ($471). Though the educated partners earned much less than the fast starters at age twenty-four, their future job prospects may have been brighter. Not only did the educated partners have much more previous education, they also were continuing to build their educations at a higher rate than the first two groups, with 27% currently enrolled in college-level courses (compared to 9% and 12%, respectively, for the first two groups).

In contrast to the other groups who lived with romantic partners, the educated partners had lived with their partners for a shorter period and their lifestyles were less distinct from those of respondents who did not live with romantic partners. Not only were the educated partners especially likely to cohabit rather than marry, but their cohabiting relationships were also newer—an average of seventeen months versus twenty-one for the entire sample. Furthermore, the average length of the marriages was only eighteen months, compared to twenty-five months for the entire sample. Nevertheless, they did date longer before marriage, an average of forty-one months versus thirty-five overall. This pattern of relative delay for entering marriage and cohabitation is consistent with the higher education of this group (see Fussell and Furstenberg, this vol., chap. 2; and Sandefur et al., this vol.; chap. 9). Adding an interesting wrinkle to this pattern, those educated partners who were married expressed the greatest satisfaction with their marriages of all six groups. In contrast, the cohabiting educated partners did not differ from the cohabiting members of the other five groups in their level of satisfaction with cohabitation. Finally, the educated partners were less likely than all other groups except the fast starters to feel that their relationship was in trouble (66% compared to 72% of all groups except fast starters).

The educated partners spent less time in household maintenance and family activities than the fast starters and parents without careers did (51% spending more than twenty hours per week, compared to 72% and 88%, respectively), and they spent more time in leisure pursuits (69% spending more than twenty hours per week, compared to 58% and 53%). Yet, like the other groups living with romantic partners, the educated partners spent relatively little time in hedonistic activities (29% spending more than twenty hours per week, compared to 39% in the full sample), and relatively few engaged in any of the illegal behaviors (44% engaging in one or more acts).

Similar to respondents in most of the other groups, the educated partners felt that they took most of the responsibility for earning their own living and paying rent. Like the first two groups, they were especially likely to feel that they were responsible for running their own household (78% vs. 66% overall), but they were somewhat less inclined to report that they bore most of the responsibility for paying their bills (78% vs. 85% overall).

In summary, despite living with a romantic partner, the educated partners in many ways exemplify the notion of emergent adulthood (Arnett 2000), for they appear to have delayed some adult commitments in favor of an extended period of exploration. The educated partners were less deeply involved in adult family roles than the fast starters and parents without careers. Furthermore, they had entered their romantic relationships more recently, they did not have children, and they spent less time in activities at home and with family. In these respects they are more similar to the groups who did not live with romantic partners. The educated partners also differed greatly from the first two groups in their employment trajectory. Their current employment profile is less stable and lower paying than the fast starters, indicating that many have not yet made strong progress in this domain. Yet their greater education and the higher prestige of their jobs suggest strong prospects for long-term success.

EDUCATED SINGLES. With their long-term schooling and later entry into family roles, the educated singles also appear to fit the mold of emergent adulthood (Arnett 2000). As defined by the latent class analysis (see fig. 10.1), the primary difference between educated singles and educated partners was that the educated singles did not live with romantic partners, and they were more likely to live with their parents. The educated singles had the highest level of education, with 61% holding bachelor's degrees.

Consistent with this high level of education, the educated singles were most likely to have high-status employment. Fifty-eight percent held jobs with status rankings above the midpoint of the prestige scale, compared to 45% for the educated partners and 31% or less for all other groups. Employment in professional positions was highly concentrated among the educated singles (34% vs. 24% for educated partners and no more than 13% for other groups). Surprisingly, their hours of employment (thirty-six per week) and earnings ($484 per week) were near the mean for the entire sample (thirty-five and $471, respectively), but this is attributable to the portion of the educated singles who were unemployed or in short-term jobs. The educated singles also tended to be on an upward trajectory that would increase their educational advantage: 30% were currently enrolled in college-level courses, the highest among the six groups.

There were few differences in relationship satisfaction among the three groups who were not living with romantic partners. In all three of these groups, however, respondents with steady dating relationships felt very differently about romantic relationships than those without. Respondents who were steadily dating were quite satisfied with their relationships (mean of 6.2 on a seven-point scale), which had lasted an average of twenty-nine months. Fifty-seven percent of those without steady relationships wanted one; and 63% felt it was somewhat to very important to have a committed relationship. Respondents without a steady relationship typically went on dates no more than once per week (72%). On the whole, respondents without a steady romantic relationship were not satisfied with their dating situation (66% responded 1–3 on a seven-point scale).

All three groups of respondents who did not live with romantic partners spent relatively little time in family and household activities. This was especially true of the educated singles, only 33% of whom devoted more than twenty hours per week to these endeavors, compared to 49% for the entire sample. Correspondingly, the educated singles spent the most time in leisure activities (80%, more than twenty hours per week), including high rates of physical activities, skill-oriented activities, and hedonistic activities. Fifty-six percent of the educated singles had engaged in at least one of the illegal behaviors, far more than any of the groups living with romantic partners (44% or less). Among the educated singles, those who lived on their own had even lower rates of family and household activities and higher rates of socializing than did the educated singles who lived with parents or relatives.

Despite their less settled lifestyle, the educated singles were just as likely as members of the other five groups to report bearing adult responsibilities in the areas of earning a living, paying their own bills, and paying rent. They were slightly less likely to report that they took the major responsibility for running their own households (60% vs. 66% overall).

The overall picture for the educated singles is of slower entry into adult roles associated with emergent adulthood. They were neither parents nor living with romantic partners, and they devoted little time to activities with family or at home. They were in the early stages of their careers, holding jobs they saw as short term or steps in careers. In accord with their high level of education, however, those jobs were more prestigious. For this group, which is by far the largest of the six (39%), there is clear evidence that the midtwenties are a period of continuing exploration and delayed commitment to adult roles. At the same time, the educated singles had gathered considerable personal capital through education and employment that should prove valuable resources for long-term economic success.

WORKING SINGLES. The combination of living with parents and career-oriented employment distinguished the working singles from the other five groups. As figure 10.1 shows, the working singles were similar to the educated singles in their pattern of romantic relationships and residence, and they were similar to the fast starters in their pattern of employment and education. Males were overrepresented in this group (53% vs. 43% overall)—the only group for which this was true.

A more detailed examination of employment illustrates the similarity of the working singles with the fast starters. The working singles earned relatively high incomes ($593 per week compared to an average of $471) and worked many hours per week (forty-two compared to thirty-five overall). Many of these respondents were employed in skilled and technical trades (33% vs. 24% overall). The average prestige of their positions was somewhat higher than the fast starters, with 31% above the scale midpoint, compared to 26% for the latter. Both of these two groups held jobs with considerably lower prestige than the educated partners and educated singles (45% and 58% above the midpoint, respectively). Thus, the working singles were well established in the world of work, with stable positions and jobs that provide moderate incomes and prestige. Sixteen percent of the working singles were currently taking college-level courses.

Our picture of the romantic relationships of the working singles is essentially the same as the educated singles and slow starters. The working singles' time use fell between that of the educated singles and the groups who lived with romantic partners. Forty-nine percent of the working singles spent more than twenty hours per week in family and household activities (compared to 50% overall), and 66% spent more than twenty hours per week in leisure activities (compared to 70% overall). The working singles spent higher than average amounts of time in physical activities and hedonistic activities but lower than average in skill-oriented activities. Their rate of illegal behavior was comparable to the educated singles (56% committed at least one of the acts). As with the educated singles, the working singles were especially likely to indicate that they were responsible for earning their own living, paying rent, and paying other bills but were less likely than groups living with partners to indicate that they were responsible for running their own households.

In sum, the working singles were similar to the fast starters in the world of work and education and similar to the educated singles in their family involvements. They invested more heavily in work than in education, and at twenty-four they had good earnings from long-term jobs that did not carry much prestige. They were less adult-like in their family relations in that they were neither married or cohabiting nor serving as parents, and they were quite likely still to live with their parents.

SLOW STARTERS. Figure 10.1 shows that the slow starters were not well established in the realms of romantic relationships, residence, employment, and education, but a moderate portion had become parents. Additional analysis showed that the slow starters worked fewer hours and earned less than all groups other than the parents without careers (thirty hours and $370 per week, respectively). They were especially likely to hold low-level service jobs (23% vs. 17% overall) and office jobs (27% vs. 22% overall); many had jobs in skilled or technical trades as well (28% vs. 24% overall). The prestige ratings of their positions were as low as those of the parents without careers, with only 18% rising above the midpoint of the scale. In contrast, a sizable portion of the slow starters was then taking college-level courses (21%, which was higher than all other groups except the educated partners and educated singles), and that should improve their future employment prospects.

It is notable that a particularly large portion of the slow starters was single, without a steady dating relationship (49%), and in all groups, respondents in this situation were those least satisfied with their romantic relationships. If slow starters did have a steady relationship, they were more likely than members of the other groups to report that their relationship was in trouble (78% vs. 68% overall). Unlike the educated singles and working singles, many of the slow starters were already parents. Among nonparents, however, the slow starters were somewhat less likely than other groups to expect that they ever would become parents.

The slow starters' time use was comparable to that of the working singles, falling between the educated singles and the groups living with romantic partners. More than half of the slow starters spent more than twenty hours per week in household and family activities (54% vs. 50% overall), and 68% spent more than twenty hours per week in leisure activities (compared to 70% overall). They devoted higher than average amounts of time to hedonistic activities (43% spending twenty hours per week or more compared to 39% in the full sample). Their rate of illegal behavior was the highest of all groups, with 63% reporting at least one of the acts.

The slow starters were about average for the amount of responsibility they reported taking for earning their own living, paying rent, and paying other bills. As with the educated singles and working singles, they were less likely than average to indicate that they took most of the responsibility for running their households.

As the label implies, the slow starters were the group least advanced in their progression into adult roles. They can be seen as representing another version of emergent adulthood (Arnett 2000), for they have not assumed most of the traditional roles of adulthood, and they are, perhaps, in an extended period of exploration. In contrast to the educated partners and singles, however, they do not seem to be placing themselves in a strong position to succeed when the time comes to enter those roles. Most had reached their midtwenties with little education, they were still living with their parents, had unsatisfactory romantic relations, and were either not working or holding jobs with poor pay and prospects.

Precursors of Alternative Pathways through the Transition to Adulthood

We have seen that these six groups represent dramatically different pathways through the transition to adulthood and that those differences were foreshadowed by social-class differences in their natal families. Next we examine information obtained from our sample at age eighteen about activities, attitudes, and expectations relating to education, employment, and family. We consider both what this information tells us about the potential precursors of group membership and how it connects earlier social-class differences to respondents' subsequent pathways to adulthood.

The MSALT study includes a wealth of information about the respondents at earlier ages. We chose age eighteen as a point of comparison because it represents the point when transitions to adult roles become acceptable under conventional standards. See table 10.B1 (app. B) for a list of the measures included in this analysis.

We found that information gathered at age eighteen strongly fore-shadows the high educational achievement of the educated partners and educated singles. Compared to all other groups, these respondents had higher self-concepts of academic ability, greater interest in academics, and stronger expectations for their future education. The educated partners and educated singles were also distinct from the other groups in spending more time in three categories of activities known to be linked to educational outcomes and positive youth development: sports, skill-oriented activities, and community activities (Barber, Eccles, and Stone 2001; Eccles and Barber 1999; Eccles and Gootman 2002). Perhaps this is a reflection that respondents on these two paths had been the most inclined to devote their time and energy to pursuits that are highly valued by white middle-class society.

In contrast to these results for attitudes about education, attitudes about employment did not differ across the six groups. At age eighteen, future members of all groups placed very high importance on successful employment (averaging 6.4 on a seven-point scale), and they held equally high expectations for future occupational success (averaging 5.9 on a seven-point scale). There was, however, a nonsignificant trend ($p = .11$) for respondents who were to become fast starters and working singles to have worked more hours at age eighteen than did the future members of other groups.

The questionnaire at age eighteen also asked about attitudes concerning marriage and family. There was a trend ($p =. 06$) for the future parents without careers to have the highest future expectations for marriage. They also wanted to get married at a younger age than any of the other five groups, with a mean desired age at marriage of twenty-three years compared to twenty-five for the full sample. Indeed, a high proportion of this group was married by age twenty-four. Despite an equally high rate of marriage among fast starters by age twenty-four, however, their future expectations for marriage at age eighteen were no different from other groups.

Future expectations about parenting failed to differentiate the groups who were to have high and low rates of parenthood at age twenty-four. All groups were highly and equally likely to have expected to become parents. When asked about the desired age for having a first child, however, respondents who would become parents without careers expressed the youngest mean age: twenty-four versus twenty-seven for the full sample. The six groups assigned very similar levels of importance to family at age eighteen. On the whole then, attitudes about marriage and family were not very predictive of future differences among the groups. Nonetheless, the two differences that did emerge were consistent with future differences in marriage and parenthood.

Simultaneously Considering Multiple Predictors of Transition Group Membership

It is also interesting to ascertain which of these precursors of group membership are still predictive after taking into account other factors. For instance, is the high rate of intact marriages for parents of the educated partners and educated singles an indirect consequence of the high level of education for those parents, or is it perhaps the other way around? We addressed questions of this sort through multinomial logistic regression analyses in which the outcome measure was membership in the six latent class groups at age twenty-four and the predictor variables were background characteristics (demographic factors and characteristics of the natal family) and selected measures from the questionnaire at age eighteen. Table 10.C1 (app. C) presents the tests of statistical significance for the independent prediction provided by each variable, controlling for others.[2]

We first consider the contributions of gender, race, and whether the respondent's parents' marriage was intact when the respondent was age twenty-four. As a set, these predictors were significantly, though not strongly, related to who fell into which of the transition groups at age twenty-four ($\chi^2 = 35.2$, 15 df, $p = .002$). Both gender ($\chi^2 = 12.0$, 5 df, $p = .034$) and parents' marital status (having parents who were still married to one another [$\chi^2 = 16.7$, 5 df, $p = .006$]) were independent predictors, controlling for the other variables.

Among the demographic and natal family variables, the factors most strongly related to transition group membership at the bivariate level had been the three measures reflecting social class: mother's education, father's education, and family income (see table 10.2). Adding these measures to the other three background factors considerably enhanced our ability to predict into which transition groups respondents would fall at age twenty-four ($\chi^2 = 65.8$, 15 df, $p = .000$). Both mother's and father's education were significant predictors, controlling for the other demographic and family background variables ($\chi^2 = 15.6$, 5 df, $p = .008$, and $\chi^2 = 18.5$, 5 df, $p = .002$, respectively). Furthermore, controlling for the social-class measures reduced to chance the predictive power of parents' marital status ($\chi^2 = 8.9$, 5 df, $p = .114$).

Next we considered whether the measures at age eighteen were associated with transition group membership after the demographic variables and family background were taken into account.[3] These same analyses are also informative about whether the respondents' adjustment at age eighteen can help explain the connection between the background variables and the paths respondents took through the transition to adulthood.

We first examined the contribution of those measures at eighteen that are relevant to future family roles, including current dating and expectations for marriage and parenting. Earlier we saw that, when considered one at a time, these measures were only modestly related to the six latent classes. Accordingly, after controlling for the background characteristics, this group of predictors was related to transition group membership at only a chance level ($\chi^2 = 26.8$, 25 df, $p = .366$). Gender was no longer a significant predictor once these characteristics were taken into account, but this resulted from redundancy due to gender differences in views about marriage and family rather than from any connection of those views to the transition to adulthood.

The earlier analysis showed that the transition groups had been more distinct in the domain of work and education at age eighteen, so we saved these measures for the last step of the analysis. We found that, indeed, the predictive contribution of these measures remained very clear, even after taking into account all other predictors ($\chi^2 = 134.7$, 30 df, $p = .000$). More specifically, the two measures concerning education—future educational expectations and high school grade point average—stood out as especially robust predictors of the latent class groups ($\chi^2 = 32.1$, 5 df, $p = .000$ and $\chi^2 = 47.9$, 5 df, $p = .000$, respectively). The two measures concerning employment did not ($\chi^2 = 8.2$, 5 df, $p = .148$ and $\chi^2 = 2.4$, 5 df, $p = .787$, respectively).

A final and especially important result emerges from this last step of the analysis: once we took educational expectations and performance into account, the natal family social-class profiles of the transition groups differed by no more than would be expected by chance. The implications are profound, for this result not only provides an explanation for the advantages of parents' social class, but it also demonstrates that those advantages are not inevitable. Children whose parents are highly educated have a much greater chance of becoming educated partners and educated singles at age twenty-four precisely because they are more likely to have done well in high school and to expect to obtain a college degree. However, students from poor families who do equally well in school and have the same high expectations are just as likely to arrive in those high trajectory groups at age twenty-four.

DISCUSSION

Our analysis has produced four main conclusions. First, we identified six quite distinct pathways into young adulthood. In a review of the life-course literature on the transition to adulthood and its relation to historical events and economic circumstances, Shanahan (2000) documented the increasing variability in pathways to adulthood over the past fifty years. Clearly the young adults in the MSALT sample show substantial diversity in the sequences of adult roles they take on as they make their transition to adulthood. Rather than everyone moving toward adulthood by getting married, having children, and securing a stable job, we found a number of different possible trajectories, all of which seem quite viable and culturally appropriate for this generation. These include a delay in many traditional domains, such as marriage and parenthood, in favor of options such as extending educational paths and choosing nonmarital partnerships. Furthermore, these six paths at age twenty-four connect logically with the four paths that Sandefur and colleagues (this vol., chap. 9) found at ages twenty-six and twenty-eight.

Second, of these six pathways, our sample is overrepresented in the one that most strongly reflects "emerging adulthood" (Arnett 2000; Arnett and Taber 1994). If being an adult means being settled in all of the five domains used in our classification, as was typically thought in previous generations, our sample falls short at age twenty-four. Rather than viewing this as a failure, however, several researchers now suggest that these patterns reflect two secular trends: (1) a delay in taking on the full responsibilities of marriage and family in favor of personal exploration and educational preparation and (2) acceptance of a wider range of valued adult lifestyles. For example, rather than marry, much of our sample has chosen to cohabit or steadily date. Jobs serve as steps in a career rather than long-term positions. Although the majority of the sample expressed a desire to have a family, child rearing has largely been postponed. Residences are temporary as opposed to permanent, as, for example, with home ownership. What clearly distinguishes the large portion of our sample who appear to be on this emerging adulthood path is the commitment to education. Whereas a more traditional route to adulthood might be through securing financial independence, much of our sample places importance not on settling in a job, but on advancing their education. Thus, our latent class analysis shows clear evidence both of a diversification of pathways to adulthood and of a tendency toward a period of emerging adulthood.

Third, our analysis of other lifestyle variables shows that it is useful to go beyond the traditional markers of role transitions (i.e., marriage, employment, parenthood, etc.) to see how people taking particular paths are experiencing life in their midtwenties. Again, such an examination shows a pattern consistent with Arnett's concept of emerging adulthood. The educated singles, our largest group, and the educated partners, the next largest, appear to be more devoted to educational and professional advancements than the other four groups. This emphasis on investment in education and on an upward trajectory of employment suggests that these groups are more concerned with improving themselves individually and professionally than with settling into traditional family-oriented adult roles. Although the fast starters and parents without careers seem more "adult," their lifestyles seem to lack the emphasis on growth and exploration present in two of the other groups. For example, fast starters are quite settled in the domain of employment, yet their jobs tend to be skilled rather than professional and are of low prestige. In contrast, personal exploration and advancement in all areas of life seems to be highly valued, particularly by the educated singles. Although this group places importance on committed relationships, a smaller proportion of individuals in this group are currently in committed relationships. Members of this group still seem to be "trying out" partnerships. They spend their free time in leisure activities with an emphasis on having fun and learning new things.

The lifestyles of the educated partners and educated singles contrast with the emphasis on home and family found in the groups that have settled into families. The educated partners and working singles are similar to the educated singles in that they are more likely than the other groups to engage in leisure activities. With their emphasis on personal and professional growth, as well as being settled romantically, the educated partners appear to combine the emerging adulthood stage with settled adult life. The slow starters, by way of contrast, have made little to no progress in any domain. Thus, they certainly have not moved into the role of an adult, nor do they appear to be delaying adulthood in favor of personal advancement. As far as we can determine from our data, this group does not seem to be engaged in positive exploration or on a forward-looking path of any kind. They demonstrate that a delay in entering traditional adult roles does not necessarily imply investment in future prospects.

Our fourth conclusion concerns the precursors of these paths through the transition. Clearly there is more than one pathway into adulthood, but what leads individuals to take these different paths? Our analyses suggest that the nature of one's transition to adulthood is strongly linked to the social-class characteristics of one's natal family. Our findings support the notion that individuals are "both constrained and enabled by socially structured opportunities and limitations" (Shanahan 2000, 675). The social-class characteristics of the groups' natal families differ in quite predictable ways. The educated singles and educated partners are more likely to have come from families of higher social class. With more education and higher incomes, these natal families have the resources necessary for young adults to pursue the kind of personal and professional advancement characteristic of these two groups. These two groups also had strong academic abilities, attitudes, and values during high school, which in turn have been shown to be related to the resources and the value placed on education in families of higher social class (Eccles, Wigfield, and Schiefele 1998). In contrast, having high expectations for marriage and family at an earlier age rather than for future education, as did the parents without careers, is consistent with a pathway into adulthood characterized more by family roles of marriage and parenthood than by education and employment (Schneider and Coleman 1993; Sewell and Hauser 1980). The path one takes, therefore, typically reflects the social-class values and resources of one's natal family.

We close by noting that our findings also refute any implication that family background is destiny. Despite the strong link between parents' social class and the transition groups at age twenty-four, the connection of future group membership to academic factors at age eighteen is even stronger. When poor children whose parents have little education succeed in high school and expect to continue to succeed in college, they are just as likely as children of privileged backgrounds to reach age twenty-four on a promising pathway through the transition to adulthood.

APPENDIX A
LATENT CLASS ANALYSIS

We conducted the latent class analysis using Vermunt and Magidson's (2000) Latent Gold program. This sophisticated program provides solutions to some of the most common difficulties of latent class analysis, such as a Bayesian approach to preventing boundary solutions and automatic generation of multiple starting values to avoid local maxima. Latent Gold also permits the use of cases with missing values on some variables, which allowed us to maintain a sample size of 1,410 respondents for the analyses reported in this chapter. Because including cases with missing data reduces the power of tests for model fit, analyses to determine the number of latent classes

TABLE 10.A1

FIT OF LATENT CLASS SOLUTIONS FOR DIFFERING

NUMBERS OF CLASSES OR CLUSTERS

	MODEL χ^2	BIC	df	p VALUE
1 cluster	1,243.73	−679.15	276	1.2E − 122
2 clusters	611.13	−1,249.05	267	5.1E − 29
3 clusters	477.82	−1,319.66	258	2.5E − 15
4 clusters	382.58	−1,352.19	249	1.1E − 7
5 clusters	292.88	−1,379.20	240	.011
6 clusters	261.33	−1,348.04	231	.083
7 clusters	241.69	−1,304.98	222	.17
8 clusters	221.15	−1,262.81	213	.34

Note. BIC = Bayesian information criteria.

and restrictions on the solution were limited to the 1,061 cases with complete data. The latent classes were virtually identical for analyses with and without cases that had missing values.

Examination of preliminary results suggested that employment and education might well be treated as ordinal rather than categorical variables. Model comparisons indicated that doing so yielded the best balance of parsimony and model fit, so we included this restriction in our final analysis.

The summary of model fit in table 10.A.1 indicates that six latent classes or clusters are necessary to provide a summary that does not significantly differ from the data. Yet these results indicate that four or five clusters would be more parsimonious (i.e., yield lower values of Bayesian information criteria). Furthermore, comparison of log likelihood values indicates that seven and eight cluster solutions significantly improve upon six clusters. We chose six clusters as providing an optimal combination of model fit, parsimony, and most important, interpretable and interesting clusters.

Latent class analysis does not directly assign each respondent to one and only one of the groups or clusters. Instead, this method yields a probability that any respondent is a member of each group. Some respondents have a very high probability of membership in one group and very low probability in all others, while other respondents have moderate probabilities of belonging in two or more groups. This presents a difficulty in comparing the groups on other dimensions, which is the major purpose of this chapter.

The most common approach for comparing groups is to assign respondents to the group for which they have the highest probability of membership. Though doing so will generally provide a reasonable approximation to the latent groups, there is a risk of distorting the portrayal of some groups. For instance, suppose that respondents with a certain profile of characteristics have a .55 probability of belonging to group A and a .45 probability of belonging to group B. All of these respondents would be assigned to group A, overrepresenting their attributes for that group, while underrepresenting them in group B.

We used a relatively simple approach for avoiding this type of bias in our comparisons among the paths through the transition to adulthood. We treated each respondent as a member of each path with a case weight equal to the probability membership in that group. Thus, respondents contributed to each group profile to the degree that they were representative of that path. This method of assignment bears some similarity to multiple imputation methods for missing data (Schafer 1997) as a way of avoiding bias. Unlike the most sophisticated multiple imputation methods, however, we do not attempt to assess the variability in results stemming from uncertainty about group membership. This may be compensated for by a tendency to underestimate group differences resulting from the negative dependence created by including the same individual as part of both groups being compared. We are confident, however, that our approach is superior to normal standards and that its limits will not present problems for the largely descriptive purposes of our analyses.

APPENDIX B

TABLE 10.B1

MEASURES INCLUDED IN ANALYSES OF CONCURRENT CORRELATES OF LATENT CLASS MEMBERSHIP

AT AGE 24 AND OF PRECURSORS OF LATENT CLASS MEMBERSHIP

VARIABLE	QUESTIONNAIRE ITEM	CODING FOR ANALYSIS
Age 24:		
Employment:		
Occupation	What is your main occupation or job?	Professional, skilled, sales, administrative support, service, other[a]
Salary	Approximately how much do you earn in this job?	Dollars earned per week
Hours	How many hours per week do you work at this job?	Hours worked per week
Prestige	What is your main occupation or job?	Socioeconomic status score from 0–100[b]
Education:		
College	Are you currently taking any undergraduate or graduate college courses?	0 = no; 1 = yes
Relationship variables:		
Satisfaction	*Single:* How satisfied are you with your dating life?	1–7 scale, 1 = not at all satisfied/very unhappy; 7 = very satisfied/very happy
	Other: How do you feel about being involved/living with/being married to your partner?	
Trouble	Have you ever thought your relationship might be in trouble?	0 = no; 1 = yes
Ending	Have you or your partner ever seriously suggested the idea of ending your relationship?	0 = no; 1 = yes
Abuse	How many times in the past 12 months did your partner or date throw something at you?	Recoded to number of times, 0–20

Variable	Question	Coding
Length	*Cohabiting:* How long have you lived together? *Married:* How long have you been married?	Recoded to number of months
Length of dating	*Cohabiting:* How long did you date your partner before you began living together? *Married:* How long did you date your spouse before you were married?	Recoded to number of months
Time use	"About how many hours do you usually spend each week doing [specified activity]"	
Family		Time with children; indoor and outdoor chores at home; family based leisure
Leisure		The sum of the following:
Physical	...	Athletic, sports, or fitness activities
Skill oriented	...	Reading; musical instrument; hobbies
Hedonistic	...	Hanging out with close friends
Passive	...	Watching TV; using a computer at home
Organizations	...	Clubs or organizations
Deviance:		
Illegal	About how many times in the last 6 months did you: damage property; have a physical fight; drive when drunk; use marijuana; use other drugs; do something else illegal?	0 = no illegal acts; 1 = at least one act
Responsibility:		
Earning	How much responsibility do you take for: earning own living; paying rent; paying other bills; making sure your household runs smoothly	1 = somebody else does this for me all of the time; 5 = I am completely responsible for this all of the time
Rent		
Bills		
Household		

(continued)

TABLE 10.B1.

(CONTINUED)

VARIABLE	QUESTIONNAIRE ITEM	CODING FOR ANALYSIS
Background variables:		
Demographic variables:		
Gender	...	0 = female; 1 = male
Race	...	0 = nonwhite; 1 = white
Family of origin		
Structure	Are your biological parents: married and living together; divorced; separated; never married and living together; never married and not living together; widowed?	0 = nonintact; 1 = intact
Income	About how much is your current family income each year?	0 = low ($0–$40,000); 1 = high (>$40,000)
Parents' education		1 = high school or less; 2 = some postsecondary; 3 = bachelors or more
Age 18:		
Employment:		
Job	Do you have a regularly paying part-time job?	0 = no; 1 = yes
Importance	How important will each of the following be to you in your adult life? Able to find steady work; being successful in work; being financially independent. Before you get married, how important is it to you to____: Have a secure job? Save a lot of money?	Scale scored as mean across items, alpha = .75. 1 = not at all important; 7 = extremely important
Expectations	When you think about your future, how likely do you think each of the following will be in the next 10 to 15 years: You will have a job you enjoy doing; you will	Scale scored as mean across items, alpha = .76. 1 = very unlikely; 7 = very likely

be a success in your line of work; you will have a job that pays well; (reversed) you will be laid off from your job; (reversed) you will have difficulty supporting your family financially.

Education:		
GPA	Grade point average	Continuous measure of GPA
Interest	Items asked for specific subjects—e.g., math, English: I find working on ____ assignments: How much do you like doing ____? For me, being good at ____ is:	Scale scored as mean across 14 items, alpha = .81. 1 = very boring/a little/not at all; 7 = very interesting/a lot/very useful/very important
Ability	Items asked for specific subjects—e.g., math, English: How good at ____ are you? Compared to most of your other school subjects, How good are you at learning ____?	Scale scored as mean across 11 items, alpha = .80. 1 = not at all/worse/not at all/much worse; 7 = very good/much better/very good/much better
Educational expectations	How likely do you think each of the following will be in the next 10 to 15 years: You will graduate from college (4 year); you will attend graduate or professional school	Scale scored as mean across items. alpha = .64. 1 = very unlikely; 7 = very likely
Relationship variables:		
Future marriage	When you think about your future, how likely do you think each of the following will be: You will get married; you will have a successful, happy marriage	Scale scored as mean across items, alpha = .73. 1 = very unlikely; 7 = very likely
Marry age	At what age would you like to marry?	Continuous measure of age in years
Future parent	When you think about your future, how likely do you think each of the following will be: You will have children; you will be a successful parent	Scale scored as mean across items, alpha = .85. 1 = very unlikely; 7 = very likely

(continued)

TABLE 10.B1
(CONTINUED)

VARIABLE	QUESTIONNAIRE ITEM	CODING FOR ANALYSIS
Parent age	At what age would you like to start having children?	Age in years
Family importance	How important will each of the following be to you in your adult life? Getting married; having children; having a successful/happy marriage; being a successful parent; spend a lot of time with your children; want to have children	Scale scored as mean across items; alpha = .86. 1 = not at all important; 7 = very important
High school date	Are you currently going out with only one person?	0 = no; 1 = yes
Time use	About how many hours do you usually spend each week doing ____.	The following time use variables recoded to hours per week.
Friends	Hanging out with friends	
Community service	Providing volunteer or community service	
Work	Working for pay	
Sports	Taking part in organized sports; doing other athletic or sports activities	
Family based	Doing things with your family; taking care of younger brothers or sisters; fixing family meals; other indoor housework chores at home; yard work and other outdoor chores at home	
Skilled	Reading for fun; playing a musical instrument	

[a] Occupations classified using the 1980 U.S. Census Standard Occupational Classification.

[b] As derived by Nakao and Treas (1992), who determine socioeconomic status of occupations based on both educational attainment and income of occupational categories listed by the census.

TABLE IO.CI

MULTINOMIAL LOGIT ANALYSIS OF PRECURSORS: LIKELIHOOD RATIO TESTS

	χ^2	df	SIGNIFICANCE
Model 1:			
Gender	12.0	5	.034
Race	4.8	5	.444
Intact family	16.7	5	.006
Total model	35.2	15	.002
Model 2:			
Gender	11.2	5	.048
Race	5.1	5	.406
Intact family	8.9	5	.114
Mother's education	15.6	5	.008
Father's education	18.5	5	.002
Family income	2.9	5	.717
Total model	101.0	30	.000
Model 3:			
Gender	8.4	5	.137
Race	4.8	5	.441
Intact family	7.1	5	.216
Mother's education	12.6	5	.027
Father's education	16.8	5	.005
Family income	3.4	5	.632
Marriage expectations	2.1	5	.830
Parenting expectations	4.4	5	.492
Dating at age 18	5.5	5	.358
Total model	127.8	55	.000
Model 4:			
Gender	7.9	5	.159
Race	4.1	5	.540
Intact family	5.3	5	.376
Mother's education	6.7	5	.242
Father's education	5.0	5	.411
Family income	3.9	5	.565
Marriage expectations	3.3	5	.654
Parenting expectations	4.7	5	.455
Dating at age 18	3.6	5	.603
Job at age 18	8.2	5	.148
Future education likely	32.1	5	.000
Positive occupation expectations	2.4	5	.787
High school grade point average	47.9	5	.000
Total model	262.5	85	.000

Note. Models 3 and 4 also include dummy variables reflecting missing value substitutions for a total of four predictors.

NOTES

1. Means for hours of employment and earnings are based on all respondents in a group, whether employed or not. Mean prestige scores are limited to respondents who are employed.

2. Our presentation of these results focuses on which differences among groups remain after controlling for other factors. When differences remain, their pattern across groups is essentially the same as reported for the bivariate relationships above. Therefore we do not report the rather overwhelming set of eighty regression coefficients that result from this analysis (five for each of the thirteen predictors). Due to missing data from these various time points, the analyses were conducted on a reduced sample of 605.

3. Though the data set includes many more measures taken at age eighteen, we limited the analysis to a subset that provide a good representation of major concepts in these domains, that were more related to group membership at the bivariate level, and that had the least missing data. This strategy enhances statistical power while reducing problems of collinearity.

REFERENCES

Arnett, Jeffrey Jensen. 2000. Emerging Adulthood: A Theory of Development from the Late Teens through the Twenties. *American Psychologist* 55 (5):469–80.

Arnett, Jeffrey Jensen, and Susan Taber. 1994. Adolescence Terminable and Interminable: When Does Adolescence End? *Journal of Youth and Adolescence* 23 (5):517–37.

Barber, Bonnie L., Jacquelynne S. Eccles, and Margaret R. Stone. 2001. Whatever Happened to the Jock, the Brain, and the Princess? Young Adult Pathways Linked to Adolescent Activity Involvement and Social Identity. *Journal of Adolescent Research* 16:429–55.

Clogg, Clifford C. 1995. Latent Class Models. Pp. 311–59 in *Handbook of Statistical Modeling for the Social and Behavioral Sciences*, edited by Gerhard Arminger, Clifford C. Clogg, and Michael E. Sobel. New York: Plenum.

Eccles, Jacquelynne. S., and Bonnie L. Barber. 1999. Student Council, Volunteering, Basketball, or Marching Band: What Kind of Extracurricular Involvement Matters? *Journal of Adolescent Research* 14:10–43.

Eccles, Jacquelynne. S., and Jennifer Gootman, eds. 2002. *Community Programs to Promote Youth Development.* Washington DC: National Academy Press.

Eccles, Jacquelynne. S., Allan Wigfield, Constance A. Flanagan, Christy Miller, David A. Reuman, and Doris K. Yee. 1989. Self-concepts, Domain Values, and Self-esteem: Relations and Changes at Early Adolescence. *Journal of Personality* 57:283–310.

Eccles, Jacquelynne S., Allan Wigfield, and Ulrich Schiefele. 1998. Motivation. Pp. 1017–95 in *Handbook of Child Psychology,* edited by Nancy Eisenberg. Vol. 3. 5th ed. New York: Wiley.

Lazarsfeld, Paul. F., and Neil W. Henry. 1968. *Latent Structure Analysis.* Boston: Houghton Mifflin.

Magnusson, David, ed. 1988. *Individual Development from an Interactional Perspective.* Hillsdale, NJ: Erlbaum.

Nakao, Keiko, and Judith Treas. 1992. The 1989 Socioeconomic Index of Occupations: Construction from the 1989 Occupational Prestige Scores. *General Social Survey Methodological Report* no. 74. Chicago: University of Chicago, National Opinion Research Center.

Schafer, Joseph L. 1997. *Analysis of Incomplete Multivariate Data.* London: Chapman & Hall.

Schneider, Barbara, and James S. Coleman. 1993. *Parents, Their Children, and Schools.* Boulder, CO: Westview Press.

Sewell, William, and Robert Hauser. 1980. The Wisconsin Longitudinal Study of Social and Psychological Factors in Aspirations and Achievements. Pp. 59–100 in *Research in the Sociology of Education and Socialization,* edited by Alan Kerckoff. Vol. 1. Greenwich, CT: JAI.

Shanahan, Michael J. 2000. Pathways to Adulthood in Changing Societies: Variability and Mechanisms in Life Course Perspective. *Annual Review of Sociology* 26:667–92.

Vermunt, Jeroen K., and Jay Magidson. 2000. *Latent Gold: User's Guide.* Belmont, MA: Statistical Innovations.

CHAPTER 11

IS IT GETTING HARDER TO GET AHEAD?

Economic Attainment in Early Adulthood for Two Cohorts

MARY CORCORAN AND JORDAN MATSUDAIRA

Moving out of the childhood bedroom, setting up one's own household, and paying for it with one's earnings have always been major markers of a successful transition to adulthood for men and are increasingly becoming ones for women. Achieving residential and financial independence is usually contingent on finding employment. In this chapter, we ask whether transitions into the labor market have changed for young adults. We also ask whether such changes have differed by race and sex and whether sex-based economic inequality, race-based economic inequality, and intergenerational income inequality have increased, decreased, or remained constant over time. We compare the economic trajectories of young adults born in the 1950s to those of young adults born in the 1960s. Children born in the 1950s grew up in the 1950s and 1960s and turned twenty in the 1970s, while children born in the 1960s were raised in the 1960s and 1970s, and turned twenty in the 1980s.

Labor market conditions at the beginning of individuals' work careers can have long-term effects on their economic trajectories (Beaudry and Di-Nardo 1991), and the labor market faced by entering workers in the 1970s was different from that faced by entering workers in the 1980s. Between 1949 and 1973, during the postwar boom, men's real mean earnings doubled and income inequality narrowed (Blank 1997; Danziger and Gottschalk 1995; Levy 1998). The mid- to late 1970s, a period Levy (1998) calls the "quiet depression," was characterized by back-to-back recessions, rapid inflation, and slower economic growth. During the 1980s, recessions in 1981 and 1982 were followed by a seven-year economic expansion and lower rates of inflation (Blank 1997; Danziger and Gottschalk 1995; Levy 1998). Globalization, deindustrialization, and technological upgrading in the 1970s and 1980s were associated with a decline in the supply of manufacturing jobs, a decline in the number of unionized jobs, and an increase in the supply of service jobs (Blank 1997; Danziger and Gottschalk 1995; Levy 1998; Wilson 1996). Earnings differences between the highly educated and those with low levels of schooling widened during the 1980s (Bound and Johnson 1992). In the late seventies, male college graduates' earnings were 33% higher than those of high school graduates; by the end of the eighties this advantage had increased to 53% (Gottschalk 1997). Thus, the economy changed during the 1980s in ways that favored the better educated over the less educated. According to Levy (1998), the economy remained skill-biased throughout the mid-1990s as well.

These increases in returns to schooling during the 1980s are likely to benefit women more than men, and whites more than African Americans, given that women, on average, have more schooling than men and that whites, on average, have more schooling than African Americans (Charles and Luoh 2002). In fact, wage differences by race widened in the 1980s, and wage differences by gender narrowed over this same period (Blau 1998; Bound and Dresser 1999; Bound and Freeman 1992; Corcoran 1999; Holzer and LaLonde 2000; Juhn 2000). Evidence is mixed on whether intergenerational economic inequality widened, narrowed, or was unchanged during this time (Mayer and Lopoo, forthcoming; Nam 2002).

At the same time that the economy was expanding during the 1980s, the distribution of income became more unequal. The share of total income that went to the families in the bottom income quintile dropped, and the share that went to families in the top quintile rose. The drop in the poverty rate during the 1980s expansion was smaller than in prior expansions. Whites are more likely than African Americans to benefit from these changes in the income distribution given that whites are more likely to come from high-income families and less likely to be poor than are African Americans.

Most of the income gains in the 1980s went to households in the upper half of the income distribution. Schoeni and Ross (this vol., chap. 12) report that high-income parents provide more resources to their children than do low-income parents. One would expect that as the income gap between rich and poor parents widens, rich parents' investments in children would increase relative to those of poor parents. Of course, the distribution of income was not the only factor that changed in the 1980s; returns to schooling increased sharply, thereby increasing the payoffs to this parental investment. This increase in returns to human capital would lead to a decrease in intergenerational mobility (Solon 2003) unless the higher potential payoff somehow induced poor parents to increase investments in their children's schooling despite the decline in their own resources.

In addition to economic changes, policy changes, increased immigration, the movement of manufacturing jobs to the suburbs, and the deterioration of inner-city neighborhoods may have influenced young adults' early economic outcomes. During the course of the 1980s, the real value of the minimum wage dropped sharply, and this probably had the strongest impact on the wages and earnings in low-wage jobs, many of which are held by women or minorities. Bound and Freeman (1992) and Bound and Dresser (1999) find that part of the increased African American/white wage gap in the 1980s was due to erosion in the value of the minimum wage. During the 1980s, the Reagan administration reduced funding and support for the enforcement of affirmative action and equal employment opportunity legislation, which also could have negatively affected employment and wage opportunities for women and minorities who entered the labor market in the 1980s. Furthermore, high rates of immigration in the 1970s and 1980s meant increasing competition for jobs in the low-skilled labor market. The movement of manufacturing jobs to the suburbs during this same period likely further reduced the number of jobs available to low-skilled inner-city minority residents. Poor African American inner-city children's exposure to nonworking adults and to disadvantaged neighborhoods grew steadily throughout the 1970s and 1980s, and this could have led to increases in adult nonwork for minority children raised in such inner-city communities (Wilson 1996). Mead (1992) also argues that inner-city neighborhoods became increasingly disorganized throughout the 1970s and 1980s and that nonwork grew among young women and men growing up in these communities. He attributes the growth in nonwork, however, to the growth of a "welfare culture" that damaged work ethics, not to a loss of economic opportunities.

The probability that a woman would be divorced and/or a single mother at some point rose steadily throughout the 1960s–80s (Wu and Li, this vol., chap. 4). Children born in the 1960s were more likely than children born ten years earlier to spend time in single-parent families (Wu and Li, this vol., chap. 4). Growing up in a nonintact family is positively correlated with dropping out of high school, male idleness, and teen pregnancy, all of which might be detrimental to young adults' economic prospects (McLana-han and Sandefur 1994). At the same time, the increasing instability of mar-riage in the 1960s–80s should have led young women who were coming of age to value economic self-sufficiency more and to focus more on their own careers than did past cohorts (Eggebeen and Hawkins 1990; Leibowitz and Klerman 1995; Noonan 2001; Spain and Bianchi 1996). Relying on a man for financial support was a much riskier proposition for women than it used to be, and as a result women born in the 1960s may have been more career oriented than previous cohorts of women had been. Although the need to be financially independent may have encouraged female labor force participa-tion, the increase in the occurrence of single parenthood may have reduced it because single mothers were less able to work full time on a regular basis.

Fertility rates have declined since the 1950s. According to Wu and Li (this vol., 124) there has been "a general shift away from women bearing large numbers of children toward their bearing no children, one child, or two children." One implication of this shift is that more recent cohorts of women may need to devote less time to childbearing and child rearing than their earlier cohorts. This, in turn, might free up time for paid market work with the result that women's employment rates would increase and nonwork time would decrease.

Gender roles have also changed (Smith, this vol., chap. 6). Attitudes about the appropriate roles of men and women in the family and in the workplace differed substantially from the 1960s to the 1990s. Most notably, it became more acceptable for mothers of young children to work for pay (Brewster and Padavic 2000; Melville 1988; Thornton, Alwin, and Camburn 1983). Support for the traditional division of labor within the home (husband as breadwinner and wife as responsible for child rearing and housework) steadily dropped between the 1970s and 1990s, and support for husbands and wives sharing responsibilities for providing income and for raising chil-dren rose (Ciabattari 2001; Goldscheider and Waite 1991; Jump and Haas 1987; Noonan 2001; Radcliffe Public Policy Center 2000; Smith, this vol., chap. 6; Wilkie 1993). These attitudinal changes are reflected in maternal work patterns and in current welfare policies. Leibowitz and Klerman (1995) report that employment of mothers of very young children rose steadily from 22% in 1971 to 55% in 1990 (cited in Noonan 2001). Noonan (2001) and O'Connell (1990) report similar trends. The most recent Bush admin-istration proposal for welfare reauthorization would require welfare recipi-ents, even mothers of young children, to work forty hours per week.

Other things being equal, increases in the likelihood of divorce and/or single parenting and changing attitudes about male and female work and family roles should lead women to invest more in human capital and to increase their paid work. As male and female employment patterns converge, gaps in wages and earnings should shrink, which indeed began to occur throughout the 1980s (Altonji and Blank 1999; Blau 1998).

In sum, many factors may have affected young adults' transitions into the labor market across cohorts, including changes in economic conditions, income inequality, minimum wage and equal employment policies, competition from immigrant workers, education-based labor market inequalities, nonwork experiences, neighborhood resources, family structures, and sex roles. On balance, cross-cohort changes in early employment and income outcomes were probably more positive for women than for men, for whites than for African Americans, and for high-income children than for low-income children. White women were particularly well placed to benefit from the economic and social changes of the 1980s and early 1990s. In contrast, many of these social and economic changes might be expected to restrict the economic prospects of African American men. We would expect to see white women, on average, taking more jobs as professionals and administrators, while African American men, on average, would suffer wage losses due to the decline in manufacturing industries.

Understanding how and whether transitions into the labor market have changed over time is important because most young adults should have launched their careers by their mid- to late twenties. Three-quarters of men's wage growth occurs in their first ten years of work (Topel and Ward 1992) and because of this, labor market conditions at the time young adults begin work may have enduring effects on their later wage growth and incomes (Beaudry and DiNardo 1991). Labor market problems, such as excessive nonwork, frequent job losses, or poor pay early in their careers, may mean that young adults miss out on crucial on-the-job training and socialization that are prerequisites for future economic mobility and employment stability. Employment problems in the midtwenties may also harm young adults' future economic trajectories by stigmatizing them as unmotivated, lazy, or unreliable in the eyes of potential employers. For women, extended periods of nonwork to care for children may stigmatize them as lacking in career commitment if employers use past work history to predict future productivity (Noonan, Corcoran, and Courant 2003).

Mean income grew and income inequality widened between 1983 and 1989. We ask whether intergenerational income inequality also widened during this period. That is, were the chances of escaping poverty as an adult lower for poor children who came of age in the 1980s than for poor children who came of age in the 1970s? Were the chances of remaining affluent higher for children from affluent families? If so, then not only has income inequality widened within a generation but economic opportunities and mobility have declined across generations as well. This raises serious ethical questions in a society, such as the United States, that professes to value equality of opportunity.

Solon's (forthcoming) model of mobility variation predicts that as returns to human capital increase, mobility across generations ought to decrease. Unfortunately, the evidence on changes in intergenerational mobility is mixed, many studies only examine men, and results are sometimes inconsistent across studies. For example, some report that, in contrast to Solon's predictions, men's economic mobility has increased over time. Mayer and Lopoo (forthcoming) report that father-son intergenerational income correlations were higher for men born between 1951 and 1956 than for men born between 1957 and 1965. Corcoran (2001) finds that father-son income correlations were higher for men born between 1953 and 1960 than for men born from 1961 to 1970. Levine (1999) and Perucci and Wysong (2002), on the contrary, report that economic mobility has decreased rather than increased in the course of time. Nam (2002) directly examined movement into and out of low-income status and high-income status across time. She finds that the probability of escaping low income (defined as 1.5 times the poverty line) was not significantly different for young men born 1954–58 than for young men born 1964–68, but that the probability of remaining high income (defined as an income-to-needs ratio of five or more) was significantly higher for young men born 1964–68 than for young men born ten years earlier.

In this chapter we compare the early economic trajectories of two cohorts—one that came of age in the 1970s and one that came of age in the 1980s. We examine multiple indicators of early transitions into the labor market—employment rates, wages, annual earnings, and nonwork—and we measure these indicators over a three-year period. Few analysts have examined nonwork and hourly wages spanning multiple years for young adults. For instance, Haveman and Wolfe (1994), Mayer (1997), and McLanahan and Sandefur (1994) examined nonwork and/or wages over only one year; Blau (1998), Bound and Dresser (1999), Bound and Freeman (1992), and Corcoran (1999) all use point-in-time wage measures. We also examine family incomes and patterns of intergenerational income mobility to assess whether intergenerational economic inequality has increased, decreased, or remained the same across cohorts.

SAMPLE AND METHOD

We use the 1968–96 waves of the Panel Study of Income Dynamics (PSID) to examine the extent to which the timing of leaving home, years of schooling, and economic outcomes in early adulthood differed for men and women born in the 1950s and for men and women born in the 1960s. The PSID has tracked the economic fortunes of about five thousand American families on an annual basis since 1968. The PSID follows children as they leave home and start up their own households and so provides contemporaneous reports of income by parents during childhood years and children's own contemporaneous reports of their economic outcomes as adults. The head of the household (defined as the husband in husband/wife households) reports on family income—and on his own and his spouse's employment outcomes in the year prior to the interview date. Individuals interviewed at age twenty-seven, for example, report on their income during the prior year, when they were twenty-six.

Our sample consists of two cohorts of PSID respondents. Cohort 1 includes 1,170 women and 1,110 men who were born 1952–59, who were children aged nine to sixteen in PSID households in 1968, and who were observed as young adults at ages twenty-seven to thirty-four in 1986. Cohort 2 includes 832 women and 763 men who were born 1962–69, who were children aged nine to sixteen in PSID households in 1978, and who were observed as young adults aged twenty-seven to thirty-four in 1996. Individuals in cohort 1 were born in the 1950s, became adolescents in the late 1960s to mid-1970s, and became young adults (i.e., turned twenty) between 1972 and 1979—a period characterized by back-to-back recessions after 1973. Individuals in cohort 2 were born in the 1960s, became adolescents in the late 1970s to mid-1980s, and became young adults during 1982–89—mostly during an economic expansion.

The PSID has several advantages for examining early employment and income trajectories. First, the PSID enables us to compute multiyear labor market and income measures for two cohorts of young adults who entered the labor market under different economic conditions. For instance, this will be one of the first studies to compare three-year patterns of nonwork and three-year earnings averages across cohorts. Because we average earnings and wages over a multiple-year period, we have fewer problems with measurement error and selection bias than do studies that examine wages at a point in time or spanning a single year. The selection issue is important when examining women's earnings and wages since many women work part time and/or take time out from work to bear and raise children during early adulthood.[1] Point-in-time estimates of men's wages are also more likely to exclude men with erratic employment histories than are multiple-year wage estimates. This could matter for young African American men, given that some experience substantial nonwork (Juhn 2000).

Second, because the PSID obtains measures of parental economic circumstances reported by the parents when children lived at home, we can examine whether there are differences in how individuals' early economic trajectories vary by parents' three-year income status. Mazumder (forthcoming) and Solon (1992) have shown that intergenerational income and earnings correlations are larger when parental economic status is measured over multiple years.

Third, the PSID has a large African American subsample, so analyses can be run separately for African Americans and whites.[2] Traditionally, the employment of African Americans has been more sensitive to economic conditions than that of whites has. Employment, wages and incomes of African American men and women typically drop at a higher rate during recessions and grow at a higher rate during economic expansions than do the employment, wages, and incomes of white men and women (Corcoran 1999; Hoynes 1999). This large subsample of African Americans also enables us to gauge the extent to which race-based inequalities in three-year measures of labor market success have changed with time. And finally, because the PSID collected comparable employment and wage data for male household heads, wives, and female household heads, we can assess how sex-based differences in early labor market outcomes have changed across cohorts.

There are two disadvantages associated with using the PSID. First, the PSID provides a sample of children born to families who were representative of the U.S. population as of 1968. Since 1968, large numbers of families from Asia and South America have immigrated to the United States. The PSID does not include children in such immigrant families. Second, the PSID asks detailed questions about the schooling, income, and labor market experiences of heads of households and wives, which are relatively comparable across cohorts. Questions about the schooling and labor market experiences of family members other than heads or wives provide less detail and are not consistent over the two cohorts. As a result, we restrict cohort comparisons of education, income, and labor market outcomes to sons and daughters who were household heads or wives at the ages over which these outcomes are measured.

Adult economic outcomes are measured during the years 1977–86 for cohort 1 and during the years 1987–96 for cohort 2. Both periods include recession and expansion years. We examine the following outcomes: age at leaving home, years of schooling, high school and college graduation rates, employment, wages, earnings, nonwork (idleness), family income, and income quintile. We measure adult economic incomes over ages twenty-four to twenty-six years because the teens and early twenties are often a period of economic turbulence for individuals as they sort themselves into and are sorted into jobs. We examine whether cohort changes in individuals' ages at leaving home, schooling, and early economic trajectories differed by race or sex and whether there were cohort changes in rates of intergenerational income inequality.

Age at leaving home is measured as the age at which the respondent first became head of or wife to the household head of his or her own family unit. Level of education is measured when the respondent is age twenty-seven years.[3] Work and income outcomes are measured spanning ages twenty-four to twenty-six. Most researchers measure employment outcomes at a single point in time or over a one-year period. A three-year measure of employment outcomes should be less prone to measurement error than a single-year measure. A second advantage of examining economic outcomes over a three-year period is that we include individuals who worked part of the year and/or who worked in only one of the three years between ages twenty-four and twenty-six. Such individuals likely have lower mean earnings and mean wages than do individuals who work a full year on a regular basis. This means we can include more African American men and more women in wage and earnings comparisons than do analysts who examine these outcomes for shorter periods. One result of this may be that we will find larger sex-based and race-based gaps in wages and earnings than do analysts who exclude part-year workers from their analyses.

The samples used for analysis vary depending on the outcomes examined. Years of schooling and labor market outcomes have been consistently recorded for heads of households and wives but not for other household members over the two cohort periods we examined. As a result, education at age twenty-seven is only examined for respondents who were household heads or wives by age twenty-seven. For the same reason, work and income outcomes at ages twenty-four to twenty-six are examined only for respondents who were household heads or wives at ages twenty-five, twenty-six, and twenty-seven years old and who were not full-time students at ages twenty-five, twenty-six, or twenty-seven. Because wages and annual earnings are only measured for workers, we further restrict analyses of these two outcomes to employed individuals who had worked at least 250 hours in at least one year between the ages of twenty-four and twenty-six.[4]

Table 11.1 describes how each outcome measure was constructed. Earnings, income, and wage measures are measured in 1996 dollars. Our

TABLE II.I

OUTCOME VARIABLES, DEFINITIONS, AND SAMPLES

OUTCOME MEASURE	DEFINITION	SAMPLE
Home leaving	Age at which become head or wife in own household	Full sample; cohort 1 = 2,280, cohort 2 = 1,595
Education	Most recent report of completed years of schooling at age 27 (GED = 12)	Head or wife at age 27; cohort 1 = 1,968, cohort 2 = 1,281
Work/income outcomes at ages 24–26:		
Family income (1996 $)	Sum of family income plus food stamps reported at ages 25–27 divided by 3	Head or wife at ages 25–27; cohort 1 = 1,827, cohort 2 = 1,139
Income quintiles	Quintile of family income reported at ages 25–27	Head or wife at ages 25–27; cohort 1 = 1,827, cohort 2 = 1,139
Employed	1 if employed in one or more of years prior to interviews at ages 25–27; 0 if otherwise	Head or wife and not a full-time student at ages 25–27; cohort 1 = 1,739, cohort 2 = 1,139
Weeks of nonwork	156 − weeks worked + weeks on strike + weeks paid vacation + weeks on sick leave) reported at ages 25–27	Head or wife and not a full-time student at ages 25–27; cohort 1 = 1,739, cohort 2 = 1,139
Labor income (1996 $)	Mean labor income averaged over all years reported nonzero labor income between ages 25–27	Head or wife and not a full-time student at ages 25–27, reported nonzero labor income in at least one year, and worked 250 or more hours in at least one year; cohort 1 = 1,543, cohort 2 = 1,037
Hourly wage (1996 $)	Labor income divided by weeks worked, averaged over all years reported nonzero labor incomes between ages 25–27	Head or wife and not a full-time student at ages 25–27, reported nonzero labor income in at least one year, and worked 250 or more hours in at least one year; cohort 1 = 1,543, cohort 2 = 1,037

measure of weeks of nonwork differs from measures of idleness used by previous researchers. Past measures of idleness typically cover one year only and are binary measures. For instance, Mayer (1997) defines idleness as working less than a thousand hours at age twenty-four. We measure weeks of nonwork spanning the three years prior to the age twenty-seven interviews. We define weeks of work as the sum of weeks worked, weeks on strike, weeks of paid vacation leave, and weeks on sick leave for the three-year period between ages twenty-four and twenty-six. We then subtract this sum from 156 (3 × 52). Thus, sick leave, paid vacation, and time on strike count as time spent working. The nonwork variable can range from zero, for those who were working or on strike, on sick leave, or on paid vacation leave for the entire three-year period, to 156 for those who reported no weeks worked, no strike time, no sick leave, and no paid vacation leave during the entire three-year period. Our measure has two advantages. First, it is continuous and thus picks up variations in nonwork. Second, because it is a multiyear measure, we can distinguish individuals who have one "bad year" from individuals who consistently work at low levels.

Table 11.1 also reports the sample restrictions and sample sizes by cohort for each outcome we examine. As table 11.1 shows, sample sizes drop when we restrict analyses by headship (wife) status at age twenty-seven and at ages twenty-five to twenty-seven.

RESULTS

Cohort Changes in Age at Leaving Home and in Schooling

We find that age at leaving home has increased over time (see table 11.2). This pattern held true for all race/sex groups. Within racial cohorts, women left home earlier than did men. Within gender cohorts, whites left home earlier than African Americans.

Children born in the 1960s typically had higher levels of schooling than did children born in the 1950s (see table 11.3). High school dropout rates declined consistently across cohorts for all race/sex groups. Mean years of schooling and college graduation rates rose across cohorts for white men, African American men, and white women. College graduation rates and mean years of schooling declined across cohorts for African American women, but these declines were not significant and are likely due to sampling error. In both cohorts, African Americans were more likely than were whites to be high school dropouts or to have stopped schooling after receiving a high school diploma or GED. Given that returns to schooling widened

TABLE 11.2

AGE AT LEAVING HOME

	WHITE			AFRICAN AMERICAN		
	COHORT 1 (1952–59)	COHORT 2 (1962–69)	DIFFERENCES (COHORT 2 − COHORT 1)	COHORT 1 (1952–59)	COHORT 2 (1962–69)	DIFFERENCES (COHORT 2 − COHORT 1)
Men:						
<17	0	0	0	.2	.2	0
17–19	17.4	12.6	−4.8	11.4	5.0	−6.4
20–22	39.1	30.4	−8.7	31.9	24.5	−7.4
23–25	24.9	33.1	8.2	27.8	32.1	4.3
26–27	5.9	7.6	1.7	9.6	11.7	2.1
28 or older	12.6	16.4	3.8	19.2	26.5	7.3
All (%)	100	100		100	100	
n	615	457	. . .	495	306	. . .
Women:						
<17	2.0	1.0	−1.0	1.4	.8	−.6
17–19	34.3	24.2	−10.1	27.3	19.0	−8.3
20–22	36.8	35.2	−1.6	33.3	25.2	−8.1
23–25	17.7	27.6	10.1	19.5	30.8	10.3
26–27	5.5	4.9	−0.6	7.3	7.4	.1
28 or older	3.7	7.0	3.3	11.2	16.9	5.7
All (%)	100	100		100	100	
n	612	450	. . .	558	382	. . .

Notes. Data set is the Panel Study of Income Dynamics (PSID). Cohort 1 sample is men and women aged 9–16 in 1968 who were observed at age 27. Cohort 2 sample is men and women aged 9–16 in 1978 who were observed at age 27.

during the 1980s, this suggests that, on average, the whites in cohort 2 may have fared better than the African Americans did.

Cohort Changes in Employment

Working on a regular basis is often considered a necessary first step to economic independence. Table 11.4 reports on three measures of individuals' employment status: whether employed at the age twenty-seven interview; whether ever worked in the calendar year prior to the age twenty-seven interview (i.e., at age twenty-six); and whether ever employed in the three calendar years prior to the age twenty-seven interview (i.e., at ages twenty-four

TABLE 11.3

YEARS OF COMPLETED SCHOOLING AT AGE 27

	WHITE			AFRICAN AMERICAN		
	COHORT 1 (1952–59)	COHORT 2 (1962–69)	DIFFERENCES (COHORT 2 − COHORT 1)	COHORT 1 (1952–59)	COHORT 2 (1962–69)	DIFFERENCES (COHORT 2 − COHORT 1)
Men:						
<High school	15.4	11.4	−4.0	22.6	19.6	−3.0
GED or						
high school						
diploma	37.7	39.7	2.0	53.5	49.2	−4.3
Some college	26.0	22.6	−3.4	16.3	19.4	3.1
BA or more	21.0	26.2	5.2	7.6	11.9	4.3
All (%)	100	100		100	100	
n	522	368		377	199	
Women:						
<High school	11.9	8.9	−3.0	22.4	17.4	−5.0
GED or						
high school						
diploma	44.3	39.5	−4.8	39.2	44.0	4.8
Some college	21.9	26.6	4.7	27.1	34.2	7.1
BA or more	21.9	25.0	3.1	11.3	4.4	−6.9
All (%)	100	100		100	100	
n	576	398		459	288	

Note. Mean years of education (top-coded at 17 for any graduate-level education) are as follows (standard errors in parentheses): white men, 13.1 (.09) for cohort 1 and 13.3 (.11) for cohort 2; African American men, 12.2 (.09) for cohort 1 and 12.4 (.12) for cohort 2; white women, 13.1 (.09) for cohort 1 and 13.4 (.10) for cohort 2; African American women, 12.6 (.08) for cohort 1 and 12.4 (.08) for cohort 2. Data set is the Panel Study of Income Dynamics (PSID). Cohort 1 sample is men and women aged 9–16 in 1968 who were heads of households or wives at age 27. Cohort 2 sample is men and women aged 9–16 in 1978 who were heads of households or wives at age 27.

to twenty-six). The first three columns of table 11.4 report the percentages of individuals who were employed in each of these three periods for cohort 1 by race/sex group. The second three columns report the same percentages for individuals in cohort 2 by race/sex group. The third set of three columns reports the change in percentage employed across cohorts (the cohort 2 percentage minus the cohort 1 percentage).

For the most part, white men worked on a regular basis over all three periods examined, and the length of the period over which employment was measured had little effect on their employment rates. More than 92% were

TABLE II.4

EMPLOYMENT

RACE/SEX GROUP	COHORT 1 (BORN 1952–62)			COHORT 2 (BORN 1962–69)			DIFFERENCES (COHORT 2 − COHORT 1)		
	PERCENTAGE EMPLOYED AT AGE 27 INTERVIEW	PERCENTAGE EMPLOYED IN YEAR PRIOR TO AGE 27 INTERVIEW	PERCENTAGE EMPLOYED IN 3 YEARS PRIOR TO AGE 27 INTERVIEW	PERCENTAGE EMPLOYED AT AGE 27 INTERVIEW	PERCENTAGE EMPLOYED IN YEAR PRIOR TO AGE 27 INTERVIEW	PERCENTAGE EMPLOYED IN 3 YEARS PRIOR TO AGE 27 INTERVIEW	PERCENTAGE EMPLOYED AT AGE 27 INTERVIEW	PERCENTAGE EMPLOYED IN YEAR PRIOR TO AGE 27 INTERVIEW	PERCENTAGE EMPLOYED IN 3 YEARS PRIOR TO AGE 27 INTERVIEW
Men:									
White	92.5	98.8	99.7	92.6	98.8	100.0	.1	.0	.3
	(1.1)	(.5)	(.2)	(1.4)	(.6)	(.0)			
Black	79.4	91.3	99.4	71.7	88.0	94.9	−7.7*	−3.3	−4.5*
	(2.1)	(1.4)	(.4)	(3.2)	(2.3)	(1.7)			
Women:									
White	64.2	79.0	90.1	78.7	86.2	94.8	14.5*	7.2*	4.7*
	(2.0)	(1.7)	(1.3)	(2.1)	(1.7)	(1.1)			
Black	63.2	79.4	87.6	63.3	81.4	92.5	.1	2.0	4.9*
	(2.2)	(1.9)	(1.6)	(2.8)	(2.2)	(1.6)			

Notes. Standard errors (in parentheses) account for sample weights. Data set is the Panel Study of Income Dynamics (PSID).

*Statistically significant at the .05 level.

employed at the age twenty-seven interviews; about 99% were employed in the year prior to the age twenty-seven interview; and 99.7% were employed at some point between ages twenty-four and twenty-six.

Employment patterns were more erratic for African American men and for women. In cohort 1, only 79% of African American men were employed at the age twenty-seven interviews; 91% were employed in the year prior to that interview, and 99.4% were employed at some point between ages twenty-four and twenty-six. Young African American men's employment was apparently less stable than that of young white men. The variation in employment rates by length of period was even stronger for women in cohort 1: 63%–64% of white women and African American women were employed at the age twenty-seven interview date; 79% were employed in the year prior to that interview; and 88%–90% were employed between ages twenty-four and twenty-six. This variation is likely due in part to the sex division of labor within the home—that is, to the fact that women typically assumed the bulk of child-rearing responsibilities in the 1970s.

All else equal, did individuals' chances of finding and keeping jobs grow across cohorts? Did patterns of change differ by race and sex? During the 1980s, structural economic changes such as deindustrialization, the erosion in the value of the minimum wage, the movement of jobs to the suburbs, increased competition from immigrants, decreased enforcement of equal opportunity legislation, and the deterioration of inner-city neighborhoods might all have reduced employment opportunities for minority men and women. At the same time, changes in gender roles might be expected to lead to increases in women's employment relative to that of men. The last three columns in table 11.4 record the employment gains and losses of individuals across cohorts 1 and 2 on each of the three employment measures.

White men's employment was stable and did not change across cohorts; the vast majority worked in each cohort. White women's employment rose significantly across cohorts for all three employment measures, as would be expected, given changes in social norms, increases in the demand for skilled workers, decreases in the unemployment rate, decreases in fertility, and increases in the probability of divorce. The percentage of white women employed at the age twenty-seven interview rose by more than 14.5 percentage points between cohorts 1 and 2; the percentage employed in the year prior to the age twenty-seven interview rose by 7.2 percentage points, and the percentage employed at ages twenty-four to twenty-six years rose by 4.5 percentage points.

African American women's employment rose across cohorts on two of the three employment measures: the percentage of African American women who were employed in the year prior to the age twenty-seven interview rose by two percentage points (not significant), and the percentage employed at ages twenty-four to twenty-six rose by almost 5 percentage points (significant). The percentage of African American women employed at the age twenty-seven interview date was the same (63%) across cohorts 1 and 2.

Coming of age during the 1980s was associated with lower employment rates for African American men. They were the only group who experienced drops in employment rates across cohorts. African American men's employment at the age twenty-seven interview dropped significantly by 7.7 percentage points across cohort 1 and cohort 2; their employment in the year prior to the age twenty-seven interview dropped by 3.3 percentage points (not significant) across cohorts 1 and 2; and their employment at ages twenty-four to twenty-six dropped significantly by 4.5 percentage points across cohorts. These drops in African American men's employment are hardly surprising given the growing importance of skills in the 1980s economy, increased competition from immigrants, and the deterioration of inner-city communities.

The 4.5 percentage point drop in African American men's employment spanning ages twenty-four to twenty-six may affect our cohort comparisons of mean wages and mean earnings. If men who do not work at all between ages twenty-four and twenty-six tend to be those whose prospective wages fall at the bottom end of the wage distribution, then eliminating them from wage analyses may lead us to overestimate the mean wage and mean earnings available to all African American men and therefore underestimate declines in mean wages and mean earnings across cohorts (Solon, Barsky, and Parker 1994). This could also lead to underestimates of increases in race-based gaps in men's earnings and wages across cohorts.

Given changing attitudes regarding gender roles, we predicted that sex-based gaps in employment would decrease across cohorts. This did occur; with sex-based employment gaps within racial groups at age twenty-seven dropping by roughly half across cohorts. Among whites, however, the drop was entirely due to white women's increased employment, whereas among African Americans it was primarily driven by the decrease in African American men's employment.

The gap in employment between African American men and white women actually reversed across cohorts. In cohort 1, 79.4% of African American men and 64.2% of white women were employed at age twenty-seven; in cohort 2, 71.7% of African American men and 78.7% of white women were employed at age twenty-seven. Thus, the gap in employment between African American men and white women was 15.2% in favor of African American men in cohort 1 and 7.0% in favor of white women in cohort 2.

While sex-based employment inequalities narrowed across cohorts, race-based inequalities in employment often widened across cohorts. White/ African American gaps in men's employment grew from 13.1 percentage points in cohort 1 to 20.9 percentage points in cohort 2 due to the decline in the employment of African American men. Race-based gaps in men's one-year (age twenty-six) and three-year (ages twenty-four to twenty-six) employment rates also rose across cohorts. White/African American gaps in women's employment grew from only 1 percentage point for cohort 1 to 15.4 percentage points for cohort 2 due to the rise in white women's employment.

Cohort Changes in Nonwork

The midtwenties are a period during which individuals should be developing the work histories and job skills necessary for mobility. Nonwork during these years could have long-term negative repercussions for individuals' future economic trajectories. We next investigate whether patterns of nonwork at ages twenty-four to twenty-six have changed across cohorts. Table 11.5 and figures 11.1–11.4 compare the means and distributions of weeks of nonwork at ages twenty-four to twenty-six for men and women in cohort 1 to those for men and women in cohort 2. Recall that our measure of nonwork is conservative. An individual is defined as not working only if she meets all the following criteria: not attending school full time, not working for pay, not on strike, not on paid vacation, and not on sick leave. Weeks of nonwork are measured for the years 1977–86 for cohort 1 and for the years 1987–96 for cohort 2.

TABLE 11.5

MEAN WEEKS NOT WORKED (OUT OF A POSSIBLE 156) AT AGES 24–26

	COHORT 1 (BORN 1952–59)	COHORT 2 (BORN 1962–69)	DIFFERENCES (COHORT 2 − COHORT 1)
Men:			
White	12.8 (1.13)	10.2 (1.16)	−2.6
Black	35.0 (2.51)	37.7 (3.47)	2.7
Women:			
White	55.5 (2.58)	42.8 (2.43)	−12.7*
Black	51.3 (2.87)	53.5 (3.56)	2.2

Notes. Standard errors in parentheses account for sample weights. Data set is the Panel Study of Income Dynamics (PSID). Cohort 1 sample is men and women aged 9–16 in 1968 who were head or wife and not a full-time student at ages 25–27. Cohort 2 sample is men and women aged 9–16 in 1978 who were head or wife and not a full-time student at ages 25–27.

*Statistically significant at the .05 level.

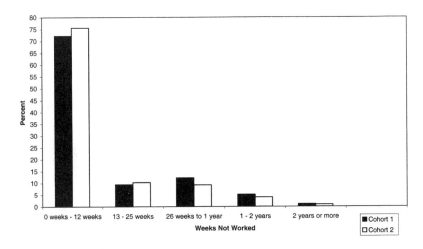

Figure 11.1. White men's frequency of weeks of nonwork over ages 24–26

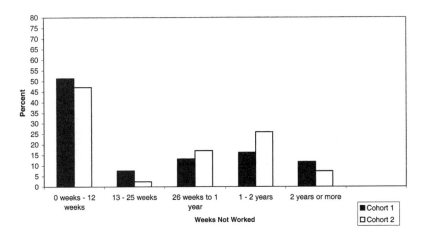

Figure 11.2. Black men's frequency of weeks of nonwork over ages 24–26

Once again we see that African American men had more erratic patterns of employment in their midtwenties than did white men, and this difference grew slightly across cohorts. The average white man in cohort 1 reported 12.8 weeks of nonwork at ages twenty-four to twenty-six. This dropped to 10.2 weeks for white men in cohort 2. The average African American man in cohort 1 reported 35.0 weeks of nonwork. This rose to 37.7 weeks for African American men in cohort 2. As a result of these changes, the white/ African American gap in men's weeks of nonwork widened from 22.2 weeks

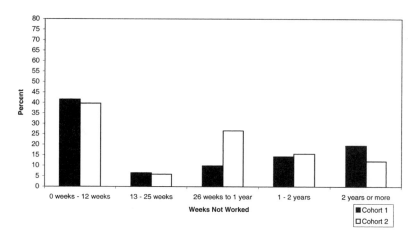

Figure 11.3. White women's frequency of weeks of nonwork over ages 24–26

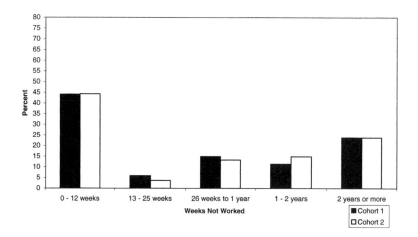

Figure 11.4. Black women's frequency of weeks of nonwork over ages 24–26

for cohort 1 to 27.5 weeks for cohort 2. Juhn (2000) also found that race differences in men's nonemployment have been growing as time goes on.

There was considerable variation in the total weeks of nonwork that men accumulated between ages twenty-four and twenty-six. For many men, amounts of nonwork were zero or small. In both cohorts, more than 70% of white men and more than 45% of African American men reported fewer than thirteen weeks of nonwork between ages twenty-four and twenty-six (see figs. 11.1 and 11.2). But a small minority of white men and a sizable minority of African American men were not employed on a regular basis in their midtwenties. In each cohort, 5%–6% of white men and 29%–33% of

African American men reported fifty-two weeks or more (out of a possible 156 weeks) of nonwork between ages twenty-four and twenty-six years. This is a lot of nonwork given that we do not include full-time students in these analyses and that sick leaves, paid vacation leaves, and strikes are not included in our measure of nonwork.

Changes in the distribution of men's nonwork across the two cohorts were small. The percentage of men who reported extensive nonwork was roughly equal across cohorts for whites and rose slightly across cohorts for African Americans. Roughly 40% of African American men in cohort 1 and 50% of African American men in cohort 2 reported twenty-six weeks or more nonwork; about 29% of African American men in cohort 1 and 33% of African American men in cohort 2 reported one year or more of nonwork.

The employment and nonwork numbers for African American men in cohort 2 are disquieting given that the midtwenties are the period when they should be establishing their careers. More than 28% of African American men were not employed at the age twenty-seven interview. One in three African American men did not work for more than a year between ages twenty-four and twenty-six. An African American male born in the 1960s averaged thirty-eight weeks of nonwork between ages twenty-four and twenty-six.

Given that women spend more time than men caring for children and doing housework, we expected that, on average, women would have accumulated more nonwork and that extensive nonwork would be more common for them. Both predictions proved true. In cohort 1, the average woman had accumulated roughly one year of nonwork between the ages of twenty-four and twenty-six; 35%–42% of women had reported a year or more of nonwork; and roughly one in four women had accumulated two or more years of nonwork (see table 11.5 and figs. 11.3 and 11.4).

We also expected that changes in gender roles would lead women in cohort 2 to devote more time to paid work than did women in the earlier cohort. This held true for white woman but not for African American women. White women's mean weeks of nonwork dropped from 55.5 weeks for cohort 1 to 42.8 weeks for cohort 2. About 42% of white women in cohort 1 reported one year or more of nonwork, and about 28% reported 2 years or more of nonwork. About 28% of white women in cohort 2 reported a year or more of nonwork, and about 12% reported two years or more of nonwork.

African American women, in contrast, did not experience a decrease in nonwork across cohorts. In each cohort, African American women averaged about one year of nonwork; more than 35% of African American women reported one year or more of nonwork; and almost one in four reported two years or more of nonwork. One reason African American women's nonwork did not drop in response to changing social norms may be that other factors—the increasing importance of skills, competition from immigrants, the suburbanization of manufacturing jobs, the decline of unions, and the erosion of the minimum wage—reduced employment incentives and opportunities for minority women who came of age in the 1980s (see Bound and Dresser 1999).

Race-based differences in nonwork changed across cohorts for women. White and African American women in cohort 1 had similar means and distributions of nonwork. But in cohort 2, white women's mean on weeks of nonwork was 10.7 weeks lower than that of African American women, and white women were less likely than were African American women to report nonwork of a year or more. This widening was driven primarily by reductions in white women's nonwork across cohorts. This result is consistent with those of Blau (1998), Corcoran (1999), and Corcoran and Heflin (2002), who found that the gap between the labor force participation rates and employment rates of white women and African American women widened between 1979 and the early 1990s.

Sex-based gaps in nonwork dropped across cohorts for white women, but not for African-African women. In cohort 1, white men and African American men averaged far fewer weeks of nonwork than did either white or African American women. The gap in average weeks of nonwork between white men and white women dropped from 42.7 weeks in cohort 1 to 32.6 weeks in cohort 2; and the gap in average weeks of nonwork between African American men and white women dropped from 20.5 weeks in cohort 1 to only 5.1 weeks in cohort 2.

Cohort Changes in Earnings and Wages

We examine cohort changes in mean wages, mean earnings and mean incomes of young adults in table 11.6. The means for annual labor income, hourly wages, and annual family income at ages twenty-four to twenty-six for cohort 1 are reported in the first three columns of table 11.6; the comparable means for cohort 2 are reported in the second three columns; and the cross-cohort differences in means are reported in the last three columns. Labor income, hourly wages, and family income are expressed in 1996 dollars. We discuss wage and earnings results in this section and family income results in a later section.

We predicted that the economic, demographic, and social changes of 1980s and early 1990s would lead to better labor market outcomes for women and whites than for men and for African Americans. In fact, the news for both white and African American women's earnings was good:

TABLE 11.6

MEANS ON LABOR INCOME, HOURLY WAGE, AND FAMILY INCOME AVERAGE OVER AGES 24–26 (1996 $)

	COHORT 1 (BORN 1952–59)			COHORT 2 (BORN 1962–69)			DIFFERENCE (COHORT 2 − COHORT 1)		
	LABOR INCOME	HOURLY WAGE	FAMILY INCOME	LABOR INCOME	HOURLY WAGE	FAMILY INCOME	LABOR INCOME	HOURLY WAGE	FAMILY INCOME
Men:									
White	29,077	13.99	38,369	28,888	13.15	39,305	−189	−.84*	936
	(594)	(.261)	(773)	(754)	(.323)	(1,153)			
Black	20,491	11.12	26,813	17,948	9.49	22,165	−2,543*	−1.63*	−4,648*
	(653)	(.273)	(927)	(734)	(.326)	(1,159)			
Women:									
White	16,953	10.52	39,511	19,427	10.77	42,928	2,474*	.25	3,417*
	(482)	(.230)	(809)	(651)	(.295)	(1,324)			
Black	13,938	8.72	24,046	15,820	9.19	22,333	1,882*	.47	−1,713
	(425)	(.219)	(735)	(668)	(.299)	(866)			

Note. Standard errors in parentheses account for sample weights.

*Statistically significant at the .05 level.

their mean labor incomes rose significantly by 14%–15% across cohorts. White men's mean labor income did not change across cohorts. However, African American men's mean labor income dropped significantly by 13% across cohorts.

As a result of these changes, sex-based earnings inequality narrowed; race-based inequality in women's earnings did not change; and race-based inequality in men's earnings widened across cohorts. The increases in women's mean earnings across cohorts substantially reduced the gaps between white men's mean earnings and those of white women and African American women. For instance, the gap between white men and white women's mean earnings dropped from $12,124 to $9,461. The large drop in African American men's mean earnings across cohorts increased the white/African American gap in men's mean earnings (from $8,586 to $10,940); reduced the male/female gap in African Americans' mean earnings (from $6,553 to $2,228); and reversed the gap between African American men's and white women's mean earnings (from $3,538 in favor of African American men to $1,474 in favor of white women).

Labor incomes can grow for two reasons: increases in annual work hours and increases in wages. Cross-cohort increases in women's mean hourly wages were smaller than were increases in their mean labor incomes, suggesting that mean hours worked per year increased across cohorts for women. Mean wages rose slightly ($.25 to $.47 per hour) for white and African American women across cohorts but these changes were not significant. Men's mean wages, on the contrary, declined significantly across cohorts— by $.84 per hour for white men and by $1.63 per hour (15%) for African American men.

Changes in sex-based and race-based wage inequalities mirrored the changes in earnings inequalities. Sex-based wage gaps narrowed; the race-based gap in women's wages did not change; and the race-based gap in men's wages widened across cohorts. In cohort 1, African American men had higher mean wages than did either white women or African American women. In cohort 2, white women's mean wage exceeded that of African American men, and African American women's mean wage had almost caught up to that of African American men.

We have seen that race-based gaps in men's mean labor incomes and mean earnings widened across cohorts. The comparisons reported in table 11.6 may understate the deterioration in African American's fortunes relative to those of white men. Virtually all white men in both cohorts worked between ages twenty-four and twenty-six. This was not true for African American men: 99.4% in cohort 1 and 94.9% in cohort 2 worked at ages twenty-four to twenty-six. That is, 5% of African American men in cohort 2 neither worked nor attended school full time between the ages of twenty-four and twenty-six. If, as is likely, the 5% of African American men who did not work in cohort 2 were disproportionately men who would have received low wage offers, then the numbers in table 11.6 will underestimate the decline in African American men's relative and absolute economic prospects.

Race/Sex Ordering of Labor Market Outcomes

Cross-cohort changes in young adults' employment, nonwork, wages, and earnings were all positive for white women, mostly positive for African American women, negligible for white men, and mostly negative for African American men. In this section, we compare the labor market outcomes of African American men, white women, and African American women to those of the most advantaged group, white men (see table 11.7).

We examine three outcomes: percentage employed between ages twenty-four and twenty-six, mean labor income, and mean hourly wage. We compare outcomes by constructing the ratio of a group's score on an outcome to the score of white men on the same outcome. The first three columns of table 11.7 report the ratios of a group's labor market outcome to the white male outcome for individuals in cohort 1. The second three columns report the same ratios for individuals in cohort 2. The last three columns report the difference between the cohort ratios, which measures the extent to which white men's average labor market advantage relative to that of another group grew or dropped across cohorts. Thus, row 2 of table 11.7 shows that, in cohort 1, African American men's mean labor income was 70% that of white men; in cohort 2, African American men's mean labor income was 62% that of white men; and the mean labor income advantage of white men vis-à-vis African American men widened by 8 percentage points between cohort 1 and cohort 2.

There is a clear ordering of labor market success by race and sex. White men are at the top of the labor market hierarchy in cohort 1. They have the highest employment rates, the highest mean labor income, and the highest mean wage on each of these outcomes. African American men are in second place, followed by white women, and then African American women. Note that the ratios of African American's mean labor incomes and mean wages to those of white men are much higher than are the comparable ratios of African American women's mean labor incomes and mean wages to those of white men.

The ordering of labor market success across the four race/sex groups changed between cohort 1 and cohort 2, primarily because African American men lost ground relative to white men, and white and African American

TABLE 11.7

THE RATIOS OF MEAN LABOR OUTCOMES AT AGES 24–26 OF EACH RACE-SEX GROUP TO WHITE MALE MEANS BY COHORT

| | COHORT 1 (BORN 1952–59) | | | COHORT 2 (BORN 1962–69) | | | DIFFERENCE (COHORT 2 − COHORT 1) | | |
	EMPLOYED	LABOR INCOME	HOURLY WAGE	EMPLOYED	LABOR INCOME	HOURLY WAGE	EMPLOYED	LABOR INCOME	HOURLY WAGE
Men:									
White	1.00	1.00	1.00	1.00	1.00	1.00	...	...	...
Black	.95	.70	.79	.91	.62	.72	−.04	−.08	−.07
Women:									
White	.90	.58	.75	.95	.67	.82	.05	.09	.07
Black	.87	.48	.62	.92	.55	.70	.06	.07	.08

women gained ground. The ratio of African American men's employment to that of white men dropped from 0.95 in cohort 1 to 0.91 in cohort 2; the ratio of the mean wage of African American men to that of white men dropped from 0.79 to 0.72 across cohorts; and the African American male/white male mean earnings ratio dropped from 0.70 to 0.62. In contrast, cross-cohort changes in the ratios of both white and African American women's employment rate, mean earnings, and mean wages relative to those of white men were positive and increased from 0.05 to 0.09 across cohorts. As a result of these cohort changes, white women moved into second place after white men in the labor market hierarchy; and African American men fell to third place. African American women remained at the bottom of the hierarchy, but their employment rates now equaled those of African American men and their mean labor incomes and mean wages approached those of African American men.

Cohort Changes in Income and Income Mobility

We next examine changes in mean income and in rates of intergenerational income mobility across cohorts. Wu and Li (this vol., chap. 4) report that age at first marriage and fertility have declined, and rates of out-of-wedlock childbearing and single parenthood have risen with the passage of time. While cohort changes in income will reflect changes in labor market status, changes in income will also reflect these changes in family structure, marriage, and fertility. The changes in mean family income (measured spanning ages twenty-four to twenty-six) across cohorts are reported in the third, sixth, and ninth columns of table 11.6.

Cross-cohort changes in labor market outcomes were positive for white women, mostly positive for African American women, negligible for white men, and mostly negative for African American men. Cross-cohort changes in mean incomes did not follow this pattern. Instead, mean family income rose across cohorts for whites and declined across cohorts for African Americans. Income gains were significant for white women but not for white men. Mean annual family income rose by $3,417 for white women and by $936 for white men. Income losses were significant for African American men but not for African American women. Mean family income declined by $4,648 (23%) per annum for African American men and by $1,713 (13%) for African American women.

How did these changes affect race-based and sex-based income inequalities? Race-based gaps in mean income at ages twenty-four to twenty-six were larger for both men and women in cohort 2 than for men and women in cohort 1. Sex-based income gaps within racial groups narrowed across cohorts, but the gap between white men's and African American women's mean incomes widened.

Despite a large increase in African American women's mean earnings across cohorts, their mean family incomes did not increase and actually dropped across cohorts. This is probably due to the drop in African American men's earnings and to declines in marriage. The decline in African American men's mean family incomes (23%) is larger than the decline in their mean earnings (13%). This difference is likely due partly to declines in African American men's employment from age twenty-four to twenty-six and to differences in marriage rates.

It is well documented that the distribution of income became more unequal during the 1980s and remained so through the mid-1990s (Danziger and Gottschalk 1995; Levy 1998). We next investigate whether intergenerational income inequality also widened during this period and whether intergenerational mobility was, therefore, less likely in cohort 2 than in cohort 1. One advantage of the PSID data is that they enable us to compare rates of intergenerational income mobility across our two cohorts.

African American children grew up in more disadvantaged economic circumstances than did white children, and this was true in both cohorts. Table 11.8 compares by race and cohort the quintile distributions of three-year parental income when respondents were fifteen to seventeen years old and still living in their parents' household. African Americans were 3.5 times as likely as whites to have been raised in low-income families, and whites were many times more likely than African Americans to have been raised in affluent families. More than half of African Americans in each cohort were

TABLE 11.8

THE DISTRIBUTION OF INDIVIDUALS ACROSS INCOME QUINTILES

AT AGES 15–17 BY RACE AND COHORT

INCOME QUINTILE AT AGES 15–17	WHITES		AFRICAN AMERICANS	
	COHORT 1 (BORN 1952–59)	COHORT 2 (BORN 1962–69)	COHORT 1 (BORN 1952–59)	COHORT 2 (BORN 1962–69)
1 (lowest)	14.9	15.0	54.1	55.3
2	18.7	19.7	26.9	21.8
3	22.2	20.8	7.4	15.5
4	21.9	21.7	8.0	6.2
5 (highest)	22.5	22.8	3.6	1.2

TABLE 11.9

DISTRIBUTION OF INDIVIDUALS ACROSS INCOME QUINTILES AT AGES 24–26 FOR INDIVIDUALS
WHO WERE IN THE BOTTOM INCOME QUINTILE AT AGES 15–17

INCOME QUINTILE AT AGES 24–26	WHITES			AFRICAN AMERICANS		
	COHORT I (BORN 1952–59)	COHORT 2 (BORN 1962–69)	CHANGE (COHORT 2 − COHORT I)	COHORT I (BORN 1952–59)	COHORT 2 (BORN 1962–69)	CHANGE (COHORT 2 − COHORT I)
1 (lowest)	22.0	26.7	4.7	55.4	61.2	4.8
2	26.1	27.6	1.5	22.1	12.2	−9.9
3	21.1	18.4	−2.7	8.3	19.6	11.3
4	17.5	19.3	1.8	10.0	4.7	−5.3
5 (highest)	13.2	8.0	−5.2	4.2	2.3	−1.9
All (%)	100	100		100	100	

in the bottom income quintile as teenagers; more than three out of four African Americans were in the bottom two income quintiles; and less than 4% were in the top income quintile. In comparison, only 15% of whites in each cohort were in the bottom income quintile as teenagers, and 22%–23% of whites were in the top income quintile.

The United States is often called the land of opportunity. This depiction implies that one's economic future is not strongly predetermined by one's economic origins and by one's race. One way to assess equality of economic opportunity is to estimate the extent to which individuals change income quintiles between childhood and adulthood. If there were no change in income quintiles between the teenage years and early adulthood, this would indicate complete income immobility, with economic origins perfectly predicting economic destinations. If one's income quintile as a teenager were unrelated to one's income quintile as an adult, this would indicate complete mobility, with economic destination completely independent of economic origin. Since the distribution of income inequality widened during the 1980s, primarily because the share of total income going to the bottom income quintile dropped and the share going to the top income quintile rose, we focus on mobility out of the top and bottom income quintiles.

Has it become easier or harder to escape low income? We begin by asking whether rates of mobility out of the bottom income quintile dropped, stayed the same, or rose across cohorts. That is, were low-income teenagers born in the 1960s less likely to escape low income as adults than low-income teenagers born in the 1950s? Table 11.9 shows, by race and cohort, income quintile at ages twenty-four to twenty-six for those who were in the bottom income quintile at ages fifteen to seventeen. This shows the extent to which individuals who were in the bottom income quintile during their teenage years in their parents' households had moved into higher income quintiles as young adults, aged twenty-four to twenty-six years, after they had established their own households.

Rates of mobility out of low-income status were not significantly different across cohorts (see table 11.9). Nam (2002) reports similar results. The more striking finding in table 11.9 is that, in each cohort, the chances that a low-income teenager remained in the bottom income quintile in his or her midtwenties were more than twice as high for African Americans than for whites. More than half of African Americans who were in the bottom income quintile as teenagers, ages fifteen to seventeen years, were still in the bottom income quintile at ages twenty-four to twenty-six years. In contrast, only one in four whites who were in the bottom income quintile as teenagers were still in the bottom income quintile at ages twenty-four to twenty-six years. Other research has found similar race differences in intergenerational mobility for those of low-income status (Hertz, forthcoming, Mazumder, forthcoming). Some have also found that African Americans and whites also have different rates of intragenerational mobility (Gottschalk and Danziger 1995). They tracked the incomes of individuals aged twenty-three to thirty-nine throughout the course of the twenty-three-year period 1968–91. They report that 72% of nonwhites who started in the bottom income quintile were still in that income quintile twenty-three years later compared to 46% of whites.

The high degree of income inequality in the United States is often excused by the argument that the United States is a highly mobile society—that is, that everyone has a chance of ending up at the top, regardless of where they started. What percentage of teenagers in low-income households had made it into the top income quintile by their midtwenties? Among low-income white teenagers, the percentages were not awful—13.2% for cohort 1 and 8.0% for cohort 2. Among low-income African American teenagers, the percentages were quite low—4.2% for cohort 1 and only 2.3% for cohort 2. Note that for both whites and African Americans, the chances that a low-income teenager would make it to the top income quintile by his or her twenties dropped across cohorts.

We next ask whether it became easier to stay rich—whether downward mobility out of the top income quintile dropped, stayed the same, or grew across cohorts. Were affluent teenagers born in the 1960s more likely to remain affluent as adults than were affluent teenagers who were born in the 1950s? Table 11.10 reports income quintiles at ages twenty-four to

TABLE 11.10

THE DISTRIBUTION OF WHITES ACROSS INCOME QUINTILES

AT AGES 24–26 FOR WHITES WHO WERE IN THE TOP

INCOME QUINTILE AT AGES 15–17

INCOME QUINTILE AT AGES 24–26	COHORT 1 (BORN 1952–59)	COHORT 2 (BORN 1962–69)	CHANGE (COHORT 2 – COHORT 1)
1 (lowest)	15	8	−7
2	17	11	−6
3	17	11	−6
4	24	29	5
5	27	42	15

twenty-six for whites who were in the top income quintile at ages fifteen to seventeen by cohort. This shows the extent to which whites who were in the top income quintile as teenagers had dropped out of that income quintile as young adults. We do not examine African American downward mobility out of the top income quintile because so few African Americans were in the top income quintile at ages fifteen to seventeen (3.6% in cohort 1 and 1.2% in cohort 2).

Chances of remaining rich were higher for white children born in the 1960s than for white children born in the 1950s (see table 11.10). About 27% of whites in cohort 1 who were in the top income quintile as teenagers were still in the top income quintile at ages twenty-four to twenty-six years; about 42% of whites in cohort 2 who were in the top income quintile as teenagers remained in the top quintile at ages twenty-four to twenty-six years. Nam (2002) also finds that the probability that teenagers from wealthy backgrounds remain affluent has increased over time. This result is consistent with the predictions of Solon's (forthcoming) model that increases in earnings inequality should lead to increases in intergenerational inequality.

DISCUSSION

We began this chapter by asking whether young adults' economic trajectories had changed with the passage of time, whether changes varied by race and sex, and whether intergenerational economic inequality had widened or narrowed across time. We have compared the early economic fortunes of two cohorts of young adults. The first cohort came of age during the early to late

1970s, a period Levy (1998) calls "the quiet depression." The second cohort came of age during the 1980s, a period characterized by a widening of income inequality and by increases in returns to schooling.

Cross-cohort changes in economic fortunes differed considerably for the four groups of young adults we examined: white men, African American men, white women, and African American women. As a result, race-based economic inequality typically widened, and sex-based economic inequality typically narrowed across cohorts. There is suggestive evidence that it became easier for high-income families to pass their economic advantages on to their children.

One troubling finding is that a small minority of white men and sizable minorities of African American men had accumulated significant amounts of nonwork in their midtwenties, a period when young adults should be developing the job skills and work records that lead to long-term stable employment and wage growth and that protect against poverty (Freeman 2001; Holzer and LaLonde 2000; Topel 1991). More than 14% of white men and more than 40% of African American men had accumulated twenty-six or more weeks of nonwork in the three years between ages twenty-four and twenty-six. Few white men, 5%–6%, but almost one in four African American men reported fifty-two or more weeks of nonwork between ages twenty-four and twenty-six. Five percent of African American men in cohort 2 did not work for pay at all between the ages of twenty-four and twenty-six. These levels of nonwork among men are high, given that our nonwork measure is conservative and does not include full-time students, strikes, sick leaves, and paid vacation time.

Women were more likely than men to report extensive nonwork. Roughly 27%–42% of white women and 35% of African American women had accumulated more than a year of nonwork in the three years between ages twenty-four and twenty-six. Part of this nonwork may be voluntary: women may postpone labor market work to spend more time on child rearing. But, whether voluntary or due to restricted job opportunities, nonwork has a cost in terms of future economic mobility. Noncontinuous work is associated with lower levels of wage growth among women (Johnson 2002).

It is also troubling that white women were the only group whose chances of experiencing a year or more of nonwork dropped much during the two time periods we examined. The incidence of high levels of nonwork either rose or changed very little across cohorts for white men, African American men, and African American women.

White women were uniquely well placed to benefit from the economic and social changes of the 1980s. Their economic fortunes improved across cohorts on every economic outcome we examined. Their employment rates, average earnings, and average income rose sharply across cohorts; their mean hourly wages rose slightly across cohorts. Their mean weeks of non-work and their probabilities of accumulating extensive nonwork declined sharply across cohorts. White women's economic gains far outpaced those of the other three race/sex groups.

White men's economic fortunes did not change much across cohorts. Their employment rates, mean earnings, and mean weeks of nonwork were roughly the same; their mean wages dropped slightly; and their mean incomes rose slightly across cohorts. In both cohorts, white men's means on every labor outcome examined were more positive than those of the other three race/sex groups.

Cohort changes in African American women's economic fortunes were mixed. On the positive side, African American women's mean earnings and mean wages rose across cohorts. But unlike those of white women, African American women's mean levels of nonwork did not drop across cohorts. And on the negative side, mean family income was 13% lower for African American women who came of age in the 1980s than for those who came of age in the 1970s, perhaps because opportunities to marry a man with a steady income had declined.

It became harder for African American men to establish economic autonomy by their midtwenties. Virtually all of the cross-cohort changes in African American men's labor market outcomes were negative. African American men continued to stay home and out of work at a rate that was alarmingly high relative to their white peers. Roughly 28% of African American men born in the 1960s were not working for pay at the age twenty-seven interview; one in three accumulated more than fifty-two weeks of nonwork between ages twenty-four and twenty-six; and 5% did not work at all between ages twenty-four and twenty-six. Working African American men experienced large drops in mean earnings, mean wages, and mean incomes across cohorts. Furthermore, the observed wage and earnings declines may understate actual declines in the wages and earnings opportunities available to African American men since the percentage of men employed dropped across cohorts. Other researchers using different data sets have reported similar declines in African American men's absolute and relative economic fortunes (see Bound and Freeman 1992; Danziger and Gottschalk 1995; Freeman 2001; Mead 1992; Wilson 1996). These researchers attribute these declines to a number of economic and social factors including: the growing importance of skills, changes in industrial structure, decline in unionization, erosion of the minimum wage, deterioration in inner-city neighborhoods, and increasing social isolation of inner-city minority residents.

One encouraging finding is that sex-based labor market inequalities narrowed on most dimensions across cohorts. Within racial groups, sex-based differences in employment rates, mean wages, and mean earnings narrowed across cohorts. Gaps between white women's and African American men's labor market outcomes narrowed as well and often reversed across cohorts. Gaps between white men and African American women's mean wages and mean earnings also narrowed across cohorts.

On a more discouraging note, race-based labor market and income inequalities among men increased across cohorts. Race differences in men's employment rates, mean wages, mean earnings, mean weeks of nonwork, and mean incomes all widened across cohorts. We suspect that within-cohort race differences in men's schooling are a primary reason that African American men's relative labor market outcomes have deteriorated. African American men in cohort 2 are much more likely to be high school dropouts and much less likely to be college graduates than are white men in cohort 2. Furstenberg, Rumbaut, and Settersten (this vol., chap. 1), Fussell and Furstenberg (this vol., chap. 2), and Sandefur, Eggerling-Boeck, and Park (this vol., chap. 9) all report that education, particularly a college degree, increasingly became a prerequisite for labor market success in the 1980s.

The relative labor market positions of the four race/sex groups we examined changed across cohorts. In cohort 1, white men had the highest employment rates, the highest mean labor income, the highest mean wage, and the lowest mean weeks of nonwork. African American men were next on the economic ladder. African American men's employment rates, mean labor incomes, and mean hourly wage were all lower than those of white men, but much higher than those of white and African American women. White women and African American women were third and fourth, respectively, on the economic ladder in cohort 1. White women and African American women in cohort 1 reported roughly the same levels of employment and nonwork, but white women's mean earnings and mean wages exceeded those of African American women.

The ordering of labor market outcomes was very different in cohort 2. Although white men in cohort 2 remained at the top of the labor market hierarchy, the gaps between white men's labor market outcomes and those of white women and African American women narrowed across cohorts, while the gaps between the labor market outcomes of white men and African American men widened across cohorts. White women moved to second place on the economic ladder in cohort 2. White women's mean earnings and mean wages now exceeded those of African American men; their employment rate had caught up to that of African American men; and the gap in mean weeks of nonwork between white women and African American men had dropped to only five weeks. African American women remained fourth in the labor market hierarchy; but their employment rate now equaled that of African American men; and their mean earnings and mean wages were close to those of African American men.

Income inequality widened during the 1980s, particularly at the two ends of the income distribution (Blank 1997; Danziger and Gottschalk 1995; Levy 1998). We explored whether intergenerational income inequality had also increased by comparing rates of intergenerational income mobility across the two cohorts. We find no evidence that children raised in low-income families in cohort 2 were less likely than low-income children in cohort 1 to escape low-income as adults. But children of the rich were more likely to remain rich. There was a large and significant decrease in downward mobility out of the highest income quintile for white teenagers. These results are consistent with Levine (1999), Nam (2002), and Perucci and Wysong (2002) but not with Corcoran (2001), and Mayer and Lopoo (forthcoming). If correct, these results suggest that the passing on of economic privilege increased over the same period during which the distribution of income within a generation was becoming more unequal.

Sandefur and colleagues (this vol., chap. 9, 315) conclude that young people who are white "are more likely to start off well during the early adult period than are those who are black." We also find that African American and white children are not on an equal footing in the race for economic success. The size and persistence of race-based differences in access to economic resources as children, and in chances of escaping low income as adults, are disappointing in a society that values equal opportunity. African Americans are more likely to be born poor and to remain poor than are whites. More than half of African Americans in both cohorts were in the bottom income quintile as teenagers, compared with only 15% of whites, making African Americans 3.5 times as likely to be poor. African Americans were not only more likely to start out at an economic disadvantage; they were more likely than similarly situated whites to remain at an economic disadvantage as adults. Among teenagers in the bottom income quintile, African Americans were more likely than whites to remain there as adults. Hertz (forthcoming) and Mazumder (forthcoming) also find that African Americans have lower rates of mobility out of poverty than do whites. Furthermore, this large African American/white difference in mobility out of low-income status between the teen years and early adulthood has not dropped as time has passed. These race differences suggest to us that the current administration's emphasis on dismantling affirmative action policies and programs may be premature.

The United States has one of the most unequal distributions of income among Western industrialized countries (Burtless and Smeeding 2001). Despite this, and despite the widening of income inequality in the 1980s, there is considerably less support for governmental redistributive policies (such as child allowances or high inheritance taxes) in the United States than there is in western Europe and Canada. The higher degree of income inequality is often justified by the argument that rates of economic mobility are higher in the United States than elsewhere. That is, we may have an unequal distribution of income, but everyone, regardless of race or parental income, has a shot at becoming rich. In fact, rates of intergenerational economic mobility are no higher and may be slightly lower in the United States than in many western European countries (Solon 1999). Furthermore, as the results here show, the chances that a low-income African American child will eventually become rich are very low (2.3% in cohort 2) compared to the chances that a rich white child will remain rich (42% in cohort 2).

Our analyses of the differences in children's access to economic resources have focused on parental income during the child's teenage years. This likely understates true race differences in access to economic resources. Race differences in family wealth are at least as large as race differences in income. For instance, in 1994, median net assets were $72,000 for a white family and only $9,800 for an African American family; in addition, at every income level, whites have two or more times the assets of blacks (Conley 1999). This may be one reason African American children raised in low-income households experience less upward mobility than did white children who were raised in low-income households. Schoeni and Ross (this vol., chap. 12) examine material assistance that parents provide to children between the ages of eighteen and thirty-four—that is, as young adults make the transition to adulthood. Not surprisingly, affluent parents provide more transitional aid than do low-income parents. Schoeni and Ross estimate that parents in the top income quartile, relative to those in the bottom income quartile, provide an average of three times more material assistance to children between the ages of eighteen and thirty-four. Thus, African Americans who are many times more likely than whites to come from low-income families and many times less likely to come from affluent families, are also likely to receive less financial assistance from their families as young adults. In addition, they are not only less likely than white young adults to have parents who can provide economic resources, they are also more likely than white young adults in similar economic circumstances to have siblings who need financial assistance and less likely to have siblings who can provide economic support. Pattillo-McCoy and Heflin (2003) report that low-income African Americans are less likely than low-income whites to have a middle-income sibling and that middle-income whites are less likely than middle-income African Americans to have a poor sibling.

What do these results tell us about the question posed in the title of this chapter, "Is It Getting Harder to Get Ahead?" The answer is: It depends. White men's chances of getting ahead, as measured by the outcomes we examine, were roughly equal for those born in the 1960s and those born in the 1950s. White women's chances of getting ahead were higher for those born in the 1960s than for those born ten years earlier. The reverse was true for African American men: those born in the 1960s fared worse than their counterparts who were born ten years earlier. Changes in the economic prospects of African American women were mixed. African American women born in the 1960s had higher mean earnings and wages but had lower mean incomes than did their counterparts who were born in the 1950s. The evidence on whether family economic origins mattered more for children born in the 1960s than for children born in the 1950s is less clear. The chances of getting ahead did not drop significantly over cohorts for children raised in low-income households, but the chances of staying rich did increase significantly across cohorts for the children of the rich.

NOTES

1. Such women are not included in studies that examine wages or earnings for shorter periods of time.

2. The sample weight adjusts for the initial oversample of poor families and for nonresponse time.

3. We chose to measure education at twenty-seven years because it takes many individuals more than the standard four years to graduate from high school or to obtain a college degree.

4. When computing average earnings or average wages spanning ages twenty-four to twenty-six, we do not add in earnings from years in which respondents worked less than 250 hours.

REFERENCES

Altonji, Joseph, and Rebecca Blank. 1999. Gender and Race in the Labor Market. Pp. 3143–259 in *Handbook of Labor Economics*, edited by Orley Ashenfelter and David Card. Vol. 3C. New York: Elsevier Science Press.

Beaudry, Paul, and John DiNardo. 1991. The Effect of Implicit Contracts on the Movement of Wages over the Business Cycle: Evidence from Micro Data. *Journal of Political Economy* 99 (4):665–88.

Blank, Rebecca. 1997. *It Takes a Nation.* Princeton, NJ: Princeton University Press.

Blau, Francine. 1998. Trends in the Well-Being of American Women, 1970–1995. *Journal of Economic Literature* 36 (1):112–65.

Bound, John, and Laura Dresser. 1999. Losing Ground: The Erosion of the Relative Earnings of African-American Women during the 1980s. Pp. 61–104 in *Latinas and African American Women at Work,* edited by I. Browne. New York: Russell Sage

Bound, John, and Richard Freeman. 1992. What Went Wrong? The Erosion of Relative Wages and Employment among Young Black Men in the 1980s. *Quarterly Journal of Economics* 107 (1):201–32.

Bound, John, and George Johnson. 1992. Change in the Structure of Wages during the 1980s: An Evaluation of Alternative Explanations. *American Economic Review* 82 (3):371–92.

Brewster, Karin L., and Irene Padavic. 2000. Change in Gender Ideology, 1977–1996: The Contributions of Intracohort Change and Population Turnover. *Journal of Marriage and the Family* 62 (2):477–87.

Burtless, Gary, and Timothy Smeeding. 2001. The Level, Trend, and Composition of Poverty. Pp. 27–68 in *Understanding Poverty,* edited by Sheldon H. Danziger and Richard H. Haveman. Cambridge, MA: Harvard University Press.

Charles, Kerwin, and Ming Ching Luoh. 2002. Gender Differences in Completed Schooling. NBER Working Paper No. w9028. Ford School of Public Policy, University of Michigan, Ann Arbor. (http://papers.nber.org/papers/W9028.)

Ciabattari, Teresa. 2001. Changes in Men's Conservative Gender Ideologies: Cohort and Period Influences. *Gender and Society* 15 (4):574–91.

Conley, Dalton. 1999. *Being Black, Living in the Red.* Berkeley: University of California Press.

Corcoran, Mary. 1999. The Economic Progress of African-American Women. Pp. 35–60 in *Latinas and African American Women at Work,* edited by I. Browne. New York: Russell Sage.

Corcoran, Mary. 2001. Mobility, Persistence, and the Consequences of Poverty for Children: Child and Adult Outcomes. Pp. 127–61 in *Understanding Poverty,* edited by Sheldon H. Danziger and Richard H. Haveman. Cambridge, MA: Harvard University Press.

Corcoran, Mary, and Colleen Heflin. 2002. Race and Ethnicity-Based Inequalities in Women's Earnings. Working Paper. Ford School of Public Policy, University of Michigan, Ann Arbor.

Danziger, Sheldon, and Peter Gottschalk. 1995. *America Unequal.* New York: Russell Sage Foundation.

Eggebeen, David, and A. Hawkins. 1990. Economic Need and Wives' Employment. *Journal of Family Issues* 11 (1):48–66.

Freeman, Richard. 2001. The Rising Tide Lifts . . . ? Pp. 97–126 in *Understanding Poverty*, edited by Sheldon H. Danziger and Richard H. Haveman. Cambridge, MA. Harvard University Press.

Goldscheider, Frances K., and Linda J. Waite. 1991. *New Families, No Families.* Berkeley: University of California Press.

Gottschalk, Peter. 1997. Inequality, Income Growth, and Mobility: The Basic Facts. *Journal of Economic Perspectives* 11 (2):21–40.

Hauser, Robert M. 1998. Intergenerational Economic Mobility in the United States: Measures, Differentials and Trends. CDE Working Paper no. 98-12. University of Wisconsin, Center for Demography and Ecology, Madison. http://www.ssc.wisc.edu/cde/cdewp/98-12.pdf.

Haveman, Richard, and Barbara Wolfe. 1994. *Succeeding Generations: On the Effect of Investments in Children.* New York: Russell Sage Foundation.

Pattillo-McCoy, Mary, and Colleen M. Heflin. 2003. Poverty in the Family: Siblings of the Black and White Middle Class. IPR working paper 98-20. Institute for Policy Research, Northwestern University. http://www.northwestern.edu/ipr/publications/workingpapers/wpabstracts98/wp9820.html.

Hertz, Thomas. Forthcoming. Rags, Riches, and Race: The Intergenerational Economic Mobility of Black and White Families in the United States. In *Unequal Chances: Family Background and Economic Success*, edited by S. Bowles, H. Gintis and M. Osborne. Princeton, NJ: Princeton University Press.

Holzer, Harry, and Richard LaLonde. 2000. Job Change and Job Stability among Less Skilled Young Workers. Pp. 125–59 in *Finding Jobs: Work and Welfare Reform*, edited by D. Card and R. Blank. New York: Russell Sage Foundation.

Hoynes, Hilary. 1999. The Employment, Earnings, and Income of Less-Skilled Workers over the Business Cycle. *Focus* 20 (3):31–36.

Johnson, Rucker. 2002. Wage and Job Dynamics after Welfare Reform: The Importance of Job Skills. Chap. 3 of Essays on Urban Spatial Structure, Job Search, and Job Mobility. Ph.D. diss., University of Michigan.

Juhn, Chinhui. 2000. Black-White Employment Differentials in a Tight Labor Market. Pp. 89–109 in *Prosperity for All? The Economic Boom and African-Americans*, edited by R. Cherry and W. Rodgers. New York: Russell Sage Foundation

Jump, Teresa L., and Linda Haas. 1987. Fathers in Transition: Dual-Career Fathers Participating in Child Care. Pp. 98–114 in *Changing Men: New Directions in Research on Men and Masculinity*, edited by Michael S. Kimmel. Newbury Park, CA: Sage Publications.

Leibowitz, Arleen, and Jacob A. Klerman. 1995. Explaining Changes in Married Others' Employment over Time. *Demography* 32 (3):365–78.

Levine, David I. 1999. Choosing the Right Parents: Changes in the Intergenerational Transmission of Inequality between the 1970s and the Early 1990s. Working Paper no. 72. Institute for Labor Relations, University of California, Berkeley.

Levy, Frank. 1998. *The New Dollars and Dreams.* New York: Russell Sage Foundation.

Mayer, Susan E. 1997. *What Money Can't Buy: The Effect of Parental Income on Children's Outcomes.* Cambridge, MA: Harvard University Press.

Mayer, Susan E., and Leonard M. Lopoo. Forthcoming. Trends in the Intergenerational Economic Mobility of Sons and Daughters. In *Generational Income Mobility in North America and Europe,* edited by Miles Corak. Cambridge: Cambridge University Press.

Mazumder, Bhashkar. Forthcoming. The Apple Falls Even Closer to the Tree Than We Thought. In *Unequal Chances: Family Background and Economic Success,* edited by S. Bowles, H. Gintis, and M. Osborne. Princeton, NJ: Princeton University Press.

McLanahan, Sara and Gary Sandefur. 1994. *Growing Up in a Single Parent Family: What Works, What Doesn't.* Cambridge, MA: Harvard University Press.

Mead, Lawrence. 1992. *The New Politics of Poverty: The Nonworking Poor in America.* New York: Basic Books.

Melville, Keith. 1988. *Marriage and Family Today.* New York: Random House.

Nam, Yunju. 2002. Is America Becoming More Equal for Children? Changes in Intergenerational Economic Mobility. Ph.D. diss., University of Michigan.

Noonan, Mary. 2001. The Changing Effects of Parenthood on Men's and Women's Employment. Ph.D. diss., University of Michigan.

Noonan, Mary, Mary E. Corcoran, and Paul N. Courant. 2003. Pay Differences among the Highly Trained: Cohort Differences in the Male-female Earnings Gap in Lawyer's Salaries. Working Paper. Department of Sociology, University of Iowa.

O'Connell, Martin. 1990. Maternity Leave Arrangements: 1961–1985. Pp. 11–17 in *Work and Family Patterns of American Women,* edited by U.S. Bureau of the Census, Population Division. Current Population Reports, Series P-23, no. 165. Washington, DC: U.S. Government Printing Office.

Perucci, Robert, and Earl Wysong. 2002. *The New Class Society: Goodbye American Dream?* Lanham, MD: Rowman & Littlefield.

Radcliffe Public Policy Center. 2000. *Life's Work: Generational Attitudes toward Work and Life Integration.* Cambridge, MA: President and Fellows of Harvard College.

Reveille, Robert. 1995. Intertemporal and Life Cycle Variation in Measured Intergenerational Earnings Mobility. RAND Corporation. Unpublished mimeo.

Solon, Gary. 1992. Intergenerational Income Mobility in the United States. *American Economic Review* 82 (3):393–408.

———. 1999. Intergenerational Mobility in the Labor Market. Pp. 1761–1800 in *Handbook of Labor Economics*, edited by Orley Ashenfelter and David Card. Vol. 3A. Amsterdam: North-Holland.

———. Forthcoming. A Model of Intergenerational Mobility Variation over Time and Place. In *Generational Income Mobility in North America and Europe*, edited by Miles Corak. Cambridge: Cambridge University Press.

Solon, Gary, Robert Barsky, and Jonathan Parker. 1994. Measuring the Cyclicality of Real Wages: How Important Is Composition Bias? *Quarterly Journal of Economics* 109 (1):1–25.

Spain, Daphne, and Suzanne M. Bianchi. 1996. *Balancing Act: Marriage, Motherhood and Employment among American Women.* New York: Russell Sage Foundation.

Thornton, Arland, Duane Alwin, and Donald Camburn. 1983. Causes and Consequences of Sex-Role Attitudes and Attitude Change. *American Sociological Review* 48 (2):221–27.

Topel, Robert. 1991. Specific Capital, Mobility, and Wages: Wages Rise with Job Seniority. *Journal of Political Economy* 99 (1):145–76.

Topel, Robert, and Michael Ward. 1992. Job Mobility and the Careers of Young Men. *Quarterly Journal of Economics* 107 (2):439–79.

Wilkie, Jane. 1993. Changes in U.S. Men's Attitudes toward the Family Provider Role, 1972–1989. *Gender and Society* 7 (2):261–79.

Wilson, William J. 1996. *When Work Disappears: The Inner City, the Underclass, and Public Policy.* New York: Alfred A. Knopf.

CHAPTER 12

MATERIAL ASSISTANCE FROM FAMILIES DURING THE TRANSITION TO ADULTHOOD

ROBERT F. SCHOENI AND KAREN E. ROSS

A great deal of analysis on social stratification and the intergenerational transmission of social class has been informed by the status attainment research developed in the late 1960s and early 1970s. One of the key tenets of the status attainment model is that parents' levels of educational and occupational attainment are good predictors of their children's socioeconomic attainment. While there has been controversy over some aspects of this work, it continues to inform research agendas in many fields, including work on the nature of the transition to adulthood. In particular, one important question concerns the mechanisms by which parental education and income affect children's success or failure in the various stages of their transition to adulthood, such as leaving home, completing schooling, finding employment, and starting one's own household. The authors in this volume address the nature and timing of youth's transition to adulthood via these events, including the potential difficulties youth may experience during these critical periods of change.

During the transition to adulthood, youth may rely on different sources for information, support, and other resources. Families are perhaps the most important source of support for many youths, and studies continue to elucidate the nature and strength of the impact of family characteristics, most importantly parental education and income, on their children's successful transitions to adulthood (Duncan, Featherman, and Duncan 1972; Hogan 1981; Marini 1978a, 1978b). For example, Sandefur and colleagues (this vol., chap. 9) show that parental education and family income are positively associated with the likelihood of pursuing higher education and, in general, getting off to a good start in early adulthood. Further, Osgood and colleagues (this vol., chap. 10, 345) conclude: "The path one takes, therefore, typically reflects the social-class values and resources of one's natal family."

Families can positively influence their children's life chances and outcomes through a variety of channels: they may serve as positive role models, provide social and employment connections, facilitate access to peers with high aspirations, pay for high-quality schooling, and give direct material support (e.g., see Sandefur et al. this vol., chap. 9). There are many ways in which parents who value education may help their children attain high levels of schooling beyond simply encouraging them and being involved in the learning process. They may choose to live in an area with high-quality public schools and peer groups for their children, pay to send their children to private schools, or begin saving early for their children's college education. At the same time, the extent to which families can make these supportive choices is constrained by their resources.

As a complement to the other chapters in this volume that examine the role of young adults' families of origin in the transition to adulthood, this study examines direct material support provided by parents in the form of money, time, and shared housing. To highlight the importance of financial transfers from parents to adult children, imagine a few ways in which this form of parental help may be critical in ensuring a successful transition. As their children enter young adulthood, parents may use their own financial advantages to support their children as they pursue higher education, to help their children establish independent households by helping them with down payments for their first homes, or to lessen the financial burden involved with having their own children. Further, other parental assets, such as home ownership or help caring for children, may be used to aid adult children in difficult life stages; for example, parents may allow their adult children to live with them during times of unemployment, illness, divorce, single parenthood, or other personal hardships.

Sociodemographic trends also suggest that familial assistance may have increased over the past several decades: children are enrolled in school longer (often paid for by parents), the age at marriage is rising, and divorce and single parenthood is increasing. These trends demonstrate that individuals are delaying some of the key markers in the transition to adulthood, suggesting they may be in need of familial support for a longer period. Furthermore, shared housing is likely to be a major form of support for young adults pursuing higher levels of schooling and delaying marriage, given that both of these trends often prevent young adults from starting their own independent households.

Despite the evidence that children from advantaged familial backgrounds have smoother transitions into adulthood and the anecdotal evidence that parents provide substantial financial assistance to their children, we are aware of no scientifically based estimate of the amount of assistance that children receive during young adulthood. The primary objective of this chapter is to fill that gap. Specifically, this study will address four questions:

1. How much familial assistance do youth receive during the transition to adulthood?

2. How much more assistance do children in high-income families receive during these formative years?

3. What is the pattern of familial support during the transition years, and do life-course events such as getting married, buying a home, or attending school explain the observed age pattern?

4. Has familial support increased in the past several decades?

We begin by describing the data and approach that we use given limitations in available data. After describing the answers to the four focal questions, we interpret the findings.

SAMPLE AND METHOD

This study uses three complementary data sources to address the four research questions posed above: the 1988 Panel Study of Income Dynamics (PSID), with special supplements regarding interhousehold time and money transfers, the 1992–93 National Postsecondary Student Aid Study (NPSAS), and the decennial censuses of 1970, 1980, and 1990. Together these data allow us to examine several different forms of familial assistance at various stages: we use the PSID to examine monetary assistance and time help (e.g., child care, errands, chores, etc.) received by young adults (roughly ages eighteen to thirty-four); the NPSAS provides estimates of parental assistance received by college students; and we use census data to examine changes in the pattern of home leaving among young adults during the past thirty years.

Data

The Panel Study of Income Dynamics (PSID) is a longitudinal, nationally representative sample begun in 1968. The aim of the PSID is to collect a wide variety of information regarding household composition, residential location, employment histories, and amounts and sources of income. While the family was the original unit of study, over time individual family members have been tracked as they age and form their own families and households. In 1988 a special Time and Money Transfers Supplement was administered, and we use those data to estimate young adults' receipt of both money and time transfers in the 1987 calendar year. In addition to those data, we are able to take advantage of the longitudinal nature of the PSID in order to estimate the family income of our 1988 young adults when they were children. To approximate permanent economic status of parents, we use the average family income over the six years when the child was ten to fifteen years old. Overall, our total sample consists of 6,661 eighteen- to thirty-four-year-olds, of whom 4,848 were heads or spouses of their family in 1988.

Second, the National Postsecondary Student Aid Study (NPSAS) is a nationally representative sample of undergraduate students enrolled in postsecondary institutions during the 1992–93 school year. We use these data to estimate the amount of direct financial assistance students receive from their parents for college expenses. Specifically, we examine parental reports of direct monetary contributions to their child for expenses during the academic year, as well as how these amounts vary by parental income. In addition, the 1999–2000 wave of the NPSAS is used to estimate the degree to which the costs of postsecondary education have increased in real terms over the past decade.[1]

Third, we use the 5% sample of the census (the Integrated Public Use Microdata Series) to analyze historical trends in coresidence among young adults and their parents (Ruggles and Sobek 2003). These data include thousands of youth in each decennial census year, 1970–90, and allow us to examine the proportion of individuals aged eighteen to thirty-four who are living with at least one of their parents at each of these time points.

Method

The primary goal is to estimate the total amount of material assistance youth receive during the transition to adulthood, which we take as ages eighteen to thirty-four. Ideally one would want to follow a cohort of youth through the transition to adulthood and total up the amount of assistance they receive.

Unfortunately, high-quality data on assistance or transfers between family members is rarely collected in national surveys. The best familial transfer data for studying the population eighteen to thirty-four is the 1988 PSID, which asked respondents how much they received from friends and family during the past year.[2] Assistance in the form of direct financial transfers, reported in dollars, and assistance with chores, child care, and so forth, reported in hours, are collected. The survey does not ask respondents to report the type or use of the time help—such as child care or chores—only the amount of hours they received in total. Another limitation is that information on the services provided from the adult child to their coresident parents is not available.

Using these data, we estimate the amount that is received over an entire adult transition for the average youth by using a synthetic cohort approach. That is, we first estimate the age-specific average amount of assistance received, expressed in 2001 dollars using the Consumer Price Index for All Urban Consumers (CPI-U).[3] We then simply add the age-specific averages to obtain the total amount that we expect to be received over the entire seventeen-year period from eighteen to thirty-four. Totals are estimated for financial assistance and time help. To explore differences by socioeconomic factors, separate age-specific averages are calculated by quartiles of average parental income when the youth was ten to fifteen years old and then summed to lead to the estimates of assistance received over the transition for each income group.

Although the PSID is the best available data on familial transfers, it (and almost all other surveys) has one important limitation: transfers are only reported if they take place between people living in different households. Therefore, parental transfers received by youth while they are living with their parents will not be captured. As over half the eighteen- to twenty-two-year-olds in the 1988 PSID sample did not live independently of their parents, it is important to include estimates of intrahousehold assistance. Because of the paucity of data, there is great uncertainty for many of the assumed parameter values that are required to estimate intrahousehold assistance. We therefore devote considerable effort to examining the sensitivity of the overall estimates to various assumptions.

In order to estimate the amount of assistance youth are receiving from their parents, we differentiate between PSID sample members in two main ways: first, by whether they are living independently of their parents and, second, by whether they are enrolled in postsecondary education. For those living independently, the estimated amount of assistance they receive is captured by the PSID data on interhousehold transfers.

For those not living independently, we first estimate the implicit rental value and food expenditures saved by children because they live with their parents.[4] We estimate the value of this form of parental assistance by examining the amounts spent by PSID youth living independently on rent and food consumed at home, taking into account family size by dividing the total amount spent by the family equally across all family members; we also examine the sensitivity of this assumption to account for returns to scale in family size, with the results described in the next section.

Annually, youth are spending almost $3,000 on rent and nearly $1,700 on food at home per capita, both figures expressed in 2001 dollars. This is likely an underestimate of the true value of the assistance received by youth living at home, given that their parents are likely to provide a higher quality of housing and food than youth would be able to afford if they were living independently. Youth living at home who are not attending school are assumed to receive the full estimate of food and housing assistance, while those enrolled in college are expected to receive this assistance only during the summer months.[5] Among those enrolled in college, direct parental contributions to college expenses are based on estimates calculated by the authors using the NPSAS, which includes food and housing assistance.

An additional complication is the fact that youth who move from their parents' homes right into college are typically not treated as living in a separate household by the PSID. Because the PSID measures of time and cash transfers are restricted to interhousehold transfers, transfers received during the college years are typically not captured in the 1988 PSID data. To address this limitation, for eighteen- to thirty-four-year-olds who are considered part of their parents' PSID family and who are attending college, we estimate the amount of assistance that their parents are providing for college-related expenses. Information on parental assistance with college expenses is sparse; the best source is the National Postsecondary Student Aid Study (NPSAS) conducted by the National Center for Education Statistics. The 1992–93 NPSAS asks parents how much they contributed to their children's expenses for the school year, excluding loans or in-kind assistance. On average, students received $4,017 per school year from their parents. Finally, all values are expressed in 2001 dollars using the CPI-U.

RESULTS

Below we discuss the analyses used to address each of the four questions in turn, beginning with the central question of interest: How much do families provide to children during the transition years?

TABLE 12.1.

INTERHOUSEHOLD ASSISTANCE RECEIVED DURING THE TRANSITION TO ADULTHOOD

	ANNUAL INTERHOUSEHOLD FINANCIAL ASSISTANCE			ANNUAL INTERHOUSEHOLD TIME ASSISTANCE		
		AVERAGE DOLLARS RECEIVED			AVERAGE HOURS RECEIVED	
	PROPORTION			PROPORTION		
AGE	RECEIVING ASSISTANCE	AMONG RECIPIENTS	ALL PEOPLE	RECEIVING ASSISTANCE	AMONG RECIPIENTS	ALL PEOPLE
18–20	.41	685	282	.57	527	303
21–22	.59	1,625	976	.62	558	350
23–24	.38	1,266	477	.38	587	226
25–26	.35	4,552	1,697	.58	279	162
27–28	.43	3,243	1,378	.51	271	140
29–30	.30	4,226	1,314	.53	555	297
31–32	.32	3,777	1,239	.52	309	162
33–34	.28	5,183	1,451	.41	332	134
18–34	.34	3,410	1,173	.47	367	176
Total during transition			17,909			3,852

Source. 1988 Panel Study of Income Dynamics.

Note. All values expressed in 2001 dollars using the Consumer Price Index for All Urban Consumers (CPI-U).

How Much Assistance Is Received during the Transition to Adulthood?

We start by examining estimates of interhousehold assistance reported in the PSID (table 12.1). Many young people who are living independently from their parents receive cash assistance and time help. Thirty-four percent of youth aged eighteen to thirty-four receive cash, and 47% receive time help in a given year. Youth who receive help collect an average of $3,410 in cash and 367 hours in time help. This is a substantial amount of assistance, especially considering that the average family income for households headed by eighteen- to thirty-four-year-olds is $48,000. The amount of interhousehold cash assistance increases with age. This pattern is due in part to the fact that children from low-income families leave their parental homes at younger ages (as shown in table 12.5), and more affluent parents provide more assistance to their children. At the same time, as we will see below, the amount of assistance received for college expenses declines with age, due largely to the fact that relatively few children are enrolled in school after ages twenty-five to twenty-six.

The time help translates into nine weeks of full time, forty hours-per-week help. The last row of table 12.1 reports the total amount of interhousehold assistance received during the transition to adulthood. Over this seventeen-year period, the average amount received is $17,909, or just over $1,000 per year. In terms of time help, youth receive a total of 3,852 hours, roughly equivalent to two years of full time labor.

The estimates in table 12.1 are restricted to interhousehold transfers. Table 12.2 contains estimates that capture assistance received by youth regardless of whether they live independently from their parents. Because this is the central table of this chapter, we will discuss the estimates column by column.

The first column provides estimates from the PSID of the share of eighteen- to thirty-four-year-olds who are living independently from their parents.[6] It is important to note that in almost all cases, the PSID assumes that children who are away at college are still part of their parents' household and that they do not live independently. At ages eighteen to twenty, only 25% of youth were not considered part of their parents' household. By ages twenty-five to twenty-six, this rises to 80%, and almost all of the youth in their midthirties live independently.

Among those who live independently, economic assistance from parents, which includes assistance for any purpose, such as a home purchase, schooling, rent, or regular assistance, is reported in the interhousehold transfer questions reported in table 12.1. These estimates are replicated in table 12.2, column 2.

The majority of table 12.2 is devoted to calculating an estimate of the amount of assistance for youth who do not live independently. Columns 3 and 4 provide estimates of housing and in-home food expenses saved by living with parents, and columns 5–7 are used to calculate college assistance. Column 5 estimates the share of coresident children who are enrolled in college, either full time or part time, and shows 57% of eighteen- to twenty-year-olds in college. The amount of direct assistance to children enrolled in college, based on the NPSAS, is reported in column 6. The estimate of parental assistance from the 1992–93 NPSAS is adjusted for the rise in the cost of college between 1992–93 and 1999–2000 using the two waves of the NPSAS. That is, we assume that parental assistance for college increased by the same amount as total college costs, in proportionate terms.

Column 7 reports the estimate of help with college expenditures for all youth living with their parents. Recall that this average includes many

TABLE 12.2

ESTIMATE OF TOTAL ECONOMIC ASSISTANCE RECEIVED AMONG ALL YOUTH 18–34 (IN DOLLARS)

| AGE | PROPORTION LIVING INDEPENDENTLY (1) | YOUTH LIVING INDEPENDENTLY: DIRECT FINANCIAL ASSISTANCE (2) | YOUTH NOT LIVING INDEPENDENTLY | | | | | TOTAL AVERAGE ASSISTANCE RECEIVED (8)[b] | ALL YOUTH: TOTAL AVERAGE ASSISTANCE RECEIVED (9)[c] |
			HOUSING ASSISTANCE (3)	FOOD AT HOME (4)	PROPORTION IN COLLEGE (5)	COLLEGE ASSISTANCE FROM PARENTS AMONG STUDENTS (6)	COLLEGE ASSISTANCE FROM PARENTS AMONG ALL DEPENDENT YOUTH (7)[a]		
18–20	.25	282	2,362	1,591	.57	4,017	2,284	4,551	3,499
21–22	.47	976	2,780	1,912	.27	4,017	1,093	4,827	3,020
23–24	.64	477	3,112	1,846	.24	4,017	951	5,028	2,129
25–26	.80	1,697	3,177	1,614	.26	4,017	1,057	4,903	2,323
27–28	.87	1,378	3,043	1,597	.17	4,017	665	4,729	1,823
29–30	.92	1,314	3,087	1,651	.01	4,017	21	4,741	1,595
31–32	.93	1,239	2,787	1,675	.11	4,017	453	4,537	1,475
33–34	.97	1,451	2,740	1,655	.14	4,017	581	4,500	1,556
Total during transition									38,340

Sources. Columns 1–5 are estimated directly from the 1988 and 1990 Panel Study of Income Dynamics, inflated by Consumer Price Index for All Urban Consumers (CPI-U) to 2001 dollars; col. 6 is estimated from the 1992–93 National Postsecondary Student Aid Study (NPSAS).

Note. All values expressed in 2001 dollars using the CPI-U.

[a]Column 7 = col. 5 × col. 6.

[b]Column 8 = [col. 7 + (col. 3 + col. 4) × col. 5 × .25] + (col. 3 + col. 4) × (1.0 − col. 5).

[c]Column 9 = (col. 1 × col. 2) + [(1.0 − col. 1) × col. 8].

youth—in fact the majority of youth in all age groups except eighteen to twenty—who were not enrolled in college. So for students not enrolled in college, the assistance they receive is in the form of housing assistance (col. 3) and food at home (col. 4). College students receive the food and housing assistance for the summer months plus direct assistance with college expenses (col. 6). Column 8 adds together all parental assistance received by college and noncollege youth living with their parents. On average, youth who do not live independently receive between $4,500 and $5,000 per year.

The final column reports the average assistance for all youth, including both those who do and those who do not live with their parents. As expected, on average, assistance declines as children age. The estimated annual amount of assistance is $3,499 during ages eighteen to twenty, $2,323 during ages twenty-five to twenty-six, and, falling further, $1,556 by thirty-three to thirty-four. Over the entire seventeen-year period (ages eighteen to thirty-four), the average amount received is $38,340.

It is useful to compare estimates of expenditures by parents during the childhood years, from birth to age seventeen, with our estimates of assistance during the adult transition. The U.S. Department of Agriculture produces annual estimates of total expenditures, including housing, food, transportation, clothing, healthcare, child care, and education. For middle-income families (i.e., with income between $39,100 and $65,800) in 2001, the total expenditures during the childhood years are estimated to be $170,460. Therefore, the financial assistance provided during the transition to adulthood, ages eighteen to thirty-four, is 23% of the amount provided during the childhood years.

Because of the limited data on which to base some of the estimates, it is important to examine the sensitivity of the estimates of assistance to alternative parameter values. This information is presented in table 12.3. We begin by altering the housing assistance assumptions in two ways: a 50% increase and a 50% decrease. Because so many young people live with their parents, the value of this parameter is one of the most important. However, even with what we feel are large differences relative to our best estimates, the range in estimated total assistance during the transition is only $33,334–$43,347. Altering the remaining parameters to values that should represent high and low bounds changes the estimate of the total amount of assistance by no more than about 10%. In particular, the high and low estimates of college expenses paid for by parents lead to differences in the total amount of parental assistance during the transition of not quite $8,000–$34,485 versus $42,196.

TABLE 12.3

SENSITIVITY ANALYSIS OF ESTIMATES OF ECONOMIC ASSISTANCE RECEIVED DURING

THE TRANSITION TO ADULTHOOD (IN DOLLARS)

AGE	AS REPORTED IN TABLE 12.2 (1)	IMPLICIT HOUSING ASSISTANCE		FOOD AT HOME: INCREASE BY 50% (5)	COLLEGE ASSISTANCE FROM PARENTS, AMONG STUDENTS	
		INCREASE BY 50% (3)	DECREASE BY 50% (4)		INCREASE BY 50% (6)	DECREASE BY 50% (7)
18–20	3,499	4,009	2,988	3,843	4,359	2,638
21–22	3,020	3,607	2,433	3,424	3,310	2,730
23–24	2,129	2,594	1,665	2,405	2,302	1,957
25–26	2,323	2,572	2,074	2,450	2,427	2,220
27–28	1,823	2,000	1,646	1,916	1,867	1,779
29–30	1,595	1,721	1,469	1,662	1,596	1,594
31–32	1,475	1,567	1,384	1,530	1,491	1,459
33–34	1,556	1,599	1,514	1,582	1,566	1,546
Total during transition	38,340	43,347	33,334	41,465	42,196	34,485

Note. All values expressed in 2001 dollars using the Consumer Price Index for All Urban Consumers.

TABLE 12.4

DISPARITIES IN ECONOMIC ASSISTANCE RECEIVED DURING THE

TRANSITION TO ADULTHOOD

	ECONOMIC ASSISTANCE		
	INTERHOUSEHOLD FINANCIAL ($)	TOTAL ($)	TIME HELP (HOURS)
All youth	17,909	38,340	3,852
Average family income when youth was 10–15 years old:			
1st quartile (poorest)	9,458	23,414	3,864
2nd quartile	9,209	26,489	4,133
3rd quartile	20,761	43,546	3,662
4th quartile	33,194	70,965	3,869

Note. All values expressed in 2001 dollars using the Consumer Price Index for All Urban Consumers. Table 12.A1 contains the estimates of each component for each income quartile.

Disparities by Parental Income

While the average amount received by youth is estimated at $38,340, anecdotal evidence suggests that the variation in assistance is substantial. Some children from advantaged backgrounds attend private schools and receive generous assistance with the purchase of cars and homes. Children with less affluent parents presumably receive much less assistance. To investigate this issue we calculate separately estimates of assistance received during the transition for children from more and less advantaged backgrounds. Specifically, using the panel design of the PSID, for each eighteen- to thirty-four-year-old youth in the 1988 sample, we calculate the average income of the family in which they resided during the six years when they were ten to fifteen years old. We then ranked all youth by family income and grouped them into quartiles. The estimates for direct college assistance use the income quartiles defined within the NPSAS. For each of these groups, we produced separate estimates of columns 1–6 in table 12.2. We then recalculated the amount of assistance over the transition period based on these parameters. Table 12.4 reports the cumulative amount of assistance received by each quartile, with the detailed calculations provided in table 12.5. Also in table 12.4 is the estimate of the amount of time help, in hours, that is

TABLE 12.5

ESTIMATE OF TOTAL ECONOMIC ASSISTANCE RECEIVED AMONG YOUTH 18–34, BY INCOME QUARTILE OF PARENTS

| AGE | PROPORTION LIVING INDEPENDENTLY (1) | YOUTH LIVING INDEPENDENTLY: DIRECT FINANCIAL ASSISTANCE ($) (2) | YOUTH NOT LIVING INDEPENDENTLY | | | | | TOTAL AVERAGE ASSISTANCE RECEIVED ($) (8) [b] | ALL YOUTH: TOTAL AVERAGE ASSISTANCE RECEIVED ($) (9) [c] |
			HOUSING ASSISTANCE ($) (3)	FOOD AT HOME ($) (4)	PROPORTION IN COLLEGE (5)	COLLEGE ASSISTANCE FROM PARENTS AMONG STUDENTS ($) (6)	AVERAGE COLLEGE ASSISTANCE AMONG ALL DEPENDENT YOUTH ($) (7) [a]		
1st (bottom) quartile:									
18–20	.25	123	1,816	1,569	.52	2,219	1,151	3,219	2,432
21–22	.55	1,302	1,761	1,538	.19	2,219	432	3,250	2,173
23–24	.64	234	1,986	1,374	.06	2,219	127	3,343	1,343
25–26	.84	1,827	2,236	1,389	.09	2,219	192	3,582	2,110
27–28	.83	355	1,810	1,416	.04	2,219	84	3,218	848
29–30	.90	261	1,744	1,486	.02	2,219	46	3,227	552
31–32	.93	176	1,712	1,334	.02	2,219	41	3,045	380
33–34	.93	390	2,628	1,535	.01	2,219	20	4,155	653
Total during transition									23,414
2nd quartile:									
18–20	.25	320	2,191	1,391	.53	2,350	1,236	3,405	2,635
21–22	.49	667	2,575	1,711	.43	2,350	1,019	3,911	2,317
23–24	.46	146	2,782	1,733	.22	2,350	524	4,284	2,362

25–26	.78	1,407	2,325	1,579	.08	2,350	187	3,858	1,935
27–28	.85	891	2,891	1,429	.20	2,350	461	4,145	1,365
29–30	.00	387	3,137	1,445	.00	2,350	0	4,582	396
31–32	.94	213	2,888	1,699	.00	2,350	0	4,587	481
33–34	.99	414	2,070	1,584	.00	2,350	0	3,654	436
Total during transition									26,489
3rd quartile:									
18–20	.19	575	2,599	1,437	.61	4,013	2,430	4,633	3,868
21–22	.34	842	2,891	1,899	.20	4,013	785	4,873	3,508
23–24	.58	1,129	3,789	1,637	.09	4,013	365	5,421	2,929
25–26	.73	2,843	2,962	1,463	.38	4,013	1,520	4,687	3,345
27–28	.85	1,163	2,957	1,514	.30	4,013	1,216	4,671	1,695
29–30	.87	395	3,068	1,698	.00	4,013	0	4,765	981
31–32	.92	2,393	3,077	1,798	.00	4,013	0	4,875	2,601
33–34	.96	753	2,818	1,728	.00	4,013	0	4,546	913
Total during transition									43,546
4th (top) quartile:									
18–20	.16	252	3,742	2,126	.61	7,893	4,792	7,988	6,718
21–22	.38	873	4,965	2,821	.26	7,893	2,066	8,324	5,458
23–24	.70	549	4,296	2,554	.62	7,893	4,914	8,565	2,969
25–26	.84	905	4,474	1,888	.60	7,893	4,749	8,240	2,049
27–28	.92	2,917	4,405	2,007	.04	7,893	290	6,525	3,221

(continued)

TABLE 12.5.

(CONTINUED)

		YOUTH NOT LIVING INDEPENDENTLY							
AGE	PROPORTION LIVING INDEPENDENTLY (1)	YOUTH LIVING INDEPENDENTLY: DIRECT FINANCIAL ASSISTANCE ($) (2)	HOUSING ASSISTANCE ($) (3)	FOOD AT HOME ($) (4)	PROPORTION IN COLLEGE (5)	COLLEGE ASSISTANCE FROM PARENTS AMONG STUDENTS ($) (6)	AVERAGE COLLEGE ASSISTANCE AMONG ALL DEPENDENT YOUTH ($) (7)[a]	TOTAL AVERAGE ASSISTANCE RECEIVED ($) (8)[b]	ALL YOUTH: TOTAL AVERAGE ASSISTANCE RECEIVED ($) (9)[c]
29–30	.93	3,748	4,484	1,945	.00	7,893	0	6,430	3,941
31–32	.93	2,629	4,282	1,866	.50	7,893	3,947	7,789	3,012
33–34	.96	4,598	5,129	1,833	.66	7,893	5,206	8,724	4,754
Total during transition									70,965

Sources. Columns 1–5 are estimated directly from the 1988 and 1990 Panel Study of Income Dynamics, inflated by Consumer Price Index for All Urban Consumers (CPI-U) to 2001 dollars; col. 6 is estimated from the 1992–93 National Postsecondary Student Aid Study (NPSAS).

Note. All values expressed in 2001 dollars using the CPI-U.

[a] Column 7 = col. 5 × col. 6.

[b] Column 8 = [col. 7 + (col. 3 + col. 4) × col. 5 × .25] + (col. 3 + col. 4) × (1.0 − col. 5).

[c] Column 9 = (col. 1 × col. 2) + [(1.0 − col. 1) × col. 8].

received during the transition. We also report the amount of interhousehold financial transfers for comparison with table 12.1.

There are large differences across income groups. For interhousehold financial transfers, youth in the two lowest-income quartiles received less than one-third of the amount the top quartile received, $9,000 versus $33,194. Moreover, children with more affluent parents stay in their parents' home longer, and the imputed rental transfer is about twice as high for the highest quartile relative to the lowest quartile (table 12.5). The disparities by income for college assistance are large, both because children from higher-income families are more likely to go to college and because, when they do attend college, they receive almost four times more assistance, $8,000 compared with $2,200 (table 12.5).

Adding all the various transfers reported in table 12.5, table 12.4 reports the total amount of assistance received over the entire transition for each quartile. These figures demonstrate the extent to which differences in assistance by income levels are dramatic over youth's early years. While youth in the bottom two quartiles receive roughly $25,000 on average during the years eighteen to thirty-four, the top 25% receive nearly three times as much, or $70,965.

Although less affluent families may not have resources to provide financial assistance to their children, they may provide more time assistance. In fact, a simple theoretical model of time value would suggest that families with low wages—who are typically low-income families—would be more likely to provide time help, all else equal. We, however, find no evidence in support of this hypothesis; youth from low- and high-income families receive almost identical amounts of time help: 3,864 and 3,869 hours (see table 12.4).

Pattern of Receipt of Familial Assistance during the Transition to Adulthood

The age pattern of assistance reported in table 12.2 shows that, for the most part, assistance falls substantially with age. Average assistance is $3,499 during ages eighteen to twenty and $1,556 for adult children thirty-three to thirty-four. While this is a substantial decline, on average adult children still receive a significant amount of assistance in their midthirties.

But what explains the age pattern of transfers? The assumption is that assistance is triggered by life events. Given that these life events tend to be clustered at certain ages, transfers vary with age. We investigate this issue using the reports of interhousehold financial and time transfers in the PSID for people of all ages—not just youth. Specifically, reported in table 12.6 are

TABLE 12.6

LOGISTIC REGRESSIONS OF RECEIPT OF INTERHOUSEHOLD TRANSFERS

| | ODDS RATIOS | | | |
| | FINANCIAL ASSISTANCE | | TIME HELP | |
EXPLANATORY FACTORS	(1)	(2)	(3)	(4)
Age:				
<21	1.84*	1.728	2.033*	1.845*
21–25	1.387**	1.396**	1.158	1.144
26–30[a]	. . .	. . .	. . .	. . .
31–35	.717**	.728**	.84*	.896
36–40	.646**	.667**	.549**	.623**
41–45	.507**	.526**	.325**	.377**
46–50	.307**	.32**	.194**	.23**
51–55	.252**	.262**	.189**	.222**
56–60	.162**	.17**	.168**	.198**
61–65	.132**	.138**	.204**	.237**
66–70	.149**	.157**	.172**	.201**
71–75	.09**	.093**	.206**	.237**
76–80	.165**	.170**	.329**	.365**
80+	.072**	.073**	.395**	.426**
Currently a student		1.446		1.056
Marital status:				
Married[a]		. . .		. . .
Single		.815*		.782*
Separated/divorced/widowed		1.097		1.294**
Have child under 3 in family		1.195*		2.01**
Bought home in last year		1.602**		1.125
Number of observations	9,584	9,584	9,624	9,624

[a] Reference group.
*Statistically significant at the .05 level.
**Statistically significant at the .01 level.

estimates of odds ratios from logistic regression models of transfer receipt with and without accounting for various major life events: being in school, being married, having a child under three years old, and buying a home in the past year.

Models 1 and 3 demonstrate that assistance declines virtually monotonically with age. Compared to someone in his or her late twenties, someone in his or her early twenties is 39% more likely to have received cash assistance, and someone eighteen to twenty years old is 84% more likely to receive help. The major life events we adjust for in the multivariate analyses, however, do not account for much of the observed age pattern; that is, the age effects change very little when we add in controls for being a student, being married, having a young child, and having bought a home in the past year. These factors have the expected effect. For example, individuals with young children and those who have bought a home recently are more likely to receive cash assistance. Presumably grandparents and other relatives provide assistance to help with the added expenses of a new child or new home. But the measured factors simply do not account for the strong age gradient. Most likely there are other events that account for some of the age gradient that are not included in our model; however, given the size of the age gradient and the fact that it changed very little when these controls were included, it is quite likely there is an underlying pattern with age that drives some assistance decisions.

Is Familial Assistance on the Rise?

Estimating the amount of assistance received from parents requires many assumptions, even with the advantage of relatively generous data available in modern surveys. Estimating changes in assistance over the past several decades is yet more challenging. While we do not attempt to estimate changes over time in all forms of assistance as we did for the point-in-time estimates in table 12.2, we can examine changes in living arrangements, which is a substantial source of assistance.

For each single-year age group between the ages of eighteen to thirty-four, figure 12.1 reports the proportion of youth living with their parents. In 1990, 70% of eighteen-year-olds lived with their parents, falling to 30% by age twenty-four and to 10% by age thirty. Between 1970 and 1990 there was a monotonic rise in shared housing. Between the ages of twenty and twenty-six, there was a roughly 10 percentage point rise in the share of children living at home. On average among people in their twenties, this amounted to an increase of 50%. It should be noted that this rise does not necessarily imply that parents are now more likely to live with a child. This is true because today's parents had lower fertility than parents several decades ago, so that even if the odds of a given child living with their parents has increased, today's parents simply have fewer children. Therefore, the total burden to parents may not have increased even though the average child receives more assistance today than they did decades ago.

One way to assess the magnitude of this change is to use the parame-

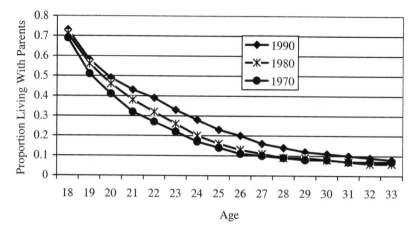

Figure 12.1. Trends in young adults living with parents

ters in table 12.2, but alter the estimates of the proportion living independently in column 2 based on the 1970 and 1990 census tabulations. This exercise provides an estimate of the increase in assistance simply due to the increase in shared housing, assuming the value of that shared housing remains the same. This change alone leads to an estimate of total transfers of $35,841 for 1990 versus $31,665 for 1970, or a 13% increase (not shown in table).[7] The rise in college attendance and college costs no doubt caused assistance to rise even further.

DISCUSSION

Almost all children are completely economically dependent on their parents for their first fifteen to eighteen years of life. Their parents' resources will help determine where they live, who their neighbors are, the quality of the schools they attend, the food and medical care they receive, and the developmental opportunities that they experience. But quite often, parental material assistance continues for some years into early adulthood as children begin to make their way and establish themselves economically. Our best estimate implies that on average parents provide roughly $38,000 in material assistance—housing, food, educational expenses, or direct cash assistance—during the transition to adulthood. This averages over $2,200 in each year from ages eighteen to thirty-four, although assistance diminishes with age.

There is substantial variation among youth in the amount of assistance they receive, with some youth receiving many tens of thousands of dollars, while others receive very little or no support. We find that children in the top one-fourth in terms of family income received three times more material assistance than children in the bottom one-fourth.

One policy option for addressing the low levels of assistance received by children from low-income families is for the government to expand assistance to needy youth. It must be realized, however, that government intervention risks the possibility of displacing or crowding out assistance that some families are already providing to youth. Any policy must take this factor into account. The goal is to identify policies that complement, or at least do not displace, the strong network that is already in place for some families.

Moreover, government assistance is already targeted toward low-income youth through, for example, income-based student aid programs. A natural extension of our work here would be to estimate—for low- and high-income youth separately—the amount of assistance they receive from familial and governmental sources combined. To what degree do government assistance programs already offset the disparities we observed?

The implicit assumption of this study is that familial assistance is key to a successful transition. The evidence from many studies, including ones in this volume, implies that children from more advantaged families have more successful transitions. However, the important aspect of family background might not be the direct material assistance that families provide. Government intervention may be able to help level material assistance across young adults, but this may not substantially reduce disparities in the transition to adulthood because it may not be the material assistance per se that leads to a successful transition. It may be some other mechanism transmitted through families—such as early childhood experiences and opportunities—that lead more advantaged youth to a smoother transition. A richer understanding of the exact mechanism by which families affect the transition is necessary. With this knowledge in hand, we can then consider ways to encourage and promote these practices.

NOTES

We acknowledge financial support from the National Institute of Aging, grant #K01 AG00670.

1. We do not use the 1999–2000 wave to estimate parental assistance because it does not ask for exact amounts of parental transfers—only if parental support for nontuition expenses is greater or less than $1,000.

2. The PSID has included a single question on financial assistance from friends and family for many years that could be used to calculate assistance received during the transition. However, reports of transfers based on that question are sub-

stantially underreported. For example, in 1988 the more detailed set of questions led to an estimate of 20% of families receiving cash assistance while the one question that has been asked annually led to an estimate of just 5%.

3. Familial transfers include assistance from own parents, parents-in-law, and all other relatives (including grandparents) of persons living in the immediate nuclear family. An estimated 80% of these transfers are received from the person's parents or parents-in-law. Therefore, we will use both "familial" and "parental" transfers to refer to the assistance being measured in this study.

4. We assume that youth do not pay rent to their parents as it is rarely the case that they do.

5. For youth attending college, help with room-and-board expenses during the school year is likely captured in the college assistance measure; therefore estimates of food and housing assistance are probably only relevant during the summer months when students are not attending school.

6. More accurately, these are people eighteen to thirty-four who are heads of their own family or the wives of those household heads. Less than 3% of household heads and wives live in the same household as their parents.

7. Note that the estimates of living arrangements reported here for 1990 do not match the estimates in table 12.2 because the estimates here are based on census data, which uses a somewhat different definition of shared household than the PSID does.

REFERENCES

Duncan, Otis Dudley, David L. Featherman, and Beverly Duncan. 1972. *Socio-economic Background and Achievement.* New York: Seminar Press.

Hogan, Dennis. 1981. *Transitions and Social Change: The Early Lives of American Men.* New York: Academic Press.

Marini, Margaret Mooney. 1978a. Sex Differences in the Determination of Adolescent Aspirations: A Review of Research. *Sex Roles* 4 (5):723–51.

———. 1978b. The Transition to Adulthood: Sex Differences in Educational Attainment and Age at Marriage. *American Sociological Review* 4:484–507.

Ruggles, Steven, and Matthew Sobek. 2003. *Integrated Public Use Microdata Series.* Version 3.0. Minneapolis: Historical Census Projects, University of Minnesota. http://www.ipums.umn.edu/usa/cite.html.

CHAPTER 13
EARLY ADULT TRANSITIONS AND THEIR RELATION TO WELL-BEING AND SUBSTANCE USE

JOHN SCHULENBERG, PATRICK M. O'MALLEY,
JERALD G. BACHMAN, AND LLOYD D. JOHNSTON

In recent decades, the period between adolescence and adulthood has become extended for many segments of the population, making this period more than simply a staging ground for adulthood (Arnett 2000). At the same time, traditional sequences of events that mark adult status (e.g., complet-ing school, obtaining full-time employment and gaining financial independence, getting married, and starting a family) appear to have become less central to the definition of adulthood (if not less common). Nevertheless, embedded within this period of life are multiple and specific developmental tasks and transitions in the domains of achievement, affiliation, and identity (Oerter 1986; Schulenberg and Maggs 2002). Although there is not a single normative or prescribed pathway through these various tasks and transitions (Cohen et al. 2003; Settersten 2003; Shanahan 2000), successfully negotiating at least some of them (and particularly those viewed as central by the young person) is likely to be associated with more salutary trajectories of health and well-being and to provide a foundation for optimal development during adulthood (Masten and Curtis 2000; Ryff, Singer, and Seltzer 2002; Schulenberg, Bryant, and O'Malley, in press; Weise, Freund, and Baltes 2000).

Well-being has been found to increase during the period between late adolescence and early adulthood (Gore et al. 1997; Schulenberg et al. 2000), but questions remain about how widespread this increase may be and why it occurs and, more generally, how the course of well-being relates to the various diverse pathways out of high school. Substance use also tends to increase during this period, reaching its lifetime peak during the early twenties, depending on the given cohort and substance (Chen and Kandel 1995; Jackson et al. 2002; Johnston, O'Malley, and Bachman 2003). While it has been found that changes in substance use relate to various social role transitions during emerging adulthood (e.g., Bachman et al. 1997; Brook et al. 1999; Jessor, Donovan, and Costa 1991), questions remain about how various transitions work together in contributing to increases and decreases in substance use during this time. Well-being and substance use, while not necessarily sharing a common etiology or developmental course across the life span, may increase during the transition to adulthood in part because of the new roles and contexts that provide more freedom and selection of opportunities (Bachman et al. 1997; Schulenberg and Maggs 2002). Furthermore, while substance use has clear negative and often dangerous correlates and consequences (e.g., Hawkins, Catalano, and Miller 1992), experimental substance use during late adolescence may also serve constructive purposes in regard to developmental tasks related to, for example, peer bonding, independence striving, and identity experimentation (Chassin, Presson, and Sherman 1989; Maggs 1997; Schulenberg, Maggs, and O'Malley 2003a).

In this chapter, we analyze data from four waves of nationally representative U.S. panel data spanning ages eighteen to twenty-four, and we offer a "big picture" about the timing, sequencing, and covariation of social role transitions related to school and work, romantic involvement (specifically marriage), parenthood, and independence in the form of leaving the parental home. At wave 1 in our study, young people were nearing the end of their senior year of high school (modal age of eighteen), allowing us to follow their "launching" into post–high school transitions. During this important launching period, initial plans first combine with new experiences to place individuals on paths that will lead them into adulthood (Clausen 1991; Gore et al. 1997). In aggregating across these specific transitions at wave 2 (modal ages of nineteen to twenty) to construct mutually exclusive transition groups, we focus on both the number of transitions and the distinct patterning of various transitions, defining and offering prevalence estimates of the multiple pathways through emerging adulthood. Building on some of our previous research (Schulenberg et al. 2000), we consider associations between the wave 2 transition groups (i.e., aggregated by number and by unique patterns) and trajectories of well-being and sub-stance use across the four waves (spanning ages eighteen to twenty-four). And in the last phase of the analyses, we examine diversity within transition groups, focusing specifically on how the differential transitional experiences that occur between waves 2 and 4 relate to trajectories of well-being and sub-stance use.

In conceptualizing how the different transition groups might relate to trajectories of well-being and substance use, we draw from Coleman's focal theory (1989) regarding transition effects during early adolescence. Accord-ing to focal theory, the number of transitions a young person goes through relates to the amount of difficulty the young person experiences; that is, nu-merous and simultaneous transitions can overwhelm one's coping capacity, and well-being can suffer (Schulenberg and Maggs 2002). Thus, it might be expected that the number of transitions in the year or two immediately fol-lowing high school is negatively related to well-being and positively related to substance use. But it is also possible that those most willing to take on more transitions at once might have more psychological resources to begin with, suggesting an opposite direction of relations. More broadly, we draw from Elder's (1998) conceptualizations concerning the social life course and Rutter's (1996) conceptualizations regarding transitions as potential turning points with regard to ongoing functioning and adjustment (for additional details on our conceptual approach, see Schulenberg et al. [2003a]).

Our approach is largely descriptive, which is appropriate given that our purpose is to map the milestones of the broader critical developmental transition from adolescence to adulthood. But we also try to provide some preliminary explanations of our findings. The different pathways and their relations to trajectories of well-being and substance use may vary by gender, cohort membership, and race/ethnicity (Schulenberg et al. 2000), and we investigate these possibilities in our analyses. We take a pattern-centered (rather than single variable–centered) approach to considering the different transitions. Such an interaction-based approach to change (see Cairns and Cairns 1994; Magnusson 1995; Singer et al. 1998) seeks to extend previous main-effects findings, such as the effects of marriage and living away from parents, that we and others have demonstrated in previous analyses (Bach-man et al. 1997; Graber and Dubas 1996; Leonard and Rothbard 1999; Schulenberg et al. 2000). This pattern-centered approach is more complex than typical variable-centered (main effects) approaches, but the additional complexity is warranted given that certain transitions tend to co-occur dur-ing emerging adulthood.

METHOD

We examine national panel data spanning ages eighteen to twenty-four from the Monitoring the Future (MTF) project (Johnston et al. 2003), which is an ongoing, cohort-sequential longitudinal project funded by the National Institute on Drug Abuse. It is designed to understand the epidemiology and etiology of substance use and, more broadly, behavior and psychosocial development during adolescence and young adulthood. The project has surveyed nationally representative samples of approximately 17,000 high school seniors in the United States each year since 1975, using questionnaires administered in classrooms. Approximately 2,400 individuals are randomly selected from each senior year cohort for follow-up. Follow-up surveys are conducted by mail every two years.

Sample

The panel sample used in the present study consisted of nineteen consecutive cohorts of respondents who were surveyed as high school seniors (wave 1, age eighteen) from 1977 through 1995, and who participated in follow-up surveys one or two years after high school (wave 2, ages nineteen to twenty), three or four years after high school (wave 3, ages twenty-one to twenty-two), and five or six years after high school (wave 4, ages twenty-three to twenty-four). Differences in year of follow-up occur because the biennial follow-up surveys begin one year after high school for one random half of the panel drawn from each cohort, and two years post high school for the other. For these analyses, the two random halves were combined.

To increase the breadth of areas covered by the surveys, MTF uses six different questionnaire forms (questionnaires are distributed randomly within schools at senior year, and a given individual's questionnaire form is consistent across waves). Because the items that comprise the well-being measure are located on only one of the forms, only one-sixth of the sample was available for the present study. This included 3,912 weighted cases (1,666 males and 2,243 females). Drug users are oversampled for follow-up, and corrective weighting is used to reflect population estimates.

Measures

We focus primarily on transitions that occur during the first year or two immediately following high school (by wave 2, ages nineteen to twenty), an appropriate time frame given our emphasis on the launching into emerging adulthood. We examine longitudinal trajectories of well-being and substance use in order to try to capture the course of these constructs prior to, during, and after the wave 2 transitions. This makes it possible to consider selection effects, as well as to examine whether the transitions serve to alter the ongoing trajectories of substance use and well-being. We selected the age twenty-three to twenty-four survey as the final (fourth) wave because this age is beyond the normative ending time for full-time college attendance (age twenty-two for most of the cohorts included here), allowing us to consider postcollege experiences.

TRANSITIONS AT WAVE 2. We consider a variety of transitions that occur between wave 1 (age eighteen, senior year in high school) and wave 2 (ages nineteen to twenty), including entering college, entering the workforce, leaving the parental home, getting married, and entering parenthood. Seven transitions were examined based on items concerning full- or part-time college attendance during the past year, full- or part-time employment during the past year, current living arrangements (specifically, living in parental home), current marital status, and parenthood. This is not a list of mutually exclusive transitions, of course, nor is it a comprehensive list of all of the important milestones during this period. But it is a reasonable group of normative social-role transitions that reflects the diversity of life paths during this launching period. We aggregated across the various transitions, in terms of their number and patterning, to form mutually exclusive transition groups (details provided below).

GENDER, COHORT, AND RACE/ETHNICITY. We considered gender, cohort, and race/ethnicity effects, particularly how they impinged on relationships between transition groups and trajectories of well-being and substance use. Senior-year classes were grouped into three cohorts (1977–82, 1983–89, 1990–95). Given our emphasis on multiple transition groups, our available sample, and the national political and substance-use cycles over the two-decade period (Johnston et al. 2003; Schulenberg et al. 2000), these cohort groups reflect logical and meaningful categories. Race/ethnicity was considered in terms of white (83% of the sample), African American (8%), and other race/ethnicity groups (9%, the majority of whom were Hispanic American). This three-way grouping is less than satisfying in some ways, but given the sample size and focus on multiple transition groups, it was our best option.

OVERALL WELL-BEING. Based on previous analyses (Schulenberg et al. 2000) and the work of Ryff and colleagues on well-being during adulthood (e.g., Ryff and Keyes 1995), overall well-being was considered in terms of a composite of three interrelated constructs: self-esteem (based on Rosenberg 1965), self-efficacy (similar to Nowicki and Strickland's [1973] internal locus of control subscale), and social support (similar to Newcomb and Harlow 1986). Each item was a statement about one's self (e.g., I feel I am a person of worth); for all items, possible responses were 1 (disagree), 2 (mostly disagree), 3 (neither agree nor disagree), 4 (mostly agree), and 5 (agree), with responses reversed if necessary so that high scores reflect high well-being. The same measures were used at all four waves, and cross-sectional exploratory factor analyses of the three scales suggested one underlying dimension at each wave. Alpha coefficients for this overall score exceeded .75 at each of the four waves.

SUBSTANCE USE. Substance use measures for these analyses included binge drinking (frequency of having five or more drinks in a row during the past two weeks) and marijuana use (occasions of use in the past twelve months). The Monitoring the Future substance-use items have been shown to demonstrate excellent psychometric properties, and their reliability and validity have been reported and discussed extensively (Johnston and O'Malley 1985; Johnston et al. 2003; O'Malley, Bachman, and Johnston 1983). Possible responses for occasions of binge drinking in the past two weeks were 1 (none), 2 (once), 3 (twice), 4 (3–5 times), 5 (6–9 times), and 6 (10 or more times); for occasions of marijuana use in the past twelve months possible responses were 1 (0 occasions), 2 (1–2 occasions), 3 (3–5 occasions), 4 (6–9 occasions), 5 (10–19 occasions), 6 (20–39 occasions), and 7 (40 or more occasions). The same measures were used at all four waves.

Analysis Plan

To address the aims of this chapter, there were five phases of analysis, which dealt with (1) average trajectories of well-being and substance use (binge drinking and marijuana use) across the four waves (ages eighteen to twenty-four); (2) description of wave 2 (ages nineteen to twenty) transitions; (3) how the number of wave 2 transitions relate to trajectories of well-being and substance use; (4) how the wave 2 transition groups relate to trajectories of well-being and substance use; and (5) within specific wave 2 transition groups, how wave 4 (ages twenty-three to twenty-four) transitions relate to trajectories of well-being and substance use.

We relied typically on within-time and repeated-measures ANOVAs, considering transition groups (along with gender, cohort, and race/ethnicity) as the predictors, and substance use and well-being (within-time and across time) as the outcomes. Despite the implied causal ordering in the analyses, bidirectional influences very likely occur between the transition groups and dependent variables; ANOVAs provide a straightforward way of connecting a categorical variable (transition groups) with longitudinal trajectories of continuous variables (substance use and well-being). In the repeated-measures ANOVAs, time effects (i.e., change across the four waves) were partitioned into orthogonal polynomial contrasts to test for linear, quadratic, and cubic effects in well-being and substance use over time. The time-interaction terms provided tests of whether and how the transition groups (and gender, cohort, and race/ethnicity) were associated with different trajectories of well-being and substance use. For significant time-by-transition group interactions, comparisons were made among the change coefficients of the various subgroups to determine significant differences.

Clearly, given the wealth of findings yielded by the analyses, not all findings can be presented here. To simplify our presentation in this chapter, and consistent with the overall approach of this volume, we focus primarily on the patterns of significant findings relevant to how the transition groups relate to well-being and substance-use trajectories. (A full report of all findings and additional detail about sample and measures is provided in MTF Occasional Paper 56 [Schulenberg et al. 2003b].)

RESULTS

Findings are presented according to the five analysis phases. We limit our consideration of findings to those differences and changes over time that were significant at least at the $p < .01$ level (a level justified by the size of our sample and the number of analyses conducted).

Average Trajectories of Well-Being and Substance Use

We start by examining average trajectories of well-being and substance use (binge drinking and marijuana use) across four waves from senior year in high school to ages twenty-three to twenty-four for the total sample and by gender, cohort, and race/ethnicity.

WELL-BEING. As shown in figure 13.1, well-being increased across the waves, with a faster rate of change between earlier waves than later waves. Men and women started with identical levels of well-being, but the increase over time was significantly greater for men than for women, and the leveling off with age was stronger for men than for women. There were no significant cohort or race/ethnicity interaction effects with time.[1]

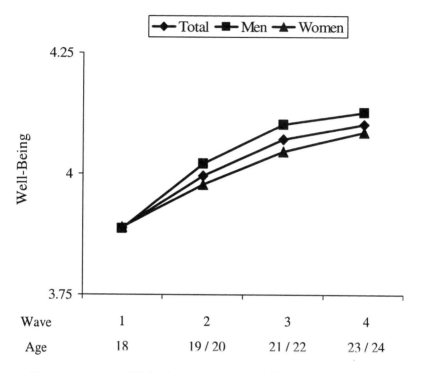

Figure 13.1. Average well-being during transition to adulthood

SUBSTANCE USE. Binge drinking tended to increase immediately following high school and was consistently higher for men than women; this gender difference increased with age, as shown in figure 13.2*a*. Figure 13.2*b* shows that binge drinking varied as a function of cohort group, with the three groups starting off quite differently in terms of initial level of binge drinking at age eighteen but then converging by ages twenty-one to twenty-two. Specifically, binge drinking for the most recent cohort group (1990–95) increased more rapidly over time than for the other cohort groups, and all groups followed a quadratic trend in which binge drinking peaked by wave 3 or 4 and then decreased. Binge drinking varied by race/ethnicity, with binge drinking being higher for whites than for African Americans and the other race/ethnicity groups; whereas the trajectory for whites increased then decreased, the trajectories for African American and other race/ethnicity groups remained flat.

The findings for marijuana use are very similar to those for binge drinking. As shown in figure 13.3*a*, marijuana use was, on average, higher for men than for women, and women decreased their use more rapidly over time than did men. Figure 13.3*b* indicates that the overall level and trajectory

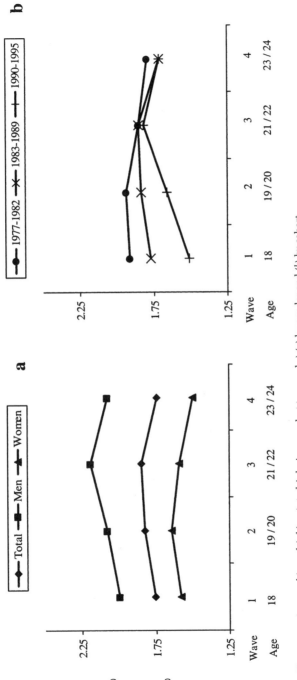

Figure 13.2. Average binge drinking (5+ drinks in a row last two weeks) (*a*) by gender and (*b*) by cohort

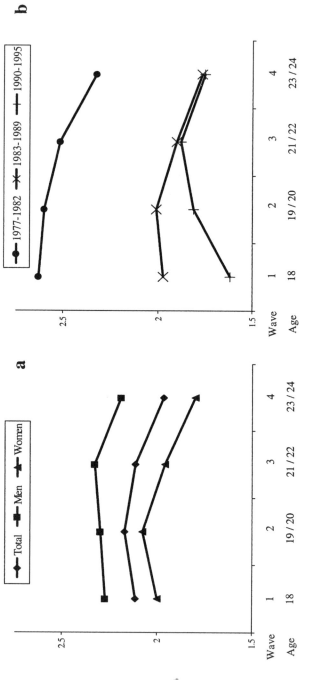

Figure 13.3. Average marijuana use (past twelve months) (*a*) by gender and (*b*) by cohort

of marijuana use varied by cohort group; the two earlier cohorts differed in level, with the 1977–82 group having the highest level, but in both cases marijuana use declined linearly across the waves. By comparison, the most recent group (1990–95) started off lowest but then increased before dropping off by wave 4. In terms of race/ethnic differences, marijuana use was highest among whites and did not change differentially for the groups over time.

SUMMARY. Overall, then, well-being was found to increase during the transition, especially over the first few years out of high school. This was true for both men and women, although the rate of increase was faster for men. These time trends held regardless of cohort or race/ethnicity. Binge drinking and marijuana use were, on average, higher for men than women, and higher for whites than African American and other race/ethnic groups. Cohort effects were striking for the trajectories of substance use (see Johnston et al. 2003), with evidence of convergence across cohorts during the mid-twenties when substance use declined for all cohorts (although the oldest cohort group maintained its higher level of marijuana use).

Transitions at Wave 2 (Ages Nineteen to Twenty)

In the second phase of the analyses, we examined the percentages of individuals in our national panels making the various post–high school transitions between waves 1 (age eighteen) and 2 (ages nineteen to twenty). These percentages are shown in figure 13.4 by gender. Note that these are not mutually exclusive transitions, with the exception of full- versus part-time work and full- versus part-time college. The most common post–high school transition was entering full-time college, with almost 60% of the sample doing this. Only 8% were attending college part time. About 33% of the men and 25% of the women made the transition into full-time work, and another 29% of the men and 35% of the women were working part time. (Part-time work does not necessarily represent a transition, given that most had worked part time during high school; however, for other purposes considered below, we wanted to include post–high school part-time work as an important activity.) Moving away from one's parents was very common, with about half the sample doing so and the other half living with one or both parents. Only about 10% of the women and 5% of the men were married by wave 2, and 7% of the women and 4% of the men had children. Significant cohort differences were evident for full-time work and full-time college, with the former decreasing and the latter increasing from earlier to more recent cohorts (see also Bachman et al. 1997). In terms of significant race/ethnicity differ-

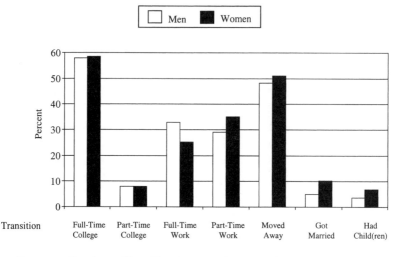

Figure 13.4. Prevalence of transitions by wave 2 (ages 19–20)

ences, whites and African Americans were more likely to have moved away from parents than those in the other race/ethnicity group.

We next considered two ways of aggregating across the individual transitions and then examined how the aggregates related to well-being and substance use. First, the number of transitions was simply summed (presented in the next section). Second, we considered all possible combinations of transitions and focused only on those combinations that encompassed sufficient portions of the sample to permit meaningful consideration.

Number of Transitions and Well-Being and Substance Use

A straightforward way of thinking of the transitions in aggregate is to sum the number of transitions a given individual makes at wave 2. As we discussed earlier, this approach draws from Coleman's focal theory (1989) in which the number of transitions a young person goes through during early adolescence is negatively related to well-being and positively related to difficulties; conversely, especially during the transition from adolescence into early adulthood, those most willing to take on more transitions at once might have more psychological resources to begin with, suggesting an opposite direction of relations.

PREVALENCE. The number of transitions any one individual could make ranged from zero to five (although there are seven possible transitions, two mutually exclusive pairs—part- and full-time work and part- and full-time school—make five the top of the range). The mode for men and women was two transitions (49% and 48%, respectively), followed by one transition (29% of men and 26% of women), and then three (15% of men and 20% of women). About 5% of the sample experienced no transitions; at wave 2 they were still living with their parents, were not married, had no children, were not enrolled in college full or part time, and were not working full or part time. Less than 2% experienced four or five transitions. There were no significant gender, cohort, or race/ethnicity differences in the average number of transitions.

WELL-BEING. Figure 13.5 shows the trajectories of well-being over time by the number of wave 2 transitions (the arrow at wave 2 signifies when transition groups are defined). Well-being increased for all groups between waves 1 and 2. It continued to increase for the one, two, and three transition groups across the waves and leveled off (quadratic effect) for the no and four/ five transition groups. With only minor exceptions, the transition groups maintained their relative ordering across the four waves, with well-being scores overall being significantly higher than average for those making two and three transitions and significantly lower than average for those making no transitions and one transition. Transition group interactions involving gender, cohort, and race/ethnicity were not significant. The fact that the differences in well-being were in place at wave 1 prior to graduating from high school indicates a selection effect: those who are higher in well-being in high

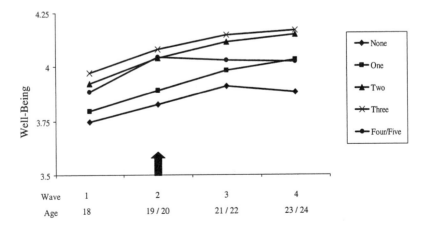

Figure 13.5. Well-being over time by number of wave 2 transitions

school are more likely to have the psychological resources and advance plans to take on more transitions following high school. As we shall see, this has a great deal to do with which transitions were involved.

SUBSTANCE USE. Figures 13.6 and 13.7 show the trajectories of binge drinking and marijuana use, respectively, for the transition groups. In contrast to what was found for the well-being trajectories, the substance-use trajectories show a fair amount of differential change as a function of number of transitions. Those in the no, one, and four/five transition groups had significantly higher binge drinking and marijuana use at wave 1 than did those in the two and three transition groups. As shown in figure 13.6, the binge drinking trajectory remained relatively flat for those in the no and one transition groups, decreased sharply for those in the four/five transition group, and increased then decreased for those in the two and three transition groups. As shown in figure 13.7, very similar results were found with regard to marijuana-use trajectories; it is noteworthy that marijuana use did not decline over time for the no transition group. For both binge drinking and marijuana use, none of the time-by-transition group interactions involving gender, cohort, or race/ethnicity was significant.

SUMMARY. Overall, there was little evidence to suggest that experiencing more transitions immediately following high school contributes to poorer functioning and adjustment. Indeed, well-being tended to be higher

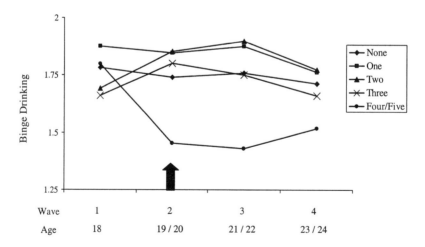

Figure 13.6. Binge drinking by number of wave 2 transitions

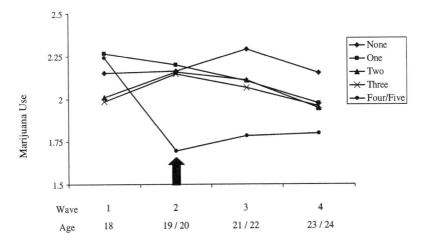

Figure 13.7. Marijuana use by number of wave 2 transitions

for those making more transitions, but these differences were in place during the senior year of high school, indicating selection effects, and the well-being trajectories were not altered by the number of wave 2 transitions. Substance use declined most for the small group experiencing four/five transitions at wave 2, tended to peak at wave 2 and then decline for those in the two and three trajectory groups, and remained relatively constant over time for those experiencing one or no transitions. Of course, interpretation of these variations depends on which transitions are experienced. Thus, while it is somewhat instructive to consider the number of transitions, considerations of process depend more on knowing which transitions one is experiencing.

Transition Groups: Well-Being and Substance Use

CONSTRUCTION AND PREVALENCE OF TRANSITION GROUPS. In this fourth phase of the analyses, we wanted to assemble a limited set of naturally occurring, mutually exclusive configurations of various transitions and then consider the trajectories of well-being and substance use as a function of these constructed transition groups. This was a potentially cumbersome process, for up to 240 unique categories (i.e., 2(5!)) were possible. But as shown in figure 13.8, we were able to construct nine mutually exclusive transition groups, with a tenth "unclassified" group (not illustrated).

Making some logical decisions, we began this analysis by isolating the

Not Married, No Children, and...

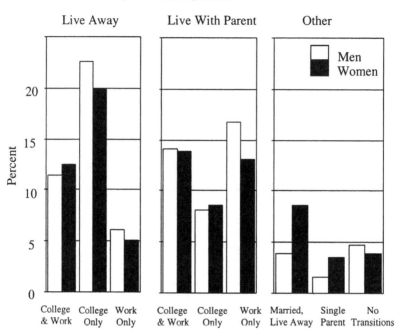

Figure 13.8. Prevalence of wave 2 transition groups by gender

small but important groups of those who were married and not living with their parents or their spouse's parents by wave 2 (most were also working full time, but this group was too small to further divide: 4% of men and 9% of women); those who were single parents by wave 2 (too small to further divide: 2% of men and 3% of women); and those who experienced no transitions by wave 2 (5% of men and 4% of women). The rationale for the first two groupings was that by age nineteen or twenty, marriage and single parenthood are sufficiently rare in our sample (which, by definition, does not include high school dropouts) as to constitute a relatively unique experience, regardless of what else the given individuals are experiencing (Schulenberg et al. 2000).

As shown in figure 13.8, the other groups that we found to encompass sufficient numbers of young people included three groups who were similar in terms of not being married, not having children, and living away from parents at wave 2: those who attended college full time and worked full or part time (11% of men and 13% of women), those who attended college full time and did not work (23% of men and 20% of women), and those who worked full or part time and did not attend college (6% of men and 5% of women). These three groups were analogous to another set of three, with the difference being that this second set of three lived home with one or both parents at wave 2: those who attended college full time and worked full or part time (14% of men and women), those who attended college full time and did not work (8% of men and women), and those who worked full or part time and did not attend college (17% of men and 13% of women).

These nine transition groups were mutually exclusive, and together, they accounted for 90% of the sample (leaving 10% in the unclassified group). Across these nine transition groups, prevalence rates did not vary significantly by gender, cohort, or race/ethnicity.

WELL-BEING. The well-being trajectories of the nine wave 2 transition groups are illustrated in figure 13.9. The trajectory for the unclassified group is not shown, but this group was included in the analyses. As is clear, well-being increased for each group, and the transition groups generally maintained their relative ranking in well-being over time, once again indicating selection effects. Compared to the total sample, well-being was significantly higher in the "not married, no children, live away, college and work," "not married, no children, live away, college only," and "not married, no children, live with parent, and college and work" groups; and it was significantly lower in the two "work-only" groups and the no transition and single parent groups. Interactions involving gender, cohort, and race/ethnicity were not significant.

SUBSTANCE USE. The trajectories for binge drinking and marijuana use for the nine wave 2 transition groups are illustrated in figures 13.10 and 13.11, respectively. In both analyses, the between-subjects effect for transition group was significant, the time-by-transition interaction was significant for both linear and quadratic trends, and none of the interactions involving gender, cohort, or race/ethnicity was significant.

Overall across the waves, compared to the total sample, binge drinking was significantly higher in the two "work-only" groups (who also had the highest level of binge drinking at wave 1) and the "live away, college only" group. It was significantly lower in the "married, live away" group. Compared to the total sample trajectory (see figure 13.2*a*), the binge-drinking trajectory decreased for the "not married, no children, live away, work-only group," decreased sharply then leveled off for the "married, live away" group, and increased then decreased for the "not married, no children, live away, college only" and "not married, no children, live away, college and work"

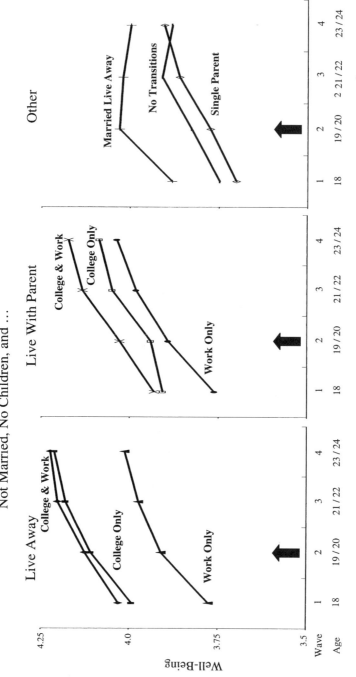

Figure 13.9. Well-being over time by wave 2 transition groups

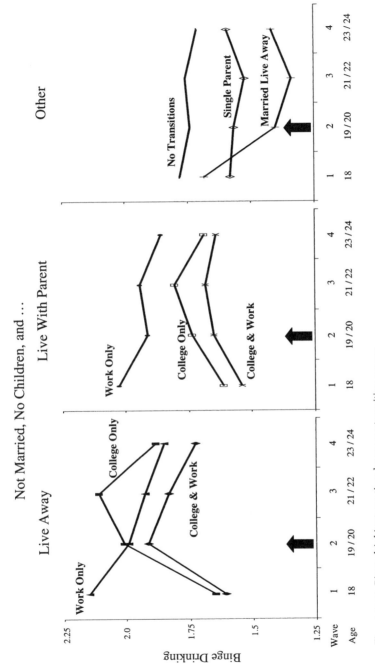

Figure 13.10. Binge drinking over time by wave 2 transition groups

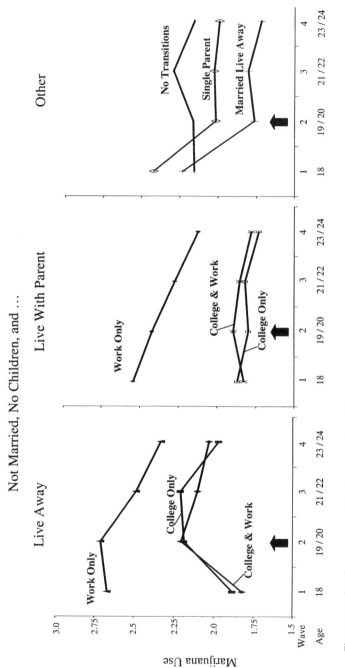

Figure 13.11. Marijuana use over time by wave 2 transition groups

groups. The trajectories for the remaining five transition groups did not differ significantly from the total sample trajectory.

Marijuana use overall—across the waves and compared to the total sample—was significantly higher in the two work-only groups and significantly lower in the two remaining groups that were "not married, had no children, and lived with parents" (the college and work, and work-only groups). Compared to the total sample trajectory (see figure 13.3a), the trajectories for the "not married, no children, live away, and college only" and "not married, no children, live away, and college and work" groups showed significantly less linear decrease and greater negative quadratic effect; the trajectory for the "not married, no children, live with parent, and work-only" group showed a significantly greater linear decrease; and the trajectory for the "married, live away" group showed a positive quadratic effect, reflecting the sharp decrease with marriage at wave 2 with this group.

SUMMARY. While differences were evident in well-being trajectories across the nine transition groups, these differences were in place at wave 1, indicating selection effects. In general, well-being was higher for those who, at wave 2, were not married, did not have children, and were in college. More differential change as a function of the nine transition groups was evident in the trajectories of binge drinking and marijuana use. In particular, for both binge drinking and marijuana use, there are sharper increases then decreases over time for those who at wave 2 are attending full-time college, not living with parents, not married, and have no children and sharper decreases for those who at wave 2 were married and not living with parents.

Examining Wave 4 Transitions within Wave 2 Transition Groups

In the final set of analyses, we wanted to examine what happened at wave 4 for some of the key wave 2 transition groups. In keeping with our pattern-centered approach, we looked within specific wave 2 groups, or appropriate combinations of "adjacent groups," and examined how wave 4 transitions related to variations in well-being and substance-use trajectories. We considered two groups that involved sufficiently large segments of the sample: (a) the wave 2 "living away, not married, no children, full-time college" combined group, which included working and nonworking subgroups and contained about 33% of the sample (1,294 individuals); and (b) the wave 2 "not married, no children, no college, work-only" combined group, which included both those living away and those living with parents and contained about 20% of the sample (787 individuals). In these analyses, we considered gender-by-transition-by-time interactions, none of which was significant, but were unable to consider interactions involving cohort and race/ethnicity due to sample size limitations.

WAVE 2 "LIVE AWAY, NOT MARRIED, NO CHILDREN, FULL-TIME COLLEGE" GROUP. All individuals in this group were (at wave 2) enrolled full time in college, lived away from home, were not married, and had no children ($n =$ 1,294). Based on the transitions that had occurred at wave 4 (ages twenty-three to twenty-four), we formed six groups and a seventh unclassified group. Three of the groups were similar in that their members still lived away from parents, were not married, did not have children, and either worked only (27%), attended college/graduate school only (12%), or worked and attended college/graduate school (14%). The remaining groups were the following: lived away from parents, married, no children, working (13%); moved back with parent(s), not married, no children (most completed college and were working full time) (20%); lived away from parents, with children (5%); and unclassified (9%).

Figures 13.12–13.14 show the trajectories of well-being, binge drinking, and marijuana use, respectively, for the six different wave 4 trajectory groups (the arrow at wave 4 signifies when transition groups are defined). As shown in figure 13.12, well-being increased for all six groups, especially across the earlier waves. The six groups did not differ from each other in their levels or trajectories of well-being, with one exception: the trajectory for those who remained in college full time, including graduate school, did not level off between waves 3 and 4 (significant cubic effect).

Figures 13.13 and 13.14 demonstrate graphically that substance-use levels were fairly equivalent across the six subgroups at wave 1 and then began to diverge considerably at wave 2 when everyone was still a full-time student living away from home and was neither married nor had children. Of particular interest, binge drinking and marijuana use at wave 2 were significantly lower compared to the group total for those who subsequently got married by wave 4, suggesting that that substance use at wave 2 foreshadows a quicker subsequent entry into marriage and, for binge drinking only, a quicker subsequent entry into parenthood. This is consistent with our earlier finding that becoming engaged is associated with—and perhaps causal of—declines in substance use (Bachman et al. 1997). More generally, binge drinking increased more rapidly for those groups who at wave 4 still lived away from home, were not married, and had no children; and it decreased more rapidly for the wave 4 "live away, married, no children, working" and "live away, with children" groups. And whereas marijuana use generally

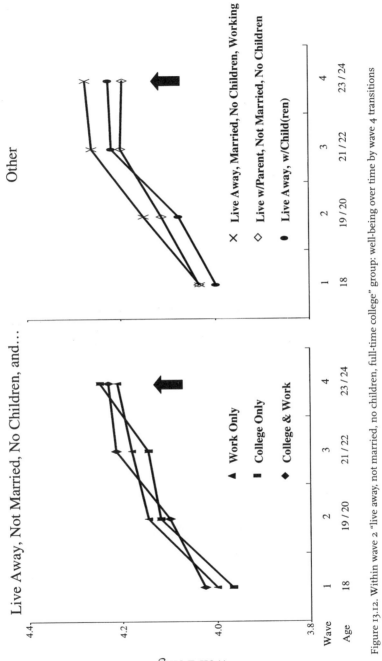

Figure 13.12. Within wave 2 "live away, not married, no children, full-time college" group: well-being over time by wave 4 transitions

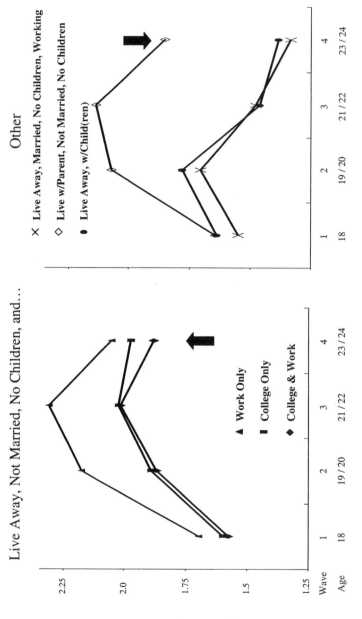

Figure 13.13. Within wave 2 "live away, not married, no children, full-time college" group: binge drinking over time by wave 4 transitions

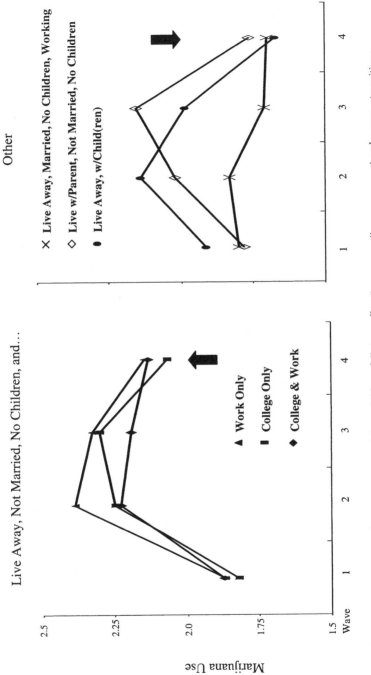

Figure 13.14. Within wave 2 "live away, not married, no children, full-time college" group: marijuana use over time by wave 4 transitions

increased then decreased for this subgroup, it remained relatively flat for the wave 4 "live away, married, no children, working" group.

WAVE 2 "NOT MARRIED, NO CHILDREN, NO COLLEGE, WORK ONLY" GROUP. All individuals in this group were (at wave 2) employed full time, were not in college full or part time, lived away from home, were not married, and had no children ($n = 787$). Based on consideration of what transitions had occurred by wave 4 (ages twenty-three to twenty-four), we formed five groups (plus a sixth unclassified group): lived away, worked full time, not married, and had no children (22%); lived away, worked full time, married, and had no children (14%); lived away, worked full time, married, had children (13%); lived away and neither attended college nor worked (10%); lived with parent(s), worked full time, not married, and had no children (22%); and unclassified (18%).

Figures 13.15–13.17 show the trajectories of well-being, binge drinking, and marijuana use, respectively, for the five different wave 4 trajectory groups. For well-being, all five groups had similar well-being scores at wave 1, and over time, only the well-being trajectory of the "live away, no college, not working" group was different than the trajectories for the other groups. Specifically, well-being declined between waves 3 and 4 to a greater extent for this group than for the total, which very likely relates to this group neither working nor attending college at wave 4.

For both the binge drinking and marijuana-use trajectories, the transition groups most different from the others were the wave 4 "live away, work, not married, no children" and "live away, work, married, with children" groups: compared to the total, the former group had significantly higher-than-average substance use across waves, and the latter group had significantly lower-than-average substance use across the waves. Of particular interest concerning the "foreshadowing" (and likely engagement effect) mentioned earlier in the other subgroup analysis, the two groups that were the same except for marriage at wave 4 (i.e., lived away, had no children, worked full time) had similar levels of binge drinking at wave 1; then they quickly diverged in binge drinking by wave 2—when both groups were working full time, were not attending college, were not married, and had no children—and remained significantly different at waves 3 and 4.

SUMMARY. On the whole, these two final analyses showed that within homogenous transition groups defined at wave 2, differences in subsequent transitional experiences between waves 2 and 4 were associated with divergences in trajectories of substance use and, to a lesser extent, of well-being.

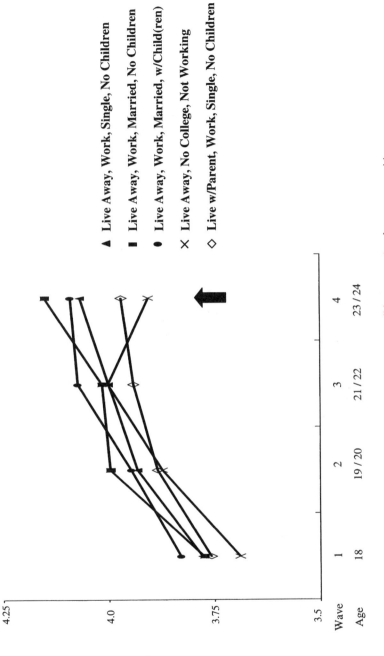

Legend:
▲ Live Away, Work, Single, No Children
■ Live Away, Work, Married, No Children
● Live Away, Work, Married, w/Child(ren)
✕ Live Away, No College, Not Working
◇ Live w/Parent, Work, Single, No Children

Well-Being

4.25
4.0
3.75
3.5

Wave   1   2   3   4
Age   18   19/20   21/22   23/24

Figure 13.15. Within wave 2 "not married, no children, work only" group: well-being over time by wave 4 transitions

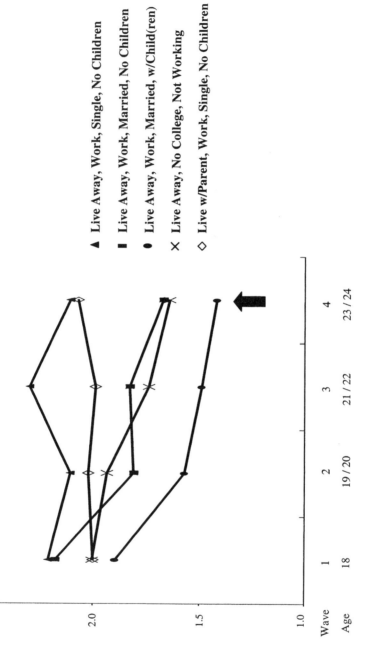

Figure 13.16. Within wave 2 "not married, no children, work only" group: binge drinking over time by wave 4 transitions

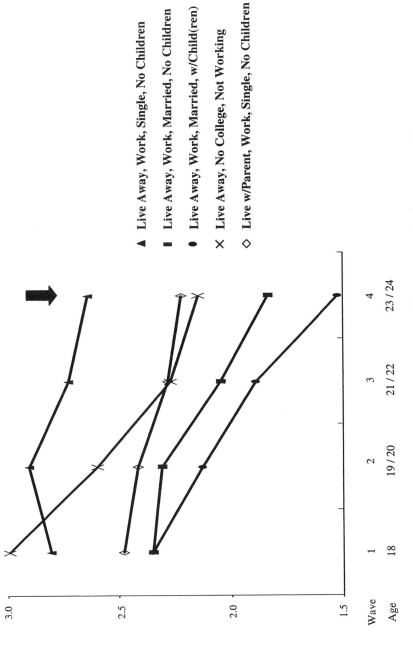

Figure 13.17. Within wave 2 "not married, no children, work only" group: marijuana use over time by wave 4 transitions

Legend:
- ▲ Live Away, Work, Single, No Children
- ■ Live Away, Work, Married, No Children
- ● Live Away, Work, Married, w/Child(ren)
- ✕ Live Away, No College, Not Working
- ◇ Live w/Parent, Work, Single, No Children

Wave	1	2	3	4
Age	18	19/20	21/22	23/24

Marijuana Use

And in the case of substance use, some of these divergences were evident at wave 2 when the groups were homogenous with respect to the various transitions; in particular, in both sets of comparisons, a greater decline in substance use—especially binge drinking—between waves 1 and 2 foreshadowed a greater likelihood of marriage by wave 4. Divergences in well-being trajectories in both sets of comparisons were limited but telling: in the wave 2 "live away, not married, no children, full-time college" group, well-being leveled off between waves 3 and 4 for all subgroups except those who remained at wave 4 in college or graduate school full time and were not working; in the wave 2 "not married, no children, no college, work-only" group, well-being dropped between waves 3 and 4 only for those who at wave 4 were neither working nor attending college and were living away from parents.

DISCUSSION

Before discussing specific findings regarding relations between various transitions and the well-being and substance-use trajectories, it is important to note first that even with the lengthening of the period between adolescence and adulthood (Arnett 2000) and the increased diversity in pathways (Shanahan 2000), our findings suggest that any attempt to understand emerging adulthood would benefit from considering traditional indicators of developmental milestones such as marriage and full-time work. Indeed, given the foreshadowing we found, these milestones represent more than simply external markers. What is especially important about these developmental milestones is how they work together—the fact that out of 240 possible combinations of transitions we were able to place 90% of our sample in one of nine mutually exclusive transition groups suggests a deliberate patterning of transitions (see Cairns and Cairns 1994). Furthermore, while there were some significant gender, cohort, and race/ethnicity differences in transitions and in trajectories of well-being and substance use, interactions with transition groups were in large part nonsignificant, indicating that the links between transition experiences and the trajectories were fairly pervasive and did not vary as a function of gender, cohort, and race/ethnicity (at least in the late twentieth century in the United States).

Trajectories of Well-Being

Looking at the sample as a whole, well-being increased during the first few years out of high school for both men and women (at a faster rate for men) and then began to level off by the midtwenties. This was true regardless of race/ethnicity or cohort. Linking well-being to the number of transitions one makes revealed some rather surprising findings. Although, as with the sample as a whole, well-being increased steadily for each group examined (i.e., those making no, one, two, three, or four or more transitions), those making more transitions had consistently higher well-being. This effect suggests that the mechanisms of stress suggested by focal theory (described previously)—in which the numerous and simultaneous transitions of early adolescence may overwhelm one's coping capacity—are not likely to be operating here. Perhaps the difference here is that, for life after high school, young people have more choice in their transitions and new social roles, thus increasing the match between what they wish to do and available opportunities. While interesting, an exclusive focus on the number of transitions falls short of offering insight into the underlying processes.

In considering the patterning of the transitions, focusing on nine mutually exclusive transition groups based on the social role changes they experienced by wave 2 (ages nineteen to twenty), we again found that well-being increased for all groups. The groups with the highest well-being were those who, at wave 2, had not yet married, had no children, lived away from home, and were attending college, with or without combining work. Those with significantly lower well-being were, at wave 2, single parents, those working without attending college, and those who had yet to make any transition. The nine transition groups tended to maintain their relative ranking in well-being over time (see fig. 13.9). This stability of intergroup differences strongly suggests a selection effect, in which well-being or a correlate of well-being, like academic achievement (Clausen 1991) during the senior year of high school or before, sets the stage for the type/patterning of transitions one plans to take on after high school. Nevertheless, when looking within groups defined at one point in time (our wave 2) to consider how within-group diversity in life paths unfolds over time (our wave 4), we learned that the course of well-being can be somewhat sensitive to the experience of transitions, particularly those related to achievement domains of school and work; such patterns suggest that the course of well-being is not entirely a function of selection effects.

The fact that nearly all transition groups, including the group that did not experience any transitions by wave 2, showed an increase in well-being over time suggests that there is some "niche picking" going on, with young people selecting the transitions or experiences that match best with their developmental needs and desires (Schulenberg and Maggs 2002). More broadly, the increase in well-being for all groups suggests the utility of Baltes's (1987) selection, optimization, and compensation life span development model for understanding how young people successfully negotiate the many changes and demands of emerging adulthood (see also Schulenberg et al., in press; Wiese et al. 2000).

Trajectories of Substance Use

For the group as a whole, substance use (marijuana and alcohol) among men and women tended to peak by the early twenties, although use among men was consistently higher than among women. The level and trajectory of substance use varied by cohort (see Johnston et al. 2003). The earlier cohorts had the highest levels of use, but within cohorts, use declined as the youth aged. Both binge drinking and marijuana use were highest among whites. The trajectory of binge drinking for whites increased and then decreased over time, while for African Americans and the other race-ethnicity groups, the trajectories were flat.

Considering the number of transitions, substance-use trajectories were a bit more varied than well-being trajectories were. Those who, by age nineteen to twenty, had already experienced four or more transitions saw the steepest decline in substance use, suggesting the effect of a combination of transitions, although marriage likely had the strongest effect (Bachman et al. 1997). It is interesting that those who made no transitions by wave 2 (ages nineteen to twenty) had a relatively high and flat trajectory of marijuana use across the waves, suggesting some effects of avoiding the tasks of early adulthood. But again, while interesting, the focus on the number of transitions is unsatisfying in regard to possible processes that connect transitions to trajectories of substance use.

As we found, trajectories of well-being are influenced considerably by the specific patterning of transitions. Certain post–high school contexts or experiences, specifically living away from home and not being married, contribute to a relative increase and delayed decrease in substance use (see Bachman et al. 1997). This provides additional evidence that the emerging adulthood period is a time of experimentation (Arnett 2000) and that once typical adulthood roles are assumed, experimentation tends to be left behind. One could also explain this pattern by means of changed willingness to take risk and/or associated changes in constraining social influences (e.g., presence of parents, fiancé, and/or spouse). Furthermore, declines in substance use appear to foreshadow upcoming transitional experiences that move the individual more firmly into adulthood status. In general, the findings that the course of substance use was more influenced by the transitions than was the course of well-being suggest that while many transitions do indeed serve as turning points, such turning point influences are not necessarily pervasive with respect to multiple indications of functioning and adjustment (Rutter 1996; Schulenberg and Maggs 2002).

Strengths and Limitations

Strengths of this study include the use of U.S. national multicohort panel data spanning the transition to young adulthood; limitations include measure limitations, the restricted set of transitions, and some degree of imprecision in defining transition groups (e.g., we may have missed some important events during the two-year lag between waves). The pattern-centered, interaction-based approach is both a strength and a limitation. Clearly, our "big picture" approach works best in combination with other more fine-grained studies that can provide more of the interesting detail about life's milestones and processes of change during this period of life.

CONCLUSION

The global transition to adulthood can serve as an important proving ground where one's accumulated talents, support, and hopes interact with the new opportunities and challenges of post–high school life. For most young people, the trajectories of functioning and adjustment established throughout childhood and adolescence likely carry into emerging adulthood and work, together with (or against) the pervasive changes that may come with this transition, yielding continuity in overall functioning and adjustment into adulthood. But this transition period can also serve as a turning point for many young people, a time when established trajectories of functioning and adjustment change direction (for better or worse) due in part to the experiences of emerging adulthood. In this study, we found extensive mean level changes in well-being and substance use during emerging adulthood, with considerable differential change in substance use as a function of transition group. We also found considerable continuity in well-being in terms of a general lack of differential change as a function of transition group. The diverse pathways from adolescence to adulthood are rooted in earlier experiences and plans that set the stage for continuity in well-being, but the experiences of the different pathways contribute to discontinuities in substance use.

NOTES

We gratefully acknowledge grant support from the National Institute on Drug Abuse (DA01411), the assistance of Ginny Laetz and Tanya Hart, and the helpful comments of the editors and reviewers.

1. This summary of the findings is based on the following ANOVA results. Among the between-subjects (i.e., ignoring time) main and interaction effects involving gender, race/ethnicity, and cohort, only the gender main effect ($p < .05$) and race/ethnicity main effect ($p < .01$) were significant. In the within-subject effects, the overall time effect was significant ($p < .001$; both linear and quadratic trends were significant, $p < .001$); the time-by-gender interaction was significant ($p < .01$; this interaction was significant for both linear and quadratic trends, $p < .05$); and none of the time-by-cohort or race/ethnicity interactions (two-, three-, and four-way) was significant. Such details are not provided in our other summaries of findings in this chapter, but they are provided in MTF Occasional Paper 56 (Schulenberg et al. 2003b).

REFERENCES

Arnett, Jeffery J. 2000. Emerging Adulthood: A Theory of Development from the Late Teens through the Twenties. *American Psychologist* 55:469–80.

Bachman, Jerald G., Katherine N. Wadsworth, Patrick M. O'Malley, Lloyd D. Johnston, and John E. Schulenberg. 1997. *Smoking, Drinking, and Drug Use in Young Adulthood: The Impact of New Freedoms and New Responsibilities.* Mahwah, NJ: Lawrence Erlbaum Associates.

Baltes, Paul B. 1987. Theoretical Propositions of Life-Span Developmental Psychology: On the Dynamics between Growth and Decline. *Developmental Psychology* 23:611–26.

Brook, Judith S., Linda Richter, Martin Whiteman, and Patricia Cohen. 1999. Consequences of Adolescent Marijuana Use: Incompatibility with the Assumption of Adult Roles. *Genetic, Social, and General Psychology Monographs* 125:193–207.

Cairns, Robert B., and Beverley D. Cairns. 1994. *Lifelines and Risks: Pathways of Youth in Our Time.* New York: Cambridge University Press.

Chassin, Laurie, Clark C. Presson, and Steven J. Sherman. 1989. "Constructive" vs. "Destructive" Deviance in Adolescent Health-Related Behaviors. *Journal of Youth and Adolescence* 18:245–62.

Chen, Kevin, and Denise B. Kandel. 1995. The Natural History of Drug Use from Adolescence to Mid-thirties in a General Population Sample. *American Journal of Public Health* 85:41–47.

Clausen, John A. 1991. Adolescent Competence and the Shaping of the Life Course. *American Journal of Sociology* 96:805–42.

Cohen, Patricia, Stephanie Kasen, Henian Chen, Claudia Hartmark, and Kathy Gordon. 2003. Variations in Patterns of Developmental Transitions in the Emerging Adulthood Period. *Developmental Psychology* 39:657–69.

Coleman, John C. 1989. The Focal Theory of Adolescence: A Psychological Perspective. Pp. 43–56 in *The Social World of Adolescents: International Perspectives*, edited by Klaus Hurrelmann and Uwe Engel. Berlin: Walter de Gruyter.

Elder, Glen H., Jr. 1998. The Life Course and Human Development. Pp. 939–91 in *Handbook of Child Psychology*. Vol. 1, *Theoretical Models of Human Development*, edited by Richard Lerner. New York: Wiley.

Gore, Susan, Robert Aseltine Jr., Mary Ellen Colten, and Bin Lin. 1997. Life after High School: Development, Stress, and Well-being. Pp. 197–214 in *Stress and Adversity over the Life Course: Trajectories and Turning Points*, edited by Ian H. Gotlib. New York: Cambridge University Press.

Graber, Julia A., and Judith Semon Dubas, eds. 1996. *Leaving Home: Understanding the Transition to Adulthood*. San Francisco: Jossey-Bass.

Hawkins, J. David, Richard F. Catalano, and Janet Y. Miller. 1992. Risk and Protective Factors for Alcohol and Other Drug Problems in Adolescence and Early Adulthood: Implications for Substance Abuse Prevention. *Psychological Bulletin* 112:64–105.

Jackson, Kristina M., Kenneth J. Sher, M. Lynn Cooper, and Phillip K. Wood. 2002. Adolescent Alcohol and Tobacco Use: Onset, Persistence and Trajectories of Use across Two Samples. *Addiction* 97:517–31.

Jessor, Richard, John E. Donovan, and Frances M. Costa. 1991. *Beyond Adolescence: Problem Behavior and Young Adult Development*. New York: Cambridge University Press.

Johnston, Lloyd D., and Patrick M. O'Malley. 1985. Issues of Validity and Population Coverage in Student Surveys of Drug Use. Pp. 31–54 in *Self-report Methods of Estimating Drug Use: Meeting Current Challenges to Validity*, edited by Beatrice A. Rouse, Nicholas J. Kozel, and Louise G. Richards. NIDA Research Monograph No. 57. Washington DC: National Institute on Drug Abuse.

Johnston, Lloyd D., Patrick M. O'Malley, and Jerald G. Bachman. 2003. *National Survey Results on Drug Use from the Monitoring the Future Study, 1975–2002*. Vol. 1, *Secondary School Students*. Vol. 2, *College Students and Young Adults*. NIH Publication No. 03–5375 and 03–5376. Bethesda, MD: National Institute on Drug Abuse.

Leonard, Kenneth E., and Julie C. Rothbard. 1999. Alcohol and the Marriage Effect. In "Alcohol and the Family: Opportunities for Prevention." Special Issue, *Journal of Studies on Alcohol* 13:139–46.

Maggs, Jennifer L. 1997. Alcohol Use and Binge Drinking as Goal-Directed Action during the Transition to Post-Secondary Education. Pp. 345–71 in *Health Risks and Developmental Transitions during Adolescence*, edited by John Schulenberg, Jennifer L. Maggs, and Klaus Hurrelmann. New York: Cambridge University Press.

Magnusson, David. 1995. Individual Development: A Holistic, Integrated Model. Pp. 19–60 in *Examining Lives in Context: Perspectives on the Ecology of Human Development,* edited by Phyllis Moen, Glen H. Elder Jr., and Kurt Lüscher. Washington DC: American Psychological Association.

Masten, Ann S., and W. John Curtis. 2000. Integrating Competence and Psychopathology: Pathways toward a Comprehensive Science of Adaptation in Development. *Development and Psychopathology* 12:529–50.

Newcomb, Michael D., and Lisa L. Harlow. 1986. Life Events and Substance Use among Adolescents: Mediating Effects of Perceived Loss of Control and Meaninglessness in Life. *Journal of Personality and Social Psychology* 51: 564–77.

Nowicki, Stephen, and Bonnie R. Strickland. 1973. A Locus of Control Scale for Children. *Journal of Consulting and Clinical Psychology* 40:148–54.

Oerter, Rolf. 1986. Developmental Tasks through the Life Span: A New Approach to an Old Concept. Pp. 233–71 in *Life Span Development and Behavior,* edited by Paul B. Baltes, David L. Featherman, and Richard M. Lerner. Vol. 7. Hillsdale, NJ: Lawrence Erlbaum.

O'Malley, Patrick M., Jerald G. Bachman, and Lloyd D. Johnston. 1983. Reliability and Consistency of Self-reports of Drug Use. *International Journal of the Addictions* 18:805–24.

Rosenberg, Morris. 1965. *Society and the Adolescent Self-image.* Princeton, NJ: Princeton University Press.

Rutter, Michael. 1996. Transitions and Turning Points in Developmental Psychopathology: As Applied to the Age Span between Childhood and Mid-adulthood. *International Journal of Behavioral Development* 19:603–26.

Ryff, Carol D., and Corey Lee M. Keyes. 1995. The Structure of Psychological Well-Being Revisited. *Journal of Personality and Social Psychology* 69:719–27.

Ryff, Carol D., Burton H. Singer, and Marsha Mailick Seltzer. 2002. Pathways through Challenge: Implications for Well-Being and Health. Pp. 302–28 in *Paths to Successful Development: Personality in the Life Course,* edited by Lea Pulkkinen and Avshalom Caspi. Cambridge: Cambridge University Press.

Schulenberg, John E., Alison L. Bryant, and Patrick M. O'Malley. In press. Taking Hold of Some Kind of Life: How Developmental Tasks Relate to Well-Being during the Transition to Adulthood. *Development and Psychopathology.*

Schulenberg, John E., and Jennifer L. Maggs. 2002. A Developmental Perspective on Alcohol Use and Heavy Drinking during Adolescence and the Transition to Young Adulthood. *Journal of Studies on Alcohol,* Suppl. 14:54–70.

Schulenberg, John E., Jennifer L. Maggs, and Patrick M. O'Malley. 2003a. How and Why the Understanding of Developmental Continuity and Discontinuity Is Important: The Sample Case of Long-Term Consequences of Adolescent

Substance Use. Pp. 413–36 in *Handbook of the Life Course,* edited by Jeylan T. Mortimer and Michael J. Shanahan. New York: Plenum Publishers.

Schulenberg, John, Patrick M. O'Malley, Jerald G. Bachman, and Lloyd D. Johnston. 2000. "Spread Your Wings and Fly": The Course of Health and Well-Being during the Transition to Young Adulthood. Pp. 224–55 in *Negotiating Adolescence in Times of Social Change,* edited by Lisa J. Crockett and Rainer K. Silbereisen. New York: Cambridge University Press.

Schulenberg, John E., Patrick M. O'Malley, Jerald G. Bachman, Lloyd D. Johnston, and Virginia B. Laetz. 2003b. How Social Role Transitions from Adolescence to Adulthood Relate to Trajectories of Well-Being and Substance Use. Monitoring the Future Occasional Paper No. 56. Ann Arbor, MI: Institute for Social Research.

Settersten, Richard A., Jr. 2003. Age Structuring and the Rhythm of the Life Course. Pp. 81–98 in *Handbook of the Life Course,* edited by Jeylan T. Mortimer and Michael J. Shanahan. New York: Plenum Publishers.

Shanahan, Michael J. 2000. Pathways to Adulthood in Changing Societies: Variability and Mechanisms in Life Course Perspective. *Annual Review of Sociology* 26:667–92.

Singer, Burton, Carol D. Ryff, Deborah Carr, and William J. Magee. 1998. Linking Life Histories and Mental Health: A Person-Centered Strategy. *Sociological Methodology* 28:1–51.

Wiese, Bettina S., Alexandra M. Freund, and Paul B. Baltes. 2000. Selection, Optimization, and Compensation: An Action-Related Approach to Work and Partnership. *Journal of Vocational Behavior* 57:273–300.

CHAPTER 14

THE EVER-WINDING PATH

Ethnic and Racial Diversity
in the Transition to Adulthood

JOHN MOLLENKOPF, MARY C. WATERS, JENNIFER HOLDAWAY,
AND PHILIP KASINITZ

The rapid pace of immigration over the past four decades has led to one out of every ten people living in the United States being foreign born, with another one in ten having an immigrant parent. These first and second-generation immigrants have settled mainly in the largest central cities of the most populous states. The two biggest metropolitan areas, New York and Los Angeles, account for almost one-third of the nation's foreign-born residents. Immigrants and their children are now a majority of their populations, further diversifying their already complicated racial and ethnic make-up and altering the social dynamics of their neighborhoods, schools, and public spaces.

This trend has evoked intense debate about whether renewed mass migration has helped or hurt the national economy, the cost of providing public services, the prospects of native minorities in the labor market, the integrity of our civic culture, and even the security of our country (Borjas 1990; 1999; Massey, Durand, and Malone 2002; Smith and Edmonston 1997). It also poses the question of how the rising number of immigrants and their children may be affecting the ways in which young people—whether immigrants, children of immigrants, or children of native-born parents—may be making the transition into young adulthood.

Has the new social context in which many young people are now growing up changed their paths into adulthood? Are young people from new immigrant backgrounds following in the same paths as their native-born counterparts, or different ones? Are they having a harder or easier time than youngsters with native parents? How much difference does racial or ethnic minority status make for them? Does the second generation enjoy special advantages (the hypothesized benefits of the ethnic enclave), face added challenges (learning a new culture, bridging the gap between two cultures), or both? And how has the growing prevalence of first- and second-generation immigrant peers changed things for young people with native-born parents? Indeed, what consequences does immigration have for the entire cohort?

Many of those with native-born and immigrant parents certainly encounter diverse peer groups as they leave school, enter the job market, form relationships, and make decisions about having children. Those with immigrant parents are suspended between the "old country" ways of their parents and the American subcultures in which they are growing up. This may produce tensions over differing values and expectations about work, family, and the meaning of success. Immigrant parents may have more traditional and restrictive notions about their children's behavior than do native parents, but they may also work long hours, have little familiarity with American mores and institutions, and thus have difficulty guiding their children. This may accelerate the second generation's transition to adulthood, because they often take on roles that parents perform in native families, but it may also retard aspects of the transition because parental strictures are strong compared to the freedoms granted to native-born youngsters. For their part, children of native parents may feel superior in some respects to their second-generation peers, but they may also be compared adversely to members of "model minority groups."

Given that the children born to the first immigrants entering the United States after the liberalization of immigration law in 1965 are now entering their midthirties, we are in a unique position to begin to answer such questions. The new second generation is a large and pivotal cohort, constituting 15.7% of all Americans under the age of thirty-six and 38.9% of those in New York City.[1] To take advantage of the opportunity to observe their entry into adulthood, we conducted the first large random sample survey of this group in a major metropolitan area.[2] Our study, which is specific to New York, includes people whose parents migrated from the Caribbean, Latin America, and Asia; we compare them to people with native white, black, and Puerto Rican parents, thus introducing a critical but often missing control factor. Consequently, we can examine how those with immigrant parents negotiate this critical stage of the life course in comparison with children of native parents with the same race, ethnicity, and gender.

Put bluntly, some scholars worry that the new second generation will not be able to continue in the path of upward mobility sought though not always achieved by their parents (Alba and Nee 2003, 230–48) but, instead, will have the vicissitudes of urban life press them—or at least those among them who are likely to be classified alongside native blacks—down into a newly multicultural ghetto poor (Gans 1992; Portes and Zhou 1993). For the children of native parents, the parallel question is how growing up among second-generation peers has affected their options and choices.

Context probably counts. We can distinguish three broad kinds of metropolitan settings in America: immigrant-receiving gateway cities like Los Angeles or Miami, declining old heartland industrial cities like Detroit or St. Louis, and rapidly growing high technology and corporate service cities like Austin, Texas, or Charlotte, North Carolina. New York clearly typifies the first category. While its black/white dichotomy is not as sharp as in Detroit, it still contains substantial African American and Puerto Rican populations, unlike such gateway cities as Boston or Seattle. It has also attracted immigrants from across the globe, including the Caribbean, Latin America, and South and East Asia, and no one national origin group makes up more than one-sixth of the immigrant population. This makes it an interesting contrast to Los Angeles and Miami, where Mexican Americans and Cuban Americans are predominant.

New York has long been connected with both the Spanish-speaking and Anglophone Caribbean. Puerto Ricans began arriving in the 1950s, followed by Dominicans and people from the Anglophone and Francophone Caribbean in the 1970s and 1980s (Kasinitz 1992). It has also attracted recent cohorts of Russian Jewish and Chinese migrants, propelled by political changes in those two countries. (The Russian Jewish parents arrived with refugee status and government assistance, while the other groups arrived largely as economic migrants.)

Our study compares young people whose parents came from the Dominican Republic and the South American countries of Colombia, Ecuador, or Peru (subsequently designated as CEP) with those whose parents were native-born Puerto Ricans. (Though many of the Puerto Rican parents were born on the island, they mostly arrived in New York themselves as youngsters, and are, of course, American citizens.) We also compare those with parents from the Anglophone Caribbean to those with native African American parents. Because of the importance of the Chinese in New York's rapidly growing Asian population, we talked to young people whose parents came from China, Taiwan, Hong Kong, and the Chinese diaspora. Finally, we compared those whose parents came from Russia with native whites, who serve as a comparison group for all the others. Our white respondents reflect the ethnic background of New York City: they are Catholics, Jews, and some white Protestants.

This rich mixture of backgrounds permits us not only to compare young people from immigrant and native backgrounds but to make these comparisons within specific ethnic and racial categories—for example, Dominicans and South Americans compared to Puerto Ricans, West Indians compared to native blacks, and Russian Jews compared to native whites. We can also compare Chinese second-generation people whose parents came from mainland China to those whose parents came from Taiwan, Hong Kong, and the Chinese diaspora. These populations give us a unique vantage point for observing the transition to young adulthood.

PATHS TO YOUNG ADULTHOOD AMONG THE SECOND GENERATION

From the fall of 1998 through the summer of 1999, we conducted telephone interviews with a random sample of 3,424 people aged eighteen to thirty-two from the eight different backgrounds described above. We interviewed roughly 400 of the Dominicans, CEPs, Puerto Ricans, native blacks, and native whites, as well as about 600 Chinese, and about 300 Russian Jews.[3] They live in New York City (not including Staten Island) and the inner suburban counties of Long Island, upstate New York, and northeastern New Jersey. Between 1999 and 2001, we followed up with 364 in-person, open-ended interviews from among the original telephone respondents. These interviews provided qualitative information on the topics raised in the telephone survey, as well as some more sensitive issues, like drug use, that it could not address. We chose the in-depth respondents partly on their willingness to participate and partly to learn about those who were particularly upwardly or downwardly mobile. Finally, six ethnographers spent the 1999–2000 academic year studying sites where native and second-generation young people interact.[4]

To appreciate how our respondents make the transition to adulthood, we must begin with an idea of who they are and where they started. Table 14.1 shows how our study groups are distributed by gender, age, where they grew up, where they live now, and how many of their parents lack college education. The Dominican, Puerto Rican, and native black respondents include more females, while the other groups are more evenly divided, reflecting both the actual prevalence of females in these minority popula-

TABLE 14.1

SAMPLE CHARACTERISTICS (ALL RESPONDENTS)

GROUP	n	FEMALE (%)	MEAN AGE	GREW UP OUTSIDE NEW YORK METRO AREA (%)	GREW UP IN NEW YORK SUBURBS (%)	LIVE IN NEW YORK CITY (%)	NO PARENT HAS B.A. (%)
CEP	410	48.3	24.0	4.9	11.5	87.3	67.3
Dominican	424	59.7	23.7	1.2	7.1	92.7	84.4
Puerto Rican	428	59.3	24.2	4.9	7.9	90.9	84.8
West Indian	404	53.0	23.4	2.7	6.2	93.6	70.3
Black	422	61.4	25.5	8.3	11.8	87.9	74.2
Chinese	607	46.3	22.5	6.8	4.3	96.9	77.1
Russian	310	49.7	22.6	5.2	4.2	100.0	28.7
White	409	54.5	25.8	36.9	22.0	87.0	41.3

Note. "CEP" stands for Colombia, Ecuador, or Peru.

tions and the difficulty of interviewing young minority males. Native blacks and whites are older, while the Russians and Chinese are the youngest, reflecting their actual age distribution in the overall population. In contrast to the other groups, a third of our native white respondents and 8% of the native blacks grew up outside metropolitan New York, mostly moving to the city as well-educated young adults pursuing their careers. The native-born groups are all more likely to have grown up in the suburbs, including a third of the native whites, 8% of native blacks, and 5% of the Puerto Ricans. Almost all of our second-generation respondents—except the CEPs—grew up in the city. (South American immigrants have clustered in Hudson and Passaic Counties in New Jersey, which are counted here as suburbs of New York City.) More than nine-tenths of our second-generation respondents attended high school in the study area. Most now live in the city itself, though many CEPs, native blacks, and native whites live in the nearest New York and New Jersey suburbs. Finally, we can see that the parents of our white and Russian respondents are much better-educated than any of the other groups, with the black and West Indian parents being somewhat more educated than the Chinese or the Hispanic groups except for the CEP.

The main objective of our study was to understand the contemporary dynamics of assimilation. Even though our respondents are young, we can see the outlines of their likely future trajectories in their experiences. Our data give a particularly good sense of how far these young people have progressed in their education, but our conclusions about their career outcomes must remain tentative. We certainly found great variation in how these different groups of young people time and sequence the key decisions they make in entering young adulthood, such as getting married, having children, getting a job, and moving outside their parents' homes. Perhaps the most consequential decision is to have a child. Although some of our respondents have made major decisions—for example, by having children—most have not. Given that they were between eighteen and thirty-two when we interviewed them (and twenty-three was the median age), most are still too young to have settled on a definitive trajectory. Yet even at this age, we can see some fascinating and important differences in their transitions. In this chapter, we examine differences across groups in the timing and sequencing of educational attainment, marriage and partnering, childbearing, and work and reflect on why these differences may have come about.

Our groups of respondents have particularly evident patterns of attending and leaving school. To understand why this might be so, we examine not only the education levels of our respondents but those of their parents as well. One rough way to characterize levels of education is to identify the median levels of achievement for both children and their parents. The median for the parents was having no education beyond a high school diploma.[5] The median for the children, our respondents, is a little higher—having a high school diploma as well as having some college experience, but no degree of any sort, whether AA or BA, and with no more than two years of college. By classifying children's experience—above or below the median—with that of their parents, we can generate a fourfold set of trajectories: (1) respondents with relatively well-educated parents who also achieved more than the median (i.e., at least an AA degree, three or more years of college, or a BA); (2) respondents from families with below-median educations who, blocked by negative experiences, also remained below the educational median; (3) respondents with poorly educated parents who nonetheless did better than the median; and (4) respondents with better-educated parents who succumbed to difficulties and failed to reach the median. Table 14.2 shows how the older members of our various groups—those aged twenty-two to thirty-two—break down across this typology.

Our respondents largely perform as expected: they tend to replicate the educational status attained by their parents. Most respondents from modestly educated families have not gotten college educations, while most of those from better-educated families have gone to college. Table 14.2 shows that most of our Hispanic respondents are clustered in the category of those who have poorly educated parents and who have not themselves gone far in

TABLE 14.2

RESPONDENT'S EDUCATION BY PARENTS' EDUCATION (RESPONDENTS AGED 22–32)

	P LOW		*P* HIGH		
	R LOW (%)	*R* HIGH (%)	*R* LOW (%)	*R* HIGH (%)	TOTAL
CEP	42.1	18.0	17.6	22.2	261
Dominican	46.9	20.4	18.0	14.7	245
Puerto Rican	52.7	14.5	21.0	11.8	262
West Indian	27.1	13.6	31.3	28.0	214
Native black	39.5	8.6	32.9	18.9	301
Chinese	14.8	47.7	5.6	31.9	304
Russian	5.7	9.5	18.4	66.5	158
Native white	16.0	9.4	11.8	62.8	331
Total	31.2	18.4	19.1	31.4	2,076

Note. P = parent; *R* = respondent. "CEP" stands for Colombia, Ecuador, or Peru.

college, ranging from 42.1% to 52.7% of these groups. As one might expect, the native white and Russian second-generation respondents are clustered in the opposite category, those with better-educated parents who are themselves making good progress in college, with 62.8% of native whites and 66.5% of Russians falling into this category. The black groups are in between, with the West Indians having slightly stronger educational profiles. But we can also see from table 14.2 that some of our groups are following trajectories that differ from what we might expect based on the experiences of their parents.

Consider members of groups that have either unexpected upward or downward mobility in table 14.2. To highlight these paths, we look at them separately in tables 14.3 and 14.4. The first shows how many respondents with less well educated parents have gotten a BA or are in the process of getting one. Quite strikingly, the two native minority groups, blacks and Puerto Ricans, show the lowest rate of college attendance, while the Russians and Chinese show the highest rates and all the other groups are clustered in between, with the CEP at the low end. Remarkably, all the immigrant minority groups are twice as likely as the native minority groups to have college experience. College attendance among the Chinese is particularly notable because so many of their parents are poorly educated; college attendance among Russians with poorly educated parents is less surprising because most parents of our Russian respondents are better educated, and thus group membership will influence them in this direction.

TABLE 14.3

UPWARD MOBILITY AMONG RESPONDENTS WITH LOW-
EDUCATION PARENTS (RESPONDENTS AGED 22−32)

	NO BA/NOT ENROLLED (%)	BA/ENROLLED FOR BA (%)	TOTAL
CEP	70.1	29.9	157
Dominican	69.4	30.3	165
Puerto Rican	78.4	21.6	176
West Indian	66.7	33.3	87
Native black	82.1	17.9	145
Chinese	24.1	75.9	191
Russian	40.0	60.0	25
Native white	63.1	36.9	84
Total	63.0	37.0	1,030

Note. "CEP" stands for Colombia, Ecuador, or Peru.

TABLE 14.4

DOWNWARD MOBILITY AMONG RESPONDENTS WITH
HIGH-EDUCATION PARENTS (RESPONDENTS AGED 22−32)

	NO BA/NOT ENROLLED (%)	BA/ENROLLED FOR BA (%)	TOTAL
CEP	44.2	55.8	104
Dominican	55.0	45.0	80
Puerto Rican	64.0	36.0	86
West Indian	52.8	47.2	127
Native black	63.5	36.5	156
Chinese	14.9	85.1	114
Russian	21.6	78.4	134
Native white	15.8	84.2	247
Total	37.8	62.2	1,048

Note. "CEP" stands for Colombia, Ecuador, or Peru.

Table 14.4 highlights those who have better-educated parents but have not gotten, or are not getting, a college degree even at age twenty-two or older. Native blacks and Puerto Ricans also stand out in this table as having the highest rates of not going to college, with their second-generation peers, the West Indians and Dominicans following their pattern. In contrast, Chinese and Russian respondents, like white respondents, have the least likelihood of not getting a college degree. Put another way, they are twice as likely to capitalize on their parents' higher educational status as the native and immigrant blacks and Hispanics, though the CEPs are significantly closer in experience to the whites and Chinese than the other groups are.

We can draw several conclusions from these tables. Most obviously, groups mostly follow the educational trajectories set by their parents. This may reflect not only the influence of individual parents on their children but also the higher expectations that parents as a group may exert on their children as a group. The opposite is most likely also true: young people are least likely to complete a college education when their own parents are not well educated and when the collective experience of the parents is one of lower educational levels. Here, too, parental status has an individual and collective negative impact on how far their children will go. This pattern has been well established by many other studies and is confirmed by other chapters in this book (Osgood et al., this vol., chap. 10; Sandefur, Eggerling-Boeck, and Park, this vol., chap. 9).

But this evidence highlights several important departures from the well-known generalization that it is beneficial to have affluent and well-educated parents. In particular, the Chinese stand out as both making strong educational careers with very little parental advantage and capitalizing on parental education when it is present. Our Chinese second-generation respondents were much more likely to get a college education than any other group with relatively poorly educated parents. Conversely, the two native minority groups are doing significantly less well than their parental levels of education might predict. The parents of our African American respondents are better educated than any of the Hispanic immigrant parents or Chinese, yet African Americans with better-educated parents are much less likely to go to a four-year college and those with poorly educated parents have especially low rates of college attendance. Although the parents of our Puerto Rican respondents are not as well educated as those of the African Americans, they are still better-educated than the Chinese parents and yet only one out of five Puerto Ricans with poorly educated parents and roughly one out of three of those with better-educated parents goes to a four-year college. (West Indians, Dominicans, and the South Americans face similar challenges to their native-born counterparts but show significantly more educational upward mobility.)

Clearly, something about the Chinese situation enables them to surmount barriers to going to college, despite their parents' lowly education, that is absent for native blacks and Puerto Ricans. Conversely, something about the black and Puerto Rican situations, and to a lesser extent the West

TABLE 14.5

EDUCATIONAL STATUS BY GROUP (RESPONDENTS AGED 22–32)

	NO HIGH SCHOOL DIPLOMA (%)	HIGH SCHOOL DIPLOMA/NO BA (%)	BA OR ENROLLED (%)	TOTAL
CEP	10.6	51.1	38.3	274
Dominican	18.6	48.5	33.0	264
Puerto Rican	23.4	52.1	24.5	282
West Indian	9.3	50.8	39.8	236
Native black	17.3	56.3	26.3	323
Chinese	1.5	21.2	77.3	326
Russian	2.5	23.3	74.2	163
Native white	5.4	23.3	71.3	335
Total	11.3	40.9	47.8	2,203

Note. "CEP" stands for Colombia, Ecuador, or Peru.

Indian and Dominican situations, not only erects an especially difficult barrier to progressing to college but actually works against them when they do have some parental advantage. Do blacks and Puerto Ricans face obstacles that Chinese youngsters do not, despite the fact that all their parents have relatively low individual and group levels of education? Or do these groups employ different strategies or have different resources for surmounting the same kinds of barriers? We return to this question below.

Will youngsters who have not yet made it into college at age twenty-two manage to do so in the coming years? We can get some evidence related to this by looking at enrollment rates for our older respondents, shown in table 14.5. Three-quarters of our white, Russian, and Chinese respondents in this age group already have a BA or are enrolled in a bachelor's degree program, suggesting that the whites and Russians will continue to build on their parents' relatively good educations, while the Chinese will maintain their upward momentum from a low starting point.

While Hispanics as a group have low rates of parental education, the Colombians, Ecuadorians, and Peruvians give every indication of going the farthest among them since they have higher parental education than Dominicans or Puerto Ricans do, they have lower high school–dropout rates, and more have completed or are enrolled in a baccalaureate program. Though they are positioned similarly to the West Indians, only two in five end up in the college degree/degree-seeking group. The situation of Puerto

Rican youngsters once again looks particularly bleak, with high dropout rates and low college attainment. It seems unlikely that they will make up the education gap in their later years, nor will native blacks close much of the gap, though they will make some progress. None of the immigrant minority groups seem likely to catch up with the trajectories of whites, Russians, or Chinese, but they definitely have higher enrollments and better prospects than do the native minority groups. Future behavior may thus soften the hard edges of table 14.2 but seems unlikely to change its basic patterns.

TRAJECTORIES INTO ADULTHOOD

What is the subjective interpretation of these experiences with the school system? Our in-depth interviews provide rich detail on the lived experience of our respondents as they enter adulthood, illuminate the barriers they face, and help us understanding whether they can overcome these barriers. One respondent, Vanessa, is a well-educated young adult from a well-educated family. An African American woman, Vanessa is currently getting her second graduate degree in biochemistry. Her father, a lawyer for the government, and her mother, a social worker, lived in middle-class white neighborhoods when Vanessa was growing up, and she went to predominantly white schools and a predominantly white college. Her parents always stressed that it was important for her to get a good education and her high school teachers expected everyone to graduate and go to college. At the same time, Vanessa often found it difficult to be one of the few black people in a white setting, particularly when her teachers stereotyped blacks as poor performers, as they frequently did in her high school, located in the South.

Vanessa said she "very easily could have been the little underachiever that I was for the first thirteen, fourteen years of life, an ego-flako headed for drugland." But she developed a strong interest in music and later in science and pursuing these subjects avidly helped her to block out negative signals from her teachers or peers and prove that they had wrongly stereotyped her. She went to a good, science-oriented college, then to a top law school. Her goal is to practice patent law for the pharmaceutical industry.

At the other end of the intergenerational mobility spectrum are people with poorly educated parents who also do not get much education. Tom's parents were only high school graduates and he grew up in a white working-class neighborhood of the Bronx. His mother, an Italian American, worked several jobs after divorcing his alcoholic father. By working two jobs, she was able to put Tom and his brothers and sisters into a Catholic grade school, but she could not afford a Catholic high school for them. Tom attended a multiethnic public high school. He was held back several times in grade school during the time his parents were divorcing and subsequently dropped out of high school after attending for only a year. Later, after getting a GED, he tried to enter a community college but found that it did not hold much attraction compared to the well-paying jobs he got in a printing factory, tending bar, and working construction. Access to a job in a unionized industry shields him from economic insecurity and makes college less meaningful.

Our educationally downwardly mobile respondents generally had fallen victim to the dangers of urban life—or were born to parents who had succumbed to them. Sean, a twenty-four-year-old African American, never knew his father. His mother had a college education, but she began using drugs heavily when he was small. By the time he was an adolescent, he was using and dealing drugs and living in and out of shelters. He had begun dealing drugs in order to support his mother. Arrested several times, he dropped out of school in the tenth grade. Life continues to be a struggle for Sean. Another example of downward mobility is Andrew, a twenty-six-year-old child of immigrant parents from Trinidad. His dad had studied at the University of the West Indies, had worked as a real estate agent and an airline shipping clerk in New York City, and had recently retired. His mother, a high school graduate, worked off and on as a nurse's aide. They split up when Andrew was a teenager, and his mother moved to Florida, while his father headed back to Trinidad. Left behind with an older sister, Andrew went to his neighborhood public high school in Brooklyn, a tough inner-city institution, ended up cutting a lot of classes, and never got his diploma. After getting a GED, he tried a City University of New York (CUNY) college serving the West Indian neighborhoods of Brooklyn but once more dropped out at the end of his first year. Even though his parents stressed the importance of education, he had more fun hanging out with his girlfriends. He fathered a son with one girl but sees him only about once a month. Presently, he is driving for a trucking company. His life is much better than Sean's, but, at twenty-six, he is not likely to achieve his dream of going to a four-year college and becoming a lawyer.

Many of these young people had nowhere to go but up from the poor education levels of their parents. But they, too, faced the dangers of drugs, the lure of the streets, and the lack of family resources that might help them overcome such challenges. George, for example, is the son of two Ecuadorian immigrants, neither of whom had more than a few years of grade school. In New York, his father got a steady job as a meatpacker, while his mother was a seamstress. Like many other parents, they stressed education as the key to success in America. George went to local public schools and did well but got into drugs as a teenager and dropped out. His parents had enough money to set him up in a video business upstate, but his drug problem persisted, and he was arrested. This experience led to a drug rehabilitation and enrollment in a four-year college, where he is now getting along and is, at least for the time being, clean.

Sophia, a twenty-four-year-old woman whose mother was from Barbados, presents a more clear-cut picture of upward mobility. Like Sean, she faced many tough situations growing up in Brooklyn, where drug use was common among the kids in her neighborhood. At seventeen, she was hit by a stray bullet from a shoot-out between drug dealers down the street from her home. Her mother, who had fled family trouble in Barbados as a teenager, arriving in Brooklyn when Sophia was only two, attended community college in Manhattan, became a nurse's aide, and held two jobs for many years in order to support her children. Sophia grew up with her mother, grandmother, and a much younger half-sister. Even though she grew up in a female-headed household, lived in a tough neighborhood, and had been shot, Sophia stayed away from drugs and focused on her schoolwork. Her mother told Sophia, "You're not going to be an idiot. I'm not going to raise no fools. You come out of this house; you're going to be smart. You're going to thank me later." Sophia's reaction was "I do [thank her], because she stuck on me. She might not have understood a lot of the work that I was doing but she made sure that I did it." Clearly, having a committed and vigilant mother helped Sophia get an education. Though Sophia had a child as a teenager and was abandoned by the child's father, she persevered in her education. She did well in gifted and talented classes in elementary school, got through high school on time, and graduated from Long Island University. Now working full time, she aspires to get a master's degree in social work from a nearby university, something that seems well within her reach.

SUBJECTIVE UNDERSTANDING OF SUCCESS

So far, we have discussed how our respondents have negotiated the most important institution in their adolescent lives—the educational system. But how do they understand this experience? How do they define a good outcome? What role do they think education plays in determining overall success? We asked our respondents: "How would you define success for someone your age?" "Did your parents ever give you advice about how to be successful in life?" "What would you like to be doing in ten years?" We also asked what each respondent thought about education: "Some people say education will help you find a good job. Others say that whether you have a high school diploma or college degree it does not matter much these days. What do you think?"

Our respondents use very different frameworks to judge their own situations, they have different goals for themselves, and they have different priorities for reaching those goals. Their answers reflect their different class origins as well as the collective experiences of their group in New York and of their parents in their countries of origin. The Chinese respondents, for example, evaluated their circumstances based on occupation, money, education, discrimination, and knowledge of future goals. Not one Chinese respondent mentioned having friends, just meeting basic needs, or having money at the end of your pay period as examples of success, answers that were common among African Americans. Nor did any Chinese person express the opinion sometimes heard from other groups that education might not lead to success. Despite their positive approach to achievement, the Chinese respondents were the most likely to mention discrimination. They said their parents made a point of telling them that they should expect to encounter discrimination but should not let it keep them from being successful. However, they did think that they would have to try harder than a white person would to be successful in the United States.

> Interviewer: How would you define success for somebody your age?
> Respondent: In what way? Economically?
> Interviewer: Just take your pick, what do you think for a person like you?
> Respondent: Well, you have to look at successful business people like in the headlines like people dealing with computers, people by the age of thirty to thirty-five are multibillionaires. You really small compared to what they achieved by the time you were that age. Maybe it's too unrealistic but it causes you to think that I'm over thirty and I'm a failure. Because you have the media that blares out these headlines about how successful they are. How much money they have and how old are they. It does drive you down in a small way. Personally, I wish I were that successful. I wish I was that motivated. I wish a lot of things by that time but what can you do? Sometimes some things work out for them, sometimes it doesn't. In my case, it doesn't.
> (*thirty-one-year-old Chinese male*)

African Americans, by contrast, commonly mentioned education, money, fun, material goods, stability, discrimination, and being the boss as signs of success. A few defined success as just being alive or avoiding trouble. Many said their parents pushed education and considered themselves successful because of their education, but a considerable number also doubted whether education led to success. Several reported knowing of highly successful people with poor educations and highly educated people who were having very hard times (e.g., CEOs who were high school dropouts and homeless people with PhDs, respectively). A number of African Americans mentioned "having their own business" and "wanting to be their own boss." This theme appears to cut across class lines and is pronounced in this group, despite the fact that their parents have the lowest rates of self-employment among the groups in our study. For this group autonomy, rather than economic benefits, seems to make self-employment attractive. Consider, for instance, the twenty-seven-year-old African American male in the interview excerpt that follows.

> Interviewer: How would you define success for someone your age?
>
> Respondent: Now? Their own business. That's the only thing I can see. One of my friends will come home soon 'cause he got some money put away and I wish I had some money and I'm waiting for the State [to pay what] they owe me. Open a barber shop or something. That's the only thing I can see. I mean, I'm for real. I'm being honest. If I had money, I would be in the Laundromat. Put my money into it. That's the only thing I can see, some kind of your own business. Not the drug business.
>
> Interviewer: Some people say education will help you find a good job. Others say that whether you have a high school diploma or college degree it doesn't matter much these days. What do you think?
>
> Respondent: I say 50/50, man. 'Cause I have a lot of friends that have a college education now and they got shit. They try. They got a nice little degree and some of them ain't got nothing, some of them do. That's why I can't say yes to that question. I would say yes and no. Some do, some don't.

Neither the Chinese respondents nor the African Americans ever mentioned having children and only one mentioned being married (because her mother was concerned about it) as milestones of success. Yet respondents whose parents came from Colombia, Ecuador, and Peru frequently mentioned these topics and often linked them to stability, which was one of the other common themes for this group, as well as education and material goods. As a group, they reported mixed attitudes toward education; many said their parents wanted them to finish high school, but fewer talked about college. They talked about having a trade, getting a "good job," and, most of all, stability.

Interviewer: How would you define success for someone your age?

Respondent: Probably somebody who has a nice stable job, that's not hopping around from job to job. Who, at this point, is either close to being settled down as far as marriage and family. Probably, by now, at almost twenty nine, I'd say to probably have children by this point.

Interviewer: Do you think school has to be part of that?

Respondent: No. I don't think so. I think that the opportunities are out there in a lot of different companies, but it depends on what you do. . . . You just got to know the right people and do the right things while you're there. Be confident and do your best and you can get ahead very far.

(twenty-eight-year-old CEP female)

Dominicans frequently reported concerns with discrimination, education not mattering, avoiding trouble, being the boss, knowing your goals, and occupation. Avoiding trouble was a large part of how they talk about success, as was getting out of New York. They reported even more ambivalence about education than African Americans.

Interviewer: How would you define success for someone your age?

Respondent: Being able to say that you're alive.

Interviewer: Why do you say that?

Respondent: Look at the news, you know. Look at the newspaper. You don't hear about too many twenty five-, twenty-six-year-old males—Hispanic, African American, you know—doing anything with their lives other than dying or going to jail, so you know.

Interviewer: Some people say that education helps you find a job. Other people say that whether you have a high school diploma or a college degree doesn't matter much. What do you think?

Respondent: It doesn't. It doesn't at all. I don't think education has a thing to do with success.

Interviewer: Tell me why?

Respondent: I think education, being educated is a condition, you know. I think that your own success comes through your own determination and your own will to be successful. You know, I know college graduates that are drug dealers.

Interviewer: Why do you think they're doing that?

Respondent: Because they can't get jobs!

(twenty-five-year-old Dominican male)

Puerto Ricans also mentioned that education does not matter and focused on being the boss and not being dependent. They were not sure education is the right route to success, telling many stories about highly educated people who were not successful. They used the idea of family to refer
to an extended family, not just a spouse. As one twenty-six-year-old put it:

> How would I define success? I don't know; I don't know if I'm there
> yet. For me it's like being able to own your own home, having re-
> sponsibilities that you know you can handle, having a good family
> support, maybe a girlfriend or wife who I can always have somebody
> stand by me. Where I'm happy.

Among Russian Jews, the most common themes were money, occupation, discrimination, education, and being aggressive. They were distinct in thinking that "being aggressive" was a good way to become successful. While the Chinese said that their parents told them all the time that education was the key to success, the Russian Jews almost could not understand the question. They took it completely for granted that they would
proceed through school to an advanced degree. Interestingly, Russian Jews
included the only respondents who felt that success might be due to good
luck. When asked about discrimination, they said their parents told them
how much they experienced in Russia, but that they were not subject to it
here in the United States. Starting a family was also important to our Russian respondents.

> Interviewer: Did your mother or father give you advice about how to
> be successful?
> Respondent: Sure. They wanted me to go to college, finish college,
> and get a nice job.
> Interviewer: Did they encourage you to pursue a particular major or
> career?
> Respondent: Of course every Jewish person wants you to be a doctor,
> if you're very smart. If you're not so smart, maybe a lawyer. If you're real
> stupid, then an accountant. That is what I would teach my son. Go to
> college, get your degree and if you want to sweep the streets, that's fine,
> but you got to get a degree. Even when you get a degree, 90% of the
> time, you're going to pursue a better life. Nobody spends four or five
> years in college and then does nothing.
> (*thirty-two-year-old Russian Jewish male*)

Interviewer: How do you define success for someone your age?

Respondent: Should be already at least a college graduate, living independent from their parents, either married or relationship, starting a family and stuff, with their own career already at this point. I would think they would be successful.

(*twenty-seven-year-old Russian Jewish female*)

The most common themes for West Indians were discrimination, education not mattering, getting into a good occupation, being happy, being alive, avoiding or getting out of trouble, and being the boss. This group was the most likely spontaneously to mention conflict with parents over what it meant to be successful, with people talking about how their parents were pushing them to succeed. Showing ambivalence about her chances, a twenty-three-year-old West Indian female responded,

Respondent: Success would be if I had a father that worked in a big corporation that would pull strings for me to get a good job.

Interviewer: That's how you would define success for someone your age?

Respondent: Opportunities for success. That's how to define it. I mean what the hell is success anyway. When you get to whatever you think you're successful, it's probably not going to be fulfilling to you emotionally. I don't even know if I know the answer to that question.

Another West Indian woman expressed skepticism about the value of education.

Respondent: I think [education] matters but you have to have more than a college degree to get a good job now. You have to be super smart and even if you're super smart, which I'm super smart now in this industry, would be if you're a computer whiz, that would be, you know. There's no guarantee that if you have a college degree that you're going to get a good job. Because I know people with a college degree and I remember I saw this girl. I saw her a couple of days ago and she just graduated from Brooklyn College and she was working at Macy's as a cashier. So I know. And my son's father, his sister graduated from school and she still hasn't gotten a good job yet. She's still working in school and she graduated from school. But I mean, I know you have to know where the opportunities are. Like for a long time I looked for a job in the newspaper. You have to go to an employment agency. That's the only way. And they're so racist there too.

This twenty-eight-year-old West Indian male expressed another perspective.

> Interviewer: How would you define success for someone your age?
> Respondent: Be alive. Not in jail. I can't say that, I know some—a lot of—guys who've got criminal records, come out and doing better than me right now. Just being alive. Just being able to look back. Just knowing what you want and not being on drugs or sick or something like that . . . Just because you've got a PhD don't mean you know nothin' about life. I know guys who got all this college education. They don't know the first thing about if you was to drop them in the middle of Manhattan, they would not have enough common sense to know how to get from point *A* to point *B*. So what's a piece of paper?

Native whites showed great concern for being the boss, having money, an education, and an occupation, setting future goals, and getting married and having a family. Native whites were also the only ones to mention concern for inner goals, such as being happy, being a good person, and making the world a better place. Whites expressed concern that success should not be defined through material goods, which a number of them saw as being shallow.

> Interviewer: How would you define success for somebody your age?
> Respondent: My age, I would say you have a solid foundation as far as education goes. You have a good job that you're well into, that you're comfortable with, you're settled in. That you have a good personal life, you have good home social life and all that. I would not necessarily say that we're all, in my age I mean, married and have family and all that, but a good personal and professional life.
> Interviewer: It would be the priority at this age?
> Respondent: Yes, I would say so.
> (*twenty-five-year-old white male*)

THE IMPACT OF FAMILY, NEIGHBORHOOD CONTEXT, AND PARENTING CHOICES ON EDUCATIONAL ACHIEVEMENT

As we've just seen parental level of education had a strong impact on how far our respondents went through the educational system, though this was not dispositive for every group. One of the major factors that influenced their progress was whether they had children themselves. This in turn was dependent on the kinds of families in which they had grown up and the ways family dynamics shaped their thinking about being a parent. Moreover, their families of origin provided a matrix of assets and deficits for helping them manage and respond to the risks of childhood and young adulthood.

Family background cannot be summed up in one simple, static characteristic, such as household income or number of parents present. Our respondents came from many different kinds of families, the dynamics of which shifted over time. Some had two working parents and an extended kin network, while others had a single mother on welfare and did not know their father. Some parents worked in ethnic niches in the labor market, such as Chinese fathers working in restaurants or Dominican mothers working in the garment industry, while others worked in the mainstream economy. Class positions varied a great deal. Obviously, such factors deeply influence the resources that parents can deploy to help their children get a start in life.

Social scientists have also increasingly noted ways in which families are embedded in social contexts that have an impact on their lives (Putnam 2000; Sampson, Raudenbush, and Earls 1997). That context begins with a kinship network that may help young people get a summer job or that supply them with religious values. It puts the person in a social position that accords them a specific social status and to which other groups may react with stereotypes. Our respondents tell many stories about how they have experienced prejudice and disrespect from other groups. Finally, groups may be concentrated in neighborhood contexts that may include a rich or sparse set of institutions, such as churches, neighborhood schools, community organizations, and political leaders, that connect to broader opportunities.

These contextual factors interact with family background, and the effects may be indirect and conditional. Sophia's mother's insistence, for example, that she stay away from neighborhood dangers and focus on her schoolwork ultimately counteracted the prevalence of drug use and violence on her block. Eventually, Sophia's mom moved to a better neighborhood to distance her from these problems. New York City's successful effort to reduce the level of violent crime in the years when many of our respondents were growing up probably also made life easier for Sophia and her neighbors, but there was clearly a time in their lives when life was quite dangerous in many New York neighborhoods. Racial, ethnic, and income segregation consigned some parents and respondents to neighborhoods that exposed many, if not all, young people to risks and hazards.

Other respondents grew up in safer middle-class neighborhoods or suburban enclaves where the biggest complaint was that they were bored and had nothing to do. Many young whites came to New York as young adults with a good college education to search for professional job opportunities. Many respondents, including minorities, were able to grow up in New York City neighborhoods chosen by their parents to provide good schools and other neighborhood amenities. Such contextual factors clearly do shape the broad levels of risk and opportunity that our respondents encountered.

In a previous study, we found that one important way that neighborhood context affects individual outcomes is the quality of the high school that individuals attended (Mollenkopf et al. 2002). In New York City, children generally attend grade schools and middle schools in their neighborhood, then go either to a high school zoned for their neighborhood, to another high school for which they seek entrance, or they exit the public system. Seven high schools choose students through competitive entry, including the three famous science high schools such as the Bronx High School of Science. The zoned high schools have the worst performance records and a high school quality measure has a strong impact, net of many other factors, on how far youngsters go in their education. When people living in poor minority neighborhoods get channeled into poor schools, they suffer, although some find their way to better public schools and others exit for private alternatives. This choice is affected by the ways in which school authorities categorize, channel, and reward or sanction different kinds of students.

Family origin and neighborhood context do not explain everything, however. Within these broad background constraints, young adults from different backgrounds seem to have distinctive ways of sequencing and combining life events like getting a job, going to school, and having children. To see these differences, we categorize our respondents according to work and school status (i.e., whether they are doing one, the other, neither, or both) and whether they have had children. Table 14.6 shows how our groups of respondents are distributed across this typology.

Most of our respondents are working and not attending school, ranging from 62.6% of our oldest and most established group, native whites, down to 36.9% for the Chinese and 35.8% for the Russians—our youngest and most recently arrived groups. By and large, few of these respondents have had children, although that ranges from only 7.2% for the Chinese to fully 61.7% of the native blacks, with West Indians, Dominicans, and Puerto Ricans toward the high end of the range. A sizable minority in each group, from 15% to 30%, are combining school and work; this is particularly true for the immigrant second-generation groups compared to the native white,

TABLE 14.6

WORK, SCHOOL, AND PARENTING STATUS BY GROUP

(ALL RESPONDENTS)

	NO CHILD (ROW %)	HAS CHILD (ROW %)	COLUMN %
CEP:			
Work no school	67.5	32.5	47.5
Work and school	86.4	13.6	25.2
School no work	89.0	11.0	17.8
No school no work	48.7	51.3	9.5
Total	74.3	25.7	409
Dominican:			
Work no school	57.3	42.7	42.1
Work and school	74.1	25.9	25.5
School no work	69.4	30.6	14.7
No school no work	32.0	68.0	17.7
Total	58.9	41.1	423
Puerto Rican:			
Work no school	52.7	47.3	47.5
Work and school	76.0	24.0	17.6
School no work	70.6	29.4	11.9
No school no work	35.7	64.3	23.0
Total	55.0	45.0	427
West Indian:			
Work no school	54.4	45.6	39.5
Work and school	77.5	22.5	25.5
School no work	83.1	16.9	22.3
No school no work	60.8	39.2	12.8
Total	67.5	32.5	400
Native black:			
Work no school	38.3	61.7	46.6
Work and school	60.3	39.7	15.0
School no work	67.9	32.1	12.6
No school no work	29.4	70.6	25.9
Total	43.0	57.0	421
Chinese:			
Work no school	92.8	7.2	36.9
Work and school	98.7	1.3	25.1
School no work	100.0	0	31.7
No school no work	94.9	5.1	6.4
Total	96.7	3.3	605

(continued)

TABLE 14.6

(CONTINUED)

	NO CHILD (ROW %)	HAS CHILD (ROW %)	COLUMN %
Russian:			
Work no school	77.5	22.5	35.8
Work and school	97.9	2.1	30.3
School no work	95.0	5.0	25.8
No school no work	72.0	28.0	8.1
Total	87.8	12.2	310
Native white:			
Work no school	87.1	12.9	62.6
Work and school	90.6	9.4	15.6
School no work	93.8	6.3	11.7
No school no work	61.0	39.0	10.0
Total	85.8	14.2	409

Note. "CEP" stands for Colombia, Ecuador, or Peru.

black, and Puerto Rican respondents. Relatively few of these busy people have children, with the Chinese, Russians, native whites, and CEPs the least likely and native blacks the most likely to combine work, school, and parenting. Relatively few devote themselves solely to school, although this course is somewhat more common among the Chinese and Russians. No Chinese and few Russian students are also parents, but a third of the native black students are.

A significant minority of our respondents are neither working nor attending school. This condition is least prevalent among the Chinese, Russians, and CEPs (6.4%, 8.1%, and 9.5%, respectively) and most prevalent among Dominicans, Puerto Ricans, and native blacks (17.7%, 23%, and 25.9%, respectively). Most of the Chinese, Russian, native white, and West Indian young people do not have children, but two-thirds or more of the Puerto Ricans, Dominicans, and native blacks who are neither working nor in school are parents. For them, being a parent may have helped to push them out of the workplace and schools. Although the causal arrow probably runs mainly from being a parent to not holding a job or going to school, it may point in the other direction as well: parenting may be an alternative to these pursuits, especially if no decent job seems available and educational opportunities do not seem likely to provide one. By contrast, parental status does not seem related to not having a job and not going to school for the Chinese and Russians.

Stepping back from this detail, being a parent clearly reduces school attendance for every group, although the strength of the relationship varies. Whether or not they are also working, school-going Russians, Chinese, and native whites are least likely to have children. In other groups, people are more likely to combine parenting with going to school or working. For these groups, however, parenting is even more strongly associated with not working or going to school. African Americans are by far the most likely to have children and neither be working nor going to school: of the ten African American respondents who neither work nor go to school (a quarter of our African American respondents), seven have children. Thus almost one-fifth of our African American respondents are nonworking parents who are not enrolled in school. In this sense, they offer the negative role model suggested by segmented assimilation theory (Portes and Zhou 1993; see also Kasinitz, Mollenkopf, and Waters 2002a). (This is a sharp contrast with West Indians, only one out of twenty of whom fit this description, or even Puerto Ricans, of whom one out of seven can be so described.)

Given the large impact of having a child on other outcomes, especially educational attainment, and given that our groups have very different ways of combining school, work, and family decisions, what can we say about how the different groups approach the timing of having children? Figure 14.1 shows the percentage of women who have had children at different age points for each of our groups. Three different patterns can be discerned. Chinese women have the lowest fertility rates across the whole age span—virtually nil. By contrast, native black, Puerto Rican, and Dominican women are more likely to begin having children early and to continue to do so, with West Indian women lagging somewhat behind the other groups. Two other groups—the CEPs and Russians—exemplify the third pattern of those who start with low fertility rates that increase over time, with the uptick coming sooner for the CEPs than the Russians. (This parallels the importance of family discussed by CEP respondents above.) Native white women also begin to be more likely to have children in the oldest cohort. The early and relatively high fertility among African Americans, Puerto Ricans, and Dominicans may pose a risk to long-term educational attainment, while the immigrant second-generation groups are delaying parenting so as to pursue educations and careers and whites and Chinese (at least between the ages of eighteen and thirty-two) have avoided the burdens (and also the pleasures) of having children.

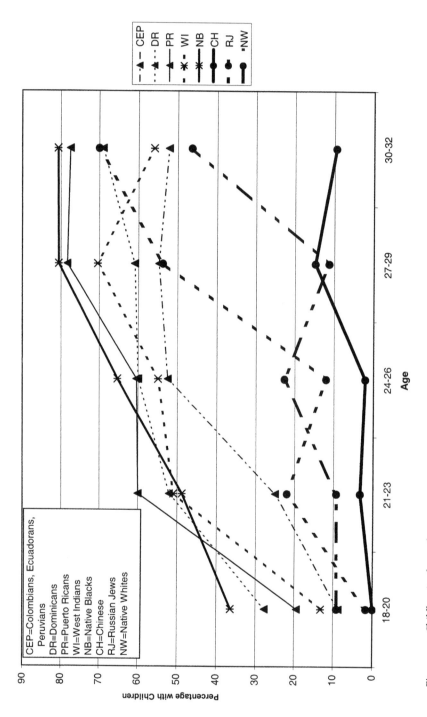

Figure 14.1. Childbearing by age by group

TABLE 14.7

PARTNERING AND PARENTING STATUS BY GROUP

(ALL RESPONDENTS AGED 22–32; ROW PERCENT)

	UNMARRIED NONPARENT (%)	MARRIED NONPARENT (%)	UNMARRIED PARENT (%)	MARRIED PARENT (%)	TOTAL
CEP	52.6	15.1	5.5	26.8	272
Dominican	33.2	14.3	10.2	42.3	265
Puerto Rican	29.3	11.1	20.7	38.9	280
West Indian	41.3	11.9	18.3	28.5	235
Native black	24.1	8.8	32.9	34.2	319
Chinese	76.5	17.6	1.5	4.3	323
Russian	54.0	24.5	.6	20.9	163
Native white	58.3	25.3	3.0	13.6	332
Total	46.4	15.9	12.1	25.7	2,189

Note. "CEP" stands for Colombia, Ecuador, or Peru.

Partnering, shown for the older respondents in table 14.7, follows a related pattern. Native blacks and Puerto Ricans are least likely to be unmarried people without children and most likely to be unmarried parents. Almost as many black parents are unmarried as married. By contrast, most native whites, Russians, Chinese, and CEPs remain unmarried and childless. These differences are clear in table 14.8, which shows whether our respondents live with older adults. African Americans and Puerto Ricans are least likely to live with both parents and most likely (except for native whites) to be on their own, although they are also more likely to live with one parent or other older person, such as a grandparent.[6] The Chinese, Russians, and to a lesser extent, the South Americans stand out from the other groups in living with two parents.

These data prompt several important, if obvious, conclusions. The decision to have a child has huge consequences for other aspects of the transition to young adulthood. It slows down educational attainment, speeds exit from schooling, and hampers entry into the labor force, especially for those who are teenage or single parents. Unmarried mothers, whether living on their own or with their mother, grandmother, or other relatives, face worse odds in going to school or getting a job, although Sophia's case shows that these odds are not insuperable. Native blacks, Puerto Ricans, West Indians, and Dominicans are far more likely to have children, and to have them com-

TABLE 14.8

PRESENCE OF OLDER GENERATION IN HOUSEHOLD BY GROUP

(ALL RESPONDENTS AGED 22−32; ROW PERCENT)

	PROBABLE CURRENT FAMILY				
	LIVING WITHOUT ELDERS (%)	LIVING WITH ONE PARENT (%)	LIVING WITH OTHER ELDERS (%)	LIVING WITH BOTH PARENTS (%)	TOTAL
CEP	49.1	16.8	4.8	29.3	273
Dominican	62.6	14.7	6.4	16.2	265
Puerto Rican	66.4	16.6	4.6	12.4	283
West Indian	60.2	18.2	5.9	15.7	236
Native black	66.6	20.1	6.5	6.8	323
Chinese	41.7	9.5	1.2	47.5	326
Russian	55.2	19.0	1.2	24.5	163
Native white	71.9	17.0	1.5	9.6	335
Total	59.5	16.3	4.0	20.1	2,204

Note. "CEP" stands for Colombia, Ecuador, or Peru.

paratively early, while other groups, particularly the Chinese and native whites do not. These patterns both reinforce the significant difficulty the former groups have in staying in school, going to college, and finding a good job and reflect the skepticism these groups have expressed about whether sticking it out in school will lead to a good job. Such findings, of course, echo much other work (see chaps. 2, 8, and 10 in this vol.).

In keeping with other research, our qualitative data also suggest that circumstance has as much impact on who becomes a parent as volition and rational decision making do. Some of our respondents became pregnant by accident because they did not use birth control or it did not work. Some chose pregnancy, sometimes with support from parents who offered to help raise the child. Some married young and felt pressure from older partners. Yet others hoped that having a child early would make their relationship more secure. For these young women, becoming a mother was often itself a marker of reaching adulthood. Especially for young mothers, this decision sometimes evoked regret later. Said one thirty-one-year-old African American woman, "If God was gonna say, 'OK, we're gonna start you back at eighteen,' I wouldn't have a kid!" But motherhood motivated other women to go back to school and provide a good start in life for their own children.

Avoiding early parenthood is not a surefire ticket to success. Many who do not become parents also encountered difficulties, dropped out of school, and could not keep a job. In these cases, parental resources often made the difference in enabling our respondents to survive and, ultimately, reach a better situation. Kathleen, a twenty-six-year-old white woman from a well-off family, dropped out of college, where she had been a film major, got help from her parents as she sought a job in film production. Tarance, a twenty-four-year-old African American, dropped out of his last year of high school and entered the military, but was discharged after breaking a series of minor rules. He has been living at his mother's place in the Bronx, unsuccessfully looking for a job. Although Kathleen and Tarance both hit obstacles that they have not yet overcome, family support is helping them get by for the time being. Many of our respondents relied on this kind of support well into their young adult years.

Finally, our study groups have what might be called distinctive "family strategies of human capital accumulation." In some groups, the young people live with their parents until an older age, get more support from parents and other older family members, feel less pressure to work, and above all delay or forgo childbearing so they can concentrate on making progress through school and college. The Chinese among our respondents most clearly follow such a strategy, allowing them to rise rapidly through the educational system, often from modest beginnings. Native white and Russian respondents also follow such a pattern, although the latter have children sooner than the two former groups. Members of other groups, however, leave the parental home earlier, get less parental support in the first place, and have children earlier. This slows or even stops their educational progress. Such a path often reinforces the initial educational disadvantage of their parents and promotes downward mobility even when parents have relatively good educations. The native minority groups were most likely to follow this pattern.

RESILIENCE IN THE FACE OF PERVASIVE HAZARDS

New York City is a tough place to grow up and most of our respondents who grew up in the city faced significant hazards, ranging from prejudice against their ethnic group to the prevalence of drug use and violence in their neighborhoods. While most of our respondents were exposed to such hazards, some were more resistant to damage than others, especially when family resources helped them rebound. In other cases, parents were separated or had significant difficulties of their own. Some respondents lived in neighborhoods that provided pathways for recovery, while others did not.

Hazards that befall many young people—such as getting arrested—are evidently interpreted more negatively by society when they happen to members of a minority group. Many of our native white male respondents encountered an unresponsive school system, got involved with drugs, or were arrested. But these events had a less severe and lasting impact on them than they did for young men from black, West Indian, and Dominican backgrounds, who reported the highest rates of discrimination and harassment by the police. (Once more, such experiences helped to generate the different conceptions about success discussed above.) While most respondents agreed that success meant getting a good job by first getting a good education, more than a few of our young minority male respondents told us they would be grateful "just being alive and not in jail" and did not think education would yield them a decent job.

We gathered data on exposure to such hazards as being raised by a single parent, parents' marital break-up, death of a parent, number of times the family has moved, childhood neighborhood problems with racial conflict, youthful disrespect for authority, drug use and drug dealing, crime, and unwillingness of neighbors to help each other. We also asked our respondents whether they had been held back in school, placed in special education or English as a second language classes, received various forms of welfare, or were ever arrested or incarcerated. Table 14.9 shows the incidence of these hazards across our entire sample. While the most common problem was youthful disrespect for authority, which could happen in any community, a great many of our respondents were exposed to drugs, crime, the lack of after-school activities, and frequent family moves. The death of a parent, arrest, and incarceration were also critical.

These hazards were not evenly distributed across people or the places where they grew up. Table 14.10 shows that native blacks and Puerto Ricans consistently had the highest exposure to growing up without both biological parents, growing up in neighborhoods with open drug use, being held back in school, and being arrested. Among the second-generation groups, West Indians and Dominicans had high rates of exposure to risk, while the South Americans had less and the Chinese and Russians very little, even lower than the exposure rates for native whites. Finally, table 14.11 shows that those growing up in New York's inner suburbs did not fare much better than those growing up in the city; only growing up outside the metropolitan area (the preserve of our white respondents) afforded some protection from risk.

It is hardly surprising that exposure to such risks is associated with becoming a single parent and getting less education. In particular, growing up with a single parent in a drug-infested neighborhood is highly associated

TABLE 14.9

EXPOSURE TO HAZARDS GROWING UP (TOTAL SAMPLE)

HAZARD	PERCENTAGE
Did not grow up with both parents	37.9
Grew up with both parents but they are now divorced	15.3
A parent is now dead (voluntary response)	8.0
Moved 2+ times between ages of 6 and 18	45.5
Problem with youths not respecting authorities in neighborhood growing up[a]	62.9
Problem with lots of crime in neighborhood growing up[a]	61.7
Problem with people dealing/using drugs in the open in neighborhood growing up[a]	55.9
Problem with lack of after-school activities growing up[a]	42.7
Problem with neighbors not willing to help in neighborhood growing up[a]	37.9
Problem with neighbors not knowing each other growing up[a]	33.3
Problem with racial groups not getting along in neighborhood growing up[a]	28.7
Ever held back a grade in school	22.2
Received Medicaid growing up	34.6
Received SSI/disability growing up	12.7
Received TANF (AFDC) growing up	10.6
Ever arrested	13.9
Ever in reform school, detention center, jail, or prison	6.0

Note. Results are weighted to reflect size of sample groups in overall population.

[a] Percent answering "a big problem" or "somewhat of a problem."

with becoming a single parent and getting less education, while having a better-educated mother is negatively associated with those outcomes (Mollenkopf et al. 2002). Nevertheless, net of these factors, the group to which one belongs still has an independent impact on outcomes. It seems that group-wide characteristics, not just individual family background characteristics, make a considerable difference. The contrast between second-generation Chinese respondents, who are highly unlikely to become single mothers, and blacks and Puerto Ricans, who are much more so, despite the fact that all come from families with relatively low educations, makes this point clearly.

Multivariate analysis of how individual choices, family background, and neighborhood context contribute to the potential for educational mobility clearly shows that individual choices, particularly having a child, and fam-

TABLE 14.10

EXPOSURE TO HAZARDS GROWING UP BY GROUP AND PLACE GROWING UP

(PERCENT OF TOTAL SAMPLE)

	NOT TWO PARENTS (%)	NEIGHBORHOOD HAD OPEN DRUG USE (%)	HELD BACK (%)	ARRESTED (%)
CEP	31.3	55.1	24.4	11.3
Dominicans	40.3	69.0	27.4	10.0
Puerto Ricans	45.3	73.8	33.0	14.8
West Indians	48.4	57.6	25.0	14.0
Native blacks	58.5	68.1	26.8	17.4
Chinese	12.4	37.0	12.9	5.0
Russians	18.4	40.3	6.8	5.9
Native whites	27.9	31.0	9.3	13.7
Grew up in New York City[a]	39.8	63.5	25.9	13.4
Grew up in suburbs[a]	34.3	43.6	14.8	19.8
Grew up outside New York metro area[a]	30.7	26.1	8.4	11.5
New York City males[a]	38.1	63.7	29.9	25.1

Note. "CEP" stands for Colombia, Ecuador, or Peru.

[a] Weighted to reflect size of sample groups in overall population.

ily background contribute far more than neighborhood circumstances. Above all, the decision to bear a child substantially increases the chances of downward mobility and limits upward mobility. As table 14.11 shows for our older respondents, being a parent reduces the likelihood of getting a BA by two-thirds and increases the likelihood of being a high school dropout five-fold. This impact seems most damaging to Puerto Ricans, who have both the lowest college rate and the highest dropout rate after having a child.

From our perspective, family background ought to influence the transition to young adulthood, but the Chinese and Puerto Rican cases both seem exceptional. Many of our Chinese second-generation respondents had poorly educated parents, low family incomes, and little familial proficiency with English. Yet they remained in their parents' households, put off getting married and having children, and instead pursued higher education and occupational mobility at an astonishing rate. These poor families produced upwardly mobile children. In contrast, even though two-fifths of our Puerto Rican respondents had parents born on the U.S. mainland, and were thus third-generation New Yorkers and, of course, all are citizens, they have ended

TABLE 14.11

EDUCATIONAL OUTCOMES BY GROUP BY PARENTING STATUS

(RESPONDENTS AGED 22–32)

	NO HIGH SCHOOL DIPLOMA (%)	HIGH SCHOOL DIPLOMA, NO BA (%)	BA OR ENROLLED (%)	TOTAL
No child:				
CEP	4.3	47.6	48.1	185
Dominican	7.9	46.5	45.7	127
Puerto Rican	8.8	50.9	40.4	114
West Indian	7.9	49.2	42.9	126
Native black	8.5	45.3	46.2	106
Chinese	1.3	18.9	79.8	307
Russian	2.3	17.2	80.5	128
Native white	2.8	18.9	78.2	280
Total	4.5	32.6	62.9	1,373
Has child:				
CEP	23.9	59.1	17.0	88
Dominican	28.3	50.7	21.0	138
Puerto Rican	33.7	52.4	13.9	166
West Indian	11.0	52.3	36.7	109
Native black	21.9	61.9	16.3	215
Chinese	5.6	61.1	33.3	18
Russian	5.7	42.9	51.4	35
Native white	17.9	46.4	35.7	56
Total	22.8	54.7	22.5	825

Note. "CEP" stands for Colombia, Ecuador, or Peru.

up with lower educational outcomes than Dominicans, CEPs, or native blacks. These moderately well-off families produced downwardly mobile children. What might explain these divergent outcomes?

CONTRASTING PARADOXES: THE CHINESE AND PUERTO RICANS

We argue that the answer lies in the distinctive familial strategies that these groups have developed about how to help their children accumulate human capital—in other words, how families seek to ensure that their children get a good education and the degree to which concentrating on improving the human capital of the next generation is a prime family objective. Neighborhood qualities contribute to this difference since the groups cluster in neighborhoods with rather different educational opportunities.

In Chinese families, more adults support fewer children, the children remain in the home until older ages, the families seek out (and are more accepted by) neighborhoods with better schools, they move less frequently, and they relentlessly stress public schools as a path for upward mobility. As we have seen, very few of even our oldest Chinese respondents have had children. In most Puerto Rican families, in contrast, mothers often support several children, who have only tenuous connections to their fathers. The Puerto Ricans in our study were most likely to reproduce the pattern of young single motherhood. Even though they live in poor neighborhoods with bad public schools, many Puerto Rican parents are evidently reluctant to allow their children, especially their daughters, to travel to better but more distant schools. For these families, the preferred strategy for educational attainment is exiting the public system for Catholic schools or leaving New York City.

The Chinese

The success of our Chinese respondents is partly explained by the fact that many had better-educated parents from Taiwan or Hong Kong who themselves may have come to the United States for higher education or career advancement. (More than a third of these families had a parent with a BA, twice the rate for parents from mainland China.) Looking only at respondents with parents from the mainland, they are more likely to have come as small children (only a third were born here). Still, nine out of ten of our respondents grew up with both parents, and nine out of ten of those parents are still together. Life was difficult for these families, as both parents often worked full time and many spoke little English. For a quarter of these respondents, both parents lacked a high school degree, and in 60% of the cases neither had a college degree. Yet of those aged twenty-two to thirty-two, only three were high school dropouts and three-quarters had a BA or were enrolled in a four-year college. This is an extraordinary achievement for someone having started from modest circumstances.

Coming to New York City was a long, arduous journey for mainland parents that represented a huge break with their past lives. They knew it would be tough to get a job, make a living, and adapt to the new setting but expected their children to accrue the benefits of immigration. Aware that they are poor people in a rich society, they work hard, scrimp, and save, transferring part of the pressure to "make it here" onto their children. One Chinese respondent, Darryl, typifies this experience. Darryl's parents came from Guangdong in the early 1960s. Like many of his peers, he felt that their decision was as much for him as for themselves:

> I think constantly as a kid I was reminded of this . . . the fact that their mindset for coming here to the United States was to have a better life, sure. But they were very realistic in the fact that they felt how much of a better life can we have here in the United States. Great, we have a house or a car or whatever. But it's that next part; it's the next generation that's really going to have an impact. And so for them, I think they have. They don't have a house. They don't have a car. The first car in my family was bought by me and so I think they have made a tremendous sacrifice.

Although most Chinese parents never delivered the message this explicitly, Darryl remembers the evening when he became painfully aware of his father's sacrifice and hopes for his son's future.

> Darryl: So, in fact, one of the turning points in my life, I think, was when he one day came into my room and "Okay, we're going to have a talk." "Talk? Talk about what? What is this?" He never did that. And he came in, and I was in bed and I was about to go to sleep, and he goes, "look, my life is hard." I said, "Yeah, I kind of realized that." He said, "I don't want you to grow up like me." So it was his story of shape up in school, do well and be like your uncle. . . . He was like, "Be like your uncle who is an engineer. He's a professional. He makes good money. He's out in society. He's well respected in society." And that's when it hit me and that I still remember that. Because I was, "Wow, okay." And that's why I majored in engineering in college.
>
> Interviewer: How old were you at that time, that night when you had that talk?
>
> Darryl: I think I wasn't in high school yet, probably eighth grade or something like that. It was right after the restaurant was sold. My grandfather's restaurant was sold, and he was having a difficult time finding work, and I guess he was at that time—he felt, "I don't want my son to do that."

Working-class mainland Chinese parents generally cannot help their children with their homework, but they make an effort to live in neighborhoods with better schools and leaving those with gangs and other dangers. Their understanding that school quality is crucial to later outcomes derives partly from experience in the home country and partly from ethnic media and networks. Chinese parents not only buy property in the right school districts, but they also use false addresses to register their children in better schools, let their children travel to more distant schools, and encourage them to go to after-school programs to prepare for the science high school test. Darryl's parents made the unusual choice to send him to Catholic school after he was sent to his public high school principal for a minor infraction.

The system has rewarded these parental efforts: one out of five children of mainland Chinese families went to a public magnet school, and more than half went to high schools in the top two performance quintiles for New York City schools. Once there, second-generation mainland Chinese young people took more honors courses, put in more time at homework, got higher grades, and were more likely to receive a regents' diploma than any other group.

Chinese children clearly benefit from the stereotype of Asians as a "model minority," with many garnering an added layer of support on top of that provided by parents. In other cases, guidance counselors and teachers sought out and encouraged students whose families were troubled or less focused on their education. This could be a curse for lower-achieving youngsters, but it helped many others. Darryl's comments are typical of how our Chinese respondents talk about the high expectations of their families and teachers:

> Well, I guess this could be a good and a bad. Being Chinese and being among all the different racial groups, I was always pointed out as, "He's Chinese; he must be the smart one. If he's not, oh man is he in trouble." Or there's something wrong. He must be retarded or something. And it is bad. I think we carry that as being Chinese. Hard working, comes from a very good family background and really, really smart. And in a way that has helped me because that has always pushed me. I have a standard to uphold. And also, from my parents, "You got to do better. You got to do better."
>
> A good story for that is my grandmother who takes care of my cousins, and my cousin came home one day and got off the bus, "Grandma, Grandma oh man I got a 98 on my math test." He's thinking before the math test, "I'm going to fail this." Or "I'm going to get an 80 or whatever and it's going to be bad." So he comes home running, "Grandma, I got a 98." And my grandmother without

blinking an eye goes, "Alright, what happened to those two points?" That's how I see Chinese parents. And he is like, "Oh, I don't know." Let me savor this.

So that can be a blessing and it can be. . . . It's hard. It's hard to live to that type of standard. But I think growing up I guess I had a free pass, especially in a Catholic school. I was there for discipline, but they didn't know how bad I was. They were, "He's from a Chinese family, he must be pretty good." So I was asked to do a lot of different things. I was asked to tutor kids, especially immigrants, Chinese immigrants who came here and they don't understand the language. So I can translate. I also tutored Hispanic kids, if they understood English. So I was put up, doing many different things which benefits me now because I think with[out] that type of background, I wouldn't be as involved.

Chinese families may also be more able to protect their children from risk. Although the children of our working-class mainland families were often not particularly close to their parents, who often worked long hours, the family was a stable unit and divorce infrequent.[7] The ratio of working people to school-going children is generally 1 to 1 or better in mainland Chinese households. Not only are both parents working, but so are younger family members. Older relatives may also be present to help with child care. Chinese families tend to have fewer children, with only the Russian and native white respondents having fewer siblings.

Chinese families can therefore invest more in any given child and pool resources to buy homes or businesses. Many of our respondents mentioned receiving financial support or help in finding work from relatives and child care from grandparents. Darryl's father worked for several years in his grandfather's restaurant after coming to New York and his grandparents looked after him and his cousins after school. Such strong familial ties carry an expectation of reciprocity; many respondents said they felt obligated to give back in later life and some were already caring for grandparents or planning to provide financially for their parents, many of whom have jobs that will bring no pension. These family networks have been a source of strength during most respondents' early lives and helped them to get off to a good start.

The Puerto Ricans

Despite the fact that they are U.S. citizens who were born in New York to parents who had also resided in the city most of their lives, our Puerto Rican respondents experienced an entirely different set of family forms and dynamics. Almost half grew up without two parents, and of those who did grow up with both, two-fifths of those parents are no longer together. In two-parent families, mothers were far less likely to work than in Chinese families. As a result, far fewer Puerto Rican respondents grew up with two working parents. Parents also had to support more children than in the Chinese families. And Puerto Rican respondents left home earlier. Reflecting their parents' difficult economic circumstances, our Puerto Rican respondents were also far more likely to move during their adolescent years. As with the mainland Chinese parents, the Puerto Rican parents had quite modest educations; in more than four out of five families, neither parent had a BA. Unlike the Chinese, however, a quarter of the Puerto Rican respondents aged twenty-two to thirty-two are high school dropouts and only a quarter have a BA or are enrolled in a four-year college. Even more troubling, two-thirds of the Puerto Ricans with better-educated parents are no more than high school graduates. Strikingly, a quarter of those whose mothers have a college degree are high school dropouts. What factors contribute to this outcome?

Puerto Rican families are under severe economic stress. Single parents with few resources struggle to raise their children in some of New York City's poorest neighborhoods. Though one Puerto Rican mother in ten had gotten a college degree—many of whom went to college later in life—few could convert that degree into a professional position. Puerto Rican families were less able to pool resources to buy homes in neighborhoods with better schools. Racial and class segregation funneled Puerto Rican families into neighborhoods with bad schools. Puerto Ricans went predominantly to high schools in the lowest two quintiles of school performance in New York City. Some female Puerto Rican respondents told us that their parents were so fearful of what might happen to them if they got on the subway that they actively discouraged them from going to better, but more distant, schools. They often described the teachers in their nearby schools as having little interest in students. Cutting class was common among these respondents, and when they began to get behind in class work, it seemed more difficult and less worth trying to graduate.

In these lower performing schools, our Puerto Rican respondents took fewer honors classes, did less homework, and were more likely to drop out. Aside from native whites, Puerto Ricans were the group least likely to do two hours or more of homework per week. A third were held back at some point. When they went on to college, they often attended a CUNY community college and rarely reached a nationally ranked four-year institution. The lucky youngsters escaped the New York City school system for a parochial school or moved to the suburbs.

Our Chinese respondents, who could often speak and understand Chinese fairly well but not read or write it, generally developed a good command of English. Our Puerto Rican respondents grew up speaking Spanish, but are not entirely fluent and prefer to speak English, although they also have less facility with that language. Being less prepared for school in English, |going to weaker schools, and doing less well conforms to a negative stereotype about Puerto Rican abilities held by many teachers and guidance counselors. Just as a positive stereotype can be self-reinforcing for Chinese youngsters, the negative stereotype for Puerto Rican students pushed them out of school.

In reaction to such experiences, as well as to the example of their own families, almost half of our Puerto Rican respondents have had their own children, often at relatively young ages. One-sixth of our Puerto Rican respondents are single parents. This factor alone greatly hampers educational mobility among our Puerto Rican respondents. While people who drop out of school and have children may be able to catch up later by getting a GED, enrolling in a two- or four-year CUNY campus, and working their way through school, most cannot follow this arduous path, much as they might want or intend to.

Melinda grew up in a South Bronx neighborhood where she feels she cannot look directly at a person without provoking hostility. Her father died of asthma when she was four and her mother was on welfare until she began working as a nurse's aide when Melinda was six. Her mom moved to Puerto Rico for a while, then later remarried, and often left Melinda with her grandmother there. When her stepfather abandoned the family, they moved back to New York. Her mother and grandmother had low expectations for Melinda, though they encouraged her to complete high school.

> Melinda: Well, they only suggested, they didn't tell me how, but they told me more or less what would be better, and to always finish school, and get a good job, a good career, don't depend on nobody . . . you have your own . . . you don't have to worry about where am I going to sleep. It was to be independent.
>
> Interviewer: Did they ever encourage you to choose a certain career?
>
> Melinda: No, they just said whatever makes me happy, whatever I think is best for me.

Melinda did not feel that moving back to New York was good for her and believed that New York's permissive atmosphere was detrimental to young people: "Honestly, I think in Puerto Rico it would have been better, because the schools are strict there, and family values are more put down than here.

Here, everybody comes here and they go crazy, they go wild, they want to do whatever they want, you know, they're in the United States you can do whatever. Over there it's like a little more laid down than it is here." In talking about how she might raise her own child, Melinda felt her mother and grandmother had not put enough pressure on her regarding school: "A couple of things, like if I didn't want to go to school, if I was tired, they would be like, 'OK, stay.' That I wouldn't do—unless she's sick or she's got a doctor's appointment or something, she will be going to school. Because that's what made me get lazy. But she will have to go to school."

Although Melinda had started out in a gifted group in school, she started cutting class in the eighth grade and could only go to her zoned high school.

> Just because you're in that school, they make you look like a truant or something, and they just pass the lesson and that's it. And if anybody was flunking they would . . . they would just sit down and wouldn't do anything. So why am I going to go to school for to sit down? For that I stay home. I didn't really have problems with anyone . . . I would just go to the class that I would have to go to, and that's it. Most of the teachers, I didn't get along with them, because they thought that because they were the teachers they could talk down to you. I'm sorry, but . . . you disrespect me, I disrespect you. They would always send me to the dean's office. I mean, there were people pulling knives on teachers and they wouldn't send them; me, because I talk back and I'm sarcastic, I get sent to the dean's office. So I just said forget it.

Melinda became pregnant at seventeen when her birth control did not work. Her mother had told her she shouldn't have a child until she was married, but she later embraced the baby.

> Melinda: I was taking my GED, because I had asked for a transfer from the school I was in and the district told me no three times, and I gave up, I didn't like the school, so I just didn't go, and I decided to go for my GED. That's when I came up pregnant, and I was working and I stopped working because I worked standing up, I was a waitress and I couldn't do it, so I just dropped everything to have my baby.
> Interviewer: But when you were pregnant, how did your family react to that?
> Melinda: Well, at first they were like "you're too young," and all this other stuff, but then they considered, they thought back to everybody

else in my family, twelve, thirteen, fourteen with kids, you know, and they said at least I was older, I was maybe eighteen already—I could sign my own baby at the hospital, it's my responsibility. I'm old enough to go out there and get a job, but I have to depend on my mother.

Interviewer: Was your mother generally supportive?

Melinda: Yeah. At first she was a little upset because she figures, you're finally going to school, you're getting your own stuff—now she's crazy about her, she doesn't let me do anything with her—"she's mine."

So many women in the community have children when they are young that it has become an acceptable option, especially for those with problems in school. Ivette, a case study in educational success, actually considered herself to be "too old" to be starting a family at thirty. Raised in a tough neighborhood by parents without much education, Ivette graduated from college, is working on her master's, and teaches public school. Yet she expresses regret that she didn't have children earlier in life:

> Oh boy. I think there are two sides of how I feel about that. I am going to be thirty in two months so I see the majority of my friends have had children when they were younger and went through life difficulties. But they made it through and now their kids are a little older and it seems like they are having a second life. Things are a little different for them, which is good. Now, here I am, I've had a good time when I was younger, I've traveled. I've gone out. I've gone to school. I've had different jobs. I've dated different people of all nationalities and I have a boyfriend now and I'm thinking, "Is it too late to have kids?" No, it is not too late biologically. Biologically it is not too late to have a child but do I want to have an eighteen-, nineteen-, twenty-year-old when I'm fifty-three? Do I want to be a grandparent at sixty or seventy?

CONCLUSION

Respondents who come from working-class families with modest educations face a labor market where a college education is a prerequisite for access to a good job. Whether they know it or not, success at school is critical to their future. The New York City public school system is a complex mechanism that sorted our respondents across varied settings for elementary and high school education. Our respondents either had to chart a clear strategy for getting into better schools, as the Chinese did, or had to exit the system, as most whites and many Hispanic respondents did. Those who were channeled into poor schools often rightly questioned the value of the education they were getting. They described classrooms where teachers did not bother to teach and could hardly keep order. (This may not be the norm, but it is a common experience, nevertheless.) Despite hearing from their parents that they must get a good education, students in such schools often cut class, hang out with their friends, and get into drugs. Adults may be absent or fail to intervene. Such bad options for school interact with initial disadvantage to produce many of the outcomes we have observed here. Our respondents clearly begin from different family starting points and face different opportunity structures, leading to their varied trajectories into young adulthood.

Our data suggest that group characteristics strongly shape these outcomes. Even members of groups that have some disadvantages, can, through determined effort, achieve surprisingly high rates of intergenerational upward mobility, as the mainland Chinese case demonstrates. Children in families where more working adults support fewer children, that convey high educational expectations to their children, and that gain access to the better parts of school system—aided by teachers and counselors who favor children from some ethnic groups over others—are more likely to succeed than children in families where fathers do not support their children, young people drift into bad schools that expect little of them, and many drop out or see early parenthood as a preferable alternative.

In saying this, we are not advancing a "cultural explanation," at least in the narrow sense. Our Chinese respondents know little about traditional Chinese culture. But working-class Chinese parents do have traditional ideas about parenting and place heavy expectations on their children in terms of school performance. Awareness of their parents' grueling existence leads most of them to comply with their parents' expectations. Chinese families have more supportive social networks that include relatives who migrated earlier who can provide financial or other support. Finally, because Chinese migration has included well-educated professionals from Taiwan as well as poorly educated people from rural mainland China, the community has better sources of information and more examples of success than is available to Puerto Ricans. Prejudice and housing discrimination shunt Puerto Rican families into neighborhoods with concentrated poverty, declining city services, and poor public schools. The prevalence of single mothers with few resources leaves them less able to share community resources with each other.

The contrast between these two groups also underscores the selective nature of the migration process. The first-generation parents of our Chinese respondents had to make a significant effort to get to New York City and survive the difficult process of entering and remaining in the country. By definition, they are determined and hardy. The first- and second-generation parents of our Puerto Rican respondents, however, are not "positively selected" in the same sense. As they can travel back to Puerto Rico far more easily than the Chinese can go to China (Kasinitz et al. 2002b), immigration is a less momentous decision and less hangs on how it turns out for the children. Indeed, there is some evidence that the Puerto Rican migration to New York City was the result of "negative selection" and that the people who came were disproportionately poor (Ramos 1992). As they enter the third generation, more successful Puerto Rican families have moved out of New York City to suburban locations and smaller cities where they face less labor market competition from new immigrants. In short, the differences between the Chinese and Puerto Rican experiences, which seem to exemplify over- and underachievement compared to their parents, reflect not cultural differences but the profound impact of family strategy as it interacts with social inequality.

NOTES

1. We define "new second generation" here as all those born in the United States to one or two post-1965 immigrant parents and those who were born abroad but arrived here by age twelve and have lived in the United States for at least a decade, the so-called 1.5 generation. Figures were computed from the March 2001 Current Population Survey. The figure for Los Angeles County is 47.8%.

2. This study was initiated by the Russell Sage Foundation and received additional support from the Ford Foundation, the Andrew W. Mellon Foundation, the Rockefeller Foundation, the United Jewish Appeal-Federation, and the National Institute of Child Health and Human Development, all of whom we thank. The opinions expressed here do not reflect those of the sponsoring organizations. Our study complements the other major study of the second generation, the Children of Immigrants Longitudinal Study (CILS), which conducted three waves of interviews with respondents who were originally grade-school students in San Diego and Miami. It does not include native-born comparison groups (Portes and Rumbaut 2001).

3. This sample includes "1.5ers" as well as those born here to foreign parents, the second generation. About 60% of our Dominican and CEP respondents are American born, as are 53% of the West Indians, 44% of the Chinese, and, owing to their recent arrival, 13% of the Russians. While we do not report in this chapter the breakdown between the 1.5 and 2.0 generations for the relationships shown in the following tables, we have examined them to make sure that the differences between these subgroups do not qualify our conclusions. We oversampled Chinese youth in order to distinguish those whose parents were from mainland China and elsewhere and had a smaller sample of Russians because of their relatively recent arrival. We were also compelled to relax the age-of-arrival criterion to eighteen for Russians. We

used a different method to interview a supplemental sample of 657 Chinese, black, West Indian, Puerto Rican, Dominican, and South American respondents from outer suburban areas, but these data are not analyzed here.

4. For more detail on the study design, see Kasinitz et al. (2004).

5. We use mother's or father's education for those who grew up with only one parent and the highest level attained by either parent for those who grew up with both parents.

6. We do not have information about the exact relationship between the respondent and other older members of the household in all cases.

7. Of respondents whose parents came from the mainland, 92.7% grew up with both parents, compared with 79.7% of those who had at least one parent from Taiwan.

REFERENCES

Alba, Richard, and Victor Nee. 2003. *Remaking the American Mainstream: Assimilation and Contemporary Immigration.* Cambridge, MA: Harvard University Press.

Borjas, George. 1990. *Friends or Strangers: The Impact of Immigrants on the U.S. Economy.* New York: Basic Books.

———. 1999. *Heaven's Door: Immigration Policy and the American Economy.* Princeton, NJ: Princeton University Press.

Gans, Herbert. 1992. Second Generation Decline: Scenarios for the Economic and Ethnic Futures of the Post-1965 American Immigrants. *Ethnic and Racial Studies* 15 (2):173–93.

Kasinitz, Philip. 1992. *Caribbean New York: Black Immigrants and the Politics of Race.* Ithaca, NY: Cornell University Press.

Kasinitz, Philip, John Mollenkopf and Mary C. Waters. 2002a. Becoming Americans/Becoming New Yorkers: The Experience of Assimilation in a Majority Minority City. *International Migration Review* 36, no. 4 (winter): 1020–36.

Kasinitz, Philip, John Mollenkopf, and Mary C. Waters, eds. 2004. *Becoming New Yorkers: The Second Generation in a Global City.* New York: Russell Sage Foundation 2004.

Kasinitz, Philip, Mary C. Waters, John Mollenkopf, and Merih Anil. 2002b. Transnationalism and the Children of Immigrants in Contemporary New York. Pp. 96–122 in *The Changing Face of Home: The Transnational Lives of the Second Generation,* edited by Mary C. Waters and Peggy Levitt. New York: Russell Sage Foundation.

Massey, Douglas, Jorge Durand, and Nolan J. Malone. 2002. *Beyond Smoke and Mirrors: Mexican Immigration in an Era of Economic Integration.* New York: Russell Sage Foundation.

Mollenkopf, John, Aviva Zeltzer-Zubida, Jennifer Holdaway, Philip Kasinitz, and Mary Waters. 2002. Chutes and Ladders: Educational Attainment among Young Second Generation and Native New Yorkers. Paper prepared for the Mellon Foundation Project on Immigrants in New York City, Milano School, New School University.

Portes, Alejandro, and Rubén Rumbaut. 2001. *Legacies: The Story of the New Second Generation.* Berkeley: University of California Press; New York: Russell Sage Foundation.

Portes, Alejandro, and Min Zhou. 1993. The New Second Generation: Segmented Assimilation and Its Variants. *Annals of the American Academy of Political and Social Science* 530:74–97.

Putnam, Robert D. 2000. *Bowling Alone: The Collapse and Revival of American Community.* New York: Simon & Schuster.

Ramos, Fernando A.1992. Out-Migration and Return Migration of Puerto Ricans. Pp. 49–66 in *Immigration and the Work Force: Implications for the United States and Source Areas,* edited by George Borjas and Richard Freeman. Chicago: University of Chicago Press.

Sampson, Robert J., Stephen W. Raudenbush, and Felton Earls. 1997. Neighborhoods and Violent Crime: A Multilevel Study of Collective Efficacy. *Science* 277 (5328):918–24.

Smith, James P., and Barry Edmonston. 1997. *The New Americans: Economic, Demographic, and Fiscal Effects of Immigration.* Washington, DC: National Academy Press.

PART FOUR

POLICY AND PRACTICE FOR LIVES IN TRANSITION

CHAPTER 15

THE TRANSITION TO ADULTHOOD FOR YOUTH LEAVING PUBLIC SYSTEMS

Challenges to Policies and Research

E. MICHAEL FOSTER AND ELIZABETH J. GIFFORD

Like all youth who are moving from adolescence into adulthood, individuals whose lives have touched the foster care, juvenile justice, and special education systems are faced with a series of critical choices. As discussed in other chapters (e.g., Fussell and Gauthier, this vol., chap. 3; Mouw, this vol., chap. 8; Osgood et al., this vol., chap. 10; Wu and Li, this vol., chap. 4), these decisions involve education, employment, residential independence and self-sufficiency, and early family formation. Shaping these choices are young people's own preferences, the norms of their families and communities, and their emotional and financial resources. The consequences of choices made at these critical transitions can be long-lasting.

The transition to adulthood is also marked by changes in one's legal status. As individuals grow older, they gain the right to drive and then to vote. They become eligible for the draft and are permitted to drink alcohol. Their relationship to public programs changes as well. As young people begin to live on their own, their eligibility for Medicaid and other safety net programs begins to depend on their own employment, resources and marital status rather than on that of their parents. Their involvement with the public institutions that have been responsible for their education may end as well.

For youth in public systems that serve children, the nature of their relationship to public policies and programs changes even more fundamentally. Public involvement in their lives has been pervasive and profound and, as they approach adulthood, that involvement diminishes or ends. For youth in foster care, for example, the state has often been primarily responsible for their housing and sustenance and has regulated when and whether they lived with their biological family. For youth in juvenile justice, the state has controlled when and whether they lived in institutions and has monitored their activities when they lived in the community. For children in special education, the state's involvement in their lives has been more intensive as well. For some of these youth, this involvement has meant that the child lived apart from his or her family in residential schools.

Therefore, as these youth become adults, the role of the state in shaping their lives changes. These changes are especially important given that they occur in the context of many challenges, including learning disabilities, limited life skills, and health or emotional and behavioral problems. Furthermore, their families may offer only limited support during the transition; their economic resources are often limited, and the quality of their relationships with the youth may be poor. As a result, outcomes for these young people are often dreadful. They are more likely than other young people to drop out of high school, experience joblessness, rely on public assistance, give birth while unmarried and unprepared for parenthood, and undergo periods of homelessness or residential instability.

Recognizing their vulnerability, policymakers have attempted to create a transitional period during which young people's involvement in these programs is phased out. During that time, special services are offered that target key outcomes, such as life skills, emotional and behavioral problems, and employment. These services involve educational opportunities (including vocational training), counseling and support services, training in daily living skills, outreach services, and a range of other services (such as family planning and parenting classes).

In this chapter, we examine the transition to adulthood among adolescents leaving three child-serving systems in the United States—foster care, juvenile justice, and special education. We begin by describing the ways in which children enter those systems and the ways in which they exit them prior to late adolescence. We then describe the ways in which the transition to adulthood affects their involvement with those systems, review the literature on how these youth fare over time, and consider the special challenges they face. We examine their transition out of these programs, describe services designed to facilitate it, and review the little that is known about the effectiveness of those services. We conclude with an evaluation of these programs from a life-course perspective and offer some reflections on why available evidence is so limited and on directions for future research.

HOW DO CHILDREN AND YOUTH ENTER THESE THREE SYSTEMS?

One cannot understand the youth who leave these systems in late adolescence without understanding the ways they entered them in the first place. As discussed below, many children and youth encounter these systems but not all are eligible for the transition services they provide. Some youth exit the systems before reaching the age at which services are available or never participate to the degree required to receive transition services.

Foster Care

Many children encounter the various programs and services of the child welfare system. Established through Titles IV and V of the 1935 Social Security Act, this system helps parents care for their children and removes children from their homes when their parents have died or are otherwise unable to care for them (U.S. Congress 2000). The provisions of Title IV establish a range of services and provide federal matching funds for administering and delivering those services. Title IV-B, for example, provides funds for services that prevent child neglect, abuse, exploitation, or delinquency or that prevent the separation of youth from their families. States vary widely in how they actually use those funds.

This variation is typical. While the federal government provides considerable funding, child welfare services are administered at the state level and delivered at the local level. In order to receive federal funds, states are required to comply with a series of federal provisions that are intended to protect children. In practice, the federal government appears to monitor state compliance only loosely (U.S. Congress 2000). Even within states, the ways in which child welfare services are delivered vary substantially from one community to the next. Local agencies are important in providing services, finding safe adoptive and foster care families and monitoring the well-being of children who are in state custody.

Best known among the programs encompassed by the child welfare system is foster care. Foster care is regulated and supported through Title IV-E and provides funds to support children and youth who have been placed out of their home with foster parents or in other institutional settings. For these children, the state assumes "custody" and, therefore, has the right to determine where and with whom the child lives. The state is responsible for providing the child with essentials (food, shelter, education, emotional support, and basic medical care), as well as for the child's protection and discipline. (Parents, however, retain parental rights. A key implication of this arrangement is that a child cannot be adopted until those rights are terminated through legal proceedings.) For children in custody, federal law requires that states establish a permanency plan. Those plans are to be reviewed as part of periodic permanency hearings. The permanency plans and hearings provide the state an opportunity to determine the best possible long-term living arrangement for the child given his or her individual circumstances and to plan appropriate services. For example, a child may be reunified with his or her family, live with relatives, remain in long-term foster care, or be placed for adoption. This decision influences the services that the child and the child's family receive. In order to promote reunification, the child or the family may receive counseling, substance abuse treatment services, mental health services, assistance addressing domestic violence, temporary child care and therapeutic services such as crisis nurseries, and transportation to and from these activities (U.S. Congress 2000).

Note that federal support for foster care is limited to children from low-income families who otherwise would have received cash assistance through the former Aid to Families with Dependent Children program (AFDC). Many other children are in state custody at the state's expense. These children represent about half of all children in foster care (U.S. Congress 2000).

Different paths lead children into foster care. At birth, some children are abandoned or placed for adoption. Some older children may be placed into foster care because their special needs exceed their parents' resources. Other children are referred to foster care through the juvenile justice system (a process that is discussed below). The most common path to foster care, however, involves investigations for abuse and neglect (U.S. Congress 2000).

Suspicions of child abuse or neglect are reported to the child protective services (CPS) unit of the local child welfare office. This unit investigates reports of child maltreatment, may remove children from their homes, and then may petition the court for permanent custody of the child. In 2000, CPS fielded 3 million reports of child maltreatment involving 5 million children (U.S. Department of Health and Human Services [U.S. DHHS] 2002b). Most reports of child maltreatment are not substantiated—only 62% were "screened in" by CPS agencies and thus formally investigated or assessed to determine the validity of the allegations. Of the screened-in cases, approximately 879,000 children were found to be victims of maltreatment (63% experienced neglect, 19% were physically abused, 10% were sexually abused, and 8% were psychologically maltreated).

Typically, youth exit foster care by being reunited with their families (57%) or through adoption (17%). Others are placed in the home of a relative who is not their parent (10%). The advantage of this type of care is that the parent does not have to relinquish legal rights, yet the child may feel a sense of stability and family belonging. Smaller percentages of children exit through guardianship arrangements (4%); by transfers to other agencies (such as juvenile justice) (3%); by running away (2%); or by dying (less than 1%). Only a small minority of all foster care children "age out" of the system (7%).

Few youth who encounter the child welfare system spend time in out-of-home placements such as foster care. For instance, only one-fifth of the youth that CPS found to be abused or maltreated were removed from their homes (Walter R. McDonald and Associates 2000). Still, approximately 556,000 youth were in foster care in 2000 (U.S. DHHS 2002a). This number is based on information collected from state child welfare organizations by the Administration for Children and Families through the Adoption and Foster Care Analysis and Reporting System (AFCARS).

Of youth who enter foster care, about one-third spend two or more years there (U.S. DHHS 2002a). Reducing the amount of time youth spend in foster care has been a goal of recent state and federal efforts. The most recent of these has been the Adoption and Safe Families Act (ASFA), which has reduced the length of time that the state could hold a youth in custody, without holding a permanency hearing, from eighteen months to one year. This act also required states to provide permanency plans that detailed the necessary steps for placing the youth in a permanent home. In addition, ASFA included financial incentives for states that raised their adoption rates.

Juvenile Justice System

The juvenile justice system typically has jurisdiction over youth who commit crimes or other offenses prior to their eighteenth birthdays. As with child welfare, youth enter and exit the juvenile justice system in a variety of ways. The way in which the system deals with a particular youth varies substantially depending on the youth's age, the nature of the offense committed, and the state and locality involved.

This variation reflects the fact that, like child welfare, responsibility for juvenile justice is shared across different levels of government. Within guidelines established through the U.S. Constitution, states and local jurisdictions shape the juvenile justice system. The Constitution protects youth's rights to "due process and fair treatment." States determine key features of the system, such as the age at which juvenile court authority ends. In some states, for example, juvenile courts are allowed to impose sanctions that extend beyond age eighteen. This arrangement is known as "extended sentencing" (Snyder and Sickmund 1999). In some states, the juvenile court may impose sanctions in the adult correctional facility for youth who would "age out" of juvenile court jurisdiction. This arrangement is known as "blended sentencing" (Sickmund, Snyder, and Poe-Yamagata 1997). Local courts and agencies are typically responsible for matters that occur prior to court appearance and for ordinary probation services (intake, investigation, and supervision). State-level agencies are generally responsible for secure confinement of delinquent youth and aftercare services (Griffin 2000). In contrast to child welfare, the role of the federal government is relatively minor.

Youth enter the juvenile justice system after committing an offense reported by their teachers or family or observed by a police officer. In most communities, a youth's subsequent path through the juvenile justice system depends on whether his or her offense is a delinquent act or a status offense. The latter refers to behaviors that would not constitute a crime if committed by an adult (e.g., curfew violations or truancy), whereas delinquency involves offenses that would be considered crimes regardless of the offender's age. This distinction has important implications in many states. Some states view a status offense as indicating that the youth needs supervision rather than punishment. In these states, status offenses are referred not to the courts but to child welfare.

If an individual is referred to the juvenile courts, his or her case can be handled in a variety of ways. Many youth are processed without an official hearing. An officer of the court (the intake officer) may dismiss the case, may manage it informally, or may require a formal adjudication or waiver hearing. About half of juvenile cases are handled informally whereby the case is officially dismissed after the youth signs a "consent decree" (Snyder and Sickmund 1999). In this document, the youth agrees to a set of specific conditions lasting for a period of time (e.g., victim restitution, school attendance, drug counseling, or a curfew). A probation officer may monitor these conditions. Failure to adhere to these conditions may lead to a formal hearing.

If the case is handled formally, the case may be adjudicated by the juvenile court or waived to the criminal (adult) court. Again, the distinction is important because the former is much less formal. Whereas the adult system bases prosecution decisions solely on legal facts, the juvenile system also considers a youth's personal and social circumstances (e.g., the severity of the offense, offense history, and family characteristics).

Depending on the state, young offenders may enter the adult system in several ways. Many states have statutes that require a case to be handled in the adult system depending on the youth's age and the severity of the crime. For example, in Connecticut, any youth above the age of thirteen who has committed a capital felony, certain other classes of felonies, or an arson murder must be tried in an adult court (Griffin, Torbet, and Szymanksi 1998). In many states, the intake officer or the prosecutor also retains some discretion: they may file a waiver petition requesting that other cases be tried in an adult court. Nonetheless, the adjudication of minors in adult court is still relatively rare. In 1998, eight out of every thousand delinquency cases were waived to the criminal courts (Puzzanchera 2002).

A youth who is found guilty by the juvenile justice system proceeds through a series of steps. Through interviews with individuals who know the youth (parents, teachers, neighbors, counselors, etc.), a probation officer investigates the youth's social circumstances. This investigation assesses the youth's environment, familial relationships, attitude, and behavior in various settings, as well as the ability of the child's parents to provide supervision at home (Trojanowicz, Morash, and Schram 2001). The results of this investigation, along with recommendations by the prosecutor or even the youth, are presented to a judge. In a disposition hearing, the judge determines the best course of action for the youth, who may be released to his or her parents, placed on probation, or institutionalized.

Of the disposition hearings held in 1998, the youth was adjudicated delinquent in 63% of cases (Stahl 2003). Of these, 58% received probation, while 26% received out-of-home placement. According to the 1997 Census of Juveniles in Resident Population data, 106,000 individuals were in residential placement on a given day in 1997. A large percentage of individuals who were in out-of-home placement were adjudicated delinquents (93%), with the remaining being status offenders. Of those receiving out-of-home placements, delinquent youths are typically placed in higher security facilities than status offenders. Three-quarters of confined delinquent youth were in a locked facility compared with one-quarter of confined status offenders.

States differ in how they determine the length of time that an individual spends in such facilities. In some states, the agencies that operate commitment facilities determine the length of confinement. In other states, the court or a juvenile parole board may monitor agency release decisions (Griffin 2000). Typically, when a youth is released from secure confinement, a disposition plan has been designed that involves decreasing amounts of supervision as the youth proves his or her ability to remain in the community.

Special Education

In 1975 Congress determined that approximately 1 million "handicapped" children were receiving no education and that another 3.5 million were not receiving an education appropriate to their level of need (U.S. Department of Education 2002). As a result, Congress enacted the Education for All Handicapped Children Act (EAHCA) in that year. This act gave all children the right to a free and appropriate education and established regulations governing the terms under which this education would be provided. For example, the law requires that each child have an individualized education plan (IEP) that specifies goals for the child's education, as well as a services plan for attaining those goals. The meaning of a "free and appropriate education" has continued to evolve through lawsuits and subsequent laws, such as the Individuals with Disabilities Act (IDEA), the successor to EAHCA.

Like child welfare and juvenile justice, responsibility for special education is shared across levels of government. Like general education, special education is largely funded using state and local funds. The federal allotment for special education accounts for only about 10% of the cost of special education (Chambers, Parrish, and Harr 2002).

During the 2001–2 school year, special education programs served more than 6 million children ages three to twenty-one (Westat 2002b). Eligible youth are those who have one of the thirteen conditions listed in IDEA and need services in order to benefit from their education. Special education students receive services in a variety of settings: regular classrooms, separate classrooms, special schools, residential facilities, or their own homes. The particular configuration of services received must be outlined and justified in his or her IEP. That plan must be developed in consultation with a child's parents and must be reviewed periodically. The law also specifies a series of steps for resolving disputes between parents and schools.

Children and youth leave special education in a variety of ways. Of the nearly 375,000 students aged fourteen to twenty-one who exited special education during the 2000–2001 school year, only about 70,448 returned to regular education. Others left by dropping out (89,672), graduating with a diploma (173,523), receiving a certificate (33,427), reaching the maximum age (5,959), or dying (1,791). The majority of individuals who dropped out were ages sixteen or older.

In sum, for a variety of reasons a large number of children and youth encounter the three systems considered here. At least for juvenile justice and child welfare, however, only a minority remains in those systems long enough and/or participate to such a degree that they become eligible for transition services. The processes by which individuals move through these systems vary across communities and evolve over time.

HOW MANY CHILDREN ARE INVOLVED?

The three groups considered vary substantially in size. The best available estimates suggest that children leaving foster care represent the smallest of the three groups. The U.S. Department of Health and Human Services estimates that nearly 20,000 adolescents are emancipated from foster care each year. In fiscal year 2000, 19,895 were reported as emancipated according to AFCARS data.

The next largest group involves children leaving the juvenile justice system. A complete count of this group includes individuals leaving either a juvenile or an adult facility. The Census of Juveniles in Residential Placement, which provides information on the former, reveals that an estimated 37,880 individuals aged seventeen to twenty were in residential placement in 1997 (Sickmund 2000). The majority of these youth are released within a relatively short time period. For instance, data reveal that the length of stay in these facilities averages less than six months (Sickmund 1997).

The Census of Juveniles in Residential Placement figures do not include individuals residing in adult facilities who were admitted prior to their eighteenth birthdays. Data for these individuals are available from the National Corrections Report Program. These data reveal that 9,300 individuals who had been admitted to state prisons prior to their eighteenth birthdays were released from state prisons in 1997 (Storm 2000).[1] Combining the two sets of figures, we estimate that roughly 45,000 adolescents exit juvenile or adult facilities each year.

Clearly, the largest of the three groups involves individuals exiting special education. Department of Education data reveal that approximately 375,000 adolescents exited special education in the 2000–2001 school year (Westat 2002a). This figure includes students both in and out of residential settings.

WHY FOCUS ON THESE GROUPS?

As discussed above, these three groups are fairly sizable in absolute terms but still involve only a minority of all adolescents. (According to the 2000 census, 20,219,890 youths were aged fifteen to nineteen in 2000.) The special attention they receive, however, exceeds their actual numbers. This importance derives from the challenges they face and from the problematic outcomes they experience as they enter adulthood.

Series of Challenges

Individuals leaving the foster care, juvenile justice, and special education systems face a variety of challenges, including learning disabilities, limited life skills, and health or emotional and behavioral problems.

First, learning disabilities are quite common among children and adolescents in these three groups. Among children in the juvenile justice system, 30%–50% of all youth in the correctional system have an identified learning disability (Rutherford et al. 2002). As one might expect, such problems are quite common among children in special education as well. Sixty percent of these children have been diagnosed with a learning disability.

Obviously, these problems hinder school performance, but these children have limited life skills more generally. For example, in a study of youth leaving foster care (described below), approximately 30% of respondents felt unprepared for managing their own money, living on their own, obtaining housing, or getting a job. Forty percent felt unprepared for parenting (Courtney et al. 2001). Despite being in high school, almost a third (32%) of adolescents exiting foster care were at or below an eighth-grade reading level (Dworsky and Courtney 2001). Another study of forty-six youth who had been in foster care revealed that 90% reported difficulty budgeting their earnings and saving after discharge (Mallon 1998).

A third category of challenges involves health and emotional and behavioral problems. Based on Medicaid claims data from Pennsylvania and California, Rosenbach and colleagues (2000) found that between 30% and 40% of children in foster care had physical or emotional problems (Rosenbach, Lewis, and Quinn 2000). Another analysis of adolescents aging out of the system (described in more detail below) found that 47% of survey respondents had received some form of mental health or social services while in care (Courtney et al. 2001). A 1990 study of foster care youths who were leaving care found that 38% were emotionally disturbed (Cook 1991).

Similarly, youth involved in the juvenile justice system were more likely to have psychosocial disorders as well as physical problems than were a comparison group of similarly aged males (Forrest et al. 2000). This analysis of 202 children consecutively admitted to a Maryland juvenile residential facility revealed that these youth had more acute injuries (broken bones, head injuries, and gunshot wounds), more physical discomfort, more chronic disorders, lower self esteem, and were less likely to report being in good or excellent health. In a study of detainees in Cook County, Illinois, Teplin and colleagues (2002) found high rates of affective disorder (19% and 28% for males and females, respectively) and of attention-related disorders (17% and 21% for males and females, respectively). Nearly half of enrollees were identified as having a behavior disorder (41% and 46% for males and females, respectively).

Data from the Office of Special Education Programs indicate that 12% of children leaving special education meet the criteria for emotional disturbance (Westat 2002a). According to IDEA, emotional disturbance is a condition that adversely affects a youth's education and is marked by at least one of the following persistent conditions: (1) an inability to learn that is not explained by intellectual, sensory, or health factors; (2) an inability to build or maintain relationships with peers or teachers; (3) inappropriate behaviors or feelings under normal conditions; (4) pervasive mood of unhappiness or depression; or (5) a tendency to develop physical symptoms or fears associated with personal or school problems (IDEA Practices 2002).

These data reveal high rates of mental and physical health problems among youth in these three systems. In interpreting these figures, one should bear in mind two additional factors. First, the children in these groups often face multiple disabilities. As a result, information on individual disabilities understates the difficulties facing some youth. Medicaid data on children in foster care, for example, indicate substantial overlap between mental and physical conditions. Second, abuse of alcohol and other drugs is common among these groups as well. Roughly half of both males and females in the Cook County study of juvenile justice youth had a substance use disorder (51% and 47%, respectively [Teplin et al. 2002]). Among children exiting foster care, 42% had used alcohol in the previous thirty days, and 13% had used marijuana in the previous thirty days (Cook 1990).

Limited Familial Support

Family resources often smooth the transition to adulthood. In contrast, adolescents in these special populations often come from families whose economic resources are limited. In other instances, the quality of the relationships in their families is degraded or poor.

Little information is available on the families of individuals exiting juvenile justice, but a long series of studies link delinquency and family resources, such as poverty (e.g., Browning and Loeber 1999). Those studies suggest that these individuals are likely to be from poor single-parent families.

Similarly, children from poor single-parent families are overrepresented in special education as well. Wagner and colleagues (1993) report that 68% of those in special education are from families with incomes of less than $25,000 compared with only 40% of students in the general population. Moreover, special education students were 50% more likely to come from a single-parent home (37% vs. 25% for other children). Low levels of parental education are also common among these students (Wagner et al. 1993).

Family resources encompass more than financial means. A variety of studies have examined the link between parent-child relationships and delinquency. The Rochester Youth Study, for example, found that delinquents were less likely to have warm and involved parents. If the quality of parent-child relationships does not improve over time, then children in these special populations will have fewer emotional resources as they age (Browning, Thornberry, and Porter 1999). These problems are most stark among children leaving the foster care system. Courtney and colleagues (2001) report that 66% of youth reported having been neglected, 57% having been physically abused, and 31% having been sexually abused.

Poor Outcomes

While limited, available evidence suggests that youth in these special populations fare poorly across a range of outcomes—school completion, employment, public assistance, early fertility, and homelessness and residential stability. Table 15.1 describes outcomes for each group. We briefly review the studies on which the table is based.

For youth leaving foster care, four studies provide the best evidence. The first involves interviews with a sample of 810 youth in eight states conducted by Westat (Cook 1991). Individuals were eligible for the study if they were sixteen years or older and discharged from foster care between January 1987 and July 1988. Outcomes were measured thirty to forty-eight months after exiting foster care when the youth were ages eighteen to twenty-four. A wide range of outcomes was examined, such as education, employment, access to health care, social support, and mental health.

A second study, the Foster Youth Transitions to Adulthood Study, involved a sample of 113 youth in Wisconsin (Courtney et al. 2001). The study comprised three waves of interviews—while the youth were residing in out-of-home care, twelve to eighteen months after exiting foster care, and three years after exiting foster care. A third study was larger in size but relied exclusively on administrative data. That study analyzed employment, earnings, and public assistance among former foster care youth. Individuals were eligible for the study if they exited out-of-home care between 1992 and 1998 and were at least age seventeen at the time they exited the system (Dworsky and Courtney 2001). Employment and earnings information was taken from the Wisconsin unemployment insurance file; these data were used to describe employment and earnings during the first eight quarters following exit (Dworsky and Courtney 2001). State administrative data were used to describe the use of AFDC/Temporary Aid to Needy Families and food stamps during the same period. Employment and public assistance outcomes were also followed until the year 2000.

In a fourth study, Goerge and colleagues (2002) examined employment outcomes using administrative data. The sample included youth who reached their eighteenth birthdays during the study period (1996–97 in Illinois and South Carolina and 1995–96 in California) and who were emancipated at age eighteen. Data were extracted from Child Welfare Information Systems, unemployment insurance files, and the income maintenance program eligibility and tracking systems. Employment outcomes were tracked for thirteen quarters and included the amount each youth earned and number of quarters each youth was employed.

For youth exiting special education, the best source of data is the National Longitudinal Transition Study of Special Education Students (NLTS). The study interviewed a nationally representative sample of 8,000 youth who were thirteen to twenty-one and in secondary school in 1985. The weighted sample generalizes to youth served with disabilities nationally and separately to each of the eleven disability categories at that time. Data collection occurred between 1987 and 1990. Information was obtained from multiple sources—telephone interviews, analyses of high school transcripts, and surveys of teachers and principals. The NLTS also included more than 800 youth who exited special education between 1985 and 1987.

In addition to the evaluations discussed below, we identified two studies tracking individuals exiting juvenile justice. The first study tracked 759 individuals who were exiting two Wisconsin high schools (both of which were correctional facilities) in 1979. Data were gathered from school transcripts (including schools that the youth had previously attended), computerized records from the Division of Corrections as well as the youth's test scores, educational plans on release, social service records, and parole officers. This study tracked youth's educational attainment (high school completion and acquisition of a general equivalency degree [GED]) for three years postrelease. A second study, the Transition Research on Adjudicated Youth in Community Settings, involved a five-year longitudinal study of 531 incarcerated youth in Oregon. Participants were recruited from two large juvenile correction programs and three correctional camps. Interviews were conducted at six-month intervals after return to the community for one to four years. The study examined employment, schooling, living arrangements, and level of independence.

Table 15.1 draws on these studies to describe a range of outcomes for the three populations. Note that figures for different groups and from different studies are only roughly comparable because of differences in the way the outcomes were measured. One can see that, regardless of the outcome considered, these individuals fare poorly during early adulthood. Looking first at education, between 37% and 46% of individuals leaving foster care had not finished high school at follow-up. This rate is roughly comparable to that for youth leaving special education (38%). The figure for youth leaving juvenile justice is especially high: 54% of youth leaving the juvenile justice system had not completed a high school degree or GED after returning to the community.

Not surprisingly (given their education), youth leaving the three systems show high levels of joblessness. Roughly half of individuals exiting foster care and juvenile justice were jobless during early adulthood. The picture for youth exiting special education is somewhat better. Only about 20% of these youth who were looking for employment lacked a job three to five years after exiting services.

Public assistance figures for youth exiting foster care suggest that roughly one-third of these youth were receiving AFDC cash benefits at the follow-up interview. Similarly, our tabulations of the NLTS suggest that about one-fifth of youth exiting special education receive public assistance three to five years after exiting school. One explanation of these figures for women involves high rates of early fertility. In the Westat study, nearly 60% of young women had given birth by the follow-up interview. Other studies of youth exiting foster care reveal high rates of early fertility as well. Figures available for juvenile justice and special education also suggest early parenthood.

Finally, as the low levels of education and high rates of joblessness suggest, individuals leaving these three systems have problems living on their own or even finding a stable place to live. Nearly two out of three individuals leaving special education had not achieved residential stability, meaning that they lived with family members, in a foster home, or in some type of supervised living facility (Wagner et al. 1993). These figures also include individuals who have experienced bouts of homelessness. Among

TABLE 15.1

OUTCOMES DURING EARLY ADULTHOOD FOR SPECIAL POPULATIONS

	FOSTER CARE		JUVENILE JUSTICE		SPECIAL EDUCATION	
	STUDY	%	STUDY	%	STUDY	%
School failure	Courtney et al. 2001	37	Habermann and Quinn 1986	54	Wagner et al. 1993; Wagner and Blackorby 1996	38
	Cook 1990, 1991	46				
Joblessness	Goerge et al. 2002	14	Bullis et al. 2002	69	Wagner et al. 1993; Wagner and Blackorby 1996	19–36
	Cook 1990, 1991	51				
Public assistance	Courtney et al. 2001	31	N.A.		Author's tabulations (NLTS exiter-substudy)	19
	Cook 1990, 1991	34				
Early fertility	· · ·		Thornberry et al. 2000	25	Wagner et al. 1993; Wagner and Blackorby 1996	24
Men	Cook 1990, 1991	23	· · ·		· · ·	
Women	Cook 1990, 1991	60	· · ·		· · ·	
Residential instability	Courtney et al. 2001	12	N.A.		Wagner et al. 1993; Wagner and Blackorby 1996	63[a]
	Cook 1990, 1991	25[b]				

[a] Had not achieved residential independence.
[b] Homeless.

those who had been in foster care, for example, fully one in four had been homeless at some point since leaving that home (Cook 1990, 1991).

RELATIONSHIP TO PROGRAMS CHANGES
ON APPROACHING ADULTHOOD

Clearly, youth exiting these three systems face challenges and experience poor outcomes in adulthood. These problems need to be viewed in the context of their administrative transition out of programs that have often shaped their lives for long periods of time. Children in foster care, for example, remain in state care for nearly three years on average (thirty-three months [U.S. DHHS 2002a]). Similarly, youth exiting special education and juvenile justice often have a long history of involvement with those systems.

The administrative transition to adulthood differs in some critical ways among the three systems. For juvenile justice, this period signals a change from a child-oriented system (juvenile justice) to an adult system (criminal justice). For youth in foster care or special education, involvement in the child-oriented programs ends, and their future well-being depends on their ability to connect with various programs targeted at adults, such as vocational rehabilitation. However, young people in all three groups enter a transitional period during which their involvement with the system is reduced or transformed.

Children in foster care, for example, are required to leave state care between the ages of eighteen and twenty-one. In most states, individuals remaining in care after age eighteen must be working or in school for the equivalent of full-time hours. Starting at age sixteen, preparation for exiting the system begins as youth become eligible for transition services (described below).

Involvement in the juvenile justice system is also governed by the maximum age at which individuals can remain in a juvenile justice facility. In most states, youth sentenced in the juvenile justice system can remain in system facilities through age twenty. Some of these youth have a blended sentence and are then transferred to the adult criminal system.

As they approach adulthood, special education students also enter a transitional period. IDEA mandates that public K–12 education systems provide services until an individual receives a high school diploma or until the individual reaches his or her twenty-first birthday. The IEP team may decide that a student's education or transition services should continue beyond the time that the student has completed graduation requirements. The student may continue to receive services with the stipulation that he or she has not actually received his or her diploma (Morningstar, Lattin, and Sarkesian 1998). Many school districts do allow special education youth reaching age eighteen to participate in high school graduation ceremonies.

TRANSITION IS FACILITATED BY PROGRAMS

Unlike most youth, the three groups examined here are eligible for services designed to improve the transition to adulthood. These programs cover a wide range of services and vary substantially across communities. In this section, we review the origins of these programs, their goals, the types of services provided, and recent developments as well as evidence of effectiveness.

Transition Services for Children Leaving Foster Care

Services are provided to individuals exiting the foster care system under the Independent Living Program (ILP). These programs were first authorized under a temporary program in 1985 and then made permanent in 1993. As originally authorized, eligibility was limited to youth ages sixteen to eighteen who qualified for the federal Title IV-E program, and funds could not be used for housing or living expenses. Federal funds provide the majority of the dollars for ILP. In 1996, this program served approximately 67,600 individuals (Goldman, Capitani, and Archambault 1999).

The ILP was recently reorganized and expanded under the Foster Care Independence Act of 1999 (FCIA; also known as the John H. Chafee Foster Care Independence Program). Under FCIA, adolescents up to age twenty-one who are in foster care or have aged out of foster care are eligible for services without regard to their Title IV-E status. In addition, FCIA increased federal funding from 70 million dollars under the ILP to 140 million dollars and requires states to match 20% of the federal dollars.

Among the types of assistance provided by ILP are educational opportunities (including vocational training), counseling and support services, training in daily living skills, outreach services, and a range of other services such as family planning and parenting classes (U.S. General Accounting Office 1999). According to a review of annual state reports on ILPs, the services most commonly offered include postsecondary education support, education and career resources, home maintenance, personal care, medical care, education, teen parenting classes, substance abuse, and youth advisory boards and newsletters (Goldman et al. 1999). States also have focused on building life skills such as decision making, communication, and conflict resolution (Goldman et al. 1999). The FCIA has had a significant effect on service delivery, and the Chaffee program expanded available services greatly. In addition, states now can use up to 30% of program funds for room and board.

In general, very little is known about the effectiveness of ILP offerings (U.S. General Accounting Office 1999). The only national assessment of independent living services was conducted in the late 1980s (Cook 1990, 1991). This study examined the link between specific services and key youth outcomes such as employment, education, health care, social costs (such as using welfare or being in jail), and life satisfaction. The study was observational; no effort was made to assign individuals randomly to different services. It compared outcomes for individuals who did and did not receive specific services, such as managing money, obtaining health insurance, obtaining car insurance, finding housing, and doing house chores (Cook 1991). To control for preexisting differences among individuals receiving different services, the study did adjust for a variety of individual factors. Covariates included demographics (e.g., race and ethnicity), the youth's health (e.g., emotional disturbance), history of involvement in foster care (e.g., age-entered care and reason for placement), and youth problems (e.g., use of drugs and pregnancy prior to leaving foster care).

This study generally found that receipt of services improved relevant outcomes. For instance, youth who received training on accessing health care were less likely to have problems obtaining needed health care. In some instances, the link between the type of training and the outcome was not obvious. Obtaining consumer training, for example, was positively associated with avoiding early parenthood. One explanation for this is that service use is confounded with characteristics not included in the extensive list identified above. This weakness is inherent in a study of this sort.

A range of smaller studies also considers the nature and impact of ILP services, but these studies suffer from a variety of limitations (Lindsey and Ahmed 1999; McMillen and Tucker 1999; Scannapieco, Schagrin, and Scannapieco 1995). These studies are reviewed in detail in Courtney and Bost (2002), and we do not review them here. In general, they did not measure self-sufficiency outcomes such as employment and residential independence, lacked a reasonable comparison group, were limited by small sample sizes, and poorly measured the services and interventions that youth received (Courtney and Bost 2002).

Transition Services for Individuals Leaving Juvenile Justice

A range of programs addresses the needs of individuals moving from residential placement in the juvenile justice system to the community. Included among these are aftercare programs, one of several forms of parole or non-custodial supervision for juveniles (Altschuler and Armstrong 1994a, 1994b; Altschuler, Armstrong, and Mackenzie 1999). These programs can involve a variety of services, including job training, counseling or tutoring, which may be provided in residential or nonresidential settings and often involve a case management component (Altschuler and Armstrong 1994a, 1994b; Altschuler et al. 1999). The programs promote goals that communities identify as important (such as reductions in recidivism or substance abuse or increases in school completion).

Federal initiatives have stimulated the growth of these programs. In 1987, the Office of Juvenile Justice and Delinquency Prevention began designing and implementing the Intensive Community-based Aftercare Program. This model targets youth most likely to be reincarcerated, such as those who were arrested at young ages, who have a history of arrests, or who are property offenders. The philosophy of the model includes three components: each youth should receive services that match his or her needs; the youth must be held accountable for his or her actions; and public safety must be maintained (Altschuler and Armstrong 1994a, 1994b).

To achieve these goals, these intensive aftercare programs (IAPs) provide a continuum of support and supervision through a series of phases. Support begins at system entry when the individual's needs are assessed and programs are identified to meet those needs. During incarceration, youth may receive educational, vocational, or mental health counseling, drug/alcohol treatment, and life-skills training services (Wiebush, McNulty, and Le 2000). On release, youth receive supervision and support. Problems that may hinder reintegration, such as family, peer, or school problems are identified and addressed by connecting the youth with the appropriate community resources. During this phase, youth may continue to receive services delivered while incarcerated as well as counseling and monitoring of school attendance (Clouser 1996). Finally, in the "long-term reintegration" phase, youth are weaned from the support provided by the aftercare team.

Rigorous evaluations are somewhat more common for aftercare programs than for ILP and special education programs. In a review of early programs, Altschuler and colleagues (1999) identified four evaluations: (1) the Philadelphia Intensive Probation Aftercare Program; (2) Juvenile Aftercare in a Maryland Drug Treatment Program; (3) the Skillman Intensive Aftercare Project in Detroit and Pittsburgh; and (4) the Michigan Nokomis Challenge Program.

The Philadelphia program targeted serious, violent, and habitual offenders (Sontheimer and Goodstein 1993). Aged seventeen on average, participants were males and had at least one prior adjudication for a serious crime or multiple adjudications for burglary. Individuals were randomly assigned to either the control group ($n = 53$) or an experimental group ($n = 53$). The former received traditional treatment, which involved meeting with a probation officer twice a month. For the experimental group, contact with the probation officer was to be much more frequent. In particular, the program required probation officers to meet in person with each youth three times per week during the first six weeks, at least twice a week during the second six weeks, and once a week thereafter. Probation officers were also encouraged to contact the youth's family and friends. The evaluation tracked participants for three to seventeen months after release.

The Maryland program targeted male and female juvenile offenders with a history of drug abuse (Sealock, Gottsfredson, and Gallagher 1997). Both the control group and the experimental group entered a residential treatment facility immediately after being released from the detention facility. During residential treatment, the youth participated in Alcoholics Anonymous, academic courses, recreational activities, vocational education, work assignments, and social activities. The study employed a quasi-experimental design. The control group ($n = 132$) lived in areas surrounding Baltimore and did not receive aftercare services. The treatment group involved youth living in Baltimore, and these individuals received aftercare services on leaving residential treatment ($n = 120$). Those services were delivered in three phases, beginning while the youth was still in residential treatment. During this initial, prerelease phase, a family therapist met with the family to develop a family treatment participation contract. On release to the community, the youth began the intensive aftercare phase, which included intensive supervision by aftercare staff: daily in-person contacts, group support meetings and family support meetings. Meanwhile, the youth met individually with an addiction counselor. During the final phase, the transitional aftercare phase, youth met with a case manager twice per week and with an addiction counselor at least twice per month. Family support groups were continued and links with the appropriate community-based services were established.

The Skillman program examined whether IAP could lessen the length of time that adjudicated youth spend in residential placement. This program focused on male juvenile offenders from Detroit and Pittsburgh. Youth from each site were randomly assigned to either a control group ($n = 87$) or an experimental group ($n = 96$). While the former spent the traditional length of time in residential placement, the latter received intensive aftercare supervision in lieu of the last two months of residential care. Caseworkers provided a host of services for youth in the experimental group. Prior to release, the caseworker contacted the youth and family. After release, the caseworker would contact the youth frequently (several times a day in the beginning and then diminishing with time), monitoring the youth's whereabouts and behaviors, as well as providing guidance. When possible, the caseworker would work with family members, providing counseling and striving for improved family functioning/stability. The caseworker also helped the youth identify and pursue potential job or education opportunities (Greenwood, Deschenes, and Adams 1993). Study participants averaged age sixteen, and follow-up data collection continued for twelve months.

Finally, the Michigan Nokomis Challenge Program targeted medium- to low-risk juvenile offenders (Deschenes, Greenwood, and Marshall 1996). The intervention involved three months of wilderness camp followed by nine months of aftercare treatment and surveillance. The evaluation compared youth who received the intervention ($n = 102$) with a matched sample of youth who spent roughly sixteen months in a residential training school ($n = 97$). Study participants were age sixteen and a half on average; outcomes were tracked for twenty-four months.

For the most part, these studies show few if any benefits of aftercare (Altschuler et al. 1999). Given that the control or comparison groups received alternative services, one would anticipate small effects. Only in the Philadelphia program did aftercare reduce subsequent arrests (1.65 vs 2.79) and convictions.[2] The lack of statistically significant findings may also reflect a lack of precision stemming from small sample sizes. In two of the four studies, nonequivalent comparison groups pose unknown problems. Nonrandom sample attrition was also a substantial limitation of these analyses. Because some of the programs were not implemented as intended, it is difficult to know the specific reason for failure to find an effect of aftercare. For example, staff turnover or funding issues may also have played a role.

Transition Services for Adolescents Leaving Special Education

The Individuals with Disabilities Act requires that transition services be provided to special education students starting at age fourteen. As discussed above, individuals remain eligible for services until they receive their high school diplomas.[3] Under the original special education law (the Education for All Handicapped Children Act [EAHCA] 1975), no special provisions were made for children exiting special education. However, IDEA amended EAHCA and mandated that the IEP for students' age sixteen and older include transition-related goals and services. The 1997 law extends the age range downward to age fourteen. The current disabilities act mandates that

IEPs specify transition goals and identify transition services that target those goals. Those services should reflect the youth's needs and preferences as well.

One can think of transition services as falling roughly within three age ranges: ages fourteen to sixteen, ages sixteen to eighteen, and eighteen and older. In the first period, the transition goals must focus on the student's course of study (e.g., vocational education), and services are largely school-based. For those age sixteen and older, these goals must not only address instruction but also provide community experiences, employment, daily living skills, and vocational evaluation. The plan must include other related services, such as rehabilitation counseling or other services necessary to achieve the plan's goals (Morningstar et al. 1998). During the third period, students increasingly receive services away from the school. These services may even be provided by other agencies, such as a state department of vocational rehabilitation (Morningstar et al. 1998). The local school district remains responsible for ensuring that adolescents receive the services that they need regardless of how they are arranged or delivered (Wright and Wright 1999). School districts differ enormously in the services they provide.

To date, there have been no evaluations of transition services. As with the Westat study of ILP services, the NLTS has been used to examine the link between transition services and planning and posttransition outcomes. In particular, Wagner and Blackorby (1996) examined the predictors of post-school employment and education. They find that many individuals, especially those with mild impairments, benefit from vocational education. The benefits of work experience programs were limited to a smaller group, those with physical impairments and mild disabilities. Regular education placement improved outcomes for those with physical disabilities but was less helpful for others. In particular, the benefits of regular education accrued only to those who were able to complete those courses successfully. Simply taking—and struggling in—regular classes was not inherently beneficial.

CONCLUSION

We began this chapter by arguing that youth leaving special education, juvenile justice and child welfare—while relatively small in number—deserve special attention. Although limited, the available data clearly indicate that these youth face special challenges as they enter adulthood. The discussion above also demonstrates that a wide range of programs and services are targeted to these individuals at this critical stage. The data on outcomes illustrate that this attention is not misplaced. Given that the United States lacks a clear, cohesive infrastructure for facilitating the transition to adulthood for all youth, it seems appropriate that the limited resources available are targeted to these special populations.

We have also reviewed here the rather limited evidence on the programs serving these youth. With the exception of special education, even drawing a nationally representative picture of the services youth receive is difficult, if not impossible. Information about these programs and the youth they serve is mostly limited to specific communities and, given the potential variation within and across states, it is difficult to generalize. Even less is known about the effectiveness of those services. The research on juvenile justice is most developed among the three groups, but only a handful of studies have rigorously examined the impact of aftercare services.

The Need for and Barriers to Future Research

Many questions remain unanswered. Transition programs, for example, include various services targeted to a range of goals, including improved literacy, vocational training, job search, and living skills as well as reductions in substance abuse. Little is known about whether some components are more effective than others, the appropriate sequence and duration with which these components should be delivered, and how to match an individual's needs to the appropriate services.

Questions remain at the macro or community level as well. Clearly, the type and extent of services available vary substantially within and across states. Relatively little is known about the reasons why communities adopt certain strategies, about how those services evolve over time, or about how the transition programs stimulate or stunt the development of the services context.

Why don't we know more? One can identify at least four reasons. First, existing data sources (like those analyzed for the other chapters in this volume) are often inadequate for examining special populations. Second, developing new data sources is particularly difficult and expensive for these special populations. Third, while essential to these analyses, administrative data pose special challenges. Fourth, and finally, this research requires a multidisciplinary research team composed of service providers, policymakers, and researchers, which is hard to assemble.

The first challenge involves the inadequacy of national surveys for examining the lives of these special populations. Many studies, such as the National Longitudinal Survey of Youth, the National Survey of America's Families, the Survey of Income and Program Participation, and the Panel Study of Income Dynamics omit (at least some) institutionalized populations from their initial sampling frame and/or from follow-up data collection. As a result, many or most youth in foster care and juvenile justice are excluded. Also missing are many of the most interesting (and most costly) individuals in special education, those attending special residential schools.

When national surveys do include institutionalized populations, the information that is collected is often insufficient. For example, the National Longitudinal Study of Adolescent Health ("Add Health") included institutionalized persons in its initial sampling frame. However, it is impossible for the researcher to identify the type of facility involved. (A wide range of facilities are lumped together as "group quarters.")

Similarly, many national surveys rely on interviews with youth and their parents. Such reports may be an inadequate source of information for key constructs. For example, the Panel Study of Income Dynamics collects information on special education from parental interviews. Parents, however, may have difficulty distinguishing special education per se from remedial services or those provided under Section 504 of the Rehabilitation Act of 1973.[4] Parents may not even know that their child is receiving special education services.[5] Likewise, the National Longitudinal Survey of Youth includes self-reported information on involvement with the police and juvenile justice systems. Yet, the stigma associated with such involvement may lead individuals to underreport their involvement. Moreover, national studies may omit key constructs altogether, such as whether a caregiver is the child's legal guardian. Given that these constructs are irrelevant for most respondents (especially given the sampling frame) and the need to keep interviews at a manageable length, such omissions are reasonable. For the populations of interest here, however, those omissions represent critical limitations.

As a result, studies mounted specifically to study special populations may represent the best source of data on these groups. Developing such studies is difficult and costly. Simply obtaining a cost-effective sampling frame and recruiting study participants may be challenging. In the case of juvenile justice and child welfare, a random community sample would yield relatively few individuals who are involved with at least one of these systems especially if limited to those eligible for transition services. Other sampling strategies, such as oversampling the relevant agencies (e.g., the foster care rolls) or facilities (e.g., youth detention centers), also pose problems. The facilities may be unable to produce a list of youth under their care and contact information for their families. In the case of child welfare, for instance, lawsuits filed against the agencies involved often cite a failure to track the children in state custody as evidence of the system's failure. Furthermore, obtaining a list of eligible participants may pose legal and ethical challenges if students' rights are to be respected. Juvenile justice or other agencies cannot simply release the names of individuals in their care. In many cases, before the research team can contact the family, the agency must obtain permission from the child's legal guardian. An added challenge involves maintaining adequate response rates. The Westat study of individuals leaving foster care, for example, had follow-up rates below 50% (Cook 1991).

A third challenge involves the difficulties associated with administrative data. Such data are necessary to document key features of the individual's involvement with the systems of interest. These data, however, have key limitations and must be combined with interview data for many purposes. Administrative data lack key outcome measures (such as measures of mental health status) and provide no information on children or youth who have left the systems. Furthermore, the data may be difficult to access (e.g., paper records) or of low quality, reflecting the limited resources of the systems involved. Even if good on average, quality and content likely vary across sources. For example, a review of ILPs revealed that agencies did not use a standardized format for reporting information. Reports consequently differed in content, depth, breadth, and methodology. As a result, the reports defined essential terms such as "served," "eligible," "completed services," "needs assessment," "counseling," and "aftercare" differently (Goldman et al. 1999). This variation complicates comparing service delivery across communities. Still other problems are posed by a desire to link records from different service systems (e.g., juvenile justice records and welfare caseload data five years post exit).

The fourth and final challenge involves assembling the right research team. That team should involve researchers, service providers, and representatives of the public agencies involved. Developing a cohesive whole from these parts is difficult. Often strapped for resources, public agencies may be unwilling to invest in research. Furthermore, those agencies may be reluctant to release data, especially in an environment where lawsuits are common. They may have had negative experiences with researchers and perceive them as asking for data (and funding) but offering little in return. Over time, these fears may be allayed as researchers and policymakers learn to trust each other, but such relationships develop slowly.

Service providers are also essential members of the research team. They provide a sense of the aims and content of service delivery, including the barriers to effective delivery, such as why individuals drop out of services. For a program evaluation, they can provide important insights into program implementation and other information necessary for interpreting measures of effectiveness.

Researchers represent the third and final member of the research team. They provide the necessary expertise in research design and methodology and in program evaluation. Yet researchers may be unwilling to invest the time and energy to develop necessary partnerships. Furthermore, this type of research does not fit within the bounds of a single discipline. An understanding of developmental psychology and sociology provides insight into the youths' needs, while knowledge of economics and management is essential for shaping policies and service delivery approaches. Many researchers may find that such interdisciplinary work is not well rewarded in traditional academic departments.

These challenges are formidable. Recent developments, however, offer some hope. The National Longitudinal Transition Study represents a model for how descriptive information can be collected for special populations. The second generation of that study is in the field now. Furthermore, the FCIA required a national evaluation of ILP, and planning for that evaluation is underway. Finally, with regard to aftercare, federal funding recently was made available to implement and evaluate a handful of IAPs (Wiebush et al. 2000). These studies build on the lessons of the earlier studies; they rely, for example, on random assignment.

Evaluating Available Programs from a Life-Course Perspective

Much of the other material in this volume is presented and discussed from a life-course perspective. What does that framework reveal about these programs and policies? Settersten (2003) poses a series of questions for thinking about social policies. Several of these are particularly relevant here, and we discuss them below.

The first of Settersten's questions asks whether the model of the life course underlying a policy is rigid or flexible. All three of the systems described in this chapter rely largely on a model of the life course that is relatively inflexible. This rigidity is apparent in two ways. First, the key steps and stages in the process by which individuals move into and through transition services are still defined mainly by age rather than by an individual's need for services. Entry into juvenile justice aftercare is less structured; individuals receive those services when discharged from residential services. However, as discussed earlier, both entry into and exit from those facilities is strongly influenced by the youth's age. This inflexibility is particularly striking in light of the enormous diversity of experiences among typical young adults (Mouw, this vol., chap. 8; Wu and Li, this vol., chap. 4).

A second rigidity involves the degree to which families are involved in transition services. With the exception of model programs of juvenile justice aftercare, none of the programs equip families to support youth during the transition to adulthood. Both child welfare and special education presume that the youth will have to live independently of his or her family on leaving the system. In the case of special education, this assumption may be inappropriate. Many of the youth have disabilities and will rely on their parents and families for support well into adulthood. Our tabulations of the NLTS suggest that 62% of students who had exited special education between 1985 and 1987 and who were over the age of twenty-three in 1990 were living with family members. In the case of child welfare, the assumption that family support and involvement will be lacking may appear reasonable. That a youth has been in foster care suggests that his or her family was poorly equipped to care for the child and that their involvement in his or her life will be minimal. However, research indicates that a significant proportion of youth leaving foster care continue to have contact with their families (Courtney et al. 2001). In that light, the problems of the past only accentuate the need to prepare families and youth for life together in early adulthood.

The limited support these programs offer for families highlights a second of Settersten's questions: Does the vision of the life course lag "behind the times"? The other chapters in this volume make it clear that families offer key support to their children as they enter early adulthood (e.g., Corcoran and Matsudaira, this vol., chap. 11; Mouw, this vol., chap. 8; Schoeni and Ross, this vol., chap. 12). The assumption that youth live "independently" in early adulthood seems outdated.

Settersten poses a third question that is particularly relevant here: What are the program's underlying assumptions about who is at risk? As discussed above, all three systems use the degree of involvement in the system as a measure of risk or need. The educational, child welfare and juvenile justice systems all provide transition services to only some of the youth who potentially need those services. Individuals with IEPs get transition services; those served under section 504 or remedial programs do not. Individuals in detention facilities may receive aftercare; those who were diverted earlier do not. Individuals who spend time in foster care are eligible for independent living programs; those who otherwise encounter the child welfare system are not. In a world of scarce resources, some rationing is necessary. However, involvement in these systems is shaped by many factors other than the youth's need for transition services. In some instances, these other factors are quite salient; individuals may be diverted from juvenile justice because of their family's perceived ability to monitor and care for them. To the extent these families would offer greater resources to their child during the transition to adulthood, that youth's needs for transition services would be less than those of a youth placed in detention. At the same time, other factors less related to the family's ability to offer transition support (such as their race) may influence involvement in these systems and have unintended implications for access to transition services.

That these systems act as the gateway to transition or independent living services has other implications as well. The children and youth in these three systems overlap substantially. Many youth are involved with more than one system or share common problems and challenges, but in many communities the systems operate fairly independently. For this reason, the system into which a child enters and stays has important implications for their access to transition services. While this lack of coordination across systems may simplify program administration, it violates a central feature of life-course studies: that of the person-oriented perspective. Such a perspective requires that an individual's life be considered as a whole and that a fragmented view of delinquency, education, and family circumstances is likely to offer an incomplete view of the youth's needs as he or she enters adulthood. A holistic view provides a much sounder foundation on which to plan and deliver services.

A fourth question posed by Settersten (2003) involves social costs: What are the costs associated with a policy? And for whom? As discussed earlier, the costs of these programs are substantial. The limited amount of available research makes it difficult to say whether this money is well spent. If the programs fail to serve those in greatest need or if the services themselves are ineffectual, then these programs do not represent a good use of society's resources.

However, it seems clear that the costs of doing nothing are enormous. Many of the outcomes described above (homelessness, crime, and joblessness, among others) create enormous costs for the youth, their families, and society as a whole. The costs of a failed transition may extend well into the future. Cohen (1998), for example, estimates that the social costs of a life of crime exceed $1 million in today's dollars. Those costs include government expenditures for criminal justice investigation, arrest, adjudication, and incarceration; costs to victims, such as medical costs, time missed from work, and the value of stolen property, as well as loss of life; and costs that accrue to the criminal and his or her family, such as lost wages.

Well-designed programs and policies, therefore, have the potential to be cost effective. The likelihood of reaching that potential, however, will be much greater if the programs and policies involved reflect a realistic vision of the life course, involve families appropriately, and target those persons most in need and/or most likely to benefit from transition services.

NOTES

We would like to thank Gordon Berlin, Mark Courtney, Frank Furstenberg Jr., Anne H. Gauthier, Phyllis Levine, D. Wayne Osgood, and Michael S. Wald for their comments on earlier drafts. We are responsible for any remaining errors.

1. These figures include only prisoners whose sentence exceeds one year.

2. Note that the percentage of individuals who were arrested did not differ between the experimental and control groups.

3. Local school districts may continue to provide services after that point at their own discretion (and expense).

4. Section 504 prohibits both public and private programs and activities that receive federal assistance from discriminating on the basis of disability. Public schools are subject to this law and are required to provide "free and appropriate public education" to all students, even those whose disability does not entitle them to special education services.

5. Our tabulations of the 1995 PSID suggest that fewer than 7% of individuals aged twenty to twenty-four had ever been classified as needing special education. However, this estimate seems low given that about 11% of the population aged six to seventeen is served by special education in a single year (U.S. Department of Education 2002).

REFERENCES

Altschuler, David M., and Troy L. Armstrong. 1994a. *Intensive Aftercare for High-Risk Juveniles: A Community Care Model—Program Summary.* Washington, DC: U.S. Department of Justice, Office of Justice Programs, Office of Juvenile Justice and Delinquency Prevention.

———. 1994b. *Intensive Aftercare for High-risk Juveniles: Policies and Procedures.* Washington, DC: U.S. Department of Justice, Office of Justice Programs, Office of Juvenile Justice and Delinquency Prevention.

Altschuler, David M., Troy L. Armstrong, and Doris Layton Mackenzie. 1999. *Reintegration, Supervised Release, and Intensive Aftercare.* Juvenile Justice Bulletin. Washington, DC: U.S. Department of Justice, Office of Justice Programs, Office of Juvenile Justice and Delinquency Prevention.

Browning, Katharine, and Rolf Loeber. 1999. *Highlights of Findings from the Pittsburgh Youth Study.* OJJDP Fact Sheet no. 95. Washington, DC: U.S. Department of Justice, Office of Justice Programs, Office of Juvenile Justice and Delinquency Prevention.

Browning, Katharine, Terence Thornberry, and Pamela K. Porter. 1999. *Highlights of Findings from the Rochester Youth Development Study.* OJJDP Fact Sheet no. 103. Washington, DC: U.S. Department of Justice, Office of Justice Programs, Office of Juvenile Justice and Delinquency Prevention.

Bullis, Michael, Paul Yovanoff, Gina Mueller, and Emily Havel. 2002. Life on the Outs. Examination of the Facility-to-Community Transition of Incarcerated Youth. *Exceptional Children* 69 (1):7–22.

Chambers, Jay G., Tom Parrish, and Jennifer Harr. 2002. *What Are States Spending on Special Education Services in the United States, 1999–2000?* Advance Report no. 1, Special Education Expenditure Project (SEEP). Washington, DC: U.S. Department of Education.

Clouser, Megan. 1996. Aftercare and Specialized Aftercare Services. In *Pennsylvania Progress: Juvenile Justice Achievements of the Pennsylvania Commission on Crime and Delinquency.* Harrisburg, PA: National Center for Juvenile Justice.

Cohen, Mark A. 1998. The Monetary Value of Saving a High-Risk Youth. *Journal of Quantitative Criminology* 14 (1):5–33.

Cook, Ronna. 1990. A National Evaluation of Title IV-E Foster Care Independent Living Programs for Youth, Phase 1, Final Report. Rockville, MD: Westat, Inc.

———. 1991. A National Evaluation of Title IV-E Foster Care Independent Living Programs for Youth. Phase 2 Final Report. Volumes 1 and 2. Rockville, MD: Westat Inc.

Courtney, Mark E. and Noel Bost. 2002. *Review of Literature on the Effectiveness of Independent Living Services.* Urban Institute, Chapin Hall Center for Children at the University of Chicago, The National Opinion Research Center, U.S. Department of Health and Human Services Commissioner's Office of Research and Evaluation, Administration on Children, Youth and Families.

Courtney, Mark E., Irving Piliavin, Andrew Grogan Kaylor, and Ande Nesmith. 2001. Foster Youth Transitions to Adulthood: A Longitudinal View of Youth Leaving Care. *Child Welfare* 80 (6):685–717.

Deschenes, Elizabeth Piper, Peter W. Greenwood, and G. Marshall. 1996. *The Nokomis Challenge Program Evaluation.* Santa Monica, CA: The RAND Corporation.

Dworsky, Amy, and Mark E. Courtney. 2001. *Self-sufficiency of Former Foster Youth in Wisconsin: Analysis of Unemployment Insurance Wage Data and Public Assistance Data.* Madison: University of Wisconsin—Madison, Institute for Research on Poverty.

Forrest, Christopher B., Ellen Tambor, Anne W. Riley, Margaret E. Ensminger, and Barbara Starfield. 2000. The Health Profile of Incarcerated Male Youths. *Pediatrics* 105:286–91.

Goerge, Robert M., Lucy Bilaver, Bong Joo Lee, Barbara Needell, Alan Brookhart, and William Jackman. 2002. *Employment Outcomes for Youth Aging Out of Foster Care.* Chicago: Chapin Hall Center for Children at the University of Chicago.

Goldman, Jill, Jill Capitani, and Claudette Archambault. 1999. *Title IV-E Independent Living Programs: A Decade in Review.* Washington, DC: U.S. Department of Health and Human Service, Administration for Children and Families, Administration of Children, Youth and Families, Children's Bureau.

Greenwood, Peter W., Elizabeth Piper Deschenes, and J. Adams. 1993. *Chronic Juvenile Offenders: Final Results from the Skillman Aftercare Experiment.* Santa Monica, CA: RAND.

Griffin, Patrick. 2000. National Overviews. *State Juvenile Justice Profiles.* Pittsburgh, PA: National Center for Juvenile Justice. http://www.ncjj.org/stateprofiles/overviews/faq1.asp.

Griffin, Patrick, Patricia Torbet, and Linda Szymanksi. 1998. *Trying Juveniles as Adults in Criminal Court: An Analysis of State Transfer Provisions.* Washington, DC: Office of Juvenile Justice and Delinquency Prevention.

Haberman, M, and Lois M. Quinn. 1986. The High School Re-entry Myth: A Follow-up Study of Juveniles Released from Two Correctional High Schools in Wisconsin. *Journal of Correctional Education* 37:114–17.

IDEAPractices. 2002. *IDEA '97 Final Regulations.* http://www.ideapractices.org/law/regulations/glossaryIndex.php.

Lindsey, Elizabeth W., and Fasih U. Ahmed. 1999. The North Carolina Independent Living Program: A Comparison of Outcomes for Participants and Nonparticipants. *Children and Youth Services Review* 21:318–412.

Mallon, Gerald P. 1998. After Care, Then Where? Outcomes of an Independent Living Program. *Child Welfare* 77:61–78.

McMillen, J. Curtis, and Jayne Tucker. 1999. The Status of Older Adolescents at Exit from Out-of-Home Care. *Child Welfare* 78 (3):339–60.

Morningstar, Mary E., Dana L. Lattin, and Sue Sarkesian. 1998. *Answers to Commonly Asked Questions about Transition Services and the Individualized Education Program (IEP).* Lawrence, KS: Kansas Transition Systems Change Project.

Puzzanchera, Charles M. 2002. *Juvenile Court Placement of Adjudicated Youth, 1989–1998.* Washington, DC: U.S. Department of Justice.

Rosenbach, Margo, Kimball Lewis, and Brian Quinn. 2000. *Health Conditions, Utilization, and Expenditures of Children in Foster Care.* Cambridge, MA: U.S. Department of Health and Human Services, Office of the Assistant Secretary for Planning and Evaluation.

Rutherford, Robert B., Michael Bullis, Cindy Wheeler Anderson, and Heather M. Griller-Clark. 2002. *Youth with Disabilities in the Correctional System: Prevalence Rates and Identification Issues.* Washington, DC: Center for Effective Collaboration and Practice and EDJJ, National Center on Education, Disability, and Juvenile Justice.

Scannapieco, Maria, Judith Schagrin, and Tina Scannapieco. 1995. Independent Living Programs: Do They Make a Difference? *Child and Adolescent Social Work Journal* 12 (5):381–89.

Sealock, Miriam D., Denise C. Gottsfredson, and Catherine A. Gallagher. 1997. Drug Treatment for Juvenile Offenders: Some Good News and Some Bad News. *Journal of Research in Crime and Delinquency* 34 (2):210–36.

Settersten, Richard A. 2003. Rethinking Social Policy: Lessons of a Life-Course Perspective. Pp. 191–222 in *Invitation to the Life Course: Toward New Understandings of Later Life,* edited by J. Richard A. Settersten. Amityville, NY: Baywood Publishing Co.

Sickmund, Melissa. 2000. *Census of Juveniles in Residential Placement 1997.* Pittsburgh, PA: National Center for Juvenile Justice.

Sickmund, Melissa, Howard N. Snyder, and Eileen Poe-Yamagata. 1997. *Juvenile Offenders and Victims: 1997 Update on Violence.* Washington, DC: Office of Juvenile Justice and Delinquency Prevention.

Snyder, Howard N., and Melissa Sickmund. 1999. *Juvenile Offenders and Victims: 1999 National Report.* Washington, DC: Office of Juvenile Delinquency and Prevention.

Sontheimer, Henry, and Lynne Goodstein. 1993. Evaluation of Juvenile Intensive Aftercare Probation: Aftercare versus System Response Effects. *Justice Quarterly* 10 (2):197–227.

Stahl, Anne L. 2001. *Delinquency Cases in Juvenile Courts, 1998.* OJJDP Fact Sheet no. 31. Washington, DC: U.S. Department of Justice, Office of Justice Programs, Office of Juvenile Justice and Delinquency Prevention. http://www.ncjrs.org/pdffiles1/ojjdp/fs200131.pdf.

Storm, Kevin J. 2000. *Profile of State Prisoners under Age 18, 1985–1997.* Special Report. Washington, DC: Bureau of Justice Statistics.

Teplin, Linda A., Karen M. Abram, Gary M. McClelland, Mina K. Dulcan, and Amy A. Mericle. 2002. Psychiatric Disorders in Youth in Juvenile Detention. *Archives of General Psychiatry* 59 (12):1133–44.

Thornberry, Terence P., Eveyln H. Wei, Magda Stouthamer-Loeber, and Joyce Van Dyke. 2000. *Teenage Fatherhood and Delinquent Behavior.* Washington, DC: U.S. Department of Justice, Office of Justice Programs, Office of Juvenile Justice and Delinquency Prevention.

Trojanowicz, Robert C., Merry Morash, and Pamela J. Schram. 2001. Handling the Juvenile Delinquent. Pp. 205–41 in *Juvenile Delinquency: Concepts and Control.* Upper Saddle River, NJ: Prentice Hall.

U.S. Congress. 2000. The Greenbook: Section 11—Child Protection, Foster Care, and Adoption Assistance. Washington, DC.

U.S. Department of Education Office of Special Education and Rehabilitative Services. 2002. *A New Era: Revitalizing Special Education for Children and Their Families.* Washington, DC.

U.S. Department of Health and Human Services, Administration for Children and Families, Administration on Children, Youth and Families, and the Children's Bureau. 2002a. *The AFCARS Report: Interim FY 2000 Estimates as of August 2002.* http://www.acf.hhs.gov/programs/cb/publications/afcars/report7.pdf.

U.S. Department of Health and Human Services, Administration on Children Youth and Families. 2002b. *National Child Abuse and Neglect Data System (NCANDS): Summary of Key Findings from Calendar Year 2000.* http://www.calib.com/nccanch/pubs/factsheets/canstats.cfm.

U.S. General Accounting Office. 1999. *Foster Care Effectiveness of Independent Living Services Unknown.* Washington, DC: U.S. Government Printing Office.

Wagner, Mary, Jose Blackorby, Renee Cameto, Kathleen Hebbeler, and Lynn Newman. 1993. *The Transition Experiences of Young People with Disabilities: A Summary of Findings from the National Transition Study of Special Education.* Menlo Park, CA: SRI International.

Wagner, Mary M., and Jose Blackorby. 1996. Transition from High School to Work or College: How Special Education Students Fare. *Future of Children* 6 (1): 103–20.

Walter R. McDonald & Associates. 2000. *Eleven Years of Reporting Child Maltreatment 2000.* U.S. Department of Health and Human Services, Administration for Children and Families, Administration on Children, Youth and Families, Children's Bureau. http://www.acf.hhs.gov/programs/cb/publications/cm00/cm2000.pdf.

Westat. 2002a. Table AD2: Number of Students with Disabilities Exiting Special Education by Age Year, during the 2000–2001 School Year. *Annual Report Tables.* http://www.ideadata.org/tables25th/ar_ad2.htm.

———. 2002b. Table AA1: Number of Children Served under IDEA, Part B by Age Group, during the 2001–02 School Year. *Annual Report Tables.* http://www.ideadata.org/tables25th/ar_aa1.htm.

Wiebush, Richard G., Betsie McNulty, and Thao Le. 2000. Implementation of the Intensive Community-Based Aftercare Program. *Juvenile Justice Bulletin.* Washington, DC: U.S. Department of Justice, Office of Justice Programs, Office of Juvenile Justice and Delinquency Prevention.

Wright, Peter W. D., and Pamela Darr Wright. 1999. *Wrightslaw: Special Education Law.* Hartfield, VA: Harbor House Law Press.

CHAPTER 16

SOCIAL POLICY AND THE TRANSITION TO ADULTHOOD

Toward Stronger Institutions and Individual Capacities

RICHARD A. SETTERSTEN JR.

In this chapter I draw on the findings of *On the Frontier of Adulthood* and other recent research to launch a discussion about the intersection between early adult development and social policy. I ask how social policies and institutions regulate the structure and content of early adulthood and how well the models of and routes to early adulthood promoted within institutions match the needs and everyday realities of young people. I also ask for whom the transition is helped or hindered in the process and how policies might be created or reformed to ease entry into and promote development during adulthood.

Contemporary patterns of the transition to adulthood in North America and Western Europe must be understood within the context of the dramatic changes of the latter half of the twentieth century (see also Corijn and Klijzing 2001). Significant economic and social changes include the expansion of secondary and higher education; a decline in the availability of full-time jobs; an increase in the proportion of individuals concurrently pursuing higher education and work; an increase in the labor force participation of women; an increase in cohabitation; delays in marriage and childbirth; a decline in fertility; and the expansion and retraction of welfare state policies and programs. Major cultural shifts include weaker normative controls on behavior and greater individualization, both of which have allowed young people more freedom to plan and live life in accordance with their interests and wishes, and the emergence of feminism, which has reoriented the priorities of women. Changes such as these have not only reshaped early adult life but have altered the nature of the entire life course.

Ways of thinking, feeling, and expressing oneself have also shifted (for new evidence, see Smith, this vol., chap. 6). In the United States, expectations about independence and autonomy promote a "sink-or-swim" transition to adulthood (Cook and Furstenberg 2002). Young people who "swim" are often able to do so only because families provide significant material and emotional support, making parental investments in higher education critically important in launching young adults. Yet the larger ethos in America is that once those investments have been made—if they have been or can be made—young people are to navigate markets for education, jobs, and partners using whatever knowledge and resources they have acquired. As a result, a higher proportion of young people in the United States seem to "sink" relative to those in other countries. This is especially true of racial minorities and those from disadvantaged backgrounds, whose skills and resources tend to be less adequate or relevant going into the transition. (For an overview of how the transition to adulthood is generally structured and experienced in Italy, Sweden, Germany, and the United States, which are characterized by different types of welfare states, see Cook and Furstenberg [2002].)

This is consistent with themes of recent social theories that depict the modern world as unpredictable and full of risks that must be negotiated on the individual rather than institutional or collective levels (Beck 2000; Furlong and Cartmel 1997; Giddens 1991). For young people, these risks are exacerbated by the facts that the world they know differs dramatically from that of previous generations and that the wide variety of routes taken into adulthood leave individuals feeling as if their experiences not only are unique but in reality also have uncertain outcomes. This flexibility brings new freedom to pursue personal goals but also new responsibilities and risks as the experimental nature of "do-it-yourself" biographies makes these biographies prone to "slippage or collapse" (Beck 2000). When individuals choose or find themselves on pathways that are not widely shared by others or reinforced in institutions or policies, they may lose important sources of informal and formal support. In such a scenario, personal failures are viewed as being no one's fault but one's own.

We must therefore ask how the increased strains of modern life are played out in, and created by, social settings that incorporate young people. Indeed, institutions and policies meant to help young people may actually hurt them if they are based on outdated models of life that no longer reflect actual experiences (Heinz 1996; Levy 1996; Settersten 2003a). Under these conditions, individual resources may take on even greater significance in determining early adult experiences and their consequences (Corijn and Klijzing 2001), pointing to the need to redefine and broaden the groups of young people who are at risk as they move into adulthood.

Our commitments to young people must strengthen the institutions that serve them (and the connections between institutions) as well as the skills and resources of young people themselves so that they can better navigate early adult life. In this chapter, I explore these two levels in the spheres of work, education, and family. I also consider some of the special challenges faced by vulnerable or at-risk populations, how better safety nets might be created, how more effective information and guidance might be provided, and how civic engagement might be fostered. I close by highlighting some of the complexities associated with making social policy on the transition to adulthood and with bridging science, policy, and practice.

STRENGTHENING INSTITUTIONS
AND INDIVIDUAL CAPACITIES

The authors in this book make important contributions to understanding how the transition to adulthood has changed during the last century, why these changes have occurred, and what consequences they bring. The findings they present, like those of other initiatives in the Research Network on Transitions to Adulthood and Public Policy funded by the John D. and Catherine T. MacArthur Foundation (hereafter referred to as the "network"), raise questions about how institutions, policies, and programs might be modified to improve the experiences of young people. They suggest that significant mismatches exist between the emerging and varied pathways now taken into adulthood and the institutions, policies, and programs that affect young people. It is important for institutions and policies to meet the needs of young people more appropriately, while at the same time improving the personal skills and resources of young people so that they can better take advantage of the supports available to them. Understanding what interventions work best, and for whom, is critical to the process of designing effective policies and programs that are responsive to the significant variability in early adult experiences.

Strengthening Education and Work

Education and work are central to the structure of the life course in Western societies, as lives—especially men's lives and, increasingly, women's lives—have been organized into three successive "boxes" of education, work, and retirement. Important shifts in the boundaries between the three boxes have occurred in recent decades (e.g., Hendricks and Cutler 2003; Henretta 2003). The trend toward early retirement at the end of work life, coupled with an extension of schooling at the beginning, has made the period of gainful work shorter. Education and training have been extended in most countries, particularly over the past decade, as the result of several factors: (1) markets have demanded higher levels of education and better credentials for access to good jobs; (2) institutions of higher education are often overcrowded (and students are bottlenecked at entry points as they await access); (3) students are more often working during their studies; and (4) growing numbers of dropouts are returning to secondary or tertiary education. Early retirement, coupled with increased longevity, has lengthened the period of retirement.

While the boundaries between these boxes have shifted, and even seem to be disintegrating, the three-box structure remains salient in individual and cultural thought, and roles and activities are often allocated accordingly (Settersten 2003a). This structure also underlies and is reinforced by the policies and programs of the welfare state (for examples, see Settersten 2003b). Yet for recent cohorts, growing numbers of people are beginning to experience life in ways that depart from these patterns, whether by choice or circumstance. More significant shifts are apparent in the first two boxes, as education and work are now more often, and more often must be, pursued concurrently. Modernization and rapid technological change have made it necessary for adults to update their skills and knowledge continually if they are to compete in contemporary markets, especially given that "lifetime" models of work have eroded and stable work has itself become uncertain. In the third box, a wider array of patterns into retirement are now common, though most people nonetheless desire and strive for a fairly long period of retirement (O'Rand and Henretta 1999).

The simultaneous pursuit of education and work through midlife is often hampered by policies that discourage flexibility rather than facilitate it (Settersten and Lovegreen 1998; Settersten 1999). Besides the three-box structure noted above, these constraints relate to (1) the demands of family roles (especially for women, who continue to shoulder most of the responsibility for the care and raising of children, which strongly limits their educational attainment and labor market attachment); (2) the need for health insurance (which, at least in the United States, means having a full-time job that provides benefits); (3) rules related to employer pensions and old-age welfare-state programs (which require long periods of continuous full-time work for eligibility); (4) rules related to scholarships, tuition benefits, and financial aid (which require students to be enrolled full time for eligibility); (5) the structure of educational and occupational careers (which require movement through sequences of hierarchical or "nested" experiences); (6) age biases against young and old workers, and against "nontraditional" students; and (7) the "midlife squeeze," in which middle-aged adults must invest significant time and money caring for both aging parents and young adult children. Popular discussions of the need for "lifelong learning" do not acknowledge these very real constraints, which make it difficult to add educational experiences to an already demanding mix of work and family roles. A significant challenge to overcome, then, is to break up the lockstep nature of education and work by rethinking policies that penalize individuals for cycling between or simultaneously pursuing education and work experiences.

One effective way to move in these directions is to develop more open and coherent education and training programs early in adulthood. This has become a salient policy concern in countries of the Organization for Economic Co-Operation and Development (OECD 2000).[1] For the past few decades, the approach in many countries has been focused on dealing with youth unemployment, building a "youth friendly" labor market, and improving vocational education at early ages, particularly for young people at risk for unemployment or dead-end jobs. Recent emphases in the United States have been on developing access to postsecondary education for adults by improving the quality of secondary education and by developing and investing in community colleges.

TARGETING COMMUNITY COLLEGES AS A CENTRAL INSTITUTION FOR INTERVENTION. The community college is one of the key institutions in the transition to adulthood. It touches large numbers of young people, is flexible, and offers connections to a range of potential career paths—work, four-year college, and the military, to name a few. In addition, it has the potential to respond to the needs of a wide range of young people. Community colleges play especially important roles in training as second-chance remediation programs and as vocational/technical programs that offer employer-validated degrees and certificates. These roles uniquely position community colleges to address the growing mismatch between the skills of individuals and those needed in the job market, a mismatch that creates high levels of earnings inequality.

Unfortunately, community-college dropout rates are high, and there is little student movement from remediation programs into vocational training programs, and even less into four-year colleges (Grubb 2001; Kane and Rouse 1995). There are several reasons for this. One issue is cost. Although fees are relatively low, community colleges are not free. A problem for many community-college students is that federal and state grant support is designed primarily for students who attend school full time on a nine-month academic calendar and is of little help to the majority of community-college students, who attend school part time. Moreover, these grants generally cannot be used for noncredit courses, including some remedial education. Second, institutional factors may be important, such as the fact that community colleges seldom manage to integrate students in noncredit courses with those in certificate and degree programs. As a result, the lowest skilled and most disadvantaged students end up isolated from other members of the student body. Students in remedial programs are rarely viewed (or see themselves) as candidates for certificate and degree programs. Another important institutional factor is that community colleges provide little career counseling and student advising. Nationally, the average caseload of community-college counselors is nearly a thousand students (Grubb 2001). These cost and institutional factors pose serious barriers to the recruitment and retention of students who have much to gain from education at community colleges.

Our network is collaborating with the Manpower Demonstration Research Corporation (MDRC) to design a demonstration program, called Opening Doors to Earning Credentials, to improve educational attainment and other outcomes of young adults attending community college via interventions in three areas: increased financial aid, enhanced student services, and improvements in remedial and developmental education. This will be a significant initiative of our network in the coming years. We are especially interested in strengthening attachment to community colleges so that they act less as "revolving doors" and more as routes to further education and employment. This will be an important response to the challenges faced by highly vulnerable populations, such as those exiting foster care, prisons, or the juvenile justice system.

Indeed, a small but growing group of community colleges is beginning to address challenges related to access and retention by building links between their remediation and degree programs. Many are also attempting to strengthen social resources for students by facilitating study and support groups, creating tutoring and mentoring programs, providing on-site child care, and establishing flexible course timetables. Other colleges are exploring the feasibility of working with employers to develop specialized supports for incumbent workers, for example in buying back time from employers to enable workers to spend half time in college and still receive full-time pay or in building incentive structures for students who mix work and education as they complete benchmarks (for other examples, see Shaw and Jacobs 2003).

Initiatives such as these will help young people from low-income families enter and complete degree and certificate programs at community colleges. They may also have important effects on job retention and advancement, subsequent patterns of family formation, and psychological and physical health. Focused, short-term training programs that target high-growth industries and build strong employer partnerships, coupled with linkages to mainstream accredited college programs, are a promising route to career ladder jobs.

TARGETING EDUCATION-WORK LINKAGES. Many of the points above relate to making possible the concurrent pursuit of work and education and the need to better connect educational and work experiences. While school-to-work transitions may be ideal junctures for strengthening these connections, secondary schools may provide important opportunities to couple educational and work experiences early on (see also Youniss and Ruth 2002). In fact, OECD has heralded the combination of educational and work experiences as a central factor in creating successful transition systems for young people (OECD 2000). These combinations make learning applied and interesting for young people and improve educational attainment, help develop specific occupational skills that employers want and need, foster general work habits and attitudes, and signal these skills to employers when young people are seeking work.

Such outcomes can be achieved only if the objectives of learning at school and work are clearly defined; if complimentary objectives can be recognized by young people, teachers, trainers and employers; and if teaching, training, and learning processes are organized accordingly. We rarely think about work as an opportunity for "learning," which itself demonstrates how difficult combining the two can be. These combinations can only result if policies do not penalize people for pursuing both. In the United States, for example, health insurance is tied to having a full-time job with benefits, and when one is bound to a full-time fixed-schedule job, opportunities for school enrollment are few. Furthermore, tuition assistance programs in most companies are available only to full-time employees, and only for coursework that leads directly to practical skills that can be transferred to the current job and does not interfere with predictable work schedules. Similarly, scholarships and financial aid are largely offered to those engaged in full-time study, and admission to competitive institutions at both undergraduate and graduate levels is often contingent on an ability to enroll full time. These examples illustrate some of the significant barriers to the simultaneous pursuit of work and education.

As a result, countries are faced with the challenge of expanding the availability and scope of combined education and workplace experiences, improving their quality, and encouraging young people to participate in them. This involves a careful consideration of the strengths and weaknesses of current institutional arrangements in both education and the labor market (such as those noted above) and the steps most likely to be successful in creating change. For example, OECD (2000) suggests that effective school-work linkages require:

- modifying school and work schedules so that these experiences can be more easily combined;
- creating better dialogue between employers and educators at local, regional, and national levels;
- giving employers greater say in the administration and content of programs that combine education and work;
- creating effective institutions at local and regional levels to manage, monitor, and evaluate such programs;
- providing resources to stimulate local partnerships and strengthen recruitment links between educational institutions and work organizations;
- increasing the availability of part-time and temporary employment contracts for young people and improving training wages and benefits; and
- systematically relating what students learn at work and school.

These changes seem daunting. Nonetheless, pathways that combine education and work experience can encourage lifelong learning by enabling students to see the worlds of work and study as intertwined from the start. The pace at which young people find jobs after leaving school, and the kinds of jobs they find, have a powerful effect not only on their subsequent employment (OECD 1999) but also on larger life-course patterns. In this sense, the cost of making these sizable investments upfront pales in comparison to the cumulative gains made over an entire career. Policies must therefore focus on the paths that young people follow after leaving school, for these set the stage for subsequent employment patterns. Some countries offer stable but rigid routes into work life, while others offer open but fragile ones. The former model has tended to be more successful in helping young people get their first jobs and limiting long-term unemployment. In developing future policy options, however, international experience suggests that no single approach will suffice but that a wide array of strategies are needed, as long as these strategies combine strong stable structures with flexible pathways to suit individual needs. Despite the range of factors that determine early labor market success—or, perhaps, precisely because of that range—societies must strive to develop coherent education, labor, and social policies to help young people in their transition to work and adult life.

Where the transition from education to working life is concerned, OECD (2000) recommends that all national policies should aim for:

• high proportions of young people completing secondary education with recognized qualifications for work or higher education;

• high levels of knowledge and skill among young people at the end of the transition period;

• a low proportion of young adults who are neither in education nor employed and a high proportion of young adults who have jobs at the completion of a period of education or training; and

• stable and positive employment and educational histories in the years after leaving upper secondary education and an equitable distribution of outcomes by gender and social background.

The broad policy principles described in this section can be extended to a wide range of countries, despite the distinctiveness of their traditions and institutions.

Strengthening Family Relationships and Resources

The resources of young people's families of origin, and the nature of their family relationships, can seriously help or hinder the transition to adulthood. Economic assistance, in particular, plays a central role in the successes of young people (Schoeni and Ross, this vol., chap. 12). Family background, however, encompasses more than just money and time. Government intervention may bring material assistance to young people from disadvantaged backgrounds, but it may do little to reduce disparities in outcomes if material assistance per se is not what leads to a successful transition. For example, contextual research on adolescence has shown that a host of positive factors are associated with higher economic status of families—such as more positive processes in families, peer groups, schools, and neighborhoods (e.g., Cook et al. 2002). It may be these factors, rather than money itself, that make the difference for young people as they move into adulthood. Policies and programs must complement, and not displace or crowd out, any positive relationships and helpful networks already in place for some families.

The answer to the question of whether it is getting harder to get ahead depends on family resources (Sandefur, Eggerling-Boeck, and Park, this vol., chap. 9). Not surprisingly, individuals with more highly educated parents and who attended private schools are more likely to start off on the right foot, or at least on more solid ground. Of course, parental education and type of school have long been shown to influence life chances in many ways. Increasing the availability of aid for higher education, and improving the information available to middle and high school students about higher education and jobs, could improve the chances of others for success. Definitions of success and adherence to certain pathways are also greatly influenced by the strength and consistency of expectations within nuclear and extended families. These dynamics are strikingly clear in some of the families of young people who are second-generation immigrants in New York City (see Mollenkopf et al., this vol., chap. 14). It is also important to recognize that support not only flows downward from parents to young adult children but also flows upward from young adult children to parents. We know little about such transfers, though in-depth interviews from the same project in New York City suggest that such transfers are common, especially among the Chinese. In these families, a surprising proportion of young people talk about the fact that they support—and are obligated to support—their parents in both expressive and instrumental ways. Mollenkopf and colleagues also highlight the special hazards and risks that young people face in urban neighborhoods, and the strategies individuals and families use to protect themselves, if any.

There is also great need to strengthen fragile families formed by young people themselves. For substantial numbers of economically and educationally disadvantaged young people, the transition to parenthood precedes and, in fact, never culminates in marriage or a significant union—and even if it does, that union is at greater risk of ending in separation and divorce. Partly because of the confounding of race and class in America, these youth are disproportionately African American. Recent census data, however, suggest that marriage and home ownership are on the rise for black families, though these proportions remain significantly lower than those for whites or the nation at large (McKinnon 2003).

Previous research has shed little light on the economic, social, and psychological factors and processes that transform fledgling but basically positive relations between young, economically disadvantaged, unmarried parents into stable, reasonably harmonious, satisfying unions. However, researchers are increasingly turning their attention to this question, reflecting a shift from an emphasis on deficits to assets (McLanahan and Garfinkel 2000). Complementing this trend is an expansion of state and community programs meant to strengthen fragile families during their formative years. The strategies adopted by programs to achieve this goal are highly varied and include providing a range of social supports to young unmarried, as well as married, couples with children; increasing poor, young, unmarried fathers' involvement and investment in their children; and improving the quality of children's home environments and experiences by expanding the repertoire of strategies that parents use to discipline their children and understand what children need to develop in healthy ways. Restructuring the workplace so that individuals are able to better manage work and family responsibilities also goes a long way in easing the burdens of young families. Such strategies or proposals include on-site affordable child care; flextime; part-time parity in wages, benefits, training, and advancement opportunities; a handful of paid days for family and medical leave; and limits on mandatory overtime (e.g., Heymann 2000; Williams 2000).

The delay in family formation in the United States is not excessive and is common to advanced industrial countries (Fussell and Gauthier, this vol., chap. 3). Obstacles and opportunities alike in education or employment play roles in determining the timing of marriage and parenting. The increase in nontraditional paths in both work and family formation does, however, suggest that young people today face novel and difficult challenges as they enter adulthood, despite the fact that diversity in these pathways has long existed (see Wu and Li, this vol., chap. 4). Contemporary patterns must be understood within the context of political, social, and economic changes that have in recent decades altered the social institutions that affect young people. Changes in policies and institutions may prompt changes in behavioral patterns, but behavioral patterns can also change first, with policies and institutions lagging behind the times—what Riley, Kahn, and Foner (1994) call the problem of "structural lag." In either direction, social policies and institutions have a significant influence on young people and their families.

Improving the Footing of Vulnerable Populations

In the decade following high school, youth in industrialized countries rely heavily on their families for material support to obtain the lengthy education required for professional occupations, child care when babies come sooner than steady incomes, and a place to stay when marriages fail or jobs are lost.

This pattern led members of our network to be concerned about youth who are likely to have no family on which to call, whose pasts are so troubled that they have lost their family's good will, or whose families simply do not have resources on which to draw. These issues are especially important for youth whose skills and abilities are so limited that they will always rely heavily on others. The welfare state is a critical support system for these youth and for populations that historically have had difficulty making the transition to full adulthood, such as hard-to-employ individuals with mental health and substance abuse problems. In most welfare states, particularly "liberal market states" such as the United States or the United Kingdom, support is meant to be temporary and transitional (Esping-Andersen 1997; Mayer 2001).[2]

The child welfare and criminal justice systems also have profound effects on the transition to adulthood, adding burdens of stigma and alienation to young adults who already bring low personal and social capital to this juncture (see Foster and Gifford, this vol., chap. 15). Although programs and services are available to facilitate their independence, many services are unnecessarily inflexible and defined by age rather than need. Further, few programs equip families with the resources they need to support young people during this period. As other chapters in this book make clear, families are a primary source of support to adult children, and the assumption that young adults live "independently," even for those outside of child welfare and criminal justice systems, is outdated (Goldscheider and Goldscheider 2000; Settersten 1998). Finally, many at-risk youth are simultaneously involved in more than one system, and support services are rarely interconnected, let alone integrated. This leads to a fragmented view of the needs of vulnerable populations as they enter adulthood, despite the fact that these populations have already been the targets of extensive governmental programs during childhood and adolescence.

The support offered by government programs typically ends between the ages of eighteen and twenty-one, suggesting a serious policy gap during the transition to adulthood. It is important to consider the repercussions of ending this support at a time when other youth continue to receive so much assistance from their families. The costs of services for these populations are significant, and systematic high-quality evaluation research is needed to determine whether and how these services help. But the costs of doing nothing seem far greater. When young adults with emotional, physical, learning, or behavioral problems are adrift, the cost to society in homelessness, crime, joblessness, and other negative outcomes is substantial and enduring. Programs have the potential to be cost effective, especially if they reflect a realistic vision of the life course, involve families appropriately, and target those persons most in need and most likely to benefit from the transition services.

To extend the view of vulnerable populations provided by Foster and Gifford (this vol., chap. 15), our network is producing a separate book that takes an in-depth look at the challenges faced by those populations, their success in meeting those challenges, and special policy concerns related to these populations during the early adult years. *On Your Own without a Net: The Transition to Adulthood for Vulnerable Populations* (Osgood et al., forthcoming) focuses on young adults who were, as adolescents, in the mental health, foster care, juvenile justice, or criminal justice systems; homeless or runaways; in special education; or chronically ill or physically disabled. These groups face exceptional challenges, stemming from many and often multiple sources, in making successful transitions into the major arenas of adulthood, including employment, higher education, marriage, and parenthood. Some are hampered by limited abilities or skills, such as those with physical disabilities and former special education students with learning disabilities. Some lack the support of parents in ways both emotional and instrumental, such as those who spent their teen years on the streets. Some are vulnerable because they have had other difficulties that decrease their chances for success in adulthood, such as mental illnesses or histories of crime and incarceration.

Besides these populations, and those from or in fragile families, African American youth and youth from working- and lower-class backgrounds are not on equal footing with their peers when it comes to educational and economic success (see Corcoran and Matsudaira, this vol., chap. 11; Sandefur et al., this vol., chap. 9). The United States has one of the most unequal income distributions among Western countries. Despite the large and widening gap, there is little government support for redistributive policies, partly because of the common assumption that America has a high rate of economic mobility: many believe that while there may be inequality, everyone has a shot at success, regardless of race or family resources. In fact, rates of intergenerational economic mobility are no higher in the United States than in many western European countries and are slightly lower than in some.

Establishing Safety Nets

Any discussion of vulnerable populations naturally leads to the need to build better safety nets. What is clear from the findings of this book and other research is that safety nets need to be strengthened for all young people, and strengthened still further for those at highest risk. As OECD (2000) also notes, some highly desirable outcomes, such as having relatively few young adults who are neither in education nor employed, or in unstable or low-quality jobs, can only be achieved if a large majority of young people are integrated and retained in mainstream education and training; if dropouts are closely tracked and intensely supported; and if strategies for responding to vulnerable populations include early intervention.

What can schools, municipalities, and others do to better monitor young people who are at risk of getting lost in the transition process? The OECD (2000) has highlighted a cluster of individualized and multiple supports adopted by Nordic countries that are effective in helping young people develop personal strategies for success. Such support is expensive and requires unconventional programs and forms of cooperation among publicly and privately funded agencies and organizations and the government. Many elements of the tightly knit safety nets provided in Nordic countries are now being implemented in policy initiatives of other countries. Key features include:

- keeping the number of early leavers low by making school attractive for the widest possible range of students, and providing remedial programs for the weakest students;
- developing education, labor market, and welfare policies that reduce incentives for inactivity as an attractive or plausible option;
- widening definitions of risk that extend beyond unemployment;
- managing tracking mechanisms so that those at risk can be quickly identified and provided with assistance;
- providing tailored assistance based on individual needs and built around personal action plans that are regularly reviewed;
- coordinating services across different levels of government and complementing education, training, and employment assistance with personal, health, and welfare assistance;
- securing significant local resources, given that the tasks of integration and monitoring are best conducted and ensured by bodies closest to young people; and
- targeting individuals in their early twenties or younger, given that interventions with older populations come with significantly weaker effects.

Providing Effective Information and Guidance

As the analyses in this book have attested, pathways through education and work have become more varied, and young people face more and increasingly complex choices. A task central to improving the transition is to provide effective information and guidance to vulnerable populations, and such services are increasingly being integrated with labor market and social services. But in today's world, career information and guidance should be seen as essential services for all young people. Information and guidance services must provide accurate information on future educational options, develop young people's understanding and realistic knowledge of the world of work, assist them with job searches, help them find high-quality child care, and identify strategies for balancing family, education, and work.

Some young people can make confident choices with little assistance, while others need intensive and often individual assistance. Either way, those who plan and make good decisions in adolescence make better subsequent decisions and have higher life satisfaction—what Clausen (1991) called the power of early "planful competence." These outcomes will also benefit society in the long run, reducing the drain on government programs and creating productive and satisfied workers and citizens. The complexity of education, work, and family life in modern societies complicates the demands made on information and guidance services, how best to organize and deliver them, and the roles, responsibilities, and qualifications of service providers. Nonetheless, information and guidance services must assume a much higher priority for families, schools, work organizations, and government programs, as ever widening groups will need access to these services.

Indeed, no country appears to have been able to develop fully satisfactory provision of information and guidance services for all young people, despite the fact that many examples of good practices can be found. As OECD (2000) points out, there is a clear need to (1) improve the training of personnel who provide information and guidance to young people; (2) make career information and guidance central to objectives in educational and work settings; (3) help young people better relate information to their actual talents and interests; (4) use multiple formats, including classroom experiences and one-on-one assistance; and (5) draw on multiple sources beyond teachers and counselors, including employers, coworkers, alumni, and parents. Sound transitions require effective personal relationships between young people and the adults who hope to help, relationships built on open information exchange, mutual obligations, trust, and sharing.

Clearly, there is neither a single answer to building effective transition systems nor is there a single problem. Some key features of effective transition systems are difficult to transplant across borders without modifying the institutions at their core. Other features are not as closely dependent on the nature of institutions—such as the building of safety nets and the provision of career information and guidance, which can be introduced or improved in a wide variety of contexts.

Fostering Civic Engagement

The transition to adulthood and the subsequent life course can be facilitated through opportunities for public service. These opportunities not only develop the skills and foster the integration of young people into their neighborhoods, cities, and nations, but they also further the well-being of the entities they serve. While the findings presented in this book do not explicitly address matters of civic engagement, we, as a network, wish to emphasize the great potential of these policies and programs, especially for groups of young people who have not been able to participate fully in society and the body politic. Early adulthood is a period ideally suited to wrestling with political and moral issues and a period during which experiences related to civic participation may leave a significant positive imprint on individuals. It is a time of cognitive and behavioral flexibility, when individuals are not yet firmly committed to opinions, values, roles, and responsibilities, and are often open to exploring a range of viewpoints and behaviors.

In many countries, government-organized public service, whether through military or community service, is an important and even mandatory rite of passage. In other countries, civic involvement is less formal, organized by private organizations, through private-public partnerships, or by young people themselves and grassroots efforts. The model of youth civic engagement in the United States has been that of the middle and upper classes providing service to the less advantaged (Verba, Schlozman, and Brady 1995). In contrast to the noblesse oblige orientation to civic engagement in America, many countries view civic work and national service as obligations of all citizens, young and old alike (Barber 1994).

In the United States, participation in either civilian or military service programs in the late adolescent and early adult years has been found to lead to improved labor market and civic engagement outcomes for low-income youth and to civic engagement and political activism as lifelong commitments for those from the middle or upper classes (McAdam 1989; Verba et al. 1995). Juxtaposed to these benefits is a precipitous decline over the past few decades in young adults' participation in conventional politics, such as voting or even staying informed about political issues through print and broadcast media (Keeter et al. 2002; National Association of Secretaries of State 2000). As Smith (this vol., chap. 6) shows, confidence in social institutions declined for all age groups from the 1970s through the 1990s, but the current generation of eighteen- to twenty-five-year-olds is significantly more disconnected from traditional institutions and partisan politics, less trustful of others, and more cynical about human beings and life.

While participation in partisan politics is particularly low among young Americans, there has been a significant increase in the numbers who volunteer in community service activities. When asked why they choose service over politics, youth report that they feel they can make a difference by doing direct service, whereas they feel ineffective in the political arena (Galston 2001). While civilian youth service programs, such as the Los Angeles Corps, Boston's City Year, and AmeriCorps, have been growing since the 1980s, the movement nonetheless remains small, serving only a few thousand young people each year.

Analyses of national service programs, however, suggest that there may be unique advantages of programs for disadvantaged youth that combine job training with opportunities to contribute to their communities (Flanagan 2004). For these groups, the armed services might begin to play a larger role, akin to the role it played in earlier eras, in facilitating adult transitions for the young people it now excludes on the basis of aptitude standards and/or prior involvement in the criminal justice system. The youth service movement might also be expanded by linking youth service programs and military programs.

Much remains to be learned about how civic engagement matters for the skills and development of young people; for whom it matters most; what factors prevent or promote it; the elements of good programs at local, state, and federal levels; and the opinions of participants, the public, and government officials about the effectiveness of programs. Investments in civic engagement should bring short- and long-term payoffs for both individuals and societies if these values can be instilled and commitments can be made early on. There is, in fact, convergent evidence that young adults who wrestle with social issues and participate in civic matters are more likely to be engaged citizens throughout life. Public or community service programs are models of new institutions that fill—or have the potential to fill—a developmental gap in the transition to adulthood (Flanagan 2004).

I have thus far highlighted some ways to strengthen institutions related to education, work, family, and civic engagement and to build the capacities of young people in these areas. I now close by highlighting other complexities associated with making social policy on the transition to adulthood within the context of modern welfare states and the larger life course.

Minding Other Challenges to Modern Welfare States and Policies

The first few decades of life are defined and structured by social policy systems that establish relationships between childhood, adolescence, and early adulthood. Yet young adults, like children (Brim and Phillips 1988), have been the targets of a fragmented and haphazard collection of policies and programs. How might we articulate a more coherent, coordinated, and comprehensive set of policies and programs for young people as they move into and through adult life? Policies related to young adults must be recast as opportunities for social investment, the benefits of which must not only be weighed against immediate risks and costs but against long ranging ones as well.

In the second half of the twentieth century, welfare states emerged as a (if not *the*) major creator of life-course markers in many countries via mandatory and universal programs and legal entitlements (Leisering 2003). The American emphasis on individualism comes with a preference for a smaller presence and role of government intervention relative to European nations. Nonetheless, the welfare state is, even in America, the only "overarching agency"—to use Leisering's (2003) term—that has direct and indirect bearings on the entire life course, some effects of which may be unintended. Yet welfare states rarely address the life course as a whole, instead providing spot coverage around specific periods of vulnerability and risk or specific transitions. A policy that affects the life course is not the same as a life-course policy designed with the whole of life in mind and meant to connect and integrate different life periods. With the exception of the vulnerable populations noted earlier, few people or groups have lasting or exclusive life trajectories that are enmeshed with the state. This is particularly true of liberal market states, such as the United States and the United Kingdom, whose intended coverage is, from the start, limited and temporary (see also Allmendinger and Hinz 1998; Esping-Andersen 1997; Mayer 2001; Settersten 2003b).

The research presented in this book shows that transition experiences are highly variable across social classes, gender, racial and ethnic groups, and nations—and that variability within these groups is also striking. How might social policy be used to smooth the discontinuities of increasingly fluid life courses, and manage the risks they bring, without compromising the benefits of fluidity? Ultimately, these levels of variability may demand that institutions re-create themselves in fresh ways. Indeed, one approach might be to strive for the "institutionalization of flexibility" and *re-* rather than *de*-institutionalize the life course (Leisering 2003; Settersten 1999). This is consistent with the emergent emphasis of modern welfare states on equipping individuals and families to manage their own lives through their own actions rather than on protecting individuals and families from changes and risks (Esping-Andersen 2002). From this perspective, investments in human capital (e.g., education and training) and social services (e.g., assistance with child and elder care) are primary means for achieving this because they facilitate participation in the market.

At the same time, an emphasis on human agency may be a double-edged sword, at least in liberal market states that place a high premium on autonomy and self-reliance. These states leave it up to individuals to take advantage of the opportunities they encounter or create. Collective responsibility for young people to attain their goals is minimal, and an inability to achieve positive outcomes is taken as a personal failure (Breen and Buchmann 2002). These factors result in highly competitive, risk-prone, individualistic climates. Under these conditions, young people are likely to engage in risky behaviors in an effort to achieve highly valued goals, especially when opportunities are limited. Good decision making becomes central to achieving positive adult statuses, yet this is only possible when routes into adulthood are secure and "properly signposted," to use Coles's phrase (2002).

Young adults, even those of majority age, are similar to adolescents in that they are considered capable of making decisions about their own futures but are also (at least partially) dependent on other people (particularly parents) for care, guidance, and support (see also Coles 2002). For example, full-time students in higher education are assumed to be dependent on parents when calculations are made regarding eligibility for loans or other forms of assistance, and students must provide proof of health insurance (generally through parental coverage) to enroll in classes.

Legal rights and responsibilities of adulthood are also given gradually (and in seemingly inconsistent or arbitrary ways) so that there is no clear end to adolescence and beginning of adulthood. For example, formal age-based laws determine when one can vote, drink, marry, have consensual sex, serve in the military, and be prosecuted, and these are often granted at different ages. The same is true of informal age norms for early adult transitions (Settersten 2003a) and of the views of young people themselves, who use graduated measures of the attainment of "adult" status and a wide array of markers beyond legal ages (see Furstenberg, Rumbaut, and Settersten, this vol., chap. 1; Shanahan et al., this vol., chap. 7; Mollenkopf et al., this vol., chap. 14). Given that the boundary between adolescence and adulthood is blurred, and the transition longer, a more comprehensive and protective set of entitlements and rights, similar to those offered to minors, might be extended into the early adult years.[3]

As we have seen, some of the statuses through which young people move on the way to adulthood are prescribed by law, some are driven by the economy and social agencies and institutions, some stem from the choices and resources of parents, and some result from the choices and resources of young people themselves. A central challenge to designing effective social policy, then, is to handle the many factors that work in combination to shape pathways into adulthood.

Policies and programs on early adulthood, like those on adolescence (Pittman, Diversi, and Ferber 2002), must focus on positive and not just negative processes and outcomes; address and build support in a range of settings and systems; include the voices and actions of varied groups of young people as they are developed, implemented, and evaluated; and be connected to those designed for older and younger populations. The latter point also underscores the importance of understanding the connections between experiences in adjacent life periods and calls attention to the fact that many effective interventions for responding to problems at the transition to adulthood might well occur before that juncture. For example, an effective way to address inequality in college attendance and completion across race and class lines is to improve the skills that youth develop before college; an effective way to help young people transition from the juvenile justice system into the job market is to help divert them from criminal offending in the first place; and the complications of high school completion and college attendance for teen mothers can in principle be addressed by helping teens delay fertility.[4]

Indeed, an assumption underneath most policymaking is that investments made in children bring the greatest pay offs and that by the late teen and early adult years, continued investments matter little. The evidence in this book, however, suggests that early adulthood is a critical time to continue investing in those who have had troubled beginnings and make new investments in those who have not. The early adult years are unique in that young people have ideas about the support and guidance they need, but they also want to practice making decisions and assuming responsibility for them. Many social systems are structured for either dependent children or independent adults with few examples of institutional practices that provide a scaffold for the blurry space between dependence and independence. As a result, natural support systems such as families and primary and secondary schools are charged with the responsibility of caring for or educating children, but once individuals become "adults" they are responsible for their own fate and actions. This either/or system does not take into account the fact that most young adults in their early and even late twenties are only semiautonomous, not fully autonomous.

The goals noted above require more effective methods in the policy-making process (Esping-Andersen 2002; Leisering and Walker 1998; Settersten 2003b). Normal policymaking is generally short-sighted, fragmented into specialized areas and compartments, and based on static methods that produce snapshots rather than moving pictures. Point-in-time snapshots may work when societies are stable, but modern societies are ever changing. To achieve what Ellwood (1998) calls "dynamic policy-making," dynamic data and methods must be gathered and used to peek into the future, link fragments to wholes, and capture the shifting nature of risk and resilience. This means regularly collecting data on multiple indicators of well-being and development of young people so that their problems, progress, and needs are monitored and addressed (Saraswathi and Larson 2002). Adopting a life-course perspective is critical to this task because its principles, concepts, and methods are explicitly aimed at understanding lives in time and place (Settersten 1999).

Consistent with recent OECD recommendations (OECD 2000), our network emphasizes that effective policy processes are needed to support effective institutions; that policy implementation and evaluation should be given as much attention as policy design; and that pilot projects and successful local initiatives must be deliberately used and tested as models for scaling up programs. Comprehensive multipronged reform is preferred to isolated and piecemeal reform, and national and top-down approaches need to be balanced with local and bottom-up approaches. We also place high priority on interventions that reach special populations at risk of not making successful transitions into the labor force or into stable unions, that have strong possibilities for widespread adoption, and that are likely to have powerful enough effects so that a wide range of economic, social, and psychological outcomes can be examined. We also urge policymakers to create more comprehensive policy packages that serve all young people, not just those at greatest risk.

To meet these goals, the connections between research, policy, and practice must be strengthened and coupled with solid evaluation efforts. This means that the chasms between the three separate "cultures" of science, policy, and practice, which are often at odds with one another, must be bridged (Shonkoff 2000; see also Brim and Philips 1988; Ralston et al. 2000; Settersten 2003b). These three cultures differ in their understanding of rules of evidence, in how they are influenced by ideologies and values, in the degree and nature of professional respect, and in the stability of the environments in which they work. In attempting to better integrate these three cultures, we must be open to different ways of thinking about the needs of young people and their families and how best to gather knowledge and put it into action on their behalf.

A new policy agenda will require considerable public investment, and an understandable concern about immediate financial costs must be balanced with the recognition that low levels of investment in early adult life come with large psychological, social, and economic costs, especially in the long run (see also Cohen 1998; Coles 2002). Many of the changes evidenced in this book point to both new opportunities and new risks in moving into adulthood. Among the most pressing risks in the United States and abroad are the challenges of balancing paid work and family responsibilities (especially child care), lacking the skills necessary to find adequately paid work, having skills and training become obsolete and being unable to upgrade them, and having an insufficient work history to qualify for social security (Taylor-Gooby 2004). The successful negotiation of new risks is especially important for young people not only because these risks are more common but also because failure can have substantial implications for their future life chances—and for the future of nations and our world.

NOTES

1. Established as part of a convention signed in Paris in 1960, the original OECD countries included Austria, Belgium, Canada, Denmark, France, Germany, Greece, Iceland, Ireland, Italy, Luxembourg, the Netherlands, Norway, Portugal, Spain, Sweden, Switzerland, Turkey, the United Kingdom, and the United States. Now thirty-countries strong, the core of original European and North American members has expanded to include Japan, Australia, New Zealand, Finland, Mexico, Korea, and four former communist states in Europe: the Czech Republic, Hungary, Poland, and the Slovak Republic. The OECD provides a unique forum for discussing, developing, and refining economic and social policies. The members of OECD compare experiences, seek answers to common problems, and work to coordinate domestic and international policies to help members and nonmembers deal with globalization.

2. Literature on welfare states often distinguishes between "liberal market states" (such as the United States or the United Kingdom), "continental conservative welfare states" (such as Germany or, more accurately, the former West Germany), "Scandinavian social democratic welfare states," and "southern European welfare states" (such as Italy). For an overview of the characteristics of these states, see Esping-Andersen (2002) or Mayer (2001).

3. Following Coles (2002), these might relate to basic entitlements, rights of protection, and rights of representation. Basic entitlements include rights to (*a*) knowledge about education, vocational training, housing provision, income support, health care and health promotion, and law and the operation of the criminal justice system; (*b*) social care; (*c*) privacy; (*d*) knowledge and respect for cultural and ethnic origins; (*e*) equal opportunities (and compensatory care for those without); and (*f*) sensitivity to special needs. Rights of protection include rights related to (*a*) physical abuse; (*b*) sexual abuse and sexual harassment; (*c*) abuse and harassment that stems from sources such as race, disability, or sexuality; and (*d*) work (e.g., health and safety, working hours). Representational rights include rights related to (*a*) sharing in decision making about their futures (especially education and training, residence, and health care) and (*b*) being consulted about the running of institutions of which they are part.

4. Special thanks to an anonymous reviewer for pushing this point and these examples.

REFERENCES

Allmendinger, Jutta, and Thomas Hinz. 1998. Occupational Careers under Different Welfare Regimes: West Germany, Great Britain, and Sweden. Pp. 64–84 in *The Dynamics of Modern Society*, edited by Lutz Leisering and Robert Walker. Bristol: Policy Press.

Barber, Benjamin R. 1994. *An Aristocracy of Everyone: The Politics of Education and the Future of America*. New York: Oxford University Press.

Beck, Ulrich. 2000. Living Your Own Life in a Runaway World: Individualization, Globalization, and Politics. Pp. 164–74 in *Global Capitalism*, edited by W. Hutton and A. Giddens. New York: New Press.

Breen, Richard, and Marlis Buchmann. 2002. Institutional Variation and the Position of Young People: A Comparative Perspective. Pp. 288–305 in *Annals of the American Academy of Political and Social Science: Early Adulthood in Cross-National Perspective*, edited by Frank F. Furstenberg Jr. London: Sage Publications.

Brim, Orville G., and Deborah A. Phillips. 1988. The Life-Span Intervention Cube. Pp. 277–97 in *Child Development in Life-Span Perspective*, edited by Eileen Mavis Hetherington, Richard M. Lerner, and Marion Perlmutter. Hillsdale, NJ: Lawrence Erlbaum Associates.

Clausen, John S. 1991. Adolescent Competence and the Shaping of the Life Course. *American Journal of Sociology* 96 (4):805–42.

Cohen, M. A. 1998. The Monetary Value of Saving a High-Risk Youth. *Journal of Quantitative Criminology* 14 (1):5–33.

Coles, Bob. 2002. *Youth and Social Policy: Youth Citizenship and Young Careers.* London: Routledge.

Cook, Thomas D., and Frank F. Furstenberg Jr. 2002. Explaining Aspects of the Transition to Adulthood in Italy, Sweden, Germany, and the United States: A Cross-Disciplinary, Case Synthesis Approach. Pp. 257–87 in *Annals of the American Academy of Political and Social Science: Early Adulthood in Cross-National Perspective,* edited by Frank F. Furstenberg Jr. London: Sage Publications.

Cook, Thomas D., Melissa Herman, Meredith Phillips, and Richard A. Settersten Jr. 2002. How Neighborhoods, Families, Peer Groups, and Schools Jointly Affect Changes in Early Adolescent Development. *Child Development* 73 (4): 1283–1309.

Corijn, Martine, and Erik Klijzing. 2001. Transitions to Adulthood in Europe: Conclusions and Discussion. Pp. 313–40 in *Transitions to Adulthood in Europe,* edited by Martine Corijn and Erik Klijzing, Boston: Kluwer Academic Publishers.

Ellwood, David. 1998. Dynamic Policy Making: An Insider's Account of Reforming U.S. Welfare. Pp. 49–61 in *The Dynamics of Modern Society,* edited by Lutz Leisering and Robert Walker. Bristol: Policy Press.

Esping-Andersen, Gøsta. 1997. Welfare States at the End of the Century: The Impact of Labour Market, Family, and Demographic Change. Pp. 63–80 in *Family, Market, and Community: Equity and Efficiency in Social Policy,* edited by Organization for Economic Co-Operation and Development. Paris: Organization for Economic Co-Operation and Development.

———. 2002. Towards the Good Society, Once Again? Pp. 1–25 in *Why We Need a New Welfare State,* by Gøsta Esping-Andersen with Duncan Gallie, Anton Hemerijck, and John Myles. Oxford: Oxford University Press.

Flanagan, Connie A. 2004. Volunteerism, Leadership, Political Socialization, and Civic Engagement. Pp. 721–46 in *Handbook of Adolescent Psychology,* edited by Richard M. Lerner and Laurence Steinberg. New York: John Wiley & Sons.

Furlong, Andy, and Fred Cartmel. 1997. *Young People and Social Change: Individualization and Risk in Late Modernity.* Buckingham: Open University Press.

Galston, William A. 2001. Political Knowledge, Political Engagement, and Civic Education. *Annual Review of Political Science* 4:217–34.

Giddens, Anthony. 1991. *Modernity and Self Identity: Self and Society in the Late Modern Age.* Oxford: Polity Press.

Goldscheider, Calvin, and Frances K. Goldscheider. 2000. *The Changing Transition to Adulthood: Leaving and Returning Home.* Thousand Oaks, CA: Sage Publications.

Grubb, W. Norton. 2001. *"Getting into the World": Career Counseling in Community Colleges*. Occasional Paper Series. New York: Community College Research Center, Teachers College, Columbia University.

Heinz, Walter R. 1996. Status Passages as Micro-Macro Linkages in Life-Course Research. Pp. 51–65 in *Society and Biography*, edited by A. Weymann and W. R. Heinz. Weinheim: Deutscher Studien Verlag.

Hendricks, Jon, and Stephen Cutler. 2003. Leisure in Life-Course Perspective. Pp. 107–34 in *Invitation to the Life-Course: Toward New Understandings of Later Life*, edited by Richard A. Settersten Jr. Amityville, NY: Baywood Publishing Co.

Henretta, John. 2003. The Life-Course Perspective on Work and Retirement. Pp. 85–105 in *Invitation to the Life Course: Toward New Understandings of Later Life*, edited by Richard A. Settersten Jr. Amityville, NY: Baywood Publishing Co.

Heymann, Jody. 2000. *The Widening Gap: Why America's Working Families Are in Jeopardy and What Can Be Done about It*. New York: Basic Books.

Kane, Thomas J., and Cecilia Rouse. 1995. Labor-Market Returns to Two-and Four-Year College. *American Economic Review* 85 (3):600–614.

Keeter, Scott, Cliff Zukin, Molly Andolina, and Krista Jenkins. 2002. *The Civic and Political Health of the Nation: A Generational Portrait*. College Park, MD: Center for Information and Research on Civic Learning and Engagement.

Leisering, Lutz. 2003. Government and the Life Course. Pp. 205–25 in *Handbook of the Life Course*, edited by Jeylan T. Mortimer and Michael J. Shanahan. New York: Kluwer Academic Publishers.

Leisering, Lutz, and Robert Walker. 1998. Making the Future: From Dynamics to Policy Agendas. Pp. 265–85 in *The Dynamics of Modern Society*, edited by Lutz Leisering and Robert Walker. Bristol: Policy Press.

Levy, Rene. 1996. Toward a Theory of Life-Course Institutionalization. Pp. 83–108 in *Society and Biography*, edited by A. Weymann and W. R. Heinz. Weinheim: Deutscher Studien Verlag.

Mayer, Karl Ulrich. 2001. The Paradox of Global Social Change and National Path Dependencies: Life Course Patterns in Advanced Societies. Pp. 89–110 in *Inclusions and Exclusions in European Societies*, edited by Alison Woodward and Martin Kohli. New York: Routledge.

McAdam, Doug. 1989. The Biographical Consequences of Activism. *American Sociological Review* 54:744–60.

McKinnon, Jesse. 2003. *The Black Population in the United States: March 2002*. Current Population Reports, Series P20-541. Washington, DC: U.S. Census Bureau.

McLanahan, Sara, and Irwin Garfinkel. 2000. *The Fragile Families and Child Well-Being Study: Questions, Design, and a Few Preliminary Results*. Discussion paper no. 1208. Madison: Institute for Research on Poverty, University of Wisconsin-Madison.

National Association of Secretaries of State. 2000. *The New Millennium Project*. Pt. 1, *American Youth Attitudes on Politics, Citizenship, Government, and Voting*. Lexington, KY: National Association of Secretaries of State.

O'Rand, Angela M., and John C. Henretta. 1999. *Age and Equality: Diverse Pathways through Later Life*. Boulder, CO: Westview Press.

Organization for Economic Co-Operation and Development. 1999. *Preparing Youth for the Twenty-first Century: The Transition from Education to the Labour Market*. Proceedings of the Washington D.C. Conference, 23–24 February 1999. Danvers, MA: Organization for Economic Co-Operation and Development.

———. 2000. *From Initial Education to Working Life: Making Transitions Work*. Paris: Organization for Economic Co-Operation and Development.

Osgood, D. Wayne, E. Michael Foster, Connie A. Flanagan, and Gretchen R. Ruth, eds. Forthcoming. *On Your Own without a Net: The Transition to Adulthood for Vulnerable Populations*. Chicago: University of Chicago Press.

Pittman, Karen, Marcelo Diversi, and Thaddeus Ferver. 2002. Social Policy Supports for Adolescence in the Twenty-First Century: Framing Questions. Pp. 149–66 in *Adolescent's Preparation for the Future: Perils and Promises*, edited by Reed Larson, B. Bradford Brown, and Jeylan Mortimer. Ann Arbor, MI: Society for Research on Adolescence.

Ralston, Penny A., Richard M. Lerner, Ann K. Mullis, Coby B. Simerly, and John B. Murray, eds. 2000. *Social Change, Public Policy, and Community Collaborations: Training Human Development Professionals for the Twenty-first Century*. Boston: Kluwer Academic Publishers.

Riley, Matilda W., Robert L. Kahn, and Anne Foner, eds. 1994. *Age and Structural Lag: Society's Failure to Provide Meaningful Opportunities in Work, Family and Leisure*. New York: John Wiley & Sons.

Saraswathi, T. S., and Reed W. Larson. 2002. Adolescence in Global Perspective: An Agenda for Social Policy. Pp. 344–62 in *The World's Youth: Adolescence in Eight Regions of the Globe*, edited by B. Bradford Brown, Reed W. Larson, and T. S. Saraswathi. New York: Cambridge University Press.

Settersten, Richard A., Jr. 1998. A Time to Leave Home and Never Return? Age Constraints around the Living Arrangements of Young Adults. *Social Forces* 76 (4):1373–1400.

———. 1999. *Lives in Time and Place: The Problems and Promises of Developmental Science*. Amityville, NY: Baywood Publishing Co.

————. 2003a. Age Structuring and the Rhythm of the Life Course. Pp. 81–98 in *Handbook of the Life Course,* edited by Jeylan Mortimer and Michael J. Shanahan. New York: Kluwer Academic/Plenum Publishers.

————. 2003b. Rethinking Social Policy: Lessons of a Life-Course Perspective. Pp. 191–222 in *Invitation to the Life Course: Toward New Understandings of Later Life,* edited by Richard A. Settersten Jr. Amityville, NY: Baywood Publishing Co.

Settersten, Richard A., Jr., and Loren D. Lovegreen. 1998. Educational Experiences throughout Adult Life: New Hopes or No Hope for Life-Course Flexibility? *Research on Aging* 20 (4):506–38.

Shaw, Kathleen M., and Jerry A. Jacobs, eds. 2003. *Community Colleges: New Environments, New Directions.* Thousand Oaks, CA; London: Sage Publications.

Shonkoff, Jack P. 2000. Science, Policy, and Practice: Three Cultures in Search of a Shared Mission. *Child Development* 71 (1):181–87.

Taylor-Gooby, Peter. 2004. *New Risks and New Welfare in Europe.* Buckingham: Open University Press.

Verba, Sidney, Kay Lehman Schlozman, and Henry E. Brady. 1995. *Voice and Equality: Civic Volunteerism in American Politics.* Cambridge, MA: Harvard University Press.

Williams, Joan. 2000. *Unbending Gender: Why Work and Family Conflict and What to Do about It.* New York: Oxford University Press.

Youniss, James, and Allison Ruth. 2002. Approaching Policy for Adolescent Development in the Twenty-first Century. Pp. 250–71 in *The Changing Adolescent Experience: Societal Trends and the Transition to Adulthood,* edited by Jeylan T. Mortimer and Reed W. Larson. New York: Cambridge University Press.

Index

abortion, attitudes about, 182, 183, 185, 186, 196, 201

adaptive strategies, 54

Add Health. *See* National Longitudinal Study of Adolescent Health

adolescence, 3–5, 17, 45

Adoption and Foster Care Analysis and Reporting System (AFCARS), 505

Adoption and Safe Families Act (ASFA), 505

adulthood: definition of, 226; duration of early stage of, 18; onset of, 6, 17–18, 79–80, 552–53; "psychological," 226; reversibility of markers of, 229, 259–60. *See also* adulthood, emerging; adulthood, self-perception of; getting off to a good start; individualization of transition to adulthood; paths to adulthood; timing and sequence of transition to adulthood; transition to adulthood; women's transition to adulthood, international comparison of

adulthood, emerging: conceptual basis of, 226–27; criteria for adulthood and, 239, 249, 250–51; as cultural-political construction, 253; defined, 5; paths to adulthood and, 335, 337, 339, 343, 344; substance use and well-being and, 449; as time of experimentation, 448. *See also* adulthood

adulthood, self-perception of, 225–53; autonomy and, 227; behavioral markers of adulthood, 227–28, 230, 249, 251; broad and narrow socialization and, 227–28; cognitive markers of adulthood, 226, 227, 230, 249, 251; data, 232–39; demographic transitions and, 225, 226, 230–31, 236–38, 248–50, 251, 293, 302; discussion of findings, 249–51; emotional markers of adulthood, 226, 227, 230, 249, 251; empirical evidence and, 229–31; findings, 239–49; historical considerations and, 228–29; hypotheses about, 231; independence from parents and, 314, 316–17; individualism and, 226, 227; in industrial societies, 227; versus legal markers of adulthood, 552; literature on, 225–28, 229–31; in preindustrial societies, 227; "psychological adulthood" and, 226; questionnaire, 252; research methods, 226, 231–33, 236, 239–40, 250–51; reversibility of markers of transition and, 229; single parenthood and, 480; situational considerations, 249; traditional markers of adulthood and, 225, 226, 230–31; "youthhood" and, 226. *See also* adulthood

adultolescence, 5